Biographical Directory of the Governors of the United States 1789-1978

Volume I
(Alabama-Indiana)

Biographical Directory of the Governors of the United States 1789-1978

Volume I
(Alabama-Indiana)

Edited by
Robert Sobel and John Raimo

MECKLER BOOKS
A Division of Microform Review Inc.
520 Riverside Ave.
Westport, CT 06880

Library of Congress Cataloging in Publication Data

Main entry under title:

Biographical directory of the governors of the United
   States, 1789-1978.

   1. Governors—United States—Biography. I. Sobel,
Robert, 1931 (Feb. 19)- II. Raimo, John W., 1946 (Dec. 28)-
E176.B573   973'.0992   [B]   77-10435

ISBN 0-930466-00-4

ISBN 0-930466-01-2 (Vol. I); -02-0 (Vol. II); -03-9 (Vol. III); -04-7 (Vol. IV)

Meckler Books, *A Division of Microform Review Inc.*
520 Riverside Avenue
P.O. Box 405 Saugatuck Station
Westport, Conn. 06880
Printed in United States of America

CONTENTS

Volume Three

Index to Volumes I-IV follows Pennsylvania

Volume Four

Index to Volumes I-IV follows Wyoming

PREFATORY NOTE

Of the approximately 2,000 men and women who served as a State Governor,* the great majority of these have not been the subject of full-scale, published biographies. While some have appeared as major figures in the lives of other individuals, little is known about many Governors who held office during the nation's first half century. For some, information hitherto could be found only through an archival search. Now this data will be more readily accessible.

The Biographical Directory of the Governors of the United States, 1789-1978 is arranged alphabetically by states; within each state, the order of biographical entries is chronological. Biographies of those who served more than one term of office as Governor are situated within the years of first gubernatorial term. Inserts, listing the Governor's name and terms of office, have been included in the chronological sequence in order to preserve the recording of the continuity of the governorship within each state. The general index, appearing at the end of each volume, cites the volume number and first page of each biographical entry.

Each biography has been written by an expert, usually a researcher in a state or local historical society, a librarian, or a professor of history. Wherever possible, such basic information as dates of birth and death, ancestry and family, religion and political affiliation, electoral results, and political and private careers, have been included. In addition, the biographies contain bibliographic guides for further research; many also indicate where the Governor's papers are located.

For the original thirteen states, the biographical entries begin with the Governor taking office in 1789, the year in which the new Federal Constitution was implemented, rather than in 1776, the year the American colonies declared their independence from Great Britain. Although this decision has meant that some Governors, who served both under the Articles of Confederation and the Federal Constitution, are here discussed primarily in terms of developments during their gubernatorial careers after 1788; they, and the remaining governors of the colonial period (1607 to 1789), will be subsequently treated in a single volume scheduled to appear in the near future.

Robert Sobel
New College, Hofstra University

John W. Raimo
Editor

---

*The actual number is a matter of some dispute, for some states do not include individuals who served as Acting Governor on their lists. All those who took the oath of office from 1789 have been included in this work, which means that several who served less than a week are to be found here.

The following individuals have contributed entries to *The Biographical Directory of the Governors of the United States, 1789-1978*:

Elizabeth S. Adams, Michigan Historical Commission
Thomas Appleton, University of Kentucky
Mrs. Thomas H. Baird, Western Kentucky Museum
Willard Barnes, University of Idaho
Rodney E. Bell, South Dakota State University
Arthur W. Bergeron, Jr., Louisiana Archives & Records Service
W.C. Bethea, Arkansas Historical Commission
Aaron Berman, New York City, New York
Bob L. Blackburn, Oklahoma State University
Richard Bland, University of Kentucky
Warren M. Blankenship, University of Oregon
Susan Blain, Rhode Island Historical Society
Frank Boles, Bentley Library, University of Michigan
Ruth B. Bordin, Bentley Library, University of Michigan
Roger Bridges, Illinois State Historical Library
Larry Brooks, New York City, New York
Eugene T. Carroll, Denver, Colorado
Loren B. Chan, San Jose State University
Steven Channing, University of Kentucky
Russell J. Clemens, University of Missouri-Columbia
Len G. Cleveland, Georgia Department of Archives and History
David R. Colburn, University of Florida
Bridget Collier, Vermont Historical Society
James F. Cook, Floyd Junior College
David Crosson, University of Wyoming
Phyllis David, Alaska Historical Library
Michael D'Innocenzo, Hofstra University
Richard M. Doolen, Bentley Library, University of Michigan
Michael W. Everman, Oklahoma State University
Tomas Felt, New York Office of State History
Kenny A. Franks, Oklahoma Historical Society
John A. Fribley, University of Wyoming
Russell W. Fridley, Minnesota Historical Society
Patricia C. Gaster, Nebraska State Historical Society
Christopher C. Gibbs, University of Missouri-Columbia
Judith Gildner, *Annals of Iowa*
Steven K. Gragert, Oklahoma State University
David B. Gracy, III, Texas State Library
Larry Gragg, University of Missouri-Columbia
C.L. Grant, Georgia State University
James W. Hammack, Jr., Murray State University
Mac R. Harris, Oklahoma Historical Society
Lowell Harrison, Western Kentucky University
Gordon O. Hendrickson, University of Wyoming
Patricia Hickin, Richmond, Virginia
Ann Hinckley, Utah Division of State History

Zaneta Hirst, Montana Historical Society
Melvin G. Holli, University of Illinois at Chicago Circle
James Larry Hood, Kentucky Historical Society
Hazel Hopper, Indiana State Library
Millicent S. Huff, Texas State Library
H. Draper Hunt, University of Maine at Portland
Peter Iverson, University of Wyoming
Michael Kass, Massapequa, New York
Gregory Kendrick, University of Wyoming
Tevis L. Kimball, Rhode Island Historical Society
Philip Klein, Pennsylvania State University
James C. Klotter, Kentucky Historical Society
Stanford J. Layton, Utah Division of State History
Linda Lotridge Levin, Rhode Island Historical Society
Foy Lisenby, University of Central Arkansas
Nena B. Lovinger, University of Oregon
Robert M. McBride, Tennessee Historical Quarterly
Ursula McFarland, Rhode Island Historical Society
H. Brett Melendy, University of Hawaii at Manoa
Howard L. Meredith, Oklahoma Historical Preservation Review Commission
Frank C. Mevers, New Hampshire Historical Society
Mary L. Montanye, Anna Maria College
Waddy Moore, University of Central Arkansas
Miriam Murphy, Utah Division of State History
Keith A. Murray, Western Washington State College
Alan S. Newell, Historical Research Associates
Warren H. Onken, Jr., University of Wyoming
Ruth C. Page, New Hampshire Historical Society
John C. Paige, Wyoming State Archives and Historical Department
Betsy Peters, University of Wyoming
Marsha Peters, Rhode Island Historical Society
Robert Peters, University of Oregon
Steven L. Piott, University of Missouri-Columbia
John O. Pohlman, California State College at Dominguez Hills
A. Kent Powell, Utah Division of State History
Thomas E. Powers, Bentley Historical Library, Michigan Historical Collections
George E. Pozzetta, University of Florida
Harry Readnour, University of Central Arkansas
Patrick Reed, Northern Virginia Community College
Robert W. Righter, University of Wyoming
Leonard Rogoff, University of North Carolina
John Rusmandel, Freeport, New York
A. Bower Sageser, Kansas State University
Robert K. Scher, University of Florida
Paul Alan Schmidt, Stratford, Connecticut
Robert F. Sexton, University of Kentucky
T. McNeal Simpson, University of Tennessee
J.M. Skaggs, Wichita State University
James M. Smallwood, Oklahoma State University

John David Smith, Lincoln Library and Museum
John S.H. Smith, Utah State Historical Society
Homer E. Socolofsky, Kansas State University
Stuart Sprague, Morehead State University
Michael Starr, Hiram College
Vicki Sullivan, Oklahoma Historical Society
Hambleton Tapp, Kentucky Historical Society
Linda Thatcher, Utah Division of State History
Shirley Thayer, Maine State Library
Melvina K. Thurman, Oklahoma Historical Society
Carrie M. Townley, University of Nevada-Reno
Joseph G. Tregle, Jr., University of New Orleans
Len Tucker, Massachusetts Historical Society
Louis Tucker, New York Office of State History
Kirby O. Turner, University of Oklahoma
Carl N. Tyson, Oklahoma State University
Bruce Udolf, Boston, Massachusetts
Robert M. Warner, Bentley Library, University of Michigan
Gary D. Williams, Historical Research Associates
Sylvia Wrobel, University of Kentucky
B. Michael Zuckerman, Rhode Island Historical Society
Timothy A. Zwink, Oklahoma State University

INTRODUCTION

The office of American Governor is of central significance in the structure of American political parties. Since parties are organized on a statewide rather than a national basis, the Governor is the central personality in the state party of which he is a member. His leadership position automatically makes him the key spokesman on political matters within his state. A Governor who knows how to exploit effectively the media can develop insurmountable advantages of incumbency, often guaranteeing not only himself but also his party effective dominance within his state. The wealth of patronage appointments at the disposal of the Governor further strengthens the role of his party. It is not too much to say that an effective Governor is responsible for his party's performance on the national level. His organizational effectiveness lays the foundation for both state and national performance.

No less significantly, the program that a Governor pursues on a statewide level can be a testing of its effectiveness on a nationwide basis. Typical of this process was the performance of Robert M. La Follette, whose governorship of Wisconsin between 1901-1906 was marked by innovative programs of reform that emphasized the importance of expert knowledge in the shaping of public policy. His parallel efforts to make the selection process for candidates and campaign expenditures less vulnerable to corruption turned Wisconsin into a laboratory for progressive reform. The opportunities to make a statewide mark have often made the governorship a stepping stone to the presidency. A classic instance was the incumbency of Woodrow Wilson between 1911 and 1913 in New Jersey, where his highly visible reform program gave him national exposure. In a sense, the state provides a microcosmic testing of the man and program before they are applied to the macrocosmic stage of the nation.

In addition, the health of a party depends in substantial measure on its ability to elect Governors and members of State Legislatures. A party defeated on the national level can still sustain itself so long as it holds a significant proportion of governorships and state offices. But if it fails to maintain itself on the statewide level, the party begins to atrophy and runs the serious risk of its demise. No better evidence of this consequence is to be found than the fate of either the Federalist or Whig Party, each of which disintegrated when it could no longer win governorships and state offices. This fact permits the assertion that the basic unit of American politics is the state. It is there that the critical decisions which ultimately shape national politics are made. Therefore, to understand the dynamics of American politics, one must understand its functioning on the state level. Given the importance of the governorship, it is safe to say that an understanding of the gubernatorial office, and the men and women who have held it, is a key to such dynamics. From the *Biographical Directory of the Governors of the United States, 1789-1978*, a wealth of detail can be extracted that explains the origins and nature of the office, how it has evolved over time, and how it has shaped American history. In addition, by describing the people who have held the office, one obtains not only an insight into the nature of American politicians but also a striking perception of the nature of the American electorate who have chosen them.

The office of State Governor has its roots in the colonial governorship. As such, it is the oldest executive office in the United States. Prior to the Revolution, the governorship resembled in many ways the role of the King in the parliamentary system. It had extensive appointive powers, the authority to convene and dissolve colonial assemblies, the right to veto legislation, as well as the ability to serve as commander of the colonial militia. Outside of Connecticut and Rhode Island, the Governors were chosen by the crown; in these two New England colonies, they were elected. Since many colonial grievances prior to the Revolution were directed against the exercise of executive power, one of the major results of the Revolution was a major redefinition of the power of the governorship. The principle of an elective governorship, chosen either directly or indirectly from and by the citizenry, became accepted practice. To assure a responsive governorship, terms of office of one year became commonplace. The concern for the separation of powers was apparent in the care with which the Governor was distinguished from the legislature. Public determination to keep the executive subordinate to the legislative authority was reflected in the numerous limitations that circumscribed early gubernatorial powers. Nonetheless, despite these limitations, the Governor was clearly recognized as the head of the state, as well as the commander of the state militia. In addition the dimensions of the power assigned to the post-revolutionary Governors varied from state to state. In the old charter states of Connecticut and Rhode Island, the Governor continued to be popularly elected, and remained essentially independent of the legislature. In sharp contrast was the legislatively appointed Governor of South Carolina. In the states of New York and Massachusetts, a strong Governor possessed a suspensive veto power and extensive appointive authority. For a brief time, in states such as Georgia and Vermont, the Governor did little more than preside over an executive council which exercised the powers of the executive. Whatever the dimensions of their power, by 1792, all state chief executives were known as Governor.

The emphasis on a one-year term was originally common, with the exception of New York and Delaware which gave their chief executives three-year terms, and South Carolina which authorized a two-year term. The seven states of Pennsylvania, Delaware, Maryland, Virginia, North and South Carolina, and Georgia placed limits on the re-eligibility of an incumbent Governor. The most striking restriction was in Georgia which limited the term to one single year in a three-year period. Interestingly, the modern constitution of Georgia limits an incumbent to a single term in an eight-year period, a restriction that is also true in North and South Carolina, Virginia, Tennessee and Mississippi. The one-year term restriction did not prevent the repeated election of incumbent Governors. William Livingston, the first Governor of the State of New Jersey, was elected to fourteen successive terms between 1776 and 1790. Yet the effort to keep Governors responsive to the electorate was an overriding concern in keeping the terms brief.

More important to the development of a democratically chosen governorship was the shift to a popularly elected Governor. Outside of the original thirteen states, only Kentucky and Louisiana failed immediately to establish direct gubernatorial elections, but even these two quickly reverted to popular choice. Of the original thirteen states, all but South Carolina had abandoned legislative choice of the Governor before the Civil War, and in 1865, the "Palmetto State" fell into line. A number of states made the additional requirement of either a runoff election or a legislative choice between the two top candidates when no candidate won a clear majority. Today only the southern states of Georgia, Mississippi, Arkansas, Alabama, Florida, Louisiana, North Carolina, Oklahoma, South Carolina, Texas and Virginia provide for a runoff; the other states have settled for a plurality choice. The power of the popular choice was never more strikingly demonstrated than in the 1839 election by a single vote of Marcus Morton to the governorship of Massachusetts.

Not all gubernatorial contests have been settled as peacefully. Rhode Island teetered on the edge of Civil War in 1842, as two factions, led by Thomas W. Dorr and Samuel W. King, both claimed the office. Federal intervention assured King's incumbency, but the source of the original dispute, Dorr's effort to broaden the suffrage to all whites, was resolved in 1843 with the adoption of a new constitution incorporating liberalized suffrage provisions. A more spectacular controversy erupted in Kentucky in 1899 when a bitterly fought election reached a climax when the Democratically controlled legislature chose the anti-railroad reformer William Goebel to replace the Republican William S. Taylor. Taylor was removed on the grounds that his narrow victory had been fraudulently won. Tension exploded on January 30, 1900, when Goebel was shot outside the State Capitol. The legislature then proclaimed Goebel Governor, and upon his death four days later, his Lieutenant Governor, J.C.W. Beckham, succeeded him. Eventually the Kentucky courts upheld the choice of Beckham. Taylor escaped prosecution for complicity in the assassination by fleeing to Indiana, but the Republican Secretary of State, as well as an aide, were eventually convicted and sentenced to life imprisonment. A more recent dispute was settled in Rhode Island in 1956, when the State Supreme Court invalidated some 5,000 absentee votes to assure Dennis Joseph Roberts a fourth term by a bare 711 votes. Invariably, these disputed elections have reflected the existence of deeply felt internal divisions within states.

A further complication in the choosing of Governors has been the time period during which gubernatorial candidates have been chosen. Over the years arguments have been made that candidates should be chosen at elections other than those involving presidential candidates. Obviously, so long as most Governors were chosen for one or two years, their elections would coincide with that of Presidents. But as a four-year term became the more common period, efforts were made to switch gubernatorial choices to off-year elections. This process has arrived at the point that presently only the Governors of Arkansas, Delaware, Indiana, Missouri, Montana, New Hampshire, North Carolina, North Dakota, Rhode Island, Utah, Vermont and West Virginia are to be chosen in the year of presidential election. The present Governor of Illinois, James R. Thompson, was elected to a two-year term in 1976 in order to provide for a shift to an off-year four year sequence. The five states of Kentucky, Louisiana, Mississippi, New Jersey and Virginia have futher lessened the chance that state and national issues might be confused by electing their Governors at times when no member of the federal government is being voted on.

The choosing of gubernatorial candidates during the nineteenth and well into the twentieth century had been made at conventions. The colorful, often corrupt, nature of the convention process resulted in a developing backlash that steadily displaced the convention by the direct primary system. With its compulsory application to party choices in Wisconsin in 1903, the direct primary became a central focus of Progressive political reform. Ironically, in one party states, such as those in the South, the primary election which resulted in the choice of the designated Democratic Party candidate became the key election. Once the party candidates were chosen in the primary, despite reform expectations, the election tended to attract party workers and zealots in far larger proportions than regular voters. This gave a decided advantage to candidates who had strong party worker support. In states such as California, which until 1959 allowed a candidate to cross-file for nomination by more than one party, it was possible for a candidate like Earl Warren to win both the Republican and the Democratic gubernatorial nomination in 1946. Most states have since adopted the "closed" primary that generally restricts voting in primaries to registered members of the parties. The last of the fully convention states, Indiana, has since 1976 switched to a primary. Connecticut still uses the convention method of choosing its candidates, but any losing candidate, who in convention gets 25 percent of the delegate vote, can call for a primary; Delaware also still uses conventions to select candidates. In most primaries, the plurality winner gets the nomination, a process that allowed Brendan Byrne of New Jersey to win renomination in 1977 with barely 30 percent of the vote.

The path to nomination as Governor was once considerably more difficult. In the formative stages of the republic, many states required that a Governor own substantial amounts of property. The largest amount required was in South Carolina, which specified that the candidate own no less than a £10,000 debt-free freehold. In contemporary terms that would be tantamount to requiring a Governor to be a millionaire. Most states originally placed precise requirements on the Governor's religious belief. Typical of this was New Jersey's requirement that the Governor be a member of a Protestant sect. More in line with contemporary practice, Virginia started out with neither property nor sectarian requirements. But over time, the original restrictions were steadily modified. The religious test was finally terminated in 1961 when the United States Supreme Court found a Maryland statute requiring state officials to declare their belief in Christianity, or in a future existence where the sinful were punished and the believer rewarded, an unconstitutional violation of freedom of religion. Some requirements still remain. Most Governors must be at least thirty years of age, and all are required to be American citizens and residents of the states of which they are Governor. The requirement that a Governor be a native-born United States citizen ceased in 1955 when Maine deleted that requirement from its Constitution. Similarly, gubernatorial qualifications specifically designate the conviction for certain kinds of crime as an immediate disqualification.

The question of qualification has occasionally resulted in a serious conflict over the eligibility of a gubernatorial candidate. In 1924, Miriam A. Ferguson, the Democratic candidate for the Texas governorship, was challenged on the grounds of her sex, the fact that she was married, and that her husband, James E. Ferguson, had been previously removed from the Texas governorship by impeachment. The courts decided in her favor and she went on to be elected. In the middle 1930s, William Langer of North Dakota was forced to relinquish the Governor's post on the grounds that his conviction for a felony made him ineligible to hold the office.

But given the number of past Governors, the most remarkable fact is the relatively few controversies that have surrounded gubernatorial qualifications.

An analysis of the governorship over a span of time indicates certain constants in the character of the individuals who have held the post. Most immediately, the candidates have been overwhelmingly male, with the inclusion of only five women, Nellie Tayloe Ross of Wyoming, Miriam A. Ferguson of Texas, Lurleen Wallace of Alabama, Ella Grasso of Connecticut and Dixy Lee Ray of Washington (all Democrats.) A study of the proportion of party representation finds that 35.5 percent of all Governors have been Republican; 45.1 percent Democrats; 7.9 percent Democratic-Republican, i.e. Jeffersonian Republicans, the predecessor of the Democratic Party; 6.5 percent Whigs; 2.8 percent Federalists; and the remaining 2.2 percent from a scattering of parties. The average age at which Governors have been first elected is 48.2 years. A surprising difference is found between Democrats who have averaged 46.5 years and Republicans who have averaged 50.1 years. Overwhelmingly, by 97.6 percent to 2.4 percent, Governors have been married, with Democrats, by a two to one margin, likely to be the unmarried. However, few Governors have matched the marital record of Jonas Galusha of Vermont who married and buried four wives.

Generally Governors have reflected the population composition of their home states. The preponderance of the Protestant faith is reflected in the fact that 87.5 percent of all Governors have belonged to a Protestant sect. Of the remainder, 12.1 percent were Roman Catholic, .1 percent Jewish, and the final .3 percent have noted no religion. The latter fact strongly suggests that gubernatorial candidates have found it advantageous to identify with some religious sect. Interesting evidence of recent change is the fact that among incumbent Governors, 65 percent are Protestant, 30.5 percent are Roman Catholic, 4 percent are Jewish, and .5 percent are Greek Orthodox. With regard to discernible ethnic origin, the overwhelming preponderance of incumbents have been of British, German, Irish and Scandinavian origin. More recently, candidates of Italian, Slavic, Hispanic, i.e. Mexican, and Japanese ancestry have been elected. The presence of a given group in a state, particularly if it is numerous, is no guarantee that one of its number will be quickly elected to the governorship. For example, the first Jewish Governor of New York State, Herbert Lehman, was not elected until 1932, although Idaho, Oregon and New Mexico, with negligible Jewish populations, elected the first modern Jewish Governors, Moses Alexander (1915), Julius L. Meier (1930) and Arthur Seligman (1930), respectively.[1] Similarly, New Jersey, whose Roman Catholic population approaches 40 percent, did not elect a Roman Catholic Governor (Richard J. Hughes) until 1961, while Connecticut, with its sizeable Italian population, elected its first Governor of Italian origin (Ella Grasso) in 1974. It is worth noting that no black has ever been elected to a governorship, although Pinckney B.S. Pinchback, a black, served briefly in 1872-1873 as Governor of Louisiana, when the white incumbent was impeached.

The most significant determinant in the choice of gubernatorial candidate has been his prior service in state government. No fewer than 71.3 percent of all Governors have served in the state legislature previous to their election. This strongly suggests that the connections one makes through state service have played

1. David Emanuel, Governor of Georgia (1801), was the first Jewish Governor.

a significant role in party nominations. A gubernatorial candidate with such credentials has the immense advantage of being a predictable quantity for the party leadership. It also means that an outsider, such as Woodrow Wilson was when nominated by New Jersey Democrats in 1910, is an exceptional development. Almost 14 percent of all Governors have served in either the Senate or the House of Representatives. The latter office is more likely to be held before the governorship, while the former is more likely to be held subsequently. In addition, no fewer than 31.1 percent have served on the federal level in other than Congress. Among the latter were fourteen future Presidents, a number that indicates that gubernatorial service has been an impressive advantage in seeking the presidency.[2] An odd fact was the election of the Confederate Vice President, Alexander Stephens, after the Civil War to the governorship of Georgia. In the category of the unusual fact, only Sam Houston served as Governor in more than one state, i.e. Tennessee (1827-29) and Texas (1859-61). However, a number of Governors held previous state offices in states other than those that had elected them Governor. Some examples are Ninian Edwards, an Illinois Governor, who had served in the Kentucky House of Representatives, as well as being that state's Chief Justice; George Thomas Wood of Texas who had served in the Georgia legislature; William Erskine Stevenson of New Mexico who had sat in the Pennsylvania Legislature; Arthur Calvin Mellette of South Dakota who had been a member of the Indiana House of Representatives; and William John McConnell of Idaho who had also been an Oregon State Senator.

The portrait of Governors would not be complete without noting their educational, professional, and military attainments. Although it is difficult to draw effective comparisons between contemporary and past educational facilities, it is safe to deduce that the average Governor has had a significantly more extensive educational background than his constituents. It seems that 76.8 percent of all Governors have attended colleges or universities. Interestingly, all present 50 incumbents in state governorships had received higher education, and Oklahoma's David Boren was a Rhodes scholar. Approximately 66 percent of all Governors have been practicing lawyers, a dominant characteristic of all elected officials on both the state and federal level. Among present Governors the percentage of lawyers is 52 percent. This decline in the number of lawyers has resulted in an interesting diversification of occupations among present Governors. Seven have been active in business; two have been dentists, and the present Governor of Indiana is still a practicing medical doctor; four are farmers or ranchers; one was a commercial fisherman and air taxi operator, and another a high school teacher and coach; while Dixy Lee Ray of Washington State is an oceanographer. The steady broadening of the occupational range of Governors in the past four decades reflects the widening of political parameters in the United States. One can assume that the traditional dominance in politics of lawyers will continue to decline, although as a group they are likely to remain the largest single component. Equally as striking is the fact that 68.1 percent of Governors have given military service. Americans have traditionally honored their veterans, a fact illustrated by South Dakota's election of Congressional Medal of Honor winner Joseph Foss after World War II.

2. Jefferson (VA); Monroe (VA); Van Buren (NY); Tyler (VA); Polk (TN); A. Johnson (TN); Hayes (OH); Cleveland (NY); McKinley (OH); T. Roosevelt (NY); Wilson (NJ); Coolidge (MA); F.D. Roosevelt (NY); Carter (GA).

One limitation on gubernatorial candidacy has been the inescapable expense of running for the office. It is safe to assume that the vast mass of Governors have come from solid middle class circumstances. Most Governors can expect to receive presently a salary approximating that of a middle range business executive. In addition to their salaries, they may receive the use of the Governor's residence and other perquisites of office, such as a limousine and a private plane. However, a large proportion of Governors are likely to find that an independent outside income is an essential ingredient to surviving the expenses of office. Since its earliest origins, the post has carried with it the implied idea that compensation is secondary to the distinction of the office. As a result, most governorships pay substantially less than equivalent federal offices. Present salaries range from a high of $85,000 in New York State to a low of $10,000 in Arkansas. Most Governors are paid between $25,000 and $50,000 annually. The combination of heavy campaign costs and comparatively low salaries has resulted in most candidates being people of independent means who have further access to substantial campaign contributions.

Once in office Governors have found that their office resembles the national presidency in both its structure and power. Like the President, the Governor is both the Chief Executive and Party Chief within his political bailiwick. He also is Commander-in-Chief of the state armed forces and will be expected to call them into action if circumstances dictate their use. When the Governor is sworn into office, he is expected to deliver an inaugural address that forecasts the general policies that his administration will follow. Normally, the Governor delivers an annual "state of the state" address which spells out unsettled problems and their proposed solution. Since many state responsibilities are likely to affect directly the daily lives of the average citizen, any failure to provide effective service is likely to focus criticism against the Governor. The result is that the gubernatorial post is more likely to see frequent changes in incumbents than congressional posts. Typically it can result in the Republicans, as was true in 1968, holding 31 of the 50 governorships and the Democrats in 1978 holding 36 of the posts. The vulnerability of Governors, combined with the frequent limits imposed on their terms of office, has meant that few Governors hold their offices for longer than eight years. Nonetheless, strong Governors have the power to guide their legislatures to implement legislative programs that are needed.

At the outbreak of the Civil War, Indiana's Republican Governor, Oliver P. Morton, used the State Militia to disband the Democratically controlled State Legislature. More generally, the Governor is likely to maintain good relations with the legislature by working carefully with the legislative leadership. Obviously this process is simplified if the leadership is of the Governor's party, but even a legislature dominated by the opposition is likely to deal cautiously with an incumbent Governor. They are well aware that as Chief Executive, he is in a powerful position to depict the legislature as "obstructionist." In every state but North Carolina, the Governor possesses an executive veto, a weapon that can be used to embarrass the legislature. This is particularly true since more than half the states provide the Governor with the additional time of a month or more to deal with legislation reaching him at the end of a legislative session. Since most legislation is passed in the closing days of a session, this permits the Governor to use wide-ranging consultations before he approves a measure. Only a most inept Governor is likely to fail to invoke a powerful backing before he issues his veto.

Once a veto is made, most states require that three-fifths or two-thirds of the full legislative membership vote to override it, and Alaska requires a three-fourths vote to override a veto of a money bill. In addition, in New Jersey, Massachusetts, Virginia and Alabama, the Governor can return a bill with suggestions on specific amendments that would make a bill satisfactory to him. The power of the veto is indicated by the fact that less than 2 percent of bills vetoed by Governors are presently overridden. Ironically, the public perception of this increased gubernatorial power has resulted in its holding Governors responsible for failure to meet public problems.

The final public control that can be exerted over the governorship is removal from office. With the exception of Oregon, every state provides for an impeachment procedure similar to that in the federal constitution, and even in Oregon, a Governor can be removed by a trial conducted in a manner similar to other criminal trials. In addition, Wisconsin, Michigan, California, Oregon, Arizona, Colorado, Idaho, Nevada, Washington, Louisiana, North Dakota and Kansas provide for the recall of a Governor. However, these removal procedures are used infrequently. It is as if Americans understand that removal from office involves awesome implications and must be used with care, less it degenerate into potential abuse. This is a fear that was reenforced during the Reconstruction when two Southern Governors were removed by impeachment, a third forced to resign under the threat of impeachment, and three other Southern incumbents impeached but not tried.

More recently in the twentieth century, the New York Legislature removed William Sulzer on charges that he was contemptuous of its powers. The Texas Legislature removed James E. Ferguson for abusing his appointive, fiscal and pardoning powers. A number of Governors have been removed after their conviction on criminal charges, involving most recently, in 1977, governor Marvin Mandel of Maryland. Perhaps the most extraordinary example of gubernatorial corruption was exposed when Vice President Spiro Agnew was obliged to relinquish his office in 1973 on charges that arose out of corruption dating from his prior governorship of Maryland. But given the number of past Governors, it is apparent that the process of removal is as sparingly used as in the federal executive.

Without question, the American governorship provides a profound insight into the nature of the American executive. In sheer number, Governors are the largest single component of executive power on the political level. To understand how they achieved their political position is to come to understand the vast structure of state political organization that is the hidden side of the federal system. The changes that have occurred in the shape of the American governorship during the past two centuries are the key to understanding how the American political system has evolved into an increasingly centralized democratic republic. Finally, the Governors are a reflection of the extraordinary diversity that has characterized state politics. Within the constant of one republic, the state polity has provided Americans with the opportunity to diverge from their sister states, and to experiment on a scale that allows them to confine the original risks to one state, while making subsequent benefits available to all states. In these four volumes, the reader is given an introduction to a side of the American political experiment that has been hidden — and the Governors whose biographies are contained here are the actors in that shadowed experiment.

James P. Shenton
Columbia University

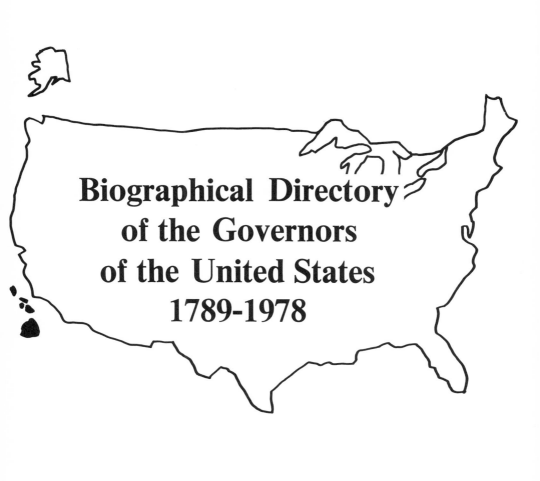

Biographical Directory
of the Governors
of the United States
1789-1978

ALABAMA

ALABAMA

BIBB, William Wyatt, 1819-1820

Born on October 2, 1781, in Amelia County, Virginia, son of William, a soldier and politician, and Sally (Wyatt) Bibb. Brother of Thomas, Benajah S., Peyton, John Dandridge, Joseph, Delia, and Martha D.; married to Mary Freeman in 1803, and father of George Bailey and Mary. Attended William and Mary College; graduated in medicine from the University of Pennsylvania in 1801. Moved to Petersburg, Georgia, in 1801 and practiced medicine. Member, Georgia House of Representatives, 1803-1805; member, United States House of Representatives, 1807-1813; member, United States Senate, 1813-1816; resigned from the office; appointed Governor of the Territory of Alabama by President James Monroe, 1817. On March 2, 1819, the United States Congress passed the Enabling Act authorizing the citizens of the Alabama Territory to call a constitutional convention in preparation for statehood. The convention was held on July 5, 1819, at Huntsville, Alabama; after the adoption of a Constitution, elections for officials were held on September 20 and 21. As a Democratic-Republican, Bibb was elected Governor by popular vote, receiving 8,342 votes against 7,140 received by another Democratic-Republican, Marmaduke Williams. Bibb was inaugurated on November 9, 1819. Alabama was admitted to the Union on December 14, 1819, and Bibb faced the challenge of implementing the new state government. He was strongly in favor of education and internal improvements, and the General Assembly provided for the sale and leasing of school lands to fund the development of both. In addition, the General Assembly passed laws against dueling, fraudulent land transactions, and usury—loans in excess of eight percent were outlawed. While Bibb was governor, Mobile was granted a city charter, and a Federal District Court was organized for the state. On July 9, 1820, Bibb died in office, after being thrown from a horse. He was buried in the family cemetery at Coosada Station, Alabama. Bibliography: Thomas M. Owen, *History of Alabama and Dictionary of Alabama Biography*, 4 vols. (Chicago, 1921); Albert B. Moore, *History of Alabama and Her People*, 3 vols. (New York, 1927); Roy Glashan, *American Governors and Gubernatorial Elections, 1775-1975* (Stillwater, Minnesota, 1975); C. E. Jones, "Gov. William Wyatt Bibb," *Publications of the Alabama Historical Society*, vol. III (1919).

BIBB, Thomas, 1820-1821

Born in 1784 in Amelia County, Virginia, son of William, a soldier and politician, and Sally (Wyatt) Bibb. Brother of William W., Benajah S., Peyton, John Dandridge, Joseph, Delia, and Martha D.; married Parmelia Thompson, and father of Adaline,

Emily, Thomas, William Dandridge, Porter, Elmira, Robert Thompson, Eliza Parmelia, and three children who died in infancy. Planter and merchant; moved to Huntsville, Alabama in 1816; member, Alabama Constitutional Convention, 1819; elected to the Alabama Senate, September, 1819; elected President of the Alabama Senate, 1819. A Democratic-Republican. The 1819 Constitution of Alabama provided that in case of the removal of the Governor from office, the President of the State Senate "shall exercise all the power and authority appertaining to the office of governor, until the time pointed out by this constitution for the election of governor shall arrive. . . ." Governor William W. Bibb died on July 9, 1820, and Thomas Bibb, as President of the State Senate, assumed the governor's office on July 15, 1820. During Thomas Bibb's term, the University of Alabama was chartered, a State Bank was authorized, and a patrol system was established to prevent the escape of slaves. On August 6, 1821, Israel Pickens was elected Governor, and on November 9, 1821, Thomas Bibb left office. Afterward, he continued to be active in state politics, and served in the Alabama General Assembly. Bibb died on December 20, 1839, and was buried in Huntsville, Alabama. Bibliography: W. Brewer, *Alabama: Her History, Resources, War Record and Public Men from 1540 to 1872* (Montgomery, 1872); Thomas M. Owen, *History of Alabama and Dictionary of Alabama Biography*, 4 vols. (Chicago, 1921); Albert B. Moore, *History of Alabama and Her People*, 3 vols. (New York, 1927); Roy Glashan, *American Governors and Gubernatorial Elections, 1775-1975* (Stillwater, Minnesota, 1975).

PICKENS, Israel, 1821-1825

Born on January 30, 1780 in Mecklenburg County, North Carolina, son of Captain Samuel Pickens, a colonial officer, and Jane (Carrigan) Pickens; a Presbyterian. Brother of Samuel; married to Martha Orilla Lenoir on June 9, 1814, and father of Julia, Andrew, and Israel, Jr. Attended private schools; graduated from Washington College, Pennsylvania, in 1802; studied law. Admitted to the North Carolina Bar, and began law practice. Member, North Carolina Senate, 1808-1810; United States House of Representatives, 1811-1817. Moved to Alabama Territory in 1817; Register in the Land Office at St. Stephens, Alabama Territory, 1817-1821; member, Alabama Constitutional Convention, 1819. As a Democratic-Republican, Pickens was elected Governor of Alabama by popular vote in the general election on August 6, 1821, defeating another Democratic-Republican, Henry Chambers, 9,114 votes to 7,129. Pickens was sworn into office on November 9, 1821. Pickens completed the organization of the new state government, which had been interrupted by the death of Governor William Bibb. During Pickens' administration the Marquis de Lafayette visited the state on a tour of America, and a survey for a possible canal at Muscle Shoals was ordered. In addition, a State Bank was organized in 1824, with a capital of approximately $200,000, and the law removing all limitations on interest rates for loans was repealed. On August 4, 1823, Pickens was reelected to a second term, defeating Chambers again by a vote of 6,942 to 4,604. Ineligible, under the 1819 Alabama Constitution, to serve as governor for more than four years in a six year period, Pickens left office on November 25, 1825. Afterward, he was appointed to the United States Senate, and served from

February 17, 1826 to November 27, 1826. Declined an appointment as a United States District Judge in 1826, and retired to Cuba because of his poor health. Pickens died on April 24, 1827, and was buried in Matanzas, Cuba; however, the Alabama Legislature later disinterred his body and removed his remains to the old Pickens homestead, near Greensboro, Alabama. Bibliography: Thomas M. Owen, *History of Alabama and Dictionary of Alabama Biography*, 4 vols. (Chicago, 1921); Thomas P. Abernathy, *The Formative Period in Alabama, 1815-28* (Montgomery, 1922); Albert B. Moore, *History of Alabama and Her People*, 3 vols. (New York, 1927); Albert B. Moore, *History of Alabama* (University, Alabama, 1934).

MURPHY, John, 1825-1829

Born about 1785, in Robeson County, North Carolina, son of Neil Murphy and a Miss Downing; a Presbyterian. Brother of Reverend Murdock Murphy. Married to Sarah Hails; married a second time to Mrs. Sarah (Darington) Carter on January 18, 1832, and father of Duncan, John Murphy, Jr., and Mary Sue. Murphy's parents moved to South Carolina, where he taught school. Graduated from South Carolina College in 1808. Clerk of the South Carolina Senate, 1810-1817. Moved to Alabama in 1818. Studied law and admitted to the Alabama Bar; planter. Member, Alabama Constitutional Convention, 1819; member, Alabama House of Representatives, 1820; member, Alabama Senate, 1822. Mason. As a Jackson Democrat, Murphy was elected Governor of Alabama by popular vote in the general election on August 1, 1825. Without an opponent, he received 12,184 votes, and was sworn into office on November 25, 1825. During Murphy's administration, the capital of Alabama was moved from Cahaba to Tuscaloosa; a through mail route to New Orleans, Louisiana, was opened; and the United States Congress granted 400,000 acres along the Tennessee River to be sold and the proceeds used to finance a canal at Muscle Shoals. After supporting Andrew Jackson in the 1824 presidential election, the people of the state were incensed, when Jackson, after receiving a plurality of the popular vote, lost the election in the United States House of Representatives. In addition the 1828 "Tariff of Abominations" lit the fire of states' rights among the citizens of Alabama. On August 6, 1827, Murphy was reelected to a second term, again without opposition, receiving 8,334 votes. Ineligible under the 1819 Alabama Constitution to serve as governor for more than four years in a six year period, Murphy left office on November 25, 1829. Afterward, Murphy was a unsuccessful congressional candidate in 1831; however, he was later elected to the United States House of Representatives and served from 1833 to 1835. In 1839, he again was an unsuccessful congressional candidate. Murphy died on September 21, 1841, and was buried on his plantation near Gosport, Alabama. Bibliography: Thomas W. Owen, *History of Alabama and Dictionary of Alabama Biography*, 4 vols. (Chicago, 1921); Thomas P. Abernathy, *The Formative Period in Alabama, 1815-28*, (Montgomery, 1922); Albert B. Moore, *History of Alabama and Her People*, 3 vols. (New York, 1927); Roy Glashan, *American Governors and Gubernatorial Elections, 1775-1975* (Stillwater, Minnesota, 1975).

MOORE, Gabriel, 1829-1831

Born about 1785, in Surray (present-day Stokes) County, North Carolina, son of Matthew and Letitia (Dalton) Moore. Married to Mary P. Callier, but was soon divorced. Moore was graduated from the University of North Carolina in 1810; studied law. Admitted to the North Carolina Bar in 1810. Moved to Huntsville, Mississippi Territory, and began law practice in 1810. Represented Madison County, Mississippi, in the Mississippi Territorial Legislature; however, in 1817 this county was separated from the Mississippi Territory and added to the Alabama Territory. Member, Alabama Territory House of Representatives, 1817; Speaker, Alabama Territory House of Representatives, 1817; member, Alabama Constitutional Convention, 1819; member, Alabama Senate, 1819-1820; President, Alabama Senate, 1820; member, United States House of Representatives, 1821-1829. As a Jackson Democrat, Moore was elected Governor of Alabama by popular vote in the August 3, 1829 general election. Without an opponent, Moore received 10,956 votes, and was sworn into office on November 25, 1829. During Moore's administration, a constitutional amendment was adopted, which placed a six year term on the justices of the Alabama Supreme Court; the Treaty of Dancing Rabbit Creek, ceding Choctaw land in Alabama, was signed; and work on the state's first railroad was begun between Tuscumbia and Decatur. While governor, Moore advocated the graduated sale of public lands, disapproved of the nullification movement in South Carolina, and opposed the establishment of the Bank of the United States. In addition, he took an active interest in the construction of the canal at Muscle Shoals, urged a revision of the penal code, and worked for the establishment of a state penitentiary. Moore resigned from the governorship, after being elected to the United States Senate, and was succeeded as chief executive by the President of the Alabama Senate on March 3, 1831. He served in the United States Senate from 1831 to 1837, and was an unsuccessful candidate for the United States House of Representatives in 1836. Afterward, in 1843, he moved to Caddo, Texas. Moore died in Caddo on June 9, 1845. Bibliography: Thomas M. Owen, *History of Alabama and Dictionary of Alabama Biography*, 4 vols. (Chicago, 1921); Albert B. Moore, *History of Alabama and Her People*, 3 vols. (New York, 1927); Albert B. Moore, *History of Alabama* (University, Alabama, 1934); Roy Glashan, *American Governors and Gubernatorial Elections, 1775-1975* (Stillwater, Minnesota, 1975).

MOORE, Samuel B., 1831

Born in 1789, in Davidson County, North Carolina (present-day Franklin County), Tennessee. Son of Matthew and Letitia (Dalton) Moore. Brother of Gabriel. Moore was not married, and received a limited education. He was a planter in Jackson County, Alabama. In 1823, Moore was elected to the Alabama House of Representatives from Jackson County; in 1828, he was elected to the Alabama Senate and served until 1831; President, Alabama Senate, 1828-1831. He was a Democrat. On March 3, 1831, Governor Gabriel Moore resigned to enter the United States Senate, and according to the Alabama Constitution of 1819, Samuel Moore, as President of the State Senate, succeeded to the governor's office. During his administration, the University of Alabama opened, and the first railroad in the state was begun. Moore was an unsuccessful gubernatorial candidate in the August 1, 1831 general election. He polled only 12.2 percent of the votes cast, and received 3,354 votes, compared to the National Republican candidate Nicholas Davis' 8,923, and the winner, another Democrat, John Gayle's 15,309. Defeated in his bid for election in his own right as Governor, Samuel Moore completed the term of resigned Governor Gabriel Moore, and then left office on November 26, 1831. Afterward, Samuel Moore was elected from Pickens County, Alabama to the State Senate, and served from 1834 to 1838. In 1835, he was once again elected President of the Alabama Senate, and later served as Judge of the Pickens County Court from 1835 to 1841. Moore died on November 7, 1846, and was buried in an unmarked grave near Carrollton, Alabama. Bibliography: Albert B. Moore, *History of Alabama and Her People*, 3 vols. (New York, 1927); Albert B. Moore, *History of Alabama* (University, Alabama, 1934); Congressional Quarterly, Inc., *Guide to U.S. Elections* (Washington, 1975); Roy Glashan, *American Governors and Gubernatorial Elections, 1775-1975* (Stillwater, Minnesota, 1975).

GAYLE, John, 1831-1835

Born on September 11, 1792 in Sumter County, South Carolina, son of Matthew, a businessman and planter, and Mary (Reese) Gayle; a Presbyterian. Brother of Billups, Pamela Cunningham, Levin, Matilda, Lucinda, and Maria; married to Sarah Ann Haynsworth on November 14, 1819; married a second time to Clarissa Stedman on November 1, 1830; father of Matthew, Sarah Ann, Amelia Ross, Mary Reese, Richard Haynsworth, Anna Maria, Frederick, Helen, John Marshall, and Edmond Dargan. Educated at Newberry Academy; graduated from South Carolina College in 1813. Moved to Alabama Territory. Studied law, and was admitted to the Alabama Bar in 1818. Began private law practice in Mobile, Alabama. Elected a member of the Alabama Territorial Council, 1817; elected Solicitor of the First Alabama Judicial District, 1819; member, Alabama House of Representatives, 1822-1823; became Judge, Third Circuit Court, 1823; appointed a member of the Alabama Supreme Court in 1828, but resigned the position in 1829; member, Alabama House of Representatives, 1829-1831; Speaker, Alabama House of Representatives. A Democrat, Gayle was elected Governor of Alabama on August 1, 1831 in the general election, receiving 15,309 votes to National Republican candidate Nicholas Davis' 8,923, and Samuel B. Moore's 3,354. He was sworn into office on November 26, 1831. During his administration, the majority of Creek Indians in Alabama were removed to the West; the first railroad in the state was constructed between Tuscumbia and Decatur; and the first cotton factory was incorporated by the State Legislature. The question of the removal of the Creeks resulted in a clash between state and federal authorities, as federal officials attempted to enforce the provisions of the removal treaties. Gayle was reelected to a second term on August 5, 1833. Without an opponent, he received 9,750 votes. Ineligible under the 1819 Alabama Constitution to serve as governor for more than four years in a six year period, Gayle left office on November 21, 1835. Afterward, he served as Presidential Elector, 1836 and 1840; member, United States House of Representatives, 1847-1849; and United States District Judge for Alabama, 1849-1859. Gayle died on July 28, 1859, and was buried in Magnolia Cemetery, Mobile. Bibliography: Thomas M. Owen, *History of Alabama and Dictionary of Alabama Biography*, 4 vols. (Chicago, 1921); Albert B. Moore, *History of Alabama and Her*

People, 3 vols. (New York, 1927); Albert B. Moore, *History of Alabama* (University, Alabama, 1934); Roy Glashan, *American Governors and Gubernatorial Elections, 1775-1975* (Stillwater, Minnesota, 1975).

CLAY, Clement Comer, 1835-1837

Born on December 17, 1789, in Halifax County, Virginia, son of William, a planter, and Rebecca (Comer) Clay. Married to Susanna Claiborne Withers in 1815, and father of Clement Claiborne, John Withers, and Hugh Lawson. Educated in public schools; was graduated from East Tennessee College in 1807; studied law under Hugh Lawson White in Knoxville, Tennessee. Admitted to the bar in December, 1809. At the beginning of the Creek Indian War in 1813, he volunteered in the Madison County, Alabama Battalion as a private; promoted to Adjutant; served on the frontier south of the Tennessee River. His parents moved to Tennessee when he was a child; he moved to Alabama in 1811; began a private law practice in Huntsville, Alabama. Member, Alabama Territorial Council, 1817-1819; member, Alabama Constitutional Convention, 1819; Chief Justice of the Alabama Supreme Court, 1820-1823; resigned the position to return to his private law practice; member, Alabama House of Representatives, 1827-1828; Speaker, Alabama House of Representatives; member, United States House of Representatives, 1829-1835. Author: *Digest of the Laws of Alabama* (1843). As a Democrat, Clay was elected Governor of Alabama on August 3, 1835 in the general election, receiving 25,491 votes to the State's Rights Whig candidate Enoch Parsons' 13,760. He was sworn into office on November 21, 1835. During his administration, the Creek Indians became hostile, and Clay, as Commander-in-Chief of the Alabama Militia, ordered the troops into the field and took personal command. Also while Clay was governor, the Cherokee Indians signed the Treaty of New Echota; the legislature abolished direct taxation; and the Alabama State Bank was charged with all governmental expenses. Near the end of this term, he was faced with an economic crisis resulting from the Panic of 1837. On July 17, 1837, Clay resigned from the governorship after being elected to the United States Senate. He served in the United States Senate from 1837 until his resignation in 1841. Clay was appointed to compile a digest of the laws of Alabama in 1842 and 1843, and served as an Associate Judge of the Alabama Supreme Court in 1843. Afterward, he resumed his law practice in partnership with two of his sons. He favored the secession movement in Alabama, and during the Civil War he was placed under military arrest by Federal Army troops. Clay died on September 9, 1866, and was buried in Maple Hill Cemetery in Huntsville. Bibliography: Thomas M. Owen, *History of Alabama and Dictionary of Alabama Biography*, 4 vols. (Chicago, 1921); Albert B. Moore, *History of Alabama and Her People*, 3 vols. (New York, 1927); Albert B. Moore, *History of Alabama* (University, Alabama, 1934); Roy Glashan, *American Governors and Gubernatorial Elections, 1775-1975* (Stillwater, Minnesota, 1975).

McVAY, Hugh, 1837

Born in 1788 in South Carolina, son of Hugh, a soldier in the Revolutionary Army and a farmer; Methodist Episcopalian. Brother of Zadoc; married to Mary Hawks from South Carolina, and father of five children. He received a limited education.

Moved to what was later Madison County, Alabama, in 1807; became a planter. Represented the region in the Mississippi Territorial Legislature, 1811-1818; member, Alabama Constitutional Convention, 1819; member, Alabama House of Representatives, 1820-1825; member, Alabama Senate, 1825-1844; elected President of the Alabama Senate, 1836. He was a Democrat. On July 17, 1837, Governor of Alabama Clement C. Clay resigned to take a seat in the United States Senate, and according to the 1819 Alabama Constitution, McVay, as President of the Senate, succeeded to the governor's office. Completing Clay's term, McVay left office after only about five months on November 21, 1837. Afterward, he returned to the Alabama Senate, where he served until 1844. McVay died in Lauderdale County, Alabama, on May 9, 1851. Bibliography: Thomas M. Owen, *History of Alabama and Dictionary of Alabama Biography*, 4 vols. (Chicago, 1921); Albert B. Moore, *History of Alabama and Her People*, 3 vols. (New York, 1927); Albert B. Moore, *History of Alabama* (University, Alabama, 1934); Roy Glashan, *American Governors and Gubernatorial Elections, 1775-1975* (Stillwater, Minnesota, 1975).

BAGBY, Arthur Pendleton, 1837-1841

Born in 1794 in Louisa County, Virginia, son of James and Mary (Jones) Bagby; a Baptist. Married to Emily N. Steele; married a second time to Anne Elizabeth Connell in 1828; father of Mary, Adelaide, Arthur Pendleton, Virginia, Anna, Alabama, Simon Connell, John Hampden, and Ellen. Was well educated in Virginia; moved to Alabama in 1818; studied law; admitted to the Alabama Bar. Began private law practice in Tuscaloosa, Alabama in 1819. Member, Alabama House of Representatives, 1821-1822, 1824, and 1834-1836; Speaker, Alabama House of Representatives, 1822 and 1836; member, Alabama Senate, 1825. As a Democrat, Bagby was elected Governor of Alabama on August 7, 1837 in the general election, receiving 23,902 votes to the anti-Martin Van Buren Democratic candidate Samuel W. Oliver's 20,605. He was sworn into office on November 21, 1837. While Bagby was governor, Alabama's economy suffered under the Panic of 1837, and he was faced with great financial distress and a disastrous drought. During his administration, the Cherokees were removed from the state to new homes in the West; the Chancery Court system was reorganized, and imprisonment for debt was abolished. In addition, Judson College was opened; and the Choctaws ceded to Alabama all their land east of Mississippi. Bagby was reelected to a second term on August 5, 1839, defeating Whig candidate Arthur F. Hopkins, receiving 22,681 votes to Hopkins' 2,532. Ineligible, under the 1819 Alabama Constitution, to serve as governor for more than four years in a six year period, Bagby left office on November 22, 1841. Afterward, he was appointed to the United States Senate, and served from 1841 until he resigned from the office in 1846 to accept the position as United States Minister to Russia, a post he held until 1849. Returning to Alabama, he served as a member of the Commission to Codify the Laws of Alabama. He later moved to Mobile, Alabama. Bagby died on September 21, 1858, and was buried in Magnolia Cemetery in Mobile. Bibliography: Thomas M. Owen, *History of Alabama and Dictionary of Alabama Biography*, 4 vols. (Chicago, 1921); Albert B. Moore, *History of Alabama and Her People*, 3 vols. (New York, 1927); Albert B. Moore, *History of Alabama* (University, Alabama, 1934); Roy Glashan, *American Governors and Gubernatorial Elections, 1775-1975* (Stillwater, Minnesota, 1975).

FITZPATRICK, Benjamin, 1841-1845

Born on June 30, 1802 in Green County, Georgia, son of William, a member of the Georgia Legislature for nineteen years, and Anne (Phillips) Fitzpatrick. Brother of Joseph, Phillips, and a sister; married to Sarah Terry Elmore on July 19, 1827; married a second time to Aurelia Rachel Blassingame on November 29, 1846; father of Elmore Joseph, Phillips, Morris Martin, James Madison, Thomas Sumpter, John Archer, Aurelia, and Benjamin. Fitzpatrick was left an orphan when he was seven years old, and was taken to Alabama in 1815 by a brother. He received a limited education in the public schools; studied law. Admitted to the Alabama Bar in 1821. Managed the land belonging to his brothers along the Alabama River, north of Montgomery, Alabama; trading house clerk; plantation owner in Autauga County, Alabama; partner with Henry Goldthwaite in private law firm. Deputy Sheriff, Autauga County; Solicitor, Montgomery Circuit, 1819-1823. As a Democrat, Fitzpatrick was nominated for Governor by a caucus of the Democratic members of the State Legislature. On August 2, 1841 he was elected Governor in the general election, receiving 38,808 votes to the Independent Whig candidate James W. McClung's 22,777. Fitzpatrick was sworn into office on November 22, 1841. During his administration, Howard College was chartered, and state taxation was restored by the Legislature. However, the most important event of Fitzpatrick's term was the failure of the Alabama State Bank in 1843. The state became liable for the indebtedness of the bank, and for a time was on the brink of financial ruin. A commission was appointed to adjust the affairs of the bank, and the situation was alleviated. Fitzpatrick was reelected to a second term on August 7, 1843 without opposition. Ineligible, under the 1819 Alabama Constitution to serve as governor for more than four years in a six year period, Fitzpatrick left office on December 10, 1845. Afterward, he served in the United States Senate from 1848 to 1849 and from 1853 to 1861. He was chosen President Pro Tempore of the United States Senate from 1857 to 1860. Fitzpatrick was nominated for Vice President by the Democratic National Convention in 1860; however, he declined. He resigned from the United States Senate when Alabama seceded in 1861, and was President of the Alabama Constitutional Convention of 1865. Fitzpatrick died on November 25, 1869, and was buried in Oakwood Cemetery in Montgomery. Bibliography: Thomas M. Owen, *History of Alabama and Dictionary of Alabama Biography*, 4 vols. (Chicago, 1921); Albert B. Moore, *History of Alabama and Her People*, 3 vols. (New York, 1927); Albert B. Moore, *History of Alabama* (University, Alabama, 1934); Roy Glashan, *American Governors and Gubernatorial Elections, 1775-1975* (Stillwater, Minnesota, 1975).

MARTIN, Joshua Lanier, 1845-1847

Born on December 12, 1799 in Blount County, Tennessee, son of Warner, a farmer, and Martha (Bailey) Martin. Brother of William B. and Peter; married to Mary Gillam Mason; married a second time to Sarah Ann Mason; father of John M., Peter, Charles James, two other sons, and two daughters. Attended country schools, and studied under the Reverend Isaac Anderson of Maryville, Tennessee and the Reverend Gideon Blackburn. Moved to Alabama in 1819, and continued to study law with his brother in Russellville, Alabama. Admitted to the Alabama Bar, and began private law practice in Athens, Alabama. Member, Alabama House of

Representatives, 1822-1828, with the exception of one year; Solicitor, Fourth Judicial Circuit, 1829-1834; Judge of the Circuit Court, 1834; member, United States House of Representatives, 1835-1839; elected Chancellor, Middle Chancery Division, 1841. As an Independent, Martin was elected Governor of Alabama on August 4, 1845 in the general election, receiving 29,261 votes to Democrat Nathaniel Terry's 25,472. He was sworn into office on December 10, 1845. In 1843, the State Bank had failed, and during Martin's administration, the affairs of the bank had to be settled; a system of public finance had to be adopted, and measures taken to provide a sound currency. Liquidation of the bank started in February, 1846. Also while Martin was governor, the state capital was moved from Tuscaloosa to Montgomery; the Medical Association of Alabama was founded; and the war between the United States and Mexico broke out. Martin's political appeal was the result of the problems incurred with the State Bank of Alabama and its failure. In 1847, the major political parties regained control of state politics, and Martin left office on December 16, 1847. Afterward, he resumed his law practice in Tuscaloosa, and served in the Alabama House of Representatives for one additional term in 1853. Martin died on November 2, 1856, and was buried in Evergreen Cemetery in Tuscaloosa. Bibliography: Thomas M. Owen, *History of Alabama and Dictionary of Alabama Biography*, 4 vols. (Chicago, 1921); Albert B. Moore, *History of Alabama and Her People*, 3 vols. (New York, 1927); Albert B. Moore, *History of Alabama* (University, Alabama, 1934); Roy Glashan, *American Governors and Gubernatorial Elections, 1775-1975* (Stillwater, Minnesota, 1975).

CHAPMAN, Reuben, 1847-1849

Born on July 15, 1799 in Bowling Green, Virginia, son of Colonel Reuben, a Revolutionary War veteran, and Ann (Reynolds) Chapman; a Protestant Episcopal. Brother of Samuel; married to Felicia Steptoe Picket on October 17, 1838, and father of Stephen P., Reuben, Juliet, Felicia Corbin, Ellelee, and Alberta Picket. Attended high school in Bowling Green. Moved to Alabama in 1824; studied law with his brother. Admitted to the Alabama Bar in 1825. Began private law practice in Sommerville, Alabama; later moved to Huntsville, Alabama. Member, Alabama Senate, 1832-1835; member, United States House of Representatives, 1835-1847. After being nominated by the Democratic State Convention in May, 1847, Chapman was elected Governor on August 2, 1847 in the general election, receiving 35,880 votes to Whig candidate Nicholas Davis' 28,565. He was sworn into office on December 16, 1847. During his administration, the main issue in the state was the Wilmot Proviso, which prohibited slavery from all territory purchased from Mexico at the end of the Mexican War. Even though the Proviso was defeated in the United States Congress, it caused a considerable amount of concern in Alabama. At a Democratic State Convention, which convened in Montgomery, Alabama in February, 1848, the "Alabama Platform" was adopted. The platform demanded that slavery in the territories be protected by the United States Congress, and that no one who did not share this view should be nominated by the Democratic Party for the presidency. Also while Chapman was governor, the popular election of judges was adopted and the State Capitol burned. Chapman was not renominated by the Democrats for the 1849 gubernatorial election, and he left office on December 17, 1849. Afterward, he retired to his estate and resumed his law practice. Chapman was a member of the Alabama House of Representatives in 1855; a delegate to the Democratic National Convention in 1856, 1860, and 1868;

and the Confederate States' representative to France from 1862 to 1865. Chapman died on May 16, 1882, and was buried in Maple Hill Cemetery in Huntsville. Bibliography: Thomas M. Owen, *History of Alabama and Dictionary of Alabama Biography*, 4 vols. (Chicago, 1921); Albert B. Moore, *History of Alabama and Her People*, 3 vols. (New York, 1927); Albert B. Moore, *History of Alabama* (University, Alabama, 1934); Roy Glashan, *American Governors and Gubernatorial Elections, 1775-1975* (Stillwater, Minnesota, 1975).

COLLIER, Henry Watkins, 1849-1853

Born on January 1, 1801 in Lynchburg County, Virginia, son of James, a planter, and Elizabeth (Bouldin) Collier; Methodist Episcopal. Brother of Bouldin, Wyatt, Martha, James Bouldin, Eliza Wyatt, William Edward, Thomas Bouldin, and Charles Ephriam; married to Mary Ann Battle on April 25, 1826, and father of Mary W., Evelyn H., and James W. Educated at Moses Waddell's Academy, Willington, South Carolina. General, South Carolina Militia. Moved with his parents to Alabama Territory in 1818. Studied law in Nashville, Tennessee; admitted to the Alabama Bar, 1822. Began private law practice in Huntsville, Alabama; moved to Tuscaloosa, Alabama, in 1823; partner with Sion L. Perry in a law firm. Elected to the Alabama Legislature, 1827; Judge, Supreme Bench, 1828-1832; Judge Circuit Bench, 1832-1836; Justice, Alabama Supreme Court, 1836-1837; Chief Justice, Alabama Supreme Court, 1837-1849. President, Alabama Historical Society. Collier was nominated in the Alabama Democratic primary and was elected on August 8, 1849 in the general election. Without an opponent, he received 37,221 votes, and was sworn into office on December 17, 1849. Three days before Collier assumed office, the State Capitol at Montgomery was burned; it was rebuilt during his term. Also while Collier was governor, the Alabama Historical Society was formed, and the Alabama Hospital for the Insane at Tuscaloosa was authorized. The most important issue of Collier's administration was the Compromise of 1850, which became a major topic in the 1851 election. That same year the Southern Rights Party held its convention in Montgomery. Collier was reelected to a second term on August 4, 1851, defeating Whig candidate James Shields, 38,517 votes to 5,760. Ineligible, under the 1819 Alabama Constitution, to serve as governor for more than four years in a six year period, Collier left office on December 20, 1853. Afterward, he declined the offer of a seat in the United States Senate, and retired to private life. Collier died on August 28, 1855, at Bailey's Springs, Alabama. Bibliography: Thomas M. Owen, *History of Alabama and Dictionary of Alabama Biography*, 4 vols. (Chicago, 1921); Albert B. Moore, *History of Alabama and Her People*, 3 vols. (New York, 1927); Albert B. Moore, *History of Alabama* (University, Alabama, 1934); Roy Glashan, *American Governors and Gubernatorial Elections, 1775-1975* (Stillwater, Minnesota, 1975).

WINSTON, John Anthony, 1853-1857

Born on September 4, 1812 in the Mississippi Territory (present-day Madison County, Alabama), son of William, a planter, and Mary Bacon (Cooper) Winston. Married to Mary Angus Walker in 1832; married a second time to Mary W.

Logwood in 1842; father of Mary Angus. Educated in common schools; attended LaGrange College; attended Cumberland College, Nashville, Tennessee. Organized a company for service in the Mexican War, but did not see active service; at the beginning of the Civil War, he joined the Confederate States Army; appointed Colonel, Eighth Alabama Infantry; forced to resign his commission because of illness. Became a planter in Sumter County, Alabama, in 1835; member of John A. Winston and Company, Cotton Commission House, 1844-1871. Elected to the Alabama House of Representatives in 1840 and 1842; member, Alabama Senate, 1843-1853; President, Alabama Senate, 1843-1849; delegate, Democratic National Convention held in Baltimore, Maryland, 1848; delegate, Nashville, Tennessee, Convention, 1849; Presidential Elector, 1852. As a Democrat, Winston was elected Governor of Alabama on August 1, 1853 in the general election, receiving 30,862 votes to Whig W. Earnest's 9,499 and Union Democrat A. Nick's 7,096. The first native born Alabama governor, Winston was sworn into office on December 20, 1853. During his adminsitration, the Louisville and Nashville Railroad was chartered; a public school system was established; and the Alabama Educational Association was organized. Also while Winston was governor, the Kansas-Nebraska Act, which repealed the limitations on the expansion of slavery as provided in the Missouri Compromise, was passed by the United States Congress; and the Republican Party was organized. On August 6, 1855, Winston was reelected to a second term, defeating the American Party candidate, George D. Shortridge, 43,936 votes to 31,864. Constitutionally prohibited from being governor for more than four years in a six year period, Winston left office on December 1, 1857. Afterward, he remained active in politics. Winston was a delegate to the Charleston, South Carolina Convention in 1860; on the ticket as a Presidential Elector for Stephen A. Douglas in 1860; Alabama Commissioner to Louisiana in 1861; member, of the 1865 Alabama Constitutional Convention; and was elected to the United States Senate in 1867, but was not allowed to take his seat. Winston died in Mobile, Alabama on December 21, 1871. Bibliography: Thomas M. Owen, *History of Alabama and Dictionary of Alabama Biography*, 4 vols. (Chicago, 1921); Albert B. Moore, *History of Alabama and Her People*, 3 vols. (New York, 1927); Albert B. Moore, *History of Alabama* (University, Alabama, 1934); Roy Glashan, *American Governors and Gubernatorial Elections, 1775-1975* (Stillwater, Minnesota, 1975).

MOORE, Andrew Barry, 1857-1861

Born on March 7, 1807 in Spartanburg County, South Carolina, son of Charles, a planter, and Jane (Barry) Moore; a Presbyterian. Married to Mary Gorree in 1837, and father of two daughters and one son. Moore was considered well educated for the time; studied law in the office of Elisha Young and Sidney W. Goode. Admitted to the Alabama Bar in 1833. Moore came to Perry County, Alabama in 1826, and was induced to become a school teacher there. Justice of the Peace for eight years; member, Alabama House of Representatives, 1839 and 1842-1845; Speaker, Alabama House of Representatives, 1843-1845; on the ticket as a Whig Presidential Elector in 1848; Judge of the Alabama Circuit Court, 1851-1857. As a Democrat, Moore was elected Governor of Alabama on August 3, 1857 in the general election. Having no opponent, he received 41,871 votes, and was sworn into office on December 1, 1857. During his administration, the Alabama Institute for Deaf, Dumb, and Blind was opened and the Medical College of Alabama was founded in Mobile, Alabama. The sectional controversy was reaching a climax while Moore was governor. On August 1, 1859, he was reelected to a second term, defeating the Southern Rights Democrat candidate, William F. Samford, 47,293 votes to 18,070. Moore called for a State Convention to discuss the question of secession, scheduled to convene on January 7, 1861, and elections were held for delegates to the meeting on December 24, 1860. Moore ordered Alabama troops to seize the Federal Army forts and other military installations within the state. On January 11, 1861, the Secession Convention adopted the Ordinance of Secession, and in February, the Provisional Congress of the Confederate States convened in Montgomery, Alabama. Also while Moore was governor, the legislature appropriated $500,000 for defense, and authorized an indebtedness of $3,000,000 for war. Constitutionally prohibited from being governor for more than four years in a six year period, Moore left office on December 2, 1861. Afterward, he served as a special aide-de-camp to Governor John G. Shorter. In 1865, Moore was imprisoned by Federal officials, but was soon released because of his poor health. He resumed his law practice in Marion, Alabama. Moore died in Marion on April 5, 1873. Bibliography: Thomas M. Owen, *History of Alabama and Dictionary of Alabama Biography*, 4 vols. (Chicago, 1921); Albert B. Moore, *History of Alabama and Her People*, 3 vols. (New York, 1927); Clarence P. Denman, *The Secession Movement in Alabama* (Montgomery, 1933); Albert B. Moore, *History of Alabama* (University, Alabama, 1934).

SHORTER, John Gill, 1861-1863

Born on April 23, 1818 in Monticello, Georgia, son of Reuben Clarke, a physician, and Mary Butler (Gill) Shorter; a Baptist. Brother of Eli Sims, Reuben C., Henry Russell, Emily, Sarah, Martha, Mary, Sophia, and William; married to Mary Jane Battle in 1843, and father of Mary Jane. Shorter graduated from Franklin College, Athens, Georgia in 1837; studied law. Admitted to Alabama Bar, 1838. Moved to Eufaula, Alabama, in 1837; began private law practice in Eufaula, 1838. Appointed Solicitor, Eufaula Judicial District, 1842; member, Alabama Senate, 1845; member, Alabama House of Representatives, 1851; appointed, and later elected, Alabama Circuit Court Judge, 1852-1861; appointed Alabama Commissioner to the Georgia Secession Convention, 1861; member, Provisional Congress of the Confederacy, 1861. As a Democrat, Shorter was elected Governor of Alabama by popular vote in the general election on August 5, 1861, defeating the Whig candidate, Thomas H. Watts, 38,221 votes to 28,117. Shorter was sworn into office on December 2, 1861. An ardent secessionist, Shorter was a staunch supporter of the Confederacy. Much of his administration was spent in efforts to provide aid to the families of Confederate soldiers, and to adequately fortify Mobile, Alabama. In 1863, Federal troops invaded Alabama, and the resulting battles produced much suffering and hardship for the citizens of the state. Much of the blame for the military reversals was placed on Shorter, and he was defeated in his bid for reelection on August 3, 1863. Shorter left office on December 1, 1863, and returned to his law practice in Eufaula. At the end of the Civil War, he was arrested and imprisoned by Federal authorities. After being released he returned to Eufaula. Shorter died on May 29, 1872, and was buried in Eufaula. Bibliography: Walter L. Fleming, *Civil War and Reconstruction in Alabama* (New York, 1905); Thomas M. Owen, *History of Alabama and Dictionary of Alabama Biography*, 4 vols. (Chicago, 1921); Albert B. Moore, *History of Alabama and Her People*, 3 vols. (New York, 1927); Clarence P. Denman, *The Secession Movement in Alabama* (Montgomery, 1933).

WATTS, Thomas Hill, 1863-1865

Born on January 1, 1819 near Greenville, Alabama Territory, son of John Hughes, a planter, and Prudence (Hill) Watts; a Baptist. Married to Elize B. Allen on January 1, 1842; married a second time to Mrs. Ellen (Noyes) Jackson in September, 1875; father of John Wade, Thomas Henry, Florence, Catherine, Alice, and Minnie Garrett. Educated in the public schools of Butler County, Alabama; attended Airy Mount Academy, Dallas County, Alabama; graduated with honors from the University of Virginia in 1840. Admitted to the Alabama Bar, 1841. At the outbreak of the Civil War, he organized the Seventeenth Alabama Infantry, 1861. Took an active role in the 1840 presidential campaign in Alabama; began private law practice, Greenville, Alabama, 1841. Member, Alabama House of Representatives, 1842, 1844-1845, and 1849; Presidential Elector, 1848; member, Alabama Senate, 1853-1856; unsuccessful congressional candidate, 1856; member, Alabama Secession Convention, 1861; unsuccessful gubernatorial candidate, 1861. As a Whig, Watts was elected Governor of Alabama by popular vote in the general election on August 3, 1863, defeating incumbent Governor John G. Shorter, 28,201 votes to 9,664. Watts was sworn into office on December 1, 1863. When Watts became governor, Alabama and the remainder of the Confederacy were slowly crumbling under the superior power of the Union. As military prospects for a victory dimmed, discontent toward the authority of the Confederate States began to spread. While Watts was governor, the state militia clashed with conscription officers of the Confederacy, and a meeting of Confederate governors was held to protest the Southern government's restriction on trade. As a result, Watts spent much of his administration calling on the citizens of Alabama to renew their efforts against the invading Federals. With the end of the Civil War in April, 1865, Watts was removed from office. Afterward, he was arrested by Federal authorities and imprisoned. After being released, he opened a law office in Montgomery. In 1880-1881, he represented Montgomery County in the Alabama House of Representatives, and from 1889 to 1890, he served as President of the Alabama Bar Association. Watts died in Montgomery, on September 16, 1892. Bibliography: Walter L. Fleming, *Civil War and Reconstruction in Alabama* (New York, 1905); Thomas M. Owen, *History of Alabama and Dictionary of Alabama Biography*, 4 vols. (Chicago, 1921); Albert B. Moore, *History of Alabama and Her People*, 3 vols. (New York, 1927); Albert B. Moore, *History of Alabama* (University, Alabama, 1934).

PARSONS, Lewis E., 1865

Born on April 28, 1817 in Lisle, New York, son of Erastus Bellamy, a farmer, and Jennett (Hepburn) Parsons; a Presbyterian. Married to Jane Ann Boyd McCullough on September 16, 1841, and father of George Wake, Jennett Hepburn, Lewis Eliphalet, Erastus Jonathon, Celia, Joseph Hepburn, and Jessamine Kentucky. Educated in public schools; studied law in the office of Frederick Tallmadge in New York and G. W. Woodward in Pennsylvania. Moved to Talladega, Alabama, in 1840; law partner with Alexander White. Presidential Elector, 1856; member, Alabama House of Representatives, 1859 and 1865. Mason. Whig; Democrat; Republican. President Andrew Johnson appointed Parsons Provisional Governor of Alabama on June 21, 1865. Parsons appointed a staff of department heads, and began organization of a civil government under President Johnson's concept of

Reconstruction. The laws of 1861, except those pertaining to slavery, were declared valid, and the courts were called upon to help end lawlessness. However, Parsons could find few officials who could qualify for positions in the new government because of the "Iron Clad Oath." In September, 1865, a Constitutional Convention was called to organize a permanent government. Slavery was abolished, and elections were scheduled. On November 6, 1865, Robert M. Patton was elected Governor, and when he was inaugurated on December 20, 1865, Parsons left office. Afterward, Parsons was elected to the United States Senate, but was refused his seat by the Radical Republicans. In addition, he served as United States District Attorney for Northern Alabama. Parsons died on June 8, 1895, and was buried at Talladega. Bibliography: Walter L. Fleming, *Civil War and Reconstruction in Alabama* (New York, 1905); Thomas M. Owen, *History of Alabama and Dictionary of Alabama Biography*, 4 vols. (Chicago, 1921); Albert B. Moore, *History of Alabama and Her People*, 3 vols. (New York, 1927); Albert B. Moore, *History of Alabama* (University, Alabama, 1934).

PATTON, Robert Miller, 1865-1868

Born on July 10, 1809 in Russell County, Virginia, son of William, a planter and merchant, and Martha Lee (Hayes) Patton; a Presbyterian. Brother of Eliza; married to Jane Locke on January 31, 1832, and father of John Brahan, William Anderson, Mary J., Mattie H., Robert Weakley, John Simpson, Charles Hayes, Thomas, and Andrew Beirne. In 1818, Patton and his parents moved to Huntsville, Alabama. Attended Green Academy, Huntsville; business education in a commercial house. Moved to Florence, Alabama, in 1829; engaged in the mercantile business; planter. Elected to the Alabama House of Representatives, 1832; member, Special Alabama Legislature, 1837; almost continuously a member of the Alabama Legislature from 1837 to 1861; President, Alabama Senate; member, 1860 Charleston, South Carolina Convention; member, Alabama Secession Convention, 1860; member, Alabama Constitutional Convention, 1865. Trustee, University of Alabama; Trustee, Alabama Normal College. As a Whig, Patton was elected Governor of Alabama on November 6, 1865 in a special non-partisan election, receiving 20,611 votes to Democrat Michael J. Bulger's 16,380 and Union Party candidate William R. Smith's 8,557. He was sworn into office on December 20, 1865. Patton later joined the Republican Party. During his administration, the legislature ratified the Thirteenth Amendment to the United States Constitution, and it was generally assumed that by complying with President Andrew Johnson's Reconstruction Plan, the state would resume its place in the Union. However, the Radical Republicans in the United States Congress refused to ratify the Fourteenth delegation. In December, 1866, the legislature refused to ratify the Fourteenth Amendment to the United States Constitution, and in March, 1867, Alabama was placed under military rule. While Patton was governor, he issued $500,000 worth of state notes to pay the expenses of government. Though the Alabama Constitution of 1867 was rejected by the citizens of the state, the United States Congress passed an act on June 25, 1868, declaring that the Constitution had been adopted, and that as soon as the Fourteenth Amendment to the United States Constitution was ratified by the legislature, Alabama would once again be entitled to representation in Congress and to establish a new state government. On July 13, 1868, the legislature ratified the Fourteenth Amendment, and on July 14, Patton left office as the provisional government came to an end. Afterward, Patton engaged in railroad construction, and was active in rebuilding the University of Alabama, which had been destroyed during the Civil War. Patton died on February 28, 1885, and was buried in Huntsville. Bibliography: Walter L. Fleming, *The Civil War and Reconstruction in Alabama* (New York, 1905); Thomas M. Owen, *History of Alabama and Dictionary of Alabama Biography*, 4 vols. (Chicago, 1921); Albert B. Moore, *History of Alabama and Her People*, 3 vols. (New York, 1927); Albert B. Moore, *History of Alabama* (University, Alabama, 1934).

SMITH, William H., 1868-1870

Born on April 26, 1826 in Fayette County, Georgia, son of Jeptha Vinnen, a planter, and Nancy (Dickson) Smith. Brother of David, Robert T., Charles A., John, James M., Andrew J., Dallas, and two sisters; married to Lucy Wortham on January 29, 1856, and father of William H. Jr., David Dixon, J. A. Winston, and five daughters. Received an academic education; studied law with John T. Heflin in Wedowee, Alabama. Admitted to the Alabama Bar in 1850. Moved to Randolph, Alabama with his parents in 1839; partner in a private law practice with James Aiken. Member, Alabama House of Representatives, 1855-1859; on the ticket as a Stephen A. Douglas Presidential Elector, 1860; unsuccessful candidate for the Provisional Congress of the Confederate States, 1861. In December, 1862, Smith entered the lines of the Federal forces and remained there until the end of the Civil War. Appointed a Judge of the Circuit Court, 1865; appointed Chief of the Alabama Registration Bureau under the Congressional Reconstruction Acts. As a Republican, Smith was elected Governor of Alabama in a special five day election beginning on February 4, 1868, and held under the provisions of the 1865 Alabama Constitution. Having no opposition, he received 62,067 votes, and was sworn into office on July 14, 1868. During his administration, corruption was rampant among members of the government, and most of the time spent by the legislature was in passing special acts to exempt its members from legal penalites. However, some constructive measures were forthcoming. In 1869, the University of Alabama reopened, and the legislature ratified the Fifteenth Amendment to the United States Constitution. Smith was defeated in an attempt for reelection, and left office on November 26, 1870. Smith died on January 1, 1899, and was buried in Birmingham, Alabama. Bibliography: Walter L. Fleming, *The Civil War and Reconstruction in Alabama* (New York, 1905); Thomas M. Owen, *History of Alabama and Dictionary of Alabama Biography*, 4 vols. (Chicago, 1921); Albert B. Moore, *History of Alabama and Her People,* 3 vols. (New York, 1927); Albert B. Moore, *History of Alabama* (University, Alabama, 1934).

LINDSAY, Robert Burns, 1870-1872

Born on July 4, 1824 in Dumfriesshire, Scotland, son of John and Elizabeth (McKnight) Lindsay; a Presbyterian. Brother of David R.; married to Sarah Miller in 1854, and father of Mamie, Minnie Burns, Mattie I., Maud, and five others. Educated in parochial schools; attended the University of St. Andrews in Scotland. Came to the United States in 1844; placed in charge of a boy's academy in North Carolina; studied law under Robert T. Paine in North Carolina; moved to Tuscumbia, Alabama to teach school in 1849; continued his study of law while in

Alabama. Admitted to the Alabama Bar in 1852. During the Civil War, Lindsay served in Confederate General Philip D. Roddy's cavalry force. Began private law practice, Tuscumbia, 1852; member, Board of Visitors, West Point Military Academy, 1857. Elected to the Alabama House of Representatives, 1853; elected to the Alabama Senate, 1857, 1865, and 1870; Presidential Elector, 1860. Odd Fellow. The 1867 Alabama Constitution contained no prohibition against a foreign born citizen serving as Governor, and, as a Democrat, Lindsay was elected Governor of Alabama by popular vote in the general election on November 8, 1870. Receiving 77,723 votes to Republican incumbent Governor William H. Smith's 76,282, Lindsay was sworn into office on November 26, 1870. Lindsay had opposed secession, but nonetheless had remained loyal to Alabama during the Civil War. After the results of the 1870 election became known, Smith refused to leave office, and attempted to prevent Lindsay's inauguration. For two weeks, there were two governors of the state; however, Smith did not receive the support of Federal troops, and when he was ordered to leave office by a writ from the Montgomery, Alabama, Circuit Court, he did so. During Lindsay's administration, Birmingham, Alabama was granted a charter by the State Legislature, and Alabama Polytechnic Institute was opened. Lindsay refused to seek a second term, and left office on November 17, 1872. Two months after leaving office, Lindsay was stricken with paralysis and remained an invalid. Nevertheless, he returned to his law practice in Tuscumbia, where he died on February 13, 1902. Bibliography: Walter L. Fleming, *Civil War and Reconstruction in Alabama* (New York, 1905); Thomas M. Owen, *History of Alabama and Dictionary of Alabama Biography*, 4 vols. (Chicago, 1921); Albert B. Moore, *History of Alabama and Her People*, 3 vols. (New York, 1927); Albert B. Moore, *History of Alabama* (University, Alabama, 1934).

LEWIS, David Peter, 1872-1874

Born in 1820 in Charlotte County, Virginia, son of Peter C., a farmer, and Mary Smith (Buster) Lewis. He was not married. Moved to Madison County, Alabama, with his parents while he was a child. Received a college education; studied law in Huntsville, Alabama. Admitted to the Alabama Bar. Private law practice in Lawrence County, Alabama. Member, Alabama Secession Convention, 1861; he voted against Alabama leaving the Union, but signed the Secession Ordinance after it was passed; elected to the Provisional Confederate States Congress, but resigned the post; appointed Judge of the Alabama Circuit Court in 1863. After serving as judge for several months, Lewis entered the United States Army lines, and traveled to Nashville, Tennessee, where he remained until the end of the Civil War. In 1865, he returned to Huntsville, and resumed his law practice. As a Republican, Lewis was elected Governor of Alabama on November 5, 1872, in the general election, receiving 89,868 votes to the Liberal Republican candidate Thomas H. Hendon's 81,371. He was sworn into office on November 17, 1872. During his administration, the Democrats regained control of the legislature; however, Lewis refused to recognize it as the lawful representative of the people. Calling in Federal troops, he declared a body of Radical Republicans—the "Courthouse Legislature"—as the true legislative body. Eventually, the United States Attorney General intervened and restored the Democrats to power. Lewis' term as governor was the last so-called "carpetbag and scalawag" administration in Alabama, as the Democrats were returned to the governor's office in 1874. Lewis was defeated in his attempt for reelection in 1874, and left office on November 24, 1874. Afterward, he resumed his law practice in Huntsville. Lewis died on July 3, 1884 in Huntsville. Bibliography: Walter L. Fleming, *The Civil War and Reconstruction in Alabama* (New York, 1905); Thomas M. Owen, *History of Alabama and Dictionary of Alabama Biography*, 4 vols. (Chicago, 1921); Albert B. Moore, *History of Alabama and Her People*, 3 vols. (New York, 1927); Albert B. Moore, *History of Alabama* (University, Alabama, 1934).

HOUSTON, George Smith, 1874-1878

Born on January 17, 1811 in Williamson County, Tennessee, son of David, a farmer, and Hannah Pugh (Reagan) Houston. Married to Mary I. Beatty in 1835; married a second time to Ellen Irvine in April, 1861; father of David, George Smith, Jr., John P., Mary E., Emma, Maggie Lou, and four others. Moved to Lauderdale County, Alabama, with his parents about 1821. Educated in the Academy in Lauderdale County; studied law with Judge George Coalter in Florence, Alabama; completed his studies in Boyle's Law School, Harrodsburg, Kentucky. Admitted to the Alabama Bar in 1831. Elected to the Alabama House of Representatives, 1832; moved to Athens, Alabama, 1835; appointed District Solicitor, Florence Judicial District, 1836; moved to Limestone County, Alabama and began a private law practice, 1836; elected Solicitor, 1837-1841; member, United States House of Representatives, 1841-1849 and 1851-1861; private law practice in partnership with Egbert Jones, 1849-1851; withdrew from the United States Congress in 1861 because of the secession of Alabama; elected to the United States Senate in 1866, but was not allowed to take his seat; delegate, National Union Convention, 1866. As a Democrat, Houston was elected Governor of Alabama on November 3, 1874 in the general election, receiving 107,118 votes to Republican incumbent Governor David P. Lewis' 93,928. He was sworn into office on November 24, 1874. The election of Houston marked the end of "carpetbag-scalawag" rule in Alabama, and during his administration, the public school system was reorganized, and the 1875 Alabama Constitution was ratified. The new constitution abolished the office of Lieutenant Governor, gave all citizens equal civil and political rights, established biennial legislative sessions, and moved state elections from November to August. On August 7, 1876, Houston was reelected to a second term, defeating Republican candidate N. Woodruff, 96,401 votes to 55,682. In August, 1878, Houston was elected to the United States Senate, and as a result left the governor's office on November 28, 1878. He served in the United States Senate until his death. Houston died on December 31, 1879, and was buried in the City Cemetery of Athens. Bibliography: Thomas M. Owen, *History of Alabama and Dictionary of Alabama Biography*, 4 vols. (Chicago, 1921); Albert B. Moore, *History of Alabama and Her People*, 3 vols. (New York, 1927); Albert B. Moore, *History of Alabama* (University, Alabama, 1934); Roy Glashan, *American Governors and Gubernatorial Elections, 1775-1975* (Stillwater, Minnesota, 1975).

COBB, James Edward, 1878-1882

Born on February 25, 1829 in Ashville, Alabama, son of John W., a farmer, merchant, and politician, and Catherine (Stevens) Peak Cobb; a Baptist. Married to Margaret McClung in February, 1850; married a second time to Frances Fell on

December 31, 1866; father of John W. Dora, Edith, and Richard C. Educated at an academy in Ashville; graduated from the University of Tennessee at Knoxville in 1850; studied law with John C. Thomasson. Admitted to the Alabama Bar in 1855. In 1861, at the beginning of the Civil War, he enlisted in the Confederate States Army as the Captain of Company C, Tenth Alabama Infantry; assigned to Confederate General Joseph Wheeler's Cavalry in Tennessee in 1863. Partner with Thomasson in a private law practice in St. Clair County, Alabama; moved to Shelby County, Alabama in 1867, and became a law partner of B. B. Lewis; at the end of the Civil War, he moved to Marion, Alabama and opened a law office; in 1868, Cobb moved to Columbiana, Alabama; in 1873, he moved to Helena, Alabama. President, Central Iron Works, 1873-1891; engaged in cotton planting; attorney for the Louisville and Nashville Railroad; mining developer. Elected to the Alabama Senate, 1872 and 1876. Mason. As a Democrat, Cobb was elected Governor of Alabama on August 5, 1878 in the general election. Having no opposition, he received 88,255 votes and was sworn into office on November 28, 1878. During his administration the State Bar Association was organized; the Alabama Board of Health was established; and the state Board of Dental Examiners was created. Also while Cobb was governor, the cost of state government was reduced approximately $40,000, and at the end of his term, there was a net surplus in the Alabama Treasury of $386,427. In 1881, the Tuskegee Normal and Industrial Institute for Negroes was founded. On August 2, 1880, Cobb was reelected to a second term, defeating the Greenback candidate J. Pickens, 134,905 votes to 42,363. Cobb left office on December 1, 1882. Afterward, he briefly retired from public life, and returned to his business investments. In 1888, he was appointed Probate Judge of Shelby County. Soon after his term as judge expired, he moved to Birmingham, Alabama. Cobb died at Birmingham on November 26, 1913. Bibliography: Thomas M. Owen, *History of Alabama and Dictionary of Alabama Biography*, 4 vols. (Chicago, 1921); Albert B. Moore, *History of Alabama and Her People*, 3 vols. (New York, 1927); Albert B. Moore, *History of Alabama* (University, Alabama, 1934); Roy Glashan, *American Governors and Gubernatorial Elections, 1775-1975* (Stillwater, Minnesota, 1975).

O'NEAL, Edward Asbury, 1882-1886

Born on September 20, 1818, in Madison County, Alabama Territory, son of Edward, a farmer, and Rebecca (Wheat) O'Neal; a Methodist. Brother of Basil; married to Oliva Moore on April 12, 1838, and father of Alfred M., Edward A., Rebecca, Julia, Emmet, Georgia C., and Sydney. Received a B.A. degree from La Grange College, 1836. O'Neal read law with James W. McClung; was admitted to the Alabama Bar in 1840. Began law practice in Florence, Alabama, 1840. Enlisted in the Confederate States Army, 1861; Major, Ninth Alabama Infantry, 1861; promoted to Lieutenant Colonel, October, 1861; Colonel, Twenty-sixth Alabama Infantry, 1862. Solicitor, Fourth Alabama Circuit, 1841-1845; unsuccessful congressional candidate, 1848; secessionist leader in northern Alabama; member, Alabama Constitutional Convention, 1875. As a Democrat, O'Neal was elected Governor of Alabama by popular vote in the general electon on August 7, 1882, receiving 102,607 votes to Republican J. L. Sheffield's 46,742. He was sworn into office on December 1, 1882. During O'Neal's administration, Alabama began to prosper and develop for the first time since the Civil War and Reconstruction. Normal schools were established; appropriations were increased for public schools;

a Board of Convict Inspectors was created; and prison reform implemented. In addition, while O'Neal was governor, a State Board of Agriculture was organized. On August 4, 1884, he was reelected to a second term. Without an opponent, O'Neal received 143,229 votes. O'Neal left office on December 1, 1886, and returned to his home in Florence, Alabama where he died on November 7, 1890. Bibliography: Thomas W. Owen, *History of Alabama and Dictionary of Alabama Biography*, 4 vols. (Chicago 1921); Albert B. Moore, *History of Alabama and Her People*, 3 vols. (New York, 1927); Albert B. Moore, *History of Alabama* (University, Alabama, 1934); Edward A. O'Neal Papers, Alabama State Department of Archives and History, Montgomery, Alabama.

SEAY, Thomas, 1886-1890

Born on November 20, 1846 in Greene (present-day Hale) County, Alabama, son of Reuben, a planter, and Ann Green (McGee) Seay. Brother of Sarah, Mary M., Susan, Francis, Roina, Martha A., and Napoleon B. Married to Ellen Shaw on July 12, 1865; she died on February 15, 1879; married a second time to Clara De Lesdernier on March 22, 1881; father of Fanny, Reuben, Frank, Amy, Annie, and Howard. Educated in country schools; at approximately twelve years of age, he was sent to Greensboro, Alabama for his preparatory education; entered Southern University, but his studies were interrupted by the Civil War. Enlisted in the Confederate States Army in 1863, at seventeen, as a private; prisoner of war. Returned to Southern University at the end of the war, and received an A.M. degree in 1867; studied law in the office of Judge A. A. Coleman in Greensboro. Admitted to the Alabama Bar, 1869. Began private law practice in 1869 as a junior partner in Coleman and Seay Law Firm in Greensboro; continued to practice law until 1885; planter. Elected to the Alabama Senate, 1876; reelected to the Alabama Senate twice; President, Alabama Senate, 1884; delegate, Democratic National Convention, 1880 and 1884; Vice President, National Prison Association. As a Democrat, Seay was elected Governor of Alabama by popular vote in the August 2, 1886 general election, receiving 145,095 votes to Republican Arthur Bingham's 36,793. He was sworn into office on December 1, 1886. During Seay's administration, the general tax rate was reduced; the Savannah and Western Railroad was opened to Birmingham, Alabama; the first Alabama steel was produced at North Birmingham, Alabama; and pensions were authorized for disabled Confederate veterans. In addition, while Seay was governor, the Farmers' Alliance was organized in the state in 1887, and in 1889 the Farmers' Alliance consolidated with the Agricultural Wheel to form the Alabama Farmers and Labourers Union of America. Seay was reelected to a second term in the August 6, 1888 general election, defeating Republican W. T. Ewing, 155,973 votes to 44,707. In the August, 1890 election, Seay was an unsuccessful candidate for the United States Senate; afterward, he left the governor's office on December 1, 1890. Seay returned to Greensboro, where he died on March 30, 1896. Bibliography: Thomas M. Owen, *History of Alabama and Dictonary of Alabama Biography*, 4 vols. (Chicago, 1921); Albert B. Moore, *History of Alabama and Her People*, 3 vols. (New York, 1927); Albert B. Moore, *History of Alabama* (University, Alabama, 1934); Roy Glashan, *American Governors and Gubernatorial Elections, 1775-1975* (Stillwater, Minnesota, 1975).

JONES, Thomas Goode, 1890-1894

Born on November 26, 1844 in Macon, Georgia, son of Samuel G., engaged in railroad construction, and Martha (Goode) Jones; Episcopalian. Brother of Mary Virginia, Samuel Jr., Lucy Spottswood, Edwin Francis, Carter, Martha Goode, and Charles Pollard; married to Georgena C. Bird on December 20, 1866, and father of Marshall Bird, Gena Moore, Thomas Goode, Martha Goode, Carrie Bird, Madeleine Clitherall, Gordon Houston, Lucy Spottswood, Eliza Clitherall, Thomas Goode, Samuel Goode, Walter Burgwyn, and Netta. Educated by private tutors; attended Montgomery, Alabama public schools; attended Dr. Charles Minor's School; attended Gesner Harrison School; attended Virginia Military Institute, 1859-1862; withdrew from school to join the Confederate States Army; studied law. Admitted to the Alabama Bar in 1866. Served as First Sergeant, Company K, Fifty-third Alabama Infantry; First Lieutenant and aide-de-camp to Confederate Brigadier General John B. Gordon, Army of Northern Virginia; Captain and aide-de-camp to Major General Gordon; later promoted to the rank of Major; wounded four times; after the Civil War, he was commissioned a Lieutenant Colonel by Alabama Governor George S. Houston; Captain of the "Montgomery Greys," Alabama State Troops; Colonel, Second Infantry Regiment, Alabama State Troops, 1880-1890. Returned to Montgomery after the Civil War and engaged in agriculture; editor, Montgomery *Daily Piqayune*, 1868. Alderman, Montgomery, 1868-1884; member, Alabama House of Representatives, 1884-1888; Speaker, Alabama House of Representatives, 1886-1888. Trustee, Hamner Hall School for Girls; Knights of Pythias; Elk. Author: *Alabama Supreme Court Reports, 1870-1880; Last Days of the Army of Northern Virginia;* and *Code of Ethics of the Alabama State Bar Association.* As a Democrat, Jones was elected Governor of Alabama on August 4, 1890 in the general election, receiving 139,912 votes to Republican Benjamin M. Long's 42,391. He was sworn into office on December 1, 1890. During his administration, Alabama Polytechnic Institute became coeducational, and the University of Alabama opened some classes to women. On August 1, 1892, Jones was reelected to a second term, defeating Populist candidate R. F. Kolb, 126,955 votes to 115,732. Jones left office on December 1, 1894. In 1901, he was elected President of the Alabama Bar Association, and that same year he was appointed United States District Judge for the Northern and Middle Districts of Alabama. Jones died in Montgomery, on April 28, 1914. Bibliography: Thomas M. Owen, *History of Alabama and Dictionary of Alabama Biography*, 4 vols. (Chicago, 1921); Albert B. Moore, *History of Alabama and Her People*, 3 vols. (New York, 1927); Albert B. Moore, *History of Alabama* (University, Alabama, 1934); Roy Glashan, *American Governors and Gubernatorial Elections, 1775-1975* (Stillwater, Minnesota, 1975).

OATES, William Calvin, 1894-1896

Born on December 1, 1835 in Pike (present-day Bullock) County, Alabama, son of William, a planter, and Sarah (Sellers) Oates. Married to Sally Toney on March 28, 1882, and father of William Calvin. Educated in old field schools; attended high school at Lawrenceville, Alabama; studied law with Pugh, Bullock and Buford Law Firm, Eufaula, Alabama, 1858-1859. Admitted to the Alabama Bar, 1859. Entered the Confederate States Army, 1861; Captain, Fifteenth Alabama Infantry; promoted to Colonel, Forty-eighth Alabama Infantry, 1863; lost an arm in battle, 1864; commissioned by President William McKinley as a Brigadier General of United States Volunteers, 1898; served in the Spanish-American War. Taught school in Henry County, Alabama, 1851-1855; private law practice, Abbeville, Alabama, 1859-1861; newspaper editor, 1860; resumed his legal practice in Abbeville in 1865. Delegate, Democratic National Convention, 1868; member, Alabama House of Representatives, 1870-1872; unsuccessful gubernatorial candidate, 1872; Chairman, Judiciary Committee, Alabama Constitutional Convention, 1875; member, United States House of Representatives, 1881-1894. Author: *The Confederate War—Lost Opportunities: The Fifteenth Alabama Regiment in Forty-seven Battles*; articles in *North American Review* and *Forum*. As a Democrat, Oates was elected Governor of Alabama by popular vote in the general election on August 6, 1894, receiving 110,875 votes to Populist R. F. Kolb's 83,292. He was sworn into office on December 1, 1894. The 1894 election was bitterly contested, and Kolb charged that he lost the election only because of extensive frauds in the balloting process. Mass meetings of Kolb supporters were held to protest the election results, and on December 1, they held their own inauguration ceremony for Kolb in front of the capitol. Nonetheless, Oates became Governor, and during his administration, he devoted much time to state finances and prison reform. Also while Oates was governor, a Free-Silver Convention was held in Birmingham, Alabama in 1895 to urge the free and unlimited coinage of silver. Instead of seeking reelection as Governor in the August 3, 1896 election, Oates made an unsuccessful race for the United States Senate. He left office on December 1, 1896. After serving in the military during the Spanish-American War, he returned to his law practice. In the 1901 Alabama Constitutional Convention, Oates was Chairman of the Legislative Department Committee, and a member of the Committee on Suffrage and Elections. Oates died on September 9, 1910, in Montgomery, Alabama, and was buried in Oakwood Cemetery. Bibliography: Thomas M. Owen, *History of Alabama and Dictionary of Alabama Biography*, 4 vols. (Chicago, 1921); Albert B. Moore, *History of Alabama and Her People*, 3 vols. (New York, 1927); Albert B. Moore, *History of Alabama* (University, Alabama, 1934); Roy Glashan, *American Governors and Gubernatorial Elections, 1775-1975* (Stillwater, Minnesota, 1975).

JOHNSTON, Joseph Forney, 1896-1900

Born on March 23, 1843 in Lincoln County, North Carolina, son of Dr. William, a physician, and Nancy (Forney) Johnston. Brother of Robert Daniel and William H.; married to Theresa Virginia Hooper on August 12, 1869, and father of Edward Douglas, Forney, and another son. Educated in public schools; attended high school in Talladega, Alabama; studied law with W. H. Forney at Jacksonville, Alabama. Admitted to the Alabama Bar in 1866. Enlisted as a private in the Eleventh Alabama Regiment, Confederate States Army in 1861; rose to the rank of Captain in the Twelfth North Carolina Regiment; wounded four times. Moved to Alabama when he was seventeen years of age. Moved to Selma, Alabama in 1866 where he practiced law for seventeen years; moved to Birmingham, Alabama in 1884; president, Alabama State Bank for ten years; became president of the Sloss Iron and Steel Company in 1887. Chairman, Alabama State Democratic Executive Committee. As a Democrat, Johnston was elected Governor of Alabama on August 3, 1896 in the general election, receiving 128,549 votes to Populist candidate Albert T. Goodwyn's 89,290. He was sworn into office on December 1, 1896. During his administration, the office of State Tax Commissioner was created; the State Department of Insurance was established; and the office of Chief Mine Inspector was organized. Also while he was governor, Alabama experienced renewed industrial growth, as the export of iron to foreign countries was inaugurated; the first open hearth steel was manufactured in the state; and hydroelectric power development on the Tallapoosa River was implemented. In addition during Johnston's term, the Confederate Monument on Capitol Hill in Montgomery, Alabama was unveiled. Johnston was reelected to a second term on August 1, 1898, defeating Populist Gilbert B. Dean, 110,551 votes to 50,052. Johnston left office on December 1, 1900. Afterward, he was elected to the United States Senate, and served from 1907 until his death. Johnston died on August 8, 1913, and was buried in Elmwood Cemetery in Birmingham, Alabama. Bibliography: Thomas M. Owen, *History of Alabama and Dictionary of Alabama Biography*, 4 vols. (Chicago, 1921); Albert B. Moore, *History of Alabama and Her People*, 3 vols. (New York, 1927); Albert B. Moore, *History of Alabama* (University, Alabama, 1934); Roy Glashan, *American Governors and Gubernatorial Elections, 1775-1975* (Stillwater, Minnesota, 1975).

JELKS, William Dorsey, 1900, 1901-1904, 1905-1907

Born on November 7, 1855 in Warrior Stand, Alabama, son of Joseph William Dorsey, who was killed while serving in the Confederate States Army during the Civil War, and Jane Goodrum (Frazier) Jelks. Married to Alice Shorter on June 7, 1883, and father of Cathrine. Spent his early life in Union Springs, Alabama. Educated in the public schools of Bullock County, Alabama; graduated from Mercer University, Macon, Georgia in 1876; received an A.M. degree from Mercer University. Returned to Union Springs, and became a bookkeeper; became owner of the Union Springs *Herald* in 1879; owner of the Eufaula, Alabama *Times*. Member, Common Council of Union Springs; member, Eufaula City School Board; member, Alabama Senate, 1898-1900; President, Alabama Senate, 1900-1901. He was a Democrat. Governor Elect William J. Samford was too ill to assume the governor's office after the August, 1900 general election. As a result, under the provisions of the 1875 Alabama Constitution, Jelks, as President of the Alabama Senate, succeeded to the office on December 1, 1900, and served as Governor until December 26, 1900 when Samford became well enough to be inaugurated. On June 11, 1901 Samford died in office, and Jelks, as President of the State Senate, once again succeeded to the governor's office. After winning the Democratic gubernatorial primary, Jelks was elected Governor of Alabama on November 4, 1902, receiving 67,748 votes to Republican John A. W. Smith's 24,150. However, on April 25, 1904, Jelks relinquished his duties because of an illness which forced him to travel to the West for his health. Under the provisions of the 1901 Alabama Constitution, Lieutenant Governor Russell M. Cunningham succeeded to the governor's office, and served until March 5, 1905, when Jelk's health permitted him to return to office. During his administration, the 1901 Alabama Constitution was ratified. The new constitution reestablished the office of Lieutenant Governor; extended the term of elective state officers from two to four years, with the provision that they were ineligible to succeed themselves; and substituted quadrennial for biennial sessions of the legislature. Also, while Jelks was governor, the Alabama Power Company was organized. Constitutionally prohibited from succeeding himself, Jelks left office on January 14, 1907. Afterward, he organized the Protective Life Insurance Company of Birmingham, Alabama, and served as its president. In 1912, he was a delegate to the Democratic National Convention, and was elected a Democratic National Committeeman for Alabama. Jelks died on December 13, 1931. Bibliography: Thomas M. Owen, *History of Alabama and Dictionary of Alabama Biography*, 4 vols. (Chicago, 1921); Albert B. Moore, *History of Alabama and Her People*, 3 vols. (New York, 1927); Albert B. Moore, *History of Alabama* (University, Alabama, 1934); Roy Glashan, *American Governors and Gubernatorial Elections, 1775-1975* (Stillwater, Minnesota, 1975).

SAMFORD, William James, 1900-1901

Born on September 16, 1844 in Greenville, Georgia, son of William F., a professor and political writer, and Susan Lewis (Dosdell) Samford; Methodist Episcopal. Married to Caroline Elizabeth Drake in October, 1865, and father of William Hodges, Thomas Drake, Willie Jamie, Richard Lewis, Susan George, Caroline E., Crawford, Walter Robert, and Mary K. His parents moved to Chambers County, Alabama when he was a child. Educated in private schools in Auburn, Alabama; attended East Alabama Male College in Auburn for one year; attended the University of Georgia, Athens; studied law. Admitted to the Alabama Bar in 1867. Enlisted in the Confederate States Army in 1862, as a private in the Forty-sixth Alabama Regiment; promoted to First Lieutenant. Engaged in cotton planting, 1865; began private law practice in Opelika, Alabama in 1867. Alderman, Opelika, 1872-1873; Presidential Elector, 1872 and 1876; member, Alabama Constitutional Convention, 1875; member, United States House of Representatives, 1879-1881; resumed his law practice; member, Alabama House of Representatives, 1882; member, Alabama Senate, 1884-1886 and 1892; President, Alabama Senate, 1886. President, Board of Trustees, University of Alabama; Mason; Knight of Pythias; American Legion of Honor; Alabama Historical Society. As a Democrat, Samford was elected Governor of Alabama on August 5, 1900 in the general election, receiving 115,167 votes to Republican John A. Steele's 28,305 and Populist G. B. Crowe's 17,444. Samford was ill when it was time for his inaugural, and as a result the President of the Alabama Senate, William D. Jelks, served as Governor from December 1, 1900 until December 26, 1900, when Samford was sworn into office. Only governor for approximately six months, Samford died in office on June 11, 1901. He was buried in Rosemere Cemetery in Opelika. Bibliography: Thomas M. Owen, *History of Alabama and Dictionary of Alabama Biography*, 4 vols. (Chicago, 1921); Albert B. Moore, *History of Alabama and Her People* 3 vols. (New York, 1927); Albert B. Moore, *History of Alabama* (University, Alabama, 1934); Roy Glashan, *American Governors and Gubernatorial Elections, 1775-1975* (Stillwater, Minnesota, 1975).

JELKS, William Dorsey, 1900, 1901-1904, 1905-1907

CUNNINGHAM, Russell McWhortor, 1904-1905

Born on August 25, 1855 in Mount Hope, Alabama, son of Moses W., a farmer, and Caroline (Russell) Cunningham; a Baptist. Married to Sue L. Moore on August 13, 1876; married a second time to Annice Taylor; father of Moses. Educated in the public schools; began studying medicine under Dr. John M. Clark in March, 1871; attended lectures at the Louisville, Kentucky, Medical College, 1874-1875; entered Bellevue Hospital Medical College, New York City, New York in 1878, and graduated in 1879. When his education was interrupted by the Civil War, he taught school and farmed; began medical practice in Newburg, Alabama, after his graduation from medical school; appointed physician of the Alabama State Penitentiary in 1881; appointed physician and surgeon for the Tennessee Coal, Iron, and Railroad Company in 1885; physician for the Alabama Steel and Ship Building Company; established a private hospital at Ensley, Alabama; later moved to Birmingham, Alabama, and established a private practice. Member, Alabama House of Representatives, 1880-1881; member, Alabama Senate, 1896-1900; President, Alabama Senate, 1899; delegate, Alabama Constitutional Convention, 1901; Lieutenant Governor of Alabama, 1901-1904. Author of a number of articles and papers on "Croupous Pneumonia," "Tuberculosis," "Morbidity and Mortality of Negro Convicts," "General Practitioner in Gynecology," and "Relation of the Cause to the Prognosis and Treatment of Fracture." Mason; Knight Templar, President, Tri-State Medical Association; President, Alabama State Medical Association; President, Alabama State Medical Association; Professor of Principles and Practice of Medicine, Birmingham Medical College; County Health Officer, Jefferson County, Alabama. A Democrat. Incapacitated by illness, Governor William D. Jelks was forced to go west because of his health, and as Lieutenant Governor, Cunningham succeeded to the office on April 25, 1904. Governor for approximately ten months, Cunningham relinquished the office on March 5, 1905, when Jelks returned to the governor's office after regaining his health. Cunningham reverted to Lieutenant Governor, and served until 1907. Cunningham was an unsuccessful candidate in the 1906 Democratic gubernatorial primary, and afterwards, returned to his medical practice. Cunningham died on June 6, 1921. Bibliography: Thomas M. Owen, *History of Alabama and Dictionary of Alabama Biography*, 4 vols. (Chicago, 1921); Albert B. Moore, *History of Alabama and Her People*, 3 vols. (New York, 1927); Albert B. Moore, *History of Alabama* (University, Alabama, 1934); Roy Glashan, *American Governors and Gubernatorial Elections, 1775-1975* (Stillwater, Minnesota, 1975).

JELKS, William Dorsey, 1900, 1901-1904, 1905-1907

COMER, Braxton Bragg, 1907-1911

Born on November 7, 1858 in Barbour County, Alabama, son of John Fletcher, a judge and planter, and Catherine (Drewry) Comer; a Methodist. Brother of George L., Hugh M., John W., Fletcher, and Edward; married to Eva Jane Harris on October 1, 1872, and father of Sally Bailey, John Fletcher, J. McDonald, Eva Mignon, Catherine, Braxton, Bevelle, Braxton Bragg, Jr., and Hugh M. Educated in the common schools; attended the University of Alabama, Tuscaloosa, 1864-1865; attended the University of Georgia, Athens; received both the A.B. and the A.M. degree from Emory and Henry College, Emory, Virginia in 1869; awarded an honorary LL.D. degree from Southern University, Greensboro, Alabama. Engaged as a planter, merchant, banker, and cotton manufacturer; moved to Comer Station, Alabama in 1872; member, Commissioners Court of Barbour County, 1874-1880; moved to Anniston, Alabama, 1885; moved to Birmingham, Alabama, 1890; President, City National Bank, Birmingham; President, Birmingham Corn and Flour Mills; President, Avondale Cotton Mills; President, Railroad Commission of Alabama, 1905-1906. Comer won the Democratic gubernatorial primary election on August 27, 1906, and on November 6, he was elected Governor in the general election, receiving 61,223 votes to Republican Asa E. Stratton's 9,981. He was sworn into office on January 14, 1907. During his administration, an extensive series of railroad legislation was enacted; the State Board of Assessors was established; and the Child Labor Law was revised. Also, while Comer was governor, taxes were placed on public utilities, following the principle utilized in the taxation of other properties; a system of county high schools was established; and liberal appropriations were made for all levels of education within the state. Prohibited by the 1901 Constitution from succeeding himself, Comer left office on January 17, 1911. Afterward, he returned to his business investments. Comer was appointed to the United States Senate on March 5, 1920, and served until November 2, 1920. Comer died in Birmingham on August 15, 1927, and was buried in Elmwood Cemetery. Bibliography: Thomas W. Owen, *History of Alabama and Dictionary of Alabama Biography*, 4 vols. (Chicago, 1921); Albert B. Moore, *History of Alabama and Her People*, 3 vols. (New York, 1927); Albert B. Moore, *History of Alabama* (University, Alabama, 1934); Roy Glashan, *American Governors and Gubernatorial Elections, 1775-1975* (Stillwater, Minnesota, 1975).

O'NEAL, Emmet, 1911-1915

Born on September 23, 1853 in Florence, Alabama, son of Edward Asbury, lawyer and Governor of Alabama from 1882-1886, and Olivia (Moore) O'Neal; a Presbyterian. Brother of Alfred M., Edward A., Rebecca, Julia, George C., and Sydney; married to Lizzie Kirkman on July 21, 1881, and father of Elizabeth, Kirkman, and Olivia. Attended public schools in Florence, Alabama; graduated from Wesleyan University of Alabama with a B.A. degree in 1873. Privately studied law in his father's office and was admitted to the Alabama Bar in 1875. Partner in his father's law firm in Florence until 1882; practiced individually after that. Presidential Elector, 1884 and 1892; appointed District Attorney by President Grover Cleveland in 1893 and served until 1897; City Attorney, Florence, Alabama; member, Alabama Constitutional Convention, 1901. Elk; Knight of Pythias. After winning the Democratic gubernatorial primary, O'Neal was elected Governor of Alabama by popular vote in the November 8, 1910 general election, receiving 77,694 votes to Republican Joseph O. Thompson's 19,210. He was sworn into office on January 17, 1911. During O'Neal's administration, liberal appropriations were made for education; prohibition was repealed; local liquor option was adopted; and a State Highway Department was created. In addition, the State Legislature passed a series of labor acts directed at the protection of miners and the improvement of child labor laws. O'Neal's term was marred by two embezzlement scandals, one in the State Convict Department and one in the Department of Agriculture and Industries, which proved embarrassing to O'Neal who was not personally involved. Prohibited by the 1901 Alabama Constitution from succeeding himself, O'Neal left office on January 18, 1915. Afterward, he returned to his home in Florence, Alabama and died on September 7, 1922. Bibliography: Joel E. DuBuose, *Notable Men of Alabama* (Atlanta, 1904): Thomas M. Owen, *History of Alabama and Dictionary of Alabama Biography*, 4 vols. (Chicago, 1921); Albert B. Moore, *History of Alabama and Her People*, 3 vols. (New York, 1927); Albert B. Moore, *History of Alabama* (University, Alabama, 1934).

HENDERSON, Charles, 1915-1919

Born on April 26, 1860 in Henderson, Alabama, son of Jeremiah Augustus, a merchant, and Mildred (Hill) Henderson; an Episcopalian. Brother of Fox, Ella, Jere Clemens, Willis J., J. E., and Julia; married to Laura Parker Montgomery on November 7, 1888. Educated in the schools of Troy, Alabama; entered Howard College, Marion, Alabama in 1875, but did not graduate. Appointed Inspector General on Governor William J. Samford's staff; aide-de-camp to Governor William D. Jelks. Merchant in Troy; Director, Standard Chemical and Oil Company, Troy; Director, Troy Compress Company; Director, Farmers and Merchants National Bank, Troy; principal stockholder, Standard Telephone and Telegraph Company. Mayor of Troy for thirteen years; appointed President, Alabama Railroad Commission, 1906; elected President, Alabama Railroad Commission, 1908-1912. One of the founders and Trustees of Troy State Normal College; Mason; Knight Templar. After winning the Democratic gubernatorial primary election, Henderson was elected Governor of Alabama on November 3, 1914, receiving 61,307 votes to Republican John B. Shields' 11,773. He was sworn into office on January 18, 1915. During his administration, the State Legislature enacted a Prohibition law, a primary election law, and a tax revision law. In addition, the State Board of Purchase was created and the State Child Welfare Department established. Also while Henderson was governor, far-reaching educational reforms were adopted, and a Workmen's Compensation Measure was enacted. Governor when the United States entered World War I, Henderson helped mobilize Alabama's resources for the war effort. Constitutionally prohibited from succeeding himself, Henderson left office on January 20, 1919. Afterward, he returned to his business investments. Henderson died on January 7, 1937, and was buried in Troy. Bibliography: Thomas M. Owen, *History of Alabama and Dictionary of Alabama Biography*, 4 vols. (Chicago, 1921); Albert B. Moore, *History of Alabama and Her People*, 3 vols. (New York, 1927); Albert B. Moore, *History of Alabama* (University, Alabama, 1934); Roy Glashan, *American Governors and Gubernatorial Elections, 1775-1975* (Stillwater, Minnesota, 1975).

KILBY, Thomas Erby, 1919-1923

Born on July 9, 1865 in Lebanon, Tennessee, son of Peyton Phillips and Sarah Ann (Marchant) Kilby; an Episcopalian. Married to Mary Elizabeth Clark on June 5, 1894, and father of Anne Horry, Oscar Marchant, and Thomas Erby, Jr. Educated in the public schools of Atlanta, Georgia. Afterward, he moved to Anniston, Alabama. Colonel and Inspector General on the staff of Governor Braxton B.

Comer. Agent, Georgia-Pacific Railroad; organizer, operator, and President of Kilby Locomotive and Machine Plant; Vice President, Kilby Frog and Switch Company, Birmingham, Alabama; President, City National Bank of Anniston. Member, Anniston City Council, 1898-1900; member, Anniston Board of Education, 1900-1905; Mayor of Anniston, 1905-1909; member, Alabama Senate, 1911-1915; Lieutenant Governor of Alabama, 1915-1919. Mason; Shriner; Knight of Pythias. After winning the Democratic gubernatorial primary, Kilby was elected Governor of Alabama on November 5, 1918 in the general election, receiving 54,746 votes to Republican candidate D. Smith's 13,497. He was sworn into office on January 20, 1919. During his administration, a state budget system was adopted; the taxation system was revised; a Workmen's Compensation Law was enacted; and a progressive educational code was enacted. Also while Kilby was governor, a Board of Control and Economy was created; a Home for Feeble-Minded Children was established; and the authority of the Public Service Commission was extended. A special session of the legislature was called in the fall of 1920 to amend Alabama's election laws, so they would comply to the Nineteenth Amendment to the United States Constitution providing for Women's Suffrage. Constitutionally prohibited from succeeding himself, Kilby left office on January 15, 1923. Afterward, he returned to his business investments. Kilby died on October 22, 1943, and was buried in Anniston. Bibliography: Thomas M. Owen, *History of Alabama and Dictionary of Alabama Biography*, 4 vols. (Chicago, 1921); Albert B. Moore, *History of Alabama and Her People*, 3 vols. (New York, 1927); Albert B. Moore, *History of Alabama* (University. Alabama, 1934); Roy Glashan, *American Governors and Gubernatorial Elections, 1775-1975* (Stillwater, Minnesota, 1975).

BRANDON, William Woodward, 1923-1927

Born on June 5, 1868 in Talladega, Alabama, son of the Reverend Frank T. J. and Carrie (Woodward) Brandon; a Methodist. Brother of Francis W., Edward W., Forney, John Marvin, and Carolyn; married to Mrs. Elizabeth (Andrews) Nabors on June 27, 1900. Educated at Cedar Bluff Institute; attended Tuscaloosa, Alabama High School; took the law course at the University of Alabama in 1891. Admitted to the Alabama Bar. Lieutenant and later Captain of the Warrior Guards; appointed Adjutant-General of Alabama, 1899 and 1901-1906; during the Spanish-American War, he served as Major, Third Alabama Volunteer Infantry, 1900-1901. Elected Clerk of the City of Tuscaloosa, 1891; appointed Justice of the Peace, 1891; began private law practice in Tuscaloosa in 1892; published *The Citizen Soldier*. Member, Alabama House of Representatives, 1896-1899. Reading Clerk, Alabama Constitutional Convention, 1901; Alabama State Auditor, 1907-1911; elected Probate Judge of Tuscaloosa County, 1911. Mason; Knight of Pythias;; Odd Fellow; Elk. After winning the 1922 Democratic gubernatorial primary election, Brandon was elected Governor of Alabama on November 7, 1922 in the general election, receiving 113,605 votes to Republican C. D. Street's 31,175. He was inaugurated on January 15, 1923. During his administration, a Tax Commission was established; the tax-exemption privilege of the Alabama Power Company was repealed; and appropriations were increased for Confederate pensions. In addition, the State Docks Commission was created to develop the port of Mobile, Alabama, and the State Capitol was renovated. Also while Brandon was governor, there was extensive highway construction throughout the state. Ineligible under the provisions of the 1901 Alabama Constitution to succeed himself, Brandon left office on

January 17, 1927. Afterward, he again served as Probate Judge of Tuscaloosa County. Brandon died on December 7, 1934, and was buried in Tuscaloosa. Bibliography: Thomas M. Owen, *History of Alabama and Dictionary of Alabama Biography*, 4 vols. (Chicago, 1921); Albert B. Moore, *History of Alabama and Her People*, 3 vols. (New York, 1927); Albert B. Moore, *History of Alabama* (University, Alabama, 1934); Roy Glashan, *American Governors and Gubernatorial Elections, 1775-1975* (Stillwater, Minnesota, 1975).

GRAVES, David Bibb, 1927-1931, 1935-1939

Born April 1, 1873, at Hope Hull, Alabama, son of David, a planter, and Mattie (Bibb); a member of the Christian Church. Married to Dixie Bibb on October 10, 1900; they had no children. Educated in the public schools of Texas; received a B.C.E. degree from the University of Alabama in 1893; took law courses at the University of Texas, 1893-1894; received an LL.B. degree from Yale University in 1896. Admitted to the Alabama Bar in 1897. Served as Captain, Alabama Corps of Cadets, 1892-1893; aide-de-camp, with the rank of Captain, on the staff of Brigadier General Louis V. Clark; Assistant Adjutant General of Alabama, with the rank of Major; Adjutant General of Alabama, 1907-1911; assisted in the organization of the 1st Alabama Cavalry Regiment, Alabama National Guard; Lieutenant Colonel, 1st Alabama Cavalry Regiment; Colonel, 1st Alabama Cavalry Regiment. The regiment was mustered into federal service in September, 1916, and served on the Mexican border from December, 1916 until March, 1917; when it returned to Alabama, the United States had entered World War I, and the regiment remained in federal service. The 1st Alabama Cavalry Regiment was transformed into 116th and 117th Field Artillery, a part of the 51st Artillery Brigade; Graves commanded the 117th Field Artillery; he graduated from the School of Fire for Field Artillery, Fort Sill Oklahoma; served in France during World War I; discharged in January, 1919. Began private law practice in Montgomery, Alabama in 1897. Member, Alabama House of Representatives, 1898-1899 and 1900-1901; Chairman, Alabama State Democratic Executive Committee; unsuccessful candidate for the Democratic gubernatorial nomination, 1922. Organized the Alabama Department of the American Legion. After winning the 1926 Democratic gubernatorial primary election, Graves was elected Governor of Alabama on November 2, 1926 in the general election, receiving 93,432 votes to Republican J. A. Bingham's 21,605. He was sworn into office on January 17, 1927. During his administration, an amendment to the Alabama Constitution was ratified, which authorized a $25,000,000 bond issue for road construction; a gasoline tax was enacted; and a $5,000,000 bond issue was approved for completion of the docks at Mobile, Alabama. Constitutionally prohibited from succeeding himself, Graves left office on January 19, 1931; however, he won the 1934 Democratic gubernatorial primary and runoff elections, and was reelected to a second term on November 6, 1934 in the general election, receiving 155,197 votes to Republican Edmund H. Dryer's 22,621. He was inaugurated on January 14, 1935. During his second term, the State Department of Public Health was established; a two percent sales tax was enacted; and a Civil Service system was implemented in counties with 200,000 or more population. Prohibited by the Alabama Constitution from succeeding himself, Graves left office on January 17, 1939. Graves died in Sarasota, Florida, on March 14, 1942. Bibliography: Thomas M. Owen, *History of Alabama and Dictionary of Alabama Biography*, 4 vols. (Chicago, 1921); Albert B. Moore, *History of Alabama*

(University, Alabama, 1934); Alabama State Planning Commission, *Alabama: A Guide to the Deep South* (New York, 1941); Roy Glashan, *American Governors and Gubernatorial Elections, 1775-1975* (Stillwater, Minnesota, 1975).

MILLER, Benjamin M., 1931-1935

Born on March 13, 1864 in Oak Hill, Wilcox County, Alabama, son of the Reverend John Miller and Sara (Pressly) Miller; a member of the Associate Reform Presbyterian Church. Married to Otis Duggan on September 21, 1892, and father of Benjamin M. and Margaret. Received an A.B. degree from Erskine College, Due West, South Carolina in 1884; graduated in law from the University of Alabama, University, Alabama in 1888. Admitted to the Alabama Bar in 1888. Served as a member of the Wilcox Mounted Rifles, 1887-1889. Principal, Lower Peach Tree, Alabama High School, 1884-1887; private law practice in Camden, Alabama, Democratic Executive Committee, Wilcox County, 1901-1902; Judge, Fourth Alabama Judicial Circuit, 1904-1921; Associate Justice, Alabama Supreme Court, 1921-1928. Knight of Pythias. After winning the 1930 Democratic gubernatorial primary election, Miller was elected Governor of Alabama on November 4, 1930 in the general election, receiving 155,034 votes to Independent candidate Hugh A. Lock's 95,745. He was sworn into office on Janaury 19, 1931. During his administration, the Tennessee Valley Authority was created by the United States Congress and authorized to construct dams and power plants, and to develop the economic and social well-being of the Tennessee Valley region. Previously, during World War I, the federal government had constructed a large hydroelectric power plant at Muscle Shoals, Alabama, and in 1933 this installation was transferred to the Tennessee Valley Authority. Eventually, three dams and three steam power plants were established within Alabama. Also while Miller was governor, the State Planning Commission was appointed. Constitutionally prohibited from succeeding himself, Miller left office on January 14, 1935. Afterward, he returned to his home in Camden, Alabama. Miller died on February 6, 1944. Bibliography: Alabama State Planning Commission, *Alabama: A Guide to the Deep South* (New York, 1941); Charles G. Summersell, *Alabama History for Schools* (Northport, Alabama, 1965); Congressional Quarterly Incorporated, *Guide to U.S. Elections* (Washington, 1975); Roy Glashan, *American Governors and Gubernatorial Elections, 1775-1975* (Stillwater, Minnesota, 1975).

GRAVES, David Bibb, 1927-1931, 1935-1939

DIXON, Frank Murray, 1939-1943

Born on July 25, 1892 in Oakland, California, son of Frank and Launa (Murray) Dixon; a Baptist. Married to Juliet Jolly Perry on November 3, 1920, and father of Sam Perry and Launa Murray. Received a preparatory education at Phillips Academy, Exeter, New Hampshire, 1906-1909; attended Columbia University, New York City, New York, 1915; received an LL.B. degree from the University of Virginia, Charlottesville, Virginia, 1916; awarded an LL.D. degree from Birmingham-

Southern College, Birmingham, Alabama, 1930. Admitted to the Alabama Bar in 1917. During World War I, he served as a Second Lieutenant in the Coast Artillery Corps, United States Army; attached to the French Army as an aerial observer; decorated with the Chevalier Legion of Honor and the Croix de Guerre with Palm. Private law practice in Birmingham, Alabama. American Legion; Commander, Department of Alabama, American Legion, 1926-1927; Veterans of Foreign Wars; Disabled American Veterans; Mason. Dixon was the leader in a three man Democratic gubernatorial primary election in 1938; however, the need for a runoff election was eliminated by the withdrawal of the runner-up. He was elected Governor of Alabama on November 8, 1938 in the general election, receiving 115,761 votes to Republican W. A. Clardy's 16,513. Dixon was sworn into office on January 17, 1939. During his administration, the United States was beginning to upgrade its military forces as part of President Franklin D. Roosevelt's preparedness program. As a result Mobile, Alabama was selected as the site of a $10,000,000 Army Air Corps base. Also while Dixon was governor, a State Civil Service system was established; political activity by state, county, and municipal employees and officials was prohibited; and the Alabama Department of Docks and Terminals was created. In December, 1939, the first illuminated inter-city highway in the state was opened. Governor when the United States entered World War II, Dixon helped mobilize Alabama's resources for the war effort. Constitutionally prohibited from succeeding himself, Dixon left office on January 19, 1943. Afterward, he returned to his law practice in Birmingham. Dixon died on October 11, 1965, in Birmingham. Bibliography: Alabama State Planning Commission, *Alabama: A Guide to the Deep South* (New York, 1941); Charles G. Summersell, *Alabama History for Schools* (Northport, Alabama, 1965); Congressional Quarterly Incorporated, *Guide to U.S. Elections* (Washington, 1975); Roy Glashan, *American Governors and Gubernatorial Elections, 1775-1975 (Stillwater, Minnesota, 1975).*

SPARKS, Chauncey M., 1943-1947

Born on October 8, 1884 in Barbour County, Alabama, son of George Washington and Sarah E. (Castellow) Sparks; paternal grandson of Samuel and May (Lawhon) Sparks of Barbour County; maternal grandson of William H. and Lucy (Pie) Castellow of Quitman County, Georgia. Sparks was a Baptist; he was not married. Educated in the public schools of Quitman County; received an A.B. degree from Mercer University, Macon, Georgia in 1907; received an LL.D. degree from Mercer University in 1910; honorary LL.D. degrees from Howard College, Birmingham, Alabama in 1943 and the University of Alabama in 1947. Admitted to the Alabama Bar. Served as a Second Lieutenant, Company G, Second Infantry, Alabama National Guard, 1912-1915. Began private law practice in Eufaula, Alabama in 1910. Judge, Inferior Court, Precinct Five, Barbour County, 1911-1916; Secretary, Barbour County Democratic Executive Committee, 1914-1918; member, Alabama House of Representatives, 1919-1923 and 1931-1939; runner-up in the 1938 Democratic gubernatorial primary election, but withdrew from the contest prior to the runoff election. Trustee, Alabama State Department of Archives and History, 1920-1947; Elk. After winning the 1943 Democratic primary electon—a runoff election was not necessary because of his margin of victory—Sparks was elected Governor of Alabama on November 3, 1942 in the general election, receiving 69,048 votes to Republican Hugh McEniry's 8,167. He was sworn into office on January 19, 1943. During his administration, the economy of Alabama was undergoing rapid growth resulting from the wartime defense spending of the federal government. In March, 1943, Lister Hill, United States Senator from Alabama, joined with several other senators to begin a bipartisan movement to commit the United States to participation in an international organization. Also while Sparks was governor, Alabama's first producing oil well began operation, and blacks were given the right to vote in primary elections. Constitutionally prohibited from succeeding himself, Sparks left office on January 20, 1947. He was an unsuccessful candidate in the 1950 Democratic gubernatorial primary election. After his 1950 defeat, Sparks retired from public life, and returned to his home in Eufaula. Sparks died on November 6, 1968. Bibliography: Thomas M. Owen, *History of Alabama and Dictionary of Alabama Biography*, 4 vols. (Chicago, 1921); Fred McGhee, ed., *Facts on File Five-Year Index 1946-1950* (New York, 1958); Congressional Quarterly Incorporated, *Guide to U.S. Elections* (Washington, 1975); Roy Glashan, *American Governors and Gubernatorial Elections, 1775-1975* (Stillwater, Minnesota, 1975).

FOLSOM, James Elisha, 1947-1951, 1955-1959

Born on October 9, 1908 near Elbe in Coffee County, Alabama, son of Joshua Marion, Deputy Sheriff of Coffee County, and Eulala Cornelia (Dunnavant) Folsom; a Baptist. Brother of Fred, Cecil, Robert, Carl, Ruby Ellis, and Thelma Clark; married to Sarah Albert Carnley on December 25, 1936; she died in July, 1944; married a second time to Jamelle Moore on May 5, 1948; father of Rachel and Melissa by his first wife; father of James Elisha, Jr., Andrew, Jamelle, and Thelma Ebelene by his second wife. Attended the University of Alabama, 1928; attended Howard College, Birmingham, Alabama, 1929; attended George Washington University, Washington, D.C., 1935. District Agent, Emergency and Aid Insurance Company, Elba, Alabama, 1937-1940; State Manager, Emergency and Aid Insurance Company, 1940-1946. Alabama Delegate-at-Large, Democratic National Convention, 1944. Mason; Elk. After winning the 1946 Democratic gubernatorial primary election, Folsom was elected Governor of Alabama on November 5, 1946 in the general election, receiving 174,959 votes to Republican Lyman Ward's 22,362. He was sworn into office on January 20, 1947. During his administration, betting was ruled illegal within the state; flogging, as a means of punishment in Alabama prisons, was ended; and, in an anti-Ku Klux Klan move, hoods were banned. Constitutionally prohibited from succeeding himself, Folsom left office on January 15, 1951. However, after winning the 1954 Democratic gubernatorial primary, Folsom was again elected Governor of Alabama in the November 2, 1954 general election, receiving 244,401 votes to Republican Tom Abernethy's 88,688. He was sworn in as governor for the second time on January 17, 1955. During this term, the United States Supreme Court ruled against segregation on intra-state buses; a federal court prohibited segregation in Montgomery, Alabama buses; and the United States Civil Rights Commission barred segregation in hotels. Constitutionally prohibited from succeeding himself, Folsom left office on January 19, 1959. Bibliography: Fred McGhee, ed., *Facts on File Five-Year Index, 1946-1950* (New York, 1958); Lester A. Sobel, ed., *Facts on File Five-Year Index, 1956-1960* (New York, 1960); Congressional Quarterly Incorporated, *Guide to U.S. Elections* Washington, 1975); Roy Glashan, *American Governors and Gubernatorial Elections, 1775-1975* (Stillwater, Minnesota, 1975).

PERSONS, Seth Gordon, 1951-1955

Born on February 5, 1902 in Montgomery, Alabama, son of Frank Stanford and Kate Persons. Married to Alice McKeithen on March 20, 1928, and father of Gordon, Jr. and Elizabeth. Attended Starke University School, Montgomery, Alabama; attended Alabama Polytechnic Institute, Auburn, Alabama. Employed with the Alabama Farm Bureau Cotton Association, 1922-1923; owned and operated, Persons Tire Company, 1923-1928; owned, Southern Radio Service, 1928-1930; President, Montgomery Broadcasting Company Radio Station WSFA, 1930-1939; member, Board of Directors, National Association of Broadcasters, 1935-1939; owned and operated, Gordon Persons and Company Consulting Engineers, 1939-1942. Chief Radio Consultant, Office of War Information, Washington, D.C., 1941-1943; elected to the Alabama Public Service Commission in 1943, and served four terms; President, Alabama Public Service Commission, 1947-1951. Persons was the leader in a seven man Democratic gubernatorial primary election in 1950; however, the need for a runoff election was eliminated by the withdrawal of the runner-up. He was elected Governor of Alabama on November 7, 1950 in the general election, receiving 155,414 votes to Republican John S. Crowder's 15,177. Persons was sworn into office on January 15, 1951. During his administration, Alabama suffered from a severe drought, which greatly damaged the state's agricultural economy. In addition, the legislature outlawed union shops, and enacted laws against the unionization of state employees. While Persons was governor, the United States Supreme Court rendered its judgment in the *Brown vs. Board of Education of Topeka, Kansas* case, and declared that segregation in public education was a denial of the equal protection of the law guarantee of the United States Constitution. Constitutionally prohibited from succeeding himself, Persons left office on January 17, 1955. Afterward, he returned to his home in Montgomery. Persons died in Montgomery on May 29, 1965. Bibliography: Fred McGhee, ed., *Facts on File Five-Year Index 1951-1955* (New York, 1957); Charles G. Summersell, *Alabama History for Schools* (Northport, Alabama, 1965); Congressional Quarterly Incorporated, *Guide to U.S. Elections* (Washington, 1975); Roy Glashan, *American Governors and Gubernatorial Elections, 1775-1975* (Stillwater, Minnesota, 1975).

FOLSOM, James Elisha, 1947-1951, 1955-1959

PATTERSON, John Malcolm, 1959-1963

Born on September 27, 1921, in Goldville, Alabama, son of Albert Love, a lawyer, and Agnes Louise (Benson) Patterson; a Methodist. Brother of Maurice, Samuel, Jack, and one sister; married to Mary Jo McGowin on October 19, 1947, and father of Albert L. and Barbara Louise. Attended public schools; LL.B., University of Alabama in 1949. Admitted to the Alabama Bar in 1949. Entered the United States Army as a private in 1940; served in the Field Artillery during World War II; rose to the rank of Major; discharged in 1945; recalled to active duty in 1951 for service in the Korean War; discharged in 1953; held a reserve commission as a Major. His family moved to Phenix City, Alabama, in 1935; began private law practice in

Phenix City in 1949. Patterson's father campaigned for Attorney General of Alabama in 1954, on the platform of eliminating the vice and crime in Phenix City; however, he was assassinated shortly after winning the Democratic nomination. As a result, John Malcolm Patterson took his father's place. Attorney General of Alabama, 1955-1959. Veterans of Foreign Wars; American Legion; Farrar Order of Jurisprudence; Woodman of the World; National Association of Securities Commissioners; Lion; Board of Editors, *Alabama Law Review*, 1948-1949. After winning the 1958 Democratic gubernatorial primary and runoff elections, Patterson was elected Governor of Alabama on November 4, 1958 in the general election, receiving 239,633 votes to Republican William L. Longshore, Jr.'s 30,415. He was sworn into office on January 19, 1959. Immediately after being inaugurated, Patterson called the legislature into special session, and it unanimously approved a $60,000,000 bond issue for a four-year highway construction project. During his administration, he was the leader of segregation forces in the state, and in 1960 Patterson ordered the expulsion of some students at Alabama State College for Negroes who had protested against lunch counter segregation policies. While he was governor, tension over the racial issue continued to increase as pressure for integration from Alabama blacks and the federal government grew. Constitutionally prohibited from succeeding himself, Patterson left office on January 14, 1963. Bibliography: Lester A. Sobel, ed., *Facts on File Five-Year Index, 1956-1960* (Washington, 1961); Facts on File Incorporated, *Facts on File Five-Year Index, 1961-1965* (Washington, 1966); Congressional Quarterly Incorporated, *Guide to U.S. Elections* (Washington, 1975); Roy Glashan, *American Governors and Gubernatorial Elections, 1775-1975* (Stillwater, Minnesota, 1975).

WALLACE, George Corley, 1963-1967, 1971-1972, 1972-

Born on August 25, 1919 in Clio, Alabama, son of George C., a farmer, and Mozell (Smith) Wallace; a Methodist. Brother of Jack, Gerald, and Marianne; married to Lurleen Burns on May 23, 1943 who died on May 7, 1968; married a second time to Mrs. Cornelia Ellis Snively on January 4, 1971; father of Bobbie Jo, Peggy Sue, George Corley, Jr., and Janie Lee by his first wife. Attended Barbour County, Alabama High School; received an LL.B. degree from the University of Alabama in 1942. Admitted to the Alabama Bar in 1942. Served in the United States Army Air Force, 1942-1945; rose to the rank of Flight Sergeant. Assistant Attorney General of Alabama, 1946-1947; member, Alabama House of Representatives, 1947-1953; Judge, Third Judicial District of Alabama, 1953-1958; unsuccessful candidate for the 1958 Democratic gubernatorial nomination. Private law practice, Clayton, Alabama, 1958-1962. American Legion; Veterans of Foreign Wars; Disabled American Veterans; Mason; Moose; Elk; Modern Woodman of the World. After winning the 1962 Democratic gubernatorial primary and runoff elections, Wallace was elected Governor of Alabama on November 6, 1962 in the general election. Having no opposition, he received 303,987 votes, and was sworn into office on January 14, 1963. During his administration, Wallace barred the enrollment of blacks at the University of Alabama; however, President John F. Kennedy ordered the Alabama National Guard to active duty, and forced state officials to comply with federal court orders dealing with integration. Also while Wallace was governor, the legislature ratified the Twenty-fourth Amendment to the United States

Constitution. Constitutionally prohibited from succeeding himself in office, Wallace attempted to amend the Alabama Constitution to allow him to do so; however, he was unsuccessful and left office on January 16, 1967. Though Wallace was unable to succeed himself, his wife Lurleen Wallace was elected Governor in November, 1966, and followed her husband as chief executive of Alabama. While his wife was governor, Wallace served as her $1.00-a-year Special Assistant, and actually made most important executive decisions. His wife died in office on May 7, 1968, and was succeeded by the Lieutenant Governor, Albert P. Brewer. In November, 1968, an amendment to the Alabama Constitution allowing governors to succeed themselves was ratified. Wallace was the unsuccessful American Independent Party candidate for President in 1968. In the 1970 Alabama Democratic primary election, Wallace trailed Brewer; however, Wallace won the runoff election. He was elected to a second term as Governor of Alabama on November 3, 1970 in the general election, receiving 634,046 votes to National Democratic Party of Alabama candidate, John L. Cashin's 125,491 and Independent A. C. Shelton's 75,679. He was inaugurated on January 18, 1971. Wallace was a candidate for the 1972 Democratic presidential nomination, but was wounded in an attempted assassination. As a result of his wounds, he relinquished his duties as Governor to Lieutenant Governor Jere L. Beasley on June 4, 1972; however, he had recovered sufficiently by July 7, 1972 to reassume the governor's office. Wallace won the 1974 Democratic gubernatorial primary, and was elected to a third term on November 5, 1974 in the general election, receiving 497,574 votes to Republican Elvin McCary's 88,381. Bibliography: Lester A. Sobel, ed., *Facts on File Yearbook 1963* (New York, 1964); Lester A. Sobel, ed., *Facts on File Yearbook 1972* (New York, 1973); Congressional Quarterly Incorporated, *Guide to U.S. Elections* (Washington, 1975); Roy Glashan, *American Governors and Gubernatorial Elections, 1775-1975* (Stillwater, Minnesota, 1975).

WALLACE, Lurleen Burns, 1967-1968

Born on September 19, 1926 in Tuscaloosa, Alabama, daughter of Henry Morgan, a lumber grader and shipyard worker, and Estelle (Burroughs) Burns; a Methodist. Sister of Cecil; married to George Corley Wallace on May 23, 1943, and mother of Bobbie Jo, Peggy Sue, George Corley, Jr., and Janie Lee. Educated in public schools; attended Tuscaloosa Business College in 1942. Employed in a Tuscaloosa variety store; moved to New Mexico while her husband served in World War II; returned to Clayton, Alabama, where she was a housewife and mother for the next twenty years; participated in her husband's 1962 gubernatorial campaign. Her husband was elected Governor of Alabama in 1962, and held the office from 1963 to 1967; however, he was prevented from succeeding himself by the 1901 Alabama Constitution. After failing to amend the state constitution to allow successive gubernatorial terms, George C. Wallace announced on February 24, 1966 that his wife, Lurleen B. Wallace, would enter the gubernatorial contest. During the campaign, she promised to continue her husband's programs, and it was acknowledged that he would be her principal adviser. After winning the 1966 Democratic gubernatorial primary election with a large enough majority to eliminate the need for a runoff election, Wallace was elected Governor of Alabama on November 8, 1966 in the general election, receiving 537,505 votes to Republican James Martin's 262,943 and Independent C. R. Robinson's 47,653. She was sworn into office on

January 16, 1967. As Alabama's first woman governor, she was only the third female in United States history to serve as governor of a state. During Wallace's administration, her husband served as the governor's $1.00-a-year Special Assistant. While she was governor, a federal court ordered the Alabama State Board of Education to implement desegregation of all public schools. Wallace asked the legislature for full control over state schools and an increase in the number of state troopers. In addition, she urged that state funds be withdrawn from Tuskegee Institute because it was the site of civil rights demonstrations, and sought increased funds for state mental hospitals. Governor Lurleen Wallace died in office on May 7, 1968, and was buried in Montgomery, Alabama. Bibliography: Lester A. Sobel, ed., *Facts on File Yearbook 1967* (New York, 1968); Lester A. Sobel, ed., *Facts on File Yearbook 1968* (New York, 1969); Congressional Quarterly Incorporated, *Guide to U.S. Elections* (Washington, 1975); Roy Glashan, *American Governors and Gubernatorial Elections, 1775-1975* (Stillwater, Minnesota, 1975).

BREWER, Albert Preston, 1968-1971

Born on October 26, 1928 in Bethel Springs, Tennessee, son of Dan A. and Clara (Yarber) Brewer; a Baptist. Married to Martha Farmer on January 31, 1951, and father of Rebecca Ann and Beverly Alison. Received an A.B. degree from the University of Alabama in 1952; received an LL.B. degree from the University of Alabama in 1952; honorary degree from Jacksonville State University and Stamford University. Admitted to the Alabama Bar in 1952. Began private law practice in Decatur, Alabama in 1952. Member, Alabama House of Representatives, 1956-1966; Chairman, Decatur City Planning Commission, 1956-1963; Speaker, Alabama House of Representatives, 1963-1966; became a member of the Alabama Democratic Executive Committee in 1964; Lieutenant Governor of Alabama, 1967-1968. Member, Democratic Party; American Legion; Phi Alpha Delta; Delta Sigma Phi; Mason. On May 7, 1968, Governor of Alabama Lurleen B. Wallace died, and as Lieutenant Governor, Brewer succeeded to the office. During his administration, state agencies were sued by civil rights supporters to force an end to employment bias; the United States Supreme Court ordered the Montgomery, Alabama public schools to integrate; and the United States Justice Department implemented legal action to end the housing bias within the state. In addition, the United States Supreme Court placed several restrictions on Alabama voting laws. Also while Brewer was governor, two blacks were elected to the State Legislature. In February, 1970, former Alabama Governor George C. Wallace announced his intention to seek reelection as chief executive. Brewer also hoped to be elected governor in his own right. In the Democratic gubernatorial primary election, Brewer received 428,146 votes to Wallace's 416,443 and Charles Woods' 149,887. However, in the runoff election Wallace outpolled Brewer 559,832 votes to 525,951. As a result, Brewer completed the remainder of Lurleen Wallace's term, and then left office on January 18, 1971. Bibliography: Lester A. Sobel, ed., *Facts on File Yearbook 1969* (New York, 1970); Lester A. Sobel, ed., *Facts on File Yearbook 1970* (New York, 1971); Congressional Quarterly Incorporated, *Guide to U.S. Elections* (Washington, 1975); Roy Glashan, *American Governors and Gubernatorial Elections, 1775-1975* (Stillwater, Minnesota, 1975).

WALLACE, George Corley, 1963-1967, 1971-1972, 1972-

BEASLEY, Jere Locke, 1972

Born on December 12, 1935 in Tyler, Texas, son of Browder L., a farmer, and Florence (Camp) Beasley; a Methodist. Brother of William Martin; married to Sara Baker on March 15, 1958, and father of Jere Locke, Jr., Julia Anne, and Linda Lee. Received a B.S. degree from Auburn University, Alabama in 1959; received an LL.B. degree from the University of Alabama in 1962. Admitted to the Alabama Bar in 1962. Served as a Captain in the United States Army Reserve. Private law practice in Tuscaloosa, Alabama, 1962-1964; private law practice in Clayton, Alabama, 1964-1971; member, Beasley, Williams and Robertson Legal Firm, 1969-1971; Director and Legal Counsel, Bank of Commerce, Clayton; became engaged in farming in 1971. Lieutenant Governor of Alabama, 1971—. Lion. Incapacitated by wounds received in an assassination attempt during the 1972 presidential contest, Governor of Alabama George C. Wallace surrendered his authority to Lieutenant Governor Beasley on June 4, 1972. Beasley served as Governor of Alabama until July 7, 1972, when Wallace had recovered sufficiently to resume office. Beasley was reelected to a second term as Lieutenant Governor of Alabama on November 4, 1974. Bibliography: Henry H. Schulte, Jr., *Facts on File Yearbook 1972* (New York, 1973); Roy Glashan, *American Governors and Gubernatorial Elections, 1775-1975* (Stillwater, Minnesota, 1975).

WALLACE, George Corley, 1963-1967, 1971-1972, 1972-

ALASKA

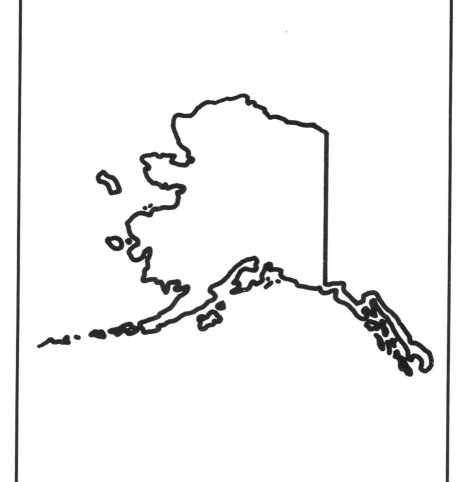

ALASKA

EGAN, William Allen, 1958-1966, 1970-1974

Born on October 8, 1914 in Valdez, Alaska, son of William Edward Egan, a miner, and Cora (Allen) Egan; brother of Clinton, Emmett, Ethel, Alaska, Alice, and Francis; a Catholic. Married to Desdia Neva McKittrick on November 16, 1940; father of Dennis William. Graduated from Valdez High School in 1932 and awarded LL.D. (honorary) from Alaska Methodist University in 1965 and the University of Alaska in 1972. After graduation from high school, Egan became a pilot, and engaged in private flying; was a member of the Alaska Road Commission; worked in a mine, 1932-43; and became owner of Valdez Supply, general store, 1946-1950. Served in AUS 1943-46 and was discharged as Sergeant. A lifelong Democrat, he was elected to the Valdez City Council in 1937; Mayor of Valdez in 1946. Egan served terms in the Alaska Territorial House in 1941, 1943, 1947, 1949, and 1951. He was Speaker of the House in 1951. He was a member of the Alaska Territorial Senate in 1953 and 1955. Egan was a delegate to the Alaska Statehood Constitutional Convention and served as presiding officer. In 1956 he was elected to be a "Tennessee Plan" provisional senator to go to Washington, D.C. to promote statehood for Alaska. When Congress approved the Alaska Statehood Act on June 30, 1958, Egan returned to Alaska as a candidate for Governor. His opponents were John Butrovich, Jr. (Republican) and Mike Dollinter (Independent). The votes cast for each were: Egan, 29,189; Butrovich, 19,299; and Dollinter, 480. Egan took office on January 3, 1959. Following his inauguration he launched Alaska on a period of transition and growth which led to his reelection in 1962. He was opposed in 1962 by Mike Stepovich. The votes cast for each were: Egan, 29,627, and Mike Stepovich, 27,054. He was inaugurated on Janaury 26, 1963. Egan ran for reelection again in 1966 and was defeated by Walter J. Hickel. The candidates in the 1966 election were Egan, John Fichtner Grasse (NP) and Walter J. Hickel (R). The votes cast for each were: Egan, 33,065; Grasse, 1,084; and Hickel, 33,145. Egan then moved to Anchorage and entered the insurance business. Egan became a gubernatorial candidate again in 1970 and was opposed by Keith H. Miller (R) who had succeeded Hickel when the latter moved to Washington, D.C. as Secretary of Interior, and Ralph Milton Anderson (AIP). The votes cast for each were: Egan, 42,309; Anderson, 1,206; and Miller, 37,264. Egan was sworn in for his third term on December 7, 1970. He ran for reelection in 1974 and was narrowly defeated. His opponents were Jay S. Hammond (R) and Joseph E. ("Joe") Vogler (AIP). The votes cast as reflected by the official recount were: Egan, 45,553; Hammond, 45,840; and Vogler, 4,770. Egan resides in Anchorage where he is associated with the Teamsters' Union. Bibliography: *Alaska Blue Book* (Anchorage, 1963); *Alaska Official Returns for the Special Statehood Referendum*

Election August 16, 1958 and the General Election November 25, 1958. (Juneau, 1958); *Bill Egan and Alaska: A Pictorial Tribute to a Gallant Leader of a Courageous State* (1965); *First Official Inaugural Program January 26, 1963* (Juneau, 1963); Elaine Mitchell, ed., *Alaska Blue Book, 1973* (Juneau, 1973); Thomas G. Morehouse, *An Electoral Profile of Alaska* (Fairbanks, 1973); *State of Alaska Official Returns By Election Precinct* (Juneau, 1962, 1966, 1970, 1974).

HICKEL, Walter Joseph, 1966-1969

Born on August 18, 1919 in Claflin, Kansas, son of Robert A. Hickel, a farmer, and Emma (Zecha) Hickel; brother of Maxine, Gertrude, Viola, Catherine, Patricia, Jeanette, Elmer, Vernon and Robert; a Catholic. Married to Janice Cannon on September 22, 1941 who died in August 1943; father of Theodore J.; remarried to Ermalee Strutz on November 22, 1945; father of Robert J., Walter J., Jr., Jack Edward, Joseph W. and Karl. Graduated from Claflin High School. Hickel's business experience includes Travelers' Inns in Anchorage and Fairbanks, Hickel Construction Company, Hotel Captain Cook, Northern Lights Shopping Center and Hickel Investment Company, all in Anchorage. A Republican, he was a Republican National Committeeman, Alaska, 1954—64, and a delegate to the Republican National Convention in 1968. Hickel was a candidate for Governor in 1966 and opposed William A. Egan (Democrat) and John Fichtner Grasse (NP) in the general election. The votes cast for each were: Hickel, 33,145; Egan 32,065; and Grasse, 1,084. He was inaugurated Governor of Alaska January 14, 1967. Hickel was appointed Secretary of Interior by President Richard M. Nixon on December 11, 1968 and resigned as Governor of Alaska on January 23, 1969 to accept that position. Hickel was Secretary of the Interior until November 25, 1970. He was a candidate in the primary race for Governor in 1974 but was defeated by Jay S. Hammond (R). He resides in Anchorage, Alaska and is engaged in private business. Bibliography: Robert E. Hickel, *The Trip That Had To Be* (Clarion Press, 1969); Walter J. Hickel, *Who Owns America?* (New Jersey, 1971); *Inaugural Program 1967* (Juneau, 1967); *State of Alaska Official Returns by Election Precinct* (Juneau, 1966, 1974).

MILLER, Keith Harvey, 1969-1970

Born on March 1, 1925 in Seattle, Washington, son of Hopkins Keith Miller and Sarah Margaret (Harvey) Miller; a Methodist. Married to Diana Mary Doyle on December 26, 1953. Graduated fro Bothell, Washington High School in 1943; received a B.A. in Business Administration from the University of Washington in 1952. Business experience includes credit and collection business; Internal Revenue Service; retail supply firm; and heating oil firm. Served in AUS Air Force, 1943-45, and was discharged as a Private First Class. Miller served a term in the Alaska House of Representatives from 1963 to 1965. He was elected Secretary of State in 1966 and served from 1967-1969. When Walter J. Hickel, Governor, was confirmed Secretary of the Interior in 1969 and resigned as Governor of Alaska, Miller, as Secretary of State, succeeded Hickel as set forth by the Constitution of the State of

Alaska. He was sworn in as Governor on January 24, 1969. Miller was a candidate for Governor in the 1970 election and was defeated by former Governor Egan. He was opposed in the general election by William A. Egan (Democrat) and Ralph Milton Anderson (Alaska Independent Party). The votes cast for each were: Miller, 37,264; Anderson, 1,206; and Egan, 42,309. Miller was elected to the Alaska State Senate in 1972 and served as a member from 1973-75. He lives in Anchorage and is engaged in private business. Bibliography: *Inaugural Program 1967* (Juneau, 1967); *Know Your Legislators* (Juneau, 1975); *Meet Your Governor* (Juneau, 1970); *National Association of Secretaries of State Handbook*, "Keith Harvey Miller" (1968); *State of Alaska Official Returns by Election Precinct* (Juneau, 1970).

EGAN, William Allen, 1958-1966, 1970-1974

HAMMOND, Jay Sterner, 1974-

Born on July 21, 1922 in Troy, New York, son of Morris Adelbert Hammond, a Methodist minister, and Edna Brown (Sterner) Hammond; a Protestant. Married to Bella Gardiner on September 21, 1952; father of Heidi Lee and Dana E. Graduated from Scotia High School, New York in 1940 and received a B.S. from the University of Alaska in 1968. Business and professional experience includes pilot-agent for the U.S. Fish and Wildlife Service, and air taxi and guiding business. Served in U.S. Marine Corps Reserves, 1942-46, and was discharged as a Captain. A Repubican, he was a member of the Alaska State House of Representatives 1959-65. Hammond was manager of the Bristol Bay Borough, 1965-66. He served in the Alaska State Senate, 1967-73, and was President of the Senate from 1971-1973. He served as Mayor of the Bristol Bay Borough from 1972 to 1974. Hammond was a candidate for Governor of Alaska in 1974 and was opposed by William A. Egan (Democrat) and Joseph E. ("Joe") Vogler (Alaska Independent Party). The votes shown by the official recount of the governor's race were as follows: Hammond, 45,840; Egan, 45,553; and Vogler, 4,770. Bibliography: *Election Candidate Pamphlet* (Juneau, 1974); "Governor Recalls Days on Fairbanks Campus," *Alaska Alumnus* (Spring, 1975); *Inaugural Program 1975* (Juneau, 1975); *Jay S. Hammond Quick Reference Biography* (Juneau, n.d.); Elaine Mitchell, ed., *Alaska Blue Book*, 2nd ed. (Juneau, 1975); *State of Alaska Official Returns by Election Precinct* (Juneau, 1974).

ARIZONA

ARIZONA

Born on November 1, 1859, in Huntsville, Missouri, son of George Washington Hunt, a "Forty-Niner" in the gold rush to California, and Sarah Elizabeth Yates Hunt, a Methodist; brother of Irby, Daniel, Robert, and Juel. Married Duett Ellison on February 24, 1905; father of Virginia. Educated in both public and private schools for about eight years. Rancher near the Salt River in Arizona, 1881-1891; associated with the Old Dominion Commercial Company, 1890; Secretary, Old Dominion Commercial Company, 1896; President, Old Dominion Commercial Company, 1900. First Mayor of Globe, Arizona; Treasurer, Gila County, Arizona; member, Arizona Territorial Legislature, 1892, 1894; member, Arizona Territorial Council, 1896, 1898, 1904, 1906, 1908; President, Arizona Territorial Council, 1905, 1909; Delegate, Democratic National Convention, 1900; President, Arizona Constitutional Convention, 1910; United States Commissioner of Conciliation, 1917; United States Envoy Extraordinary and Minister Plenipotentiary to Siam, 1920-1921; President, Anti-Capital Punishment League; Chairman, Arizona Colorado River Commission, 1927, 1931; S. A. R.; Mason; Odd Fellow. On October 24, 1911, Hunt won the Democratic gubernatorial primary and on December 12, 1911, he was elected Governor, receiving 11,123 votes to Republican Edward W. Wells' 9,166 and Socialist P. W. Gallentine's 1,247. He was sworn into office on February 14, 1912. Hunt believed that the Constitutional Convention had given the governor too little power, and during his first term, he worked to make the various state agencies more responsive to the chief executive. In addition, a pension plan for teachers who had taught more than twenty-five years was enacted. In September, 1914, Hunt won the Democratic gubernatorial primary and on November 3, 1914, he was reelected Governor, receiving 25,226 votes to Republican Ralph H. Cameron's 17,602, Progressive George U. Young's 5,206, and Socialist J. R. Barnette's 2,973. During his second term, Arizona's agricultural and mining interests underwent tremendous growth as a result of the outbreak of World War I. However, some miners dissatisfied over wages organized a strike against the copper mines, and Hunt moved quickly to crush the strike with the National Guard. Also during this administration, the Legislature enacted a Prohibition statute: the State Bureau of Mines was established; and the State Law Library was created. In September, 1916, Hunt won the Democratic gubernatorial primary, but was apparently defeated in the general election by Republican Thomas E. Campbell, 27,976 votes to 27,946. Hunt left office on January 1, 1917. However, he protested Campbell's thirty vote victory and on December 22, 1917, the Arizona Supreme Court ruled in a recount that Hunt had received 28,094 votes to Campbell's 28,051. On December 25, 1917, Hunt was sworn into office for the third time. He left office on January 6, 1919. Nonetheless, in September, 1922, he again won the Democratic gubernatorial primary and on November 7, 1922, Hunt was elected to his fourth term as Governor, defeating Campbell 37,310 votes to

30,599. He returned to the governor's office more popular than ever. He won the Democratic gubernatorial primary again in September, 1924, and was reelected on November 4, 1924 to a fifth term, defeating Republican Dwight B. Heard 38,372 votes to 37,571. Two years later, he again won the Democratic gubernatorial primary and was reelected to a sixth term when he defeated Republican E. S. Clark in the November 2, 1926 general election, 39,979 votes to 39,580. During these terms, Hunt's problems were reduced by the general boom of the "Roaring Twenties," and he continued his program of expanding the system of paved roads by using convict labor. In addition, the Bureau of Statistics was created and a new compulsory compensation law was enacted. Though Hunt won the 1928 Democratic gubernatorial primary, he was defeated in the general election and left office on January 7, 1929, announcing his retirement from politics. When the Great Depression struck, Hunt came out of retirement because of the unpopularity of Republican Governor John C. Phillips. Though he was seventy-one years of age, he won the September, 1930 Democratic gubernatorial primary. On November 4, 1930, he was elected to his seventh term, receiving 48,875 votes to Phillips' 46,231. He was sworn into office on January 5, 1931. Hunt's final term as Governor was marred by charges of political patronage in the newly created Arizona Highway Patrol. As a result, and because of his age, Hunt once again retired from politics and left office on January 2, 1933. Hunt died on December 24, 1934, and is buried in Phoenix, Arizona. Bibliography: John S. Goff, *George W. P. Hunt and His Arizona* (Pasadena, 1973); Richard E. Sloan, *History of Arizona*, 4 vols. (Phoenix, 1930); Douglas D. Martin, *Arizona Chronology, 1913-1936* (Tucson, 1966); Menzo E. Hatter, "Major Issues in Arizona's Gubernatorial Campaigns," unpublished Master's Thesis, Arizona State University, 1951.

CAMPBELL, Thomas Edward, 1917, 1919-1923

Born on January 18, 1878, in Prescott, Arizona, son of Daniel Campbell, a general service clerk at Whipple Barracks, and Eliza O'Flynn; a Catholic; brother of Harry and Joseph. Married Eleana Gayle Allen on June 18, 1900, and father of Thomas Allen and Alex Brodie. Educated in public schools; attended St. Mary's College, Oakland, California for one year. Assistant Postmaster, Prescott, Arizona 1894-1898; Acting Postmaster, Jerome, Arizona, 1898-1900; Postmaster, Jerome, Arizona, 1902-1905; President, Rio Verde Cattle Company; Director, Jerome-Verde Copper Company. Enlisted in the Rough Riders at the outbreak of the Spanish-American War, but was refused muster because he was a minor. Member, Arizona Territorial Legislature, 1900-1901; County Assessor, Yavapai County, Arizona, 1907-1911, 1912-1915; Republican candidate for United States Congress, 1914; State Tax Commissioner, 1915-1916; Councillor, National Highways Association; President, League of the Southwest; Chairman, Committee of the Western Governors, Colorado River Basin Project. In September, 1916, Campbell won the Republican gubernatorial primary, and on November 7, 1916, he was elected Governor, receiving 27,976 votes to Democrat George W. P. Hunt's 27,946. He was sworn into office on January 1, 1917. However, Hunt protested the election results, and on December 22, 1917, the Arizona Supreme Court ruled that a recount gave Hunt 28,094 votes and Campbell 28,051 — a 43 vote victory for Hunt. Campbell left office on December 25, 1917. Afterward, he served under President Herbert Hoover in the United States Food Administration and the United States Treasury Department. In September, 1918, Campbell again won the Republican gubernatorial primary and on November 5, 1918, was again elected Governor receiving 25,927 votes to Democrat Fred T. Colter's 25,588. He was sworn into office on January 6, 1919. Two years later, he defeated Democrat Mit Simms in the November 2, 1920 general election, 37,060 votes to 31,385—thus becoming Governor a third time. During Campbell's two terms, Arizona ratified the 19th Amendment to the United States Constitution, and adopted a budgeting system for state expenditures. In addition, a Workmen's Compensation Act was passed, and a comprehensive Water Code adopted. On November 7, 1922, Campbell was defeated in the general election and left office on January 1, 1923. Afterward, Campbell served as Chairman of the Fact Finding Commission on Federal Reclamation, 1923-1924; Chairman of the Board of Survey and Adjustments, Federal Reclamation Projects, 1925; member of the Republican National Committee, 1924-1928; and President of the United States Civil Service Commission, 1930-1933. Campbell died on March 1, 1944, and is buried in Phoenix, Arizona. Bibliography: Richard E. Sloan, *History of Arizona*, 4 vols. (Phoenix, 1930); Douglas D. Martin, *Arizona Chronology, 1913-1936* (Tucson, 1966); "Origins of the Colorado River Controversy in Arizona Politics, 1922-1923," *Arizona and the West*, vol. IV, no. 1 (Spring, 1962); Menzo E. Hatter, "Major Issues in Arizona's Gubernatorial Campaigns," unpublished Master's Thesis, Arizona State University, 1951.

HUNT, George Willey Paul, 1912-1917, 1917-1919, 1923-1929, 1931-1933

CAMPBELL, Thomas Edward, 1917, 1919-1923

HUNT, George Willey Paul, 1912-1917, 1917-1919, 1923-1929, 1931-1933

PHILLIPS, John C., 1929-1931

Born on November 13, 1870, near Vermont, Illinois, son of William Henry Phillips, a farmer, and Elizabeth Wood Phillips; a Methodist; brother of Bertha, Willard, Hensey H., and Mary E. Married Minnie Rexroat on October 24, 1895; father of Ralph, Aubrey, Marian, and Elizabeth. Attended Hedding College, Abingdon, Illinois, 1889-1893; privately studied law; legal courses from Sprague Correspondence School. Admitted to the Illinois Bar, 1896; private law practice, Vermont, Illinois. 1896-1898; moved to Phoenix, Arizona, 1898; member, Phillips, Holzworth, and Phillips Law Firm. Probate Judge, Maricopa County, Arizona, 1902-1912; Superior Court Judge, Maricopa County, 1912; member, Arizona House of Representatives, 1916-1922; member, Arizona Senate, 1922-1924. In September, 1928, Phillips won the Republican gubernatorial primary, and on November 6, 1928, he was elected Governor, receiving 47,829 votes to Democrat George W. P. Hunt's 44,552. He was sworn into office on January 7, 1929. Phillips' administration was characterized by public works programs and opposition to the Colorado River Project. In addition, a free county library system was established; the State Bureau of Criminal Identification was organized; and the Colorado River Commission was created. Unfortunately for Phillips, he was in office when the Great Depression struck. As a result many of the chaotic economic conditions were blamed on his administration. He was defeated in a bid for reelection in the 1930 general election, and left office on January 5, 1931. Afterward Phillips returned to his private legal practice. Phillips died on June 25, 1943, and is buried in Phoenix. Bibliography: Richard E. Sloan, *History of Arizona*, 4 vols. (Phoenix, 1930); Douglas D. Martin, *Arizona Chronology, 1913-1936* (Tucson, 1966); Lenard E. Brown, "Arizona's State Governors," *Arizoniana*, vol. III, no. 1 (Spring, 1962), Menzo E. Hatter, "Major Issues in Arizona's Gubernatorial Campaigns," unpublished Master's Thesis, Arizona State University, 1951.

HUNT, George Willey Paul, 1912-1917, 1917-1919, 1923-1929, 1931-1933

MOEUR, Benjamin Baker, 1933-1937

Born on December 22, 1869, in Decherd, Tennessee, son of John Baptist Moeur, a physician, and Ester Kelly Knight Moeur; a Congregationalist; brother of Mattie and John K. Married Honor G. Anderson on June 15, 1896, and father of John Kelly, Vyvyan Bernice, Jessie Belle and Benjamin Baker. Received an M.D. degree from Arkansas Industrial University in 1896, and began a medical practice in Tempe, Arizona that year. Member, Arizona Constitutional Convention, 1910; Secretary, Board of Education, Arizona State Teachers College for twelve years; Mason; Modern Woodman; Woodman of the World; Elk. In September, 1932, Moeur won the Democratic gubernatorial primary and on November 8, 1932, he was elected Governor, receiving 75,314 votes to Republican J. C. Kinney's 42,202. He was sworn into office on January 2, 1933. The economic crisis caused by the Great Depression was the major problem facing Moeur when he took office. To alleviate the situation, he reduced property taxes by forty percent, and instituted sales, luxury, and income taxes to eliminate the deficit in state finances. Also, the 21st Amendment to the United States Constitution was ratified by Arizona, and work began on the Yuma-Gila Reclamation Project. In addition, the spillway of Boulder Dam was officially opened to provide irrigation water to 500,000 acres of land within the state. In September, 1934, Moeur won the Democratic gubernatorial primary, and on November 6, 1934, he was elected to a second term, defeating Republican Thomas Maddock by a vote of 61,355 to 39,242. Moeur's second term was uneventful; however, in a bid for a third term, he was defeated in the 1936 Democratic gubernatorial primary by Rawghlie C. Stanford. Moeur left office on January 4, 1937. He died soon afterward on March 16, 1937, and is buried in Tempe. Bibliography: Douglas D. Martin, *Arizona Chronology, 1913-1936* (Tucson, 1966); Lenard E. Brown, "Arizona's State Governors," *Arizonian*, vol. III, no. 1 (Spring, 1962); Anna Mae Griggs, "Arizona's New Governor: Benjamin B. Moeur," *Arizona Highways*, vol. IX, no. 4 (April, 1933); Menzo E. Hatter, "Major Issues in Arizona's Gubernatorial Campaigns," unpublished Master's Thesis, Arizona State University, 1951.

STANFORD, Rawghlie Clement, 1937-1939

Born on August 2, 1879, in Buffalo Gap, Texas, son of Monroe Ogee Stanford, a merchant, and Margaret Johannah Gamble Stanford; a Presbyterian; brother of E. Stanford and A. Stanford. Married Ruth Butchee on December 26, 1907, and father of Lois, Mary, Martie, Rawghlie Clement, Roscoe, and Sharon. Moved to Arizona in 1881. Attended public schools; student, Arizona Normal School at Tempe for two years. Rancher, 1895-1899; when the Spanish-American War started, he joined the Army and served in the Philippines from 1899 to 1901; returned to Arizona and privately studied law; admitted to the Arizona Bar, 1907. Superior Court Judge, Maricopa County, Arizona, 1915-1922; member, Board of Education, Phoenix Union High School, 1920-1936; Chairman, State Democratic Central Committee, 1928-1929; Judge Advocate General, Spanish-American War Veterans; Veterans of Foreign Wars; Mason; Elk; Lion. In September, 1936, Stanford won the Democratic gubernatorial primary, and on November 3, 1936, he was elected Governor, receiving 87,678 votes to Republican Thomas E. Campbell's 36,114. He was sworn into office on January 4, 1937. Much of Stanford's administration was taken up in combating the effects of the Great Depression on Arizona's economy. However, during his term a Minimum Wage Law was enacted and unfair sales practices were outlawed. In addition, the Federal Social Security Act was implemented in the state. Stanford did not seek reelection and left office on January 2, 1939. Afterward, he served as Chairman of the State Council of Civilian Defense, 1941-1942; Justice of the Arizona Supreme Court, 1942-1944; and Chief Justice of the Arizona Supreme Court, 1944-1953. Stanford died on December 15, 1963, and is buried in Phoenix, Arizona. Bibliography: Douglas D. Martin, *Arizona Chronology, 1913-1936* (Tucson, 1966); Lenard E. Brown, "Arizona's State Governors," *Arizoniana*, vol. III, no. 1 (Spring, 1962); Bert Fireman, "Our New Governor, Rawghlie C. Stanford," *Arizona Highways*, vol. VIII, no. 1 (January 1937); Menzo E. Hatter, "Major Issues in Arizona's Gubernatorial Campaigns," unpublished Master's Thesis, Arizona State University, 1951.

JONES, Robert Taylor, 1939-1941

Born on February 8, 1884, in Rutledge, Tennessee, son of Samuel Jones, a farmer, and Sarah Legg Jones; brother of Cora, Claud, Girtrude, and Johnson. Married to Elon Armstrong and father of Albert, Claud, and Katherine. Self-educated as an engineer; worked as an engineer in Mexico; employed for one year on the construction of the Panama Canal; mining engineer in Nevada. Moved to Arizona in 1909, and was employed on several shortline railroads, before establishing the Jones Drug Company in Superior, Arizona. He later expanded his drug business into a chain of stores throughout the state. Elected to the Arizona Senate, 1930-1934, 1936-1938. In September, 1938, Jones won the Democratic gubernatorial primary, and on November 8, 1939, he was elected Governor, receiving 80,350 votes to Republican Jerrie W. Lee's 32,022. He was sworn into office on January 2, 1939. Jones had campaigned on the promise of a business-like administration of state government; however, Jones' friendliness toward some members of the Arizona Senate so infuriated members of the Arizona House of Representatives that few of his proposals were passed. Nonetheless, during his term a Minimum Wage Law for public works employees was enacted, and pardoning and paroling of convicts was regulated with more stringent rules. In addition, the office of State Historian and State Librarian were combined. Jones chose not to seek reelection and retired from politics after one term. He left office on January 6, 1941. Afterward he returned to his investments and drug company. Jones died on June 11, 1958, and is buried in Phoenix, Arizona. Bibliography: Raymond Carlson, "Arizona Greets a New Governor, Robert T. Jones," *Arizona Highways*, vol. XV, no. 1 (January, 1939); Lenard E. Brown, "Arizona's State Governors," *Arizoniana*, vol. III, no. 1 (Spring, 1962); Odie B. Faulk, *A Short History of Arizona* (Norman, 1975); Menzo E. Hatter, "Major Issues in Arizona's Gubernatorial Campaigns," unpublished Master's Thesis, Arizona State University, 1951.

OSBORN, Sidney Preston, 1941-1948

Born on May 17, 1884, in Phoenix, Arizona, son of Neri Ficklin Osborn, newspaperman, and Marilla Murray Osborn; a Methodist; brother of Gordon, Neri, Ambra, Alma, and Katheryn. Married to Marjorie Grant in September, 1912; she died in December, 1918; married to Gladys Smiley on June 1, 1925, and father of Marjorie Grant. Attended public schools, and was graduated from Phoenix High School in 1903. Editor and owner of *Dunbar's Weekly*, 1925-1941; Collector of Internal Revenue, 1933-1934. Page, Arizona Territorial Legislature, 1898; secretary to J. F. Wilson, Arizona Delegate to the United States Congress, 1903-1905; member, Arizona Constitutional Convention, 1911; Arizona Secretary of State, 1912-1919. In September, 1940, Osborn won the Democratic gubernatorial primary and on November 5, 1940, he was elected Governor, receiving 97,606 votes to Republican Jerrie W. Lee's 50,358. He was sworn into office on January 6, 1941. During Osborn's terms, Arizona's economy recovered from the Great Depression as a result of the World War II industrial boom. For the first time industry moved into the state in a significant way. Another economic boon to the state was several military installations constructed during the war years. The new economic boom caused the state population to double, and this resulted in increased social and educational needs. In addition, the state's chronic water shortage became severer. Under Arizona's Constitution, the Governor has little power in dealing with the Legislature. To overcome this disadvantage, Osborn relied on radio appeals to the public. Though popular with the people, Osborn did not get along well with the legislature, and in September, 1945, the solons met in special session to consider impeachment charges against the governor. Though he was charged with misuse of public funds, Osborn was vindicated and remained in office. An extremely popular chief executive, Osborn won reelection three times. He defeated Republican Jerrie W. Lee, 63,484 votes to 23,562 on November 3, 1942, and again by 100,202 votes to 27,262 on November 7, 1944. On November 5, 1946, Osborn was reelected to a fourth term by defeating Republican Bruce D. Brockett, 73,595 votes to 48,867. Osborn died in office on May 25, 1948, and is buried in Phoenix. Bibliography: Odie B. Faulk, *A Short History of Arizona* (Norman, 1975); Raymond Carlson, "Governor Sidney P. Osborn," *Arizona Highways*, vol. XVII, no. 1 (January, 1941); Lenard E. Brown, "Arizona's State Governors," *Arizoniana*, vol. III, no. 1 (Spring, 1962); Menzo E. Hatter, "Major Issues in Arizona's Gubernatorial Campaigns," unpublished Master's Thesis, Arizona State University, 1951.

GARVEY, Dan E., 1948-1951

Born on June 19, 1886 in Vicksburg, Mississippi, son of Andrew F., a police judge, and Johanna (Horrigan) Garvey; a Catholic; brother of Josephine, Catherine, and six others now deceased. Married to Thirza Jannette Vail on February 20, 1912; father of Dan E., Dorothy, and Annette. Attended parochial schools; graduated from St. Aloysius College in 1901. Railroad accountant in Mississippi, 1903-1909; moved to Arizona, 1909; railroad accountant in Arizona and Mexico, 1909-1927; manager, Phoenix, Arizona bank; Councilman, City of Tucson, Arizona, 1930-1931; County Treasurer, Pima County, Arizona, 1935-1938; Treasurer, City of Tucson, 1938; Assistant Arizona Secretary of State, 1939-1942. Arizona Secretary of State, 1942-1948. On May 25, 1948, Governor Sidney P. Osborn died in office, and Garvey as Secretary of State succeeded him as Acting Governor. During the time Garvey was finishing the unexpired term, the Arizona Supreme Court ruled that Indians on reservations within the state should be allowed to vote in primary elections. And in the September, 1948 Democratic gubernatorial primary, which Garvey won, the Indians were allowed to cast their ballots for the first time. However, prior to the November 1948 general election, an amendment to Arizona's Constitution was adopted establishing the line of succession to the governorship. As a result, Garvey was inaugurated as chief executive. On November 4, 1948, Garvey was elected Governor by defeating Republican Bruce Brockett in the general election, 104,008 votes to 70,419. He was sworn into office on January 3, 1949. During Garvey's second administration a Children's Colony was established; greater financial support was given to higher education; and a new Highway Code was enacted. Defeated in the 1950 Democratic gubernatorial primary, Garvey left office on January 1, 1951. Sixty-four years of age when he left the governor's office, Garvey returned to his business investment in Tucson. Garvey died on February 5, 1974, and was buried in Tucson. Bibliography: Ann M. Peck, *The March of Arizona History* (Tucson, 1962); Odie B. Faulk, *A Short History of Arizona* (Norman, 1975); Raymond Carlson, ed., "Dan E. Garvey, Governor," *Arizona Highways*, vol. XXV, no. 1 (January, 1949); Lenard E. Brown, "Arizona's State Governors," *Arizoniana*, vol. III, no. 1 (Spring, 1962).

PYLE, John Howard, 1951-1955

Born on March 25, 1906, in Sheridan, Wyoming, son of the Reverend Thomas Miller Pyle, and Marie Anderson Pyle; a Baptist. Married to Lucile Hanna on August 9, 1930; father of Mary Lou and Virginia Ann. Received an honorary LL.D. degree from Redlands University in 1950; an honorary LL.D. degree from Chapman College in 1953; an LL.D. degree from Arizona State University in 1954; an honorary L.H.D. degree from Lebanon College in 1956; an LL.D. degree from Bradley University in 1957. During World War II, Pyle served in the Pacific Theatre as a war correspondent for the Arizona Broadcasting Company, NBC. Realtor; Secretary, Tempe, Arizona Chamber of Commerce; engaged in advertising and promotion; Program Director, KTAR radio station; Vice President, KTAR; radio reporter, World Security Conference, San Francisco, California, 1945; Trustee, Redlands University; co-founder, Annual Grand Canyon Easter Sunrise Service; Rotary. In September, 1950, Pyle won the Republican gubernatorial primary and on November 7, 1950, he was elected Governor, receiving 99,109 votes to Democrat Ana Frohmiller's (the only woman to date to run for Governor of Arizona) 96,118. He was sworn into office on January 1, 1951. During Pyle's administration, the Arizona Development Board was formed; legal districts for junior colleges were drawn; the Underground Water Commission was organized; a Civil Defense Act was passed; and the Compact for Western Regional Cooperation in Higher Education was ratified. In addition, while Pyle was Governor, President Harry Truman signed an amendment to the Arizona Statehood Enabling Act which permitted long-term leases on Arizona land to allow for gas pipelines. Pyle won reelection on November 4, 1952 by defeating Democrat Joe D. Haldiman in the general election, 156,592 votes to 103,693. Though otherwise a popular governor, Pyle offended the Mormon vote in Arizona by using the Highway Patrol to disband a small sect of polygamists at Short Creek, Arizona. As a result, when he sought a third term, he was defeated in the November 2, 1954 general election by Democrat Earnest W. McFarland. Pyle left office on January 3, 1955. Afterward he served as Deputy Assistant to the President from 1955 to 1959, and was appointed to the National Safety Council in 1959. In addition, Pyle served as Chairman of the Advisory Council, President's Committee on Highway Safety from 1959 to 1960, before returning to his business investments and home in Tempe, Arizona. Bibliography: Ellen L. Trover, ed., *Chronology and Documentary Handbook of the State of Arizona* (Dobbs Ferry, New York, 1972); Odie B. Faulk, *A Short History of Arizona* (Norman, 1975); Raymond Carlson, ed., "Howard Pyle, Governor," *Arizona Highways*, vol. XXVII, no. 1 (January, 1951); Lenard E. Brown, "Arizona's State Governors," *Arizoniana*, vol. III, no. 1 (Spring, 1962).

McFARLAND, Earnest William, 1955-1959

Born on October 9, 1894, near Earlsboro, Oklahoma, son of William Thomas McFarland, a farmer, and Keziah Smith McFarland; a Methodist; brother of Forest C., Sterling C., and Etta Pearl. Married to Edna Eveland Smith in 1938; father of Jewel. Educated in public schools; attended East Central Oklahoma Teachers' College, 1913-1914; B.A., University of Oklahoma, 1917; J. D., Stanford University, 1921; honorary LL.D., University of Arizona; honorary LL.D., Arizona State University. Served as a seaman with the United States Naval Reserve during World War I, and afterward moved to Arizona. Admitted to the Arizona Bar in 1920; private legal practice in Casa Grande, Arizona; Arizona Assistant Attorney General, 1923-1924; County Attorney, Pinal County, Arizona, 1925-1930; Judge, Superior Court, Pinal County, 1936-1940; member, United States Senate, 1941-1953; Majority Leader, United States Senate, 1951-1952; defeated in a bid for reelection to the Senate in 1952. American Legion; Veterans of Foreign Wars; Mason; Lion; Odd Fellow; Elk; K.P. In September, 1954, McFarland won the Democratic gubernatorial primary and on November 2, 1954, he was elected Governor receiving 128,104 votes to Republican Howard Pyle's 115,866. He was sworn into office on January 3, 1955. During McFarland's administration, the Interstate Oil Compact was ratified; the Colorado River Boundary Commission was created; and the State Racing Commission was given legal powers. In addition, the State Parks System was initiated and state aid to schools was increased. On November 6, 1956, McFarland won a second term, defeating Republican Horace B.

Griffen 171,848 votes to 116,744 in the general election. In 1958, he chose not to seek a third term as governor, but instead campaigned for reelection to the United States Senate. However, he was unsuccessful and left office on January 5, 1959. Afterward McFarland served as Chief Justice of the Arizona Supreme Court, 1965-1970, and currently is president of KTVK Arizona Television Company. Bibliography: Odie B. Faulk, *A Short History of Arizona* (Norman, 1975); Raymond Carlson, "Earnest W. McFarland, Governor of Arizona," *Arizona Highways*, vol. XXXI, no. 2 (February, 1955); Lenard E. Brown, "Arizona's State Governors," *Arizoniana*, vol. III, no. 1 (Spring, 1962).

FANNIN, Paul Jones, 1959-1965

Born on January 29, 1907, in Ashland, Kentucky, son of Thomas Newton Fannin, dairy farmer and proprietor of a harness shop, and Katherine Davis Fannin; a Methodist; brother of Ernest. Married to Elma Addington on May 6, 1934, and father of Thomas, Robert, Paul, William, and Linda. Attended the University of Arizona; B.A. degree from Stanford University, 1930. Vice President, Fannin's Gas and Equipment Company, 1930-1956; President, Fannin's Gas Supply Company, 1956-1958; President, Fannin's Service and Supply Company, 1945-present. In September, 1958, Fannin won the Republican gubernatorial primary and on November 4, 1958, he was elected Governor, receiving 160,136 votes to Democrat Robert Morrison's 130,329. He was sworn into office on January 5, 1959. One of the major goals of Fannin's administration was the attraction of more industry to the state. In addition, he advocated the enactment of a statewide tax equalization program, and pushed for an increased allotment of water for Arizona from the Colorado River Project. On November 8, 1960, Fannin won reelection to a second term as Governor by defeating Democrat Lee Ackerman in the general election, 235,502 votes to 161,605. Continuing the same policies and choosing qualified advisors regardless of their political affiliation, Fannin continued to be very popular in the state. On November 6, 1962, he was elected to the governorship for a third term with 200,578 votes to Democrat Sam Goddard's 165,263 in the general election. In the November, 1964 general election, Fannin won a United States Senate seat from Arizona. As a result he left the governor's office on January 4, 1965. Fannin was reelected to the United States Senate in the 1970 general election and declined to run in 1976. Bibliography: Charles Farrington, Jr., "Paul Fannin, Governor of Arizona," *Arizona Highways*, vol. XXXV, no. 3 (March, 1959); Lenard E. Brown, "Arizona's State Governors," *Arizoniana*, vol. III, no. 1 (Spring, 1962); Odie B. Faulk, *A Short History of Arizona* (Norman, 1975).

GODDARD, Samuel Pearson, 1965-1967

Born on August 8, 1919 in Clayton, Missouri, son of Samuel Pearson, a wholesale grocer, and Florence Hatch (Denham) Goddard; a Unitarian. Married to Julia Hatch on July 1, 1944; father of Samuel Pearson,III, Pascal Hatch, and William Denham. Received an A.B. degree from Harvard University in 1941; received an LL.B. degree from the University of Arizona in 1949. Served in the United States

Army Air Force and rose to the rank of Major, 1941-1946; Brigadier General, United States Air Force Reserve. Admitted to the Arizona Bar, 1949; private law practice, Tucson, Arizona, 1949-1964; became Executive Vice President, Niles Radio Corporation, 1952; became Vice President, Movie Center, Incorporated, 1958; became senior partner, Goddard, Gin Hanshaw, and Gianas Legal Firm, 1960; became President, Catalina Leasing Corporation, 1963. Chairman, Democratic Party of Arizona, 1960-1962; Democratic National Committeeman, Arizona; member, Executive Section, Charter Commission, 1972-1976. Tucson Man of the Year, 1959; Reserve Officers Association; V.F.W.; Air Force Association; American Legion; Phi Alpha Delta; Rotarian. In September, 1964, Goddard won the Democratic gubernatorial primary and on November 3, 1964, he was elected Governor, receiving 252,098 votes to Republican Richard Kleindienst's 221,404. He was sworn into office on January 4, 1965. Goddard, a Democrat, was elected despite the fact that the 1964 Republican presidential candidate was Barry Goldwater, an Arizonian. During Goddard's administration, a three judge Federal Court ordered the Arizona Legislature reapportioned and changes made in two House of Representative districts within the state. In addition, the United States Supreme Court declared the State Employees Loyalty Oath was unconstitutional. Also, during Goddard's term, the Arizona Liquor Control Board was marred by a series of scandals. Goddard was the Democratic nominee for reelection in the 1966 general election; however, he was defeated by Republican Jack Williams. Goddard left office on January 2, 1967. Afterward he returned to his law practice and investments. Bibliography: Roanna Winsor, "Sam Goddard, Arizona's New Governor," Arizona's Highways, vol. XLI, no. 2 (February, 1965); Ellen L. Trover, *Chronology and Documentary Handbook of the State of Arizona* (Dobbs Ferry, New York, 1972); Odie B. Faulk, *A Short History of Arizona* (Norman, 1975).

WILLIAMS, John Richards, 1967-1975

Born on October 29, 1909 in Los Angeles, California, son of James Maurice Williams, an employee of Wells Fargo Company, and Laure (LaCositt) Williams; an Episcopalian. Married to Vera May on June 5 1942; father of John Richard, Jr., Michael M., and Nikki. Attended Phoenix Junior College, 1928-1929. Became Director, KOY radio station, 1929; Secretary-Treasurer, Key Investment Company, KYO, Incorporated; Vice President, Phoenix Housing Authority, 1944-1947; President, Phoenix Elementary School Board, 1948-1953; Councilman, City of Phoenix, 1953-1954; Mayor of Phoenix, 1956-1960. Phoenix Man of the Year, 1953; member, Phoenix Junior Chamber of Commerce; Kiva. After winning the Republican gubernatorial primary, Williams was elected Governor on November 8, 1966, receiving 203,438 votes to Democratic incumbent Governor Samuel P. Goddard's 174,904. He was sworn into office on January 2, 1967. During Williams' first administration, both houses of the Arizona Legislature were dominated by Republicans for the first time in state history; this administration also contained the first Indian elected to the Arizona House of Representatives. With legislative support, Williams secured a reevaluation of the state tax structure, increased aid to both public schools and universities, and began construction on the Central Arizona Project, which would provide more water for agricultural and municipal purposes. On November 5, 1968, Williams was elected to a second term, defeating Goddard once again in the general election, 279,923 votes to 204,075. During this administration, the governor's term of office was increased from two years to four years. On November 3, 1970, Williams was elected to a four year term by defeating Raul H. Castro in the general election, 209,365 votes to 212,053. In a bid for a fourth term, Williams was defeated by Castro in the November 5, 1974 general election. He left office on January 6, 1975. Afterward he returned to his business investments. Bibliography: Ellen L. Trover, ed., *Chronology and Documentary Handbook of the State of Arizona* (Dobbs Ferry, New York, 1972); Odie B. Faulk, *A Short History of Arizona* (Norman, 1975); Raymond Carlson, ed., "The New Governor of Arizona, Jack Williams," *Arizona Highways*, vol. XLIII, no. 1 (January, 1967).

CASTRO, Raul Hector, 1975-1977

Born on June 2, 1916 in Cananea, Sonora, Mexico, son of Francisco D., a miner, and Rosario (Acosta) Castro; a Catholic; brother of one sister and twelve brothers. Married to Patricia Steiner; father of Mary Pat and Beth. Castro's family moved to Pirtleville, Arizona in 1926; became a naturalized citizen in 1939. Attended high school in Douglas, Arizona; received a B.A. degree from Arizona State College in 1939; received a J.D. degree from the University of Arizona in 1949. Member, Arizona National Guard, 1935-1939. Clerk, Office of the United States Foreign Service, Agua Prieta, Sonora, Mexico, 1941-1946; Instructor of Spanish, University of Arizona, 1946-1949; senior partner, Castro and Wolfe Legal Firm, Tucson, Arizona, 1949-1955; Judge, Pima County Superior Court, 1959-1960, 1963-1964; Judge, Pima County Juvenile Court, 1960-1963; United States Ambassador to El Salvador, 1964-1968; United States Ambassador to Bolivia, 1968-1969; private law practice, Tucson, 1969-1975. Naturalized Citizen of the Year, Pima County Bar Association, 1963; Matias Delado Decoration, Government of El Salvador, 1968; Phi Alpha Delta; Rotarian. In September, 1974, Castro won the Democratic gubernatorial primary and on November 5, 1974, he was elected Governor, receiving 278,375 votes to Republican Russell Williams' 273,674. He was sworn into office on January 6, 1975. Born in Mexico, Castro was the first Spanish-American to hold the office of chief executive in Arizona. Though somewhat of a political conservative, he had campaigned on a promise to maintain the rights of minorities and those of differing political ideologies within the state. On October 20, 1977, Castro resigned from the governorship to become United States Ambassador to Argentina. Bibliography: Roy Glashan, *American Governors and Gubernatorial Elections, 1775-1975* (Stillwater, Minnesota, 1975); W. David Barnes, "Raul H. Castro," *Arizona Highways*, vol. LI, no. 2 (February, 1975); Raul H. Castro, "Biography: Governor Raul H. Castro," unpublished manuscript, Office of the Governor, Phoenix, 1975.

BOLIN, Wesley H., 1977-1978

Born on July 1, 1908 in Butler, Missouri, son of Don Strother and Margaret (Combs) Bolin; a Congregationalist. Twice married, the second time to Marion Knappenberger on August 14, 1967; father of Wesley, Bill, Thomas, Bruce and Steven. Moved to Phoenix, Arizona in 1917. Graduated from Phoenix Union High School; attended Phoenix Junior College, 1928-1929; completed the LaSalle Extension School course in law. Engaged in the dry cleaning business. Active in Young Democrats. Elected Constable of West Phoenix Precinct, serving from 1938 to 1942; appointed Justice of the Peace, West Phoenix Precinct in 1942 to complete the term of Nat T. McKee, serving to 1948. Assisted in organizing the Arizona Justices of the Peace and Constables Association, serving as its first secretary-treasurer. Elected Arizona Secretary of State in 1948 and subsequently reelected to that position for ten consecutive terms, serving until October 19, 1977. Active in the National Association of Secretaries of State, serving as its president in 1952-1953, chairman of the Arizona Code Commission in 1956. Elk; Moose; Junior Chamber of Commerce. A Democrat. As Arizona Secretary of State, Bolin assumed the Arizona governorship on October 20, 1977, upon Raul H. Castro's resignation to become Ambassador to Argentina. Wesley Bolin died of a heart attack at his home in Phoenix on March 4, 1978. Attorney General Bruce Babbitt was sworn in as Governor the same day. Bibliography: *Arizona Revised Statutes* (St. Paul, Minnesota, 1956); *Congressional Quarterly Weekly Report,* vol. XXXV, no. 35 (August 27, 1977); *Mesa Tribune* [Mesa, Arizona] (October, 19, 1977); *Facts on File, 1977* (New York, 1977).

BABBITT, Bruce, 1978-

As *The Biographical Directory of the Governors of the United States, 1789-1978* was going to the printer, Governor Babbitt was sworn in as Governor of Arizona. His full biography will appear in the first revision of *The Biographical Directory of the Governors of the United States* (1982).

ARKANSAS

ARKANSAS

CONWAY, James Sevier, 1836-1840

Born on December 9, 1798 on the family plantation in Greene County, Tennessee, son of Thomas, a planter, and Ann (Rector) Conway; an Episcopalian. Married to Mary Bradley in 1823; father of several children. Although the family lived in St. Louis, Missouri Territory for a short while and subsequently moved to Boone County, Missoure, young James attended school in Tennessee and worked with private tutors. James and his brother Henry were good surveyors, and in 1820 they went to Arkansas Territory to survey a large body of land. The brothers and two friends formed a town-site company and took over the land on which Little Rock, Arkansas was built. In 1823 Conway came to the territory to live and settled on a wide acreage on Red River in Lafayette County. In addition to working on his plantation, Conway surveyed the western boundary line of the Territory in 1825 and the southern boundary in 1831. He became surveyor-general of the Arkansas Territory, serving from 1832 until 1836. Arkansas was admitted as a state on June 15, 1836, and in preparation for statehood, the people of Arkansas were required to elect a governor. Conway, a Democrat, was nominated by his party, and the Whigs nominated Absalom Fowler. Conway won 5,338 votes to Fowler's 3,222. Governor Conway was inaugurated on September 13, 1836. Of the many problems facing the first governor of any state, one is the medium of exchange. Many people owned land in Arkansas, but few had ready money. To solve this problem, Conway directed the legislature to charter two banks, the State Bank and the Real Estate Bank. Unfortunately, both banks eventually failed, leaving Arkansas with a debt of over three million dollars. Conway was also an avid supporter of Martin Van Buren in the presidential election of 1836, the first presidential election in which the people of Arkansas could participate. Governor Conway left office on November 4, 1840 to return to his plantation on Red River. Conway died at Walnut Hills, Arkansas, March 3, 1855. Bibliography: Fay Hempstead, *A History of the State of Arkansas* (New Orleans, 1889); Roy Glashan, *American Governors and Gubernatorial Elections, 1775-1975* (Stillwater, Minnesota, 1975); Congressional Quarterly, Inc. *Guide to United States Elections* (Washington, D.C., 1975); John G. Fletcher, *Arkansas* (Chapel Hill, North Carolina, 1947).

YELL, Archibald, 1840-1844

Born in August 1797, near Waxhow, North Carolina. Little is recorded about his parentage or early years; a Baptist. Married three times: to Mary, who died in 1830; to Nancy, who died October 3, 1835; and to Marie, who died October 14, 1838. As a youth, Yell moved to Tennessee and became a Captain in the Jackson Guards. He served under Andrew Jackson against the Creek Indians, against the British at New Orleans, and against the Seminoles in Florida. Yell then studied law, was admitted to the bar, and enjoyed a successful practice in Fayetteville, Tennessee. Yell, a Democrat, served one term in the Tennessee Legislature. In 1830 he moved to Little Rock, Arkansas to take charge of the Federal Land Office. President Andrew Jackson offered him a choice of two appointments: the governorship of Florida or a territorial judgeship in Arkansas. Yell chose the latter, moved to Fayetteville, Arkansas, and served as a judge from 1835 to 1837. Although widely mentioned as a possible candidate for Arkansas' first state governor, Yell was barred from nomination by the state constitution's four-year residency requirement. In 1837 he ran for Congress, was elected, and served until 1839. In 1840 Yell was unopposed in his campaign for Governor. He received 10,554 votes. Governor Yell was inaugurated on November 4, 1840. His administration urged stronger control of the State Bank and the Real Estate Bank. He wanted a Board of Internal Improvements to bring more railroads to the state, to make waterways more navigable, and to improve the system of roads for trade and public mobility. He also recommended more funds for education, and the establishment of agricultural schools to fill the needs of Arkansas' rural society. Yell resigned the governorship on April 29, 1844 to run for Congress. Elected, he took his seat in 1845; left Washington (without resigning his post) to accept the colonelcy of the 1st Arkansas Volunteer Cavalry during the Mexican War. When Yell stayed in the field, Governor Thomas Drew considered his Congressional seat vacant and ordered a special election. Made Brigadier General for conspicuous gallantry, Yell was killed in the Battle of Buena Vista, February 22, 1847. Bibliography: Fay Hempstead, *A History of the State of Arkansas* (New Orleans, 1889); Roy Glashan, *American Governors and Gubernatorial Elections, 1775-1975* (Stillwater, Minnesota, 1975); Congressional Quarterly, Inc., *Guide to United States Elections* (Washington, D.C., 1975); John G. Fletcher, *Arkansas* (Chapel Hill, North Carolina, 1947).

ADAMS, Samuel, 1844

Born on June 5, 1805 in Halifax County, Virginia, son of Sylvester, a farmer, and Fanny (Smith) Adams; a Baptist. Married to Rebecca May in 1824, who died in 1840; father of six children. In 1810 the Adams family moved to Humphrey County, Tennessee, where young Samuel grew up in the frontier wilderness. Consequently, he had few social or educational opportunities and was self-taught. After his marriage in 1824, Adams and his family lived in Tennessee until 1835, when they moved to western Arkansas to settle in what is now Johnson County; there Adams became a planter and a respected resident of the area. Adams, a Democrat, was elected in 1840 to the State Senate, during his second term, he was chosen President of the Senate. When Governor Archibald Yell resigned his office on April 29, 1844 to run for Congress, Adams, by virtue of his office as President of the Senate, became Governor. Governor Adams was inaugurated on April 29, 1844, and served until November 5, 1844, when Thomas S. Drew who had been elected in August, took office. During his short tenure, Adams supported Yell's policies of education, internal improvements and fiscal responsibility, leaving $125,420 in the state treasury at the end of his term. On the national scene, Adams advocated the annexation of Texas, because he feared that the British might influence the Texans to abolish slavery; the disposition of public lands; and James K. Polk's bid for the presidency. After leaving the governor's chair, Adams returned to his plantation. In 1846 he was elected State Treasurer and moved to Little Rock. He served in that capacity until his death on February 27, 1850 in Saline County, Arkansas. Bibliography: Fay Hempstead, *A History of the State of Arkansas* (New Orleans, 1889); Roy Glashan, *American Governors and Gubernatorial Elections, 1775-1975* (Stillwater, Minnesota, 1975); Congressional Quarterly, Inc., *Guide to United States Elections* (Washington, D.C., 1975); John G. Fletcher, *Arkansas* (Chapel Hill, North Carolina, 1947).

DREW, Thomas Stevenson, 1844-1849

Born on August 25, 1802 in Wilson County, Tennessee, son of Newton, a farmer, and Jane (Stevenson) Drew; a Baptist. Married to Fanny Akins in 1822; father of several children. Attended the local grammar school. Drew moved to Arkansas in 1818 and found work as a travelling salesman. He then settled in what is now Ouachita County, about eighteen miles from Camden, and there taught school. When Drew and Fanny Akins were married, her father gave them a small farm and a dozen slaves, and Drew became a prosperous farmer. A Democrat, Drew was not politically ambitious. His only experience for the governorship was the two years that he had served as county clerk and the ten days that he had spent at the state's Constitutional Convention in 1836. In 1844 the Democratic State Convention nominated Elias N. Conway, brother of Arkansas' first governor, who declined the nomination because of personal obligations. When asked to name a substitute, Conway suggested Drew. He ran and defeated the Whig candidate, Lawrence Gibson, 8,859 votes to 7,244. Richard C. Byrd, an Independent, polled 2,507 votes in the election. In 1848 Drew was unopposed and received 15,962 votes. Governor Drew was inaugurated on November 5, 1844. During his administration the managers of the Real Estate Bank had gained control of the state's finances and Drew seemed powerless to regain control. After serving a little more than a year of his second term, he resigned, giving as his reason that the salary of $1,800 a year was insufficient to support his family. Drew left office on January 10, 1849. President of the State Senate, Richard C. Byrd, became Acting Governor. Drew's fortunes deteriorated further. He returned home to his farm, but his crops failed. He went to California, hoping to discover gold, but again failed. Ill and broken in spirit, Drew died near Lipan, Hood County, Texas in 1879. Bibliography: Fay Hempstead, *A History of the State of Arkansas* (New Orleans, 1889); Roy Glashan, *American Governors and Gubernatorial Elections, 1775-1975* (Stillwater, Minnesota, 1975); Congressional Quarterly, Inc., *Guide to United States Elections* (Washington, D.C., 1975); John G. Fletcher, *Arkansas* (Chapel Hill, North Carolina, 1947).

BYRD, Richard C., 1849

Born in Hawkins County, Tennessee in 1805 of pioneer stock; married to Mary E.; father of William. A Protestant. Moved to Arkansas about 1826; a merchant and farmer in Pulaski County, Arkansas Territory. Byrd served as Auditor of the Arkansas Territory from 1829-1831; he was elected Representative for Pulaski County in the Territorial Legislature in 1833, and State Representative in 1836. He served as State Senator for

Pulaski County, 1840 and 1842; and State Senator from Arkansas, Jefferson and Desha counties, 1846 and 1848. Defeated in the 1844 election for Governor of Arkansas. Byrd served as president of the Arkansas State Senate in 1848 and, in that capacity, succeeded to the office of Governor after the resignation of Thomas S. Drew. A Democrat. Byrd assumed the duties of governor on January 11, 1849. During his brief term, he called a special election for Governor of Arkansas to be held on March 14, 1849. Governor Byrd left office on April 19, 1849 after the election of John S. Roane. He then returned to his mercantile business in Jefferson County, Arkansas. Byrd died on June 1, 1854. Bibliography: Roy Glashan, *American Governors and Gubernatorial Elections, 1775-1975* (Stillwater, Minnesota, 1975); Congressional Quarterly, Inc., *Guide to U.S. Elections* (Washington, D.C., 1975); Arkansas History Commission, "Sketch on Richard C. Byrd" (Little Rock, Arkansas); Walter Scott McNutt, Olin Eli McKnight, and George Allen Hubbell, *A History of Arkansas* (Little Rock, 1932).

ROANE, John Selden, 1849-1852

Born on January 8, 1817 in Wilson County, Tennessee, son of John, a storekeeper, and Mattie (Selden) Roane; a Baptist. Married to Mary K. Smith on June 5, 1855; father of three daughters. Roane attended the local schools in Wilson County and went to Cumberland College in Princeton, Kentucky. He later studied law and was admitted to the bar in 1837. He then moved to Pine Bluff, Arkansas and began to practice law. From November 5, 1840 to September 19, 1842, Roane, a Democrat, served as Prosecuting Attorney for the Second Judicial District. He was a representative to the State Legislature from 1842 to 1843. At the end of the year, he moved to Van Buren, Crawford County, serving as its representative from 1844 until the outbreak of the Mexican War. He then volunteered and served as Lieutenant Colonel of the Arkansas regiment commanded by former Governor Archibald Yell. At the Battle of Buena Vista, Colonel Yell was killed and Roane took command. After the war, Roane returned to his law practice in Pine Bluff. When Governor Thomas S. Drew resigned his office on January 10, 1849, Acting Governor Richard C. Byrd called a special election. Roane defeated the Whig candidate, Charles Wilson, 3,317 votes to 3,228. Governor Roane was inaugurated on April 19, 1849. He urged more railroads, better roads and greater funds for education. Among the counties created during Roane's administration were Calhoun and Sebastian. In the national census of 1850, the population of Arkansas was 209,897, an increase of 112,323 since 1840. In the presidential election of 1852, Governor Roane supported Franklin Pierce. Roane left office on November 15, 1852 to return to his private law practice. When the Civil War broke out, Roane joined the Confederacy. He knew Jefferson Davis and Robert E. Lee, who had been impressed by his military prowess during the Mexican War. Roane was commissioned a Brigadier-General and raised troops in the Trans-Mississippi Department. After the war he returned home. Roane died in Pine Bluff, Arkansas on April 17, 1867. Bibliography: Fay Hempstead, *A History of the State of Arkansas* (New Orleans, 1889); Roy Glashan, *American Governors and Gubernatorial Elections, 1775-1975* (Stillwater, Minnesota, 1975); Congressional Quarterly, Inc., *Guide to United States Elections* (Washington, D.C., 1975); John G. Fletcher, *Arkansas* (Chapel Hill, North Carolina, 1947).

HAMPTON, John R., 1851, 1857

Born on April 1, 1807 in Charlotte, Mecklenburg County, North Carolina, son of a county sheriff; a Presbyterian. Was orphaned at an early age; received only three months' education in public schools. Eventually learned the printer's trade and published a newspaper in Macon, Mississippi. Moved to Tuscaloosa, Alabama, where he married Frances Ann Webb. In 1843, he settled in Union County, Arkansas, near the present El Dorado. His wife died three weeks after their arrival in Arkansas, leaving him with two young children, Susan and Henry. Hampton later remarried Nancy Gabeen; they had four children, J. E., Charlotte, Fannie and George. In 1843 Hampton was appointed as a commissioner to select a central location for the county seat of Union County. A few years later, he moved to Bradley County, settling on a profitable plantation, "Forest Home," comprising approximately 1,300 acres. In 1846, Hampton was elected to the General Assembly of Arkansas as a Democratic senator from Bradley County. From 1848 to 1849, and again from 1850 to 1851, Hampton was a member of the Arkansas Senate, representing Union County. In 1850 he was elected President of the Arkansas Senate. In September 1851, during chief executive John Roane's term of office, Hampton served as Acting Governor of Arkansas. He was again elected senator from Union County in 1852. From 1856 to 1857, Hampton was senator from Dallas and Bradley counties, and was elected President of the Arkansas Senate during that term. During his term in office, Hampton served as governor of the state from April 21 to September 14, 1857, since Governor Elias Conway was then in poor health and needed to move to the East. After his service as governor, Hampton was elected again to the Arkansas Senate from Dallas and Bradley counties in 1858 and 1862. In 1861, he was chosen as one of the six presidential electors from Arkansas who were instructed to vote for Jefferson Davis. Hampton served as a delegate from Bradley and Dallas counties to a special session of the Confederate Legislature held in Washington, Arkansas from September 22 to October 2, 1864. In 1874 Hampton was a delegate from Bradley County to the State Constitutional Convention in Little Rock. He was elected senator from the 18th District to the 21st General Assembly in 1877 and to the 22nd General Assembly in 1879. Hampton was one of the original incorporators of the Cairo and Fulton Railroad in 1853. The county seat of Calhoun County, Arkansas was named for Hampton and in 1858, the town of Johnsville was named for Hampton, John Martin, John Pagan and John Brady. The date of Hampton's death cannot be verified. Bibliography: Josiah H. Shinn, *The History of Arkansas* (Richmond, Virginia, 1900); Dallas T. Herndon, ed., *Annals of Arkansas, 1947*, 4 vols. (Little Rock, 1947); Margaret Ross, *Arkansas Gazette: The Early Years, 1819-1866* (Little Rock, 1969); Roy Glashan, *American Governors and Gubernatorial Elections, 1775-1975* (Stillwater, Minnesota, 1975).

CONWAY, Elias Nelson, 1852-1860

Born on May 17, 1812 near Greenville, Green County, Tennessee, son of Thomas, a planter, and Ann (Rector) Conway; an Episcopalian. Never married. Brother of James S. Conway, the first governor of Arkansas. When Elias was six years old he moved with his family to Boone County, Missouri, where he was educated by private tutors. He later studied surveying, and in October 1833, joined his older brothers, Henry and James, in the Arkansas Territory. Reaching Little Rock in November, he contracted to survey public lands in the northwest part of the territory. From 1835 to 1849, Elias served as Auditor of Arkansas. In 1840 he outlined to the legislature a plan for opening public lands to settlement, an idea which was adopted and became state policy. In addition to his work as surveyor and state auditor, Conway, a Democrat, was active in politics. In 1844 he declined the Democratic gubernatorial nomination, but he accepted it in 1852. Conway defeated the Whig candidate, Allen Smith, 15,932 votes to 12,955. Renominated in 1856, Conway won 28,159 votes while James Yell, his Whig opponent, received 15,436. Governor Conway was inaugurated on November 15, 1852. One of his greatest problems was the questionable management of the Real Estate Bank, whose directors, it appeared, were manipulating its assets in ways detrimental to the public good. Unable to control the bank in any other way, Governor Conway created a Court of Chancery which finally destroyed the bank's financial stranglehold on the state. Conway also encouraged the state's railroad system by giving large grants. In addition, he secured a geological survey of the state. When he left office on November 16, 1860, the treasury held a surplus of $420,000. After leaving the governor's chair. Conway spent the rest of his life looking after his land interests. He died in Little Rock, Arkansas on February 28, 1892. Bibliography: Fay Hempstead, *A History of the State of Arkansas* (New Orleans, 1889); Roy Glashan, *American Governors and Gubernatorial Elections, 1775-1975* (Stillwater, Minnesota, 1975); Congressional Quarterly, Inc., *Guide to United States Elections* (Washington, D.C., 1975); John G. Fletcher, *Arkansas* (Chapel Hill, North Carolina, 1947).

HAMPTON, John R., 1851, 1857

RECTOR, Henry Massey, 1860-1862

Born on May 1, 1816 in Fountain's Ferry near Louisville, Kentucky, son of Elias, landowner and postmaster of St. Louis, Missouri, and Fanny (Thurston) Rector; a Presbyterian. In 1838 married Jane Elizabeth Field,who died in 1857; father of four sons and three daughters; remarried in 1859 to Ernestine Flora Linde, by whom he had one daughter. Rector's father died in 1822, leaving him land in Arkansas. His mother soon remarried, and he received his elementary education from her; his practical experience he obtained driving teams and hauling loads from his stepfather's salt works in Missouri. He attended school in Louisville, Kentucky for a year, read law for several years, and was admitted to the bar in 1854. In 1835 Rector moved to Arkansas to see after his inheritance. A Democrat, he worked as a teller of the State Bank, farmed, and took an interest in politics. He was U.S. Marshall for the District of Arkansas from 1842 to 1843, a State Senator from 1848 to 1850, and U.S. Surveyor-General of Arkansas from 1851 to 1854. Having been admitted to the bar, Rector specialized in criminal law. From 1855 to 1859, he was a representative to the State Legislature, and from 1859 to 1860, he served as a judge on the Arkansas Supreme Court. In 1860 he ran for Governor on the Independent Democratic ticket. He defeated R.H. Johnson, the Regular Democratic candidate, 31,578 votes to 28,622. Governor Rector was inaugurated on November 16, 1860. After Fort Sumter had surrendered in April 1861, President Abraham Lincoln called for 75,000 volunteers to save the Union and requested that Arkansas send her quota. Heretofore, sentiment in Arkansas had been pro-Union. Governor Rector's reply to the Secretary of War, Simon Cameron, reflected the shift in public opinion: "In answer to your requisition for troops from Arkansas to subjugate the southern states, I have to say that none will be furnished. The demand is only adding insult to injury. The people of this state are freemen, not slaves, and will defend to the last extremity their honor, lives, and property against northern mendacity and usurpation." In May, 1861, a convention passed the Ordinance of Secession by a vote of sixty-nine to one, and Arkansas was admitted to the Southern Confederacy on May 20, 1861. Since no provision had been made for continuing the governor's office, Rector left office on November 4, 1862. He was succeeded by Thomas Fletcher, who was president of the Confederate Senate. Rector died in Little Rock, Arkansas on August 12, 1899. Bibliography: Fay Hempstead, *A History of the State of Arkansas* (New Orleans, 1889); Roy Glashan, *American Governors and Gubernatorial Elections, 1775-1975* (Stillwater, Minnesota, 1975); Congressional Quarterly, Inc., *Guide to United States Elections* (Washington, D.C., 1975); John G. Fletcher, *Arkansas* (Chapel Hill, North Carolina, 1947).

FLETCHER, Thomas, 1862

Born April 8, 1819, in Randolph County, Arkansas, son of Henry, a farmer, and Mary (Lindsey) Fletcher; a Baptist. Married Lucinda Beavers on September 4, 1841, and father of nine children. In 1825 the Fletchers moved to Saline County, where Thomas attended school. In 1839 he moved to Little Rock, Pulaski County, to teach school; in the summers he worked on his farm. A Democrat, Fletcher served as Sheriff of Pulaski County from 1858 to 1861. Before the people of Arkansas had time to vote on whether the state should withdraw from the Union, the Civil War had begun. Unwilling to fight against fellow Southerners, Governor Henry Rector refused President Abraham Lincoln's request for troops, and Arkansas seceded from the Union. The convention that met in May 1861 prepared a new constitution, which included the state's resolve to join the Southern Confederacy. From 1862 to 1864 Fletcher served as a member of the Confederate Senate. As President of this body, he became Acting Governor when Governor Rector resigned. Inaugurated on November 4, 1862, Governor Fletcher served until November 15, 1862. His function was to call a gubernatorial election and to serve until the new governor could take office. After Harris Flanagin was elected and sworn in, Fletcher returned to private life. He continued to farm and to read law, and in 1866 was elected sheriff. From 1868 to 1884 he practiced law; he was also an unsuccessful candidate for Governor in 1876 and 1878. In 1885 President Grover Cleveland appointed him U.S. Marshall for the Eastern District of Arkansas, a position he held until 1889. Fletcher became interested in the Populist Party and was a Populist leader until his death. He was also associated with the Farmers' Alliance and Industrial Union, the Masons, and the Patrons of Husbandry. Fletcher died at his home in Little Rock, Arkansas on February 21, 1900, at the age of eighty. Bibliography: Fay Hempstead, *A History of the State of Arkansas* (New Orleans, 1889); Roy Glashan, *American Governors and Gubernatorial Elections, 1775-1975* (Stillwater, Minnesota, 1975); Congressional Quarterly, Inc., *Guide to United States Elections* (Washington, D.C., 1975); John G. Fletcher, *Arkansas* (Chapel Hill, North Carolina, 1947).

FLANAGIN, Harris, 1862-1864

Born on November 3, 1817 in Roadstown, Cumberland County, New Jersey, son of James, a farmer, and Mary F. Flanagin; a Catholic. Married to Martha E. Nash on July 23, 1851; father of three children: Duncan, Nash, and Laura. Flanagin attended the local schools in Roadstown, New Jersey; studied law; and was admitted to the bar in 1837. That same year he moved to Greenville, Clark County, Arkansas, to open a law office. In 1842 Arkadelphia became the county seat, and Flanagin moved there to expand his practice. A Democrat, Flanagin served as a representative to the State Legislature from 1842 to 1844. When the Civil War began, he joined the Confederate Army as Captain of Company E, 2nd Arkansas Regiment of Mounted Rifles. He later became Colonel of this regiment. When Arkansas seceded from the Union in May, 1861, Henry M. Rector was governor. He resigned his office on November 4, 1862, and Thomas Fletcher, president of the Confederate Senate, became Acting Governor. He had called a special gubernatorial election for September 6, 1862, under the new Confederate State Constitution. Flanagin, then commanding his regiment in the field, was elected with 18,139 votes. Governor Flanagin was inaugurated on November 15, 1862. During his administration, he had the difficult task of trying to maintain civil order during the war, to coordinate and assist Confederate forces fighting Union armies in Arkansas, and to relieve the suffering of the wounded, the widowed, and the orphaned. By the end of 1862, the rigid Union blockade had effectively cut off such imported supplies as tea, coffee, pepper, drugs, and medicines. In addition to the scarcity of goods, Confederate money was so greatly depreciated that a pound of pepper, if it could be had, cost $300. President Abraham Lincoln's Emancipation Proclamation which affected about 111,000 slaves in Arkansas also had an economic impact on the state. Among the battles fought on Arkansas soil were those at Pea Ridge, Prairie Grove, Pine Bluff, Arkansas Post, Helena, Jenkin's Ferry, and Little Rock, the capital, which was captured on September 10, 1863. The capture of Little Rock paved the way for a Union provisional government, with Isaac Murphy, the only man who had voted against the Ordinance of Secession, Governor. Flanagin left office on April 18, 1864 to return to his private law practice. He died in Arkadelphia, Arkansas, September 23, 1874. Bibliography: Fay Hempstead, *A History of the State of Arkansas* (New Orleans, 1889); Roy Glashan, *American Governors and Gubernatorial Elections, 1775-1975* (Stillwater, Minnesota, 1975); Congressional Quarterly, Inc., *Guide to United States Elections* (Washington, D.C., 1975); John G. Fletcher, *Arkansas* (Chapel Hill, North Carolina, 1947).

MURPHY, Isaac, 1864-1868

Born on October 16, 1802 near Pittsburgh, Pennsylvania, son of Hugh, a paper manufacturer, and Jane (Williams) Murphy; a Congregationalist. Married to Angelina A. Lockhart on July 31, 1830; father of five children. Received a classical education at the local schools in Pittsburgh. In 1830 Murphy moved to Montgomery County, Tennessee, taught school, and married. In November 1834, he moved his wife and two daughters, Mitilda and Mary, to Fayetteville, Arkansas. They later moved to Mount Comfort, where he taught school, studied law, and passed the bar examination in 1835. In addition to practicing law and teaching, Murphy worked on the public land surveys in northwest and eastern Arkansas. A Democrat, Murphy served in the State Legislature from 1848 to 1849. After prospecting for gold in California for four years, Murphy returned to Arkansas and settled in Huntsville, Madison County. From 1856 to 1857, he served as a State Senator. Sent as a Union delegate to the State Convention to decide on the question of secession, Murphy alone voted negatively. He joined the Union forces in Missouri and became Major of the 1st Arkansas Infantry (Federal). Murphy was with the command that captured Little Rock on September 10, 1863. Governor Flanagin, a Confederate sympathizer, was removed; Murphy became Provisional Governor on January 20, 1864. Running unopposed, he received 12,418 votes from forty counties under Union Army control and was inaugurated Governor on April 18, 1864 according to the provisions of a new Federal state constitution. Although hated by his constituents, Governor Murphy managed to keep the civil peace. His conservative administration was frugal, and he left a surplus of $270,000 in the state treasury when he left office on July 2, 1868. His administration was marked by being neither punitive nor corrupt. Murphy returned to his home in Huntsville to practice law until his death on September 8, 1882. Bibliography: Fay Hempstead, *A History of the State of Arkansas* (New Orleans, 1889); Roy Glashan, *American Governors and Gubernatorial Elections, 1775-1975* (Stillwater, Minnesota, 1975); Congressional Quarterly, Inc., *Guide to United States Elections* (Washington, D.C., 1975); John G. Fletcher, *Arkansas* (Chapel Hill, North Carolina, 1947).

CLAYTON, Powell, 1868-1871

Born on August 7, 1833 in Bethel County, Pennsylvania, son of John, a surveyor, and Ann (Clark) Clayton; a Presbyterian. Married to Adaline McGraw on December 14, 1865; no children. Attended the common schools in Bethel County and Partridge Military Academy in Bristol, Pennsylvania. From 1859 to 1861, he was an engineer in Leavenworth, Kansas. When the Civil War began, Clayton joined the 1st Kansas Infantry as Captain. He was promoted Lieutenant-Colonel of the 5th Kansas Cavalry on February 27, 1862 and Colonel on March 30. He saw action in Missouri and Arkansas, and received command of Pine Bluff in March 1864, where he repulsed the Confederate attack led by General John S. Marmaduke. For his defense of Pine Bluff, Clayton was made Brigadier-General. Leaving the Union Army on August 24, 1865, he bought a plantation near Pine Bluff and settled there as a cotton planter. A Republican, Clayton campaigned for the adoption of the State Constitution of 1868 which would readmit Arkansas to the Union; he also campaigned for the governorship. Since former Confederates were barred from voting. Clayton ran unopposed. The Republicans approved the constitution and elected the Republican candidates; Arkansas was restored to the Union; and Governor Clayton was inaugurated on July 2, 1868. The Democrats despised Clayton as a "carpet-bag" governor for several reasons. First, he placed Arkansas under martial law and called out a black militia to hunt down the Ku Klux Klan at a cost of $330,675. Second, the Republican State Senate acquitted him on charges of corruption (for using bonds to aid railroads) and election fraud. Elected to the U.S. Senate in 1871, Clayton refused to resign because he did not want J.M. Johnson, the Lieutenant-Governor, to become governor. Clayton "persuaded" R.J.T. White to resign as Secretary of State, and he appointed Johnson to this post. Clayton then resigned, and O.A. Hadley, president of the Senate, became Acting-Governor. Soon after, Clayton sent White a certificate of deposit, and undisclosed persons gave him railroad bonds worth $25,000. Many Democrats supported Clayton's U.S. Senate race to get him out of Arkansas. He left the governor's chair on March 17, 1871. Clayton served in the U.S. Senate from 1871 to 1877. He then returned to Arkansas, settling in Little Rock. In 1882 he built and became manager of the Eureka Springs Railway, and a director of the Missouri & North Arkansas Railroad. From 1897 to 1905, he was U.S. Ambassador to Mexico. He then returned to Arkansas and lived until 1912, when he moved to Washington, D.C. Clayton died in Washington, D.C. on August 25, 1914. Bibliography: Fay Hempstead, *A History of the State of Arkansas* (New Orleans, 1889); Roy Glashan, *American Governors and Gubernatorial Elections, 1775-1975* (Stillwater, Minnesota, 1975); Congressional Quarterly, Inc., *Guide to United States Elections* (Washington, D.C., 1975); John G. Fletcher, *Arkansas* (Chapel Hill, North Carolina, 1947).

HADLEY, Ozra A., 1871-1873

Born on June 30, 1826 in Cherry Creek, Chautauqua County, New York. Records reveal nothing about his parentage; a Universalist. Unmarried. Educated in the local schools of Chautauqua County. In 1855 Hadley moved to Colfax County, Minnesota where he farmed. From 1859 to 1865, he was Auditor of Colfax County. After leaving this office, he moved to Little Rock, Arkansas, and opened a general store. A Republican, Hadley was elected to the State Senate, serving from 1869 to 1871. On January 10, 1871, Governor Powell Clayton was elected to the U.S. Senate, a position he wished to accept. However, Governor Powell did not want the Lieutenant-Governor, J.M. Johnson, to succeed him. Accordingly, Powell persuaded R.J.T. White to resign his post as Secretary of State, and appointed Johnson to White's job. The presidency of the Senate thus being vacant, Hadley was selected to fill it. After accomplishing these maneuvers, Governor Clayton resigned on March 17, 1871. Hadley, as President of the Senate, became Governor. Hadley was inaugurated on March 17, 1871. His administration marked a turbulent period in Arkansas history. Hadley supported the radical view of Reconstruction and refused to help reenfranchise whites, most of whom were Democrats. Soon after Senator Clayton arrived in Washington, D.C., a scandal concerning the alleged bribery of White broke out in Arkansas. Clayton had sent him a certificate of deposit, and undisclosed persons had given him railroad bonds worth $25,000. A Senate committee investigated the charges; Clayton received a qualified exoneration, but the people of Arkansas believed Hadley had used his influence to clear Clayton. In addition, Hadley continued to issue railroad bonds. The bonded debt of the state was $10,618,166, and $6,900,000 of this had gone for railroad bonds, which many considered a major source of corruption in the state. Hadley left office on January 6, 1873. He was later appointed Registrar of the U.S. Land Office. He was Postmaster at Little Rock from 1878 to 1882. After leaving this post, he moved to Wartrous, New Mexico, bought a large ranch and acquired cattle. Hadley died at his ranch on July 18, 1915. Bibliography: Fay Hempstead, *A History of the State of Arkansas* (New Orleans, 1889); Roy Glashan, *American Governors and Gubernatorial Elections, 1775-1975* (Stillwater, Minnesota, 1975); Congressional Quarterly, Inc., *Guide to United States Elections* (Washington, D.C., 1975); John G. Fletcher, *Arkansas* (Chapel Hill, North Carolina, 1947).

BAXTER, Elisha, 1873-1874

Born on September 1, 1827 in Rutherford County, North Carolina, son of William, a farmer, and Catherine (Lee) Baxter; a Catholic. Married to Harriet Patton in 1849; father of six children. Baxter attended the local schools in Rutherford County. After trying storekeeping and farming with little success, he moved to Batesville, Independence County, Arkansas and opened a store. He went bankrupt within three years. He then worked for a printing house, read law, and in 1856 was admitted to the bar. An old-line Whig, Baxter served as a State Senator from 1854 to 1856 and from 1858 to 1860. As the Civil War approached, he became a Unionist. When hostilities broke out, Baxter proclaimed himself neutral and refused to fight against his Confederate friends. Nevertheless, the community showed such hostility towards him that he fled to the Federal troops in Missouri for protection. Captured by the Confederates, Baxter was brought to trial at Little Rock for treason and was imprisoned. He escaped, raised the 4th Arkansas Mounted Infantry Regiment (Union), and was assigned Batesville, his hometown, as his command. In 1864, was made Chief Justice of the Arkansas Supreme Court by Governor Isaac Murphy, the provisional chief executive. Elected to the U.S. Senate that year, Baxter was refused his seat, and all subsequent attempts to seat him failed. In 1868 he became Judge of the Third Circuit under the Reconstruction government of Governor Powell Clayton, serving until 1872. In the gubernatorial election of 1872, the Republicans were split into two factions. One group chose Baxter, the other selected Joseph Brooks. Although they were nearly all disfranchised, the Democrats favored Brooks. Baxter won the election with 41,808 votes, with Brooks receiving 38,909. Brooks contested the election, but since the legislature supported Baxter, he was inaugurated on January 6, 1873. Governor Baxter had promised an administration of reform, and once in office he submitted an amendment reenfranchising whites. Baxter, convinced that the railroad bonds were a major source of state corruption, opposed a bill to issue more bonds, and in March 1874, refused to issue any more at all. The decision caused Baxter's party to desert him. Brooks took the matter to the Supreme Court and after receiving a decision in his favor, seized the governor's office. Both men called out the militia and appealed to President U.S. Grant to settle the matter. The President referred the dispute to the Arkansas Legislature, which decided for Baxter. The Legislature called a convention which formed a new constitution, vacated all state offices, and cut two years off of Baxter's term. Baxter agreed to this, leaving office on November 12, 1874. In 1874 Baxter declined the Democratic nomination for Governor. In 1878 he ran for the Arkansas Legislature but was defeated. He then retired to private life. He died at his home in Batesville, Arkansas on June 2, 1899. Bibliography: Fay Hempstead, *A History of the State of Arkansas* (New Orleans, 1889); Roy Glashan, *American Governors and Gubernatorial Elections, 1775-1975* (Stillwater, Minnesota, 1975); Congressional Quarterly, Inc., *Guide to United States Elections* (Washington, D.C., 1975); John G. Fletcher, *Arkansas* (Chapel Hill, North Carolina, 1947).

GARLAND, Augustus Hill, 1874-1877

Born on June 11, 1832 in Covington, Tennessee, son of Rufus and Barbara (Hill) Garland. His father died when he was young, and his mother married a second time to Thomas Hubbard, a lawyer. Brother of John, Rufus, and Elizabeth; married to Virginia

Sanders in 1853; father of Sanders, E. Cummings, William, and Daisy Garland. Educated in private schools; attended St. Mary's College, Lebanon, Kentucky; graduated from St. Joseph's College, Bardstown, Kentucky in 1849; studied law under Thomas Hubbard. Admitted to the Arkansas Bar in 1853. Garland's family moved to Arkansas in 1833. Taught school; began private law practice in Washington, Arkansas; moved to Little Rock, Arkansas, three years later; became partner with Ebenezer Cummins in a legal firm; admitted to practice before the United States Supreme Court in 1860. Presidential Elector on the Constitutional Union Party ticket, 1860; delegate, Arkansas Secession Convention, 1861; delegate, Confederate States Provisional Congress; member, Confederate States House of Representatives, 1861-1864; member, Confederate States House of Representatives, 1864-1865; pardoned by President Andrew Johnson, July 1865; applied for reinstatement of license to practice before the United States Supreme Court; elected to the United States Senate in 1866, but not allowed to take his seat; Acting Arkansas Secretary of State, 1874. Author: *Experiences in the Supreme Court of the United States* (1898). As a Democrat, Garland was elected Governor of Arkansas on October 13, 1874 in a special election held under the provisions of the 1874 Arkansas Constitution. Having no opponent, he received 76,552 votes and was sworn into office on November 12, 1874. Shortly after Garland's inauguration, former Lieutenant Governor Volney V. Smith declared himself Governor of Arkansas, and asserted that the Constitution of 1874 was null and void. However, President Ulysses S. Grant appointed Smith as United States Consul to St. Thomas. During Garland's administration, a U.S. Congressional committee examined the method of the adoption of the 1874 Arkansas Constitution, and reported that no interference by the federal government was advisable. Thus, Reconstruction in Arkansas came to an end. In 1876, Garland was elected to the United States Senate, and as a result, he left the governor's office on January 11, 1877. He served in the United States Senate from 1877 until 1885. In March, 1885, Garland was appointed Attorney General of the United States by President Grover Cleveland, a position he held until March, 1889. Afterward, he practiced law in Washington, D.C. Garland died in Washington, D.C. on January 26, 1899, and was buried in Mount Holly Cemetery in Little Rock. Bibliography: Dallas T. Herndon, *Centennial History of Arkansas*, 3 vols. (Chicago, 1922); David Y. Thomas, ed., *Arkansas and Its People*, 4 vols. (New York, 1930); Walter S. McNutt, Olin E. McKnight, and George A. Hubbell, *A History of Arkansas* (Little Rock, 1932); Roy Glashan, *American Governors and Gubernatorial Elections, 1775-1975* (Stillwater, Minnesota, 1975).

MILLER, William R., 1877-1881

Born on November 23, 1823 in Batesville, Independence County, Arkansas, son of John, a farmer, and Clara (Moore) Miller. Married to Sarah Susan E. Bevers on January 27, 1849; father of William R., Hugh, Mrs. W. J. Joblin, and Mrs. J.E. Williams. Miller lived on his father's farm until he was twenty-one years old. Attended local schools; studied law. Admitted to the Arkansas Bar in 1868. Private law practice in Batesville. Elected Clerk of Independence County in 1848, and served until 1854; State Auditor of Arkansas, 1854-1855, 1857-1864, and 1874-1878. After being nominated by the State Democratic Convention, Miller was elected Governor of Arkansas on September 4, 1876 in the general election. Receiving 69,775 votes to Republican A.W. Bishop's 36,272,

Miller was sworn into office on January 11, 1877. Miller was reelected to a second term on September 2, 1878. Without an opponent, he polled 88,726 votes. During his administration, Arkansas began to return to normalcy after the chaos and confusion of the Civil War and Reconstruction; the State Legislature appropriated funds for the maintenance of the Arkansas Industrial University and the State Blind Asylum; and counties were authorized to issue bonds to fund outstanding indebtedness. In 1878, a yellow fever epidemic swept the South, and Miller authorized a committee of the State Medical Society to take measures to keep the disease out of Arkansas. The Arkansas Constitution was amended to prohibit the Legislature from either levying a tax or making an appropriation for the principal on the interest of James Holford and Company bonds issued in 1840. Miller left office on January 13, 1881. In 1886, he was again elected State Auditor of Arkansas. Miller died in Little Rock, Arkansas on November 29, 1887, and was buried in Mount Holly Cemetery. Bibliography: Dallas T. Herndon, *Centennial History of Arkansas*, 3 vols. (Chicago, 1922); David Y. Thomas, ed., *Arkansas and Its People*, 4 vols. (New York, 1930); Walter S. McNutt, Olin E. McKnight, and George A. Hubbell, *A History of Arkansas* (Little Rock, 1932); Roy Glashan, *American Governors and Gubernatorial Elections, 1775-1975* (Stillwater, Minnesota, 1975).

CHURCHILL, Thomas J., 1881-1883

Born on March 10, 1824 near Louisville, in Jefferson County, Kentucky, son of Samuel C., a farmer, and Abby (Oldham) Churchill. Married to Ann Sevier on July 31, 1849, and father of Samuel J., Abbie, Mrs. John B. Calef, a Mrs. Langhorne, and Mrs. M.M. Hankins. Graduated from St. Mary's College in Kentucky in 1847; took a course in law at Transylvania College, Lexington, Kentucky. At the outbreak of the Mexican War, he enlisted as Lieutenant in the First Kentucky Mounted Riflemen; captured and made a prisoner of war in January 1847; exchanged near the end of the conflict. At the outbreak of the Civil War, he raised the First Arkansas Mounted Riflemen, a cavalry regiment, for service with the Confederate States Army; rose to the rank of Major General in the Confederate States Army. Moved to Arkansas in 1849; owner of a plantation near Little Rock, Arkansas. Appointed Postmaster of Little Rock by President James Buchanan in 1857 and served until 1861; State Treasurer of Arkansas, 1874-1881. After being nominated by the State Democratic Convention in June, 1880; Churchill was elected Governor of Arkansas on September 6, 1880 in the general election. Receiving 84,815 votes to Greenback candidate W.P. Park's 31,424, he was sworn into office on January 13, 1881. During his administration, money was appropriated for an asylum for the insane, and for construction of a normal school at Pine Bluff, Arkansas. In addition, regulations were adopted for the practice of medicine and surgery; a Medical Department was established at Arkansas Industrial University in Little Rock; and a State Board of Health was created. While he was governor, Churchill sent the state militia to Perry County, Arkansas to assist the civil authorities in maintaining order. Churchill left office on January 13, 1883. In 1881, the State Legislature had appointed a special committee to audit the books of the State Treasury for the period when Churchill was treasurer. A deficit in state funds was discovered, and in May, 1883, the Arkansas Attorney General brought suit against Churchill for the missing money. Eventually, Churchill was ordered to repay the funds. Afterward, he returned to his law practice. Churchill died at Little Rock, on March 10,

1905. Bibliography: Fay Hempstead, *Historical Review of Arkansas*, 3 vols. (Chicago, 1911); Dallas T. Herndon, *Centennial History of Arkansas*, 3 vols. (Chicago, 1922); Walter S. McNutt, Olin E. McKnight, and George A. Hubbell, *A History of Arkansas* (Little Rock, 1932); Roy Glashan, *American Governors and Gubernatorial Elections, 1775-1975* (Stillwater, Minnesota).

BERRY, James Henderson, 1883-1885

Born on May 15, 1841 in Jefferson County, Alabama, son of James M. and Isabella Jane (Orr) Berry. Berry was fourth of ten children; married to Lizzie Quaile in October, 1865. In 1848, he moved to Carrollton in Carroll County, Arkansas, with his parents. Educated in the county's schools; attended Berryville Academy, Berryville, Arkansas for one year; studied law. Admitted to the Arkansas Bar in 1866. Enlisted in the Confederate States Army in 1861; Second Lieutenant, Company E, Sixteenth Arkansas Infantry; lost a leg in the Battle of Corinth, Mississippi in 1862. After recovering from his wound, he went to Texas, where he remained until the end of the Civil War; returned to Arkansas; taught school; began private law practice in Berryville in 1866; moved to Bentonville, Arkansas in 1869, and continued to practice law. Elected to the Arkansas House of Representatives, 1866, 1872, and 1874; Speaker, Extraordinary Session of the Arkansas House of Representatives, 1874; Chairman, Democratic State Convention, 1876; Judge of the Circuit Court, Fourth Arkansas Judicial District, 1878-1882. After being nominated by the State Democratic Convention, Berry was elected Governor of Arkansas on September 4, 1882 in the general election. Receiving 87,669 votes to Republican W.D. Slack's 49,372 and Greenback candidate R.K. Garland's 10,142, Berry was sworn into office on January 13, 1883. During his administration, the Arkansas Bar Association was formed; Cleburne County, Arkansas was organized; and the State Hospital for Nervous Disease was opened. Also while Berry was governor, the legislature dissolved the State Finance Board, provided for a revision and digest of Arkansas statutes, and enacted laws regulating the state's labor system. Berry left office on January 17, 1885. In March, 1885, he was elected to the United States Senate to fill the vacancy created when Augustus H. Garland resigned. Berry served in the United States Senate from 1885 unitl 1907, when he left the post after being defeated for reelection. He then returned to Bentonville. In 1910, he was appointed by President William H. Taft to the commission responsible for the marking of the graves of Confederate soldiers who had died in Northern prisoner of war camps, a task which was completed in 1912. Berry died in Bentonville on January 30, 1913, and was buried in the Knights of Pythias Cemetery. Bibliography: Dallas T. Herndon, *Centennial History of Arkansas*, 3 vols. (Chicago, 1922); David Y. Thomas, ed., *Arkansas and Its People*, 4 vols. (New York, 1930); Walter S. McNutt, Olin E. McKnight, and George A. Hubbell, *A History of Arkansas* (Little Rock, 1932); Roy Glashan, *American Governors and Gubernatorial Elections, 1775-1975* (Stillwater, Minnesota, 1975).

HUGHES, Simeon P., 1885-1889

Born on April 14, 1830 in Smith County, Tennessee, son of Simeon P., a farmer, and Mary H. Hughes. Married to Ann E. Blakemore on June 2, 1857, and father of William B., Robert, George, John, Sallie, and Lillian. Hughes moved to Pulaski County, Arkansas with his parents in 1844. Attended Sylvan Academy in Tennessee, 1846-1847; attended Clinton College, 1848-1849; studied law. Admitted to the Arkansas Bar in 1857. Enlisted in the Twenty-third Arkansas Infantry Regiment, Confederate States Army in 1861; Captain of a company in the Twenty-third Arkansas Infantry; promoted to Lieutenant Colonel, Twenty-third Arkansas Infantry; when the regiment was reorganized, he enlisted as a private in a Texas Cavalry Battalion, and served until the end of the Civil War. Began farming in Monroe County, Arkansas in 1849; private law practice in Little Rock, Arkansas, 1877-1885. Sheriff, Monroe County, 1854-1856; member, Arkansas House of Representatives, 1866-1867; delegate, Arkansas Constitutional Convention, 1874; Attorney General of Arkansas, 1874-1877. In June, 1884, Hughes was nominated by the State Democratic Convention on the thirty-sixth ballot, and on September 1, 1884 in the general election, he was elected Governor of Arkansas. Receiving 100,875 votes to Republican Thomas Boles' 55,388, Hughes was sworn into office on January 17, 1885. During his administration, the office of State Geologist was created; the Bureau of Mines, Manufactures, and Agriculture was established; and the State Debt Board was organized. Also while Hughes was governor, bauxite was discovered south of Little Rock; the Agricultural Experiment Station was opened at Arkansas Industrial University; and the state militia was used to keep the peace during a railway strike in Miller County, Arkansas. Hughes was elected to a second term on September 6, 1886 in the general election, receiving 90,650 votes to Republican Lafayette Gregg's 54,063 and the Agricultural Wheel Party candidate, C.E. Cunningham's 19,169. Hughes left office on January 17, 1889. Afterward, he was elected an Associate Justice of the Arkansas Supreme Court in 1889 and 1896. Hughes died on June 29, 1906. Bibliography: Dallas T. Herndon, *Centennial History of Arkansas,* 3 vols. (Chicago, 1922); David Y. Thomas, ed., *Arkansas and Its People,* 4 vols. (New York, 1930); Walter S. McNutt, Olin E. McKnight, and George A. Hubbell, *A History of Arkansas* (Little Rock, 1932); Roy Glashan, *American Governors and Gubernatorial Elections, 1775-1975* (Stillwater, Minnesota, 1975).

EAGLE, James P., 1889-1893

Born in 1837 in Maury County, Tennessee, son of James, a farmer, and Charity (Swain) Eagle, both of whom were Baptists. Brother of William, Rosanna, Joseph, Robert, Mary, Mattie, and Sally; married to Mary Kavanaugh Oldham in January, 1882; no children. After serving in the Civil War with the 5th Arkansas Infantry and the 1st Arkansas Regiment, he attended Mississippi College at Clinton. He became a farmer, and was president of the Baptist State Convention (1880-1904). As a Democrat, he served in the Arkansas Legislature of 1873-1878 and 1885, when he was Speaker of the House. In 1888, Eagle was nominated on the 137th ballot for Governor by the Democrats and narrowly defeated the Union Labor Party candidate, Charles Norwood, 92,214 votes to 84,213. In 1890, he defeated the Union Labor candidate, N.B. Fizer, by a larger majority, 106,267 to 85,181. In response to charges of discrepancies in his own election, a State

Board of Election Commissioners was created. Eagle urged that the convict lease program be ended and that the state work its own convicts. An act was passed by the legislature in 1893, but it simply substituted a contract lease system which continued most of the undesirable features of pure leasing. After the completion of two terms, Eagle declined to seek a third. He then returned to his plantation at Lonoke and his duties as president of the Arkansas Baptist State Convention. In 1902, Eagle became president of the Southern Baptist Convention, a position he held until his death. Eagle also remained active in politics as a member of the controversial Capitol Commission, from which he was removed by Governor Jeff Davis, after disagreeing with Davis over reelection plans and the building of the capitol. Eagle died on December 19, 1904 and was buried in Mt. Holly Cemetery, Little Rock. Bibliography: *Baptist Advance* [Little Rock] (January 5, 1905); Clifton Paisley, "The Political Wheelers and Arkansas' Election of 1888," *Arkansas Historical Quarterly*, vol. XXV, no. 1 (Spring, 1966); J.B. Searcy, "Governor James P. Eagle," *Baptist Advance* [Little Rock] (October 2, 1913); Jane Zimmerman, "The Convict Lease System in Arkansas and the Fight for Abolition," *Arkansas Historical Quarterly*, vol. VIII, no. 3 (Autumn, 1949). A small selection of Eagle's correspondence is available at the Arkansas History Commission in Little Rock.

SLOAN, Clay, 1893

Born in 1861 in Smithville, Arkansas, son of James F. and Margaret (Raney) Sloan. Married to Kittie Matthews in 1888; father of Lawrence, Eugene, James F. and Ralph M. and one other son who died at birth. Moved with his parents to Powhatan, Arkansas, where he attended public schools; later attended Arkansas College at Batesville, graduating in 1881. Following graduation, he taught in Smithville until 1886; he was also the Democratic county examiner from 1884 to 1886. In 1884 he ran for the office of county clerk, but lost the election. Two years later, he ran again for the office and was elected. He was reelected in 1888. From 1891 to 1893 Sloan represented Lawrence County in the lower house of the State Legislature, and from 1893 to 1897 he was a State Senator. At the close of his first term in the Senate, he was chosen President Pro Tempore, by virtue of which position he became Lieutenant Governor. Consequently, he served as Governor for thirty days while the elected chief executive was out of the state. During his term of service, Sloan performed all the duties and actions of the governor's office; he appointed a Justice of the Peace, vetoed a bill, and issued a pardon. Afterwards, Sloan had no further ambition to be governor. From 1897 to 1901, Sloan was State Auditor. He later served as Commissioner of Agriculture, Mines and Manufacture. He was on the Board of Charities, and he served for several years as chairman of the County Democratic Committee of Lawrence County. In 1917 Sloan was a delegate from Lawrence County to the State Constitutional Convention. Sloan and his family lived at Powhatan until 1900, when they moved to a home on a farm near Black Rock, Arkansas. Clay Sloan died at his home in Strawberry, near Walnut Ridge, Arkansas, on February 14, 1942, at the age of eighty-one. Bibliography: Josiah H. Shinn, *The History of Arkansas* (Richmond, Virginia, 1900); Walter E. McLeod, *Centennial Memorial History of Lawrence County* (Russellville, Arkansas, 1936); Dallas T. Herndon, ed., *Annals of Arkansas, 1947*, 4 vols. (Little Rock, 1947); Roy Glashan, *American Governors and Gubernatorial Elections, 1775-1975* (Stillwater, Minnesota, 1975).

FISHBACK, William M., 1893-1895

Born on November 5, 1831 in Jefferson, Virginia, son of Frederick, a farmer, and Sophia A. (Yates) Fishback, both of whom were Episcopalians. Brother of Frederick, Sally, Harrison, Lucy, Fanny, Benjamin, Henry Ward, and Yates; married to Adelaide Miller on April 4, 1867, and father of Louis, William E., Mary, Bertha, and Herbert. Attended University of Virginia and graduated in 1855. Admitted to the bar in 1858, after which he practiced law in Fort Smith and Greenwood, Arkansas. During the Civil War, he founded the *Unconditional Union* in Little Rock and raised the Union 4th Arkansas Cavalry. In 1861, he was a Union sympathizer as a member of the Secession Convention; he was elected to the U.S. Senate in 1864 but was refused the seat; in 1874, he was a member of the State Constitutional Convention; he served in the Legislature, 1871-1881, and was defeated for the U.S. Senate by James Berry in 1884. He was defeated for the Democratic nomination for Governor in 1888, but received the nomination in 1892. In the general election, J.P. Carnahan of the People's Party received 31,177 votes, W.G. Whipple, the Republican candidate, received 33,644 votes, and Fishback received 90,115 votes. In 1879, as a legislator, Fishback introduced an amendment to the Constitution prohibiting the state from paying Holford railroad and levee bonds. As governor, he refused to recognize claims of the U.S. government against the state resulting from real estate bank bonds held in trust by the U.S. Treasury. Fishback had little part in the legislature's program, and chiefly worked on a publicity program for the state. Although a Democrat, he was not widely trusted because of his earlier connection with the Union cause. He was also unpopular with the Democratic establishment and so allowed Attorney General James P. Clarke to capture the gubernatorial nomination in 1894, while he made an abortive attempt to capture the senatorial nomination from James Berry. After leaving office, he worked to expand industrial development in Arkansas, and in 1896 he assisted in the presidential campaign of W. J. Bryan. He died on February 9, 1903 at Fort Smith and was buried in Oak Cemetery. Bibliography: Garland E. Bayliss, "Post-Reconstruction Repudiation: Evil Blot or Financial Necessity?," *Arkansas Historical Quarterly*, vol. XXIII, no. 3 (Autumn, 1964); *Fort Smith News Record* (February 9, 1903); Dallas T. Herndon, "Repudiation or Thumbing the Nose-Which?," *Arkansas Historical Review*, vol. 1, no. 1 (March, 1934); Ralph Wooster, "The Arkansas Secession Convention," *Arkansas Historical Quarterly*, vol. XIII, no. 2 (Summer, 1954).

CLARKE, James P., 1895-1897

Born on August 18, 1854 in Yazoo City, Mississippi, son of Walter, an architect and civil engineer, and Ellen (White) Clarke; a Methodist. Married to Sallie Moore Wooten on November 15, 1883, and father of James P., Jr., Julia and Marian (Clarke) Williams. Attended University of Virginia Law Division and graduated in 1878. Editor of a newspaper in Yazoo City, Mississippi, and after college practiced law in Helena, Arkansas. In 1886, he was elected to the Arkansas House of Representatives. In 1888, he was elevated to the State Senate, and in 1891, was chosen President Pro Tempore; he served one term as Attorney General (1893-1895) before becoming Governor. Clarke defeated three candidates, D.E. Barker (Populist, 24,541 votes), H.L Remmel (Republican, 26,085 votes), and J.W. Miller (Prohibitionist, 1,551 votes) to win the election in 1894. As governor, Clarke favored a new constitutional convention to consider both a four-year gubernatorial term of office and a limitation of one term. However, the legislature did not call a convention. Clarke was the first governor of any state to stop a prize fight with an injunction. He did not seek a second term. In 1896, Clarke was defeated for the U.S. Senate by James K. Jones, but in 1902, he defeated Jones in a popular election for the office. In 1913, he became President Pro Tempore of the U.S. Senate. Clarke died on October 1, 1916 and is buried at Oakland Cemetery in Little Rock. Bibliography: *Arkansas Reports*, vol. 129 (1917); B.F. Fly, *Ex-Gov. James P. Clarke and his Attitude in the Hudson Bank Claim* (Little Rock, (1902); Walter Scott McNutt, *Great Statesmen of Arkansas* (Jefferson, Texas, 1954).

JONES, Daniel Webster, 1897-1901

Born on December 15, 1839 in Bowie County, Texas, son of Isaac N., a physician, and Elizabeth (Littlejohn) Jones, both of whom were Episcopalians. Brother of Mary C., Annie R., Thomas L., Robert, Sarah, Issac, Elizabeth, and Mollie; married to Maggie P. Hadley on February 9, 1864; father of Claudius, Elizabeth, Bobbie, Daniel, Howard, and two children who died during infancy. Attended Washington Academy in Washington, Arkansas. During the Civil War, Jones served in the Arkansas Confederate Infantry, from which he retired as a Colonel. He then practiced law in Hempstead County, and was elected Prosecuting Attorney for the Ninth Circuit in 1874; in 1884, he was elected to one term as Attorney General; afterwards, he practiced law in Little Rock, until the election of 1890, which sent him to the State House of Representatives for a term. In 1896, he was elected Governor, receiving 91,114 votes. He defeated J.W. Miller (Prohibitionist) who received 851 votes; A.W. Files (Populist) with 13,990 votes; and H.L. Remmel (Republican), who polled 35,836 votes. In the election of 1898, Jones received 75,362 votes to defeat the Republican, H.F. Austen, who received 27,524 votes and two other candidates (W.S. Morgan-Populist-8,332), and Alexander McKnight-Prohibitionist-679). Legislation passed under Jones' administration provided for a system of uniform textbooks in public schools, and the appropriation of money for a new State Capitol. Jones proposed to give the minority party the exclusive right to name the third member of the State Election Commission, the County Election Board, and one judge and one clerk in every voting precinct, but these recommendations were rejected. After his years as governor, Jones returned to the practice of law in Little Rock, and was later elected to the Arkansas House of Representatives in 1914. Jones died on December 25, 1918 and was buried in Oakland Cemetery, Arkansas. Bibliography: Dallas T. Herndon, *Centennial History of Arkansas*, 3 vols. (Chicago, 1922); David Y. Thomas, ed., *Arkansas and Its People*, 4 vols. (New York, 1930); Walter S. McNutt, Olen E. McKnight and George A. Hubbell, *A History of Arkansas* (Little Rock, 1932). Jones' correspondence at the Arkansas History Commission.

DAVIS, Jefferson, 1901-1907

Born on May 6, 1862 near Richmond, in Little River County, Arkansas, son of Lewis W., a lawyer, and Mary D. Davis; a Baptist. Married to Ina McKenzie in 1882; married a second time to Leila Carter in October, 1911; father of twelve children by his first wife.

Moved to Dover in Pope County, Arkansas with his parents. Educated in common schools of Russellville, Arkansas; for two years, he attended the Preparatory Department of the University of Arkansas, Fayetteville, Arkansas; graduated from Vanderbilt University, Nashville, Tennessee in 1884; received a degree in law from Cumberland University, Lebanon, Tennessee. Admitted to the Arkansas Bar at age nineteen. Began private law practice in partnership with his father in Russellville. Prosecuting Attorney, Fifth Judicial District of Arkansas, 1892-1896; Attorney General of Arkansas, 1898-1900. After winning the Democratic gubernatorial primary, Davis was elected Governor of Arkansas on September 3, 1900 in the general election, receiving 88,636 votes to Republican H.L. Remmel's 40,701. Davis was sworn into office on January 8, 1901. Davis was reelected as Governor on September 1, 1902, polling 77,354 votes to Republican Harry H. Meyers' 29,251 and Populist Charles D. Greaves' 8,345. On September 5, 1904, Davis became the first governor to hold more than two consecutive terms, when he defeated Republican Meyers, 90,262 votes to 53,898. During his administration, the Arkansas Constitution was amended to require bondsmen for state officials to be Arkansas residents, and fixing a definite salary for members of the State Legislature. Also, natural gas was discovered near Fort Smith, Arkansas, and diamonds were found in Pike County, Arkansas. While Davis was governor, the Arkansas Supreme Court declared the poll tax amendment to the State Constitution invalid; laws were enacted for segregation of street cars; and the Boys' Industrial School was established. In 1904, Davis was a delegate to the Democratic National Convention. Elected to the United States Senate in September, 1906, Davis left office on January 8, 1907. He served in the United States Senate from March, 1907, until his death. Davis died in Little Rock on January 3, 1913, and was buried in Mount Holly Cemetery. Bibliography: L.S. Dunaway, *Jeff Davis, Governor and United States Senator* (Little Rock, 1913); Dallas T. Herndon, *Centennial History of Arkansas*, 3 vols. (Chicago, 1922); David Y. Thomas, ed., *Arkansas and Its People*, 4 vols. (New York, 1930); Walter S. McNutt, Olin E. McKnight, and George A. Hubbell, *A History of Arkansas* (Little Rock, 1932).

LITTLE, John Sebastian, 1907

Born on March 14, 1851 in Jenny Lind, Sebastian County, Arkansas, son of Jessie, a farmer, and Mary E. (Tatum) Little. Married to Elizabeth J. Irwin in January, 1887; father of Paul, Thomas E., Jesse E., Mrs. H.B. Patterson, and Mrs. N.W. Wallace. Educated in common schools; attended Cane Hill College, Cane Hill, Arkansas; studied law under C.B. Neal. Admitted to the Arkansas Bar in 1874. Began private law practice in Greenwood, Arkansas in 1874. Elected District Attorney in 1877, and reelected for four successive terms; member, Arkansas House of Representatives, 1884; elected Arkansas Circuit Judge in 1886 for a four-year term; Chairman, Arkansas Judicial Convention, 1893; was elected to the United States House of Representatives to fill the vacancy caused by the resignation of Clifton R. Breckinridge, and served from 1894 until 1907. As a Democrat, Little was elected Governor of Arkansas on September 3, 1906 in the general election, receiving 105,586 votes to Republican John I. Worthington's 41,689; he was sworn into office on January 8, 1907. Shortly after being inaugurated Governor, Little suffered a complete physical and mental breakdown. As a result he resigned from the governorship on February 11, 1907. Little did not recover, and he died at the Arkansas Hospital for Nervous Diseases in Little Rock, Arkansas on October 29, 1916. He was buried in the City Cemetery in Greenwood, Arkansas. Bibliography: Dallas T. Herndon, *Centennial History of Arkansas*, 3 vols. (Chicago, 1922); David Y. Thomas, ed., *Arkansas and Its People*, 4 vols.(New York, 1930); Walter S. McNutt, Olin E. McKnight, and George A. Hubbell, *A History of Arkansas* (Little Rock, 1932); Roy Glashan, *American Governors and Gubernatorial Elections, 1775-1975* (Stillwater, Minnesota, 1975).

MOORE, John I., 1907

Born on February 7, 1856 near Oxford, Mississippi, son of Esam, a farmer, and Nancy Moore. Brother of Elizabeth, Mattie, and Sally. Moore was brought to Phillips County, Arkansas by his parents when he was one year old. His father served in the Confederate States Army, and was killed in the Civil War. Moore was raised by his uncle. Educated in Phillips County; received A.B. degree from the University of Arkansas, Fayetteville, Arkansas in 1881; studied law. Began private law practice in Helena, Arkansas in 1884; Director, People's Savings Bank and Trust Company; Director, Guarantee Loan and Trust Company. Member, Arkansas House of Representatives, 1883, 1901, and 1903; Phillips County Judge, 1894-1900; Speaker, Arkansas House of Representatives, 1903; member, Arkansas Senate, 1906-1907; President, Arkansas Senate, 1907. He was a Democrat. Shortly after being inaugurated, Governor John S. Little resigned, after suffering a complete physical and mental breakdown. The 1874 Arkansas Constitution provided that in the "case of the . . . resignation . . . of the governor, the powers, duties, and emoluments of the office for the remainder of the term . . . shall devolve upon and accrue to the president of the senate." As a result, Moore became Governor of Arkansas on February 11, 1907. Moore served as governor until May 11, 1907, when the Arkansas Senate elected Xenophon O. Pindall as President Pro Tempore. No longer in line of succession to become chief executive, Moore left office. Afterward, he served as a member of the Arkansas Board of State Capitol Commissioners. Moore died on March 13, 1937. Bibliography: Dallas T. Herndon, *Centennial History of Arkansas*, 3 vols. (Chicago, 1922); David Y. Thomas, ed., *Arkansas and Its People*, 4 vols. (New York, 1930); Walter S. McNutt, Olin E. McKnight, and George A. Hubbell, *A History of Arkansas* (Little Rock, 1932); Roy Glashan, *American Governors and Gubernatorial Elections, 1775-1975* (Stillwater, Minnesota, 1975).

PINDALL, Xenophon O., 1907-1909

Born on August 21, 1873 near Middle Grove, Missouri, son of L.A. and Nora (Snell) Pindall; a member of the Disciples of Christ. Married to Mae Ruth Quelling on September 15, 1902. Attended Central College in Missouri; received LL.B. degree from the University of Arkansas, Fayetteville, Arkansas in 1896. Private law practice in Arkansas City, Arkansas. Member, Arkansas House of Representatives, 1902-1906; unsuccessful candidate for Attorney General of Arkansas; member, Arkansas Senate, 1907; President, Arkansas Senate, 1907. He was a Democrat. Shortly after Arkansas Governor John S. Little was inaugurated in January, 1907, he suffered a complete nervous breakdown. As a result he resigned, and the President of the Arkansas

Senate, John I. Moore, became Governor under the provisions of the Arkansas Constitution of 1874. However, Pindall was elected President Pro Tempore of the Arkansas Senate (just before the Legislature adjourned) and succeeded Moore in the governor's office. Pindall was inaugurated on May 15, 1907. During his administration, the Arkansas Constitution was amended to require every voter to show a receipt for the poll tax before being permitted to vote. Also while he was governor, the Ozark National Forest was established. Pindall completed the remainder of Little's term, and then left office on January 11, 1909. Afterward, he returned to his law practice. Pindall died on January 2, 1935, and was buried in Arkansas City. Bibliography: Dallas T. Herndon, *Centennial History of Arkansas*, 3 vols. (Chicago, 1922); David Y. Thomas, ed., *Arkansas and Its People*, 4 vols. (New York, 1930); Walter S. McNutt, Olin E. McKnight, and George A. Hubbell, *A History of Arkansas* (Little Rock, 1932); Roy Glashan, *American Governors and Gubernatorial Elections, 1775-1975* (Stillwater, Minnesota, 1975).

DONAGHEY, George W., 1909-1913

Born on July 1, 1856 in Oakland, Union Parish, Louisiana, son of Columbus, a farmer, and Elizabeth (Ingram) Donaghey; a Methodist Episcopalian; married Louvenia Wallace on September 20, 1883; father of several children. Donaghey attended the local schools in Oakland and the University of Arkansas, where he took a degree in civil engineering. Beginning as a carpenter, Donaghey became a successful contractor. He erected buildings in Arkansas, Texas, Louisiana, and Oklahoma. For five years he was the contractor on the Choctaw, Oklahoma, & Gulf Railroad. A resident of Little Rock, Arkansas, Donaghey was a Democrat and interested in politics. He accepted his party's nomination for the gubernatorial race in 1908, and went on to defeat John I. Worthington, the Republican candidate, by 110,418 votes to 44,863. In 1910 Governor Donaghey won 101,612 votes while his Republican opponent, Andrew I. Roland, received only 39,870. Inaugurated on January 14, 1909, Governor Donaghey urged measures for education and eleemosynary institutions, railroads, and roads. He sought to rebuild the state's economy by encouraging the production of bauxite and the growth of large sawmills between West Memphis and Blytheville. He also encouraged tourism. Donaghey supported Woodrow Wilson in the presidential election of 1912. He agreed that the nation needed action on the tariff, banking, regulation of business, and conservation. Governor Donaghey left office on January 15, 1913, to return to his varied business interests. Donaghey also built the new state capitol at Little Rock and was contractor for the U.S. government's army aviation center at Lonoke. He served as president of the Board of Control of State Eleemosynary Institutions and the State Board of Education; vice president of the Bankers Trust Company and Beal-Burrow Dry Goods Company. He was also president of the First National Bank of North Little Rock. In addition, he was an active Mason. Donaghey died in Little Rock, Arkansas, December 15, 1937, at the age of eighty-one. Bibliography: Fay Hempstead, *A History of the State of Arkansas* (New Orleans, 1889); Roy Glashan, *American Governors and Gubernatorial Elections, 1775-1975* (Stillwater, Minnesota, 1975); Congressional Quarterly, Inc., *Guide to United States Elections* (Washington, D.C., 1975); John G. Fletcher, *Arkansas* (Chapel Hill, North Carolina, 1947).

ROBINSON, Joseph, 1913

Born on August 26, 1872 near Lonoke, Arkansas, one of eleven children of James and Matilda (Swaim) Robinson. Married to Ewilda Miller on December 15, 1896; they had no children. Robinson and his wife were Methodists. Robinson received a teacher's certificate and taught school for two years. He also attended the University of Arkansas for two years, and a summer session of the University of Virginia Law School, Studied law with a judge in Lonoke; admitted to the bar in 1895. Elected to the State Legislature in 1894 and served one term. Left office to practice law, and in 1902, was elected to Congress from the 6th District. Served as Congressman for five terms and supported progressive measures, such as regulation of railroads, income tax, and Women Suffrage amendments to the Federal Constitution. Elected Governor in 1912, defeating incumbent George Donaghey in the Democratic primary, 90,520 votes to 46,701, and winning over two opponents in the general election by a majority of nearly 60,000 votes. As governor, Robinson worked to secure the enactment of a Corrupt Practices Act, the establishment of a Bureau of Labor Statistics, and changes in the state's banking laws. He signed a State Prohibition Bill, although he personally preferred local option for liquor regulation. Robinson served only a few weeks as governor, since on January 28, the General Assembly elected him to the United States Senate seat vacated by the death of Jeff Davis; Robinson received 71 of the 133 votes cast by the Assembly. Robinson resigned from the governorship on March 10, 1913. As Senator, Robinson supported the Federal Reserve Bill, and Wilson's views on the Treaty of Versailles, and the League of Nations. In 1920, he was elected Permanent Chairman of the Democratic National Convention, and in 1923 became Minority Leader of the Senate; in 1933, he became Majority Leader. During the 1920s, he was a delegate at several international conferences. Robinson opposed Republican tax and tariff policies, and supported proposals for flood control of the Mississippi. He was the Democratic nominee for Vice President in 1928; he and Al Smith, the presidential nominee, were defeated. During the period 1933-1937, Robinson loyally backed Roosevelt's New Deal measures, although he was not entirely sympathetic with them. He led the fight for Roosevelt's abortive Court Reorganization Bill. Robinson died in Washington on July 14, 1937, and was buried in Roselawn Cemetery in Little Rock. Bibliography: Nevin Neal, "A Biography of Joseph T. Robinson," Unpublished Ph.D Dissertation, University of Oklahoma, 1958; Beryl Pettus, "The Senatorial Career of Joseph Taylor Robinson," Unpublished Master's Thesis, University of Illinois, 1952.

OLDHAM, William, 1913

Born on May 20, 1865, in Richmond, Kentucky, son of William K. and Kate (Brown) Oldham; a Baptist. Married to Lillian Munroe of Lonoke, Arkansas, on February 1, 1894; father of William K. and Lillian. Attended Central University in Richmond from 1882 to 1885. Moved to Arkansas in 1885, and became a planter; eventually owned a farm consisting of 2,100 acres; lived in Pettus, Lonoke County, Arkansas. Member, Arkansas House of Representatives, 1907; member, Arkansas Senate, 1911-1913; President Arkansas Senate, 1913. Trustee, Ouachita College; trustee, Oldham High School; member, Board of Directors of the Arkansas Tuberculosis Sanatorium; member, Arkansas Cotton Growers Cooperative Marketing Association. A Democrat.

On March 10, 1913, Governor of Arkansas J. T. Robinson resigned from office, and under the terms of the Arkansas Constitution of 1874, Oldham as President of the State Senate succeeded to the office. He held the position of chief executive for six days, before relinquishing the duties to J. Marion Futrell who was the newly elected President of the Arkansas Senate. After leaving office, he returned to his farm, and his home in Pettus. Oldham died on May 6, 1938. Bibliography: Dallas T. Herndon, *Centennial History of Arkansas*, 3 vols. (Chicago, 1922); Walter S. McNutt, *History of Arkansas* (Little Rock, 1932); John G. Fletcher, *Arkansas* (Chapel Hill, North Carolina, 1947); Roy Glashan, *American Governors and Gubernatorial Elections, 1775-1975* (Stillwater, Minnesota, 1975).

FUTRELL, Junius Marion, 1913, 1933-1937

Born on August 14, 1872, in Greene County, Arkansas, son of Jeptha and Arminia Futrell. Married to Tera Ann Smith on September 14, 1893, and father of Bill Nye, Selma Prentiss, Junis Bryon, Ernie Exah, Olive Janice, and Daniel Wood. Attended the University of Arkansas, Fayetteville, Arkansas, 1892-1893; studied law. Admitted to the Arkansas Bar in 1913. Began teaching school in 1892; engaged in farming; Circuit Clerk. Member, Arkansas House of Representatives, 1897-1899, 1901-1903; member, Arkansas Senate, 1913-1917; President of the Arkansas Senate, 1913-1915. He was a Democrat. On March 10, 1913, Governor of Arkansas Joseph T. Robinson resigned, and was succeeded by the President of the Arkansas Senate, William K. Oldham, who was serving the last half of his legislative term. In the meantime, Futrell was selected as President Pro Tempore of the Arkansas Senate. On March 13, 1913, the Arkansas Legislature adjourned; however, Oldham maintained that he was entitled to remain as governor because Robinson had resigned while he was still holding his legislative office. Though an opinion by the Arkansas Attorney General supported Oldham's contention, Futrell argued that he was the actual chief executive, and he established his own governor's office. Finally, on March 27, 1913, the Arkansas Supreme Court ruled that Futrell was Governor, and had been so since March 13. Futrell remained in office until July 23, 1913. when, after a special gubernatorial election, he was succeeded by George W. Hayes. After leaving office, Futrell served as a Circuit Judge in 1922, and as State Chancellor of Arkansas from 1923 to 1933. In 1932, he won the four-man Democratic gubernatorial primary, and on November 8, 1932, Futrell was elected Governor of Arkansas, receiving 200,096 votes to Republican J.O. Livesay's 19,717. He was sworn into office on January 10, 1933. Arkansas was in the midst of the Great Depression, and Futrell urged a plan of strict economy in government; he began a policy of slowly refunding the state's highway debt. Also during his administration, the Arkansas Prohibition Act was repealed; a State Planning Board was established; and the state observed its centennial celebration. After winning the 1934 Democratic gubernatorial primary, Futrell was reelected to a second term on November 6, 1934, polling 123,918 votes to Republican C.C. Ledbetter's 13,083. Futrell left office on January 12, 1937. Afterward, he engaged in special legal work for Dyess Colony Incorporated. Futrell died in Little Rock, Arkansas on June 20, 1955. Bibliography: Walter S. McNutt, Olin E. McKnight, and George A. Hubbell, *A History of Arkansas* (Little Rock, 1932); Arkansas State Planning Board, *Arkansas: A Guide to the State* (New York, 1941); Leland DuVall, *Arkansas: Colony and State* (Little Rock, 1974); Roy Glashan, *American Governors and Gubernatorial Elections, 1775-1975* (Stillwater, Minnesota, 1975).

HAYS, George, 1913-1917

Born on September 23, 1863 near Camden, Arkansas, the son of Thomas and Parthena (Ross) Hays. Brother of J.M. Hays; married to Ida Virginia Yarbraugh on February 26, 1895, and father of Grady and William Hays. Hays and his wife were Missionary Baptists. Received common school education, then studied law at Washington and Lee University in Lexington, Virginia, from which he graduated in 1894. Practiced law in Quachita County, and served as County and Probate Judge, 1900-1904. Served as Judge of the 13th Judicial Circuit from 1906 to 1913. In January, 1913, Governor Joe T. Robinson resigned after being elected by the legislature to the United States Senate seat vacated by the death of Jeff Davis. In the spring, Acting Governor James Futrell announced a special election for July 23 to choose a successor for Robinson's unexpired term. Hays won the Democratic primary election on June 22 by a small margin (802 votes), but his opponent, Stephen Brundidge, challenged the results. This controversy was settled when the State Supreme Court declared Hays to be the Democratic nominee. Hays then won the general election on July 23, receiving 53, 655 votes--over 64 per cent of the total. His opponents were Harry Meyers (Republican, 16,842 votes); George Murphy (Progressive,8,431 votes); and Emil Webber (Socialist, 4,378 votes). As governor, Hays urged participation by Arkansas in the Pan-American Exposition in California in 1915. There being no state appropriation for this purpose, Hays organized a committee which raised money for the Arkansas exhibit. Another of Hays' favorite projects was the improvement of Arkansas' roads. During his administration, a statewide Prohibition Law was passed; construction of the new State Capitol was completed; and a Board of Control for Charitable Institutions was established. In 1914, Hays was unopposed in his campaign for renomination as Democratic candidate for Governor, and in the general election he defeated Audrey Kinney (Republican), and Dan Hogan (Socialist), receiving 94,143 out of a total of 125,524 votes cast. Hays did not seek a third term, but returned to his law practice. In the two years immediately preceding his death, he wrote several articles, most of them on the Democratic prospects for winning the presidency in 1928. Hays died at his home in Little Rock on September 18, 1927, and was buried at Camden, Arkansas. Bibliography: Dallas T. Herndon, *Centennial History of Arkansas*, 3 vols. (Chicago, 1922); David Y. Thomas, ed., *Arkansas and Its People*, 4 vols. (New York, 1930); Walter S. McNutt, Olin E. McKnight and George A. Hubbell, *A History of Arkansas* (Little Rock, 1932). Hays' Papers are on deposit in the University of Arkansas Library in Fayetteville.

BROUGH, Charles, 1917-1921

Born on July 9, 1876 in Clinton, Mississippi, son of Charles Milton and Flora (Thompson) Brough. Brother of Knight Brough; married to Anne Roark on June 17, 1908; they had no children. Brough and his wife were Baptists. Graduated from Mississippi College at Clinton in 1894; received Ph.D. degree from John Hopkins University in 1898. Taught philosophy, economics, and history at Mississippi College, 1898-1901. Attended University of Mississippi Law School and received degree in 1902. Taught at Hillman College in Clinton for one year; then joined faculty of the University of Arkansas, where he taught economics and sociology, 1903-1915. Resigned professorship to seek Democratic nomination for Governor in 1916, and won the nomination by a plurality of

15,000 votes. In the general election, he defeated the Republican candidate, Wallace Townsend, by a majority of 68,000 votes. Brough was renominated and reelected in 1918, defeating Clay Fulks (Socialist) in the general election by a vote of 68,192 to 4,792. Governor Brough sponsored a bill to allow women to vote in primary elections, and during his second term, he called a special session of the Legislature to ratify the Women Suffrage Amendment to the Federal Constitution. Brough supported various other progressive measures, including the creation of an Illiteracy Commission and the establishment of a girls' industrial school and a State Reformatory for Women. A gifted orator, Brough delivered numerous speeches in support of the American cause in World War I. He chose not to seek a third term. Following his governorship, Brough spent four years as lecturer for the Redpath Chautauqua. From 1925 to 1928, he was Director of the State Public Information Bureau. He served as President of the Central Baptist College, 1928-1929, and then became a special lecturer for the General Extension Service of the University of Arkansas. Brough ran unsuccessfully for the U.S. Senate in 1932. During 1934-1935, he was chairman of the Virginia-District of Columbia Boundary Commission, charged with settling a century-old dispute. The commission completed its report two weeks before Brough's death. Brough died on December 26, 1935, and was buried in Roselawn Cemetery in Little Rock. Bibliography: Elizabeth Bierwirth, "A Rhetorical and Semantic Study of Charles Hillman Brough's Major Chautauqua Address," Unpublished Master's Thesis, University of Arkansas, 1958; Charles W. Crawford, "Charles H. Brough: Educator and Politician," Unpublished Master's Thesis, University of Arkansas, 1957. Papers of Brough in the Special Collections Division of the University of Arkansas Library, Fayetteville, Arkansas.

McRAE, Thomas Chipman, 1921-1925

Born on December 21, 1851 in Mount Holly, Arkansas, son of Duncan L., a farmer, and Mary Ann (Chipman) McRae; a Presbyterian. Married to Amelia A. White on December 17, 1874; father of Ethel, Herbert C., Mary L., and Carrie. Attended private schools in Shady Grove, Mount Holly, and Falcon, Arkansas; graduated from Soule Business College, New Orleans, Louisiana in 1869; graduated from the Law School of Washington and Lee University, Lexington, Virginia in 1872. Admitted to the bar in 1873. Private law practice in Rosston, Arkansas, 1873-1877; moved his law practice to Prescott, Arkansas in 1877. Appointed Arkansas Election Commissioner in 1874; member, Arkansas House of Representatives, 1877-1879; member, United States House of Representatives, 1885-1903; member, Arkansas Constitutional Convention, 1918. Presidential Elector on the Democrat ticket, 1880; Chairman, Arkansas Democratic State Convention, 1884 and 1902; delegate, Democratic National Convention, 1884; member, Democratic Congressional Committee, 1888-1902; member, Democratic National Committee, 1896-1900. Resumed his law practice in Prescott after leaving the United States House of Representatives; engaged in banking in Prescott; President, Arkansas Bankers' Association, 1909-1910; President, Arkansas Bar Association, 1917-1918. After winning the five-man 1920 Democratic gubernatorial primary election, McRae was elected Governor of Arkansas on November 2, 1920, receiving 123,637 votes to Republican Wallace Townsend's 46,350. He was sworn into office on January 11, 1921. During his administration, the Railroad Commission was reestablished; women were given the right to hold civil offices in the state; the Arkansas War Memorial was created; a State Tuberculosis Sanitorium for Negroes was established; and a severance tax for schools enacted. Also while McRae was governor, oil production began in southern Arkansas; an Arkansas Service Bureau to aid disabled World War I veterans was organized; and the office of State Geologist was established. After winning the 1922 Democratic gubernatorial primary, McRae was reelected to a second term on November 7, 1922, polling 99,987 votes to Republican John W. Grabiel's 28,055. McRae left office on January 13, 1925. Afterward, he was appointed Special Chief Justice of the Arkansas Supreme Court, and was elected a life member of the Arkansas State Convention in 1926. He also returned to his private law practice and banking interests in Prescott. McRae died at Prescott on June 2, 1929, and was buried in De Ann Cemetery. Bibliography: David Y. Thomas, ed., *Arkansas and Its People*, 4 vols. (New York, 1930); Walter S. McNutt, Olin E. McKnight, and George A. Hubbell, *A History of Arkansas* (Little Rock, 1932); Olin E. McKnight and Boyd W. Johnson, *The Arkansas Story* (Oklahoma City, 1960); Roy Glashan, *American Governors and Gubernatorial Elections, 1775-1975* (Stillwater, Minnesota, 1975).

TERRAL, Thomas J., 1925-1927

Born on December 21, 1882 in Union Parish, Louisiana, son of George W., a farmer, and Celia E. Terral. Married to Eula Terral on February 14, 1914. Terral moved to Arkansas in 1907. Educated in public schools; attended Kentucky State University; received an LL.B. from the University of Arkansas. Admitted to the Arkansas Bar. Taught school. Assistant Secretary of the Arkansas Senate, 1911; Assistant to the Deputy State Superintendent of Public Instruction, 1912-1916; resigned from this position each session of the Arkansas Senate, so he could serve as Secretary of the Arkansas Senate; Secretary of the Arkansas Senate, 1913 and 1915; Arkansas Secretary of State, 1917-1921. After winning the six man 1924 Democratic gubernatorial primary, Terral was elected Governor of Arkansas on November 4, 1924 in the general election. Receiving 99,598 votes to Republican John W. Grabiel's 25,152, Terral was sworn into office on January 13, 1925. During his administration, the State Legislature voted to give the federal government authority to establish fish and game rules for Arkansas; the boards of directors of several state institutions were abolished; the Board of Charities and Corrections was created; and the office of Commissioner of Insurance and Revenues was established. Also while Terral was governor, the Arkansas Constitution was amended to allow the initiative and referendum, and to fix the number of justices of the State Supreme Court at seven. During his term, the State Legislature ratified the Child Labor Amendment to the United States Constitution, and Petit Jean State Park, Arkansas' first state park was created. Terral was defeated in the 1926 Arkansas Democratic gubernatorial primary election, polling 101,981 votes to John E. Martineau's 117,232. As a result, Terral left office on January 11, 1927. Afterward, he engaged in private law practice. He made his home in Little Rock, Arkansas. Terral died on March 9, 1946. Bibliography: Walter S. McNutt, Olin E. McKnight, and George A. Hubbell, *A History of Arkansas* (Little Rock, 1932); Arkansas State Planning Board, *Arkansas: A Guide to the State* (New York, 1941); Congressional Quarterly, Inc., *Guide to U.S. Elections* (Washington, D.C., 1975); Roy Glashan, *American Governors and Gubernatorial Elections, 1775-1975* (Stillwater, Minnesota, 1975).

MARTINEAU, John Ellis, 1927-1928

Born on December 2, 1873 in Clay County, Missouri, son of Gregory, a farmer, and Sarah Hettie (Lamb) Martineau; a Methodist. Brother of Andrew C., James A., and Valentine; married to Mabel Erwin Thomas on May 1, 1919. When he was two years old, Martineau's family moved to Lonoke County, Arkansas. Attended public schools in Lonoke County; received an A.B. degree from the University of Arkansas, Fayetteville, Arkansas in 1896; received LL.B. degree from the University of Arkansas in 1899. Admitted to the Arkansas Bar in 1899. Principal, Chickasaw Male Academy, Tishomingo, Chickasaw Nation; Principal, North Little Rock High School, 1897-1900; began private law practice in Little Rock. Member, Arkansas House of Representatives, 1903-1905; Chancellor, First Chancery Circuit of Arkansas, 1907-1927. Mason. After winning the 1926 Democratic gubernatorial primary, Martineau was elected Governor of Arkansas on November 2, 1926, receiving 116,735 votes to Republican M.D. Bowers' 35,969. He was sworn into office on January 11, 1927. During his administration, one of the most disastrous floods in Arkansas history inundated nearly one-fifth of the state. Also while Martineau was governor, pensions were provided for Confederate soldiers, sailors, and widows; the State Equalization Fund was created; the Arkansas Tax Commission was organized; the Normal School of the Ozarks was established; and a Board of Conservation for preservation of oil and gas was created. In October 1926 the Arkansas Constitution was amended to exempt textile mills from taxation for a period of seven years, and to prohibit passage by the State Legislature of local or special acts. On March 4, 1928, Martineau resigned from the governorship to be appointed Judge of the Federal District Court for Eastern Arkansas, a position he held until his death. Martineau died in Little Rock on March 6, 1937. Bibliography: David Y. Thomas, ed., *Arkansas and Its People*, 4 vols. (New York, 1930); Walter S. McNutt, Olin E. McKnight, and George A. Hubbell, *A History of Arkansas* (Little Rock, 1932); Olin E. McKnight and Boyd W. Johnson, *The Arkansas Story* (Oklahoma City, 1960); Roy Glashan, *American Governors and Gubernatorial Elections, 1775-1975* (Stillwater, Minnesota, 1975).

PARNELL, Harvey, 1928-1933

Born on February 28, 1880 in Cleveland County, Arkansas, son of William R., a farmer, and Mary (Martin) Parnell; a Methodist. Brother of James H., Lovet L., and George W.; married to Mable Winston on June 2, 1903, and father of Martha Dell and Mary Francis. Attended rural schools; attended the Warren, Arkansas High School. Worked on a farm until he was about eighteen years of age; clerk in a hardware store in Warren; moved to Dermott, Arkansas in 1900; bookkeeper and clerk for E.P. Remley and Company in Dermott; in 1902, he purchased E.P. Remley and Company; farmed on a small scale; in 1910, he began farming on a large scale, and later he gave up his business investment to devote his full time to farming; operated a 1,750 acre farm in Chicot County, Arkansas. Member, Arkansas House of Representatives, 1919 and 1921; member, Arkansas Senate, 1923-1925; Lieutenant Governor of Arkansas, 1927-1928. He was a Democrat. On March 4, 1928, Arkansas Governor John E. Martineau resigned, and as Lieutenant Governor, Parnell succeeded to the office. After winning the 1928 Democratic gubernatorial primary election, Parnell was elected Governor of Arkansas on November 6, 1928 in the general election, receiving 151,743 votes to Republican M.D. Bowers' 44,545. During his administration, the State Highway Department was given the right of eminent domain; a tobacco tax was adopted; and legislation for the adoption of uniform school textbooks was passed. Also, a State Highway Fund was created; a State Bureau of Commerce and Industry was established; an Arkansas State Park Commission was organized; and a State Commissioner of Education was appointed. While he was governor, Parnell vetoed a bill calling for a State Constitutional Convention, but he did call the Legislature into special session in March, 1932. In April, all specified items of the special session had been acted upon, and the State Senate voted to adjourn; however, the State House of Representatives refused to comply. Eventually, Parnell issued a proclamation declaring the Legislature adjourned, but sixty-nine representatives still refused. Finally, the Arkansas Supreme Court ruled the session over. Parnell was reelected when, after winning the 1930 Democratic gubernatorial primary, he defeated Republican J.O. Livesay in the November 4th general election, 112,847 votes to 26,126. Parnell left office on January 10, 1933. Afterward, he returned to his farming interests. Parnell died on January 16, 1936. Bibliography: Walter S. McNutt, Olin E. McKnight, and George A. Hubbell, *A History of Arkansas* (Little Rock, 1932); Olin E. McKnight and Boyd W. Johnson, *The Arkansas Story* (Oklahoma City, 1960); Leland DuVall, *Arkansas: Colony and State* (Little Rock, 1974); Roy Glashan, *American Governors and Gubernatorial Elections, 1775-1975* (Stillwater, Minnesota, 1975).

FUTRELL, Junius Marion, 1913, 1933-1937

BAILEY, Carl Edward, 1937-1941

Born on October 8, 1894 in Bernie, Missouri, son of William Edward, a farmer, and Margaret Elmyra (McCorkly) Bailey; a member of the Christian Church (Disciples). Married to Margaret Bristol on October 10, 1915, and father of Carl Edward, Frank Albert, Reginald Eugene, Elizabeth Dixon, Alfred Bristol, and Richard Robert. Graduated from Campbell, Missouri High School in 1912; attended Chillicothe Business College, Chillicothe, Missouri in 1915; studied law; awarded a Litt. D. degree from Subiaco College, Subiaco, Arkansas in 1935; awarded an LL.D. degree from Arkansas State College, Jonesboro, Arkansas in 1938. Admitted to the Arkansas Bar in 1923. Began teaching school in 1913; worked as a laborer, farmer, and railway brakeman; became a clerk for a lumber company in Augusta, Arkansas in 1917; became involved in the cotton industry in 1923; private law practice, 1924-1935. Deputy Prosecuting Attorney, Sixth Judicial District of Arkansas, 1927-1935; Prosecuting Attorney, Sixth Judicial District of Arkansas, 1931-1935; Attorney General of Arkansas, 1935-1937. Assistant secretary of the Arkansas Cotton Growers Cooperative Association, 1923-1924; a Mason. After winning the four-man 1936 Democratic gubernatorial primary, Bailey was elected Governor of Arkansas on November 3, 1936, receiving 155,152 votes to Republican Osro Cobb's 26,875. He was sworn into office on January 12, 1937. During his administration, all state-owned bridges were made toll free; laws were enacted to protect 15,000,000 acres of timberland within Arkansas; a free textbook law was passed;

and a free library service was established. Also while Bailey was governor, a retirement system for teachers was formulated, and a new Agricultural Experiment Station was established at Batesville, Arkansas. After winning the 1938 Democratic gubernatorial primary, Bailey was reelected to a second term on November 8, 1938, polling 118,696 votes to Independent candidate, Charles S. Cole's 12,077. Bailey left office on January 14, 1941, and returned to his private law practice in Little Rock, Arkansas. Bailey died on November 23, 1948. Bibliography: Dallas T. Herndon, *The Arkansas Handbook, 1939-1940* (Little Rock, 1940); Olin E. McKnight and Boyd W. Johnson, *The Arkansas Story* (Oklahoma City, 1960); Leland DuVall, *Arkansas: Colony and State* (Little Rock, 1974); Roy Glashan, *American Governors and Gubernatorial Elections, 1775-1975* (Stillwater, Minnesota, 1975).

ADKINS, Homer Martin, 1941-1945

Born on October 15, 1890 near Jacksonville, Arkansas, son of Ulysses, a farmer, and Lorena (Wood) Adkins; a Methodist. Married to Estelle Elise Smith on December 18, 1921. Attended school in Little Rock, Arkansas; graduated from Draughon's Business College in 1908; graduated from the Little Rock College of Pharmacy in 1911. A registered pharmacist. Served as Captain, Medical Corps, United States Army, 1917-1919; stationed in both the United States and France. Pharmacist, Little Rock, 1911-1916; salesman, Darragh Company, Little Rock, 1916-1917; engaged in the general insurance business with the firm Adkins and Williams, 1926-1933. Sheriff and Collector of Pulaski County, Arkansas, 1923-1926; Federal Internal Revenue Collector at Little Rock, 1933-1940. American Legion; Woodmen of the World; Mason; Elk. After winning the 1940 Democratic gubernatorial primary, Adkins was elected Governor of Arkansas on November 5, 1940, receiving 184,578 votes to Republican H.C. Stump's 16,600. He was sworn into office on January 14, 1941. During Adkins' administration, a program was adopted to refinance the $137,000,000 state highway debt by means of a new bond issue; the entire issuance was purchased by the Reconstruction Finance Corporation. While Adkins was governor, Arkansas' economy emerged from the Great Depression, and received a tremendous boost from the increase in military spending during World War II and from the completion of the Grand River Dam in Oklahoma, which provided a vast amount of badly-needed electrical power to northwestern Arkansas. In 1943, a disastrous flood swept the Arkansas River Valley, causing over $200,000,000 worth of damage. After winning the 1942 Democratic gubernatorial primary, Adkins was reelected to a second term on November 3, 1942. Running without an opponent, he polled 98,871 votes. Adkins left office on January 9, 1945, and maintained an Arkansas residence in Little Rock. Adkins died on February 2, 1964. Bibliography: Dallas T. Herndon, *The Arkansas Handbook, 1941-1942* (Little Rock, 1942); John G. Fletcher, *Arkansas* (Chapel Hill, North Carolina, 1947); Congressional Quarterly, Inc., *Guide to U.S. Elections* (Washington, D.C., 1975); Roy Glashan, *American Governors and Gubernatorial Elections, 1775-1975* (Stillwater, Minnesota, 1975).

LANEY, Benjamin T., 1945-1949

Born on November 25, 1896, in "Cooterneck" Community, Ouachita County, Arkansas, son of Ezra, a farmer, and Carolyn (York) Laney; a Baptist; one of five boys and six girls; unmarried. Attended public schools in Ouachita County; also attended Hendrix College, and Arkansas State Teachers College. The outbreak of World War I interrupted his studies. Laney enlisted in the Navy, and after the war completed his degree. Known as "Business Ben," he bought a drugstore in Conway, Arkansas, and entered the real estate business. While specializing in farm land, he also bought some choice property for himself. When oil was discovered on some land he had bought near Camden, he moved there to look after his interests. A Democrat, Laney was also interested in politics. In 1935 he was elected Mayor of Camden, was reelected in 1937, and served until 1939. When he decided to enter the gubernatorial race in 1944, he was hardly known outside the Camden area. So vigorous was his campaign, however, that he won his party's nomination and defeated his Republican opponent, H.C. Stump, 186,401 votes to 30,442. In the election of 1946, Governor Laney defeated W.T. Mills, the Republican candidate, 139,029 votes to 24,133. In 1948 Laney lost the Democratic gubernatorial nomination to Sidney S. McMath. Governor Laney was inaugurated on January 9, 1945. When he came to the governor's office, Arkansas was in the midst of the war boom. Although there was the inconvenience of rationing, price controls kept down inflation and high prices; jobs in the war plants and other industries were plentiful. Among the accomplishments of Governor Laney's administration were the following: passage of the Stabilization Act—the pooling of separate tax funds into a single fund which paid the costs of government; the increase of funds for public education; construction of the War Memorial Stadium in Little Rock; and provision for the construction of a Governor's Mansion and for restoration of the "State House," the Captiol building from 1836 to 1911. On January 11, 1949, Laney left office to return to his many business interests. Bibliography: Roy Glashan, *American Governors and Gubernatorial Elections, 1775-1975* (Stillwater, Minnesota, 1975); Congressional Quarterly, Inc., *Guide to United States Elections* (Washington, D.C., 1975); John G. Fletcher, *Arkansas* (Chapel Hill, North Carolina, 1947).

McMATH, Sidney Sanders, 1949-1953

Born on June 14, 1912 in Magnolia, Arkansas, son of Hal P. and Nettie (Sanders) McMath; a Methodist. Married to Elaine Braughton on May 6, 1937; she died in 1942; married a second time to Anne Phillips on October 6, 1945; father of Sidney by his first wife; father of Phillip and Bruce by his second wife. Received LL.B. degree from the University of Arkansas, Fayetteville, Arkansas in 1936. Admitted to the Arkansas Bar in 1936. Served as a Second Lieutenant in the United States Marine Corps, 1940-1946; rose to the rank of Lieutenant Colonel; awarded the Silver Star; awarded the Legion of Merit; recommended for the Navy Cross. Private law practice in Hot Springs, Arkansas, 1936-1940; Prosecuting Attorney, Eighteenth Judicial District of Arkansas, 1947-1949. Veterans of Foreign Wars; American Legion; Blue Key; Mason; Elk; Kiwanis. After winning the Democratic gubernatorial primary and runoff elections, McMath was elected Governor of Arkansas on November 2, 1948, receiving 217,771 votes to Republican C.R. Black's 26,500. He was sworn into office on January 11, 1949. During his administration, the state's Anti-Strike Law was upheld by the courts; the Democrats ended their ban against blacks in the party; prohibition was voted down; and the Arkansas Legislature ratified the Twenty-second Amendment to the United States Constitution. After winning the 1950 Democratic gubernatorial primary, McMath was reelected to a second term on November 7, 1950, polling 266,778 votes to Republican Jefferson W. Speck's 50,303. Though he finished first in the five-man 1952 Democratic gubernatorial primary, McMath was defeated in the runoff election by Francis Cherry, 237,448 votes to 139,052. He left office on January 13, 1953. Afterward, McMath engaged in private law practice in Little Rock, Arkansas. Bibliography: Fred McGhee, ed., *Facts on File Five-Year Index, 1946-1950* (New York, 1958); Fred McGhee, ed., *Facts on File Five-Year Index, 1951-1955* (New York, 1957); Congressional Quarterly, Inc., *Guide to U.S. Elections* (Washington, D.C., 1975); Roy Glashan, *American Governors and Gubernatorial Elections, 1775-1975* (Stillwater, Minnesota, 1975).

CHERRY, Francis Adams, 1953-1955

Born on September 5, 1908 in Fort Worth, Texas, son of Haskille Scott, a railroad conductor, and Clara Belle (Taylor) Cherry; a Presbyterian. One of five children; married to Margaret Frierson on November 10, 1937, and father of Haskille Scott III, Charlotte Frierson, and Francis A., Jr. Cherry's family moved first to El Reno, Oklahoma, and then to Enid, Oklahoma while he was a child. Graduated from Enid High School in 1926; graduated with a major in pre-law from Oklahoma Agricultural and Mechanical College, Stillwater, Oklahoma, 1930; received LL.B. degree from the University of Arkansas, Fayetteville, Arkansas in 1936. Secured a commission in the United States Navy in 1944, and served for two years. After graduating from college in 1930, in the midst of the Great Depression, Cherry worked as a dishwasher and truck driver; began private law practice in Little Rock, Arkansas in 1936 in the office of Leffel Gentry; became a junior law partner with Marcus Feitz in Jonesboro, Arkansas in 1937. Served as a United States Commissioner; Referee, Workmen's Compensation Commission; elected Chancellor and Probate Judge of the Twelfth Arkansas Chancery District, 1942 and 1946. Delta Theta Phi; Little Rock Consistory; Shriner; United Commercial Travelers; American Legion; Fraternal Order of Eagles; Order of Amaranth; Lion. Cherry finished second in the five-man 1952 Democratic gubernatorial primary, but won the runoff election. On November 4, 1952 in the general election, he was elected Governor of Arkansas, defeating Republican Jefferson W. Speck, 142,292 votes to 49,292. Cherry was sworn into office on January 13, 1953. After being inaugurated, Cherry put into operation his legislative program which called for adoption of a new State Fiscal Code, revision of the Revenue Stabilization Act, and the encouragement of industrial development. To aid in industrial growth, the University of Arkansas dispatched representatives to various communities to determine what types of industry would best suit their economies. In addition, representatives were sent to other states to urge the use of Arkansas' raw materials. Also while Cherry was governor, Arkansas was struck by a severe drought, which damaged the state's agricultural production. Though he finished first in the four-man 1954 Democratic gubernatorial primary, he lost the runoff election to Orval E. Faubus, 191,328 votes to 184,509. As a result, Cherry left office on January 11, 1955. Cherry died on July 15, 1965. His Arkansas residence was in Jonesboro. Bibliography: Fred McGhee, ed., *Facts on File Five-Year*

Index, 1951-1955 (New York, 1957); Leland DuVall, *Arkansas: Colony and State* (Little Rock, 1974); Congressional Quarterly, Inc., *Guide to U.S. Elections* (Washington, D.C., 1975); Roy Glashan, *American Governors and Gubernatorial Elections, 1775-1975* (Stillwater, Minnesota, 1975).

FAUBUS, Orval Eugene, 1955-1967

Born on January 7, 1910 in Combs, Arkansas, son of John Samuel, a farmer, and Addie (Joslen) Faubus; a Baptist. Married Alta Haskins on November 21, 1931; father of Farrel Eugene. Educated in public schools; graduated from the State Vocational High School, Huntsville, Arkansas. Served as an infantry officer in Europe during World War II; rose to the rank of Major; Assistant Judge Advocate, Camp Campbell, Kentucky, 1946; discharged in 1947; awarded the Bronze Star. Rural school teacher, 1928-1938; engaged in the lumber industry in the state of Washington; Acting Postmaster, Huntsville, 1946-1947; became owner and editor of the Madison County, Arkansas *Record*, 1947; Postmaster, Huntsville, 1953-1954; owner, *Arkansas Statesman*, Little Rock, Arkansas, 1960-1969. Unsuccessful candidate in the 1936 Democratic primary for local representative in the Arkansas General Assembly; Madison County, Circuit Clerk and Recorder, 1939-1942; named to the Arkansas Highway Commission in 1949; Administrative Advisor to Arkansas Governor Sidney S. McMath; appointed Director of Highways for the State of Arkansas in 1951. Member, Madison County Chamber of Commerce; American Legion; Veterans of Foreign Wars; Disabled American Veterans; Mason; Elk; Lion. Though he was second in the four-man 1954 Democratic gubernatorial primary, Faubus won the runoff election, and on November 2, 1954, he was elected Governor of Arkansas, receiving 208,201 votes to Republican Pratt C. Remmel's 127,004. He was sworn into office on January 11, 1955. Faubus was reelected Governor of Arkansas five times: on November 6, 1956, he defeated Republican Roy Mitchell, 321,797 votes to 77,215; on November 4, 1958, Faubus polled 236,598 votes to Republican George W. Johnson's 50,288; on November 8, 1960, he received 292,064 votes to Republican Henry M. Britt's 129,921; on November 6, 1962, he defeated Republican Willis Ricketts, 225,743 votes to 82,349; on November 3, 1964, Faubus polled 337,498 votes to Republican Winthrop Rockefeller's 254,561. During his administration, a Geological and Conservation Commission was established; a single State Medical Board was created; and the State Legislature ratified the Twenty-fourth Amendment to the United States Constitution. Also while Faubus was governor, Arkansas' public school system was integrated. Faubus believed that the segregation question should be settled at the local community level; however, in 1957 he ordered the Arkansas National Guard to prevent the integration of Central High School in Little Rock. The federal courts enjoined the use of the National Guard for such purposes, and in September, 1957, after a series of local disorders, President Dwight D. Eisenhower ordered the Arkansas National Guard into federal service for the purpose of enforcing the desegregation of Central High School. At the same time, regular United States Army troops were dispatched to Little Rock to reinforce the National Guard. The troops were finally withdrawn in May, 1958. Faubus left office on January 10, 1967. In 1970 he won the largest number of votes in the five-man Democratic gubernatorial primary; however, he was defeated in the runoff election by Dale Bumpers, 259,780 votes to 182,732. Again in 1974, Faubus was a candidate for the Democratic gubernatorial election, but was defeated by David H. Pryor in the primary election, 297,673 votes to 193,105, with Bob

Riley polling 92,612 votes. President, Recreational Enterprises Incorporated, 1969-1970. Bibliography: Lester A. Sobel, ed., *Facts on File Five-Year Index, 1956-1960* (New York, 1961); Lester A. Sobel, ed., *Facts on File Five-Year Index, 1961-1965* (New York, 1966); Congressional Quarterly, Inc., *Guide to U.S. Elections* (Washington, D.C., 1975); Roy Glashan, *American Governors and Gubernatorial Elections, 1775-1975* (Stillwater, Minnesota, 1975).

ROCKEFELLER, Winthrop, 1967-1971

Born on May 1, 1912 in New York City, New York, son of John D. Rockefeller, Jr., a philanthropist and an heir to the fortune of John D. Rockefeller, Sr., and Abby Greene (Aldrich) Rockefeller; a Baptist. Brother of Abby, John D., III, Nelson A., Laurence S., and David; married to Barbara (Paul) Sears on February 14, 1948; divorced in 1954; married a second time to Jeanette Edris on June 11, 1956; father of Winthrop Paul by his first wife. Educated at Lincoln School, Columbia University Teachers College, New York City; attended Loomis School, Windsor, Connecticut, 1928-1931; attended Yale University, New Haven, Connecticut, 1931-1934; studied finance at the Chase National Bank, New York City, 1937-1938; numerous honorary degrees. Entered the United States Army as a private in January, 1941; attended Officers Candidate School; served in the Pacific Theater of Operations during World War II; rose to the rank of Lieutenant Colonel before leaving the service in 1946; awarded the Bronze Star with two Oak Leaf Clusters; awarded the Purple Heart. Trainee in the Texas oil fields of the Humble Oil and Refining Company, 1934-1937; Executive Vice-President, Greater New York Fund, 1938; worked with the Foreign Department, Socony-Vacuum Oil Company, 1939-1951; Rockefeller Brothers Incorporated; Director, Rockefeller Center, Incorporated; Trustee, Industrial Relations Counselors; Chairman of the Board, Colonial Williamsburg Incorporated and Williamsburg Restoration Incorporated. Moved to Morrilton, Arkansas in 1953; established Winrock Farm on Petit Jean Mountain in Arkansas; became a member of the Republican National Committee from Arkansas in 1961. Chairman, Arkansas Industrial Development Commission, 1955-1964; unsuccessful Republican candidate for Governor of Arkansas, 1964. Trustee, National Urban League, 1940-1964; Trustee, Rockefeller Brothers Fund; Trustee, Loomis School; Trustee, Vanderbilt University, Nashville, Tennessee; Trustee, Southwest Center for Advanced Studies; member, Santa Gertrudis Breeders International Association. After winning the 1966 Republican gubernatorial primary, Rockefeller was elected Governor of Arkansas on November 8, 1966, receiving 306,324 votes to Democrat James Johnson's 257,203. He was sworn into office on January 10, 1967. During his administration, the State Legislature ratified the Twenty-fifth Amendment to the United States Constitution; Arkansas' abortion law was revised; and all death sentences were commuted. After winning the 1968 Republican gubernatorial primary, Rockefeller was reelected to a second term on November 5, 1968, polling 322,782 votes to Democrat Marion Crank's 292,813. Rockefeller again won the Republican gubernatorial primary in 1970; however, he was defeated in the November 3, 1970 general election by Democrat Dale Bumpers 375,648 votes to 197,418, while the American Party candidate, Walter L. Carruth, polled 36,132 votes. Rockefeller left office on January 12, 1971. Afterward, he returned to his farming and business investments. Rockefeller died on February 22, 1973, and was buried in Morrilton, Arkansas. Bibliography: Dorothy Kattleman, *Facts on File Five-Year Index, 1966-1970* (New York, 1971); Leland DuVall, *Arkansas: Colony and State*

(Little Rock, 1974); Congressional Quarterly, Inc., *Guide to U.S. Elections* (Washington, D.C., 1975); Roy Glashan, *American Governors and Gubernatorial Elections, 1775-1975* (Stillwater, Minnesota, 1975).

BUMPERS, Dale Leon, 1971-1975

Born on August 12, 1925 in Charleston, Arkansas, son of William Rufus and Lattie (Jones) Bumpers; a Methodist. Married to Betty Lou Flanagan on September 4, 1949; father of Dale Brent, William Mark, and Margaret Brooke. Attended the University of Arkansas, Fayetteville, Arkansas, 1943 and 1946-1948; received a J. D. degree from Northwestern University, Evanston, Illinois in 1951. Admitted to the Arkansas Bar in 1952. Served in the United States Marine Corps, 1943-1946. President, Charleston Hardware and Furniture Company, 1951-1966; private law practice in Charleston, 1952-1970; operator of an Angus cattle farm, 1966-1970. President, Charleston School Board, 1969-1970. Member, Charleston Chamber of Commerce. Though he finished second to former Governor Orval E. Faubus in the five-man 1970 Democratic gubernatorial primary, Bumpers defeated Faubus in the runoff election, 259,780 votes to 182,732. After winning the Democratic nomination, Bumpers was elected Governor of Arkansas on November 3, 1970, receiving 375,648 votes to incumbent Governor Winthrop Rockefeller's 197,418 and the American Party nominee, Walter L. Carruth's 36,132. He was sworn into office on January 12, 1971. During his administration, the State Legislature adopted a congressional redistricting plan; the lawmakers ratified the Twenty-sixth Amendment to the United States Constitution; and the United States Supreme Court upheld Arkansas' abortion law. Also while Bumpers was governor, the state's plan for college integration was approved; an Arkansas Museum and Cultural Commission was organized; an Office of Arts and Humanities was created; and a State Advisory Council for Vocational Technical Education was established. After winning the three-man 1972 Democratic gubernatorial primary, Bumpers was reelected to a second term on November 7, 1972, receiving 488,892 votes to Republican Len E. Blaylock's 159,177. In November, 1974, Bumpers was elected to the United States Senate, defeating Republican John Harris Jones, 461,056 to 82,086. Bumpers resigned as Governor of Arkansas on January 3, 1975. Bumpers' Arkansas residence is in Charleston, Arkansas. Bibliography: Lester A. Sobel, ed., *Facts on File Yearbook, 1971* (New York, 1972); Henry H. Schulte, Jr., ed., *Facts on File Yearbook, 1973* (New York, 1974); Henry H. Schulte, Jr., ed., *Facts on File Yearbook, 1974* (New York, 1975); State of Arkansas, *General Acts of the Sixty-eight General Assembly* (Little Rock, 1971); State of Arkansas, *General Acts of the Sixty-ninth General Assembly* (Camden, Arkansas, 1973); Roy Glashan, *American Governors and Gubernatorial Elections, 1775-1975* (Stillwater, Minnesota, 1975).

RILEY, Bob Cowley, 1975

Born on September 18, 1924 in Little Rock, Arkansas, son of Columbus Allen and Winnie (Craig) Riley. Married to Claudia Mercia Zimmerman on May 26, 1956, and father of Megan. Received a B. A. degree from the University of Arkansas, Fayetteville, Arkansas in 1950; received an M.A. degree from the University of Arkansas in 1951;

received a D. Ed. degree from the University of Arkansas in 1957. Served in the United States Marine Corps Reserve, 1941-1945. Instructor, Little Rock Junior College, 1951-1955; became Professor of Political Science at Ouachita Baptist University, Arkadelphia, Arkansas in 1957; became chairman of the Division of Social Studies at Ouachita Baptist University in 1960. Advancement Chairman, Ouachita Area Council, Boy Scouts of America, 1958-1966; Consultant to the National Program of College Preparatory for Blind Students; became Director, Arkansas Council Economics Education, 1966; became a member of the training staff, Rural Training Program, Office of Economic Opportunity, Little Rock, 1966; became a member, Arkansas Planning Committee on Organic Disabilities, 1967; member, United States Senate Advisory Committee on Veterans Affairs; Director, National Accreditation Council for Agencies Serving the Blind and Visually Handicapped. Member, Arkansas House of Representatives, 1946-1951; Mayor of Arkadelphia, 1966-1967; Lieutenant Governor of Arkansas, 1971-1975. Delegate, Democratic National Convention, 1968. Recipient National Achievement Award of the Disabled American Veterans; Certified Professional Parliamentarian; member, Blinded Veterans Association. Author: *Committee Systems of the Arkansas General Assembly* (1954); *They Never Came Back* (1957). He is a Democrat. After being elected to the United States Senate, Arkansas Governor Dale L. Bumpers resigned on January 3, 1975 and as Lieutenant Governor, Riley succeeded to the office. He served as Governor of Arkansas for the remaining twelve days of Bumpers' term. Riley left office on January 14, 1975. Afterward, he returned to Arkadelphia, and a position with Ouachita Baptist University. Bibliography: Congressional Quarterly, Inc., *Guide to U.S. Elections* (Washington, D.C., 1975); Roy Glashan, *American Governors and Gubernatorial Elections, 1775-1975* (Stillwater, Minnesota, 1975); *Arkansas Democrat* [Little Rock, Arkansas]; *Arkansas Gazette* [Little Rock, Arkansas].

PRYOR, David, 1975-

Born on August 29, 1934 in Camden, Arkansas, son of Edgar and Susie (Newton) Pryor; a Presbyterian. Married to Barbara Lunsford on November 27, 1957, and father of David, Mark, and Scott. Attended Henderson State College, Arkadelphia, Arkansas; received a B. A. degree from the University of Arkansas, Fayetteville, Arkansas in 1957; received an LL.B. degree from the University of Arkansas in 1961. Admitted to the Arkansas Bar in 1964. Founder and publisher of the *Ouachita Citizen* at Camden; private law practice with Pryor and Barnes legal firm in Camden. Member, Arkansas House of Representatives, 1960-1964; member, United States House of Representatives, 1965-1973. Delegate, Democratic National Convention, 1968. Chamber of Commerce; Junior Chamber of Commerce; Blue Key; Phi Alpha Delta; Delta Theta Phi. After winning the three-man 1974 Democratic gubernatorial primary, Pryor was elected Governor of Arkansas on November 5, 1974, defeating Republican Ken Coon, 358,018 votes to 187,872. He was sworn into office on January 14, 1975. During his administration, an Advisory Board on Law Enforcement Standards was organized; an Arkansas Office on Drug Abuse Prevention was created; and a State Printing Board was established. Also while Pryor was governor, a State Health Planning Agency and the Statewide Health Coordinating Council were created. During his term, Fort Chaffee, Arkansas was selected as a relocation site for several thousand Vietnamese refugees who had fled to the United States. Bibliography: Roy Glashan, *American Governors and Gubernatorial Elections, 1775-1975* (Stillwater, Minnesota, 1975); Congressional

Quarterly, Inc., *Guide to U.S. Elections* (Washington, D.C., 1975); Charles Monaghan, ed., *Facts on File Yearbook, 1975* (New York, 1976); State of Arkansas, *General Acts of the Seventieth General Assembly* (Camden, Arkansas, 1976).

CALIFORNIA

CALIFORNIA

BURNETT, Peter Hardeman, 1849-1851

Born on November 15, 1807 in Nashville, Tennessee, eldest son of George, a carpenter and farmer, and Dorothy (Hardeman) Burnett; a Catholic. Married to Harriet W. Rogers on August 20, 1828. Moved to Howard County, Missouri with his parents in 1817; returned to Nashville in 1826, where he engaged in a mercantile business. In 1832 moved to Liberty, Missouri, where he began the practice of law in 1839, and served as prosecuting attorney in Missouri from 1840 to 1842. Joined a wagon train traveling to Oregon in 1843. Chosen as a member of the Oregon Legislative Committee in 1844; appointed a Judge on the Oregon Supreme Court in 1845; elected to the Oregon Territorial Legislature in 1848. Moved to California in 1848, becoming the Attorney and General Agent of John A. Sutter, Jr.. He was appointed a Judge of the Superior Tribunal of California by Governor Bennett Riley on August 13, 1849; selected as Territorial Governor of California in December 1849, and subsequently elected Military Governor. As a non-partisan gubernatorial candidate, Burnett was elected Governor of California by popular vote on November 13, 1849, defeating his opponents, W. Sherwood and J. Sutter, by a vote of 6,783 to 3,220 and 2,201, respectively. He was inaugurated on December 29, 1849. During his administration, Burnett recommended the exclusion of free blacks from the territory. Burnett resigned as governor of California on January 9, 1851, before the news of statehood reached California, and resumed his law practice. Appointed as a Justice of the California Supreme Court in 1857, serving until October 1858; co-founder of the Pacific Bank of San Francisco, serving as president from 1863 to 1880, when he retired to private life. Author of *The Path Which Led a Protestant Lawyer to the Catholic Church* (1860) and *Recollections and Opinions of an Old Pioneer* (1880). Burnett died on May 17, 1895 in San Francisco, California. Bibliography: Robert G. Cleland, *From Wilderness to Empire, A History of California, 1854-1900* (New York, 1944); Andrew F. Rolle, *California, A History* (New York, 1963); Congressional Quarterly, Inc., *Guide to U.S. Elections* (Washington, D.C., 1975); Roy Glashan, *American Governors and Gubernatorial Elections, 1775-1975* (Stillwater, Minnesota, 1975).

McDOUGAL, John, 1851-1852

Born in 1818, in Rose County, Ohio. Moved to the vicinity of Indianapolis, Indiana during his childhood. Brother of George. Served in the Black Hawk War in 1832; Captain in the Mexican War. Superintendent of the Indiana State Prison in 1846; went to California in 1849. Member of the 1849 California Constitutional

Convention; Lieutenant Governor of California, 1849-1851. An Independent Democrat. On January 9, 1851, Governor of California Peter H. Burnett resigned and, as Lieutenant Governor, McDougal succeeded to the office. During his administration the Land Commission was appointed; Major James D. Savage discovered Yosemite Valley; and the *Flying Cloud*, a Yankee clipper ship, arrived in San Francisco, California, eighty-one days and twenty-one hours after leaving New York City. Also while McDougal was governor, the San Francisco Vigilance Committee was formed in June 1851. Eventually numbering 716 members, the group executed four criminals and condemned fifty others to banishment before it was disbanded in September 1851. McDougal served the remainder of Burnett's term, and then left office on January 8, 1852. Afterwards, he served in the California Senate. McDougal died in San Francisco on March 30, 1866. Bibliography: Theodore H. Hittell, *History of California*, 4 vols. (San Francisco, 1885-1897); Josiah Royce, *California from the Conquest in 1846 to the Second Vigilance Committee in San Francisco (1856)* (Boston, 1886); American Guide Series, *California: A Guide to the Golden State* (New York, 1939); Walton E. Bean, *California: An Interpretive History* (New York, 1973).

BIGLER, John, 1852-1856

Born on January 8, 1805, near Carlisle, Pennsylvania, son of Jacob, a farmer, and Susan (Dock) Bigler. Married, and the father of a daughter. Attended Dickinson College in Carlisle, but withdrew when his family moved to Mercer County, Pennsylvania. Apprenticed to a printer; studied law; admitted to the bar. Was editor of the *Centre County Democrat*, Bellefonte, Pennsylvania for five years, beginning in 1827; private law practice; moved to Mount Sterling, Illinois, where he continued to practice law. Joined the Gold Rush to California in 1849 and settled in Sacramento, California where he worked as an auctioneer, wood cutter, laborer on river steamers, and engaged in the manufacture of calico comforters. He was elected to the California Assembly in 1849 serving two terms, and was chosen as Speaker of the California Assembly twice. As a Democrat, Bigler was elected Governor of California on September 3, 1851, receiving 23,175 votes to Whig, P.B. Reading's 22,732. He was sworn into office on January 8, 1852. During his administration, the United States Congress authorized the survey of a railroad route from the Mississippi River to the Pacific Ocean; Sacramento was chosen as the capital of the state; and the United States opened a branch mint in San Francisco, California. Also while Bigler was governor, three new counties were created. On September 7, 1853, he was reelected to a second term, defeating the Whig candidate, William Walde, 38,940 votes to 37,454. Bigler was defeated in his bid for a third term on September 5, 1855, polling 46,225 votes to American Party candidate J.N. Johnson's 51,157. As a result, he left office on January 9, 1856. Afterwards, he was appointed by President James Buchanan as United States Minister to Chile, a post he held for four years. In 1861, Bigler returned to California, and in 1862, he was an unsuccessful candidate for the United States Congress. He was a delegate to the Democratic National Convention on three occasions. Bigler died on November 29, 1871. His California residence was in Sacramento. Bibliography: Theodore H. Hittell, *History of California*, 4 vols. (San Francisco, 1885-1897); American Guide Series, *California: A Guide to the Golden*

State (New York, 1939); Walton E. Bean, *California: An Interpretive History* (New York, 1973); Roy Glashan, *American Governors and Gubernatorial Elections, 1775-1975* (Stillwater, Minnesota, 1975).

JOHNSON, James Neely, 1856-1858

Born on August 2, 1825, in Johnson Township, Gibson County, Indiana. His father was a politician and a member of the staff of General William Henry Harrison. Married to Mary Zabriskie in June 1851; father of two children. Studied law in Evansville, Indiana. Admitted to the Iowa Bar when he was twenty-one years of age. Moved to California in 1849; drove a mule train; engaged in mining; private law practice in Sacramento, California. Elected Sacramento City Attorney in 1850 and 1851; appointed by California Governor John McDougal as a Lieutenant Colonel in the militia, and sent to quell an Indian uprising in Mariposa County, California, 1851; elected to the California Assembly in 1852. Trustee, Sacramento State Hospital, 1851. As a member of the American or "Know-Nothing" Party, Johnson was elected Governor of California on September 5, 1855, receiving 51,157 votes to incumbent Democratic Governor, John Bigler's 46,225. He was sworn into office on January 9, 1856. During his administration, California's first railroad, from Sacramento to Folsom, was completed; the first wagon road over the Sierra Nevada Mountain Range was opened; Wells, Fargo, and Company established an express office in Los Angeles, California; and the first overland stage reached San Diego, California from San Antonio, Texas. Also while Johnson was governor, the San Francisco county and city governments were consolidated. A weak governor, Johnson had great difficulty in controlling the California Legislature during his term. In 1856, the San Francisco Vigilance Committee was revived. As governor, Johnson opposed the Vigilance; however, his efforts were both feeble and fruitless. Led by William M. Coleman, the Vigilance Committee executed four men, deported twenty-five, and ordered several others to leave the state. Johnson was not the American Party's candidate in the 1857 gubernatorial election, and left office on January 8, 1858. Afterwards, he moved to Reno, Nevada, and resumed his law practice. He served as president of the Second Nevada Constitutional Convention, and was appointed as a Justice of the Nevada Supreme Court in 1867. Johnson died in Salt Lake City, Utah on August 31, 1872. Bibliography: Hubert H. Bancroft, *History of California*, 7 vols. (San Francisco, 1886-1890); Theodore H. Hittell, *History of California*, 4 vols. (San Francisco, 1885-1897); American Guide Series, *California: A Guide to the Golden State* (New York, 1939); Roy Glashan, *American Governors and Gubernatorial Elections, 1775-1975* (Stillwater, Minnesota, 1975).

WELLER, John B., 1858-1860

Born on February 22, 1812, in Montgomery, Hamilton County, Ohio. His parents were of German descent, and natives of New York State. Married to a Miss Taylor; married a second time to a Miss Bryan; married a third time to Susan McDowell Taylor; and married a fourth time to Lizzie (Brocklebank) Stanton. Moved with his parents to Oxford, Butler County, Ohio when he was a youth. Educated in the public schools; attended Miami University in Oxford, Ohio, 1825-1829; studied law in the office of Jesse Corwin. Admitted to the Ohio Bar in 1832. Enlisted as a private in an Ohio regiment during the Mexican War; rose to the rank of Colonel of United States Volunteers. Private law practice in Hamilton, Ohio; Prosecuting Attorney, Butler County, 1833-1836; member, United States House of Representatives, 1839-1845; was not a candidate for reelection to the United States Congress; unsuccessful Ohio gubernatorial candidate, 1848; chairman of the commission to determine the boundary between the United States and Mexico according to the Treaty of Guadalupe Hidalgo, 1849-1850; moved to San Francisco, California, and opened a law office, 1850; member, United States Senate, 1852-1857; defeated for reelection to the United States Senate. As a Democrat, Weller was elected Governor of California on September 2, 1857, receiving 53,112 votes to Republican Edward Stanley's 21,040 and the American Party candidate, G.W. Bowie's 19,481. He was sworn into office on January 8, 1858. During his administration, the long feud between opposing wings of the Democratic Party in California--led by two United States Senators, William M. Gwin and David C. Broderick--reached a climax. David S. Terry, a former Judge of the California Supreme Court, killed Broderick in a duel fought in September, 1859. In November 1860, Weller was appointed United States Minister to Mexico by President James Buchanan. Weller left the governor's office on January 9, 1860. He served as United States Minister to Mexico until 1861. In 1864, he was a delegate to the Democratic National Convention, and at the end of the Civil War, he participated in a long prospecting tour through Oregon, Idaho, and Utah. Later, Weller returned to Washington, D.C. In 1867, he moved to New Orleans, Louisiana, and practiced law until his death. Weller died in New Orleans on August 17, 1875, and was buried in Lone Mountain Cemetery, San Francisco. Bibliography: Theodore H. Hittell, *History of California*, 4 vols. (San Francisco, 1885-1897); Andrew F. Rolle, *California: A History* (New York, 1963); Walton E. Bean, *California: An Interpretive History* (New York, 1973); Roy Glashan, *American Governors and Gubernatorial Elections, 1775-1975* (Stillwater, Minnesota, 1975).

LATHAM, Milton Slocum, 1860

Born on May 23, 1827, in Columbus, Ohio, third son of Bela, a lawyer, and Juliana (Sterritt) Latham. Married to Sophie Birdsall in 1853; after her death in 1867, remarried to Mary W. McMullin in 1870; father of a son. Pursued classical studies, and was graduated from Jefferson College, Canonsburg, Pennsylvania in 1846; moved to Russell County, Alabama, and studied law. Admitted to the bar in 1848. Taught school in Russell County; Circuit Court clerk, Russell County, 1848-1850. Moved to San Francisco, California in 1850; clerk of the Recorder's Court, 1850; moved to Sacramento, California, and practiced law; appointed District Attorney of Sacramento and El Dorado Counties, California in 1851. Member, United States House of Representatives, 1853-1855; declined to be a candidate for renomination; appointed Collector of the Port of San Francisco by President Franklin Pierce, and held the post from 1855 until 1857. As a Democrat, Latham was elected Governor of California on September 7, 1859, receiving 61,352 votes to the Anti-Lecompton Democratic candidate, John Currey's 31,298 and Republican Leland Stanford's

10,110. He was sworn into office on January 9, 1860. Two days after his inauguration, Latham was chosen by the California Legislature to fill the vacancy in the United States Senate created by the death of Senator David C. Broderick. As a result, he resigned as governor on January 14, 1860. Latham served in the United States Senate until 1863. Afterwards, he returned to San Francisco and practiced law; became manager of the London and San Francisco Bank from 1865 until 1878. Moved to New York City, New York in 1879, where he became president of the New York Mining and Stock Exchange. Latham died on March 4, 1882 in New York City. He was buried in Lone Mountain Cemetery in San Francisco, California. Bibliography: Hubert H. Bancroft, *History of California*, 7 vols. (San Francisco, 1886-1890); Theodore H. Hittell, *History of California*, 4 vols. (San Francisco, 1885-1897); Roy Glashan, *American Governors and Gubernatorial Elections, 1775-1975* (Stillwater, Minnesota, 1975); "Journal of Milton S. Latham," MS., Stanford University Library, Stanford, California.

DOWNEY, John G., 1860-1862

Born on June 24, 1826, in County Roscommon, Ireland, the son of Dennis Downey, a stock raiser; probably a Catholic. Most likely educated in Ireland. Immigrated to California in 1849 during the Gold Rush; settled in Los Angeles, California, in 1850; engaged in stock raising and real estate operations; owner of the Santa Gertrude Ranch. Elected Lieutenant Governor of California in 1859. A Democrat. On January 14, 1860, California Governor Milton S. Latham resigned, and, as Lieutenant Governor, Downey succeeded him in office. During his administration, the first Pony Express mail arrived in San Francisco, California; the Central Pacific Railroad Company of California was organized; and the first transcontinental telegraph line linked the east and west coasts of the United States. Also while Downey was governor, the Civil War began. There was some feeling in California that there was nothing the state could do that would have any effect on the outcome of the conflict. Some California leaders even suggested that if the Federal Union was ever dissolved, the eastern boundary of the Pacific Republic, meaning California, would be the Sierra Madre and the Rocky Mountains. However, the idea of an independent Pacific Republic was quickly crushed, and in San Francisco, on February 22, 1861, a mass meeting was arranged to encourage support for the Union. Attended by approximately 14,000 people, this meeting ended the movement for a separate Pacific Republic. Union Clubs were formed throughout the state; sympathy for the United States government was aroused; and on May 17, 1861, the California Legislature pledged the state to support the Union. Downey completed the remainder of Latham's term, and then left office on January 10, 1862. Afterwards, Downey returned to his ranching investments, and maintained his home near present-day Downey, in Los Angeles County, California. He was an unsuccessful gubernatorial candidate in the 1862 election. Downey died on March 1, 1894. Bibliography: Theodore H. Hittell, *History of California*, 4 vols. (San Francisco, 1885-1897); Andrew F. Rolle, *California: A History* (New York, 1963); Walton E. Bean, *California: An Interpretive History* (New York, 1973); Roy Glashan, *American Governors and Gubernatorial Elections, 1775-1975* (Stillwater, Minnesota, 1975).

STANFORD, Amasa Leland, 1862-1863

Born on March 9, 1824, in Watervliet, New York, the son of Josiah, a prosperous farmer and road, bridge, and railroad contractor, and Elizabeth (Phillips) Stanford. Brother of Josiah, Charles, Asa Phillips, De Witt Clinton, Thomas Welton, another brother, and a sister. Married to Jane Elizabeth Lathrop on December 30, 1850; father of Leland, Jr. Attended school until he was twelve; tutored at home for three years; attended Clinton Liberal Institute, in Clinton, New York; attended Cazenovia Seminary in Cazenovia, New York; studied law. Admitted to the bar in 1848. Began private law practice in Port Washington, Wisconsin in 1848; moved to California in 1852; operated a general store in Michigan Bluff, California; returned to Albany, New York for his wife in 1855, and the following year they moved to Sacramento, California. Engaged in the mercantile business; traveled to Washington, D.C., in 1861, to advise President-elect Abraham Lincoln on the position of the Pacific Coast in the secession controversy; became President of the Central Pacific Railroad in 1861. Justice of the Peace in Michigan Bluff; unsuccessful candidate for State Treasurer of California in 1857; unsuccessful candidate for Governor of California in 1859; delegate to the Republican National Convention of 1860, but did not attend. As a Republican, Stanford was elected Governor of California on September 4, 1861, receiving 56,036 votes to the Secession Democratic candidate, J. R. McConnell's 32,751, and the Union Democratic candidate, John Conness' 30,944. Stanford took office on January 10, 1862. During his administration, Stanford's chief task was to keep the state in the Union. Also while he was governor, he approved several public grants and four acts providing financial assistance to the Central Pacific Railroad. The first act instructed the Board of Supervisors of Placer County, California, to order a special election to consider a county subscription of $250,000 of Central Pacific stock; the second was for a similar election in the City and County of Sacramento, California, for a subscription of 3,000 shares; the third for the City and County of San Francisco, California, to submit a proposal to the voters for $1,000,000 of railroad stock; and the last act authorized the Comptroller of California to draw warrants in favor of the Central Pacific to the extent of $10,000 per mile. In 1862, the State Constitution was amended to provide for four-year gubernatorial terms. Not renominated by the Republican Party, Stanford left office on December 10, 1863. Afterwards, he continued his railway investments. He remained as President of the Central Pacific until 1893; was one of the organizers of the Southern Pacific in 1884; and served as its President from 1885 until 1890. Stanford was elected to the United States Senate in 1885, and served until his death. He founded the Leland Stanford Junior University—present-day Stanford University—in Stanford, California, in memory of his son. Stanford died on June 21, 1893, and was buried in a mausoleum on the grounds of Stanford University. Bibliography: Theodore H. Hittell, *History of California*, 4 vols. (San Francisco, 1885-1897); Zoeth S. Eldredge, ed., *History of California*, 5 vols. (New York, 1915); Walton E. Bean, *California: An Interpretive History* (New York, 1973); Roy Glashan, *American Governors and Gubernatorial Elections, 1775-1975* (Stillwater, Minnesota, 1975.

LOW, Frederick Ferdinand, 1863-1867

Born on June 30, 1828 in Frankport—present-day Winterport, Maine, the son of a small farmer in the Penobscot Valley. Married to Mollie Creed in 1850. Educated in the common schools; at the age of fifteen, apprenticed to the East Indian firm of Russell, Sturgis, and Company; broadened his education by attending lectures at Faneuil Hall and the Lowell Institute. Went to California in 1849, during the Gold Rush; after some efforts as a miner, he settled in San Francisco, California, where he began a business career as a merchant in partnership with his brother. Established a banking business in Marysville, California. Elected to the United States House of Representatives in 1861, but was not allowed to take his seat because the 1860 census disclosed that California was not entitled to another congressman; subsequently qualified under the authority of a special act of Congress and served from June 3, 1862 to March 3, 1863; he was not a candidate for reelection; appointed Collector of the Port of San Francisco in 1863. As a Union Republican, Low was elected Governor of California on September 2, 1863, defeating former Democratic Governor John G. Downey, 64,283 votes to 44,622. Low took office on December 10, 1863. He was the first governor to be elected to a four-year term under the provisions of an 1862 amendment to the California Constitution. During his administration, California continued its steadfast support of the Federal government. Many volunteers joined the Union Army, and much money was donated for the support of the troops. In the 1864 presidential election, Abraham Lincoln carried California with a 30,000 vote majority. Low left office on December 5, 1867. In December 1869, he was appointed United States Minister to China, a position he held until 1874. Afterwards, he returned to San Francisco, and served as Joint Manager of the Anglo-California Bank from 1874 until 1891. Low died on July 21, 1894, and was buried in Laurel Hill Cemetery in San Francisco. Bibliography: Theodore H. Hittell, *History of California*, 4 vols. (San Francisco, 1885-1897); Zoeth S. Eldredge, ed., *History of California*, 5 vols. (New York, 1915); Roy Glashan, *American Governors and Gubernatorial Elections, 1775-1975* (Stillwater, Minnesota, 1975). The Frederick F. Low Papers are on deposit in the Hubert H. Bancroft Library, University of California, Berkeley, California.

HAIGHT, Henry Huntly, 1867-1871

Born on May 20, 1825, in Rochester, New York, the son of Fletcher Mathews, a Judge of the United States District Court for the Southern District of California, and Elizabeth Stewart (MacLachlan) Haight. Married to Anna Bissell in January 1855. Graduated from Yale University in New Haven, Connecticut in 1844; studied law. Admitted to the bar in 1846. Haight moved with his father to St. Louis, Missouri, in 1846, where they practiced law together. He decided to move to California, and arrived in San Francisco, California, in January 1850; established a law office in San Francisco, and later was joined by his father. While in Missouri, Haight became interested in the Free Soil movement; however, in California he became affiliated first with the Democratic Party, and then the Republican Party; chairman of the California State Republican Committee in 1859; later returned to the Democratic Party. As a Democrat, Haight was elected Governor of California on September 4, 1867, defeating Republican George C. Gurham, 49,895 votes to 40,359. Haight took office on December 5, 1867. During his administration, he firmly opposed the granting of railroad subsidies; objected to the ratification of the Fifteenth Amendment to the United States Constitution; and opposed an increase in the pay of state legislators. Also while he was governor, the University of California was founded; the transcontinental railroad was completed; San Jose Teachers College was established in San Jose, California; and the Golden Gate Park was created. Haight was defeated in his bid for reelection on September 6, 1871, polling 57,520 votes to Republican Newton Booth's 62,581. He left office on December 8, 1871. Afterwards, he returned to his law practice in San Francisco. He was a member of the Board of Trustees of the University of California. In 1878, he was elected as a delegate to the State Convention called to revise the California Constitution, but died before taking his seat. Haight died in San Francisco on September 2, 1878. Bibliography: Theodore H. Hittell, *History of California*, 4 vols. (San Francisco, 1885-1897); Zoeth S. Eldredge, ed., *History of California*, 5 vols. (New York, 1915); Walton E. Bean, *California: An Interpretive History* (New York, 1973); Roy Glashan, *American Governors and Gubernatorial Elections, 1775-1975* (Stillwater, Minnesota, 1975).

BOOTH, Newton, 1871-1875

Born on December 30, 1825 in Salem, Washington County, Indiana, son of Beebe and Hannah (Pitts) Booth; a Protestant. Married to Mrs. J. T. Glover on February 29, 1892. Attended the local schools; graduated from Asbury (now DePauw) University in 1846; studied law and was admitted to the bar in 1849. Moved to Sacramento, California in 1850 and engaged in the mercantile and grocery business; returned to Terre Haute, Indiana in 1856 to practice law. Moved to Sacramento in 1860. Elected to the California Senate in 1863, serving for one term. As the Republican gubernatorial candidate, Booth was elected Governor of California by popular vote on September 6, 1871, defeating the Democratic candidate, Henry H. Haight, by a vote of 62,581 to 57,520. He was inaugurated on December 8, 1871. During his administration, Booth urged adequate protection for the Chinese already in California, but stressed the need for restrictions on further Chinese immigration; the large state debt was decreased; and the statute law was successfully revised. Booth resigned the governorship on February 27, 1875, upon his election to the United States Senate. He served as a member of the Senate from March 4, 1875 to March 3, 1881, but was not a candidate for renomination in 1880. Booth resumed his mercantile interests in Sacramento until his death. He died on July 14, 1892 in Sacramento, California and was interred in the City Cemetery. Bibliography: Andrew F. Rolle, *California, A History* (New York, 1963); Robert G. Cleland, *From Wilderness to Empire, A History of California, 1542-1900* (New York, 1944); Congressional Quarterly, Inc., *Guide to U.S. Elections* (Washington, D.C., 1975); Roy Glashan, *American Governors and Gubernatorial Elections, 1775-1975* (Stillwater, Minnesota, 1975).

PACHECO, Romualdo, 1875

Born on October 31, 1831, in Santa Barbara, California, the second son of Lieutenant of Engineers Romualdo Pacheco, an aide-de-camp to the Mexican Governor of California, and Dona Ramona Carillo; a Catholic. Brother of Mariano. Married to Mary McIntire in 1863. Pacheco's father was killed in 1831, and his mother remarried an English sea captain. Privately tutored; sent to Honolulu, Hawaii in 1840 to continue his education;he returned to California when he was fifteen years old. Served as supercargo and commanded a trading ship. When the United States acquired California, Pacheco took the oath of allegiance and became an American citizen. Engaged in agriculture. Member, California Senate, 1851 and 1861; member, California Assembly, 1853-1855 and 1868-1870; served as County Judge, 1855-1859; California State Treasurer, 1863-1866; Lieutenant Governor of California, 1871-1875. A Republican. On February 27, 1875, California Governor Newton Booth resigned, and as Lieutenant Governor, Pacheco succeeded to the office. Holding office for approximately nine months, Pacheco completed the remainder of Booth's term, and then left office on December 9, 1875. He was the Republican candidate in the 1876 election for the United States Congress, and though he was awarded the certificate of election and took his congressional seat in 1877, the election results were contested, and in 1878 he was removed and replaced by his Democratic opponent. He was subsequently elected to the United States House of Representatives, serving from 1879 until 1883. In December 1890, Pacheco was appointed United States Envoy Extraordinary and Minister Plenipotentiary to the Central American States; in July 1891, he became United States Envoy Extraordinary and Minister Plenipotentiary to Honduras and Guatemala, serving until June 1893, when he retired and returned to Oakland, California. Pacheco died on January 23, 1899, and was buried in Mountain View Cemetery in Oakland, California. Bibliography: Hubert H. Bancroft, *History of California*, 7 vols. (San Francisco, 1886-1890); Theodore H. Hittell, *History of California*, 4 vols. (San Francisco, 1885-1897); Charles E. Chapman, *A History of California: The Spanish Period* (New York, 1921); Walton E. Bean, *California: An Interpretive History* (New York,1973).

IRWIN, William, 1875-1880

Born in 1827, in Butler County, Ohio. Married to Amelia Elizabeth Cassidy on December 21, 1865. Educated in a country school; attended Carey's Academy near Cincinnati, Ohio; graduated from Marietta College, Marietta, Ohio in 1848. Taught for three years in Port Gibson, Mississippi; tutor at Marietta College; planned to study law, but instead went to Oregon for two years in 1851. Moved to Siskiyou County, California in 1854; engaged in mining and lumbering; editor of the *Yreka Union*, a newspaper in Yreka, California. Elected to the California Assembly in 1861 and 1862; Town Trustee of Yreka, 1865-1866; elected to the California Senate, 1869 and 1873; elected President Pro Tempore of the California Senate, 1873; Acting Lieutenant Governor of California, 1874. President, Mount Shasta Agricultural Association, 1867-1868. As a Democrat, Irwin was elected Governor of California on September 1, 1875, receiving 61,509 votes to Republican

T. G. Phelps' 31,322, and Independent candidates John Bidwell's 29,752. He was sworn into office on December 9, 1875. During his administration, the Southern Pacific's Los Angeles-San Francisco line was completed, which linked Los Angeles with the transcontinental railroad. Also, the oranges from California were shipped to Eastern markets. While Irwin was governor, Dennis Kearney organized the Workingmen's Party of California. Later, as violence erupted as a result of Workingmen's Party agitation, he called out the National Guard to suppress the movement, and the State Legislature authorized the arrest of "incendiary speakers" and the dispersal of "doubtful assemblages." In September 1879, a Constitutional Convention was called, and a new State Constitution was adopted which went into effect on July 4, 1879. Not being the Democratic nominee in the 1879 gubernatorial election, Irwin left office on January 8, 1880. Appointed chairman of the Board of Harbor Commissioners of California in 1883, Irwin held the post until his death on March 15, 1886 in San Francisco, California. Bibliography: Hubert H. Bancroft, *History of California*, 7 vols. (San Francisco, 1886-1890); Theodore H. Hittell, *History of California*, 4 vols. (San Francisco, 1885-1897); American Guide Series, *California: A Guide to the Golden State* (New York, 1939); Roy Glashan, *American Governors and Gubernatorial Elections, 1775-1975* (Stillwater, Minnesota, 1975).

PERKINS, George Clement, 1880-1883

Born on August 23, 1839, in Kennebunkport, York County, Maine, the son of Clement, a farmer and sailor, and Lucinda (Fairchild) Perkins. Married to Ruth A. Parker in 1864 who died in 1921; father of three sons and four daughters. Received a limited education in the local district school. Went to sea when he was twelve years old; spent the next four years at sea, and made several trips to Europe. In 1885, he sailed to San Francisco, California; traveled to Sacramento, California by boat; and then went overland to Oroville (then called Ophir), California. Member, Oroville, California National Guards; aide-de-camp to General John Bidwell. Engaged in placer-mining; became a clerk in a country store; owned a ferry; purchased a store in Oroville; built a flour mill; invested in mining; engaged in sheep-raising; and constructed sawmills. Assisted in the establishment of the Bank of Butte County in Chico, California; served as a Director of the Bank of Butte County; engaged in farming. Became a partner in the San Francisco firm of Goodall and Nelson; eventually this business became Goodall, Perkins, and Company; and finally it was incorporated as the Pacific Coast Steamship Company. This company acquired most of the coastal steamers plying between Alaska and Central America, and purchased the Oregon Railway and Navigation Company, the Pacific Steam Whaling Company, and the Arctic Oil Company. Elected to the California Senate in 1869, and served until 1876. President, Chamber of Commerce of San Francisco; president, San Francisco Art Association; trustee, California Academy of Sciences; trustee, California State Mining Bureau; trustee, State Institution for the Dumb and Blind, Berkeley; acting president of the Boys and Girls Aid Society for thirty years; Mason; Loyal Legion. As a Republican, Perkins was elected Governor of California on September 3, 1879, receiving 67,965 votes to Democrat Hugh J. Glenn's 47,667 and the Workingmen's Party or League candidate, William F. White's 44,482. He was sworn into office on January 8, 1880.

During his administration, the University of Southern California was founded in Los Angeles and the State Normal School was opened. The 1879 California Constitution had changed the election of state officials from odd-numbered years to even-numbered years, and to achieve such a change, the new Constitution provided that the first officials elected under its provisions would hold office for three years instead of four. As a result, Perkins left office on January 10, 1883. Afterwards, he returned to his business investments. In 1886, he was an unsuccessful candidate for the United States Senate; however, in 1893, he was appointed to the United States Senate by California Governor Henry H. Markham. He held the post until 1915, when he retired because of ill health and moved to Oakland, California. Perkins died on February 26, 1923, and was buried in Mountain View Cemetery in Oakland. Bibliography: Theodore H. Hittell, *History of California*, 4 vols. (San Francisco, 1885-1897); Zoeth S. Eldredge, ed., *History of California*, 5 vols. (New York, 1915); American Guide Series, *California: A Guide to the Golden State* (New York, 1939); Roy Glashan, *American Governors and Gubernatorial Elections, 1775-1975* (Stillwater, Minnesota, 1975).

STONEMAN, George, 1883-1887

Born on August 8, 1822 in Busti, Chautauqua County, New York; a Protestant. Married to Mary Oliver Hardisty of Baltimore at the close of the Civil War; father of two sons and two daughters. Attended Jamestown Academy, Jamestown, New York, and graduated from the United States Military Academy in 1846 with high honors. Served with the Mormon Battalion in the Mexican War. During the Civil War, he was promoted to the rank of Major General and commanded cavalry units. After the war, he served in Tennessee, commanding the Department of Arizona until 1871. He then retired to his ranch, "Los Robles," in California's San Gabriel Valley. In 1876, Governor William Irwin appointed Stoneman as one of California's commissioners of transportation. President Rutherford B. Hayes appointed him in 1878 as an Indian Commissioner. He sought and won his first elective office in 1879 — Railroad Commissioner for California's Third District (southern California). In 1882, he gained the Democratic nomination for Governor on the fourteenth ballot over George Hearst. He then defeated Republican Morris M. Estee, receiving 90,694 of the 164,661 votes cast for four candidates in the general election. Stoneman received fifty-five percent of the total vote. Governor Stoneman single-handedly attempted to curb the power and control the rates of the Southern Pacific Railroad. In 1884 he called a special legislative session to deal with the railroad, but most of the lawmakers, obligated to the Southern Pacific, did nothing. In 1886 he called another session to deal with the machinations of another special interest group, the large landowners. He sought to provide water rights for all Californians, based on the free use of flowing waters, but big ranchers stalled any reform. In 1885, Stoneman called for social legislation such as regulation of food and drugs, and additional state care for the blind and mental patients. Also, several state agencies were created to look after the interests of the average citizen. Stoneman was one of California's most vigorous nineteenth century governors. A person of high integrity, he was courageous in maintaining his position, but he was unable to make any headway against the railroad-controlled legislature. The Democrats in their 1886 State Convention repudiated Stoneman by not considering him for renomination. He returned to his San Gabriel Valley ranch where he resided until 1891, when he moved to Buffalo, New York to live with his sister. In April 1894, he had a stroke and never recovered. He died in Buffalo on September 4, 1894, and was buried in Lakewood, New York. Bibliography: "George Stoneman Letters," California Section, California State Library, Sacramento, California; George Stoneman, "Official Record, Executive Department," California State Archives, Sacramento, California; Hubert H. Bancroft, *History of California,* 7 vols.(San Francisco, 1886-1890); Theodore H. Hittell, *History of California,* 4 vols. (San Francisco, 1885-1897); H. Brett Melendy and Benjamin F. Gilbert, *The Governors of California* (Georgetown, Calif., 1965).

BARTLETT, Washington, 1887

Born on February 29, 1824 in Savannah, Georgia, eldest son of Cosam Emir and Sarah E. (Melhado) Bartlett. Brother of Asabella, Cosam, Julian, Franklin, Sarah, Columbus and William Tell. Did not attend college but received a common school education; apprenticed in journalism with his father's newspaper, the *Tallahassee Star.* Joined the gold rush to California in 1849. Settled in San Francisco to continue newspaper work, but read law and was admitted to the California Bar. Involved with real estate ventures. Elected County Clerk of San Francisco County in 1859, 1861, and 1867; appointed State Harbor Commissioner, 1869-1870; elected to the California State Senate in 1873 for a four-year term. With the support of the Democratic Party, he was twice elected Mayor of San Francisco, 1883-1887. Received the Democratic nomination for Governor in 1886 and defeated the Republican candidate, John Swift, in a close election, 84,970 votes to 84,311 -- a plurality of 659 votes. He was sworn into office on January 8, 1887. As governor, Bartlett's term of office was cut short by a severe stroke on August 23, 1887, which finally resulted in his death. During his eight months in office some notable legislation was passed. Most significantly, the water rights struggle between opposing doctrines of riparian rights and prior appropriation was resolved through passage of the Wright Irrigation Law, which allowed the formation of irrigation districts. Other legislation allowed the University of California greater independence from the legislature, supported the nascent viticulture industry, and aided public parks. These were positive achievements, although Bartlett did not initiate the proposals. Bartlett died on September 12, 1887 and was buried in San Francisco. He was succeeded by Lieutenant Governor Robert Waterman. Bibliography: Robert W. Righter, "The Life and Public Career of Washington Bartlett," M.A. Thesis, San Jose State University, 1963; Robert W. Righter, "Washington Bartlett: Mayor of San Francisco, 1883-1887," *Journal of the West,* vol. III, no. 2 (January, 1954); H. Brett Melendy, "California's Washington Bartlett," *Pacific Historical Review,* vol. XXX (May, 1963); *Memorial to the Life and Services of Washington Bartlett* (San Francisco, 1888). The Bartlett Papers are on deposit in the Bancroft Library, University of California, Berkeley.

WATERMAN, Robert Whitney, 1887-1891

Born on December 15, 1826, in Fairfield, New York. His father, a merchant, died when Waterman was a child, and he was raised and educated by his brothers in Sycamore, Illinois. He was a clerk in a country store until 1846 when he entered the mercantile business on his own in Belvidere, Illinois; was appointed postmaster in Geneva, Illinois in 1849. Moved to California in 1849, and engaged in mining; returned to Willmington, Illinois two years later; became publisher of the Willmington *Independent*, a newspaper, in 1853. Waterman was a delegate to the 1854 convention in Bloomington, Illinois, which founded that state's Republican Party, and took an active role in the John C. Fremont presidential campaign of 1856, and in the contest between Abraham Lincoln and Stephen A. Douglas for the United States Senate in 1858. During this period, he was engaged in several businesses. In 1873, Waterman returned to California, and settled in San Bernardino the following year. He discovered and developed several silver mines in the "Calceo District" of San Bernardino County, and was chief owner of the Stonewall Gold Mine in San Diego County, California. Waterman was president of the San Diego, Guyanaca and Eastern Railroad; he also owned extensive ranch properties. As a Republican he was elected Lieutenant Governor of California on November 2, 1886. On September 12, 1887, California Governor Washington Bartlett died, and as Lieutenant Governor, Waterman succeeded to the office. During his administration, the state's irrigation system was expanded; Long Beach, California, was incorporated, and Pomona College in Claremont, California was opened. Also while Waterman was governor, the first Tournament of Roses, known in 1890 as the Battle of Flowers, was held in Pasadena, California. Waterman served the remainder of Bartlett's term, and then left office on January 8, 1891. Afterwards, he returned to his business, mining, and ranching investments. Waterman died on April 12, 1891. His California residence was at San Bernardino. Bibliography: Zoeth S. Eldredge, ed., *History of California*, 5 vols. (New York, 1915); American Guide Series, *California: A Guide to the Golden State* (New York, 1939); Walton E. Bean, *California: An Interpretive History* (New York, 1973); Roy Glashan, *American Governors and Gubernatorial Elections, 1775-1975* (Stillwater, Minnesota, 1975).

MARKHAM, Henry Harrison, 1891-1895

Born on November 16, 1841 in Wilmington, Essex County, New York, son of Nathan B. and Susan (McLeod) Markham; a Protestant. Married to Mary A. Dana on May 17, 1876. Attended the local schools and Wheeler's Academy in Vermont. Moved to Wisconsin in 1861 and enlisted as a private in Company G, Thirty-Second Regiment, Wisconsin Volunteer Infantry; wounded at the Battle of Whippy Swamp on February 3, 1865; honorably discharged on June 12, 1865. Settled in Milwaukee, Wisconsin and studied law; subsequently admitted to the bar in 1861, practicing in Milwaukee and before the United States Courts. Moved to Pasadena, California in 1878 because of ill health and pursued mining interests. Became president of the Los Angeles Furniture Company, and a director of the Los Angeles National Bank, the San Gabriel Valley Bank, and the Southern

California Oil Supply Company. Markham was elected a Representative to the United States House of Representatives, serving from March 4, 1885 to March 3, 1887, and was unanimously renominated in 1886, but declined to run. Appointed a member of the Board of Managers of the National Home for Disabled Volunteer Soldiers on March 16, 1889, resigning upon becoming Governor of California. As the Republican gubernatorial candidate, Markham was elected Governor of California by popular vote on November 4, 1890, defeating the Democratic candidate, E. Pond, by a vote of 125,129 to 117,184. He was inaugurated on January 8, 1891. During his administration legislation was enacted to restrict the immigration of Chinese; to insure honesty of elections; and to benefit the working population. Markham left office on January 11, 1895 upon the inauguration of James H. Budd. He was appointed a member of the Board of Managers of the National Home for Disabled Volunteer Soldiers in 1904, serving in that capacity until his death. Markham died on October 9, 1923 in Pasadena, California. He was interred in Mountain View Cemetery. Bibliography: Robert G. Cleland, *From Wilderness to Empire, A History of California, 1854-1900* (New York, 1944); Andrew F. Rolle, *California, A History* (New York, 1963); Congressional Quarterly, Inc., *Guide to U.S. Elections* (Washington, D.C., 1975); Roy Glashan, *American Governors and Gubernatorial Elections, 1775-1975* (Stillwater, Minnesota, 1975).

BUDD, James Herbert, 1895-1899

Born on May 18, 1858 in Janesville, Wisconsin; son of Joseph H., a lawyer, and Lucinda (Ash) Budd. Moved with his family to California in 1858. Enrolled with the University of California's first class, graduating in 1873; admitted to the bar in 1874. Married a widow, Inez A. Merrill, in 1873. Served briefly in Stockton as a Deputy District Attorney and then joined his father's law firm. Elected to the United States House of Representatives in 1882, but declined renomination. Returned to his law practice; served as a Stockton library trustee and on the police and fire commission. Active in the Democratic Party, he was a leading contender in 1894 for the gubernatorial nomination. He was nominated on the third ballot. In a very close general election, Budd, with 111,944 votes, defeated Republican Morris M. Estee by only 1,206 votes. Estee received 110,738 votes, and two other candidates together polled 61,865. Both parties apparently stuffed the ballot boxes. The Republicans, trying to oust Budd, charged that San Francisco Democrats had resorted to fraud, but an Assembly investigation committee found no evidence of this. During his gubernatorial administration, Budd sought to reduce the state tax rate; to consolidate overlapping governmental agencies; to improve the caliber of employees; to establish a central purchasing agency; and to create a surplus in the treasury. His administration launched the Department of Highways and began the network of state roads. Budd boasted that he had rebuilt the General Fund and that state bills were being paid from cash on hand. Most of his program was handicapped because of Republican control of the legislature. Budd's health failed in 1897, and since he was the only Democrat in a major state office, he did not seek reelection. Budd opened a law office in San Francisco in 1899 and became the attorney for the Board of State Harbor Commissioners. In 1900, Governor Henry Gage appointed him a member of the University of California Board of Regents. Hoping to improve his failing health, he traveled to Europe. In 1908, he tried unsuccessfully to practice law. Budd died in Stockton on July 30, 1908. He was buried in Stockton's Rural Cemetery. Bibliography: James M. Guinn, *History of the State of California and Biographical Record of San Joaquin County*, 2 vols. (Los Angeles, 1909); H. Brett Melendy and Benjamin F. Gilbert, *The Governors of California* (Georgetown, Calif., 1965); Oscar T. Shuck, *History of the Bench and Bar of California* (Los Angeles, 1901). Papers of Budd, California State Archives, Sacramento.

GAGE, Henry Tifft, 1899-1903

Born on December 25, 1852 in Geneva, New York, son of Dewitt C., a lawyer and judge, and Catherine (Glover) Gage. Married to Frances V. Rains in 1890; father of five children. Grew up in East Saginaw, Michigan; after graduation from high school, studied law in his father's office; was admitted to the bar when he was twenty-one years old. Moved to California in 1874. In 1877, he opened a law office in Los Angeles, and soon numbered several large corporations among his clients (one in particular was the Southern Pacific Railroad.) Active in Republican politics, Gage was elected Los Angeles City Attorney in 1881. Supported by the "Southern Pacific Political Bureau," Gage secured the Republican gubernatorial nomination on the first ballot in 1898. Successful in the general election, Gage defeated Democrat James G. Maguire 148,334 votes to 129,255. Two other candidates together received 9,398 votes. The Gage administration was rife with partisan politics, as the Southern Pacific political machine tried unsuccessfully to force its candidate for United States Senator through the legislature. Gage, as part of the machine, acquiesced to the bosses, approved legislation friendly to the railroad and opposed reform groups. He also used a spoils system to reward friends and "machine workers" with state office. He became involved in the San Francisco bubonic plague controversy, which turned into a fiasco as federal, state and local authorities contradicted each other as to the actual situation. In 1901, Gage became the first California governor to mediate a labor strike. As his term ended, Gage, considered a railroad pawn, had created a host of political enemies, within and outside of his own party. At the 1902 Republican Convention, the Southern Pacific "machine" tried to renominate Gage, but when "anti-machine" forces stalemated the convention, party bosses switched to George C. Pardee as a compromise candidate. Following his one term as governor, Gage returned to Los Angeles and his law practice. In 1909, President William Howard Taft appointed Gage Minister to Portugal. He resigned in 1911 because of his wife's health and resumed his legal work. He died in Los Angeles on August 28, 1924. Bibliography: J.C. Bates, ed., *History of the Bench and Bar of California* (Los Angeles, 1912); Robert Knight, *Industrial Relations in the San Francisco Bay Area, 1900-1918* (Berkeley, 1960); H. Brett Melendy and Benjamin F. Gilbert, *The Governors of California* (Georgetown, Calif. 1965); W.W. Robinson, *Lawyers of Los Angeles* (Los Angeles, 1959).

PARDEE, George Cooper, 1903-1907

Born in San Francisco, California on July 25, 1857, son of Enoch Homer, a physician, and Mary E. Pardee. Married to Helen Newhall Penniman in 1887; father of four daughters. Graduated from the University of California in 1879 and earned his M.A. degree from the university in 1881. After attending Cooper Medical College for two years, he went to the University of Leipzig in Germany, where he received his M.D. degree in 1885. He then joined his father's medical practice. In 1891, he was elected to the Oakland City Council and was elected Mayor of Oakland in 1893. In 1899, Governor Gage appointed him a regent of the University of California. At the 1902 Republican State Convention, Pardee won the gubernatorial nomination when the Southern Pacific Railroad political bosses and reform groups stalemated each other. In the general election, Pardee defeated Franklin Lane, a Democrat, 146,332 votes to 143,783. The Socialist and Prohibition candidates together garnered 14,229 votes. Some 5,000 ballots in Los Angeles and Oakland were disallowed and the State Supreme Court settled the subsequent election dispute in favor of Pardee. As governor, Pardee faced serious fiscal problems which he solved fairly well. An advocate of conservation, he moved ahead in the areas of forest and water resources. New beginnings were made in state fiscal support of public high schools, a state textbook program, and prison reform. The most dramatic event during Pardee's administration was the 1906 earthquake. He took personal command of San Francisco's health problems, and then called a special session of the legislature to reestablish local and state government in northern California and to sustain San Francisco, the state's financial center. Pardee proved to be an able governor and earned the respect of the state newspapers. He sought a second term, but the Southern Pacific "machine" blatantly succeeded in gaining nomination for its candidate, James N. Gillett, on the first ballot. Pardee returned to his medical career in Oakland. He served on many national and state boards. He was a member of the National Conservation Commission, 1907-1911; chairman of the California State Conservation Commission, 1911; and chairman of the California Board of Forestry, 1919. He was a delegate to four national presidential conventions. In 1912, Pardee joined the Progressive Party and was one of its presidential electors that year. In 1924, he served as a Republican elector. At the local level, he was president of the Board of Directors, East Bay Municipal Utility District, 1914-1941. From 1927 to 1941, he served as a member of the Oakland Port Commission. Dr. Pardee died in Oakland, California on September 1, 1941 at the age of eighty-four, following a protracted illness. Bibliography: George Pardee, "Correspondence and Papers," Bancroft Library, University of California, Berkeley; H. Brett Melendy and Benjamin F. Gilbert, *Governors of California* (Georgetown, Calif., 1965); Alice M. Rose, "Rise of California Insurgency: Origins of the League of Lincoln-Roosevelt Republican Clubs, 1900-1907," Ph.D. dissertation, Stanford University, 1942; Edward F. Staniford, "Governor in the Middle—the Administration of George C. Pardee, Governor of California, 1903-1907," Ph.D. dissertation, University of California, Berkeley, 1955.

GILLETT, James Norris, 1907-1911

Born in Viroqua, Wisconsin on September 20, 1860, son of Cyrus Foss and Sarah Jane (Norris) Gillett; a Protestant. Married Adelaide Pratt in 1886; father of three children; after his wife's death in 1896, remarried to Elizabeth Erzgraber in 1898; father of James N., Jr. Moved to Sparta, Wisconsin, where he attended public schools; left high school in 1878 to study law, and was admitted to the Wisconsin Bar in 1881. In 1883, Gillett worked for the lumber firm of Pope & Talbot in the Washington Territory. Moved to Eureka, California in 1884, where his law practice soon flourished. Gillett was appointed Eureka City Attorney in 1889, a position he held until he was elected to two terms (1897-1900) in the California State Senate. From 1903 to 1906, he served two terms in the United States House of Representatives. In 1906, Gillett, backed by Southern Pacific political bosses, won the Republican gubernatorial nomination on the first ballot. In the 1906 general election, a split in the Democratic Party enabled Gillett to win with only forty percent of the vote. Of the votes cast, he received 125,887; Theodore Bell, Democrat, 117,645; William H. Langdon, Independence League, 45,008; and Austin Lewis, Socialist, 16,036. Governor Gillett's early months in office were spent attempting to appease both machine bosses and reformers. Political patronage increased greatly, but reformers triumphed with the passage of a direct primary election constitutional amendment. Gillett's pure food and drug proposals, modelled after recent federal laws, were passed, but railroad and gambling measures were rejected. State control of horse racing was, however, approved. State financial reserves improved, and several new state buildings were constructed — many of these replaced earthquake-destroyed facilities. Nationally, the San Francisco-Japanese controversy gained attention. Gillett worked closely with Presidents Theodore Roosevelt and William Howard Taft to prevent the California Legislature from passing anti-Japanese measures. In January 1910, faced with the new direct primary law and personal financial problems, Gillett announced that he would not seek a second term. He established his home in Berkeley, California and opened law offices in San Francisco in 1911. He served briefly as a lobbyist for the oil industry of California in Washington, D.C. In 1934, he and his son started a law practice in Oakland. Gillett died in Berkeley on April 21, 1937 of heart disease at the age of seventy-six. He was interred in the Oakland Columborium. Bibliography: James N. Gillett, "Autobiography," in Randolph A. Richards, Jr., ed., *History of Monroe County, Wisconsin* (1912); Franklin Hichborn, *Story of the Session of the California Legislature of 1909* (San Francisco, 1909); H. Brett Melendy and Benjamin F. Gilbert, *Governors of California* (Georgetown, Calif., 1965); George Mowry, *The California Progressives* (Berkeley, Calif., 1951); Alice M. Rose, "Rise of California Insurgency: Origins of the League of Lincoln-Roosevelt Republican Clubs, 1900-1907," Ph.D. dissertation, Stanford University, 1942; the Chester Rowell Papers are on deposit in the Bancroft Library, University of California, Berkeley.

JOHNSON, Hiram, 1911-1917

Born in Sacramento, California on September 2, 1866, son of Grove L., a lawyer, and Connie (Williamson) Johnson; a Protestant. Married to Minnie McNeal of Sacramento; father of Hiram, Jr. and Archibald. After graduation from high school, he worked briefly in his father's law office. Entered the University of California in 1884, but left in his junior year to marry. Admitted to the California Bar in 1888. Joined his father and brother, Albert, in a law practice. In 1900, his support of a reform candidate for mayor of Sacramento gained him appointment as city corporation counsel. In 1902, he and his brother opened law offices in San Francisco. During 1905-1906, Hiram Johnson gained fame for his part in the San Francisco graft trials. In 1910, during the first use of the direct primary in California, the Lincoln-Roosevelt League sought Johnson as its reform candidate. He gained the Republican nomination and then defeated Democrat Theodore Bell, 177,191 votes to 154,835; the Socialist and Prohibitionist contenders polled 53,626. Reform was the key word of Johnson's administration. The initiative, referendum and recall were enacted; a civil service system was installed; railroads and utilities were strictly regulated; and an eight-hour workday for women and children, and workmen's compensation were enacted into law. An advocate of the commission form of government, Johnson created many quasi-independent state boards. In 1913, he became the first United States governor to submit a unified state budget. One of the most controversial aspects of his administration was his endorsement of an anti-alien land bill over the protest of President Woodrow Wilson. In 1912, Johnson joined the Progressive revolt in the Republican Party and ran as the vice presidential nominee on the Bull Moose ticket. When Wilson won the election, Johnson returned to the governor's mansion. He ran for reelection as governor in 1914 as a Progressive. He received 460,495 votes in the general election, while his major opponents, Republican John D. Fredericks and Democrat J. B. Curtin, gained 271,990 and 116,121 votes respectively. Johnson was the only Progressive governor to be elected in 1914. In 1916, Progressive and Republican voters nominated Johnson for the United States Senate and he won easily in the general election. Although his senatorial term began on March 4, 1917, Johnson did not resign as governor until March 15, and then reluctantly, when President Wilson called a special congressional session for March 17. Reelected four times, he remained in the Senate until his death. He was a leader of staunch isolationists, Japanese exclusionists and supporters of the Colorado River Project. Hiram Johnson died on August 6, 1945 at Bethesda Naval Hospital, Maryland at the age of seventy-nine. He was buried in Cyprus Lawn Cemetery, San Francisco. Bibliography: Rogers Daniels, *Politics of Prejudice* (Berkeley, 1962); H. Brett Melendy and Benjamin F. Gilbert, *Governors of California* (Georgetown, Calif., 1965); George E. Mowry, *California Progressives* (Berkeley, 1951); Spencer C. Olin, Jr., *California's Prodigal Sons* (Berkeley, 1968). The Papers of Hiram Johnson are in the Bancroft Library, University of California, Berkeley; The Chester Rowell Papers are in the Bancroft Library, University of California, Berkeley.

STEPHENS, William Dennison, 1917-1923

Born in Eaton, Ohio, on December 26, 1859, son of Martin F. and Alvina (Leiber) Stephens; a Protestant. Graduated from Eaton High School in 1876; taught school; and read law. After 1880, worked as a railroad construction crew member. In 1887, accompanied his parents to Los Angeles. Married Flora Rawson of Los Angeles in 1891. From 1891 to 1902, was a traveling salesman in southern California. In 1902, Stephens, by then a prominent Los Angeles businessman, helped to create the wholesale and retail grocers partnership of Carr and Stephens. He served on the Los Angeles Chamber of Commerce board of directors from 1902 to 1911. In 1909, following the resignation of Los Angeles Mayor Arthur C. Harper, Stephens was appointed interim mayor. In 1910, he was one of the Lincoln-Roosevelt League's nominees for the House of Representatives. Reelected in 1912 as a Republican, he ran successfully as a Progressive in 1914. Internal party politics, following the death of Lieutenant Governor John Eshelman in April 1916, led southern California Progressives to insist upon Stephens' appointment. Stephens became Governor following Hiram Johnson's resignation (March 1917). His first term began shortly before the United States' entry into World War I. In December 1917, a bomb damaged part of the governor's mansion, and the International Workers of the World were blamed. Stephens became a conservative force against all left-wing groups and led in the passage of a criminal syndicalism law. The 1918 gubernatorial election was greatly confused because of California's cross-filing law which allowed a candidate to file for nomination by parties besides his own; however, he had to win his own party's nomination. Stephens filed for, and won, Progressive, Prohibition and Republican nominations. His major Republican opponent, Mayor James Rolph, Jr. of San Francisco, defeated Progressive Francis J. Heney for the Democratic nomination, although Rolph's candidacy was later disallowed. Meanwhile, Democrats backed Theodore Bell as an Independent. Stephens overwhelmed all opposition with 387,547 votes, against the combined total of 301,123 votes cast for the other candidates. During his full term as governor, Stephens stressed efficiency and attempted to eliminate duplication. He successfully reorganized the executive branch. New highway construction and veterans' welfare programs were launched. Stephens encountered strong opposition when he urged increased corporation taxes to fund proposed legislative programs. He sought reelection in 1922, but as a registered Republican he lost that party's nomination to Friend Richardson in the primary election. Stephens then returned to Los Angeles, where he entered private law practice. He had been admitted to the bar in 1920, while governor. He remained active in Los Angeles civic affairs until his death on April 24, 1944 at the age of eighty-five. He was buried in Rosedale Cemetery, Los Angeles. Bibliography: John Curry, "William D. Stephens, Twenty-Fourth Governor of California," M.A. Thesis, San Jose State College, 1961; H. Brett Melendy, "California's Cross-Filing Nightmare: The 1918 Gubernatorial Election," *Pacific Historical Review,* vol. XXXII (1964); H Brett Melendy, and Benjamin F. Gilbert, *Governors of California* (Georgetown, Calif., 1965); George Mowry, *California Progressives* (Berkeley, 1951); William D. Stephens, *California in the War, War Addresses, Proclamations and Patriotic Addresses of Governor William D. Stephens* (Sacramento, 1921); The Meyer Lissner Papers are on deposit in the Borel Collection, Stanford University, Stanford California.

RICHARDSON, Friend William, 1923-1927

Born in December 1865, near Ann Arbor, Michigan, the son of William and Rhoda (Dye) Richardson; a member of the Society of Friends. Married to Augusta Felder; father of Ruth, Paul W. and John A. Educated in public schools; attended San Bernardino College, San Bernadino, California. Newspaper publisher in San Bernadino, 1896-1901; newspaper publisher, Berkeley, California, 1901-1919. California State Printer, 1912-1915; California State Treasurer, 1915-1923. President, California Press Association for thirty-nine years; Mason; Odd Fellow; Elk; Modern Woodman of the World; Order of Eastern Star; Moose; Sciot. As a Republican, Richardson was elected Governor of California on November 7, 1922, receiving 576,445 votes to Democrat Thomas Lee Woolwine's 347,530. He was sworn into office on January 9, 1923. During his administration, Memorial Coliseum in Los Angeles, California was opened; the Rosecrans and Inglewood oil fields were discovered; and the California Legislature approved a new Los Angeles City Charter. Also while Richardson was governor, the improvement of the harbor at Long Beach, California was completed, and the new site of the University of California at Los Angeles was dedicated. In 1926, California voters adopted the so-called "modified federal plan," which provided that counties be utilized as the basic units for representation in the State Senate; however, some consideration was given to population statistics in the allocation of seats. Richardson was not the Republican gubernatorial nominee in 1926, and as a result he left office on January 4, 1927. Afterwards, he was the publisher of the Alameda, California *Times Star*, a newspaper, from 1931 until 1932. Richardson served as the California State Building and Loan Commissioner from 1932 to 1933, and as California State Superintendent of Banks from 1934 until 1939. Richardson died on September 6, 1943. His California residence was in Berkeley. Bibliography: American Guide Series, *California: A Guide to the Golden State* (New York, 1939); American Guide Series, *Los Angeles: A Guide to the City and Its Environs* (New York, 1941); Clyde E. Jacobs and John F. Gallagher, *California Government: One Among Fifty* (New York, 1966); Roy Glashan, *American Governors and Gubernatorial Elections, 1775-1975* (Stillwater, Minnesota, 1975).

YOUNG, Clement Calhoun, 1927-1931

Born on April 28, 1869, in Lisbon, New Hampshire, the son of Isaac E. and Mary R. (Calhoun) Young; a Congregationalist. Married to Lyla J. Vincent on March 15, 1902; father of Barbara and Lucy. Graduated from San Jose, California High School and Santa Rosa, California High School; received a B. L. degree from the University of California in 1892. Teacher in the Santa Rosa High School, 1892-1893; teacher and head of the English Department, Lowell High School, San Francisco, California, 1893-1906. Worked for Mason-McDaffle Company, a suburban development firm in Berkeley and San Francisco, California, 1906-1944. Member, California Assembly, 1909-1919; Speaker of the California Assembly, 1913-1919; *Ex-officio* Regent, University of California, 1913-1930; Lieutenant Governor of California, 1919-1927; Republican Presidential Elector, 1920; Chairman, California Electoral Board. Delegate, Republican National Convention, 1912.

Phi Beta Kappa. Co-author: *Principles and Progress of English Poetry* (1904). As a Republican, Young was elected Governor of California on November 2, 1926, receiving 814,815 votes to Democrat Justus S. Wardell's 282,451. He was sworn into office on January 4, 1927. During his administration, the effects of the nation's Great Depression began to be felt in California. Also while Young was governor, the Henry E. Huntington Library and Art Gallery opened in Los Angeles, California; the St. Francis Dam collapsed, causing an estimated $30,000,000 worth of damage; and the Metropolitan Water District, comprising thirteen cities, was formed to obtain water from the Colorado River. In addition, during his term, classes began at the new campus of the University of California at Los Angeles. Young was not the Republican gubernatorial nominee in 1930, and he left office on January 6, 1931. Afterwards, he returned to Mason-McDaffle Company until 1944. Young died on December 24, 1947. His California residence was in San Francisco. Bibliography: American Guide Series, *Los Angeles: A Guide to the City and Its Environs* (New York, 1941); Walton E. Bean, *California: An Interpretive History* (New York, 1973); Congressional Quarterly, Inc., *Guide to U.S. Elections* (Washington, D.C., 1975); Roy Glashan, *American Governors and Gubernatorial Elections, 1775-1975* (Stillwater, Minnesota, 1975).

ROLPH, James, 1931-1934

Born on August 23, 1869, in San Francisco, California, son of James and Margaret (Nicol) Rolph; an Episcopalian. Married to Annie Marshall Reid on June 26, 1900; father of Annette Reid, James and Georgina. Educated in public schools; attended Trinity Academy in San Francisco. Began working as an office boy in a shipping firm in 1888; president, James Rolph and Company, a shipping firm; chairman of the board, Mission Savings Bank; became a member of the general insurance firm of James Rolph, Jr., Landis, and Ellis in 1928. Mayor of San Francisco, 1911-1932. In 1918, Rolph, a Republican, won the Democratic nomination for governor, but under California's Cross-Filing Law, a candidate who does not win his own party's nomination cannot run on the ticket of another party, and Rolph's candidacy was disallowed. President, Merchants Exchange; president, Ship Owners Association of the Pacific Coast; Native Sons of the Golden West; Pacific Union; Union League. As a Republican, Rolph was elected Governor of California on November 4, 1930, receiving 999,393 votes to Democrat Milton K. Young's 333,973. He was sworn into office on January 6, 1931. During his administration, he was faced with the mass migration of the citizens of other states who fled to California to escape the effects of the Great Depression. Also while Rolph was governor, construction was started on Boulder Dam; the Tenth Olympiad opened at Los Angeles, California; work on the Colorado River Aqueduct began; President Herbert Hoover set aside land for the Death Valley National Monument; an earthquake centered in Long Beach, California caused $60,000,000 worth of damage; and the California Legislature ratified the Twenty-first Amendment to the United States Constitution. Rolph died in office on June 2, 1934. Bibliography: American Guide Series, *California: A Guide to the Golden State* (New York, 1939); American Guide Series, *Los Angeles: A Guide to the City and Its Environs* (New York, 1941); Walton E. Bean, *California: An Interpretive History* (New York, 1973); Roy Glashan, *American Governors and Gubernatorial Elections, 1775-1975* (Stillwater, Minnesota, 1975).

MERRIAM, Frank Finley, 1934-1939

Born on December 22, 1865, in Hopkinton, Iowa, son of Henry, a farmer, and Anna E. Merriam. One of eleven children; his brothers and sisters included Robert M., Edith L., Susan M., Zella, Henry C., Minnie and Ann. Married to Nellie E. Boronson-Day; after her death in 1931, remarried to Mrs. Jessie Steward Lipsey, who died in 1948; father of Howard. Educated at Lenox College in Hopkinton, Iowa. Taught school in Hopkinton; became principal of the school in Hopkinton; was a school principal in Nebraska. Member, Iowa House of Representatives, 1896-1898; served as State Auditor of Iowa for two terms. Engaged in the newspaper business in Iowa and Indian Territory; moved to Long Beach, California in 1910; employed on the advertising staff of the *Long Beach Press* for twelve years; president, Citizens State Bank, Long Beach, 1924-1926. Member, California Assembly for six terms; served as Speaker of the California Assembly for two terms; served as State Auditor of California for one term; elected to the California Senate in 1928; Lieutenant Governor of California, 1931-1934. Chairman, California Republican State Central Committee, 1928. A Republican. On June 2, 1934, California Governor James Rolph, Jr. died, and as Lieutenant Governor, Merriam succeeded to the office. On November 7, 1934, Merriam was elected Governor of California in his own right, receiving 1,138,620 votes to Democrat Upton Sinclair's 879,537 and the Conservative and Progressive candidate Raymond L. Haight's 302,519. During his administration, work on the All-American Canal from the Colorado River was started; construction of Parker Dam was begun; the gates of Boulder Dam, which stored the water of the Colorado River, were closed; the San Francisco-Oakland Bay Bridge was opened; a $70,000,000 flood control plan for Los Angeles County, California was authorized by the federal government; and the Golden Gate Bridge was opened. Also while Merriam was governor, he used the National Guard to keep food supplies moving during the 1934 longshoremen's strike. In February and March 1938, Los Angeles County was inundated by a flood which caused an estimated $65,000,000 worth of damage. On November 8, 1938, Merriam was defeated in his bid for reelection, polling 1,171,019 votes to Democrat Culbert L. Olson's 1,391,734. As a result, he left office on January 2, 1939. Afterwards, Merriam engaged in the real estate business in Long Beach, and served as honorary president of the California Real Estate Association. He died in Long Beach on April 25, 1955 at the age of eighty-nine. Bibliography: American Guide Series, *California: A Guide to the Golden State* (New York, 1939); American Guide Series, *Los Angeles: A Guide to the City and Its Environs* (New York, 1941); Walton E. Bean, *California: An Interpretive History* (New York, 1973); Roy Glashan, *American Governors and Gubernatorial Elections, 1775-1975* (Stillwater, Minnesota, 1975).

OLSON, Culbert L. 1939-1943

Born on November 7, 1876, in Fillmore, Utah Territory, the son of Daniel and Delilah (King) Olson. Married to Kate Jeremy on October 21, 1905; father of Richard Culbert, John Weber and Dean Jeremy. Attended Brigham Young University, Provo, Utah, 1890-1891 and 1893-1895; attended Columbian University

Law School, Washington, D.C., 1897-1899 and 1900-1901; attended the University of Michigan, Ann Arbor, Michigan, 1899-1900; received an LL. B. degree from Columbian University in 1901. Admitted to the Utah Bar in 1901. Employed as a telegraph operator, 1891; reporter and city editor of the *Ogden Standard*, an Ogden, Utah newspaper, from 1895 until 1897; Washington, D.C. correspondent for western newspapers, 1897-1899; private law practice in Salt Lake City, Utah, 1901-1920; moved to California and continued his law practice in 1920. Delegate, Democratic National Convention, 1920 and 1940. Member, Utah Senate, 1916-1920; member, California Senate, 1934-1938; Assistant United States Attorney General, 1936-1937; *ex-officio* President, Board of Regents, University of California. As a Democrat, Olson was elected Governor of California on November 8, 1938, receiving 1,391,734 votes to incumbent Republican Governor Frank F. Merriam's 1,171,019. He was sworn into office on January 2, 1939. During his administration, California's Constitution was amended to allow the use of interim committees by the State Legislature. Also while Olson was governor, the United States Fleet was moved from California ports to Pearl Harbor, Hawaii as relations between America and Japan deteriorated. When war broke out between the United States and Japan in December 1941, the federal government poured billions of dollars into California for defense projects, and the state underwent a tremendous industrial boom. During Olson's term, President Franklin D. Roosevelt ordered the internment of approximately 110,000 Japanese-Americans in California, Oregon, Washington, and Arizona. In addition, in February 1942, a Japanese submarine shelled an oil refinery near Santa Barbara, California. On November 3, 1942, Olson was defeated in his bid for reelection, polling only 932,995 votes to Republican Earl Warren's 1,275,237. As a result, he left office on January 4, 1943. Afterwards, Olson served as a delegate to the Democratic National Convention in 1944 and 1948. He maintained his California residence in Los Angeles. Olson died on April 13, 1962, and was buried at Forest Lawn Memorial Park, Glendale, California. Bibliography: Andrew F. Rolle, *California: A History* (New York, 1963); Walton E. Bean, *California: An Interpretive History* (New York, 1973); Congressional Quarterly, Inc., *Guide to U.S. Elections* (Washington, D.C., 1975); Roy Glashan, *American Governors and Gubernatorial Elections, 1775-1975* (Stillwater, Minnesota, 1975).

WARREN, Earl, 1943-1953

Born on March 19, 1891, in Los Angeles, California, son of Methias H., a master car builder for the Southern Pacific Railroad, and Crystal (Hernlund) Warren; a Baptist. Brother of Ethel. Married to Nina P. Meyers on October 14, 1925; father of James C., Virginia, Earl, Dorothy, Nina Elizabeth and Robert. Attended Kern County High School, Bakersfield, California; received a B.L. degree from the University of California at Berkeley, California in 1912; received a J.D. degree from the University of California at Berkeley in 1914; numerous honorary degrees. Admitted to the California Bar in 1914. Enlisted in the United States Army as a private in 1917; commissioned a Second Lieutenant in 1918; rose to the rank of First Lieutenant; discharged in 1918; served as a Captain in the Officers' Reserve Corps until 1935. Worked as a cub reporter for the Bakersfield *Californian*; private law practice in San Francisco and Oakland, California, 1914-1917. Clerk, Judiciary

Committee of the California Assembly, 1919; Deputy City Attorney, Oakland, 1919-1920; Deputy District Attorney, Alameda County, California, 1920-1923; Chief Deputy District Attorney, Alameda County, 1923-1925; District Attorney, Alameda County, 1925-1929; Attorney General of California, 1939-1943. Alternate Delegate, Republican National Convention, 1944. President, National Association of Attorney Generals, 1940-1941; American Academy of Arts and Sciences; trustee, National Geographic Society; American Philosophical Society; Selden Society; Mason; Elk; Moose; Odd Fellow. As a Republican, Warren was elected Governor of California on November 3, 1942, receiving 1,275,237 votes to incumbent Democratic Governor Culbert L. Olson's 932,995. He was sworn into office on January 4, 1943. During his administration, the state sales tax was reduced; old age pension payments were raised; unemployment insurance widened; and appropriations for child-care centers were made. In 1948, Warren was the Republican nominee for Vice President of the United States, and in 1952 he was a candidate for the Republican presidential nomination. Warren was reelected to a second term on November 5, 1946. As both the Republican and Democratic gubernatorial nominee, he polled 2,344,542 votes to the Prohibition candidate Henry R. Schmidt's 180,579. On November 7, 1950, Warren won a third term, defeating Democrat James Roosevelt, 2,461,754 votes to 1,333,856. In September 1953, President Dwight D. Eisenhower designated Warren to be Chief Justice of the United States Supreme Court. As a result, he resigned as governor of California on October 5, 1953. Warren served as Chief Justice of the United States until 1969. He also was Chancellor of the Board of Regents of the Smithsonian Institution from 1953 until 1969, and chairman of the board of the National Gallery of Art from 1953 until 1969. From 1963 until 1964, he was chairman of the Commission Investigating the Assassination of President John F. Kennedy. After he retired, Warren maintained his residence in Washington, D.C. He died in Washington, D.C., on July 9, 1974. Bibliography: Andrew F. Rolle, *California: A History* (New York, 1963); Walton E. Bean, *California: An Interpretive History* (New York, 1973); Congressional Quarterly, Inc., *Guide to U.S. Elections* (Washington, D.C., 1975); Roy Glashan, *American Governors and Gubernatorial Elections, 1775-1975* (Stillwater, Minnesota, 1975).

KNIGHT, Goodwin Jess, 1953-1959

Born on December 9, 1896, in Provo, Utah, son of Jesse J., a lawyer and mining engineer, and Lillie Jane (Milner) Knight; an Episcopalian. Married to Arvilla Pearl Cooley on September 9, 1925, who died in October 1952; remarried to Virginia Carlson on August 2, 1954; father of Marilyn and Carolyn. Moved with his family to Los Angeles, California, when he was eight years old. Attended Manual Arts High School, Los Angeles; entered Stanford University, Stanford, California, but withdrew to serve in World War I; returned to Stanford University, and received a B.A. degree in 1919; received the Telluride Scholarship; attended Cornell University, Ithaca, New York, 1919-1920. Admitted to the California Bar, 1921. Served in the United States Navy as an apprentice seaman, 1918-1919. Worked in the lead and zinc mines in Nevada; reporter on the Los Angeles *News*; private law practice in Los Angeles, 1921-1925; law partnership with Thomas Reynolds, 1925-1935; president and general manager, Elephant Mining Company, Mojave, California;

member, Knight, Gitelson, Ashton and Hagenbaugh Legal Firm. Judge of the Superior Court of Los Angeles County, California 1935-1946; Lieutenant Governor of California, 1947-1953. Chairman, Interstate Cooperation Commission; member, Toll Bridge Authority; member, Lands Commission; member, Council of State Governments; member, Disaster Council. American Legion; Veterans of Foreign Wars; Mason; Knight of Pythias; Elk; Shriner; Odd Fellow. Author: *Good's Budget of Boys' Stories* (1910). A Republican. On October 5, 1953, Governor of California Earl Warren resigned, and as Lieutenant Governor, Knight succeeded to the office. On November 2, 1954, Knight was elected Governor of California in his own right, defeating Democrat Richard Perrin Graves, 2,290,519 votes to 1,739,368. During his administration, the maximum unemployment insurance payment was raised; use of the Bible in public schools was limited; and a proposed right to work law was rejected. At first Knight announced his intention to seek reelection as governor; however, he changed his mind and entered the 1958 race for a United States Senate seat. He was unsuccessful, and left the governor's office on January 5, 1959. Afterwards, Knight attempted to gain the 1962 Republican gubernatorial nomination in California, but was defeated by Richard M. Nixon. Knight died on May 22, 1970. His California residence was in Los Angeles. Bibliography: Fred McGhee, ed., *Facts on File Five-Year Index, 1951-1955* (New York, 1957); Lester A. Sobel, ed., *Facts on File Five-Year Index, 1956-1960* (New York, 1961); Walton E. Bean, *California: An Interpretive History* (New York, 1973); Roy Glashan, *American Governors and Gubernatorial Elections, 1775-1975* (Stillwater, Minnesota, 1975).

BROWN, Edmund Gerald, 1959-1967

Born in San Francisco, California on April 21, 1905, son of Edmund J., who operated several small businesses, and Ida Shuckman Brown; a Catholic. Earned his nickname, "Patrick Henry," following a World War I Liberty Bonds speech. Married to Bernice Layne on October 30, 1930; father of three daughters, Barbara, Cynthia and Kathleen, and a son, Edmund G. Brown, Jr., who also became governor of California. After graduation from Lowell High School, he worked in his father's store and attended the San Francisco College of Law. He earned his LL.B. degree in 1927 and was admitted to the bar. In 1928, he unsuccessfully sought a seat in the California Assembly as a Republican. He changed his party affiliation to Democrat in 1934. Practiced law from 1927 to 1943. In 1943, he was elected San Francisco District Attorney. He ran for State Attorney General in 1946, but lost. In 1950, he became the only Democrat to gain statewide elective office as he won his bid to be Attorney General. In 1954, cross-filing on the Republican ticket, he won election in the primaries. In 1958, he became the second Democrat in the twentieth century to be elected Governor of California, as he defeated William Knowland, 3,140,176 to 2,110,011 votes. Four years later, Brown defeated Richard Nixon, 3,037,000 to 2,740,000 votes. The Brown administration undertook a major overhaul of the executive branch, the first in thirty years. The administration led in a reapportionment fight, and developed master plans for higher education and water distribution. Also, an anti-narcotic campaign was levied, and expanding social services were provided for California's exploding population. In 1968, Pat Brown sought a third term but was defeated by Ronald Reagan, 3,742,913 votes to

2,749,174. At the close of his term, Brown moved to Beverly Hills and joined a law firm. He has remained in Democratic politics and continues to serve on area and state committees and commissions. Bibliography: Edmund G. Brown, *Reagan and Reality: The Two Californias* (New York, 1970); Edmund G. Brown, "Thoughts," *City Light* (San Francisco, 1976); Gene Marine, "This 'Pat' Brown." *Frontier,* vol. IX (1959); H. Brett Melendy and Benjamin F. Gilbert, *Governors of California* (Georgetown, Calif., 1965).

REAGAN, Ronald Wilson, 1967-1975

Born in Tampico, Illinois on February 6, 1911, the younger of two sons of John Edward, a shoe salesman, and Nelle Wilson Reagan; a Protestant. Brother of J. Neil Reagan. Married to Jane Wyman on January 24, 1940; father of a daughter, Maureen, and an adopted son, Michael; remarried to actress Nancy Davis, March 4, 1952; father of Patricia and Ronald. Grew up in Dixon, Illinois; graduated from high school in 1928 and enrolled at Eureka (Illinois) College, receiving his B.A. degree in 1932. Reagan then became a sportscaster, first for WOC, Davenport, Iowa, and then for WHO of Des Moines. In 1937, Warner Brothers gave him an acting contract. He was activated from the United States Army Reserve to duty as a Second Lieutenant in 1942; discharged in December 1945 with the rank of Captain. Reagan resumed his movie career and became the president of the Screen Actors Guild from 1947 to 1952. A liberal in politics at the time, he gradually shifted to the far right wing. He remained a Democrat until 1962, when he joined the Republican Party. From 1954 to 1962, Reagan supervised, hosted and sometimes acted in T.V.'s "General Electric Theatre." He also lectured to General Electric employees about the advantages of the free enterprise system. From 1962 to 1965, he hosted T.V.'s "Death Valley Days." Having a reputation as a right-wing crusader, he sought elective office for the first time in 1966. He defeated Pat Brown for California's governorship, 3,742,913 to 2,749,174 votes. In 1970, he gained a second term by defeating Democrat Jesse Unruh, 3,391,285 to 2,887,273 votes. Reagan had promised sweeping revisions in California's government. His record as governor for eight years was uneven. While he did effect some economies, the state budget doubled in size. In one of his major target areas, social welfare, legislation tightened up qualification requirements. During his years in office, California experienced serious race riots and major campus disruptions. Although little in the way of change occurred as a consequence of the unrest, a calm was gradually restored throughout the state. Reagan did not seek a third term. Once out of office, he became a spokesman for American conservatives, preparing daily radio broadcasts and writing a syndicated news column. In November 1975, he announced that he was a candidate for the Republican presidential nomination. He lost by a narrow margin to Gerald R. Ford. Bibliography: Edmund G. Brown, *Reagan the Political Chameleon* (New York, 1976); Lee Edwards, *Reagan, a Political Biography* (San Diego, 1967); Ronald Reagan, *Creative Society* (New York, 1968); Ronald Reagan, *Where's the Rest of Me?* (New York, 1965). The Reagan Papers are on deposit in the Hoover Library, Stanford University.

BROWN, Edmund Gerald, Jr. 1975-

Born in San Francisco, California, on April 7, 1928. Known by the nickname "Jerry," he is the son of former California Governor Edmund "Pat" Brown, Sr. and Bernice (Layne) Brown; a Catholic. Brother of Barbara, Cynthia and Kathleen. Unmarried. Graduated from Saint Ignatius College Preparatory School of San Francisco in 1955. Attended the University of Santa Clara for one year and then entered the Jesuits' Sacred Heart Novitiate in Los Gatos, California in August 1956. He left in January 1960 and entered the University of California at Berkeley, graduating in 1961. He then enrolled in the Yale Law School. For a time he did legal work for the civil rights movement in Mississippi. He received his J.D. degree from Yale in 1964. He worked briefly as a law clerk for California Supreme Court Justice Matthew O. Tobriner, and studied Spanish. He then traveled in Latin America, before joining a prominent Los Angeles legal firm. Brown ran for his first elective office in 1969 and gained a seat on the Board of Trustees for the Los Angeles community colleges. Elected California's Secretary of State in 1970, he changed that office's administration from one of passivity to activism. On June 7, 1974, Brown received thirty-eight percent of the Democratic vote, defeating five other major contenders for his party's gubernatorial nomination. In the November general election, Brown defeated Republican Houston I. Flournoy, 3,088,870 votes to 2,912,065. On January 6, 1975, he succeeded Ronald Reagan, who had defeated his father eight years earlier. Jerry Brown introduced a new personal style to American politics which made him popular to some voters and very suspect to others. He gave up the trappings of office to live a simple existence. Controversial farm legislation was enacted and the oil depletion allowance was eliminated. Less successful was his attempt to solve the problems of malpractice insurance. In March 1976, he announced that he would be a favorite son candidate for the Democratic presidential nomination, and went to the Chicago convention with some delegates besides Californians pledged to him. Unsuccessful in this effort, he returned to his duties as California's governor. Bibliography: *Nation* (March 27, 1971); *New York Times* (April 15, 1975, May 14, 1975); *Newsweek* (April 19, 1976, July 16, 1976); *Time* (April 26, 1976).

COLORADO

COLORADO

ROUTT, John L., 1876-1879, 1891-1893

Born on April 25, 1826 in Eddyville, Caldwell County, Kentucky, son of John, a farmer of moderate means and Martha (Haggard) Routt; a Methodist. Married to Esther A. Woodson in 1845, who died in 1872; father of Minnie, Birdie, Emma, Frank and John; remarried to Eliza Pickrell in 1875; father of Leila. Family moved to Bloomington, Illinois. Educated in the public schools, and then apprenticed to a builder and machinist to learn those trades. Began dealing in public land and town property in 1851. In 1860, Routt was elected Sheriff of McLean County, Illinois, and in 1862, he resigned to accept a captaincy in the 94th Illinois Infantry. Routt's regiment joined Grant at Vicksburg, and he distinguished himself in the personal service of General Grant. Returned to Bloomington after the war and was elected Treasurer of McLean County, serving two terms and declining nomination for a third term. In 1869, Routt was appointed United States Marshal for the Southern District of Illinois by President Grant, and in 1871, he was appointed 2nd Assistant Postmaster General, a position he held until 1875, when Grant made him Governor of the Territory of Colorado. Routt prepared the territory for admission into the Union. Without solicitation, he was nominated by the first Republican State Convention as its candidate for Governor to run against the Democrat Hughes. He won by a vote of 14,154 to 13,316. As governor, Routt established the credit of Colorado and won for the state some of the best land under grants from Congress. In 1879, he declined renomination and engaged in mining endeavors. In 1883, he was elected Mayor of Denver. In 1890, in spite of his desire not to be a candidate for Governor, Routt was nominated by the Republican Party to run against Democrat Caldwell Yeaman and Farmers' Alliance candidate, Joley G. Coy. Routt won by a vote of 41,827 to 35,359 and 5,199, respectively. During his second term Routt had to deal with the consequences resulting from the passage of the Sherman Law. Routt died in Denver on August 13, 1907. Bibliography: Albert B. Sanford, "J. L. Routt, First State Governor of Colorado," *Colorado Magazine*, vol. 3 (August, 1924). The Routt Papers are on deposit in the Division of State Archives and Public Records in Denver.

PITKIN, Frederick Walker, 1879-1883

Born on August 31, 1837 in Manchester, Connecticut, son of Eli, a prominent citizen of the town and Hannah (Torrey) Pitkin; a Methodist. Married to Fidelia M. James in 1862; father of Florence, Robert, Frederick and Samuel. Attended Wesleyan University and graduated with honors in 1858. Entered Albany Law

School and in 1859 was admitted to the bar. Moved to Milwaukee, Wisconsin and became a member of the law firm of Palmer, Hocker and Pitkin. Because of poor health, he left the firm in 1872. In an attempt to recover, he vacationed in Europe, returned to the United States, and was advised to move to Colorado to benefit from the high, dry climate of southwestern Colorado. Practiced law, and engaged in mining until 1878, when he was nominated by the Republican Party as its candidate for Governor to run against Democrat W. A. H. Loveland and Green-backer, R. G. Buckingham. He won by a vote of 14,308 to 11,535 and 2,783, respectively. As governor, he put down the uprising of the Ute Indians at White River without bloodshed. Also, he handled the strike by silver miners at Leadville in 1880 by declaring martial law, and ended the railway war between the Atchison, Topeka & Santa Fe and the Denver & Rio Grande companies. His administration was so efficient that he was renominated by the Republican Party in 1881 to run against Democrat John S. Hough. He won by a vote of 28,465 to 23,547. Pitkin's second term was peaceful. He was noted for his interest in public finance, and his close scrutinization of all legislative appropriation bills. In 1882, he was a candidate for the United States Senate. After failing to secure his party's nomination, he returned to his law practice in Pueblo, Colorado and resumed his mining interests. Pitkin died on December 18, 1886 in Pueblo, Colorado. Bibliography: The Pitkin Papers are on deposit in the Division of State Archives and Public Records in Denver.

GRANT, James Benton, 1883-1885

Born on January 2, 1848 in Russell County, Alabama, son of Thomas McDonough, a prominent physician, large planter and slave owner, and Mary (Benton) Grant; a Baptist. Married Mary Goodell on January 18, 1881; father of Lester and James. The Civil War interrupted his early education, when he was forced to help support his family by working on their plantation. During the last year of the war, he fought for the Confederate Army. After the war, he remained at home for several years, helping to rebuild the plantation. Moved to Iowa in 1871 and attended agricultural college, later going to Cornell to study civil engineering. Went to Freiburg, Germany for two years to study mining at the School of Mines. Returned to the United States in 1876 and went to Colorado. In 1878, with the assistance of his uncle, James Grant, he established a smelting works under the firm name of J. B. Grant & Co. In 1882, this company was consolidated with the Omaha Co. under the name of Omaha & Grant Smelting Co., of which he was made vice president. He was also vice president of the Denver National Bank. In 1882, Grant was nominated by the Democratic Party as its candidate for Governor to run against Republican E. L. Campbell. He won by a vote of 31,375 to 28,820. Governor Grant's influence was felt in commerce and public finance; his administration was characterized by peace and prosperity. He had no desire to run for a second term. After leaving office, Grant pursued his interests in smelting and in education, while remaining vice president of the Denver National Bank. From 1892 to 1897, he was president of the Denver Board of Education, and from 1884 to 1904, he was a trustee of the University of Denver. He organized the Colorado Scientific Society. In 1902, heart trouble curtailed his activities. Grant died on November 1, 1911 in Excelsior Springs, Missouri. Bibliography: Edgar C. McMechen, "Governor Grant,

Leader in Colorado Smelting," *Mines Magazine*, vol. XXVIII (1938). The Grant Papers are on deposit in the Division of State Archives and Public Records in Denver.

EATON, Benjamin Harrison, 1885-1887

Born on December 15, 1833 in Coshocton County, Ohio, son of Levi, a farmer, and Hannah (Smith) Eaton, both of whom were Quakers. Married to Delilah Wolfe in 1856, who died in 1857; father of Aaron; remarried to Rebecca J. Hill in 1864; father of A. Lincoln, Bruce G. and Jennie B. Attended West Bethford Academy, and three years later graduated and began teaching. Moved to Louisa County, Iowa and engaged in farming and teaching. In 1859, Eaton moved to Colorado, settling near Greeley in 1864 and becoming one of the largest farmers in the territory. In 1866, he was elected Justice of the Peace, holding office for nine years; was County Commissioner for six years, during four of which he was chairman of the board; was elected to the Territorial Legislature in 1872 and secured passage of the law forbidding the wasting of water from public streams. Was elected to the Territorial Senate in 1875 and served one term. In 1884, Eaton was nominated by the Republican Party as its candidate for Governor to run against Democrat Alva Adams. Eaton won by a vote of 33,845 to 30,743. As governor, Eaton was confronted with a public land controversy between stock raisers and home-steaders, which was resolved by an executive order from President Cleveland. After leaving office, Eaton pursued his interests in farming. Eaton died on October 29, 1904 in Eaton, Colorado. Bibliography: Helen Cannon, "First Ladies of Colorado: Rebecca Hill Eaton," *Colorado Magazine*, vol. 42 (1965). The Eaton Papers are on deposit in the Division of State Archives and Public Records in Denver.

ADAMS, Alva, 1887-1889, 1897-1899, 1905

Born in Iowa County, Wisconsin on May 14, 1850, son of John, a farmer, and Eliza (Blanchard) Adams. Married to Ella Nye in 1872; father of Alva Adams, Jr. Educated in the common schools; moved to Colorado with his family in 1871; established a hardware business in Pueblo, Colorado. Member of the first City Council of South Pueblo in 1873; elected to the first Legislature of the state in 1876; unsuccessful Colorado gubernatorial candidate in 1884. On November 4, 1886, Alva Adams was elected Governor of Colorado, defeating William H. Meyer, a Republican, by a vote of 28,129 to 26,533. A Democrat. Governor Adams was inaugurated on January 11, 1887. During his first term, he endeavored to develop the young state's institutions of learning and correction. He left office on January 10, 1889 and returned to his business interests until 1896, when he again accepted his party's nomination for Governor. On November 3, 1896, he gained 87,387 votes to Republican George H. Allen's 23,945 votes and Populist M. S. Bailey's 71,816 votes. During his second term, he helped to bring about the settlement of an extended and disastrous strike in the Leadville mines. Before his term ended, he made a plea for radical reformation of the assessment and taxation system which was under the control of a strong and influential State Equalization Board. Adams left office at the end of his second term on January 10, 1899. On November 8, 1904, he was elected to his third term as governor, defeating Republican James H. Peabody, 124,617 votes to 113,499. However, he only served in this administration from January 10, 1905 to March 18, 1905, due to an election dispute. The controversy was decided by the overwhelmingly Republican Legislature, which effected a compromise resulting in the elevation of the Republican Lieutenant Governor, Jesse J. McDonald, to the governor's office. Adams ran again for governor in 1906, but was unsuccessful. He returned to his business interests, and concurrently served as a member of the Democratic National Committee in 1908, and commissioner for the United States to procure the participation of Australia, New Zealand, Java, Siam, Cochin China, and China in the Panama-Pacific Exposition of 1915. Adams died on November 1, 1922. Bibliography: Roy Glashan, *American Governors and Gubernatorial Elections, 1775-1975* (Stillwater, Minnesota, 1975); Congressional Quarterly, Inc., *Guide to U.S. Elections* (Washington, D.C., 1975); *New York Times* (November 2, 1922); James H. Baker and LeRoy R. Hafen, eds., *History of Colorado*, 3 vols. (Denver, 1927).

COOPER, Job Adams, 1889-1891

Born on November 6, 1843 in Greenville, Bond County, Illinois, son of Charles, a mechanic and farmer, and Maria (Hadley) Cooper; a Baptist. Married Jane O. Barnes on September. 17, 1867; father of Olivia, Mary Louise, Genevieve and Charles. Attended Knox College in Greenville, until he enlisted in Company "C" of the 137th Illinois Infantry, in which he achieved the rank of Second Sergeant. After a short stay in the army, Cooper returned to Knox College and was graduated in 1865 with a B.A. degree; three years later he received an M.A. degree from Knox College. Entered the law offices of Judge S. P. Moore, and read law until he was admitted to the bar in 1867. In 1868, Cooper was elected Clerk and Recorder of Bond County and served in that position until he resigned in 1872 to move to Denver. Formed a law partnership under the firm name of Phelps and Cooper. In 1876, he accepted the vice presidency of the German National Bank. Cooper was one of the biggest cattle dealers in the state. In 1888, he was nominated by the Republican Party as its candidate for Governor to run against Democrat Thomas Patterson. Cooper won by a vote of 49,490 to 39,197. As governor, Cooper's influence was felt in mining, stock raising and commerce. Although he was considered honest, efficient and progressive, during his administration the General Assembly was noted for its extravagant spending and corruption. Retiring from the office of chief executive, Cooper began construction of the Cooper Building, one of the finest buildings in Denver, and in 1893 he was elected President of the Chamber of Commerce, a position which he filled until his retirement in 1897. He had extensive property holdings in mining in the Cripple Creek District. Cooper died on January 20, 1899 in Denver. Bibliography: Helen Cannon, "First Ladies of Colorado: Jane Olivia Barnes Cooper," *Colorado Magazine*, vol. 44 (1967). The Cooper Papers are on deposit in the Division of State Archives and Public Records in Denver.

ROUTT, John L., 1876-1879, 1891-1893

WAITE, Davis Hanson, 1893-1895

Born on April 9, 1825 in Jamestown, New York, son of Joseph, a lawyer, and Olive (Davis) Waite. Brother of F. H. Waite. Married to Frances E. Russell on September 15, 1851; after her death, remarried to Celia O. Crane on January 5, 1885; father of Arthur B., Jessie Francelia, Olive I., Earnest Kimball and May Josephine. Attended common schools and graduated from Jamestown Academy; studied law under his father. Moved to Wisconsin and worked with his brother in the dry goods business; elected to the Wisconsin State Legislature in 1856, as a Republican; moved to St. Louis, Missouri in 1857, and soon after to Houston, Texas County, Missouri, where he taught high school. After the outbreak of the Civil War, he moved to Warren, Pennsylvania and later to Jamestown, New York, where he was admitted to the bar and became editor of a paper. In 1876 he moved to Larned, Kansas, where he practiced law and engaged in ranching. In 1879 he was elected to the Kansas State Legislature. He moved to Leadville, Colorado in 1879, where he practiced law; in 1881 he settled in Aspen, Colorado. Here he practiced law and edited the *Union Era*, a reform paper, until 1891. In 1892 he was a delegate to the St. Louis Conference which organized the People's Party. On July 27, 1892, Waite was nominated for Governor of Colorado on the People's ticket, and on November 8, 1892 in the general election, he gained 41,344 votes to Republican J. Helmes' 38,812 votes, and Democrat J. Maupin's 8,938 votes. Governor Waite was inaugurated on January 11, 1893. The Panic of 1893 brought great distress to Colorado during his term. The repeal of the Sherman Act was a blow to silver mining and added to the state's already acute unemployment problems. On November 2, 1893, Colorado became the second state to extend suffrage to women. In 1894 the State Capitol building was completed. Governor Waite was renominated in 1894, but was defeated by Albert W. McIntire, a Republican. Governor Waite continued to reside in Denver, where he lectured and published a Populist newspaper. On November 27, 1901, Governor Waite died in Denver, Colorado. Bibliography: Roy Glashan, *American Governors and Gubernatorial Elections, 1775-1975* (Stillwater, Minnesota, 1975); LeRoy Hafen, *Colorado: The Story of a Western Commonwealth* (Denver, 1933); Percy Stanley Fritz, *Colorado: The Centennial State* (New York, 1941); Leon W. Fuller, "A Populist Newspaper of the Nineties," *Colorado Magazine*, vol. IX (May, 1932).

McINTIRE, Albert Wills, 1895-1897

Born in Pittsburgh, Pennsylvania, on January 15, 1853, son of Joseph Phillips, a businessman, and Isabella A. (Wills) McIntire. Married to Florence Johnson on July 16, 1873; remarried to Ida Noyes on January 2, 1899; father of Joseph Phillips, Elizabeth Lord and Dorothy Lord. Attended Newell's Institute in Pittsburgh; graduated from Yale University in 1873; LL.D. in 1875; admitted to the Pennsylvania Bar in 1875; practiced law in Pittsburgh, 1875-1876. Moved to Colorado in 1876, where he continued his law practice. Began ranching in the San Louis Valley, 1880. McIntire was elected County Judge in 1883 of Conejos County, Colorado and served until 1886. He then returned to his law practice, until being selected Judge of the Twelfth Judicial District by Governor John Routt, 1891-1894. A Republican. McIntire was named by acclamation as the Republican candidate for Governor of Colorado in September 1894. In the general election held on November 6, 1894, he received 93,502 votes to 74,894 for Governor David Waite, a Populist, and 8,337 for Charles Thomas, a Democrat. During his administration, leasing of state land was limited to ten years; the State Bureau of Mines was created; the age of consent for girls was raised from sixteen to eighteen; and a state commission was appointed to promote uniformity of legislation among the states of the Union. When in June 1896, the Western Federation of Miners went on strike against the silver mines of Leadville, Governor McIntire sent in the militia to stop the strike. During his term, an international dispute arose over the lynching of three Italian nationals. Governor McIntire's term ended on January 12, 1897. McIntire returned to his ranching and law practice upon the completion of his term. He died on January 30, 1935 in Colorado Springs, Colorado. Bibliography: Bernice FitzSimmons Hathaway, ed., *The Colorado Genealogist* vol. XVIII, no. 4 (April, 1957); Carl Ubbelohde, *A Colorado History* (Boulder, 1965); Roy Glashan, *American Governors and Gubernatorial Elections, 1775-1975* (Stillwater, Minnesota, 1975); Frank Hall, *History of the State of Colorado*, 4 vols. (Chicago, 1895).

ADAMS, Alva, 1887-1889, 1897-1899, 1905

THOMAS, Charles Spalding, 1899-1901

Born on December 6, 1849 in Darien, Georgia, son of William Bradley, a planter, and Caroline (Wheeler) Thomas. Brother of Mary C., Moore B. and William B. Married to Emma Fletcher on December 29, 1873; father of Helen T., Edith Marie, Charles Sewell, Hubert Fletcher and George Kenneth. Graduated with an LL.B. degree from the University of Michigan, 1871; LL.D. degree, University of Michigan, 1916. Admitted to the Colorado Bar in 1871, and began a law practice in Denver, Colorado the same year; Denver City Attorney, 1875-1876. Thomas moved to Leadville, Colorado, where he continued his law practice, 1879-1885; returned to Denver in 1885; Democratic National Convention delegate, 1880, 1896, 1900, 1904, and 1908. Thomas was unsuccessful in a bid for United States Senator from Colorado in 1888, and for governor of Colorado in 1894. As the candidate of the Democrat and Populist Fusion Party, Charles S. Thomas was elected Governor of Colorado on November 8, 1898. He received 92,274 votes to 50,880 for Henry R. Wolcott, a Republican, and was inaugurated on January 10, 1899. During his administration, Teller County was established; party emblems were removed from election tickets; an eight-hour day was established in the smelter and refining ore industries; and an appropriation was made to finish the Colorado State Capitol. Governor Thomas' major problem during his term of office was the lack of state funds for education and correctional institutions. He left office on January 8, 1901. Thomas then returned to his law practice until being selected to complete the term of United States Senator Charles Hughes in 1913. He was reelected to the Senate in 1914 and served until 1921. Served as special assistant to the United States Attorney General in 1922; returned to Denver in 1925 and resumed his law practice. Governor Thomas died on June 24, 1934 and was interred in Fairmount Cemetery, Denver. Bibliography: Roy Glashan, *American Governors and Gubernatorial Elections, 1775-1975* (Stillwater, Minnesota, 1975); James H. Baker and LeRoy Hafen, *History of Colorado*, 3 vols. (Denver, 1927); Bernice FitzSimmons Hathaway, *The Colorado Genealogist*, vol. XXI, no. 2, (April, 1960); Percy Stanley Fritz, *Colorado: The Centennial State* (New York, 1941).

ORMAN, James Bradley, 1901-1903

Born on November 4, 1849 in Muscatine, Iowa, son of John, a farmer, and Sarah (Bradley) Orman. Brother of William, Sarah, Mary and Caroline. Married to Nellie Martin on September 27, 1876; father of Edna and Frederick B. Orman. Received a common school education in Chicago, Illinois; moved to Denver, Colorado in 1866 and engaged in the buying and selling of mules and horses to the freighting business. Orman and his brother, William, formed a partnership as contractors in the railroad construction business in 1869. The partnership eventually grew into one of the largest railroad construction companies in the West, building sections for the Kansas Pacific Railroad, the Denver & Rio Grande, and the Canadian Pacific. Orman also organized and served as president of the Pueblo Horse Railroad beginning in 1879. His business interests later expanded into mining, cattle and brick manufacturing; he served as vice president of the Bessemer Ditch Company; City Councilman of Pueblo, Colorado; Representative to the Third General Assembly, 1880; and State Senator, 1883-1885. He was chosen United States Senator by the State Legislature in 1883. A Democrat. Orman was chosen as the Populist-Democratic candidate for Governor of Colorado in 1900. On November 6, 1900, he defeated Frank C. Goudy, a Republican, 121,995 votes to 93,245. He was inaugurated on January 8, 1901. During his administration, the Australasian land-tax system was adopted; South Arapahoe and Adams Counties were established; a Food and Dairy Commission was created; and a normal school in Gunnison, Colorado was founded. He left office at the end of his term on January 13, 1903. Orman later returned to his business interests and also served as Receiver of the United States Land Office, Pueblo, Colorado. Orman died on July 21, 1919 and was buried in Pueblo, Colorado. Bibliography: Roy Glashan, *American Governors and Gubernatorial Elections, 1775-1975* (Stillwater, Minnesota, 1975); Bernice FitzSimmons Hathaway, *The Colorado Genealogist*, vol. XVIII, no. 4 (October, 1957); LeRoy Hafen, *Colorado: The Story of a Western Commonwealth* (Denver, 1933); Carl Ubbelohde, *A Colorado History* (Boulder, 1965).

PEABODY, James Hamilton, 1903-1905

Born on August 21, 1852 in Topsham, Vermont, son of Calvin, a farmer, and Susan Lucinda (Turner) Peabody; an Episcopalian. Brother of Jesse W., Luther, Calvin, Hannah and one other. Married to Frances L. Clelland on March 19, 1878; father of Calvin, James Clelland, Cora May and Jessie Anne. Educated in the public schools in Topsham, Vermont; moved to Colorado with his family in 1871, where he was employed in a dry goods business. Moved to Denver, Colorado in 1875, and worked as manager of James Clelland's dry goods store. Peabody accepted a partnership with Clelland, and in 1885 purchased the business. Elected County Clerk, Fremont County, Colorado, 1885-1889; served as vice president and later president of the First National Bank of Canon City, Colorado; elected City Treasurer and City Clerk; served on the City Council of Canon City; was Mayor of Canon City for two terms. A Republican. In 1902, Peabody was chosen as the Republican candidate for Governor of Colorado. In the general election, he received 87,684 votes to 80,727 for Edward C. Stimson, a Democrat, and 7,177 for J. Provost, a Socialist. Peabody was inaugurated on January 13, 1903. During his administration, Colorado was hit by a series of strikes: the Reduction Mill employees strike in February, 1904; the Cripple Creek strike, August, 1903; and the coal strike of November, 1903. Peabody was forced to call out the National Guard to restore order. The strikes resulted in the break up of the Western Federation of Miners in Colorado and the establishment of the eight hour work day. Peabody lost in his bid for reelection to Alva Adams, a Democrat, in 1904. The election was contested and on March 18, 1905, Peabody took office, only to resign on the same day. A compromise had been reached whereby he would resign in favor of the Republican Lieutenant Governor, Jesse F. McDonald. Peabody then returned to Canon City and his business interests. He died on November 23, 1917 and was buried in Canon City, Colorado. Bibliography: Percy Stanley Fritz, *Colorado: The Centennial State* (New York, 1941); James H. Baker and LeRoy Hafen, eds., *History of Colorado*, 3 vols. (Denver, 1927); Roy Glashan, *American Governors and Gubernatorial Elections, 1775-1975* (Stillwater, Minnesota, 1975).

ADAMS, Alva, 1887-1889, 1897-1899, 1905

McDONALD, Jesse Fuller, 1905-1907

Born on June 30, 1858 in Ashtabula, Ohio, son of Lyman Mixer, a farmer, and Carolyne (Bond) McDonald; a Protestant. Married to Flora Collins on April 26, 1900. Moved to Springfield, Pennsylvania at the age of seven, where he completed his public school education. Moved to Leadville, Colorado in 1879 and found employment with George M. Robinson, a civil and mining engineer, 1879-1890. He invested wisely in mining property and soon became a miner-owner; he operated several large mines including the El Dorado, Penrose and the Gold Placer. He served as Mayor of Leadville from 1899 to 1905; elected to the Colorado State Senate in1902; later unseated. Elected Lieutenant Governor of Colorado in 1904. A

Republican. Jesse F. McDonald became Governor of Colorado on March 18, 1905, upon the ouster of Alva Adams, the Democratic Governor, due to election frauds and the subsequent resignation of Republican Governor James H. Peabody. Peabody took office and then resigned in favor of the Lieutenant Governor; thus Colorado had three governors in one day. During McDonald's term in office, the legislature passed a law making it illegal for employees to picket and interfere with workers who were trying to enter the mines. However, problems continued in the mining camps, due in part to the slow recovery of silver prices from the depression in 1890. Also during McDonald's administration, several large sugar beet companies began to expand into the Colorado area, bringing an additional source of income to the state, Governor McDonald's term ended on January 8, 1907. He again ran for Governor in 1908, but lost in the general election to John Shafroth. He then returned to his business and mining interests in Leadville and served as vice president of the American National Bank of Leadville; chairman of the Republican State Central Committee from 1910 to 1914, and again in 1931. Governor McDonald died on February 25, 1942 in Denver, Colorado. Bibliography: Roy Glashan, *American Governors and Gubernatorial Elections, 1775-1975* (Stillwater, Minnesota, 1975); Congressional Quarterly, Inc., *Guide to U.S. Elections* (Washington, D.C., 1975); *New York Times*, (February 26, 1942); Carl Ubbelohde, *et al.*, *A Colorado History, Revised Centennial Edition* (Boulder, Colorado, 1976).

BUCHTEL, Henry Augustus, 1907-1909

Born near Akron, Ohio on September 30, 1847, son of Jonathan B., a physician, and Eliza (Newcomer) Buchtel; a Methodist Episcopalian. Married to Mary Nelson on February 4, 1873; father of Frost Craft, Emma Stevenson, Henry Augustus II and Mary Stevenson. Educated in private schools; received his A.B. degree from Indiana Asbury University (later DePauw) in 1872; honorary degrees of M.A. in 1875, D.D. in 1884, and LL.D. in 1900. Engaged in the wholesale drug business and grocery business until being called to the ministry; served as missionary in Bulgaria and Turkey, 1872-1873. Buchtel returned to the United States in 1873 and served as pastor of churches in Indiana, New Jersey, and Colorado, 1873-1899; he became Chancellor of the University of Denver in 1900 and served in that capacity until retiring in 1921 as Chancellor Emeritus. Buchtel's administrative abilities at the University of Denver led to his nomination on the Republican ticket for Governor of Colorado in 1906. A Republican, Buchtel won the general election held on November 6, 1906, receiving 96,646 votes to 74,512 for Alva Adams, a Democrat, and 17,640 for B. Lindsay, an Independent League candidate. He was inaugurated on January 8, 1907. During his administration, a law was passed for the inspection of savings and loan associations; a pure food act was also passed; the state budget was balanced, with a surplus left to the new administration; prison labor was used on highway construction; a law was passed regulating insurance companies, banks, and railroads; meat and slaughterhouse inspection laws were enacted; and juvenile courts and detention houses were established. Buchtel left office on January 12, 1909. Buchtel had served in the unique capacity of Governor of Colorado and Chancellor of the University of Denver at the same time. After he left office he resumed his duties as chancellor, serving until 1921. Buchtel died on October 22, 1924 in Denver, Colorado. Bibliography: Bernice FitzSimmons Hathaway, ed., *The*

Colorado Genealogist, vol. XIII, no. 4 (October, 1952); Roy Glashan, *American Governors and Gubernatorial Elections, 1775-1975* (Stillwater, Minnesota, 1975); Carl Ubbelohde, *A Colorado History* (Boulder, 1965); LeRoy Hafen, *Colorado: The Story of a Western Commonwealth* (Denver, 1933).

SHAFROTH, John Franklin, 1909-1913

Born on June 9, 1854 in Fayette, Missouri, son of John, a merchant, and Anna (Awl) Shafroth. Brother of Sophia, William, Laura, Louisa and Caroline. Married to Virginia Morrison on October 26, 1881; father of Sudie, John Franklin, Jr., Morrison and two others. Attended the common schools and graduated from the University of Michigan at Ann Arbor in 1875; LL.D. in 1909; studied law; was admitted to the bar in Missouri in 1876 and commenced practice in Fayette, Missouri. Moved to Denver, Colorado in October 1879 and continued law practice. City Attorney, 1887-1891; elected as a Republican to the United States Congress in 1896, 1898, and 1900. His election in 1902 was contested, and when he found evidence of fraud, he immediately resigned on February 15, 1904. He ran again for Congress in 1904, but was defeated. Shafroth, who had changed his allegiance to the Democrats, was chosen as the party's gubernatorial candidate at the Democratic State Convention in 1908. On November 3, 1908, John Franklin Shafroth gained 130,141 votes to Republican Jesse McDonald's 118,953 and Socialist H. Darrah's 7,972. Governor Shafroth was inaugurated on January 12, 1909. He was reelected on November 8, 1910 by gaining 115,627 votes to Republican J. Stephen's 97,648 and Socialist H. Pinkham's 7,844. During Shafroth's administration, there was much progressive legislation. Particularly significant were the constitutional amendments providing for the initiative, the referendum, and the direct primary. Other achievements included statutes providing for the regulation of child and women's labor, and an eight-hour day for hazardous or dangerous occupations; a labor disputes act; the creation of a State Conservation Commission; and a factory inspection law. Shafroth's second term expired on January 14, 1913. He was chosen by the legislature for a seat in the United States Senate in January, 1913. Shafroth served in the United States Senate from March 4, 1913 to March 3, 1919. He was defeated for reelection in 1918. He then served as chairman of the War Minerals Relief Commission from 1919 to 1921. He died in Denver, Colorado, February 20, 1922, and was buried in Fairmount Cemetery. Bibliography: Bernice FitzSimmons Hathaway, ed., *The Colorado Genealogist*, vol. XIX, no. 4 (October, 1958); Carl Ubbelohde, *A Colorado History* (Boulder, 1965); E. K. MacColl, "John Franklin Shafroth, Reform Governor of Colorado, 1909-1913," *Colorado Magazine*, vol. XXIX (January, 1952); Roy Glashan, *American Governors and Gubernatorial Elections, 1775-1975* (Stillwater, Minnesota, 1975).

AMMONS, Elias Milton, 1913-1915

Born on July 28, 1860 near Franklin, North Carolina, son of Jehu Richard, a farmer and miner, and Margaret Caroline (Brendie) Ammons; a Baptist. Brother of Theodosia Grace, Farita H., Anna J., Gwendolyn and one other. Married to Elizabeth Fleming on January 29, 1889; father of Bruce, Elizabeth, Teller and two others. Ammons moved with his family to Colorado in 1871, and worked at various jobs while going to school; graduated from East Denver High School in 1880. Worked in the newspaper business, 1881-1885, until failing eyesight caused him to give up journalism. With Thomas P. Dawson, Ammons formed a partnership in the cattle business. Organized the First National Bank of Littleton, Colorado; vice president of the Board of Agriculture until 1909; clerk of the District Court of Douglas County, Colorado, 1890; elected to Colorado House of Representatives as a Republican, 1890-1896; served as Speaker of the House, 1894-1896; elected to Colorado State Senate as a Democrat, 1898-1902. Ammons was defeated for Lieutenant Governor in 1904 and 1906. A Democrat. Ammons won the Democratic primary in 1912 for Governor of Colorado. In the general election held on November 5, 1912, Ammons received 114,044 votes to 63,061 for Charles Parks, a Republican, and 66,132 for Edward Costigan, a Progressive. He was inaugurated on January 14, 1913. During his administration, agricultural schools were established at Fort Collins and Fort Lewis; a public utilities law was passed; and a new highway system was begun. United States Senators from Colorado were to be elected by the people, and not chosen by the legislature, and the state was reapportioned for congressional districts. Violence in the coal miners' strike in northern Colorado resulted in Ammons calling on the federal government to send troops into the area to assist in quelling the riots. Ammons' entire term was hampered by the coal strike, and it was not until the close of his administration that order was restored. Governor Ammons left office on January 12, 1915 and returned to his business interests. Bibliography: Carl Ubbelohde, *A History of Colorado* (Boulder, 1965); Roy Glashan, *American Governors and Gubernatorial Elections, 1775-1975* (Stillwater, Minnesota, 1975); Bernice FitzSimmons Hathaway, ed., *The Colorado Genealogist,* vol. XIII, no. 3 (July, 1952); LeRoy R. Hafen, *Colorado: The Story of a Western Commonwealth* (Denver, 1933).

CARLSON, George Alfred, 1915-1917

Born on October 23, 1875 near Alta, Iowa, son of Charles August, a miner, and Louisa Piternilla (Gustafson) Carlson; a Presbyterian. Brother of Charles J., and William A. Married to Rose Lillian Alps on August 29, 1906; after her death, remarried to Louise Avery Crose on March 11, 1924; father of Elaine B., George Alfred, John Swink and Junita Rose. Attended Colorado Agricultural College, Colorado Normal School, and graduated from Colorado State University in 1902; LL.B. degree from Colorado State University, 1904; practiced law in Lewiston, Indiana, 1905; returned to Colorado and settled in Fort Collins, Colorado, where he practiced law. Carlson served as Deputy District Attorney and District Attorney, 8th Judicial District of Colorado, 1908-1915. A Republican. Carlson won the Republican nomination for Governor of Colorado in 1914. On November 3,

1914, he won the general election, polling 129,096 votes to defeat T. M. Patterson, a Democrat, who received 95,640 votes, and Edward Costigan, a Progressive, who received 33,320. He was inaugurated on January 12, 1915. During his administration, a prohibition law was enacted; a workmen's compensation law was passed; a mining strike was settled, and law and order reestablished. Also an Industrial Relations Commission was established; a law was passed whereby the legislature could not appropriate more money than the state had capital available; and a commission was established to survey the state government. In the general election on November 7, 1916, Carlson lost his bid for reelection to John Gunter, a Democrat. Carlson left office on January 9, 1917 and resumed his law practice in Denver. He died on December 6, 1926 in Denver, Colorado. Bibliography: Roy Glashan, *American Governors and Gubernatorial Elections, 1775-1975* (Stillwater, Minnesota, 1975); Bernice FitzSimmons Hathaway, ed., *The Colorado Genealogist* vol. XIV, no. 1 (January, 1953); LeRoy Hafen, *Colorado: The Story of a Western Commonwealth* (Denver, 1933); Percy Stanley Fritz, *Colorado: The Centennial State* (New York, 1941).

GUNTER, Julius Caldeen, 1917-1919

Born on October 31, 1858 in Fayetteville, Arkansas, son of Thomas Montague, a lawyer and Congressman, and Marcella (Jackson) Gunter; an Episcopalian. Brother of Walker and Lou. Married to Elizabeth (Bettie) Brown on April 30, 1884; no children. Attended the University of Virginia until poor health forced him to withdraw; moved to Colorado and studied law; admitted to the bar in 1881; received an LL.D. degree from the University of Colorado in 1926. Formed law partnership in Trinidad, Colorado with James M. John; was the first lawyer to be admitted to practice before the 10th Circuit Court on a motion of the court; served as Judge of the Third Judicial District of Colorado, 1889-1895; Judge of the Colorado Court of Appeals, 1901-1905; served as Supreme Court Justice of Colorado, 1905-1907. Returned to private practice in Denver, Colorado in 1907. In 1916 Gunter won Colorado's Democratic gubernatorial nomination. Gunter won the general election for Governor held on November 7, 1916, receiving 151,912 votes to 117,723 for incumbent Governor George A. Carlson, a Republican; Gunter was inaugurated on January 9, 1917. During his administration, the United States entered the war in Europe. Gunter was the first governor to mobilize the National Guard and was instrumental in the first State Council of National Defense. He called the first extra legislative session in the United States to fund the war effort, and levied a tax on corporations for national defense. The war also brought about a mining boom in rare metals. In addition, state institutions were funded for a ten-year period, and an army hospital was built in Denver. Gunter left office on January 14, 1919. He later declined an appointment to the Colorado Supreme Court and continued in his private law practice. Gunter died on October 26, 1940 in Denver, Colorado. Bibliography: Roy Glashan, *American Governors and Gubernatorial Elections, 1775-1975* (Stillwater, Minnesota, 1975); Percy Stanley Fritz, *Colorado: The Centennial State* (New York, 1941); Bernice FitzSimmons Hathaway, *The Colorado Genealogist*, vol. XVI, no. 2 (April, 1955); LeRoy Hafen, *Colorado: The Story of a Western Commonwealth* (Denver, 1933).

SHOUP, Oliver Henry Nelson, 1919-1923

Born on December 13, 1869 near Boggs Corner, Champaign County, Illinois, son of William R., a farmer and school teacher, and Delia J. (Ferris) Shoup; a Presbyterian. Married to Unetta Small on September 18, 1891; father of Reba, Oliver Henry, Jr., Merrill E. and Verner R. Shoup. Moved with his family to Colorado Springs, Colorado in 1882 and finished his education at Colorado College, Colorado Springs, 1886-1888. He began working for the Colorado Springs Company, and in 1895 was employed by Verner Z. Reed as a private secretary and later as a manager and partner in Reed's varied enterprises, 1895-1912; helped to organize the Midwest Oil Company, 1911; president of Midwest Refining Company and Midwest Oil Company, 1911-1914; served as director of several banks in Colorado; chairman of the War Savings Stamps and Liberty Loan campaigns for El Paso County during World War I. A Republican. Shoup was chosen as the Republican candidate for Governor of Colorado in 1918. He won the November 5, 1918 general election by a margin of 112,096 to 102,307 for Thomas Tynan, a Democrat. Shoup was inaugurated on January 14, 1919. He won reelection on November 2, 1920, receiving 174,488 votes to 108,738 for James M. Collins, a Democrat. During his administration, the bonded debt of the state was reduced; the National Guard was called to assist in controlling mining strikes and the Denver trolley car strike; duplication of departments in the state government was eliminated; and a special session of the legislature was called in 1921 to assist the southern counties devastated by floods. Also out of this 1921 special session came the Pueblo Flood Conservancy District and the Moffat Tunnel Improvement District, which would finance a tunnel through the Continental Divide. Governor Shoup refused nomination for a third term and left office on January 9, 1923. Shoup later returned to his business interests; he ran for Governor again in 1926, but lost to William Adams. Shoup died on September 30, 1940 and was buried in Colorado Springs, Colorado. Bibliography: Bernice FitzSimmons Hathaway, ed., *The Colorado Genealogist*, vol. XX, no. 1 (January, 1959); Roy Glashan, *American Governors and Gubernatorial Elections, 1775-1975* (Stillwater, Minnesota, 1975); Carl Ubbelohde, *A Colorado History* (Boulder, 1965); Edgar Carlisle McMechen, *The Moffat Tunnel of Colorado* (Denver, 1927).

SWEET, William Ellery, 1923-1925

Born on January 27, 1869 in Chicago, Illinois, son of Channing, a lawyer, and Emeroy L. (Stevens) Sweet; a Congregationalist. Married to Joyeuse L. Fullerton on October 19, 1892; father of Lennig Sweet, Channing Fullerton, Joyeuse Elise and William Ellery, Jr. Graduated Phi Beta Kappa from Swarthmore College, Pennsylvania, 1890; received an LL.D. from the same institution, 1936. Sweet worked as an apprentice in business until 1894, when he established his own investment banking firm in Denver, Colorado. Sweet, Causey, Foster and Co. grew to be a multi-million dollar business operating throughout the Rocky Mountain states. Sweet retired from active business in 1921. A Democrat. Sweet received the Democratic nomination for Governor of Colorado in 1922. In the general election held on November 7, 1922, he defeated Benjamin Griffith, a Republican, 138,098 votes to 134,353. Sweet was inaugurated on January 9, 1923. During his administration, a cooperative marketing law was passed; the Colorado State Rangers were abolished; and the Ku Klux Klan began gaining political power in Colorado. Governor Sweet left office at the end of his term on January 13, 1925, after losing the 1924 gubernatorial election to Clarence J. Morley. Sweet returned to private life and later served on the Board of Trustees of the University of Denver. He was active in the Young Men's Christian Association and served as president of the Denver branch for twenty-five years. Sweet lost in his bid for election to the United States Senate in 1926. He died on May 9, 1942 in Denver. Bibliography: Bernice FitzSimmons Hathaway, ed., *The Colorado Genealogist*, vol. XX, no. 3 (July, 1959); James H. Baker and LeRoy Hafen, eds., *History of Colorado*, 3 vols. (Denver, 1927); Roy Glashan, *American Governors and Gubernatorial Elections, 1775-1975* (Stillwater, Minnesota, 1975); Percy Stanley Fritz, *Colorado: The Centennial State* (New York, 1941).

MORLEY, Clarence J., 1925-1927

Born in Dyersville, Dubuque County, Iowa, on February 9, 1869, son of John, a railway man, and Mary D. (Plaister) Morley; a Methodist Episcopalian. Brother of Harold J. and William P. Married to Maud M. Thompson on August 2, 1893; father of Katherine, Harold Thompson, Clarence J., Jr. and Mary Clarissa. Educated in the public schools of Cedar Falls, Iowa; official court reporter, 1887-1891; moved to Trinidad, Colorado and served as court reporter for the Tenth Judicial District until 1895. Graduated from the University of Denver Law School and was admitted to the bar in 1899. Practiced law in Denver, Colorado for twenty years; elected Judge of the District Court of the Second Judicial District for six years. Member of the State Board of Pardons, 1915-1919. On November 4, 1924, Clarence J. Morley was elected Governor of Colorado by defeating incumbent Governor William Sweet, a Democrat, by a vote of 178,078 to 151,041. A Republican. Governor Morley was inaugurated on January 13, 1925. He headed a Ku Klux Klan state administration during the secret order's brief period of power. His term was a very turbulent one, as he was criticized for his acts of executive clemency to criminals and for his political appointments. In addition he fought for economy in all branches of state government. Morley's term ended on January 11, 1927. He left the state shortly afterwards, and established C. J. Morley & Company, a stock brokerage, in Indianapolis, Indiana. Morley died in Oklahoma City, Oklahoma on November 15, 1948. He was buried in Fairmount Cemetery, Denver, Colorado. Bibliography: Roy Glashan, *American Governors and Gubernatorial Elections, 1775-1975* (Stillwater, Minnesota, 1975); Congressional Quarterly, Inc., *Guide to U.S. Elections* (Washington, D.C., 1975); *Denver Post* (November 16, 1948); Wilbur F. Stone, *History of Colorado*, vol. 2 (Chicago, 1918).

ADAMS, William Herbert, 1927-1933

Born on February 15, 1861 at Blue Mounds, Wisconsin, son of John, a farmer, and Elizabeth (Blanchard) Adams; a Congregationalist. Brother of Alva A., John, Frank, Elizabeth, and four others. Married to Emma Ottaway in 1891; remarried to Hattie D. Mullins in 1916; no children. Adams moved with his family to Greeley, Colorado in 1871; moved to Denver and then to Colorado Springs, where he completed his common school education. Moved to Alamosa, Colorado after 1877; became treasurer of Alamosa, 1883; elected Mayor of Alamosa in 1885, and County Commissioner of Conejos County. Elected to the lower house of the Colorado State Legislature, 1886; elected to the State Senate, 1888-1927. Adams was one of the promoters of the San Luis Canal near Alamosa, designed to bring needed water to the county's cattle raisers. A Democrat. Adams was the Democratic candidate for Governor of Colorado in 1926. He won the general election held on November 2, 1926, defeating Oliver Shoup, a Republican, 183,342 votes to 116,756. Adams was inaugurated on January 11, 1927. Reelected on November 6, 1928 by defeating Republican William L. Boatright, 240,160 votes to 144,167. Adams won reelection to a third term on November 4, 1930, defeating Republican Robert F. Rockwell by a margin of 197,067 to 124,157. During his administration, he was concerned with the state's finances, and was credited with saving the state $500,000 by economizing after the legislature had over-appropriated its revenues by more than $1,000,000. During his second term, he was able to convince the legislature that only through sharp curtailment of appropriations could the state meet its obligations. He helped to create the Colorado Agricultural College, Colorado Teachers' College, and Western State College. He also obtained appropriations to benefit the University of Colorado, and the Colorado School of Mines. Governor Adams' term ended on January 10, 1933. He retired from active participation in politics in 1933, refusing to run again on the Democratic ticket, but remained a leading figure in Democratic politics in the state until his death. Adams died in Alamosa, Colorado on February 4, 1954. Bibliography: R. Ewing Stiffler, ed., *The Colorado Genealogist*, vol. VIII, no. 1 (January, 1947); Roy Glashan, *American Governors and Gubernatorial Elections, 1775-1975* (Stillwater, Minnesota, 1975); LeRoy Hafen, *Colorado and Its People*, 4 vols. (New York, 1948); Percy S. Fritz, *Colorado: The Centennial State* (New York, 1941).

JOHNSON, Edwin Carl, 1933-1937, 1955-1957

Born in Scandia, Kansas on January 1, 1884, son of Nels, a farmer, and Annabelle (Lunn) Johnson; a Lutheran. Married to Fern Claire Armitage in February 1907; father of Janet Grace and Gladys Marie. Moved with his parents to a cattle ranch near Elsie, Nebraska in 1884. Graduated from Lincoln High School in 1903; worked as a railroad laborer, telegrapher, and train dispatcher, 1901-1909; homesteaded on government land in Colorado in 1910; operated the Farmers' Cooperative Milling Elevator and also engaged in the produce business, 1920-1930. Member of the State House of Representatives, 1923-1931; Lieutenant Governor of Colorado, 1931-1933. Served in the United States Senate from 1937 to 1955. Johnson was elected Governor of Colorado on November 8, 1932, defeating James Parriot, a Republican, by a vote of 257,188 to 183,258. A Democrat. Governor Johnson took the oath of office on January 10, 1933. He was reelected on November 6, 1934, defeating Nate C. Warren, a Republican, by a vote of 237,026 to 162,791. During his administration the legislature provided funds to help the destitute by imposing an excise tax on gasoline; also many of the federal government's New Deal programs were implemented in Colorado during these years. Johnson left office on January 1, 1937 to assume his seat in the United States Senate. Johnson served in the United States Senate from 1937 to 1955, and did not seek reelection in 1954. Instead, on November 2, 1954, he was again elected Governor of Colorado, receiving 262,205 votes to Republican David Brotzman's 227,335. He assumed the duties of governor on January 11, 1955. During this term the Colorado Anti-Discrimination Commission was created; an equal pay for equal work bill was passed; reorganization of the state government was begun; and the first class of the United States Air Force Academy was enrolled, and construction of the Academy was started at Colorado Springs. Also, a vocational training bill for the blind was passed. Governor Johnson left office on January 8, 1957. Johnson retired from public life after his second period of gubernatorial service; however, he did serve on the Colorado Commission on the Aged, and the Upper Colorado River Basin Commission. Edwin C. Johnson died on May 30, 1970 and was buried in Fairmont Mausoleum, Denver, Colorado. Bibliography: Roy Glashan, *American Governors and Gubernatorial Elections, 1775-1975* (Stillwater, Minnesota, 1975); Congressional Quarterly, Inc., *Guide to U.S. Elections* (Washington, D.C., 1975); *New York Times* (May 31, 1970); LeRoy F. Hafen, *Colorado: The Story of a Western Commonwealth* (Denver, 1933).

TALBOT, Ray H., 1937

Born in Chicago, Illinois on August 19, 1896, son of Herbert A., an electrician, and Annie (Sollitt) Talbot; a Methodist. Married to Junista L. Wilson on June 1, 1915; father of Ray H., Jr. and Adah Mae. Educated in the public schools of Pueblo, Colorado; became an electrical engineer through extension courses; employed by the Colorado Fuel and Iron Company until 1919, at which time he went to Chicago to work for the American Spiral Pipe Works in Cicero, Illinois. He returned to Pueblo in 1920 to work for the Southern Colorado Power Company, and taught vocational training in collaboration with the Colorado Agricultural College. Elected to the State Legislature in 1926 and 1928; elected Lieutenant Governor of Colorado in 1933 and 1935. A Democrat. When Governor Edwin C. Johnson resigned on January 1, 1937, Ray H. Talbot succeeded him. Governor Talbot served for ten days until Teller Ammons was inaugurated on January 12, 1937. After leaving the office of governor, Talbot served as president of the State Fair Commission; served as City Commissioner of Pueblo from 1932 to May, 1946; and became postmaster of Pueblo in May, 1946. Talbot died on January 31, 1955 in Pueblo, Colorado. Bibliography: Roy Glashan, *American Governors and Gubernatorial Elections, 1775-1975* (Stillwater, Minnesota, 1975); Congressional Quarterly, Inc., *Guide to U.S. Elections* (Washington, D.C., 1975); *Denver Post* (February 1, 1955); LeRoy F. Hafen, *Colorado: The Story of a Western Commonwealth* (Denver, 1933).

AMMONS, Teller, 1937-1939

Born on December 3, 1895 in Denver, Colorado, son of Elias Milton, insurance executive and ex-governor of Colorado, and Elizabeth (Fleming) Ammons. Brother of Bruce, Elizabeth, and two others. Married to Esther Davis on September 9, 1933; father of Davis. Ammons served in the 154th Infantry during World War I; graduated from the University of Denver in 1921; received his LL.B. from Westminister Law School, 1929; admitted to the Colorado Bar in 1929. Ammons was elected to the Colorado State Senate in 1930; reelected in 1934; resigned in 1935 to accept appointment as City Attorney of Denver. He became a leader in the Democratic Party in Denver, which resulted in his receiving the Democratic nomination for Governor of Colorado in 1936. Ammons won the general election held on November 3, 1936, defeating Republican Charles M. Armstrong, 263,311 votes to 210,614. He was inaugurated on January 12, 1937. During his administration, the Big Thompson Highway was opened; the State Industrial School was reorganized due to the excessive cost of operation; over 43,000 Coloradans found work through the Works Progress Administration in 1936; and platinum-bearing ore was discovered in southwestern Colorado. Also, a study of state government was begun during Ammons' term by an out-of-state research firm, which sought ways to eliminate waste in government. Governor Ammons' administration was hit by scandal in 1937, when he discovered listening devices in his office, hidden there by three men trying to prove misconduct among high officials in state government. Governor Ammons was proven innocent and the three men were found guilty of eavesdropping and conspiracy. Nonetheless, he was defeated in his attempt for reelection in 1938. Ammons returned to his law practice upon leaving office. On January 16, 1972, he died in Denver, Colorado. Bibliography: *Denver Post* (January 17, 1972); Roy Glashan, *American Governors and Gubernatorial Elections, 1775-1975* (Stillwater, Minnesota, 1975); Bernice FitzSimmons Hathaway, ed., *The Colorado Genealogist*, vol. XIII, no. 3 (July, 1952); Percy Stanley Fritz, *Colorado: The Centennial State* (New York, 1941).

CARR, Ralph, 1939-1943

Born on December 11, 1887 in Rosita, Colorado, son of William Frank, a mining man, and Mattie (Kimberlin) Carr; a Christian Scientist. Married to Gretchen Fowler on February 1, 1913; remarried to Eleanor Fairall on May 26, 1934; father of Cynthia Joanne and Robert Frank. Graduated with an A.B. degree from the University of Colorado in 1910 and received an LL.B. degree from the same institution in 1912. Carr worked as a correspondent for the *Rocky Mountain News* and later for the *Cripple Creek Times* while attending college. Started his law practice in Victor, Colorado, 1912; manager and editor of the *Victor Daily Record*, 1912-1913. Carr moved to Trinidad, Colorado in 1915 and continued his dual role as both a lawyer and newspaper editor, this time of the Trinidad *Picketwire*. County Attorney of Conejos County, Colorado, 1922-1929; first Assistant Attorney General of Colorado, 1927-1929; United States District Attorney for Colorado, 1929-1933. A Republican. Carr, the Republican candidate for Governor of Colorado in the general election of November 8, 1938, defeated the incumbent

Democratic Governor, Teller Ammons, 255,159 votes to 199,562. He was inaugurated on January 10, 1939. Carr won reelection on November 5, 1940, defeating Democrat George Saunders 296,671 votes to 245,292. Carr was able to reorganize the state government, which strengthened the office of the governor; he also eliminated a state deficit of $8,800,000, and called out the state National Guard in the Green Mountain Dam project strike. During his administration, highway employees went unpaid pending settlement of a controversy between the department engineer and the state auditor. Carr left office on January 12, 1943 and returned to his private law practice. Carr again received the Republican nomination for Governor of Colorado in 1950, although he was very ill and confined to bed. He died before the November general election, on September 22, 1950, in Denver, Colorado. Bibliography: Roy Glashan, *American Governors and Gubernatorial Elections, 1775-1975* (Stillwater, Minnesota, 1975); Congressional Quarterly, Inc., *Guide to U.S. Elections* (Washington, D.C., 1975); *New York Times* (September 24, 1950); Carl Ubbelohde, *A Colorado History* (Boulder, 1965).

VIVIAN, John Charles, 1943-1947

Born on June 30, 1887 in Golden, Colorado, son of John Frederick, federal prohibition administrator, and Mary (Tresidder) Vivian; an Episcopalian. Brother of Chauncey H. Married to Maude Charlotte Kleyn on June 15, 1925; no children. Served in the United States Marine Corps as a corporal during World War I; attended the University of Colorado, 1905-1911; received an LL.B. degree from the University of Denver, 1913; admitted to the Colorado Bar, 1913. Vivian worked as a correspondent for the *Denver Republican* while going to school; was also state editor for the *Denver Times*, 1911-1912, and Special Counsel for Denver City and County Attorney, 1913-1914. Vivian established a private law office in Denver, 1914; served as Federal Food Administrator for Jefferson County, Colorado, 1917-1919. Golden, Colorado City Attorney, 1922-1925; Jefferson County Attorney, 1922-1932; and special assistant to the Attorney General of the state, 1925-1929. Elected Lieutenant Governor of Colorado in 1938 and reelected in 1940. A Republican. Vivian was chosen as the Republican candidate for Governor of Colorado in 1942. In the general election, he defeated Homer F. Bedford, a Democrat, 193,501 votes to 149,402. He was inaugurated on January 12, 1943. He won reelection on November 7, 1944 by defeating Roy Best, a Democrat, 259,862 votes to 236,086. Governor Vivian's first term was characterized by great economies and substantial savings to the taxpayers of the state. Also during his first term, a beginning was made in state aid to schools; satisfactory compacts were made between Colorado and the state of Nebraska over the distribution of the waters of the Republican River, and with New Mexico over the Conejos River; an increase of up to eighteen percent in pay was given state employees; the supervision of industrial loan companies by the state bank commissioner was achieved through the passage of the Small Loans Act; and the number of state employees was reduced. Vivian's second term ended on January 14, 1947. After leaving public office, Governor Vivian began a law practice and engaged in public speaking. On February 10, 1964, he died and was buried in Golden, Colorado. Bibliography: Roy Glashan, *American Governors and Gubernatorial Elections, 1775-1975* (Stillwater,

Minnesota, 1975); Bernice FitzSimmons Hathaway, ed., *The Colorado Genealogist*, vol. XXI, no. 3 (July, 1960); Colorado State Historical Society, CWA Name File, Documentary Resources, Denver, Colorado; "Ridin' the Range with the Red Fenwick," *Denver Post* (September 22, 1963).

KNOUS, William Lee, 1947-1950

Born on February 2, 1889 in Ouray, Colorado, son of John Franklin and Julia (Bain) Knous; an Episcopalian. Married to Elsie Marie Grabow on July 1, 1915; father of William John, Robert Lee and Merle Ray. Received his LL.B. degree from the University of Colorado in 1911; LL.D. degree from Colorado College, 1952; University of Denver, 1954. Admitted to the Colorado Bar in 1911 and became a member of the law firm of Moynihan, Hughes, and Knous. Department of the District Attorney, Ouray County, 1913-1918. Representative in Colorado General Assembly, 1928-1930; State Senator, 1930-1936; President Pro Tempore of the Senate, 1935-1936; Mayor of the city of Montrose, 1926-1930; Associate Justice of the Colorado Supreme Court, 1937-1946; Chief Justice of the Colorado Supreme Court, 1946-1947. On November 5, 1946, Knous won the general election for Governor of Colorado by defeating Leon E. Lavington, a Republican, by a vote of 174,604 to 160,483. A Democrat. Governor Knous was inaugurated on January 14, 1947. He was reelected on November 2, 1948, defeating Republican David A. Hamil, by a vote of 332,752 to 168,928. While he was governor, two major interstate compacts were devised to settle the controversy over water; one was with Kansas over the division of the Arkansas River water; the other was among the states of the Upper Colorado Basin (Wyoming, New Mexico, Utah, and Colorado). A series of legislative acts known as the "Sabin Health Bills" was also passed. These included the reorganization of the Department of Public Health; the creation of local public health units; state encouragement with regard to the training of public health personnel; and special enactments to combat specific diseases. Governor Knous resigned on April 15, 1950, and was succeeded by Lieutenant Governor Walter W. Johnson. Knous served as Judge of the United States District Court for the District of Colorado, 1950-1954, and served as Chief Judge from 1954 until his death. He died on December 13, 1959 in Denver, Colorado. Bibliography: Roy Glashan, *American Governors and Gubernatorial Elections, 1775-1975* (Stillwater, Minnesota, 1975); Congressional Quarterly, Inc., *Guide to U.S. Elections* (Washington, D.C., 1975); Carl Ubbelohde, *A Colorado History* (Boulder, 1965); Fred McGhee, *Facts on File, Five Year Index, 1946-1950* (New York, 1958).

JOHNSON, Walter Walfred, 1950-1951

Born on April 16, 1904 in Pueblo, Colorado, son of John L. and Minnie Johnson; a Congregationalist. Married to Neva M. Morrow on April 6, 1922; father of Wally M. and Winnifred. Received his education in the public schools of Pueblo; engaged in the insurance and real estate business in Pueblo from 1930 onwards; elected to the Colorado State Senatorial District, 1941-1949; elected Lieutenant Governor of Colorado in 1949-1950. A Democrat. Johnson assumed the duties of Governor of

Colorado upon the resignation of Governor Walter L. Knous. He took the oath of office on April 15, 1950. Johnson was defeated for election to the governor's office in the November 7, 1950 general election. He was again elected to the State Senate in 1951 and served until 1959; he also served as the Colorado Commissioner on the Western Interstate Commission for Higher Education, 1955-1959. Johnson was a member of the Board of Managers to the Council of State Governments, 1958-1963. He is engaged in real estate and insurance in Pueblo, where he makes his home. Bibliography: Roy Glashan, *American Governors and Gubernatorial Elections, 1775-1975* (Stillwater, Minnesota, 1975); Congressional Quarterly, Inc., *Guide to U.S. Elections* (Washington, D.C., 1975); LeRoy Hafen, *Colorado: A Story of the State and Its People* (Denver, 1943); *Denver Post* (April 15, 1950).

THORNTON, Daniel Isaac J., 1951-1955

Born on January 31, 1911 in Hall County, Texas, son of Clay C., and Ida (Fife) Thornton. Brother of Leecy, Hollis, Truitt and Clarence. Married to Jessie Willock in 1934. Attended Texas Technological College and the University of California at Los Angeles; left college and worked as a bit player for Warner Brothers, as a gas station operator, and as a "roughneck" and derrick man. In 1937 he borrowed money from his father-in-law to buy a ranch in Arizona, and began breeding Herefords. He moved to Gunnison, Colorado in 1941 and purchased a 4,000 acre ranch. He became very successful and was nationally recognized for his "Triumphant Type" Herefords. Thornton was elected State Senator in 1948 and served two terms. At the end of the legislative session, he wanted to leave politics and return to ranching. However, the Republican candidate for Governor, Ralph Carr, died five weeks before the November 7, 1950 general election, and Thornton was selected to succeed him. He defeated Walter W. Johnson by a vote of 236,472 to 212,976. Thornton was inaugurated on January 9, 1951. During his first term, he secured passage of legislation to control Bang's cattle disease; to effect workmen's compensation; and to enact a Fair Employment Practices Act in state government hiring. He was reelected on November 4, 1952, defeating John W. Metzger, a Democrat, 349,924 votes to 260,044. During his second term, he established a severance oil tax; developed civil defense; raised the surtax exemption on intangibles; put penal and charitable affairs under a Board of State Institutions headed by a paid director; secured the enactment of comprehensive legislation to finance schools; and started a state advertising program. He also organized an efficient patrol administration; promoted mining in the state; revised the coal mining laws; reorganized the State Highway Commission, and formulated long-range highway plans. Governor Thornton's second term ended on January 11, 1955. After leaving office, he returned to his ranching interests in Gunnison, Colorado. Bibliography: Bernice FitzSimmons Hathaway, ed., *The Colorado Genealogist*, vol. XXIII, no. 3 (July, 1962); Roy Glashan, *American Governors and Gubernatorial Elections, 1775-1975* (Stillwater, Minnesota, 1975); Carl Ubbelohde, *A Colorado History* (Boulder, 1965); Colorado State Planning Division, *Yearbook of the State of Colorado, 1952* (Denver, 1952).

JOHNSON, Edwin Carl, 1933-1937, 1955-1957

McNICHOLS, Stephen L. R., 1957-1963

Born on March 17, 1914 in Denver, Colorado, son of William H., a State Senator, and Cassie F. (Warner) McNichols; a Catholic. Brother of three others. Married to Marjory Roberta Hart on June 27, 1942; father of Stephen L. R., Jr., Robert M., William H., Mary Elizabeth and Marjory Roberta. Received Ph.B. degree from Regis College, Denver in 1936; earned LL.D. degree at Catholic University of America, Washington, D.C. in 1939. Admitted to the Washington, D.C. Bar in 1939 and worked as a field agent for the FBI, chiefly in the Baltimore and Boston offices. Returned to Colorado in 1940 and was admitted to the Colorado Bar that same year. Served as Deputy District Attorney in Denver in 1941. In February, 1942, McNichols enlisted in the navy. He was discharged as a Lieutenant Commander in 1946. After the war, he was a special assistant to the Attorney General in the Department of Justice until 1948. He then became a partner in the law firm of McNichols, Dunn, & Nevans. He served as State Senator, 1948-1954. He became Lieutenant Governor under Governor Edwin C. Johnson in 1954. A Democrat. As the Democratic candidate for Governor of Colorado, McNichols won the general election held on November 6, 1956, defeating Donald G. Brotzman, a Republican, 331,283 votes to 313,959. He was inaugurated on January 8, 1957. McNichols won reelection on November 4, 1958, defeating Republican Palmer L. Burch, 321,165 votes to 288,643. During his administration, he tried to improve conditions for migrant workers; created an administrative department to study and supervise Colorado's resources development; encouraged lengthening of the gubernatorial term from two to four years; and called a special legislative session to enact a grasshopper-control bill. Governor McNichols lost his bid for reelection in the 1962 general election. He left office on January 8, 1963. McNichols then returned to his law practice in Denver and his other business interests. Bibliography: Roy Glashan, *American Governors and Gubernatorial Elections, 1775-1975* (Stillwater, Minnesota, 1975); Carl Ubbelohde, *A Colorado History* (Boulder, 1965); Bernice Fitz-Simmons Hathaway, ed., *The Colorado Genealogist*, vol. XVIII, no. 4 (1957); Congressional Quarterly, Inc., *Guide to U.S. Elections* (Washington, D.C., 1975).

LOVE, John A., 1963-1973

Born near Gibson City, Illinois on November 29, 1916, son of Arthur C., an accountant, and Mildred (Shaver) Love; a Congregationalist. Brother of Richard Love and Mrs. A. Morrell. Married to Ann Daniels on October 23, 1942; father of Dan, Andy and Becky. Received his B.A. degree from the University of Denver in 1938; graduated from the Denver Law School with an LL.B., 1941. Love served in the Naval Air Corps during World War II, and received the Air Medal and two Distinguished Flying Crosses. After returning to Colorado Springs in 1945, he practiced law with the firm of Love, Cole, and Mullett, until he sought the office of Governor of Colorado in 1962. On November 6, 1962, John A. Love defeated incumbent Democratic Governor Stephen L. R. McNichols, by a vote of 348,790 to 262,456. A Republican. Governor Love was inaugurated on January 8, 1963. On November 8, 1966, he gained reelection by defeating Robert Knous, a Democrat, 356,730 votes to 287,132. On November 3, 1970, he defeated Mark Hogan, a Democrat, 350,690 votes to 302,432, to win his third term. During these three terms as governor, the following occurred: the state personal income tax was cut by 15 percent on 1962 earnings and by 12½ percent on 1963 earnings; also, the state unemployment and workmen's compensation laws were revised; several state agencies were reorganized; and the state's election code was completely revised, all in 1963. In 1964 the State Assembly completed reorganization of the state courts under a constitutional amendment adopted in 1962. The legislative session of 1965 was highlighted by the enactment of a Fair Housing Bill and a bill to provide state support for birth control education. A Water Pollution Control Law and a law setting strict standards for control of air pollution were passed in 1966; in 1967 the Assembly was reapportioned, to become effective at the 1968 general election; reorganization of some 130 state agencies into twenty departments was also enacted. Bills were approved in 1969 allowing the state's takeover of the District and County Court Systems and creating a state Public Defender's System and a six-member Colorado Court of Appeals. A Land-Use Commission was created in 1970; eighteen year-olds were given the right to vote, and a uniform consumer credit code was created in 1971. The 1972 Legislature was mainly concerned with the reapportionment of legislative and congressional districts, as required by the state constitution every ten years. On July 16, 1973, Governor Love resigned to become Director of the Office of Energy and Natural Resources. Love is now president of Ideal Basic, Incorporated in Denver, Colorado. Bibliography: Roy Glashan, *American Governors and Gubernatorial Elections, 1775-1975* (Stillwater, Minnesota, 1975); Bernice FitzSimmons Hathaway, ed., *The Colorado Genealogist*, vol. XXVI, no. 4 (October, 1965); Congressional Quarterly, Inc., *Guide to U.S. Elections* (Washington, D.C., 1975).

VANDERHOOF, John David, 1973-1975

Born on May 27, 1922 in Rocky Ford, Colorado, son of Roy Elvin, and Irene (Church) Vanderhoof, a Methodist. Married to Lois June Taggart on April 3, 1943; father of Bruce and Linda. Vanderhoof received his A.A. degree from Glendale College, Glendale, California; served in the United States Naval Reserve to Lieutenant (j.g.) during World War II, 1942-1945; received the Air Medal with Oak Leaf Cluster, Purple Heart, and Distinguished Flying Cross. Vanderhoof was the owner of Van's Sporting Goods in Glenwood, Colorado from 1946 to 1955; President of Glenwood Industrial Bank, 1955—; President of the Bank of Glenwood, 1963—; elected to the Colorado House of Representatives, 1955-1970; served as Minority Leader of the House from 1955-1962; Vanderhoof served as Speaker of the House from 1963-1964 and 1967-1970; Colorado delegate to the Republican National Convention, 1968; served as Lieutenant Governor of Colorado, 1971-1973. A Republican. Vanderhoof became Governor of Colorado on July 16, 1973 upon the resignation of Governor John Love. Soon after assuming office, Vanderhoof removed the warden at the State Penitentiary due to a scandal. Also, state support of public education was increased by $221 million; an increase in the cigarette tax was passed by the State Legislature; and a No-Fault Insurance Law was passed by the State Legislature. Vanderhoof was defeated in his bid for election to the office of Governor on November 5, 1974. He left office on January 14, 1975. Governor Vanderhoof then returned to his business interests in Glenwood, Colorado. Bibliography: Roy Glashan, *American Governors and Gubernatorial Elections, 1775-1975* (Stillwater, Minnesota, 1975); Congressional Quarterly, Inc., *Guide to U.S. Elections* (Washington, D.C., 1975); Charles Monaghan, ed., *Facts on File, 1974* (New York, 1975); Colorado State Planning Division, *Yearbook of the State of Colorado, 1974* (Denver, 1974).

LAMM, Richard David, 1975-

Born on August 3, 1935 in Madison, Wisconsin, son of A. E. and Mary (Townsend) Lamm. Married to Dorothy Vennard on May 11, 1963; father of Scott Hunter and Heather. Received his B.B.A. from the University of Wisconsin, 1957; LL.B. degree from the University of California, 1961. Admitted to the California Bar in 1961. Admitted to the Colorado Bar in 1962. Lamm worked as a C.P.A. for the law firm of Ernst & Ernst in Denver, Colorado from 1961-1962; attorney for the Anti-Discrimination Commission, Denver, 1962-1963; attorney for Jones, Meiklejohn, Kilroy, Kehl, and Lyons, Denver, 1965-1975. Member of the Colorado House of Representatives, 1966-1975; served as Minority Leader, 1971-1975. On November 5, 1974, Lamm defeated John Vanderhoof, a Republican, in the general election by a vote of 441,199 to 378,907 to become Governor of Colorado. A Democrat. Governor Lamm took the oath of office on January 14, 1975. During the legislative session of 1975, a law was passed to reduce penalties for possession of less than one ounce of marijuana, and a Bilingual Education Bill was passed to provide bilingual instruction for students in kindergarten through the third grade, whose prime language was not English. In 1976 the voters of Colorado crushed efforts to repeal the State Equal Rights Amendment; restrict nuclear power; and virtually prohibit tax increases. Proposals to abolish the state sales tax on groceries and to require a nickel deposit on beverage containers were also defeated. The defeat of the food sales-tax repeal was a major setback for Governor Lamm. The issue had been his top priority, and he backed a citizen initiative to bypass the Senate to put it on the ballot. Richard D. Lamm is presently Governor of Colorado; his term will end in January, 1979. Bibliography: Roy Glashan, *American Governors and Gubernatorial Elections, 1775-1975* (Stillwater, Minnesota, 1975); Congressional Quarterly, Inc., *Guide to U.S. Elections* (Washington, D.C., 1975); Henry H. Schulte, Jr., ed., *Facts on File Yearbook, 1974* (New York, 1975); Charles Monaghan, ed., *Facts on File Yearbook, 1975* (New York, 1976).

CONNECTICUT

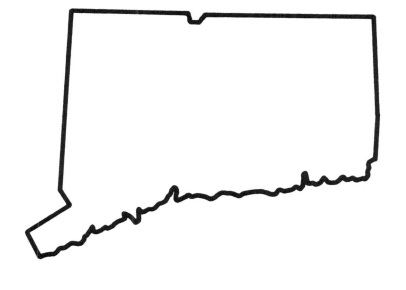

CONNECTICUT

Born on July 3, 1731 in Windham County, Connecticut, the son of Nathaniel, a farmer and clothier, and Mehetable Thurston Huntington; a Puritan; five brothers. Married to Martha Devotion in 1761; adopted his brother Joseph's children, Samuel and Francis. Attended common schools; apprenticed to a cooper; studied law; awarded an LL. D. at Dartmouth College, New Hampshire, 1785, and Yale University, New Haven, Connecticut, 1787. Admitted to the bar, 1758. Began private practice in Norwich, Connecticut, 1758. Executive Councillor, 1763; member, Connecticut Colonial Assembly, 1764; appointed King's Attorney for Connecticut, 1765; Justice of the Peace, New London County, Connecticut, 1765-1775; Judge of the Superior Court of Connecticut, 1774-1784; member, Continental Congress, 1776-1784; signer of the Declaration of Independence, 1776; President, Continental Congress, 1779-1781 and 1783; Chief Justice of the Superior Court of Connecticut, 1784; Lieutenant Governor of Connecticut, 1785-1786. As a non-partisan candidate, Huntington was elected Governor of Connecticut on April 10, 1786, defeating the incumbent, Matthew Griswold, 1,701 votes to 1,049, with 2,854 scattered votes. Because no candidate received fifty percent of the votes cast, the Connecticut Legislature decided the outcome and declared Huntington the winner. He took office on May 11, 1786. He was reelected annually for the next eleven years without significant opposition. During his administration, Connecticut ceded its western lands, with the exception of the Western Reserve, to the United States. In 1795, the Western Reserve was sold for $1,200,000 by the state and the money used to establish a school fund. Huntington supported the Federal Constitution, which was ratified by Connecticut in 1788; he also received two of the votes cast for the first President and Vice President of the United States. During his years as governor, he became a Federalist. Huntington died in office on January 5, 1796, at Norwich. He was buried in Norwichtown Cemetery in Norwich. Bibliography: George L. Clark, *A History of Connecticut; Its People and Institutions* (New York, 1914); Forrest Morgan, *Connecticut as a Colony and as a State,* 4 vols.(Hartford, 1904); Frederick C. Norton, *The Governors of Connecticut* (Hartford, 1905); Roy Glashan, *American Governors and Gubernatorial Elections, 1775-1975* (Stillwater, Minnesota, 1975).

WOLCOTT, Oliver, 1796-1797

Born on December 20, 1726 in Windsor, Hartford County, Connecticut, the youngest son of Roger, Colonial Governor of Connecticut from 1750 to 1754, and Sarah (Drake) Wolcott; a Congregationalist. Brother of Erastus and Alexander. Married to Laura Collins in 1755; father of Oliver, Frederick, Mary Ann, and an additional brother and sister. Graduated from Yale University in New Haven, Connecticut, in 1747; later studied medicine with his brother, Alexander. Commissioned a Captain by the governor of New York; raised a volunteer regiment; and served on the Canadian border during King George's War in 1748; appointed a Major in the Connecticut Militia in 1771; became Colonel of the Seventeenth Militia Regiment in 1774; appointed a permanent Brigadier General of the Sixth Militia in 1777; promoted to Major General of Militia in 1779; rose to the rank of Lieutenant General of Militia. Elected Sheriff of Litchfield County, Connecticut in 1751 and served for twenty years; elected as Deputy of Litchfield, Connecticut, 1764, 1767, 1768, and 1770; Assistant of Litchfield, 1771-1786; Judge of the Court of Probate for Litchfield, 1774-1781; Judge of the Litchfield County Court, 1774-1778; member, Connecticut State Council, 1774-1786; appointed a Commissioner of Indian Affairs for the Northern Department by the Continental Congress, 1775; member, Continental Congress, 1775-1778 and 1780-1784; appointed to the Connecticut Council of Safety, 1780; United States Commissioner at the Treaty of Fort Stanwix, 1784. Without a popular majority in the state elections of 1787, he was elected Lieutenant Governor of Connecticut by the Legislature and served until 1796. President, Connecticut Society of Arts and Sciences. He was a Federalist. On January 5, 1796, Connecticut Governor Samuel Huntington died, and as Lieutenant Governor, Wolcott succeeded to the office. On April 11, 1796, he was elected Governor without opposition, receiving 7,773 votes. Wolcott was reelected on April 10, 1797, again without an opponent. During his administration, he served as a presidential elector, and cast his vote for John Adams and Thomas Pinckney in 1796. Wolcott died in office on December 1, 1797, and was buried in Litchfield. Bibliography: George L. Clark, *A History of Connecticut; Its People and Institutions* (New York, 1914); Frederick Norton, *The Governors of Connecticut* (Hartford, 1905); Roy Glashan, *American Governors and Gubernatorial Elections, 1775-1975* (Stillwater, Minnesota, 1975).

TRUMBULL, Jonathan, 1797-1809

Born on March 26, 1740 in Lebanon, Connecticut, the son of Jonathan, a politician and lawyer, and Faith (Robinson) Trumbull; a Congregationalist. Brother of Joseph, David, John, Faith and Mary. Married to Eunice Backus in March 1767; father of Faith, Harriet, Maria, another daughter, and one son. Graduated from Harvard University in Cambridge, Massachusetts in 1759 as salutatorian of his class; awarded a master's degree in 1762, and was valedictorian. Served in the Continental Army as paymaster for the forces of the New York Department, 1776-1780; appointed secretary and aide-de-camp to Commander-in-Chief George Washington in 1780. Member, Connecticut House of Representatives, 1774-1775, 1779-1780, and 1788; Comptroller of the Treasury of the United States, 1778-1779;

Speaker of the Connecticut House of Representatives, 1788; member, United States House of Representatives, 1789-1795; Speaker of the United States House of Representatives, 1791-1793; member, United States Senate, 1795-1796; resigned from office; Lieutenant Governor of Connecticut, 1796-1797. He was a Federalist. On December 1, 1797, Governor Oliver Wolcott died, and, as Lieutenant Governor, Trumbull succeeded to the office. He was reelected Governor for the next twelve years: in 1798, he received 7,075 votes without an opponent; in 1799 and 1800, he was unopposed; in 1801, he defeated the Democratic-Republican candidate, R. Law, 11,165 votes to 1,051, with 106 scattered returns; in 1802, he received 11,383 votes to Democratic-Republican candidate, E. Kirby's 4,508, with 423 scattered votes; in 1803, he again defeated Kirby, 14,375 votes to 8,071; in 1804 he was again victorious over Kirby; in 1805, he polled 12,700 votes to the Democratic-Republican candidate, W. Hart's 7,810, with 150 scattered votes; in 1806, he again defeated Hart, 13,413 votes to 9,460; in 1807, he was victorious over Hart, 11,959 votes to 7,951; in 1808, he defeated Hart, 12,146 votes to 7,566; and in 1809 he polled 14,650 votes to the Democratic-Republican candidate, A. Spaulding's 8,159. While he was governor, Trumbull served as Chief Judge of the Supreme Court of Errors. Also during his administration, he refused a request by the United States Secretary of War, Henry Dearborn, for the use of the Connecticut Militia to enforce the Embargo Act; later, the Connecticut Legislature was called into special session to consider the situation. Trumbull died in office on August 7, 1809, and was buried in Lebanon. Bibliography: Forrest Morgan, *Connecticut as a Colony and as a State,* 4 vols. (Hartford, 1904); Frederick C. Norton, *The Governors of Connecticut* (Hartford, 1905); Roy Glashan, *American Governors and Gubernatorial Elections, 1775-1975* (Stillwater, Minnesota, 1975); "The Trumbull Papers," 4 vols., in the *Collections of the Massachusetts Historical Society,* ser. 5, vols. IX and X (1885), and ser. 7, vols. II and III (1902).

TREADWELL, John, 1809-1811

Born on November 23, 1745 in Farmington, Hartford County, Connecticut, the only son of Ephraim and Mary Treadwell; a Congregationalist. Married to a daughter of Joseph Pomeroy, who bore him one or more children. Graduated from Yale University in New Haven, Connecticut in 1767; studied law; awarded an LL. D. degree from Yale University in 1800. Elected to the Connecticut General Assembly in 1776, and remained in office, with the exception of one session, until 1798; member, Continental Congress, 1785-1786; member, Connecticut Convention which ratified the United States Constitution, 1788; became Judge of Probate in 1789, and held the post for twenty years; Judge, Supreme Court of Errors, 1789-1809; Judge of the Court of Common Pleas for three years; Lieutenant Governor of Connecticut, 1798-1809; member, Board of Managers, Connecticut School Fund, 1800-1810. Member, Corporation of Yale; founder and president, American Board of Commissioners for Foreign Missions. He was a Federalist. On August 7, 1809, Governor Jonathan Trumbull died, and, as Lieutenant Governor, Treadwell succeeded to the office. On April 9, 1810, he was elected chief executive in his own right, receiving 10,265 votes to 8,159 for A. Spaulding, a Democratic-Republican, and 3,110 for Roger Griswold, a Federalist. During Treadwell's administration, the

United States drifted closer to a war with Great Britain, which was opposed by Connecticut and the other New England states dependent on foreign trade. As a result of Macon's Bill Number Two, the Non-Intercourse Act, as applied to England, was reestablished in February, 1811. Also during Treadwell's term, the Hartford Fire Insurance Company was organized. On April 8, 1811, Treadwell was defeated for reelection by Roger Griswold. As a result, he left office on May 9, 1811. Afterward, he remained an active member of the American Board of Commissioners for Foreign Missions, and participated in other religious endeavors. He was a member of the 1818 Connecticut Constitutional Convention. Treadwell died on August 19, 1823 in Farmington. Bibliography: George L. Clark, *A History of Connecticut; its People and Institutions* (New York, 1914); Forrest Morgan, *Connecticut as a Colony and as a State,* 4 vols. (Hartford, 1904); Frederick C. Norton, *The Governors of Connecticut* (Hartford, 1905); Roy Glashan, *American Governors and Gubernatorial Elections, 1775-1975* (Stillwater, Minnesota, 1975).

GRISWOLD, Roger, 1811-1812

Born on May 21, 1762 in Lyme, New London County, Connecticut, the son of Matthew, Governor of Connecticut from 1784 to 1786, and Ursula (Wolcott) Griswold. Brother of Matthew, two other brothers, and four sisters. Married to Fanny Rogers on October 27, 1788; father of seven sons and three daughters. Graduated from Yale University in New Haven, Connecticut in 1780; studied law with his father; awarded an LL. D. degree from Harvard University in Cambridge, Massachusetts in 1811; awarded an LL. D. degree from Yale University in 1812. Admitted to the bar in 1783. Began private law practice in Lyme; moved to Norwich, Connecticut in 1785; returned to Lyme in 1794. Member, Connecticut Legislature, 1794; member, United States House of Representatives, 1795-1805; declined an offer by President John Adams to become United States Secretary of War in 1801; resigned from Congress, and resumed his law practice in 1805; Judge of the Superior Court of Connecticut, 1807-1809; presidential elector on the Charles C. Pinckney and Rufus King ticket in 1808; Lieutenant Governor of Connecticut, 1809-1811. As a Federalist, Griswold was elected Governor of Connecticut on April 8, 1811, defeating incumbent John Treadwell. Griswold took office on May 9, 1811. He was elected to a second term on April 13, 1812, polling 11,721 votes to the Democratic-Republican candidate, E. Boardman's 1,487, with 487 scattered votes. During his administration, the War of 1812 began between the United States and Great Britain. Opposed to the conflict, Griswold refused the request of William Eustis, U.S. Secretary of War, for four companies of Connecticut troops to serve with the American army. He contended that the events surrounding the conflict did not allow President Madison the constitutional power to make use of state militia, and that the fact that war had begun did not constitute an "invasion" of the country. Griswold died in office on October 25, 1812, and was buried in Griswold Cemetery at Black Hall in Lyme. Bibliography: George L. Clark, *A History of Connecticut; Its People and Institutions* (New York, 1914); Forrest Morgan, *Connecticut as a Colony and as a State,* 4 vols. (Hartford,1904); Frederick C. Norton, *The Governors of Connecticut* (Hartford, 1905); Roy Glashan, *American Governors and Gubernatorial Elections, 1775-1975* (Stillwater, Minnesota, 1975).

SMITH, John Cotton, 1812-1817

Born on February 12, 1762 in Sharon, Litchfield County, Connecticut, the son of the Reverend Cotton Mather, pastor of the Congregational Church at Sharon, and Temperance (Worhington) Gale Smith; a Calvinist. Married to Margaret Evertson on October 29, 1786; father of William Mather. Educated by his mother and local divines; graduated from Yale University at New Haven, Connecticut in 1783; studied law; awarded an LL. D. degree by Yale University in 1814. Admitted to the bar in 1786. Began private law practice in Sharon in 1787. Member, Connecticut House of Representatives, 1793 and 1796-1800; Clerk of the Connecticut House of Representatives, 1799; Speaker of the Connecticut House of Representatives, 1800; member, United States House of Representatives, 1800-1806; resigned from Congress, and returned to Sharon to resume his law practice and engage in farming; member, Connecticut Legislature, 1808-1809; Judge of the Superior Court of Connecticut, 1809; Lieutenant Governor of Connecticut, 1810-1812. Member, Northern Society of Antiquarians of Copenhagen, Denmark; member, Connecticut Historical Society; member, Massachusetts Historical Society; president, Connecticut State Bible Society; president, American Board of Foreign Missions, 1826-1841; president, Litchfield County Foreign Missionary Society; president, Litchfield County Temperance Society; president, American Bible Society, 1831-1845. Author: *The Correspondence and Miscellanies of the Hon. John Cotton Smith,* edited by W.W. Andrews (1847); contributor to scientific journals. He was a Federalist. On October 25, 1812, Connecticut Governor Roger Griswold died, and as Lieutenant Governor, Smith succeeded to the office. He was elected Governor the next four years: in 1813, he defeated the Democratic-Republican candidate, E. Boardman, 11,893 votes to 7,201; in 1814, he received 9,415 votes to Boardman's 2,619, with 687 scattered votes; in 1815, he polled 8,176 votes to Boardman's 4,876; and in 1816, he defeated the American and Toleration Party candidate, Oliver Wolcott, Jr., 11,386 votes to 10,170, with 203 scattered votes. During Smith's administration, he supported the agricultural and shipping interests of the state; was a bitter enemy of reform and of a liberal revision of the Connecticut Royal Charter; and continued his predecessor's refusal to place the state militia under federal officers. In addition, he urged Connecticut to participate in the Hartford Convention of 1814-1815. In 1817, Smith was defeated for reelection by Wolcott, 13,655 votes to 13,119. As a result, he left office on May 8, 1817. Afterward, Smith lost the 1818 and 1819 gubernatorial elections to Oliver Wolcott, and subsequently withdrew from public life; he retired to his estate near Sharon, and devoted himself to his studies. Smith died at his estate on December 7, 1845, and was buried in Hillside Cemetery. Bibliography: George L. Clark, *A History of Connecticut; Its People and Institutions* (New York, 1914); Forrest Morgan, *Connecticut as a Colony and as a State,* 4 vols. (Hartford, 1904); Frederick C. Norton, *The Governors of Connecticut* (Hartford, 1905); Roy Glashan, *American Governors and Gubernatorial Elections, 1775-1975* (Stillwater, Minnesota, 1975).

WOLCOTT, Oliver, II, 1817-1827

Born on January 11, 1760 in Litchfield, Connecticut, the son of Oliver, Governor of Connecticut from 1796 to 1797, and Laura (Collins) Wolcott; a Congregationalist. Brother of Frederick, Mary Ann, and an additional brother and sister. Married to Elizabeth Stoughton on June 1, 1785; father of Laura, five sons, and another daughter. Tutored by his mother; attended Litchfield Grammar School; graduated from Yale University in New Haven, Connecticut in 1778; studied law; awarded an LL.D. degree from Yale University, Princeton University in Princeton, New Jersey, and Brown University in Providence, Rhode Island. Admitted to the bar in 1781. Served during the Revolutionary War as a volunteer in two minor campaigns in 1777 and 1779; appointed to the Quartermaster's Department; served as an aide-de-camp to his father, General Oliver Wolcott, in 1779. Moved to Hartford, Connecticut, and became a clerk in the financial office of the Connecticut Department of State; member, Central Board of Accountants, 1782-1788; commissioned with Oliver Ellsworth in 1784 to settle the claims of Connecticut against the federal government; Connecticut Comptroller of Public Accounts, 1788-1789; Auditor of the United States Treasury, 1789-1791; refused an offer by President George Washington to be appointed President of the United States Bank; appointed Comptroller of the United States Treasury, 1791; Secretary of the Treasury of the United States, 1795-1800; Judge of the United States Supreme Court for the Second District, 1801-1802. Moved to New York City, New York in 1802, and entered the mercantile business; formed Oliver Wolcott and Company; became president of the Merchant's Bank in 1803; founder of the Bank of North America; president of the Bank of North America, 1812-1814; returned to Litchfield in 1815 and engaged in farming; became involved in the manufacturing of textiles with his brother. Unsuccessful Toleration and Reform Party candidate for Governor of Connecticut, 1816. Member of the literary circle of John Trumbull and Joel Barlow; assisted in the organization of the Hartford County, Connecticut Bar in 1783. Author: *An Address to the People of the United States* (1802). As a member of the Toleration and Reform Party, Wolcott was elected Governor of Connecticut on April 7, 1817, defeating the incumbent Federalist, John C. Smith, 13,655 votes to 13,119, with 202 scattered votes. Wolcott took office on May 8, 1817. He was reelected annually for the next nine years: in 1818, as the Constitution and Reform Party candidate, he again defeated Smith, 16,432 votes to 1,446; becoming a Democratic-Republican, he received 22,539 votes to Federalist Timothy Pitkin's 1,200 and Smith's 1,084 in 1819; in 1820, he polled 15,738 votes to Pitkin's 1,140 and the Union Republican candidate, N. Smith's 2,509; in 1821, he defeated another Democrat-Republican, E. Boardman, 10,064 votes to 580, with 304 votes cast for Federalist J. Ingersoll; in 1822, he received 8,568 votes to Federalist A. Swift's 580, and Pitkin's 492; in 1823, he polled 9,090 votes to Swift's 391 and Pitkin's 237; in 1824, he defeated Pitkin, 6,637 votes to 466, with 123 votes cast for Federalist D. Plant; in 1825, he received 7,147 votes to Federalist David Daggett's 1,342 and Federalist N. Smith's 863; and in 1826, he polled 6,780 votes to Daggett's 4,340. During his administration, a Constitutional Convention met in Hartford in August, 1818 to prepare a new instrument of government, which was adopted by the people in October, 1818. In 1823, Washington College (renamed Trinity College in 1845) was organized at Hartford; and in 1826, the boundary dispute between Massachusetts and Connecticut, dating from 1662, was resolved. Also in 1826, the

Democratic-Republican caucus rejected Wolcott as a candidate for reelection; nonetheless, he entered the April, 1827 gubernatorial election as an Independent. He was defeated by the Democratic-Republican candidate, Gideon Tomlinson, 7,681 votes to 5,295, with 175 votes cast for Daggett. As a result, Wolcott left office on May 5, 1827. Afterward, he returned to New York City. Wolcott died in New York City on June 1, 1833, and was buried in Litchfield. Bibliography: Forrest Morgan, *Connecticut as a Colony and as a State,* 4 vols. (Hartford, 1904); Frederick C. Norton, *The Governors of Connecticut* (Hartford, 1905); Roy Glashan, *American Governors and Gubernatorial Elections, 1775-1975* (Stillwater, Minnesota, 1975); "Oliver Wolcott Papers," Connecticut Historical Society, Hartford, Connecticut.

TOMLINSON, Gideon, 1827-1831

Born on December 31, 1780 in Stratford, Connecticut, eldest son of Jabez Huntington, a farmer and legislator, and Rebecca (Lewis) Tomlinson; a member of the Congregational Church. Brother of Hannah, Ann (Nancy), Sarah Lewis and Huntington Tomlinson. Married to Sarah Bradley on December 15, 1807; father of Jabez Huntington; remarried to Mrs. Lydia Ann (Wells) Wright on June 16, 1846. Graduated from Yale College in 1802. Moved to Virginia, where he served as a private tutor for one year. Studied law in Virginia and Connecticut, and was admitted to the Connecticut Bar in June 1805; set up his practice and residence in Fairfield two years later. Elected to the General Assembly in May, 1817 as a member of the Toleration Party, a Republican-based coalition which sought to withdraw special privileges from the politically powerful Congregational Church. Elected clerk of the Assembly, October, 1817; reelected the following year and served also as Speaker of the House for both sessions. Aided in the drafting of the state's first constitution in 1818; his particular contribution to it was his co-authorship of the most significant article, that dealing with the separation of church and state. From 1818 to 1827, he served in the U.S. House of Representatives. The 1826 Democratic-Republican and Toleration Party Nominating Caucus chose Tomlinson to be its gubernatorial candidate over incumbent Governor Oliver Wolcott, Jr. In the 1827 election, Wolcott ran as an Independent, but lost to Tomlinson by a vote of 7,681 to 5,295, with 627 scattered votes. In the elections of 1828, 1829 and 1830, Tomlinson was reelected, polling each time over 95 percent of the total vote. As governor, Tomlinson called for improvements in the public school system; expansion of industry, agriculture and commerce; and the districting of the state for the purpose of state senatorial representation. Only the last issue was acted upon favorably by the Legislature. The decrease in political "bossism" that resulted from the latter, coupled with the elimination of the caucus, helped create more open state nominating conventions. Prison reform was achieved with the opening of a more humane facility in 1827. The Democratic Party began to be a major force in the state during Tomlinson's term, and entered its first slate of candidates in the 1829 election. Governor Tomlinson was appointed to the U.S. Senate by the Assembly in 1830, and so resigned the governorship on March 2, 1831. Tomlinson served in the Senate from 1831 until 1837. On April 5, 1837, he became the first president of the Housatonic Railroad Company. Tomlinson died on October 8, 1854 at his Fairfield home, and was buried in Stratford's Congregational Cemetery. Bibliography: Jarvis Means Morse, *A Neglected Period of Connecticut's History, 1818-1850* (New Haven, 1933); Frederick Calvin Norton, *The Governors of Connecticut* (Hartford, 1905); Samuel Orcutt, *Henry Tomlinson, and his Descendants in America* (New Haven, 1891); William Howard Wilcoxson, *History of Stratford Connecticut, 1639-1969* (Stratford, 1969). Papers of Tomlinson are on deposit at the Connecticut Historical Society in Hartford.

PETERS, John Samuel, 1831-1833

Born on September 21, 1772 in Hebron, Connecticut, son of Bemslee, a farmer, land agent, and half-pay captain in London during the Revolutionary War, and Annis (Shipman) Peters; a member of the Protestant Episcopal Church. Brother of Clarinda, Annis, Bemslee (died in infancy), Desdemona, Mary Martha and Bemslee. Never married. He was largely self-educated. At age seven, he left home and worked on a farm; attended district schools in the winter and later taught school himself. In 1792, Peters began to study medicine and completed his education in Philadelphia four years later; he established his practice in Hebron. Served for some time as a surgeon in the state militia beginning in 1807. Peters occupied various local offices before he was elected to the Lower House of the General Assembly in May, 1810; reelected in 1816, and in 1817, became a clerk. Served in the State Senate, 1818-1823, and again in the Lower House from 1824 to 1826. Member of the State Constitutional Convention in 1818. Peters was elected Lieutenant Governor in 1827. In March 1831 Governor Gideon Tomlinson resigned to become a U.S. Senator, and Peters took over the responsibilities, but not the title of the Governor's office. That same month he was nominated for the higher post by a state convention of National Republicans. Peters was elected Governor by a vote of 12,819 out of a total 18,866 cast. As governor, Peters asked for improvement in the school system, but the legislators were more interested in national issues. There was a vacancy in the Lieutenant Governor's office in 1831, because the Senate and House were unable to agree on a winner. Governor Peters was reelected in 1832 by a large majority. The Assembly supported his ideas for internal improvements, but were unwilling to appropriate funds for that purpose. However, private enterprise was encouraged, and the state's first railroads were chartered in 1832. The following year Peters received a slight plurality of votes for reelection, but since no candidate had a majority, the choice was left to the Assembly, which awarded the office to Henry W. Edwards by a vote of 147 to 70, with ten abstentions. Peters then returned to his farm. For most of his life, he had been active in many educational, medical, and welfare organizations, which included his being president of the State Medical Society, and vice-president of the Connecticut Historical Society. Peters died on March 30, 1858, and was buried in St. Peter's Episcopal Churchyard, Hebron. Bibliography: Frederick C. Norton, *The Governors of Connecticut* (Hartford, 1905); Edmond F. and Eleanor B. Peters, *Peters of New England* (New York, 1903); Jarvis M. Morse, *A Neglected Period of Connecticut's History, 1818-1850* (New Haven, 1933); "Obituary," *New Haven Palladium* (April 1, 1858). Papers of Peters on deposit at the Connecticut State Library in Hartford.

EDWARDS, Henry Waggaman, 1833-1834, 1835-1838

Born in October 1779 in New Haven, Connecticut, son of Pierpont, a lawyer, Continental Congressman, Federal Judge, and founder of the state's Republican Party, and Frances (Ogden) Edwards; grandson of Jonathan Edwards, the Puritan theologian; a member of the Congregational Church. Brother of Mary (died young), Susan Johnson, Henry Waggaman (died young), Mary, John Stark, Moses Ogden, Henry Alfred Pierpont, Henrietta Frances, Horace and Sally. Married Lydia Miller on October 4, 1801; father of John Miller (died young), Pierpont, John Miller, Henry Pierpont, Alfred Henry Pierpont, Frances Hoyt, and Henrietta. Attended the College of New Jersey (Princeton University), and graduated in 1797. After attending Litchfield Law School, Edwards set up practice in New Haven. Served as clerk of the Lower House of the General Assembly during the October, 1818 session. Elected to the U.S. House of Representatives in 1819 as a Republican, and served until 1823, when he was appointed to the U.S. Senate. His liberal tendencies facilitated a party switch to the Jacksonian Democrats during the presidential election of 1824. Edwards remained in the Senate until the completion of his term in March, 1827. The following spring he entered the State Senate for a one-year term. In 1830, he was again elected to the Connecticut State House and served as Speaker for that year. He received the majority of votes for Lieutenant Governor in 1832, but was denied the post by a divided Assembly. In 1833, though Edwards received fewer popular votes than his opponent, Governor John S. Peters, he was elected Governor by a vote in the General Assembly of 147 to 70, with ten abstentions. As governor, Edwards gave some attention to the problems of manufacturing and the tariff. The Legislature, however, was concerned with the question of educating blacks. In 1833, they passed a discriminatory education law which was soon tested by a court case involving Prudence Crandall, the headmistress of a private academy for Negro girls in Canterbury, Connecticut. She was eventually found guilty and forced to close her school. Governor Edwards was defeated for reelection in 1834 by the Whig candidate, Samuel A. Foot, largely because of a recent business depression in the state. The final vote in the Legislature was 154 to 70, with three abstentions. Conditions had not improved by 1835, however, and Edwards was again elected Governor by a vote of 22,129 to 19,835. He was reelected in 1836 and 1837, polling each time about 53 percent of the total vote. Edwards' last three terms were marked by a substantial growth in the railroad industry; a geological survey of the state in 1835-36; and the abolition of imprisonment for debt under certain circumstances in 1837. Governor Edwards vetoed a bill in 1837 that was subsequently upheld. The first successful executive veto in twenty years, it made the legislators wary of too strong a governor. Edwards was denied the Democratic nomination in 1838. After his years as governor, Edwards returned to New Haven to live in retirement. He died on July 22, 1847 and was buried in New Haven's Grove Street Cemetery. Bibliography: F.W. Chapman, *The Trowbridge Family* (New Haven, 1872); Philip A. Grant, Jr., "Jacksonian Democracy Triumphs in Connecticut," *Connecticut Historical Society Bulletin,* vol. XXXIII, no. 4 (October, 1968); Burnham R. Moffat, *Pierrepont Genealogies from Norman Times to 1913* (privately printed, 1913); Jarvice Means Morse, *A Neglected Period of Connecticut's History, 1818-1850* (New Haven, 1933); Frederick Calvin Norton, *The Governors of Connecticut* (Hartford, 1905). There is no single repository for the "Edwards Papers."

FOOT, Samuel Augustus, 1834-1835

Born on November 8, 1780 in Cheshire, Connecticut, son of John, a Congregational minister, and Abigail (Hall) Foot. Brother of Abigail Sarah Hall, Mary Ann, Lucinda, John Alfred, Abigail Mary Ann, William Lambert, Roderick and Matilda. Married to Eudocia Hull on March 10, 1803; father of John Alfred, Andrew Hull Foote (he added an "e" to the family name), Roderick Augustus, Augustus Edwin, William Henry and Edward Dorr. Attended Yale College and graduated in 1797. Began studies at the Litchfield Law School, but severe headaches prevented his completion of them. Moved to New Haven, where he became a West Indies trader. When the Embargo Act and the War of 1812 almost destroyed him economically in 1813, he returned to the family farm in Cheshire. In 1817 and 1818, Foot was elected to the General Assembly and fought alongside the Tolerationist Republicans for a written state constitution; served as clerk of the Lower House during 1818. Elected to one term in the U.S. House of Representatives, 1819-1821, as a Republican. Returned to the State House of Representatives from 1821-23, after which he again entered Congress for another term. In May 1825 Foot returned once more to Connecticut, where he became representative from Cheshire to the General Assembly for the last time; served for that year and the next as Speaker. Member of the U.S. Senate from 1827-33; a resolution he proposed on December 29, 1829 instructing the Committee of Public Lands to inquire about limiting the sale of such lands, inspired the brilliant Webster-Hayne Debate. Foot was defeated for reelection to the Senate in 1833, but was instead elected to the House. The newly-formed Whig Party—emerging from the ruins of the National Republican Party—nominated him for Governor in 1834. Though he did not win a clear majority over Governor Henry W. Edwards, he was installed in the office by a legislative vote of 154 to 70, with three abstention. He resigned his congressional seat on May 9, 1834 to take up his gubernatorial duties. As governor, Foot was faced with a continuing economic depression which caused his defeat to former Governor Edwards in the 1835 election by a vote of 22,129 to 19,835. Foot then returned to his farm, making only one more public appearance, as a presidential elector on the Clay-Frelinghuysen ticket in 1844. Foot died in Cheshire on September 15, 1846 and was buried in Hillside Cemetery there. Bibliography: Abram W. Foote, *Foote Family* (Rutland, 1907); Nathaniel Goodwin, *The Foote Family* (Hartford, 1849); Jarvis Means Morse, *A Neglected Period of Connecticut's History, 1818-1850* (New Haven, 1933); Frederick Calvin Norton, *The Governors of Connecticut* (Hartford, 1905). There is no single repository for the "Foot Papers."

EDWARDS, Henry Waggaman, 1833-1834, 1835-1838

ELLSWORTH, William Wolcott, 1838-1842

Born on November 10, 1791 in Windsor, Connecticut, son of Oliver (Continental Congressman, delegate to the Constitutional Convention, and second Chief Justice of the U.S. Supreme Court), and Abigail (Wolcott) Ellsworth, both of whom were Congregationalists. Brother of Abigail, Oliver (died young), Oliver, Martin, William, Delia and Henry Leavitt (William's twin). Married Emily Webster, daughter of the lexicographer Noah Webster, on September 14, 1813; father of Pinckney Webster, Emily, Harriet, Oliver, Elizabeth (died young) and Elizabeth. Attended Yale College and graduated in 1810. After completing his studies at the Litchfield Law School, he was admitted to the bar in 1813, and moved to Hartford to establish a law practice. Appointed professor at Trinity College in 1827. Elected a Whig member of Congress in 1829 and served on the Judiciary Committee, which was then engaged in putting President Jackson's stand against nullification into effect; served on a Congressional Commission which investigated the U.S. Bank at Philadelphia. He resigned from Congress in June, 1834 to return to his law practice. Member of the Connecticut House of Representatives in 1835. The Whigs persuaded Ellsworth to accept their nomination for Governor in the spring of 1838. Due to the national depression, he defeated the Democratic candidate Seth Beers, by receiving 27,115 votes out of a total 50,101 cast. In the gubernatorial elections from 1839 to 1841, Ellsworth was reelected by margins ranging from 51.4 percent of the total vote in 1839 to 56 percent of the total vote in 1841. As governor, Ellsworth tried to interest the General Assembly in passing laws that would alleviate poverty and strengthen the severely weakened economy which had resulted from the Panic of 1837; however only minor legislation was enacted in this area. In 1838, the Assembly established a badly needed School Commission, but refused to make appropriations for a state normal school. A new system of voter registration was adopted in 1839. For the most part, public opinion did not support radical reform, and Ellsworth's four terms as governor were markedly conservative. By 1842, the national Whig Party was divided by President Tyler's unwillingness to heed party dictates, and this led to a loss of Whig strength in the state election that year. Though Democrat Chauncey F. Cleveland did not receive a popular majority over Governor Ellsworth, the legislature placed him in office by a vote of 139 to 68. Ellsworth then returned to his law practice and remained until 1847, when he was appointed an Associate Judge of the State Superior Court and Supreme Court of Errors. He retained this position until his retirement in 1861. Ellsworth died on January 15, 1868 and was buried in Hartford's Old North Cemetery. Bibliography: William R. Cutter, et al, eds., *Genealogical and Family History of the State of Connecticut* (New York, 1911); George H. Gould, *Sermon Preached at the Funeral of Hon. William W. Ellsworth* (Hartford, 1868); Jarvis Means Morse, *A Neglected Period of Connecticut's History, 1818-1850* (New Haven, 1933); Frederick Calvin Norton, *The Governors of Connecticut* (Hartford, 1905). Papers of Ellsworth are on deposit at Yale University in New Haven.

CLEVELAND, Chauncey Fitch, 1842-1844

Born on February 16, 1799 in Hampton, Connecticut, son of Silas, a farmer, and Lois (Sharpe) Cleveland; a member of the Congregational Church. Brother of Mason and John. Married to Diantha Hovey on December 13, 1821; father of John Cob and Delia Diantha; remarried to Helen Cornelia Litchfield on January 27, 1869. Attended public school until he started teaching in 1814. Began studying law at age seventeen and was admitted to the bar in August, 1819, establishing a practice in Hampton. A long military career culminated in his attainment of the rank of Major-General in the state infantry. He held a number of state and local offices, including State Attorney from 1833-38, and State Bank Commissioner in 1837. Elected to the Connecticut House of Representatives on the Democratic ticket in 1826, 1827, 1828, 1832, 1835 (Speaker), 1836 (Speaker), and 1838. Unsuccessful candidate for Congress in 1838 and 1840. In 1842 he was nominated for Governor by his party, and though he did not receive a popular majority over the incumbent, William W. Ellsworth, he was installed by a legislative vote of 139 to 68. Cleveland won reelection in 1843, defeating Whig Roger S. Baldwin by a vote of 27,416 to 25,401. As governor, Cleveland recommended an act abolishing imprisonment for debt, and another establishing a labor law which prevented children under fourteen from working over ten hours per day. Both of these measures were passed by the General Assembly, as was an act which authorized appropriations for an insane asylum, and an act which divided the state into four congressional districts. In another area, the legislature abolished the recently-enacted Voter Registration Law, and the newly-formed School Board, on the grounds that they were concessions to small town interests. During Governor Cleveland's second term, the Assembly liberalized divorce proceedings and extended to Jewish synagogues protective laws already applied to Christian churches. The Assembly completely ignored his pleas to eliminate capital punishment, however. Cleveland was denied reelection by the Legislature in 1844, by a vote of 116-93 in favor of Roger Sherman Baldwin, the Whig candidate. Cleveland then returned to his law practice until 1847, when he was again elected to the State House of Representatives. He retained this office until 1849, when he began a four-year term in Congress. Bitterly opposing slavery, he was an organizer of the state Republican Party. Appointed a delegate to the Washington Peace Congress, February 4-27, 1861. Member of the State House in 1863 (Speaker) and again in 1866. After the war, Cleveland returned to the Democratic Party. He remained active at the bar until the age of eighty. Cleveland died on June 6, 1887 and was buried in Hampton South Cemetery. Bibliography: Edmund James Cleveland, *The Genealogy of the Cleveland Families* (Hartford, 1899); Allen B. Lincoln, *A Modern History of Windham County, Connecticut* (Chicago, 1920); Jarvis Means Morse, *A Neglected Period of Connecticut's History, 1818-1850* (New Haven, 1933); Frederick Calvin Norton, *The Governors of Connecticut* (Hartford, 1905). There is no single repository for the "Cleveland Papers."

BALDWIN, Roger Sherman, 1844-1846

Born on January 4, 1793, in New Haven, Connecticut, son of Simeon, a lawyer, judge, congressman, and Mayor of New Haven, and Rebecca (Sherman) Baldwin. Brother of Rebecca, Ebenezer, and Simeon; stepson of Elizabeth (Sherman) Burr Baldwin, his aunt, and half-brother of Simeon, Elizabeth, Charles (died young), Martha, and Charles; grandson of Roger Sherman, the only man to have signed all of America's founding documents; a member of the Congregational Church. Married to Emily Perkins on October 25, 1820; father of Edward Law, Elizabeth Wooster, Roger Sherman, Ebenezer Simeon, Henrietta Perkins, George William, Emily Frances, Ebenezer Charles and Simeon Eben (Governor of Connecticut, 1911-15). Attended Yale University and graduated in 1811. Studied law at the Litchfield Law School, and was admitted to the bar in 1814, establishing his practice in New Haven. His most famous case involved a defense of the slaves who had mutinied against the Spanish ship, the *Amistad*, in 1839. After killing the captain and three of the crew, the slaves demanded that they be returned to Africa. However, the ship was steered into Long Island Sound, and was captured by U.S. officials. Baldwin took the case in 1840, and eventually appealed to the U.S. Supreme Court where he was aided by former President John Quincy Adams. The court finally granted the slaves their freedom in 1841. Member of the State Senate in 1837 and 1838, and of the Lower House in 1840 and 1841. Nominated for the governorship in 1843 on the Whig ticket, but was defeated. He ran again in 1844, and was installed by a legislative vote of 116-93 over incumbent Chauncey Fitch Cleveland. Baldwin won reelection in 1845, defeating Democrat Isaac Toucey by a vote of 29,508 to 26,258. As governor, Baldwin tried to persuade the Assembly to act favorably on black suffrage, but his efforts were wasted. For the most part, local political issues were forgotten in lieu of the controversy surrounding the annexation of Texas and the presidential election of 1844. The abolition of the property qualification for voting was the most important new enactment during Baldwin's second term in 1845, but the increase in the number of new voters was so nominal that it was hardly noticed. He did not stand for reelection in 1846. Baldwin returned to his law practice and remained until November 1, 1847, when he was chosen to fill an unexpired term as U.S. Senator. While in the Senate he actively opposed slavery, and made an impressive speech against the Fugitive Slave Act in 1850. Unwilling to commit himself publicly to the stand he would take on important issues in the future, Baldwin angered influential state leaders and was not reelected in 1851. He became active in the formation of the Republican Party and was a delegate to the Washington Peace Conference, February 4-27, 1861. Baldwin died on February 19, 1863 and was buried in New Haven's Grove Street Cemetery. Bibliography: Charles Candee Baldwin, *The Baldwin Genealogy: From 1500 to 1881* (Cleveland, 1881); Simeon E. Baldwin, "Roger Sherman Baldwin, 1793-1863," in *Great American Lawyers,* edited by William Draper Lewis (Philadelphia, 1908); William R. Cutter, et al, *Genealogical and Family History of the State of Connecticut* (New York, 1911); Jarvis Means Morse, *A Neglected Period of Connecticut's History, 1818-1850* (New Haven, 1933); Frederick Calvin Norton, *The Governors of Connecticut* (Hartford, 1905). Papers of Baldwin on deposit at Yale University in New Haven.

TOUCEY, Isaac, 1846-1847

Born on November 5, 1796 in Newtown, Connecticut, son of Zalmon, a farmer, and Phebe (Boothe) Toucey; a member of the Episcopal Church. Brother of Walter, Eliza, William and Phebe. Married to Catherine Nichols on October 28, 1827; no children. Received a private education before he began to study law; was admitted to the bar in 1818; moved to Hartford where he set up practice. Served as State Attorney for Hartford County, 1822-1835. Elected to Congress in 1835 on the Democratic ticket and served on the Committees of the Judiciary and Foreign Affairs; defeated for reelection in 1839; returned to his practice until 1842, when he was again State Attorney for two years. Unsuccessful gubernatorial candidate in 1845. Nominated again in 1846, and though he did not receive a popular majority, he was installed by a legislative vote of 124 to 117. As governor, Toucey pushed through an Anti-Bribery Bill aimed at stopping dishonest electoral practices. He also attempted to achieve reform in the areas of temperance, schools, and tax equalization, but was not as successful with these, and obtained only minor concessions. Toucey vetoed a bill aimed at constructing a bridge over the Connecticut River at Middletown, and though he was eventually overruled by the Legislature, he angered influential Democrats and was not renominated for Governor in 1847. Soon after completing his term, Toucey was appointed Attorney General by President Polk, serving from June 29, 1848 to March 4, 1849; he also served as Acting Secretary of State in the absence of James Buchanan for part of that time. He was elected to the State Senate in 1850 and to the Lower House of the Assembly in 1852; resigned on May 13, 1852 to become a U.S. Senator. As senator, he supported the Fugitive Slave Act; favored repeal of the Missouri Compromise; and approved the Kansas-Nebraska Bill. Toucey was appointed Secretary of the Navy at the completion of his senatorial term by President Buchanan, and repeatedly asked Congress for appropriations for building up the navy's strength. He sponsored a highly successful expedition to Paraguay in 1855. At the time of South Carolina's secession on December 20, 1860, the main strength of the navy was not available for immediate recall, and Toucey was severely criticized; however he was exonerated of any wrongdoing by a Senate investigation in 1864. Served two days as interim Secretary of the Treasury when Howell Cobb resigned to join the Southern cause on December 10, 1860. The March following the close of President Buchanan's term, Toucey returned to his law practice. Toucey died on July 30, 1869 and was buried in Cedar Hill Cemetery in Hartford. Bibliography: Jarvis Means Morse, *A Neglected Period of Connecticut's History, 1818-1850* (New Haven, 1933); Frederick Calvin Norton, *The Governors of Connecticut* (Hartford, 1905); A. Reed Schroeder, "Isaac Toucey of Connecticut," unpublished Master's Thesis, Trinity College, Hartford, 1946; "Obituary," *Hartford Courant* (July 31, 1869). Papers of Toucey on deposit at the Connecticut State Library in Hartford.

BISSELL, Clark, 1847-1849

Born on September 7, 1782 in Lebanon, Connecticut, son of Joseph William, a farmer, and Betsey (Clark) Bissell, both of whom were Congregationalists. Brother of Leverett, Emery and William. Married to Sally Sherwood on April 29, 1811;

father of Samuel Burr Sherwood, Edward Clark, George Augustus, Mary Elizabeth, Charlotte Charity and Arthur Henry. Attended Yale University and graduated in 1806. Taught school while a student, and continued his teaching after graduation, when he took a position tutoring in Maryland. After one year he returned to Connecticut, taught, and began to study law with his future father-in-law, Samuel Burr Sherwood; admitted to the bar in 1809 and established a practice in Norwalk. Elected to the State House of Representatives in 1829. That same year, he became an Associate Judge of the Supreme Court of Errors and held that office until 1839 when, because of an inadequate salary, he was forced to resign. He served in the Assembly again in 1841, and for the next two years was a member of the State Senate. Nominated for Governor in 1846 on the Whig ticket, but was defeated by a legislative vote. Elected the following year over Democrat Thomas Whittlesey by receiving 30,137 out of a total 59,674 votes cast; reelected in 1848, defeating Democrat George S. Catlin by a vote of 30,717 to 28,525. Governor Bissell requested that progressive measures be enacted in the areas of taxation, education, and liquor prohibition. His efforts, however, were all but wasted on a legislature which looked to former Governor William W. Ellsworth for guidance rather than to Bissell. Much of the 1847 session was spent in discussing a proposed bridge that was to span the Connecticut River at Middletown; nothing came of the heated debates on the subject at that time. Later that year an amendment to the Connecticut Constitution was presented to the people which permitted black suffrage. The amendment received support from Democrats, but failed to pass by a wide margin. During Bissell's second year in office, there were so many proposals for altering the thirty-year-old constitution that the Assembly actually considered drawing up a new document rather than amending the existing one. Bissell made a political blunder in 1848 when he vetoed a resolution on divorce. This was subsequently interpreted to be an attempt to undermine legislative authority, and he was not renominated for Governor in 1849. Bissell had been appointed Kent Professor of Law at Yale in 1847 and continued in that position until 1855, when age and ill health compelled him to resign. In the meantime, he also served once more in the State House in 1850. Bissell died on September 15, 1857 and was buried in Norwalk's Union Cemetery. Bibliography: D. Hamilton Hurd, *History of Fairfield County, Connecticut* (Philadelphia, 1881); Edward Payson Jones, "Genealogy of the Descendants of John Bissell of Windsor, Connecticut by 1640," Typescript at the Connecticut Historical Society, Hartford, 1939; Jarvis Means Morse, *A Neglected Period of Connecticut's History, 1818-1850* (New Haven, 1933); Frederick Calvin Norton, *The Governors of Connecticut* (Hartford, 1905). There is no single repository for the "Bissell Papers."

TRUMBULL, Joseph, 1849-1850

Born on December 7, 1782 in Lebanon, Connecticut, son of David, a farmer, legislator, and Assistant Commissary General of the United States, and Sarah (Backus) Trumbull; grandson of Jonathan Trumbull, Sr. (Governor of Connecticut, 1797-1809); a member of the Congregational Church. Brother of Sarah, Abigail, John, Jonathan and Jonathan George Washington. Married to Harriet Champion on March 6, 1818; father of Henry Champion; after his first wife's death, remarried her cousin, Eliza Brainard Storrs, on December 1, 1824; father of Eliza Storrs. Attended Yale University and graduated in 1801. Studied law with his brother-in-law, William Trumbull Williams, but soon moved to Ohio's Western Reserve and was admitted to the bar in the summer of 1802. He returned to Connecticut that fall, and was admitted to the bar in Windham County the following year. In May 1804, he moved to Hartford to practice his profession. Served as president of the Hartford Bank from 1828-39. Member of the Connecticut House of Representatives in 1832. He was chosen to fill an unexpired term in Congress from 1834-35, and was later elected to two congressional terms of his own. In 1848, he returned to the Connecticut State House. The Whig Party nominated Trumbull for Governor in 1849, and though he did not receive a popular majority over all other candidates, he was installed in office by a legislative vote of 122 to 110, with six abstentions. As governor, Trumbull's term was not particularly notable. Many public bills of little consequence were acted upon, but only the measure establishing a state normal school was of any lasting importance. He did not stand for reelection in 1850. Trumbull returned once more to the State House of Representatives in 1851, and then spent his remaining years in charitable pursuits. Trumbull died on August 4, 1861 and was buried in the Old North Cemetery in Hartford. Bibliography: Jarvis Means Morse, *A Neglected Period of Connecticut's History, 1818-1850* (New Haven, 1933); Frederick Calvin Norton, *The Governors of Connecticut* (Hartford, 1905); Francis Bacon Trowbridge, *The Champion Genealogy* (New Haven, 1891). There is no single repository for the "Trumbull Papers."

SEYMOUR, Thomas Henry, 1850-1853

Born on September 29, 1807 in Hartford, Connecticut, son of Henry, a broker and major of the Governor's Horse Guards, and Jane (Ellery) Seymour; a member of the Episcopal Church. Brother of William Ellery and Jane Ellery. Never married. Attended public school in Hartford, and in 1829 graduated from Captain Alden Partridge's Military Institute in Middletown; admitted to the bar in 1833. Served as Probate Judge for the district, 1836-39. Seymour was a member of the Hartford Light Guard for some years, and was its Commander from 1837-1841. Concurrent with his military career, he edited the *Jeffersonian,* a leading Democratic newspaper, 1837-38. Elected to the Twenty-eighth Congress, serving in the House from 1843 to 1845. During the Mexican War, Seymour distinguished himself in the Battle of Chapultepec by leading his regiment to victory, and was subsequently made a Colonel on September 13, 1847. Unsuccessful Democratic candidate for governor in 1849. Renominated the following year, running against LaFayette S. Foster, a Whig. The election focused on the issue of territorial expansion and slavery. When no candidate received a popular majority, the contest was thrown into the Assembly where states' rights Democrats were aided by anti-slavery Free Soilers in appointing Seymour Governor by a vote of 122 to 108, with seven abstentions. Seymour was reelected three times, winning by legislative vote in 1851, and by popular vote in 1852 and 1853. The Compromise of 1850, especially the measure dealing with fugitive slaves, aroused deep anti-slavery feelings in the state. Though the Assembly opposed it, the Democratic convention of 1851 subtly upheld the Compromise by affirming its constitutionality. The main issue of 1851, however, was Temperance, not slavery. In 1851, Democrats opposed prohibition as an infringement of personal rights and ignored the same issue in 1852, yet were victorious in both elections. Governor Seymour served as a presidential elector in 1852, supporting Franklin Pierce. In gratitude Pierce appointed him Minister to Russia in April, 1853, only one month into the governor's fourth term; Seymour resigned his office effective October 13, 1853. Seymour spent four years in Russia before relinquishing his post and returning home. Nominated for Governor in 1860, after a heated campaign, he lost to Republican William A. Buckingham in an extremely close election. During the entire course of the Civil War, Seymour fought for reconciliation with the South and headed the Connecticut Peace Democrats. As a member of the Assembly in 1861, he offered resolutions for peace that were heavily defeated in that body, but highly praised by the Confederacy. He was nominated for Governor in 1863, and was once more defeated by a small margin. Received thirty-eight votes for President at the Democratic National Convention in 1864. Seymour died on September 3, 1868 and was buried in Cedar Hill Cemetery in Hartford. Bibliography: Frederick Calvin Norton, *The Governors of Connecticut* (Hartford, 1905); George Dudley Seymour, *A History of the Seymour Family* (New Haven, 1939); J. Robert Lane, *A Political History of Connecticut during the Civil War* (Washington, 1941); John Niven, *Connecticut for the Union* New Haven, 1965); John E. Talmadge, "A Peace Movement in Civil War Connecticut," *New England Quarterly,* vol. XXXVII, no. 3 (September, 1964). Papers of Seymour are on deposit at the Connecticut Historical Society in Hartford.

POND, Charles Hobby, 1853-1854

Born on April 26, 1781 in Milford, Connecticut, son of Charles, a shipper and Captain in the Revolutionary War, and Martha (Miles) Pond; stepson of Kate (Dewitt) Pond; a member of the Congregational Church. Brother of Martha, Sarah, Charlotte, Mary, Adam and Susan. Married to Catharine Dickinson on March 9, 1809; father of Charles, Martha Miles, Mary F., Maria Letitia, Catharine Wales, Charlotte and Susan Augustus. Attended Yale University and graduated in 1802. Studied law with Roger Minot Sherman of Fairfield, but did not practice after being admitted to the bar because of failing health. Extended sea voyage was decided upon, and after two pleasure trips, he followed the sea for several years as a supercargo on his father's ships, and later as captain. From 1818 to 1819 Pond was an Associate Judge of the New Haven County Court. At the end of this service, he became Sheriff of that county, serving until 1834. Two years later he was again appointed an Associate Judge for that year and for the year following. A Jeffersonian Republican in his early years, Pond was a staunch Democrat in 1850 when he was elected to the office of Lieutenant Governor. Defeated in 1851 for that position, he was the successful candidate in 1852 and 1853. Governor Thomas Henry Seymour resigned his office effective October 13, 1853 to become Minister to Russia, and Pond was elevated to the governorship. Pond's term as governor was uneventful, and the only notable excitement arose in March, 1854 when the Kansas-Nebraska Bill passed the U.S. Senate, creating a furor in the state. He did not stand for reelection in 1854. Pond retired to his Milford home and spent the rest of his life in retirement. During the pre-Civil War years he was known to be a pro-slavery Democrat, but he did not publicly voice his beliefs. Pond died on April

28, 1861 and was buried in Milford Cemetery. Bibliography: Edward Doubleday Harris, *A Genealogical Record of Daniel Pond, and his Descendents* (Boston, 1873); Frederick Calvin Norton, *The Governors of Connecticut* (Hart, 1905); Daniel Streator Pond, *A Genealogical Record of Samuel Pond, and his Descendants* (New London, 1875); "Obituary," *New Haven Daily Register* (April 29, 1861). There is no single repository for the "Pond Papers."

DUTTON, Henry, 1854-1855

Born on February 12, 1796 in Plymouth, Connecticut, son of Thomas, a house joiner and farmer, and Thankful (Punderson) Dutton; a member of the Congregational Church. Brother of Matthew Rice, Chester, Anna, Betsey, Daniel Punderson, Sally, Lucy, Laura and Alma. Married to Elizabeth Elliott Joy on September 8, 1823; father of Ann Eliza, Mary Elliott, Harriet Joy and Henry Melzar. Attended Yale College, and graduated in 1818; studied law under Roger M. Sherman of Fairfield, and was admitted to the bar in 1823. Concurrent with his studies, Dutton was principal of the Fairfield Academy for two years before serving as a tutor at Yale from 1821 to 1823. He set up his law practice in Newtown and was a delegate to the Connecticut House in 1828 and 1834. Moved to Bridgeport in 1837; served in the Lower House again in 1838 and 1839, and for a time was State's Attorney for Fairfield County. After ten years in Bridgeport, Dutton moved to New Haven, where he had been appointed Kent Professor of Law at Yale in 1847. Two years later he was selected to aid in the revision of the state statutes. Member of the State Senate in 1849 and of the Lower House the following year. Judge of the New Haven County Court, 1852-53. He was the unsuccessful Whig candidate for Governor in 1853, and though he received less than one-third of the popular vote for Governor the following year, he was victorious over the Democratic candidate, Samuel Ingham; a legislative coalition of Whigs, Free Soilers, and Prohibitionists placed him in office by a vote of 140 to 93 with eight abstentions. As governor, Dutton asked for condemnation of the Kansas-Nebraska Bill, a key issue in his election; the legislature complied, though it became law in May 1854 anyway. A bill for "the Defense of Liberty in this State" was also passed in hopes of preventing the successful execution of the Fugitive Slave Law. A Prohibition measure that declared illegal all traffic in "spiritous liquors for beverage purposes" was also enacted, but soon became unpopular. Dutton was renominated for Governor in 1855, but came in last in a field of three candidates, receiving only 9,161 votes. His opponents, Democrat Samuel Ingham and William T. Minor, the American or "Know Nothing" Party candidate, polled 27,290 and 28,078 votes respectively. Minor was the eventual victor in a legislative run-off. Dutton was the last of his party to hold the governor's office in Connecticut, as the Whigs soon dissolved, and he joined the newly-formed Republicans in 1856. Judge of the Superior Court and of the Supreme Court of Errors from 1861 until 1866, when he resigned because of age. Dutton died in New Haven on April 26, 1869 and was buried in Grove Street Cemetery. Bibliography: Frederick Calvin Norton, *The Governors of Connecticut* (Hartford, 1905); Edward E. Atwater, *A History of the City of New Haven to the Present Time* (New York, 1887); Gilbert Cope, *Genealogy of the Dutton Family of Pennsylvania* (West Chester, 1871); J. Robert Lane, *A Political History of Connecticut During the Civil War* (Washington, 1941); Joshua L. Chamberlain, *Universities and Their Sons: Yale University* (Boston,

1900); Obituaries in *New Haven Register* (April 27, 1869) and *Connecticut Courant* (May 1, 1869). There is no single repository for the "Dutton Papers."

MINOR, William Thomas, 1855-1857

Born on October 3, 1815 in Stamford, Connecticut, son of Simeon Hinman, a legislator and judge, and Catharine (Lockwood) Minor; a member of the Congregational Church. Brother of James Hinman and George Albert. Married Mary Catherine Leeds on April 16, 1849; father of Charles William and Emily Catharine Lockwood. Attended Yale College, graduating in 1834. Taught school while studying law, and was admitted to the bar in 1841. That same year he began the first of four successive terms in the State House of Representatives as a Whig; again reelected in 1846, 1847, and 1852. Member of the State Senate and of the Fairfield County Court in 1854. Nominated for the governorship in 1855 on the American or "Know-Nothing" ticket; that party, largely made up of former Whigs, was strongly nativistic and anti-Catholic, and succeeded in placing Minor in office over Democrat Samuel Ingham by a legislative vote of 177 to 70. Incumbent Henry Dutton, the Whig candidate, received only 9,161 popular votes out of a total 64,551 cast. Minor took office on May 3, 1855 and immediately espoused nativist ideas, asking for a longer period of residency before naturalization. The Assembly quickly showed its support for this policy by passing a measure that denied suffrage to men unable to read the State Constitution. Governor Minor further angered immigrants by disbanding six military companies consisting mostly of Irishmen. The issue of slavery, largely ignored by the Know-Nothings, was suddenly brought to the fore in June, 1855; a national conference of the party passed certain pro-slavery resolutions, causing Connecticut's delegates to denounce the action. Reelected the following year, Governor Minor renewed his attack on foreigners, but little was accomplished during that session. The Republican Party was organized in the state in 1856 and found a coalition with Connecticut's Know-Nothings helpful in furthering their anti-slavery views. In 1857 Minor was not renominated, since there was no separate Know-Nothing Convention. Minor returned to his law practice until 1864 when he became U.S. Consul to Havana for three years. In 1868, he was appointed a judge of the State Superior Court and was once more a member of the House. Resigned his judgeship in 1873 and was the unsuccessful Republican candidate for U.S. Senator that year; the next year Minor lost an election bid for State Senator. In 1879, he was a member of a commission that settled a long-standing boundary dispute with New York. Minor died on October 13, 1889 and was buried in Stamford's Woodland Cemetery. Bibliography: Frederick Calvin Norton, *The Governors of Connecticut* (Hartford, 1905); J. Robert Lane, *A Political History of Connecticut during the Civil War* (Washington, 1941); E.B. Huntington, *History of Stamford, Connecticut* (Stamford, 1868); Frederic A. Holden and B. Dunbar Lockwood, *Colonial and Revolutionary History of the Lockwood Family in America from A.D. 1630* (Philadelphia, 1889); Alfred C. O'Connell, "The Birth of the G.O.P. in Connecticut," *Connecticut Historical Society Bulletin,* vol. XXVI, no. 2 (April, 1961). There is no single repository for the "Minor Papers."

HOLLEY, Alexander Hamilton, 1857-1858

Born on August 12, 1804 in Salisbury, Connecticut, son of John Milton, a miner and manufacturer, and Sally (Porter) Holley; a member of the Congregational Church. Brother of Maria, John Milton, Mary Ann (died young), Hannah, George W., Sally Porter, Mary Ann and an unnamed infant boy. Married to Jane M. Lyman on October 4, 1831; father of Alexander Lyman; after his first wife's death, remarried to Marcia Coffing on September 10, 1835; father of John M., Milton, William Ralston, John Coffing, George W., and Maria C.; remarried again to Sarah Coit Day, on November 11, 1856. Attended public schools in Massachusetts, Connecticut, and New York, but never entered college due to delicate health. At age sixteen, he entered his father's business and remained in that line of work for over forty years. Served in the state militia as Adjutant, Brigade Inspector, and finally Division Inspector. Delegate to the Whig National Convention of 1844. That year he began manufacturing pocket cutlery, and ten years later became president for life of the newly-organized Holley Manufacturing Company. He also had interests in banking; he was director and president of the Iron Bank at Salisbury. A railroad enthusiast, Holley promoted rail lines in New York and Connecticut, serving as director of the Connecticut Western. Holley was elected to one term as Lieutenant Governor in 1854 on the Whig ticket. Soon afterward, he joined the nativist American or "Know-Nothing" Party. In 1857 Holley was the gubernatorial candidate of the Union Party, a coalition of "Know-Nothings" and Republicans unified by the slavery issue and by a desire to defeat the Democrats. Holley was victorious over Democrat Samuel Ingham by a vote of 31,702 to 31,156, with fifty votes scattered. Inaugurated on May 6, 1857, Governor Holley immediately urged that newly-naturalized citizens be required to wait a year before receiving the vote. In another area, the governor and legislature denounced the recent Supreme Court ruling on the Dred Scott case, ascribing it to Democratic pro-slavery maneuverings. The Lecompton Constitution, currently a question in Kansas, was seen to be yet another example of slavery's aggressive expansionism, and was denounced by Connecticut Unionists. The governor's party was no longer a unified coalition by 1858; by that year it had formally adopted the name and principles of the Republican Party. Since the new organization wished to elect party stalwarts rather than former Know-Nothings, Holley was not renominated. Holley then returned to his home and spent the remainder of his life in charitable pursuits and in travelling. He died on October 2, 1887 and was buried in Salisbury Cemetery. Bibliography: Frederick Calvin Norton, *The Governors of Connecticut* (Hartford, 1905); J. Robert Lane, *A Political History of Connecticut during the Civil War* (Washington, 1941); Sarah Coit Day Holley, *Memorial of Alexander Hamilton Holley* (privately printed, 1888); Henry Porter Andrews, comp., *The Descendants of John Porter of Windsor, Conn., 1635-9* (Saratoga Springs, 1893); *History of Litchfield County, Connecticut* (Philadelphia, 1881); Alfred C. O'Connell, "The Birth of the G.O.P. in Connecticut," *Connecticut Historical Society Bulletin*, vol. XXVI, no. 2 (April, 1961). Papers of Holley are on deposit at the Connecticut Historical Society in Hartford.

BUCKINGHAM, William Alfred, 1858-1866

Born on May 28, 1804 in Lebanon, Connecticut, son of Samuel, a farmer and fisherman, and Joanna (Matson) Buckingham; a member of the Congregational Church. Brother of Abigail, Lucy Ann, Samuel Matson, Samuel Giles and Israel Matson. Married Eliza Ripley on September 27, 1830; father of William Ripley and Eliza Coit. Attended Bacon Academy, but did not attend college. Buckingham tried his hand at surveying and taught school for a year, but at eighteen, he returned to his father's farm. He served in the cavalry for a short time. In 1822, Buckingham moved to Norwich to clerk in his uncle's dry goods store. Four years later after a brief clerkship in New York, he returned to Norwich and opened his own business. In 1830 he began the manufacturing of ingrain carpeting, and eighteen years later he relinquished this enterprise to help organize the Hayward Rubber Company. Mayor of Norwich in 1849, 1850, 1856, and 1857, having previously been Town Treasurer and a member of the City Council. A Whig until the dissolution of that party in 1856, he was thereafter a Republican. In the 1858 gubernatorial election, Buckingham defeated Democrat James T. Pratt by a vote of 36,298 to 33,544, with 285 votes scattered. Governor Buckingham took office on May 5, 1858, in the midst of a financial panic and devoted much of his energy toward relieving it. In 1860 a visit to the state by Abraham Lincoln contributed to Buckingham's narrow victory over former Governor Thomas H. Seymour. Due to the voting irregularities of that year, certain vague electoral laws subsequently were repealed. For some time prior to the outbreak of the Civil War, Buckingham preached preparedness, but when the split finally came, the state was caught off guard. The governor took immediate action, and raised more than enough volunteers to fill Connecticut's share of the President's request for troops. Finances in April, 1861 were a problem, since the Assembly was not in session. Buckingham began borrowing money in his own name before the legislature came to his aid by granting him $4,000,000 to raise and outfit troops. A draft was authorized that summer, but numerous loopholes prevented its enforcement. In 1863 the Federal Conscription Act led to rioting in many states. In order to keep the peace, Buckingham emptied state arsenals and delivered weapons to responsible citizens; when ordered to give account, he successfully defended his action. Ratification of the Thirteenth Amendment was achieved in Connecticut without a dissenting vote; the Democrats however were permitted to abstain. After eight terms, Buckingham declined renomination in 1866. Buckingham entered the U.S. Senate on March 4, 1869; he served as chairman of the Committee on Indian Affairs, and was a member of the Commerce Committee. Buckingham died on February 5, 1875, before completing his term, and was buried in Yantic Cemetery in Norwich. Bibliography: Frederick Calvin Norton, *The Governors of Connecticut* (Hartford, 1905); Samuel G. Buckingham, *The Life of William A. Buckingham, the War Governor of Connecticut* (Springfield, 1894); John Niven, *Connecticut for the Union: The Role of the State in the Civil War* (New Haven, 1965); J. Robert Lane, *A Political History of Connecticut during the Civil War* (Washington, 1941); Robert G. Armstrong, *Historic Lebanon: Highlights of an Historic Town* (Lebanon, 1950); W.J. Finan, "William A. Buckingham, Civil War Governor of Connecticut," *The Lure of the Litchfield Hills,* vol. XXI, no. 1 (June, 1961); "Obituary," *New York Times,* (February 5, 1875). Papers of Buckingham are on deposit at the Connecticut State Library in Hartford.

HAWLEY, Joseph Roswell, 1866-1867

Born on October 31, 1826 in Stewartsville, North Carolina, son of Francis, a minister, and Mary (McLeod) Hawley, a member of the Congregational Church. Brother of Mary Ann, Diademia, and an unnamed infant. Married to Harriet Ward Foote on December 25, 1855; no children, though they adopted Mrs. Hawley's niece, Margaret Foote; remarried Edith Ann Horner on November 15, 1887; father of Marion and Edith. Moved to Hartford in 1837, and after studying there and in New York, he graduated from Hamilton College in 1847. He taught school and read law until he was admitted to the bar in 1850. Two years later, he was a delegate to the Free Soil National Convention and became the editor of a local abolitionist newspaper. In 1856, the state Republican Party was organized in his home. That same year, his paper merged with the *Hartford Evening Press,* the party's new organ, and by 1857 he was its editor and part owner, having quit his law practice. Hawley was one of Connecticut's first volunteers at the outbreak of the Civil War, entering the army on April 22, 1861. He participated in thirteen battles and was the Military Governor of Wilmington, North Carolina from March to June, 1865; he achieved the rank of Major General and was discharged from service on January 15, 1866. Nominated as the Republican gubernatorial candidate in 1866, Hawley defeated his Democratic opponent, James E. English, by a vote of 43,974 to 43,433 with ten votes scattered. As governor, Hawley adhered to the tenets of the Radical Republicans, opposing President Johnson's administrative policies. The legislative session that year marked the beginning of a battle between railroad and shipping interests in the state. The railroads wanted to bridge the Connecticut River at its mouth, but the shippers feared that this would interfere with their own navigation of the river, and successfully blocked the proposal. A recession hurt Governor Hawley's reelection bid in 1867, and he was defeated by James E. English by a vote of 46,578 to 47,565 with eleven votes scattered. Hawley resumed his editorial career in 1867, and that year merged his paper with the *Hartford Courant,* becoming its editor. In 1872 Hawley was appointed to the House of Representatives. Defeated for reelection in 1874, he reentered Congress in 1879 for a term. He was president of the U.S. Centennial Commission from 1872 to 1877, and also entered the U.S. Senate in 1881, serving, among other appointments, as chairman of the Civil Service Committee and of a select committee on warships. He declined renomination in 1904, completing his term two weeks before his death. Hawley died on March 18, 1905 in Washington, D.C. and was buried in Hartford's Cedar Hill Cemetery. Bibliography: Frederick Calvin Norton, *The Governors of Connecticut* (Hartford, 1905); Albert D. Putnam, editor, *Major General Joseph R. Hawley, Soldier and Editor (1826-1905): Civil War Military Letters* (n.p., 1964); Elias S. Hawley, *The Hawley Record* (Buffalo, 1890); L.P. Brockett, *Men of Our Day* (Philadelphia, 1872); John Niven, *Connecticut for the Union: The Role of the State in the Civil War* (New Haven, 1965); John Nicholson, "New England Idealism in the Civil War: The Military Career of Joseph Roswell Hawley," Unpublished Ph.D. Dissertation, Claremont College, Claremont, 1970; "Obituaries" in the *Hartford Courant* and the *Washington Post* (March 18, 1905). The Hawley Papers are on deposit in the Library of Congress in Washington and the Connecticut Historical Society in Hartford.

ENGLISH, James Edward, 1867-1869, 1870-1871

Born on March 13, 1812 in New Haven, Connecticut, son of James, a cabinet maker and farmer, and Nancy (Griswold) English; a member of the Episcopal Church. Brother of Hannah Eliza, Benjamin, John, Charles Leverett, Henry, George Doolittle, Elizabeth Hannah, Nancy Maria, and Caroline Beers. Married to Caroline Augusta Fowler on January 25, 1835; father of Edward Fowler; after his first wife's death, he remarried to Anna Robinson Morris on October 7, 1885. At age eleven, English was hired out to a local farmer for two and one-half years. From 1826 to 1828, he attended school, learning the art of architectural drawing. In 1828 he became a carpenter's apprentice, and by 1833 he was able to open his own contracting business. Two years later he left this vocation to establish the English and Welch Lumber Company. Selectman of New Haven, 1836-48; Common Council member, 1848-49; delegate to the State Assembly in 1855; State Senator in 1856, 1857, and 1858. In 1853, having retired from the lumber business, English purchased a bankrupt clock factory, eventually making it one of the largest in the world. President of the Connecticut Savings Bank, 1857-90. Unsuccessful Democratic candidate for Lieutenant Governor in 1860. English was a "War Democrat" in Congress, 1861-1865, and supported the constitutional amendment abolishing slavery. Although an unsuccessful gubernatorial candidate in 1866, he defeated Governor Joseph R. Hawley the following year, receiving 47,565 votes of a total 94,154 cast. As governor, English tried to provide benefits for immigrants and workers, but was unsuccessful in vetoing an unfair election law and in supporting an eight-hour day. In a conflict which began during his predecessor's term, shipping and railroad interests continued to quarrel over a proposed bridge spanning the Connecticut River, but the dispute was settled in June, 1868, when two bridges were approved. English lost his second reelection bid in 1869 to Republican Marshall Jewell by a vote of 45,082 to 45,493. The next election, however, found English victorious over Governor Jewell, 44,128 to 43,285. The question of abolishing one of the two existing state capitals arose in 1870, but nothing was decided upon. The 1871 gubernatorial election once more pitted English against Jewell and although English received more votes, the outcome was extremely close and fraud was charged. A canvassing committee found incorrect totals and stolen votes, and eventually awarded Jewell an eighty-six vote majority out of the 94,860 total. English served in the State House in 1872 and three years later filled an unexpired Senate term. In 1876 and 1880 he was defeated for reelection; returned to business interests. English died on March 2, 1890 and was buried in Evergreen Cemetery in New Haven.
Bibliography: Frederick Calvin Norton, *The Governors of Connecticut* (Hartford, 1905); Anna Robinson Morris English, *In Memoriam: James Edward English, March 13, 1812-March 2, 1890* (privately printed, 1891); Everett Gleason Hill, *A Modern History of New Haven and Eastern New Haven County* (New York, 1918); William Richard Cutter, editor, *Genealogical and Family History of the State of Connecticut* (New York, 1911); Rollin G. Osterweis, *Three Centuries of New Haven, 1638-1938* (New Haven, 1953); "Obituaries" in *New York Times* and *Hartford Daily Times* (March 3, 1890). There is no single repository for the "English Papers."

JEWELL, Marshall, 1869-1870, 1871-1873

Born on October 20, 1825 in Winchester, New Hampshire, son of Pliny, a tanner, and Emily (Alexander) Jewell; a member of the Congregational Church. Brother of Harvey, Maria, Pliny, Lyman B., Emily, Arthur, Charlotte A., Edmund and Charles A. Married to Esther E. Dickinson (or Dickerson) on October 6, 1852; father of Josephine M. and Florence W. He attended the common school while learning his father's trade. Left home at eighteen, and after four years in Woburn, Massachusetts, he turned his attention to telegraphy, moving to Boston in 1847. From Boston he moved to Rochester, New York, then to Akron, Ohio, where he had charge of a telegraph office. He was put in charge of constructing the line between Louisville and New Orleans and in 1849 returned north to supervise the Boston-New York line. The following year he located in Hartford, becoming a partner in his father's leather-belting business. During much of the 1850s and 1860s, he travelled worldwide for the firm. Director of the Phoenix Fire Insurance Company, the Travelers' Life Insurance Company, and the Hartford Bank; part owner of the *Hartford Evening Post;* president of the Jewell Pin Company, the Southern New England Telephone Company, and the United States Telegraph Association. Unsuccessful Republican candidate for State Senator in 1867 and for Governor in 1868. The following year Jewell defeated Governor James E. English, receiving 45,493 votes to English's 45,082 votes. Inaugurated on May 5, 1869, Jewell presided over the state's approval of the Fifteenth Amendment, guaranteeing the right to vote. When Connecticut's first Women's Suffrage Convention was held in September, the governor strongly endorsed improvements in education for women, and asked for legislation giving them equal rights to property. English regained the governor's office in 1870 by a vote of 44,128 to 43,285. The 1871 election was decided by the legislature, and a special canvassing committee report, as incorrect totals and stolen votes were discovered. Though English initially received more votes, the election went to Jewell by a vote of 47,473 to 47,373, with fourteen votes scattered. Governor Jewell's next two terms were marked by a struggle between Hartford and New Haven politicians, vying for the honor of having their city become the permanent state capital; however, no final decision was reached, and both cities continued to share this distinction until 1873. Jewell did not stand for reelection in 1873. Appointed Minister to Russia in 1873, he was recalled the next year to become President Grant's Postmaster General; served from August 24, 1874 to July 12, 1876, when he was asked to resign because of his support of a politically unpopular official. Chairman of the Republican National Convention in 1880. Jewell died on February 10, 1883 and was buried in Hartford's Cedar Hill Cemetery. Bibliography: Frederick Calvin Norton, *The Governors of Connecticut* (Hartford, 1905); Pliny Jewell and Joel Jewell, comps. *The Jewell Register* (Hartford, 1860); Orville H. Platt, *Address on the Life and Character of Hon. Marshall Jewell* (Washington, 1883); N.G. Osborn, *Men of Mark in Connecticut* (Hartford, 1908); J. Hammond Trumble, *Memorial History of Hartford County, Connecticut, 1633-1884* (Boston, 1886); William Richard Cutter, ed., *Genealogical and Family History of the State of Connecticut* (New York, 1911); "Obituary," *Hartford Daily Courant* (February 12, 1883). There is no single repository for the "Jewell Papers."

ENGLISH, James Edward, 1867-1869, 1870-1871

JEWELL, Marshall, 1868-1870, 1871-1873

INGERSOLL, Charles Roberts, 1873-1877

Born on September 16, 1821 in New Haven, Connecticut, son of Ralph Isaacs, a lawyer, Congressman and Minister to Russia, and Margaret Catherine Eleanor (Van den Heuval) Ingersoll; a member of the Episcopal Church. Brother of John Van den Heuval, Ralph Apothea, Colin Macrae, Grace Suzette, William A. and Justine Henrietta. Married to Virginia Gregory on December 18, 1847; father of Justine Henrietta, Charles V., Francis Gregory, Virginia Gregory, Margaret V. and Elizabeth Shaw. Attended Yale College; graduated in 1840; then travelled abroad for two years. Attended Yale Law School and was admitted to the bar in 1844; immediately entered his father's law office. Clerk of the State Assembly in 1846; member of that body in 1856, 1857, 1858, 1866 and 1871. Incorporator of the Connecticut Savings Bank in New Haven. Director of the New Haven Colony Historical Society from 1862. Ingersoll was the Democratic candidate for Governor in 1873 and was victorious over Republican Henry Haven by a vote of 45,075 to 39,245, with 2,542 votes going to a third candidate. Governor Ingersoll's administration was immediately beset by a serious financial panic and subsequent depression, the effects of which lasted for about six years. Hartford and New Haven had been co-capital cities until 1873, when Hartford became the sole seat of government; while a member of the Assembly in 1871, Ingersoll fought to have the honor bestowed on his native city instead. In 1875 a state constitutional amendment, doubling the governor's term of office to two years, was approved, and elections were moved back from April to November. Ingersoll declined renomination in 1876; his term was made to end in January, 1877 rather than in May, because of the recent electoral changes. Ingersoll then returned to his law practice and continued to plead cases in state and federal courts, as well as before the U.S. Supreme Court. While governor, he was an organizer of the State Bar Association in 1875 and served as its vice-president for some time. Ingersoll died on January 25, 1903 and was buried in Grove Street Cemetery in New Haven. Bibliography: Frederick Calvin Norton, *The Governors of Connecticut* (Hartford, 1905); Lillian Drake Avery, comp., *A Genealogy of the Ingersoll Family in America, 1629-1925* (New York, 1926); William Richard Cutter, ed., *Genealogical and Family History of the State of Connecticut* (New York, 1911); *Obituary Record of Graduates of Yale University Deceased during the Academical Year ending in June, 1903* (New Haven, 1903); "Obituary," *Hartford Daily Courant* (January 26, 1903). There is no single repository for the "Ingersoll Papers."

HUBBARD, Richard Dudley, 1877-1879

Born in Berlin, Hartford County, Connecticut on September 7, 1818; son of Lemuel and Elizabeth (Dudley) Hubbard. Married to Mary Juliana Morgan on December 2, 1845; father of three sons and three daughters. Graduated from Yale College in 1839; studied law; admitted to the bar in 1842; began his practice in Hartford, Connecticut. Member of the State House of Representatives, 1842-1855, and 1858; Prosecuting Attorney for Hartford County, 1846-1868; served in the United States Congress from 1867 to 1869; declined to be a candidate for renomination in 1868; resumed the practice of law in Hartford. On November 7, 1876, Hubbard was elected Governor of Connecticut, defeating H. Robinson, a Republican, by a vote of 61,934 to 58,514. A Democrat. Governor Hubbard was inaugurated on January 3, 1877. During his term legislation was passed giving a wife the right to acquire and control property equal to her husband's; other laws provided for the improvement of statutes relating to insurance companies and punished the dishonest handling of property belonging to corporations or to estates in trust. Also, a bill was passed to create a commission to supervise all reservoirs and dams in the state. Another bill created the State Board of Health, which was composed of six members to be appointed by the governor. Hubbard's term ended on January 9, 1879. He was unsuccessful in his bid for reelection in 1879, and returned to his law practice in Hartford, Connecticut. Hubbard died on February 28, 1884, and was buried in Cedar Hill Cemetery. Bibliography: Roy Glashan, *American Governors and Gubernatorial Elections, 1775-1975* (Stillwater, Minnesota, 1975); Congressional Quarterly, Inc. *Guide to U.S. Elections* (Washington, D.C., 1975); George L. Clark, *A History of Connecticut; Its People and Institutions* (New York, 1914); Frederick C. Norton, *The Governors of Connecticut* (Hartford, 1905).

ANDREWS, Charles Bartlett, 1879-1881

Born on November 4, 1836 in North Sunderland, Franklin County, Massachusetts, son of Erastus, a Baptist minister, and Almira (Bartlett) Andrews; a Baptist. Brother of Elisha B., and nine others. Married to Mary J. Carter in 1866; after her death, remarried to Sarah M. Wilson in 1870; father of one son. Attended Franklin Academy, Shelburne Falls, Massachusetts; graduated from Amherst College, 1858. Moved to Sherman, Connecticut, where Andrews taught school and studied law. he was admitted to the bar in 1861. He moved to Litchfield, Connecticut and entered into partnership with John M. Hubbard, 1863-1872. Elected to the State Senate, 1868, and 1869; served in the Lower House of the Connecticut Legislature, 1878; chairman of the Committee on Judiciary. In the November 5, 1878 general election for Governor, Andrews received 48,867 votes to 46,385 votes for Richard D. Hubbard, a Democrat, and 8,314 votes for C. Atwater, a National Party candidate. None of the candidates received a majority of the total votes cast, and the legislature decided the election in favor of Charles B. Andrews. A Republican. Governor Andrews took the oath of office on January 9, 1879. During his term the boundary line dispute between Connecticut and New York State was settled; the governor was given authority to nominate judges to the State Supreme Court; a law was passed regarding incorporation of joint-stock companies; and a new jury law was passed. Governor Andrews left office on January 5, 1881. Returned to his law practice; appointed Judge of the Connecticut Superior Court, 1882; Chief Justice, 1889-1901; delegate to the State Constitutional Convention, 1902. Andrews died on September 12, 1902 and was buried in Litchfield. Bibliography: Roy Glashan, *American Governors and Gubernatorial Elections, 1775-1975* (Stillwater, Minnesota, 1975); Congressional Quarterly, Inc. *Guide to U.S. Elections* (Washington, D.C., 1975); Frederick Calvin Norton, "The Governors of Connecticut" *The Connecticut Magazine,* vol. VIII, no. 2 (1903-1904); George L. Clark, *A History of Connecticut; Its People and Institutions* (New York, 1914).

BIGELOW, Hobart B., 1881-1883

Born in North Haven, New Haven County, Connecticut on May 16, 1834, son of Levi L., a farmer, and Belinda (Pierpont) Bigelow. Married to Eleanor Lewis on May 6, 1857; father of Frank L. and another son. Moved to Great Barrington, Massachusetts with his family about 1844; attended public schools and an academy in South Egremont, Massachusetts; left school to become an apprentice machinist; founded the Bigelow Manufacturing Company in New Haven, Connecticut, which was later organized as a corporation under the name of the Bigelow Company. Common councilman in 1863-1876. He was a member of the General Assembly in 1875, and served as Mayor of New Haven in 1879-1881. On November 2, 1880 Bigelow was elected Governor of Connecticut, defeating James E. English, a Democrat, by a vote of 67,070 to 64,293. A Republican. Governor Bigelow was inaugurated on January 5, 1881. During his administration acts were passed to prevent fraudulent registration for elections; to reduce tax on mutual life insurance companies; and to order fire-escapes built in all buildings where twelve or more persons were employed. Other legislation included the authorization of the Storrs Agricultural School and the provision for life-insurance companies to conduct accident insurance business. Governor Bigelow's term ended on January 3, 1883. He never held public office again, and devoted the rest of his life to his business interests. Bigelow died in New Haven on October 12, 1891. Bibliography: Roy Glashan, *American Governors and Gubernatorial Elections, 1775-1975* (Stillwater, Minnesota, 1975); Congressional Quarterly, Inc., *Guide to U.S. Elections* (Washington, D.C., 1975); George L. Clark, *A History of Connecticut; Its People and Institutions* (New York, 1914); Frederick C. Norton, *The Governors of Connecticut* (Hartford, 1905).

WALLER, Thomas MacDonald, 1883-1885

Born in 1840 in New York, N.Y., son of Thomas and Mary Armstrong, and brother of William, all of whom were Irish Catholic immigrants. His father was a manual worker. Both his parents and brother died before Thomas was nine years old. Married Charlotte Bishop of New London, and had six children, five of them sons (Tracey, Charles, Robert, John, and Martin) and one daughter (Elizabeth). In his youth, worked as a newsboy, and then as cabin boy on a coastwise ship. Adopted by New London, Connecticut merchant Robert Waller, who changed the boy's name. Attended Bartlett High School; read law; admitted to the bar in 1861. Served in the Connecticut Volunteers during the Civil War. Democrat. Served in Representative from New London to the State Legislature, 1867-1868. Waller was the Secretary of State of Connecticut from 1870 to 1871, and Mayor of New London from 1873 to 1879. Waller ran against Republican Morgan G. Bulkeley for the governorship in 1882, and received 59,014 votes against his opponent's 54,853. In his first term, he sought an increased budget for internal improvements and attempted to increase school levies, but in both instances, his efforts were blocked by the Republican majority in the Legislature. In 1884 he ran for reelection, receiving 67,910 votes to his Republican opponent, Henry B. Harrison's 66,274, with minor party candidates receiving 3,940. Since Waller lacked a majority of the total vote, the election was thrown into the State Legislature, which chose Harrison as Governor. Waller left office in 1885, and was appointed by President Grover Cleveland to be Consul-General in London. After his return to the United States in 1889, he formed a law firm, Waller, Cook & Wagner, with offices in New York and in New London. Waller attended the 1896 Democratic National Convention, where he was selected to respond to William Jennings Bryan's "Cross of Gold" speech. Unable to support Bryan, he left the party and joined the Gold Democrats. He returned to the mainstream Democratic Party in 1901, however, and for the rest of his life was active in its affairs, as well as in his private practice of law. Thomas Waller died on January 24, 1924, at Ocean Beach, Connecticut. Bibliography: Frederick Norton, *Governors of Connecticut* (Hartford, 1905); N. Osborn, ed., *Men of Mark in Connecticut* (Hartford, 1906); *Hartford Courant* (January 25, 1924).

HARRISON, Henry Baldwin, 1885-1887

Born on September 11, 1821 in New Haven, Connecticut, son of Ammi and Polly (Barney) Harrison; an Episcopalian. Married to Mary Elizabeth Osborne in 1856; they had no children. Attended the Lancastrian School in New Haven; privately tutored by George A. Thacher; graduated as valedictorian from Yale in 1846. Studied law at the Yale Law School and at a law office in New Haven. Admitted to the bar in 1848 and began law practice with Lucius G. Peck in New Haven. Elected as a Whig to the Connecticut House of Representatives in 1865 and 1873; unsuccessful gubernatorial candidate in 1874. Again elected to the Connecticut House of Representatives in 1884, serving as Speaker of the House. As the Republican gubernatorial candidate in the election of November 4, 1884, Harrison received 66,274 votes to 67,910 votes for his Democratic opponent, Governor Thomas M. Waller. Since neither candidate received fifty percent of the vote, Harrison was chosen Governor of Connecticut by the State Legislature; he was inaugurated on January 7, 1885. During his administration, the probate laws were compiled; compulsory education for children between the ages of eight and sixteen in the public schools (unless otherwise instructed) was initiated; a Bureau of Labor Statistics was created; and a state tax of two mills was imposed. Harrison left office in January 1887, upon the inauguration of Phineas C. Lounsbury, and retired to private life. Harrison died on October 29, 1901 at his home in New Haven, Connecticut. Bibliography: Forrest Morgan, *Connecticut as a Colony and State,* 4 vols. (Hartford, 1904); Albert E. Van Dusen, *Connecticut* (New York, 1961);

Congressional Quarterly, Inc., *Guide to U.S. Elections* (Washington, D.C., 1975); Roy Glashan, *American Governors and Gubernatorial Elections, 1775-1975* (Stillwater, Minnesota, 1975).

LOUNSBURY, Phineas Chapman, 1887-1889

Born on January 10, 1841 in Ridgefield, Connecticut, son of Nathan, a shoemaker, and Delia (Schofield) Lounsbury; a Methodist. Brother of George Edward Lounsbury, Governor of Connecticut, 1899-1901. Married Jennie Wright, daughter of Neziah Wright, in 1867; no children. Attended public and private schools in Connecticut; with his brother in 1861, established Lounsbury Brothers, Inc., a shoe factory in New Haven, Connecticut; in 1869 became a co-partner in Lounsbury, Matthewson & Company, another shoe factory, which was located in South Norwalk, Connecticut; elected to the State Legislature in 1874, representing Ridgefield until 1876. A Republican, Lounsbury sought the governorship in 1886. In the election he received 56,920 votes and his Democratic opponent, Edward Cleveland, received 58,818, while minor candidates collected 7,505. Since no candidate had received a majority, the election was decided by the Legislature, and that body chose Lounsbury as Governor. Inaugurated in January 1887, Lounsbury followed a moderate course in an attempt to placate all political factions. Notable in his administration, however, was a statute, passed by the Legislature and supported by the governor, which established a sixty-hour work week for women and for children under sixteen. Lounsbury also supported and signed the Incorrigible Criminal Act, which provided that on a third conviction, an habitual criminal would receive a sentence of twenty-five years in prison. Lounsbury chose not to seek reelection and returned to private life on January 9, 1889. After leaving the governor's office, Lounsbury became president of the Merchants' Exchange National Bank of Connecticut. He died in Ridgefield on June 22, 1925. Bibliography: Frederick C. Norton, *The Governors of Connecticut* (Hartford, 1905); Albert E. Van Dusen, *Connecticut* (New York, 1961); Forrest Morgan, *Connecticut as a Colony and as a State*, 4 vols. (Hartford, 1904); George L. Clark, *A History of Connecticut* (New York, 1914).

BULKELEY, Morgan Gardner, 1889-1893

Born on December 26, 1837 in East Haddam, Connecticut, son of Eliphalet Adams, an able lawyer who in his career held various offices, and Lydia (Morgan) Bulkeley; a Congregationalist. Married to Fannie Briggs Houghton in 1885; father of two sons and a daughter. Well educated for his time, Bulkeley attended public schools in Hartford; then joined an uncle in New York (in 1852) to become a partner in a general store; then served with the 13th New York Regiment in the Civil War. After his father's death in 1872, he returned to Hartford to found the United States Bank, of which he was president until 1879. He resigned in that year to accept the presidency of Aetna Life Insurance Company, a position he held until his death. Elected to the Hartford Common Council, 1875; placed on the Hartford Board of Aldermen in 1876; elected Mayor of Hartford in 1880 and served four terms (1880-

1888). As a Republican, Bulkeley was chosen Governor of Connecticut in 1888. Luzon B. Morris, the Democratic candidate, received 75,074 votes to Bulkeley's 73,659, but 4,915 scattered votes threw the election into the Republican Legislature, which named Bulkeley Governor. Near the end of his term, Bulkeley became involved in one of the most bitter political conflicts in the state's history. In the gubernatorial election of 1890, the Democratic candidate, Luzon B. Morris, received 67,658 votes to 63,975 for Samuel E. Merwin, the Republican. Minor candidates received 3,665. Morris appeared to be the victor, but his supporters had thrown out thousands of "specked" ballots which were defective, only because of mechanical errors. Had all ballots been counted, Morris would not have had a majority, and the Legislature would have been forced to name the Governor. The Senate and House could not agree on the legality of the "specked" ballots. Because of the deadlock, Bulkeley refused to surrender office to Morris and continued to serve as governor until 1893. After serving his second term as governor, Bulkeley retired to private life, but in 1905 he was chosen United States Senator. He held that position until 1911, when he again retired to manage his business affairs. Bulkeley died in Hartford on November 6, 1922. Bibliography: Albert E. Van Dusen, *Connecticut* (New York, 1961); Forrest Morgan, *Connecticut as a Colony and as a State,* 4 vols. (Hartford, 1904); Frederick C. Norton, *The Governors of Connecticut* (Hartford, 1905); Florence Crofut, *Guide to the History and the Historic Sites of Connecticut,* 2 vols. (New Haven, 1937).

MORRIS, Luzon Burritt, 1893-1895

Born on April 16, 1827, in Newtown, Connecticut, son of Eli Gould, a farmer, and Lydia (Bennett) Morris; a Congregationalist. Married Eugenia L. Tuttle in 1856; father of three sons and three daughters, with one son, Robert T. Morris, becoming a surgeon in New York City. Attended Connecticut Literary Institute in Suffield and Yale College, finishing his degree requirments in 1854, but lacking funds to graduate until 1858; studied law and was admitted to the bar in 1856. In 1855, while he studied for the bar, he was elected to the Connecticut House of Representatives and was reelected to the same position in 1856, 1870, 1876, 1880, and 1881; Probate Judge for the New Haven Probate Court, 1857-1863; served as State Senator from 1874 to 1876. In 1880, Morris was a member of a commission which resolved the long-standing boundary dispute between New York and Connecticut; in 1884, he served on another commission which reformed the probate laws of his state. Morris was the Democratic candidate for Governor in 1888 and again in 1890. In both races he appeared to have won but in fact lost each time due to technicalities which placed the outcome of the election into the hands of the Republican-dominated legislature, which chose the Republican standardbearers. In 1888 Morris received 75,074 votes, while Samuel Merwin received only 63,975; however, the legislature could not decide between the two candidates, and Morgan G. Bulkeley retained the governorship until January 1893. In 1892 Morris finally captured the governorship by winning 82,787 votes, while the Republican Samuel Merwin received only 76,745. Minor candidates received 5,019 votes, but Morris still maintained a majority. Inaugurated Governor on January 4, 1893, Morris carried out his duties with some success, but he failed to secure the constitutional revision of election laws which his party desired. The Panic of 1893 caused severe economic depression in Connecticut, which in turn caused Morris to lose popularity. Governor Morris' term ended on January 9, 1895. In 1895 Morris returned to private life to reopen his law practice and manage his business affairs, which included the vice-presidency of the Connecticut Savings Bank. Morris died of apoplexy on August 22, 1895 in New Haven, Connecticut. Bibliography: Frederick C. Norton, *The Governors of Connecticut* (Hartford, 1905); J.E. Johnson, *Newtown's History and Historian* (Newtown, 1917); Albert E. Van Dusen, *Connecticut* (New York, 1961); Forrest Morgan, *Connecticut as a Colony and as a State,* 4 vols. (Hartford, 1904); George L. Clark, *A History of Connecticut* (New York, 1914).

COFFIN, Owen Vincent, 1895-1897

Born on June 20, 1836 in Mansfield, New York, son of Alexander H., a farmer, and Jane (Vincent) Coffin; a Congregationalist. Married Ellen Elizabeth Coe on June 24, 1858; father of Seward Vincent Coffin, who became a successful manufacturer in Middletown, Connecticut. Attended Cortland Academy in New York and the Charlottesville Seminary in North Carolina; from 1852 until 1864, Coffin worked as a salesman in New York, representing several mercantile houses. After moving to Middletown, Connecticut in 1864, he became treasurer of the Farmers and Mechanics Savings Bank. Greatly interested in agriculture, Coffin became president of the Middlesex County Agricultural Society in 1875. In 1884 he was named president of the Middlesex Mutual Assurance Company in Middletown. A zealous Republican, Coffin served as a State Senator from 1887 to 1888 and again from 1889 to 1890. In 1894 he ran for the governorship. He received 83,975 votes, or 54.2 percent of the total votes cast. His Democratic opponent, Edward Cudy, collected only 66,287 votes, while minor candidates received 4,719. Inaugurated on January 9, 1895, Coffin presided over an administration and legislature which gave increasing attention to labor reform. During his term, legislation signed by Coffin included laws which prohibited using prison labor in the manufacture of medicine, food, and tobacco products; established a State Board of Mediation and Arbitration; banned the employment of children under fourteen years of age; guaranteed employees the right to join a labor union; and prohibited the blacklisting of union workers. Retiring from the governorship on January 6, 1897, Coffin returned to private life to manage his business affairs. He also remained interested in the social and religious life of his community. Active in the Young Men's Christian Association since his boyhood, as an older man he promoted the organization and helped found new clubs. Coffin died on January 3, 1921 at Clifton Springs, New York. Bibliography: Albert E. Van Dusen, *Connecticut* (New York, 1961); Frederick C. Norton, *The Governors of Connecticut* (Hartford, 1905); Forrest Morgan, *Connecticut as a Colony and as a State,* 4 vols. (Hartford, 1904); George L. Clark, *A History of Connecticut* (New York, 1914).

COOKE, Lorrin Alamson, 1897-1899

Born on April 6, 1831, in New Marlboro, Massachusetts, son of Levi, a farmer, and Amelia (Todd) Cooke; descendant of Resolved White, who sailed on the Mayflower; a Congregationalist; member of the Sons of the American Revolution. Married to Matilda E. Webster in 1858; she died childless in 1868; remarried to Josephine E. Ward in 1870; father of two sons and a daughter. Considered well educated; attended common schools and an academy in Norfolk, Connecticut; taught in various schools in Connecticut and became a farmer in Colebrook. He served in the State House of Representatives from 1856 to 1857; in 1869, he moved to Riverton where he became manager of a manufacturing company. A Republican, Cooke served in the State Senate from 1883 to 1885; President Pro Tempore of the Senate, 1884-1885; served as Lieutenant Governor from 1885 until 1887; again served as Lieutenant Governor from 1895 to 1897. The Republican candidate for Governor in 1896, Cooke received 108,807 votes, or 62.5 percent of the total votes cast. His Democratic opponent, James Sargent, garnered 56,524 votes, while minor candidates received 8,688. Inaugurated on January 6, 1897, Cooke found the state government in financial distress. In his first message to the Legislature, he lamented the lavish appropriations of public funds that had been made in previous years, and persuaded the legislators to implement budget reductions. Governmental costs again rose when the Spanish-American War began in 1898, but Governor Cooke responded to President William McKinley's request for men by outfitting two regiments of troops. The extra costs of the war notwithstanding, Cooke effected continued economies and left the state treasury in good financial condition. Cooke retired to private life on January 4, 1899. He made his home in Winsted, where he remained active in the Congregational Church and in civic affairs. Cooke died in Winsted on August 12, 1902. Bibliography: Frederick C. Norton, *The Governors of Connecticut* (Hartford, 1905); Forrest Morgan, *Connecticut as a Colony and as a State,* 4 vols. (Hartford, 1904); Albert E. Van Dusen, *Connecticut* (New York, 1961); George L. Clark, *A History of Connecticut* (New York, 1914).

LOUNSBURY, George Edward, 1899-1901

Born on May 7, 1838 in Poundridge, New York, son of Nathan, a shoemaker, and Delia (Schofield) Lounsbury; a Methodist; older brother of Phineas Chapman Lounsbury, Governor of Connecticut from 1887 to 1889. Married to Frances Josephine Potwin, daughter of Joseph Potwin, on November 29, 1894; no children. Attended Yale College and graduated in 1863; attended Berkeley Divinity School in Middletown, Connecticut, and graduated in 1866. While still in school, he helped his brother Phineas establish Lounsbury Brothers, a shoe factory in New Haven; from 1866 to 1868 he ministered to Episcopal parishes in Suffield and Thompsonville, but retired from the pulpit when he developed an infection of the larynx. In 1869, he became a co-partner in Lounsbury, Matthewson & Company, another shoe factory, which was located in South Norwalk, Connecticut; afterward he became president of the First National Bank of Ridgefield, Connecticut. A Republican, Lounsbury entered politics in 1894, winning election as State Senator by a 1,300 vote majority and serving until 1898. Elected Governor in 1898, he polled 81,015 votes, a 54.2 percent majority, while his Democratic opponent, Daniel Morgan, received 64,227 votes and minor candidates, 4,326. Inaugurated on January 4, 1899, Lounsbury proved to be an excellent administrator of the state's finances. He continued the frugal policy of his predecessor, Governor Lorrin Alamson Cooke, and reduced the state debt by $1,000,000. Lounsbury also vetoed several bills which he believed harmful to the general welfare, and in each case his veto was sustained by the legislature. Among the measures he stopped were the "Cash Bill," which would have reduced taxation on railroads; another proposal which would have raised the salary of the School-Funded Commissioner; and two bills which would have given private corporations the right of eminent domain. Lounsbury ended his term as governor on January 9, 1901, retired to private life, and made his home in Farmingville, near Ridgefield. He died on August 16, 1904, at his home in Farmingville. Bibliography: Albert E. Van Dusen, *Connecticut* (New York, 1961); Frederick C. Norton, *The Governors of Connecticut* (Hartford, 1905); Forrest Morgan, *Connecticut as a Colony and as a State,* 4 vols. (Hartford, 1904); George L. Clark, *A History of Connecticut* (New York, 1914).

McLEAN, George Payne, 1901-1903

Born on October 7, 1857 in Simsbury, Connecticut, son of Dudley Bestor, a farmer, and Mary (Payne) McLean; a Congregationalist. On September 18, 1873, married Leah Demarest, who died in 1918; remarried to Mrs. Isabella (Bishop) McClintock, a widow, on November 21, 1921; father, by his first wife, of four children, Helen Demarest, Graham Roweyn, Lea Demarest, and Katharine Taylor. Graduated from Hartford High School in 1877 and joined the staff of the *Hartford Post;* studied law and was admitted to the bar in 1881. A staunch Republican, McLean was elected to the Connecticut House of Representatives in 1882, serving one term, 1883-1885. From 1884 to 1901, he served as clerk of the State Board of Pardons; elected State Senator in 1888, serving one term, 1889-1891; appointed United States District Attorney in 1892 and served until 1896; nominated for Governor by the Republican party in 1900. In the gubernatorial race, McLean received 95,822 votes, a majority of 53 percent. His Democratic opponent, Samuel L. Bronson, gathered 81,421 votes, while minor candidates received 3,480. Inaugurated on January 9, 1901, Governor McLean presided over tax and administrative reforms. He supported a Constitutional Convention which met in 1902 to rewrite the state's fundamental law. One controversial issue to emerge from the convention was the question of representation. McLean and others favored democratic modifications which would give more populous areas greater representation, but the voters refused to ratify the new document. McLean succeeded in securing reform legislation, however, which created the office of Tax Commissioner and reorganized the state militia and the governor's administrative staff. Ill health forced McLean to forego any attempt to stand for a second term, and he retired from the governorship on January 7, 1903. McLean eventually recovered his health and in 1911 returned to politics. The Republican Party nominated him for the United States Senate. Running against the Democrat Homer S. Commins, McLean was elected by the State General Assembly. Reelected twice, McLean served until 1929, when he retired permanently from public life. Notable in his senatorial career was his opposition to the League of Nations covenant, his general adherence to national Republican policies in the 1920s, and his close friendship with President Calvin Coolidge. McLean died on June 6, 1932, in his home in Simsbury, Connecticut. Bibliography: Albert E. Van Dusen, *Connecticut* (New York, 1961); Frederick C. Norton, *The Governors of Connecticut* (Hartford, 1905); Forrest Morgan, *Connecticut as a Colony and as a State,* 4 vols. (Hartford, 1904); George L. Clark, *A History of Connecticut* (New York, 1914).

CHAMBERLAIN, Abiram, 1903-1905

Born on December 7, 1837 in Colebrook, Connecticut, son of Abiram, a civil engineer, and Sophronia Ruth (Burt) Chamberlain; a Congregationalist; descendant of Jacob Chamberlain, who was born in Newton, Massachusetts in 1673. Married Charlotte Roberts, daughter of Dr. Albert Roberts, on November 19, 1872; father of two sons, Albert R. and Harold B. Attended common schools in Connecticut and Williston Seminary in Easthampton, Massachusetts; studied civil engineering; settled in New Britain, Connecticut in 1856 and joined his father's engineering firm; later he joined the New Britain National Bank in Meriden, Connecticut, and was made its president in 1881; he also became vice-president of the Meriden Savings Bank and president of the Meriden Fire Insurance Company. A Republican, Chamberlain began his political career by serving on the Meriden City Council in the 1870s. He represented Meriden in the Connecticut House of Representatives in 1877-1878, and was also State Comptroller in 1901-1902. In 1902 his party nominated him for the governorship. In the contest which followed, he received 85,338 votes, a 53.4 percent majority, while his Democratic opponent, Melbert B. Cary, got 69,330 votes and minor candidates, 5,034. Inaugurated on January 7, 1903, Chamberlain proved to be an excellent administrator. He presided over the continuing urbanization and industrialization of his state. In both categories, trends in Connecticut ran well ahead of most of the nation. Chamberlain had to face increased labor problems which resulted from this rapid, somewhat haphazard growth. In one year alone, 1904, thirty-six strikes occurred in the state with workers striking for higher wages, reduced hours, and better working conditions. Chamberlain responded by taking a moderate stance, allowing labor and management to negotiate their differences, but he also supported legislation (which benefited workers) such as laws regulating sanitary conditions in factories. Chamberlain retired from the governorship on January 4, 1905, and returned to private life to manage his business affairs in Meriden. He died on May 15, 1911, at his home in Meriden. Bibliography: Albert E. Van Dusen, *Connecticut* (New York, 1961); George L. Clark, *A History of Connecticut* (New York, 1914); Florence Crofut, *Guide to the History and the Historic Sites of Connecticut,* 2 vols. (New Haven, 1937).

ROBERTS, Henry, 1905-1907

Born on January 22, 1853 in Brooklyn, New York, son of George, a manufacturer, and Elvira (Evans) Roberts; a Congregationalist. Married Carrie Elizabeth Smith on October 5, 1881; father of three children, John Taylor, Francis Thatcher, and Edward Constant. Attended public schools in South Windsor and Hartford, Connecticut; graduated from Yale University in 1877; studied at Columbia University in 1878; took a law degree at Yale in 1879, and was admitted to the Connecticut Bar. Practiced law and joined his father's manufacturing firm, the Hartford Woven Wire Mattress Company; became president of the company in 1886, and served in that capacity until the company was dissolved in 1907; made lucrative investments and became identified with many industrial enterprises in Hartford. A Republican, Roberts began his political career in 1897; he was elected to Hartford's Board of Aldermen and presided over the Ways and Means Committee; served in the Connecticut House of Representatives from 1899-1901; later served in the State Senate, 1901-1902; elected Lieutenant Governor in 1902, and served in that office from 1903 until 1905. The Republicans nominated Roberts for Governor in 1904. In the election he received 104,736 votes, a 54.9 percent majority. His Democratic opponent, A. Heaton Robertson, got 79,164 votes, while minor candidates received 6,931. Roberts was inaugurated on January 4, 1905. Governor Roberts proved progressively minded and supported many reforms which he believed to be in the general interest. During his term, the legislature framed laws which regulated the use of the automobile; protected the public from dishonest practices by representatives of private enterprise and by public officials; provided jail sentences for non-support of wives; and forbade bakeries to operate below ground level. Roberts retired from the governorship on January 9, 1907, and returned to private life to manage his business interests. Nevertheless, his public service continued in later life; he served as president of the Hartford Water Board and as a trustee of the Slater Industrial School in Winston, North Carolina. Active in social circles, he was a member of the Connecticut Society of Colonial Wars, Sons of the Revolution, Psi Upsilon, Sigma Epsilon, and Theta Psi. Roberts died in Hartford on May 1, 1929. Bibliography: Albert E. Van Dusen, *Connecticut* (New York, 1961); Florence Crofut, *Guide to the History and the Historic Sites of Connecticut,* 2 vols. (New Haven, 1937); George L. Clark, *A History of Connecticut* (New York, 1914).

WOODRUFF, Rollin Simmons, 1907-1909

Born on July 14, 1854 in Rochester, New York, son of Jeremiah, a farmer, and Clarisse (Thompson) Woodruff; a Congregationalist; a descendant of Matthew Woodruff, who emigrated from England in 1636. Never married. Attended common schools. In 1870, he moved to New Haven, Connecticut (two years after his father's death). Woodruff had a natural instinct for business; he was employed in various industries, and in 1876 joined C.S. Mersick and Company, one of the largest wholesale iron and steel dealers in New England. In 1889, he became an officer in that firm; he also became a director of several other corporations in the state, and president of the Connecticut Computing Machine Company; he served as president of the New Haven Chamber of Commerce from 1905 to 1907. Woodruff, a Republican, was elected to the Connecticut Senate in 1902, and served from 1903 until 1905, during which time he was that body's President Pro Temport. From 1905 to 1907, he served as Lieutenant Governor. In 1906 the Republican State Convention nominated him for Governor by acclamation. In the election Woodruff received 88,384 votes, a majority of 54.8 percent, while his Democratic opponent, Charles Thayer, got 67,776 votes, and minor candidates, 5,033. Inaugurated on January 9, 1907, Woodruff faced many challenges. Described as a "businessman first and a politician afterward," his policies supported traditional Republican goals, including the high tariff policy of the national leadership and aid to the business community. He disdained party bosses and refused to follow blindly the dictates of the state "machine." Woodruff frequently vetoed acts of the legislature when he believed that the state budget or state economy needed his protection. He caused friction between his executive branch and the legislature, but even his critics acknowledged that he acted in what he believed were the best interests of the state. Woodruff retired from the governor's office on January 6, 1909, and returned to private life to attend to his business activities. He remained involved in civic affairs after his years as governor, serving as a member of the Union League Club, the Quinnipiac Republican Club, and the Young Men's Republican Club of New Haven. In his later years, he spent much of his time relaxing at his summer estate in Guilford. Woodruff died on June 30, 1925. Bibliography: Albert E. Van Dusen, *Connecticut* (New York, 1961); Florence Crofut, *Guide to the History and the Historic Sites of Connecticut,* 2 vols. (New Haven, 1937); George L. Clark, *A History of Connecticut* (New York, 1914).

LILLEY, George Leavens, 1909

Born on August 3, 1859 in Oxford, Massachusetts, son of John, a farmer, and Caroline (Adams) Lilley; a Congregationalist. Married Anna E. Steele on June 17, 1884; father of three sons, Frederick, John, and Theodore: Attended common schools and Worcester High School and Technical Institute in Massachusetts. In 1877, he secured employment as a salesman for a wholesale meat house, and in 1880, moved to Waterbury, Connecticut to become a partner in Lilley Swift and Company, another meat house, which by 1900 had grown to be one of the largest in the eastern states. He developed extensive real estate holdings in Torrington, Waterbury, Winsted, and Nangatuck and was socially active, being a member of the Waterbury Club, the Union League, and various fraternal groups. A progressive Republican, Lilley entered politics in 1900 and won a seat in the Connecticut House of Representatives, serving from 1901 to 1903. From 1903 to 1909, he served in the United States House of Representatives, where he fought monopolies by conducting investigations to uncover wrongdoing. In 1908 Lilley sought the governorship. He received 98,179 votes, a majority of 51.9 percent, while his Democratic opponent, A. Heaton Robertson, got 82,260 votes, and minor candidates received 8,646. Inaugurated on January 6, 1909, Lilley continued supporting progressive programs like those he had favored as a Congressman. As governor, he supported bills which would have created a public service commission, but the legislature defeated the proposals. He conducted an investigation of, and won new appropriations for, the public school system. He also framed a statute liberalizing the State Employers' Liability Act, and he budgeted more money for the state campaign against tuberculosis. He endorsed measures which would have regulated monopolies, but was staunchly opposed by Connecticut's business community, whose lobbyists convinced the Legislature to block the governor's crusade against monopoly power. Before he could complete his term as governor, Lilley died on April 21, 1909, at the executive mansion in Hartford. Bibliography: George L. Clark, *A History of Connecticut* (New York, 1914); Albert E. Van Dusen, *Connecticut* (New York, 1961); Florence Crofut, *Guide to the History and the Historic Sites of Connecticut,* 2 vols. (New Haven, 1937).

WEEKS, Frank Bentley, 1909-1911

Born on January 20, 1854 in Brooklyn, New York, son of Daniel L., a farmer, and Frances (Edwards) Weeks; a Congregationalist. Married Helen Louise Hubbard on November 4, 1875; no children. Attended Eastman Business College in Poughkeepsie, New York, and graduated in 1872; became assistant to the superintendent of the Connecticut Hospital for the Insane in 1874; associated in 1880 with a grain and milling business in Middletown; founded the Middletown Board of Trade; a director of the Middletown Savings Bank and the Middletown Mutual Assurance Company. A Republican, Weeks entered politics in 1904 when he was chosen as a presidential elector from Connecticut; elected Lieutenant Governor in 1908 by a plurality of 40,487; became Governor upon the death of Governor George Lilley on April 21, 1909. As governor, Weeks presided over a rapidly changing state. By 1910, eighty-nine percent of Connecticut's population resided in urban areas, with industrialization occurring rapidly. Cities, such as Bridgeport and New Haven passed the 100,000 mark, with the latter registering a 109 percent growth rate from 1890 to 1910. In addition, (by 1910) the state had acquired a heavy immigrant population. That year, the foreign-born numbered 329,574, approximately thirty percent of the state's 1,114,756 people. As governor, Weeks coped with these new developments by following the policies of his predecessor Lilley, a progressive Republican. Weeks opposed monopolies and favored the regulation of industry. At the same time, he was budget-minded and practiced economy in an effort to reduce the burdens on taxpayers. His administration, while it was somewhat uneventful, was unmarred by crisis and was judged a success. Weeks left the governor's chair on January 4, 1911, but he remained active in his business career. Interested in education and historical research, he also became a trustee of Wesleyan University and was a charter member of the Middlesex Historical Society. Weeks died in Middletown on October 2, 1935, at the age of eighty-one. Bibliography: Florence Crofut, *A Guide to the History and the Historic Sites of Connecticut,* 2 vols. (New Haven, 1937); George L. Clark, *A History of Connecticut* (New York, 1914); Albert E. Van Dusen, *Connecticut* (New York, 1961).

BALDWIN, Simeon Eben, 1911-1915

Born on February 5, 1840 in New Haven, Connecticut, son of Roger Sherman, an attorney, and Emily (Perkins) Baldwin; a Congregationalist; a bachelor. Attended Hopkins Grammar School in New Haven; graduated from Yale University in 1861; from 1861 to 1863, studied law at Yale, Harvard, and in his father's office; admitted to the bar in 1863. He was a founder of the American Bar Association in 1878 and its president in 1890; he joined the law faculty at Yale in 1869 and retired Professor Emeritus in 1919. He served as president of the Association of American Law Schools in 1902, and served as a justice on the State Supreme Court from 1893 to 1910. He was appointed in 1899 as a delegate of the United States Department of State to the Sixth International Prison Congress which met in Brussels, Belgium, and in 1905 to the Twelfth International Congress which met in Budapest, Hungary. Baldwin began his career in state politics in 1867 when he ran as a Republican for the State Senate. Defeated, he temporarily abandoned politics, but in 1884 he was one of the "independents" who refused to support James G. Blaine for the presidency of the United States, and was chosen president of the Republican Party in Connecticut. After 1885 Baldwin again abandoned an active role in politics, instead devoting himself to teaching and writing, and after 1893 to his services on the State Supreme Court. Meanwhile, he made a transition politically, moving from the Republican to the Democratic Party. In 1910, after he had retired from the court, he was nominated for the governorship on the Democratic ticket. In the election he received 77,243 votes, the Republican Charles Goodwin got 73,528, and minor candidates collected 3,231. Reelected in 1912, Baldwin garnered 78,264 votes. His Republican opponent, John Studley, received 67,531, and a Progressive candidate got 31,020, while minor candidates received 13,579. Inaugurated on January 4, 1911, Baldwin's two terms proved to be successful. A reforming governor, he secured passage of a Corrupt Practices Act and a bill creating a Public Utilities Commission. Later, he persuaded the legislature to pass a Workmen's Compensation Bill, which made employers liable for industrial accidents and set rates of compensation for injured workers. In 1914 Baldwin won the Democratic nomination for the United States Senate, but he faced an incumbent Republican, Frank Bandegee, who won the election by a margin of 89,983 to 76,081. Baldwin left the governorship on January 6, 1915, and returned to Yale. He died at the age of eighty-six on January 30, 1927, in New Haven. Bibliography: Simeon Baldwin, *The Life and Letters of Simeon Baldwin* (New Haven, 1919); Simeon Baldwin, *The Young Man and the Law* (New Haven, 1919); Albert E. Van Dusen, *Connecticut* (New York, 1961); Florence Crofut, *Guide to the History and the Historic Sites of Connecticut,* 2 vols. (New Haven, 1937).

HOLCOMB, Marcus Hensey, 1915-1921

Born on November 28, 1884 in New Hartford, Connecticut, son of Carlos, a landowner, and Adah (Bushnell) Holcomb; a Baptist. Married to Sarah Carpenter Bennet on October 15, 1872; no children. Attended school in New Hartford and at Wesleyan Seminary in Wilbraham, Massachusetts; taught school and studied law in the office of Jared B. Foster of New Hartford; admitted to the bar in 1871.

Holcomb's public career began in 1893 when he became Judge of the Probate Court of the Southington District, a position he held until 1910. He also served as First Judge of the Borough Court of Southington from 1905 to 1909 and Treasurer of Hartford County from 1893 to 1908; member of the State Senate, 1893-1894; delegate, Constitutional Convention, 1902; member and Speaker of State House of Representatives, 1905 to 1906; Attorney-General, 1906-1907; Judge of the State Superior Court, 1906-1915. Holcomb ran for the governorship in 1914 on the Republican ticket. He received 91,262 votes, a 50.4 percent majority, while his Democratic opponent, Lyman Tingler, received 73,888 votes. A candidate for the Progressive Party, William Fischer, received 8,030 votes; minor candidates received 7,927. Reelected in 1916, he garnered 109,293 votes and the Democratic challenger, Morris Beardsley, received 96,787 votes, with minor candidates receiving a total of 7,727. Again reelected in 1918, Holcomb received 84,891 votes, while his Democratic opponent, Thomas Spellacy, received 76,849, and minor candidates, 5,696. Inaugurated on January 6, 1915, Holcomb conducted a successful administration which cooperated fully with the national preparedness campaign and the later war effort. Under Holcomb, a complete census of the state's men and materials was made. He created a State Council of Defense and a Food Supply Council. Also, during his term, the legislature adopted acts setting maximum working hours for women in industry; created a teachers' retirement system; and established old age pensions and health insurance programs. Holcomb's taxation policy transformed a state debt of $593,572 in 1918. Upon the expiration of his third term on January 5, 1921, Holcomb resumed his law practice. He died on March 5, 1932 in Southington, Connecticut. Bibliography: Marcus Holcomb, "Connecticut in the Van," *Review of Reviews,* LVII (May, 1918); Albert E. Van Dusen, *Connecticut* (New York, 1961); Florence Crofut, *Guide to the History and the Historic Sites of Connecticut,* 2 vols. (New Haven, 1937).

LAKE, Everett John, 1921-1923

Born on February 8, 1871 in Woodstock, Connecticut, son of Thomas, a politician and government official, and Martha (Cockings) Lake; a Congregationalist. Married to Eva Louise Sykes in 1895; after her death, remarried to Barbara Grace Lincoln; father of two children, Harold and Marjorie. Graduated from Worcester (Massachusetts) Polytechnic Institute in 1890 and Harvard University in 1892; all-American football player while at Harvard; joined the Hartford Lumber Company in 1892, became its president in 1900, and served in that capacity until 1939. A Republican, Lake began his political career after the turn of the century; served in the State House of Representatives from 1903 to 1905; was a member of the State Senate from 1905 to 1907; served as lieutenant governor from 1907-1909. Lake was elected Governor of Connecticut in 1920. He received 230,792 popular votes, a majority of sixty-three percent, while his Democratic opponent, Rollin Tyler, got 148,641 votes, and minor candidates, 13,567. Inaugurated on January 5, 1921, Lake wanted to bring the government closer to the people. He opened to the public meetings of the State Board of Control, where disbursement of funds among institutions and departmental bodies was approved. Wishing to economize, he personally inspected state institutions and found where to streamline their operation and cut their budgets, thus leaving the state treasury with a favorable balance. Lake was a conservative, but he supported laws which favored labor. During his term statutes were passed which established a maximum eight-hour day for child laborers, and permitted school officials to withhold employment certificates from children who lacked sufficient schooling. Governor Lake also tried to enforce Prohibition, but the task proved difficult; Connecticut was one of two states which never ratified the Eighteenth Amendment and large numbers of the state's citizens decided to disobey the law. The problem was one Lake could not solve and a problem that continued until Prohibition was repealed. Governor Lake retired from public office on January 3, 1923, and returned to private life. Lake died on September 16, 1948 in Hartford, Connecticut. Bibliography: Albert E. Van Dusen, *Connecticut* (New York, 1961); Florence Crofut, *Guide to the History and the Historic Sites of Connecticut*, 2 vols. (New Haven, 1937); Rowland W. Mitchell, 'Social Legislation in Connecticut, 1919-1939,' Unpublished Ph.D. Dissertation, Yale University, 1954.

TEMPLETON, Charles Augustus, 1923-1925

Born on March 3, 1871 in Sharon, Connecticut, son of Theodore, a farmer, and Ella (Middlebrooks) Templeton; an Episcopalian. Married to Martha Amelia Castle on June 17, 1897; father of three daughters, Joan, Nancy, and Lucy. Templeton attended common schools and the Episcopal School in Plainville, Connecticut; he began his business career in 1888 as a bookkeeper in a hardware store in Waterbury, and in 1890 became a partner in the business; in 1905 he dissolved his partnership and opened his own hardware store, which he managed until 1947. An active Republican, Templeton served on the Waterbury Board of Aldermen from the early 1900s to 1919. He was elected State Senator in 1918 and served in that post from 1919 to 1921. In 1920 he was a delegate to the Republican National Convention. From 1921 to 1923, he served as lieutenant governor. In 1922 he ran for the governorship. He received 170,231 votes, a majority of 52.4 percent, while his Democratic opponent, David Fitzgerald, received 148,641 votes, and minor candidates, 6,201. Inaugurated on January 3, 1923, Templeton pursued an independent course. He alienated party regulars when he refused to permit the Republican state chairman to name the governor's secretary. Then, as a matter of party politics, the General Assembly failed to confirm Templeton's choice for a vacancy on the State Superior Court. The governor was successful, however, in attempts to suspend the licenses of eclectic physicians and in securing statutes which prohibited graduates of correspondence course medical schools from practicing in the state. He obtained stricter enforcement of state liquor laws, and he cut appropriations to state institutions in order to balance the state's budget. On national issues, Templeton followed the lead of the Harding and Coolidge administrations. Templeton left the governor's chair on January 7, 1925. In later life he participated actively in civic affairs. He was a trustee of Saint Marguerite's School for Girls in Waterbury from 1920 to 1948 and aided several fund-raising drives for the institution. He was also a director of Waterbury's Young Men's Christian Association and led fund-raising drives for all of the churches in his hometown. Templeton died on August 15, 1955, at his home in Waterbury. Bibliography:

Florence Crofut, *Guide to the History and the Historic Sites of Connecticut,* 2 vols. (New Haven, 1937); Albert E. Van Dusen, *Connecticut* (New York, 1961); Roy Glashan, *American Governors and Gubernatorial Elections, 1775-1975* (Stillwater, Minnesota, 1975); Congressional Quarterly, Inc., *Guide to United States Elections* (Washington, D.C., 1975).

BINGHAM, Hiram, 1925

Born on November 19, 1875 in Honolulu, Hawaii, son of Hiram Bingham, a Congregationalist missionary, and Clarissa Brewster; a Congregationalist. Married to Alfreda Mitchell on November 2, 1900; father of Woolbridge, Hiram, Charles Tiffany, Brewster, Mitchell and Jonathan Brewster Bingham, Congressman from New York, 1965-1973; remarried to Suzanne Carroll Hill on June 28, 1937. Educated at Punahon School and Oahu College in Hawaii, 1882-1892, Phillips Academy in Massachusetts, 1892-1894, Yale University, 1894-1898, University of California at Berkeley, 1899-1900, and Harvard University, 1900-1905; taught history and political science at Harvard (1902-1905), Princeton (1905-1906), and Yale (1907-1917). Delegate to the First Pan-American Scientific Congress at Santiago, Chile in 1908; explorer of South America—Venezuela and Colombia from 1906 to 1907, Peru from 1912 to 1915; Captain in Connecticut National Guard, 1916; an aviator during World War I. A Republican, Bingham was active in politics. He served as a delegate-at-large at the Republican National Convention in 1924, 1928, 1932 and 1936. Elected Lieutenant Governor of Connecticut in 1922 and served one term from 1923 to 1925. Nominated by the Republicans for Governor in 1924, Bingham polled 246,336 votes, a majority of 66.2 percent, while his Democratic opponent, Charles Morris, received 118,676 votes, and minor candidates, 7,300. However, one month later Bingham also won election as United States Senator to fill the vacancy caused by the death of Frank B. Brandegee. When that term ended in 1927, Bingham was reelected and served until March 3, 1933. His term as governor lasted only from January 7, 1925 to January 8, 1925, as he resigned to accept the Senate seat. In state politics, Senator Bingham supported the administration of fellow Republican John Trumbull, who as lieutenant governor had been elevated to the governorship when Bingham resigned. With Bingham's encouragement, Trumbull epitomized the conservative outlook of the 1920s by balancing the state budget and creating a stable environment for business. In national politics, Bingham supported the administration of Coolidge and Hoover. The senator championed budget-minded measures and adopted a pro-business outlook. Defeated in a bid to win reelection to the Senate in 1933, Bingham became a free-lance writer in Washington, D.C., and during World War II lectured at naval training schools. Bingham died on June 6, 1956 in Washington, D.C., and was buried in Arlington National Cemetery. Bibliography: Florence Crofut, *Guide to the History and the Historic Sites of Connecticut,* 2 vols. (New Haven, 1937); Albert E. Van Dusen, *Connecticut* (New York, 1961); Rowland W. Mitchell, "Social Legislation in Connecticut, 1919-1939," Unpublished Ph.D. Dissertation, Yale University, 1954; Roy Glashan, *American Governors and Gubernatorial Elections, 1775-1975* (Stillwater, Minnesota, 1975); Congressional Quarterly, Inc., *Guide to United States Elections* (Washington, D.C., 1975).

TRUMBULL, John H., 1925-1931

Born on March 4, 1873 in Ashford, Connecticut, son of Irish immigrants; one of seven children; an Episcopalian. Married to Maud Usher; father of two daughters. Attended common schools and worked on his father's farm; in 1898 founded an electrical-contracting business; in 1899 established Trumbull Electric Company and began manufacturing appliances; served as president of the company from 1899 to 1944, when he retired; served with distinction in World War I. A Republican, Trumbull entered politics in 1921; served in the State Senate from 1921 to 1925; elected Lieutenant Governor in 1924. The day after his inauguration on January 7, 1925, he became Governor when Governor Hiram Bingham resigned to take a seat in the United States Senate. Trumbull was reelected twice. In 1926 he captured 192,425 votes, a majority of 63.2 percent, while his Democratic opponent, Charles Morris, received 107,045 and minor candidates, 3,198. In 1928 Trumbull defeated Morris again by a 296,216 to 252,209 vote margin, while minor candidates gathered 4,549. Trumbull ran for the governorship again in 1932; although he lost in the Democratic landslide of that year, he ran ahead of the national ticket. He received 277,853 votes (45.6 percent) while the Democratic victor, Wilbur Cross, received 288,633. In his years in office, Trumbull was representative of the conservative outlook of the 1920s. He balanced the state budget and created a stable environment for the expansion of business. Beginning in 1927 Trumbull presided over a massive state building program which included the construction of new facilities for a variety of institutions. He also pressed for a good roads program, which was initiated by the legislature in the late 1920s. Trumbull's last years as governor were marred by the Great Depression; he proved powerless to solve the perplexing problems brought about by increasing production cutbacks and rising unemployment. He declined to seek renomination and retired from office on January 7, 1931. After leaving office Trumbull returned to his business affairs. He again became an active officer in his manufacturing company, and also became more active civically. He was a member of the Connecticut Humane Society and the Connecticut Historical Society. Trumbull died on May 21, 1961 in Hartford, Connecticut. Bibliography: Florence Crofut, *Guide to the History and the Historic Sites of Connecticut*, 2 vols. (New Haven, 1937); Albert E. Van Dusen, *Connecticut* (New York, 1961); Rowland W. Mitchell, "Social Legislation in Connecticut, 1919-1939," Unpublished Ph.D. Dissertation, Yale University, 1954.

CROSS, Wilbur Lucius, 1931-1939

Born on April 10, 1862 in Mansfield, Connecticut, son of Samuel, a farmer and manufacturer, and Harriet (Gurley) Cross; a Congregationalist. Married to Helen Baldwin Avery on July 17, 1889, who died in 1928; father of two sons, Wilbur Lucius and Avery. Cross attended common schools and graduated from Yale College in 1885; received his Ph.D. in English literature from Yale in 1889; taught in public schools and academies in Connecticut from 1885 to 1894; returned to Yale to teach and held administrative offices there from 1894 to 1930, when he retired. After he retired as an academician, Cross became interested in politics, especially when the Great Depression, which had begun in 1929, worsened.

Nominated for the governorship in 1930 by the Democratic Party, Cross ran as a "wet" candidate who opposed Prohibition. In the election of 1930, Cross received 215,072 votes, a plurality of 49.9 percent, while his Republican opponent gathered 209,607 votes, and minor candidates received 6,223. Reelected in 1932, Cross received 288,633 votes, a plurality of 48.4 percent, and his Republican challenger, John Trumbull, got 277,853 votes, while minor candidates received 20,061. Reelected in 1934, Cross got 257,996 votes, while his Republican opponent received 249,397, and minor candidates got 44,903. Again reelected in 1936, Cross got 372,953 votes, a majority of 55.3 percent, while his Republican opponent received 277,190, and minor candidates got 24,380. Inaugurated on January 7, 1931, Governor Cross faced a hostile legislature, but adopted a conciliatory course. After 1933 a supporter of Franklin D. Roosevelt's New Deal, Cross implemented wide reform on the state level. Before he left office, he secured state laws which abolished child labor in Connecticut, established minimum wage rates and minimum safety standards for working women, and provided for state government reorganization, a balanced budget, and huge appropriations for public construction. Cross was expected to win his fifth term as chief executive in 1938, but an unexpectedly large vote cast for Jasper McLevy, Socialist mayor of Bridgeport, caused an upset. The Republican Raymond E. Baldwin won the election with 230,237 votes, a plurality of 36.4 percent, while Cross received only 227,549 votes. The Socialist McLevy got 166,253 votes, while minor candidates received 8,044. Cross left office on January 4, 1939. He again sought the Democratic nomination for Governor in 1940, but was defeated by Robert Hurley, who won the nomination. Thereafter Cross retired to devote himself to research and writing. Cross died on October 5, 1948 in New Haven, Connecticut. Bibliography: Wilbur Lucius Cross, *Connecticut Yankee: An Autobiography* (New Haven, 1943); Florence Crofut, *Guide to the History and the Historic Sites of Connecticut,* 2 vols. (New Haven, 1937); Albert E. Van Dusen, *Connecticut* (New York, 1961); Eugene A. Davidson, "A Cross for Connecticut," *Outlook and Independent,* CLVII (January 14, 1931); Roy Glashan, *American Governors and Gubernatorial Elections, 1775-1975* (Stillwater, Minnesota, 1975); Congressional Quarterly, Inc., *Guide to United States Elections* (Washington, D.C., 1975).

BALDWIN, Raymond Early, 1939-1941, 1943-1946

Born on August 31, 1893 in Rye, New York, son of Lucian Earl, a landowner, and Sarah Emily (Tyler) Baldwin; an Episcopalian. Married to Edith Lindholm on June 29, 1922; father of three sons, Lucian Earl, Raymond Earl, and Tyler Baldwin. He attended common schools in New York; graduated with a B.A. from Wesleyan University in 1916; and studied at Yale Law School, 1916-1917. He entered the United States Naval Academy for training; served on destroyers during the war; returned to Yale Law School in 1919 and graduated in 1921. In 1922 he set up a law practice in New Haven, Connecticut; from 1927 to 1930 was Public Prosecutor of Stratford, Connecticut, and from 1931 to 1933 was Judge of the Town Court. A Republican, Baldwin served in the Connecticut House of Representatives from 1931 to 1935. He ran for the governorship in 1938. In a close election he received 230,237 votes, a plurality of 36.4 percent, and defeated the incumbent governor, the Democrat Wilbur Cross, who polled 227,549. The Socialist Jasper McLevy received 166,253 votes and minor candidates got 8,044. Baldwin ran for reelection in 1940, but his 374,581 votes fell short of the Democrat Robert Hurley's total of 388,361. Minor candidates also received 27,046 votes. Baldwin ran against Hurley twice more, in 1942 and 1944, and won both elections. In 1942 Baldwin polled 281,362 votes, while Hurley received 255,166, and minor candidates got 38,473. In 1944 Baldwin received 418,289 votes and Hurley 392,417, while minor candidates got 17,873. Inaugurated for his first term on January 4, 1939, Baldwin emphasized economy in government spending. In two years he wiped out a deficit of $1,500,000 in the State Treasury and left a favorable balance of $1,000,000. He also organized an industrial training system which increased the efficiency of the state's defense plants, and later helped to coordinate the war effort in Connecticut. Baldwin faced a serious 150-day labor strike in 1945 and used troops to stop the strike because he believed it threatened national security. After the war, he established a number of boards, including a Labor-Management Council, to help ease the transition to a peace-time economy. Baldwin resigned from the governorship on December 27, 1946, after his election to the United States Senate. In 1949 Baldwin's career as a public servant entered a new phase when the Democratic governor, Chester Bowles, appointed him as an Associate Justice of the State Supreme Court, a position he held until his retirement in 1963. He was chairman of the Connecticut Constitutional Convention in 1965 and is a resident of Middletown. Bibliography: Albert E. Van Dusen, *Connecticut* (New York, 1961); Raymond E. Baldwin, *Let's Go Into Politics* (New York, 1952); Roy Glashan, *American Governors and Gubernatorial Elections, 1775-1975* (Stillwater, Minnesota, 1975); Congressional Quarterly, Inc., *Guide to United States Elections* (Washington, D. C., 1975).

HURLEY, Robert Augustine, 1941-1943

Born on August 25, 1895 in Bridgeport, Connecticut, son of Robert Emmit, a landowner and Sabina O'Hara Hurley; a Roman Catholic. Married to Evelyn Hedberg; father of three children, Robert, Joan, and Sally. He attended common schools in Connecticut and Lehigh University; worked his way through college by utilizing his training as an engineer; served in the United States Navy from 1917 to 1919 as a radio electrician with a submarine fleet and with the battleship *Pennsylvania.* He worked in private industry for many years; was named director of the Work Projects Administration for Fairfield County, Connecticut, in 1935; was the state's Public Works Commissioner from 1937 to 1940 and completed a $25 million building program. A Democrat, Hurley secured the nomination of his party in 1940 for the governorship. Running against the incumbent Republican governor, Raymond Baldwin, Hurley won the election. He received 388,361 votes to Baldwin's 374,581, while minor candidates received 27,046. Inaugurated on January 8, 1941, Hurley cooperated with the national defense effort. He appointed leaders from all fields of endeavor to the State's Defense Council. After December 7, 1941, the day of the Japanese attack on Pearl Harbor, the Governor redoubled his efforts to build the defense industry. Hurley also proved to be a reformer. He supported legislation which gave state aid to dependent children, and amendments to existing laws which gave unemployment compensation and workmen's compensation to more people. He also supported statutes which provided for annual audits of public utility companies and which established a rural electrification program. He failed in his principal labor recommendation, a proposal to create a state labor relations board, but his administration remained a marked success. Hurley's term ended on January 6, 1943. He had sought reelection but had been defeated by Baldwin, the ex-governor. In 1942 Baldwin secured 281,362 votes to Hurley's 255,166. Running again in 1944, Hurley was again defeated by Baldwin, by a count of 418,289 votes to 392,417. From 1944 to 1945, Hurley was a member of the State Surplus Property Board, but returned to private life after World War II. Hurley died in West Hartford, Connecticut on May 3, 1968. Bibliography: Albert E. Van Dusen, *Connecticut* (New York, 1961); Roy Glashan, *American Governors and Gubernatorial Elections, 1775-1975* (Stillwater, Minnesota, 1975); Congressional Quarterly, Inc., *Guide to United States Elections* (Washington, D.C., 1975).

BALDWIN, Raymond Earl, 1939-1941, 1943-1946

SNOW, (Charles) Wilbert, 1946-1947

Born on April 6, 1884 on White Head Island, St. George, Maine, son of Forest Alwin and Katharine (Quinn) Snow; a Protestant. Married to Jeanette Simmons on February 23, 1922; father of Charles Wilbert, John Forest, Nicholas, Stephen and Gregory Elisha Snow. Attended the public schools in Thomaston, Maine; received a B.A. from Bowdoin College in 1907 and an M.A. from Columbia University in 1910. He served as an Eskimo teacher and reindeer agent in Alaska during 1911 and 1912 and was a Second and First Lieutenant in the Field Artillery of the U.S. Army from 1917 to 1919. Snow was a successful teacher of English at New York University, Bowdoin College, Williams College, University of Utah, Reed College, and Indiana University until 1921; assistant and associate professor of English at Wesleyan University of Connecticut from 1921 to 1929; after 1929, he was a professor. Served as president of the Connecticut Association of Boards of Education in 1940. Snow lost the 1946 gubernatorial race to James L. McConaughy, 371,852 votes to 276,335; however as Lieutenant Governor of Connecticut, he assumed the governorship on December 27, 1946 upon the resignation of Governor Raymond E. Baldwin, and served until the inauguration of James L. McConaughy on January 8, 1947; a Democrat. He served as a State Department Lecturer in Europe and the Near East during 1951 and 1952; served as a member of the Middletown School Board and Middletown Democratic Town Committee. He was the author of a number of volumes of poetry and other writings, including *Maine Coast* (1923); *The Inner Harbor* (1926); *Down East* (1932); *Selected Poems* (1936); *Before the Wind* (1938); *Maine Tides* (1940); *Sonnets to Steve and Other Poems* (1957); *Spruce Head: Selections from His Poetry* (1958); *The Collected Poems of Wilbert Snow* (1963); *Autobiography* (1973). Snow died at his summer cottage on Spruce Island, Maine on September 28, 1977; he was ninety-three years old. Bibliography: *Facts on File Yearbook, 1946* (New York, 1947); Albert E. Van Dusen, *Connecticut* (New York, 1961); Congressional Quarterly, Inc., *Guide to*

U.S. Elections (Washington, D.C.,1975); Roy Glashan, *American Governors and Gubernatorial Elections, 1775-1975* (Stillwater, Minnesota, 1975); *New York Times* (September 29, 1977).

McCONAUGHY, James Lukens, 1947-1948

Born on October 21, 1887 in New York, son of James, a clergyman and author, and Eleanor (Underhill) McConaughy; a Congregationalist. Married to Elizabeth Townshend on June 13, 1913; father of three children, James Lukens, Pierre Rogers, and Phoebe. Attended Mount Hermon (Massachusetts) School, where his father headed the Bible Department; graduated with a B.A. from Yale University in 1909; professor of English and education at Bowdoin College from 1909 to 1915; received his M.A. degrees from Bowdoin and Dartmouth College in 1911 and 1915 respectively; received a Ph.D. from Columbia University in 1913; from 1915 to 1918, was professor of education at Dartmouth; from 1918 to 1925 was president of Knox College in Illinois; president of Wesleyan University in Connecticut from 1925 to 1943. A Republican, McConaughy entered politics while he was still president of Wesleyan. He was elected Lieutenant Governor in 1938 and served one term, 1939-1941. In 1942 he served as president of the United China Relief Fund and from 1943 to 1945 was a civilian deputy to William J. Donovan of the Office of Strategic Services (War Department). In 1946 the Connecticut Republican Party nominated McConaughy for Governor. In the election he received 371,852 votes, a majority of 54.4 percent, while the Democratic incumbent, Wilbert Snow, got 276,335 votes, and minor candidates, 35,644. Inaugurated on January 8, 1947, McConaughy supported increased appropriations for education, sponsored a state bonus for veterans of World War II, and became an advocate of integration of blacks in National Guard units. He sponsored a state sales and use tax, which effectively raised revenue but which was later modified, because it was yielding more than twice the amount required. The governor also sponsored several other reform bills: one created a Fair Employment Practices Commission; another provided for rent controls; and a third provided for more liberal unemployment benefits and old-age pensions. McConaughy's untimely death cut short a brilliant career before he finished his term as governor. He died in Hartford on March 7, 1948. Bibliography: Albert E. Van Dusen, *Connecticut* (New York, 1961); Roy Glashan, *American Governors and Gubernatorial Elections, 1775-1975* (Stillwater, Minnesota, 1975); Congressional Quarterly, Inc., *Guide to United States Elections* (Washington, D.C., 1975).

SHANNON, James C., 1948-1949

Born on July 21, 1896 in Bridgeport, Connecticut; son of Henry E. and Ellen C. Shannon; a Catholic. Married to Helen M. McMurray in 1925; father of James C., John H. and Helen C. He attended Georgetown University and Yale Law School; served in the United States Navy Air Force during World War I, and afterwards began his law practice in 1921. In 1923 he was Prosecuting Attorney for the city of Bridgeport, serving until 1931; in 1931 he was City Court and Juvenile Judge, serving until 1935; he was also counsel for the Connecticut Federation of Labor from 1939 until 1948. In 1947 he was elected Lieutenant Governor. Shannon became Governor of Connecticut on March 7, 1948 upon the death of Governor James L. McConaughy. Shannon ran for election in his own right, but was defeated in the general election by the Democratic candidate, Chester Bowles, by a vote of 431,746 to 429,071. Shannon left office on January 5, 1949. During his term of office Shannon called a special session of the legislature on housing. The governor asked for, and the legislature passed, legislation that increased the state's local housing authority bond guarantee total; lengthened the bond amortization period; and provided a seven-month moratorium on evictions. Other measures that were passed included an increase in the old-age pension. Following his term of office, Shannon served as Superior Court Judge from 1953 to 1965, and as Supreme Court Justice from 1965 to 1966. He retired in 1966. Bibliography: Roy Glashan, *American Governors and Gubernatorial Elections, 1775-1975* (Stillwater, Minnesota, 1975); Albert E. Van Dusen, *Connecticut* (New York, 1961); State of Connecticut, *Register and Manual, 1948* (Hartford, 1948); Congressional Quarterly, Inc. *Guide to United States Elections* (Washington,D.C., 1975).

BOWLES, Chester Bliss, 1949-1951

Born on April 5, 1901 in Springfield, Massachusetts, son of Charles Allen, a manufacturer, and Nellie (Harris) Bowles; a Congregationalist. Married in 1925 to Julia Fisk; then in 1934 remarried to Dorothy Stebbins; father of five children, Barbara and Chester, by his first wife, and Cynthia, Sally, and Samuel, by his second wife. Attended Choate School in Wallingford, Connecticut and graduated with a B.S. from Yale University in 1924; from 1924 to 1929, worked for a series of newspapers and advertising firms; in 1929 formed Benton and Bowles, an advertising firm in New York City; retired from his firm in 1941 and returned to Connecticut. There he served as Connecticut State Rationing Administrator from 1941 to 1942, and as state director of the Office of Price Administration from 1942 to 1943; became deputy administrator of the national OPA in early 1943 and administrator later the same year, serving until 1945, when President Harry Truman appointed him head of the new Office of Economic Stabilization. Bowles resigned from the latter position in 1946 when Congress passed a Price Control Act full of "loopholes." A Democrat, Bowles sought and won his party's nomination for Governor in 1948. In the election he captured 431,746 votes, a plurality of 49.3 percent, while his Republican opponent, James Shannon, got 429,071 votes, and minor candidates, 14,803. Inaugurated on January 5, 1949, Bowles supported a broad reform program. He demanded an end to segregation in the state National Guard and signed a law requiring that change in 1949. He persuaded the legislature to grant additional powers to the state Interracial Commission which, under the new law, could examine complaints of discrimination in hotels, public housing, and restaurants. In addition, he supported measures to increase benefits under workmen's compensation and to allow a new bond issue for construction on the campus of the University of Connecticut. He also convinced the legislature to appropriate monies for state-supported private housing. Bowles stood for reelection in 1950 but lost the election to John D. Lodge. Bowles received 419,404 votes, while Lodge gathered 436,418 and minor candidates, 22,913. Bowles retired to private life after his defeat in 1950 and made his home in Essex in Middlesex County. Bibliography: Chester Bowles, *Tomorrow Without Fear* (New Haven, 1946); Albert E. Van Dusen, *Connecticut* (New York, 1961); Roy Glashan, *American Governors and Gubernatorial Elections, 1775-1975* (Stillwater, Minnesota, 1975); Congressional Quarterly, Inc. *Guide to United States Elections* (Washington, D.C., 1975).

LODGE, John Davis, 1951-1955

Born on October 20, 1903 in Washington D.C., grandson of Henry Cabot Lodge and brother of Henry Cabot Lodge, Jr.; son of George Cabot and Mathilda Elizabeth Freylinghuysen (Davis) Lodge; a Congregationalist. Married Francesce Braggiotti on July 6, 1929; father of Lily Lodge Marcus and Beatrice (Mrs.) Antonion de Oyarzabel. Attended the Evans School in Mesa, Arizona; Middlesex School in Concord, Massachusetts; and the Ecole de Droit in Paris, France. Graduated from Harvard University in 1925 and Harvard Law School in 1929; practiced law in New York from 1933 to 1942; from 1942 to 1946, served in the United States Navy as a Lieutenant and Lieutenant Commander and was decorated with the rank of Chevalier in the French Legion of Honor and with the Croix de Guerre. A Republican, Lodge began his political career in 1946 when he was elected to the United States House of Representatives, serving for two terms from 1947 to 1951. In 1950 the Republican Party of Connecticut nominated him for the governorship. In the election Lodge received 436,418 votes, a plurality of 49.7 percent, while the incumbent governor, Chester Bowles, got 419,404 votes and minor candidates, 22,913. Lodge ran again in 1954 and received 460,528 votes, but lost the election to Abraham Ribicoff, who got 463,643 votes, while minor candidates received 12,582. Inaugurated on January 3, 1951, Lodge's first years in office were notable for the state's response to the Korean War. Connecticut ranked first in per capita value of military contracts, as the state's defense industry received $5,000,000,000 in war orders from 1951 to 1954. Lodge proved to be a reformer; he supported laws which increased workmen's compensation and unemployment benefits. Other legislation passed during his administration gave some state aid to education, and approved large bond issues for the construction of public buildings. Following his defeat in the 1954 gubernatorial contest, Lodge served as United States Ambassador to Spain from January, 1955 until January 1961; from 1964 to 1969, he served as chairman of the University of Pennsylvania's Foreign Policy Research Institute. He became Ambassador to Argentina in 1969. Since leaving that position, he is a resident of Westport, Connecticut. Bibliography: Albert E. Van Dusen, *Connecticut.* (New York, 1961); Roy Glashan, *American Governors and Gubernatorial Elections, 1775-1975* (Stillwater, Minnesota, 1975); Congressional Quarterly, Inc., *Guide to United States Elections* (Washington, D.C., 1975); Herbert F. Janick, *A Diverse People, 1914 to the Present* (New York, 1975).

RIBICOFF, Abraham Alexander, 1955-1961

Born on April 9, 1910 in New Britain, Connecticut, son of Samuel, a factory worker, and Rose (Sable) Ribicoff; of the Jewish faith. Married Ruth Siegel on June 28, 1931; father of two children, Peter and Jane. Attended public schools in New Britain; studied at New York University in 1928-1929. Graduated with an LL.B. from the University of Chicago in 1933. He was admitted to the Connecticut Bar in 1933 and set up his practice in Hartford. A Democrat, Ribicoff was elected to the Connecticut House of Representatives in 1938, where he served from 1939 to 1941; from 1941 to 1943, and again from 1945 to 1947, he served as a judge of the Hartford Municipal Court. Elected to the United States House of Representatives in 1948, and reelected in 1950, Ribicoff served from 1949 to 1953. He was unsuccessful in 1952 in an attempt to win a United States Senate seat. Ribicoff secured the state Democratic Party's nomination for Governor in 1954. In the election he received 463,643 votes, a plurality of 49.5 percent, while his leading opponent, the incumbent Republican, John D. Lodge, got 460,528, and minor candidates received 12,582. Reelected in 1958, the popular Ribicoff gathered 607,012 votes to his Republican opponent's 360,644 and to the minor candidates' 6,853. After his inauguration on January 5, 1955, Ribicoff faced an early crisis. Devastating floods struck Connecticut in August and October of 1955, and caused wide destruction. The governor personally led recovery efforts and pushed a rehabilitation program through the legislature, an action which gained bipartisan support. The leader of a reform administration, Ribicoff supported education and welfare programs. In 1957, at his urging, the legislature approved a $52,000,000 budget for expanding the state's educational system and for other welfare and humane programs. The governor also supported a state constitutional amendment which provided broader home rule powers to municipalities. Ribicoff resigned as governor on January 21, 1961, to accept a federal appointment as Secretary of Health, Education and Welfare. He assumed direction of a department with 62,000 employees and a budget of $3,750,000,000. Resigning that position in 1962, he then ran for the United States Senate. He won the election, and took his Senate seat on January 3, 1963. An ardent supporter of moderate and liberal Democratic goals, Ribicoff secured reelection to the Senate, where he still serves, in 1968 and 1974. Bibliography: Herbert F. Janick, *A Diverse People, 1914 to the Present* (New York, 1975); Albert E. Van Dusen, *Connecticut* (New York, 1961); Roy Glashan, *American Governors and Gubernatorial Elections, 1775-1975* (Stillwater, Minnesota, 1975); Congressional Quarterly, Inc., *Guide to United States Elections* (Washington, D.C., 1975).

DEMPSEY, John Noel, 1961-1971

Born on January 3, 1915 in Cahir, County Tipperary, Ireland, son of Edward Patrick, who came to the United States in 1925 and became a textile executive, and Ellen (Luby) Dempsey; a Roman Catholic. Married to Mary Madalene Frey on July 27, 1940; father of four children, Edward, John, Margaret, and Kevin. Attended public schools in Putnam, Connecticut, and Providence, Rhode Island College in 1934-35; secured employment in 1935 with Putnam Woolen Mills and later became a partner in an automobile agency. An ardent Democrat, Dempsey entered public life in 1936, winning a seat on the Putnam City Council, where he served until 1942; elected Mayor of Putnam in 1947 and served in that capacity until 1961; served as a member of the Connecticut Development Commission from 1942 to 1947; served in the Connecticut House of Representatives, 1949 to 1955; chosen executive secretary to Governor Abraham Ribicoff in 1955 and served until 1958, when he was elected Lieutenant Governor. When Governor Ribicoff resigned to accept a position in President Kennedy's cabinet, Dempsey became governor on January 21, 1961. He was reelected twice. In 1962 he received 549,027 votes, a majority of 53.2 percent, while his Republican opponent, John Alsop, received 482,582 votes, and minor candidates, 23. In 1966 Dempsey received 561,599 votes, a majority of 55.7 percent, while the Republican challenger, E. Clayton Gengras, received 446,536, and minor candidates, 422. As governor, Dempsey adopted a progressive course. He inaugurated a job-retaining program which predated the federal manpower program. He supported increased aid to education, including appropriations to build a long-needed medical school at the University of Connecticut. He also made improvements in the programs designed to care for the mentally ill and mentally retarded. In addition, the governor created a nonprofit corporation to administer a nuclear research center, which attracted new industry to the state and he influenced the legislature to earmark $150,000,000 for construction of new highways. In his views on national politics, Dempsey usually agreed with the consensus of northern liberal Democrats. Dempsey did not stand for reelection in 1971. He retired to look after his business interests in Putnam. Bibliography: Herbert F. Janick, *A Diverse People, 1914 to the Present* (New York, 1975); Roy Glashan, *American Governors and Gubernatorial Elections, 1775-1975* (Stillwater, Minnesota, 1975); Congressional Quarterly, Inc., *Guide to United States Elections* (Washington, D.C., 1975).

MESKILL, Thomas J., 1971-1975

Born on January 30, 1928 in New Britain, Connecticut, son of Thomas J., an industrial purchasing agent, and Laura (Warren) Meskill; a Roman Catholic. Married to Mary Grady; father of five children, Maureen, John, Peter, Eileen, and Thomas. Graduated from New Britain High School in 1946 and from Trinity College in Hartford, Connecticut in 1950; from 1950 to 1953, served in the United States Air Force, being discharged with the rank of First Lieutenant; received his LL.B. degree from the University of Connecticut Law School in 1956; practiced law in New Britain. A Republican, Meskill served as Mayor of New Britain from 1962 to 1964. He ran for the United States Congress in 1964 but was defeated in the Democratic landslide of that year. He ran again in 1966 and won a seat in the United States House of Representatives. Reelected once, he served a total of four years, from 1967-1971. In 1970 he received the state Republican Party nomination for Governor. In the election he gathered 582,160 votes, a majority of 53.8 percent, while his Democratic opponent, Emilio Daddario, received 500,561 votes and minor candidates, 76. Inaugurated on January 6, 1971, Meskill pursued a conservative course. He immediately faced a fiscal crisis. Connecticut in 1971 had a deficit of $260,000,000. His first act as governor was to order a ban on state hiring and on purchasing of new equipment. The governor then proposed an increase in the state sales taxes, but a Democratic-controlled legislature passed an income tax bill, a measure which became law without Meskill's signature. Intense public opposition to the income tax law led to legislative repeal and the adoption of new sales taxes which the governor had earlier advocated. By August of 1973, Meskill reported that the deficit had been overcome and that the state treasury had a surplus of $65,000,000. Under Governor Meskill, state leaders not only solved the state's financial crisis but also made much progress: a Department of Environmental Protection was created and a "no-fault" automobile insurance plan was adopted. Deciding not to seek a second term, Meskill left the governor's chair on January 8, 1975, and returned to his private law practice in New Britain. Bibliography: Herbert F. Janick, *A Diverse People, 1914 to the Present* (New York, 1975); *Wall Street Journal,* (May 3, 1973); *New York Times* (August 13, 1970; August 30, 1971); Roy Glashan, *American Governors and Gubernatorial Elections, 1775-1975* (Stillwater, Minnesota, 1975); Congressional Quarterly, Inc., *Guide to United States Elections* (Washington, D.C., 1975).

GRASSO, Ella Tambussi, 1975-

Born on May 10, 1919 in Windsor Locks, Connecticut, daughter of Giacomo, a baker, and Maria (Olivia) Tambussi; a Catholic. Wife of Thomas Grasso, a retired school principal, whom she married on August 31, 1942; mother of two children, James and Suzanne. Attended parochial school in Windsor Locks and Chaffee School in nearby Windsor; attended Mount Holyoke College in South Hadley, Massachusetts, graduating with a B.A. in 1940 and an M.A. in 1942. Worked during World War II as assistant director of research in Connecticut for the War Manpower Commission. A Democrat, Grasso began working for her party in 1943 as a speech writer and campaign supporter. She was elected to the Connecticut House of Representatives in 1952 and 1954, serving from 1953 to 1957. She served as Connecticut's Secretary of State from 1959 to 1971. Elected to the United States Congress in 1970, and reelected in 1972, Grasso served in the House of Representatives from 1971 to 1975. Nominated by the State Democratic Party to run for Governor in 1974, she faced Republican Robert H. Steele. In the election Grasso received 643,490 votes, a majority of 58.4 percent, while Steele received 440,169 votes and minor candidates, 19,054. After her inauguration on January 8, 1975, Grasso immediately proposed a record budget of $1,430,000,000. To raise needed revenue she proposed a one percent hike in the sales tax. She supported a program of social and economic reform but, at the same time, tried to economize wherever possible. She tried to reject a salary increase, and when told she could not constitutionally do so, she accepted the raise and then returned it to the state treasury in the form of a gift. She promised an "open government" and, in accordance with that promise, asked the legislature for a "right to know" statute which would open government records and meetings to the public. In her first term, Grasso also made proposals to solve the problems of ever-climbing public utility rates and of the complaints of utility executives who said that they lacked money for capital improvements. Grasso asked the legislature to pass laws enabling the state to borrow money for the construction programs of the companies. Grasso is at present serving as governor. Bibliography: Herbert F. Janick, *A Diverse People, 1914 to the Present* (New York, 1975); Hope Chamberlin, *A Minority of Members: Women in the United States Congress* (New York, 1973); *Christian Science Monitor* (July 26, 1974); Roy Glashan, *American Governors and Gubernatorial Elections, 1775-1975* (Stillwater, Minnesota, 1975); Congressional Quarterly, Inc., *Guide to United States Elections* (Washington, D.C., 1975).

DELAWARE

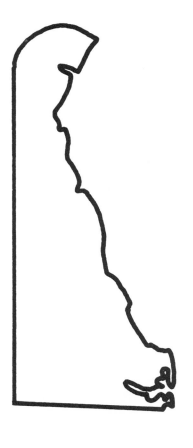

DELAWARE

CLAYTON, Joshua, 1793-1796

Born on July 20, 1744 at Bohemia Manor, Cecil County, Maryland, son of John, a miller, and Grace Clayton; a Presbyterian. Married to Rachel McCleary in 1776; father of Richard, James Lawson and Thomas Clayton. Studied medicine at the University of Pennsylvania from 1757 to 1762, afterwards practicing in Middleton, Delaware. Served as a Major in the Bohemia Battalion of the Maryland Line during the Revolutionary War; served as an aide on the staff of General Washington at the Battle of Brandywine; served as a delegate to the Provincial Congress from 1782 to 1784; elected to the Delaware House of Assembly in 1785 and 1787; served as Judge of the Court of Appeals; and elected State Treasurer of Delaware on June 24, 1786. Under the State Constitution of 1776, Clayton was elected President of Delaware by a joint ballot of the State Legislature, serving from May 30, 1789 to January 15, 1793. Under the Delaware Constitution of 1792, Clayton, the Federalist candidate, was elected the first Governor of Delaware on October 2, 1792, defeating the Independent candidates, Thomas Montgomery and G. Mitchell, by a vote of 2,209 to 902 and 458, respectively. He was inaugurated on January 15, 1793. During Clayton's administration, provisions were made for the construction of accomodations for the General Assembly at Dover; an act providing for the better relief of the poor was passed; and the lighthouse in Sussex County and the public piers opposite Reeden Island, as well as the lands belonging to them, were ceded to the United States by Delaware. Because the Delaware Constitution of 1792 prohibited a governor from succeeding himself, Clayton left office on January 13, 1796. He was elected to the United States Senate to fill the vacancy caused by the resignation of John Vining, and served from January 19, 1798 until his death. Clayton died in Philadelphia on August 11, 1798. He was first buried on his estate at Bohemia Manor, but was later reinterred in Bethel Cemetery, Cecil County, Maryland. Bibliography: John T. Scharf, *History of Delaware,* 2 vols. (Philadelphia, 1888); Paul Dolan, *The Government and Administration of Delaware* (New York, 1956); Congressional Quarterly, Inc., *Guide to United States Elections* (Washington, D.C., 1975); Roy Glashan, *American Governors and Gubernatorial Elections, 1775-1975* (Stillwater, Minnesota, 1975).

BEDFORD, Gunning, 1796-1797

Born on April 7, 1742 in Philadelphia, Pennsylvania, son of William Bedford, a farmer and landowner; a Presbyterian. Married to Mary Read in 1769; no children. Commissioned a Major in the Delaware militia on March 20, 1775, and Lieutenant-

Colonel of Colonel John Haslet's Delaware Regiment on January 19, 1776; appointed Muster Master-General in June 1776; took part in the Battle of White Plains, where he was wounded; remained in the service until 1779, when he returned to Delaware. Appointed Prothonotary of New Castle County in 1779; admitted to the bar in Sussex County, Delaware on August 4, 1779; served as a member of the Delaware House of Assembly from 1784 to 1786; elected to the Privy Council in 1783 and 1790; served as a member of the Continental Congress from 1783 to 1785, and from 1786 to 1787; chosen one of the first presidential electors in 1788; appointed Register of Wills for New Castle County on February 28, 1788; and appointed Justice of the Peace on January 24, 1789. As the Federalist gubernatorial candidate, Bedford was elected Governor of Delaware by popular vote on October 6, 1795, defeating the Democratic-Republican candidate, A. Alexander, by a vote of 2,352 to 2,142. He was inaugurated on January 13, 1796. During his administration, the Bank of Delaware was incorporated; the first act authorizing the establishment of public schools was passed; and commissioners were appointed to set the boundaries of the town of New Castle. Bedford's term came to an end with his death in Newcastle, Delaware on September 28, 1797. Bibliography: John T. Scharf, *History of Delaware,* 2 vols. (Philadelphia, 1888); Paul Dolan, *The Government and Administration of Delaware* (New York, 1956); Congressional Quarterly, Inc., *Guide to United States Elections* (Washington, D.C., 1975); Roy Glashan, *American Governors and Gubernatorial Elections, 1775-1975* (Stillwater, Minnesota, 1975).

ROGERS, Daniel, 1797-1799

Born in Accomack County, Virginia, on January 3, 1754. Rogers was a farmer and businessman near Milford, in Sussex County, Delaware. He served in the Delaware State Senate, and became its President. Upon the death of Governor Gunning Bedford on September 28, 1797, Rogers, as President of the State Senate, became Governor. Rogers, a Federalist, was succeeded on January 9, 1799 by Richard Bassett. Daniel Rogers died on February 2, 1806. Bibliography: Henry C. Conrad, *History of the State of Delaware* (Wilmington, Delaware, 1908); John A. Munroe, *Federalist Delaware, 1775-1815* (New Brunswick, New Jersey, 1954).

BASSETT, Richard, 1799-1801

Born on March 27, 1761 in Cecil County, Maryland, son of Michael, a tavern-keeper, and Judith (Thompson) Bassett; adopted by Peter Lawson, a relative; a Methodist. Married to Ann Ennalls; remarried to Miss Bruff; father of Mary and Rachel Bassett. Privately educated; studied law; admitted to the bar and afterwards practiced law in Delaware. Served as Captain of the Dover Light Horse in 1777. Served on the Council of Safety in 1776 and entered the Governor's Council during the same year, serving in that body for ten years; served as a member of the Delaware Constitutional Conventions of 1776 and 1792; served as a member of the Delaware Senate in 1782 and of the Delaware House of Assembly in 1786; served as a delegate to the United States Constitutional Convention in 1787, being one of the signers of that constitution; elected to the United States Senate; served from March 4, 1789 to March 3, 1793; appointed Chief Justice of the Court of Common Pleas of Delaware, serving from September 6, 1793 to January 8, 1799. As the Federalist gubernatorial candidate, Bassett was elected Governor of Delaware by popular vote on October 2, 1798, defeating the Democratic-Republican candidate, David Hall, by a vote of 2,490 to 2,068. He was inaugurated on January 9, 1799. The passage of the Alien and Sedition Acts of 1798 by the United States Congress resulted in considerable excitement throughout the United States during Bassett's term. However, the Virginia and Kentucky Resolutions, which denied the constitutionality of the acts and maintained that the individual states had the right to determine violations of the Constitution, were vigorously opposed by the Delaware Legislature. Bassett resigned from the governorship of Delaware on March 3, 1801 upon his appointment as United States Circuit Court Judge for the Third Circuit; he served in the capacity until 1802, when the court was abolished. Afterwards, he retired to private life. Bassett died on August 15, 1815 in Cecil County, Maryland and was buried in Wilmington and Brandywine Cemetery, Wilmington, Delaware. Bibliography: John T. Scharf, *History of Delaware,* 2 vols. (Philadelphia, 1888); Paul Dolan, *The Government and Administration of Delaware* (New York, 1956); Congressional Quarterly, Inc., *Guide to United States Elections* (Washington, D.C., 1975); Roy Glashan, *American Governors and Gubernatorial Elections, 1775-1975* (Stillwater, Minnesota, 1975).

SYKES, James, 1801-1802

Born on March 27, 1761 near Dover, Kent County, Delaware, son of James Sykes, an early Delaware politician; a Protestant. Married to Elizabeth Goldsborough; father of two sons, Samuel and William Sykes, and a daughter. Studied medicine with Dr. Clayton of Bohemia Manor and attended the lectures of Drs. Shippen, Morgan, Kuhn, and Rush. Began his medical practice in Cambridge, Maryland, where he remained for four years until he returned to Dover to establish himself as a renowned physician and surgeon. Elected to the Delaware Senate, serving as its Speaker from 1786 to 1801. A Federalist. As Speaker of the Delaware Senate, Sykes assumed the governorship of Delaware on March 3, 1801, upon the resignation of Governor Richard Bassett. During his administration, Sykes made several official appointments and continued the policies of Governor Bassett. Sykes left office on January 19, 1802 after the inauguration of David Hall, and returned to his medical practice in Dover. He moved to New York in 1814 and stayed there until 1820, when he returned to Dover. He remained in Dover until his death on October 18, 1822. Bibliography: John T. Scharf, *History of Delaware,* 2 vols. (Philadelphia, 1888); Paul Dolan, *The Government and Administration of Delaware* (New York, 1956); Congressional Quarterly, Inc., *Guide to United States Elections* (Washington, D.C., 1975); Roy Glashan, *American Governors and Gubernatorial Elections, 1775-1975* (Stillwater, Minnesota, 1975).

HALL, David, 1802-1805

Born on January 4, 1752 in Lewes, Sussex County, Delaware; a Protestant. Married to Catherine Tingley; father of Joseph Hall. Received a classical education. Was admitted to the bar on August 18, 1773. Enlisted as a private during the Revolutionary War; recruited a company which became a part of Haslet's Regiment; commissioned a Captain and participated in the battles of Long Island and White Plains; commissioned a Colonel on April 5, 1777; severely wounded at the Battle of Germantown, after which he returned to Lewes, where he resumed his law practice. As the Democratic-Republican gubernatorial candidate, Hall was elected Governor of Delaware by popular vote on October 6, 1801, defeating the Federalist candidate, Nathaniel Mitchell, by a vote of 3,475 to 3,457. He was inaugurated on January 19, 1802. During his administration, the Chesapeake and Ohio Canal Company was organized, with Joseph Tatnall of Delaware as president; an appropriation was passed to finance the securing of certain papers remaining in the land office of Pennsylvania; and several official appointments and commissions were made. Because the Delaware Constitution of 1792 prohibited a governor from succeeding himself, Hall left office on January 15, 1805. He was appointed a Judge of the Court of Common Pleas on March 5, 1813. Hall died on September 18, 1817 in Lewes, Delaware. Bibliography: John T. Scharf, *History of Delaware,* 2 vols. (Philadelphia, 1888); Paul Dolan, *The Government and Administration of Delaware* (New York, 1956): Congressional Quarterly, Inc., *Guide to United States Elections* (Washington, D.C., 1975); Roy Glashan, *American Governors and Gubernatorial Elections, 1775-1975* (Stillwater, Minnesota, 1975).

MITCHELL, Nathaniel, 1805-1808

Born in 1753 near Laurel, Sussex County, Delaware, son of James and Margaret (Dagworthy) Mitchell; a Protestant. Married to Hannah Morris; father of Theodore Mitchell. Served as an officer during the Revolutionary War with the rank of Captain in Colonel Samuel Patterson's Delaware Battalion of the "Flying Camp;" transferred to Colonel William Grayson's Additional Continental Regiment on January 20, 1777; promoted to rank of Major on December 23, 1777; appointed Brigade Major and Inspector to General Peter Muhlenberg; captured and made prisoner of war during the latter part of 1780, and was paroled on May 10, 1781. Served as a delegate to the Continental Congress; appointed as prothonotary of Sussex County, Delaware in 1788, serving in that capacity until 1805. As the Federalist gubernatorial candidate, Mitchell was elected Governor of Delaware by popular vote on October 2, 1804, defeating the Democratic-Republican candidate, Joseph Haslet, by a vote of 4,391 to 4,050. He was inaugurated on January 15, 1805. The overriding concern of Mitchell's administration was the passage of "an Act authorizing a detachment for the Militia of the United States." The act required Delaware to supply 814 men, fully equipped and organized, as its quota for the United States militia. Since the 1799 act to establish a uniform militia throughout the state had never been complied with, much time and effort was devoted to this enterprise. Because the Delaware Constitution of 1792 prohibited a governor from succeeding himself, Mitchell left office on January 19, 1808. He served as a member of the Delaware House of Assembly from 1808 to 1810, and as a member of the Delaware Senate from January 2, 1810 to May 1812. Mitchell died on February 21, 1814 and was buried in the Old Brick Church Cemetery near Laurel, Delaware. Bibliography: John T. Scharf, *History of Delaware*, 2 vols. (Philadelphia, 1888); Paul Dolan, *The Government and Administration of Delaware* (New York, 1956); Congressional Quarterly, Inc., *Guide to United States Elections* (Washington, D.C., 1975); Roy Glashan, *American Governors and Gubernatorial Elections, 1775-1975* (Stillwater, Minnesota, 1975).

TRUITT, George, 1808-1811

Born in 1756 near Felton, Kent County, Delaware, a Protestant. Married to Miss Hodgson, the daughter of Joseph and Mary Hodgson; father of Sarah Truitt. Privately educated. Served as a member of the Delaware House of Assembly for four terms, and of the Delaware Senate for one term. As the Federalist gubernatorial candidate, Truitt was elected Governor of Delaware by popular vote on October 6, 1807, defeating the Democratic-Republican candidate, Joseph Haslet, by a vote of 3,309 to 3,062; he was inaugurated on January 19, 1808. During his administration, the State Legislature appropriated funds for the purchase of arms for the state; passed a resolution requesting that fortifications be built at or near Wilmington, Delaware by the United States Government; and authorized the senators and representatives in Congress from Delaware to cede to the United States jurisdiction over those areas which were chosen as sites for forts, batteries and fortifications. Because the Delaware Constitution of 1792 prohibited a governor from succeeding himself, Truitt left office on January 15, 1811 and retired to private life. He died on October 8, 1818 and was buried in Kent County, Delaware. Bibliography: John T. Scharf, *History of Delaware*, 2 vols. (Philadelphia, 1888); Paul Dolan, *The Government and Administration of Delaware* (New York, 1956); Congressional Quarterly, Inc., *Guide to United States Elections* (Washington, D.C., 1975); Roy Glashan, *American Governors and Gubernatorial Elections, 1775-1975* (Stillwater, Minnesota, 1975).

HASLET, Joseph, 1811-1814, 1823

Born c. 1769 in Kent County, Delaware, only son of John Haslet, a member of the State Assembly and a military officer; a Presbyterian. Brother of Jemima and one other sister. Became a ward of Chief Justice William Killen after his parents' deaths in 1777. Privately educated. Moved to Cedar Creek Hundred, Sussex County, Delaware c. 1790, where he engaged in agricultural pursuits. Unsuccessful candidate for Governor in 1804 and 1807. As the Democratic-Republican gubernatorial candidate, Haslet was elected Governor of Delaware by popular vote on October 2, 1810, defeating the Federalist candidate, Daniel Rodney, by a vote of 3,664 to 3,593. He was inaugurated on January 15, 1811. During his administration, the Wilmington and Kennet Turnpike Company was incorporated in order to construct a turnpike from Wilmington to the Delaware-Pennsylvania boundary;

the Farmers' Bank of the State of Delaware was established; the State Legislature enacted several war measures; and the State Militia was reorganized, which enabled Delaware to defend itself successfully from the British in the War of 1812. Because the Delaware Constitution of 1792 prohibited a governor from succeeding himself, Haslet left office on January 18, 1814 and returned to his agricultural pursuits. He was reelected governor in a special election held on October 1, 1822, defeating his Federalist opponent, J. Booth, by a vote of 3,784 to 3,762. He was inaugurated on January 21, 1823. During this administration, Haslet made several official appointments, commissions and pardons. Haslet died on June 20, 1823 in Wilmington, while still in office. Bibliography: John T. Scharf, *History of Delaware,* 2 vols. (Philadelphia, 1888); Paul Dolan, *The Government and Administration of Delaware* (New York, 1956); Congressional Quarterly, Inc., *Guide to United States Elections* (Washington, D.C., 1975); Roy Glashan, *American Governors and Gubernatorial Elections, 1775-1975* (Stillwater, Minnesota, 1975).

RODNEY, Daniel, 1814-1817

Born on September 10, 1764 in Lewes, Sussex County, Delaware, son of John, a member of the Council of Safety and a judge of the Court of Common Pleas, and Ruth (Hunn) Rodney; an Episcopalian. Brother of Caleb Rodney. Married to Sarah Fisher on March 5, 1788; father of five sons and two daughters. Self-educated. Engaged in business in Lewes. Appointed Associate Judge of the Court of Common Pleas, serving from 1793 to 1806; served as a Federalist Presidential Elector in 1808; an unsuccessful candidate for Governor in 1810. As the Federalist gubernatorial candidate, Rodney was elected Governor of Delaware by popular vote on October 5, 1813, defeating the Democratic-Republican candidate, J. Riddle, by a vote of 4,643 to 3,768. He was inaugurated on January 18, 1814. During his administration, the United States was deeply embroiled in the war with Great Britain, and Rodney believed that the federal government should be responsible for expenses incurred in the defense of Delaware from the British. Legislation passed during his administration included a state tax and the granting of a license to the Wilmington and Philadelphia Turnpike Company to construct gates on the turnpike between Wilmington and the Delaware-Pennsylvania boundary. Because the Delaware Constitution of 1792 prohibited a governor from succeeding himself, Rodney left office on January 21, 1817 and returned to private life. He was elected to the United States House of Representatives to fill the vacancy caused by the resignation of Caesar A. Rodney, serving from October 1, 1822 to March 3, 1823; appointed to the United States Senate to fill the vacancy caused by the death of Nicholas Van Dyke, serving from November 8, 1826 to January 12, 1827, when a successor was elected. Rodney died on September 2, 1846 in Lewes, Delaware and was buried in St. Peter's Churchyard. Bibliography: John T. Scharf, *History of Delaware,* 2 vols. (Philadelphia, 1888); Paul Dolan, *The Government and Administration of Delaware* (New York, 1956); Congressional Quarterly, Inc., *Guide to United States Elections* (Washington, D.C., 1975); Roy Glashan, *American Governors and Gubernatorial Elections, 1775-1975* (Stillwater, Minnesota, 1975).

CLARK, John, 1817-1820

Born on February 1, 1761 in Smyrna, Kent County, Delaware, son of William Clark, a military officer; a Presbyterian. Married to Sarah Cook on September 16, 1784; father of Mary Clark. Self-educated. Appointed a Justice of the Peace on September 5, 1805; appointed a Lieutenant Colonel of the Third Regiment, Delaware militia on October 5, 1807; resigned on April 22, 1808 and returned to his farm in New Castle County, Delaware. As the Federalist gubernatorial candidate, Clark was elected Governor of Delaware by popular vote on October 1, 1816, defeating the Democratic-Republican candidate, Mansen Bull, by a vote of 4,008 to 3,517. He was inaugurated on January 21, 1817. During his administration, Clark recommended revision of "an act for the more easy and speedy recovery of small debts," and organized the Society of the State of Delaware for the Promotion of American Manufactures. Also, "an act for the interchange of laws," providing for the transmittal of three copies of the laws enacted by the Delaware Legislature to the executive of each state of the United States (and requesting a similar exchange in return), was passed. A difficult situation presented itself with the death of Governor-Elect Henry Molleston, on November 11, 1819. Since the Delaware Constitution of 1792 made no provision for the transfer of executive power in the case of the death of a Governor-Elect, Clark resigned as Governor of Delaware on January 15, 1820 to avoid any difficulties which might have arisen because of these circumstances. Clark died on August 14, 1821 in Smyrna, Delaware and was buried in the old Presbyterian graveyard near Smyrna. Bibliography: John T. Scharf, *History of Delaware,* 2 vols. (Philadelphia, 1888): Paul Dolan, *The Government and Administration of Delaware* (New York, 1956); Congressional Quarterly, Inc., *Guide to United States Elections* (Washington, D.C., 1975); Roy Glashan, *American Governors and Gubernatorial Elections, 1775-1975* (Stillwater, Minnesota, 1975).

MOLLESTON, Henry, [1820]*

Born in Kent County, Delaware, Molleston was a doctor in Mispillion Hundred. A Federalist, he was elected Governor on October 5, 1819, defeating Democratic-Republican M. Bull by a vote of 3,823 to 3,185, but died on November 11, 1819, before taking office. His office was taken by the President of the Senate, Jacob Stout. Bibliography: Henry C. Conrad, *History of the State of Delaware* (Wilmington, Delaware, 1908); John A. Munroe, *Federalist Delaware, 1775-1815* (New Brunswick, New Jersey, 1954).

*The above date for the term of office refers to when Governor-Elect Molleston's term would have begun.

STOUT, Jacob, 1820-1821

Born in 1764 near Leipsic, Kent County, Delaware; a Methodist. He was involved with business and farming interests. Stout was the Federalist President of the Delaware Senate when he assumed the office of Governor of Delaware on January

20, 1820. He succeeded Federalist Governor Henry Molleston from Kent County, Delaware, who had been the Governor-Elect. However, Molleston had died before his inauguration, after having defeated the Democratic-Republican M. Bull, by a vote of 3,823 to 3,185, in an election held on October 5, 1819. Stout served as Acting Governor of Delaware from January 20, 1820 to January 16, 1821, when John Collins, a Democratic-Republican, took office, filling the position left vacant by Molleston. In a special election held on October 3, 1820, Collins had defeated Federalist J. Green, by a vote of 3,965 to 3,520. During Stout's brief service as governor, the Missouri Compromise became a national issue. When the admission of Missouri as a state was proposed in 1820, a lively discussion arose in the Delaware General Assembly as to whether Missouri should be a free or a slave state. In the Assembly the question of the power of the United States Congress over slavery in the territories was referred to a committee, whose report favored Congress's right to regulate the status of slavery in the territories. The report was followed by a resolution stating that in the opinion of the General Assembly the future introduction of slaves into the territories of the United States and into any new states admitted into the Union should be prohibited by Congress. Slavery was not a partisan issue in Delaware, and some members of both the Federalist and Democratic-Republican parties argued against this act of the General Assembly. Eventually, the Missouri Compromise of 1820 passed the United States Congress under the direction of Henry Clay, and Missouri was admitted as a slave state, Maine was admitted as a free state, and slavery was prohibited in all territories west of the Mississippi River and north of latitude 36' 30''. After leaving office in 1821, Stout lived a productive life until his death in November 1855 at the age of ninety-one. Bibliography: Roy Glashan, *American Governors and Gubernatorial Elections, 1775-1975* (Stillwater, Minnesota, 1975); Henry C. Conrad, *History of the State of Delaware,* 3 vols. (Wilmington, Delaware, 1908); John A. Munroe, *Federalist Delaware, 1775-1815* (New Brunswick, New Jersey, 1954); Congressional Quarterly, Inc., *Guide to United States Elections* (Washington, D.C., 1975).

COLLINS, John 1821-1822

Born in 1775 in Nanticoke Hundred, Sussex County, Delaware, son of John, a military officer, and Sarah Collins; a Protestant. Brother of Robert and Nancy Collins. Father of Theophilus Collins. Self-educated. Appointed a Justice of the Peace of Sussex County on August 6, 1803; resigned on February 11, 1807. Appointed a Lieutenant in the Third Company, Third Brigade of the Delaware militia on October 28, 1807; commissioned a First Lieutenant of the Cavalry, Third Brigade of the Delaware militia on March 7, 1808. Upon the death of his father in 1804, Collins inherited a one-third interest in a mill built in Nanticoke and built a charcoal forge upon the Gravelly Branch, c. 1812, while continuing his business interests in the Nanticoke mill. Appointed a Major of the First Batallion, Seventh Regiment of the Delaware militia on March 15, 1815. As the Democratic-Republican gubernatorial candidate, Collins was elected Governor of Delaware by popular vote on October 3, 1820, defeating the Federalist candidate, Jesse Green, by a vote of 3,965 to 3,520. He was inaugurated on January 16, 1821. During his administration, a road, extending from the Philadelphia and Lancaster Turnpike Road in

Lancaster County to Newport, Delaware, was completed. Also, numerous official appointments and commissions were made. Collins died in Wilmington, Delaware on April 15, 1822, while still in office. Bibliography: John T. Scharf, *History of Delaware,* 2 vols. (Philadelphia, 1888); Paul Dolan, *The Government and Administration of Delaware* (New York, 1956); Congressional Quarterly, Inc., *Guide to United States Elections* (Washington, D.C., 1975); Roy Glashan, *American Governors and Gubernatorial Elections, 1775-1975* (Stillwater, Minnesota, 1975).

RODNEY, Caleb, 1822-1823

Born on April 29, 1767 in Lewes, Sussex County, Delaware; a Methodist. He was involved with business activities. Rodney was the Federalist President of the Delaware Senate when he became Acting Governor of Delaware on April 15, 1822, at the age of fifty-four. He served in that position until January 21, 1823, filling the seat left vacant by the death of Governor John Collins. A special election was held on October 1, 1822 and Democratic-Republican Joseph Haslet defeated Federalist James Booth by the narrow margin of 3,784 votes to 3,762. Haslet replaced Rodney as Governor. Earlier in Rodney's political career, he and Democratic-Republican Phillips Kollock were chief officers of an abolitionist society that first appeared in 1809 in Sussex County, Delaware. At the time slavery was not a partisan issue, although Federalists did hold enough power in the legislature to emancipate the slaves. While many Federalists in Delaware urged abolition, sponsorship of this move would have meant the dissolution of their party, for the greatest Federalist strength was in Sussex County, where slaveholding was popular. Consequently, abolitionist efforts failed and slavery remained. In 1816 Rodney ran as a Federalist candidate for a seat in the United States House of Representatives. There resulted a serious split in the Federalist Party during the campaign, when Thomas Clayton of Kent County and Thomas Cooper of Sussex County ran as independent candidates for Congress, and drew enough votes away from Rodney, who was the regular Federalist nominee, to insure a Democratic-Republican victory. Caleb Rodney died on April 29, 1840, at the age of seventy-three. Bibliography: Roy Glashan, *American Governors and Gubernatorial Elections, 1775-1975* (Stillwater, Minnesota, 1975); Henry C. Conrad, *History of the State of Delaware,* 3 vols. (Wilmington, Delaware, 1908); John A. Munroe, *Federalist Delaware, 1775-1815* (New Brunswick, New Jersey, 1954); Congressional Quarterly, Inc., *Guide to United States Elections* (Washington, D.C., 1975).

HASLET, Joseph, 1811-1814, 1823

THOMAS, Charles, 1823-1824

Born on June 23, 1790 in New Castle, New Castle County, Delaware. A lawyer. Thomas became Governor of Delaware on June 20, 1823, at the age of thirty-two. Prior to that time he had been the President of the Delaware Senate. A Democrat-Republican, Thomas filled the vacant seat of Governor Joseph Haslet, a Democrat-Republican, who had died in office after serving five months of his second term. Thomas served in the governor's office from June 20, 1823 until January 20, 1824, when Samuel Paynter of Sussex County, Delaware, took over the position. In a special election on October 7, 1823 to fill Haslet's vacated seat, the Federalist candidate Paynter had defeated the Democratic-Republican David Hazzard, by a vote of 4,348 to 4,051. Charles Thomas died on February 8, 1848, at the age of fifty-seven. Bibliography: Roy Glashan, *American Governors and Gubernatorial Elections, 1775-1975* (Stillwater, Minnesota, 1975); Henry C. Conrad, *History of the State of Delaware,* 3 vols. (Wilmington, Delaware, 1908); American Guide Series, *Delaware: A Guide to the First State* (New York, 1938); Congressional Quarterly, Inc., *Guide to United States Elections* (Washington, D.C., 1975).

PAYNTER, Samuel, 1824-1827

Born in 1768 at Paynter's Drawbridge, near Lewes, Delaware, son of Samuel, a member of the Delaware Assembly and colonel of militia, and Elizabeth (Stockley) Paynter; an Episcopalian. Married to Elizabeth Rowland; father of two daughters and two sons, among whom was Samuel Rowland Paynter. Privately educated. Appointed a Commissioner of Tax for Sussex County, Delaware on February 25, 1805; appointed director of the Farmers' Bank of Delaware on May 11, 1807; appointed State Treasurer and Trustee of the Loan Office, serving from January 1817 to January 1818; appointed a Judge of the Delaware Supreme Court on February 24, 1818, and served in that capacity until his resignation on October 6, 1820. As the Federalist gubernatorial candidate, Paynter was elected Governor of Delaware by popular vote on October 7, 1823, defeating the Democratic-Republican candidate, David Hazzard, by a vote of 4,348 to 4,051. He was inaugurated on January 20, 1824. During his administration, a public college was established in Newark; a law which gave in-state creditors of deceased persons preference over out-of-state creditors was repealed; and numerous official appointments and commissions were made. Because the Delaware Constitution of 1792 prohibited a governor from succeeding himself, Paynter left office on January 16, 1827 and returned to his business interests. He was elected to the Delaware Legislature in 1844. Paynter died on October 2, 1845 in Lewes, Delaware. Bibliography: John T. Scharf, *History of Delaware,* 2 vols. (Philadelphia, 1888); Paul Dolan, *The Government and Administration of Delaware* (New York, 1956); Congressional Quarterly, Inc., *Guide to United States Elections* (Washington, D.C., 1975); Roy Glashan, *American Governors and Gubernatorial Elections, 1775-1975* (Stillwater, Minnesota, 1975).

POLK, Charles, 1827-1830, 1836-1837

Born on November 15, 1788 near Bridgeville, Sussex County, Delaware, son of Charles, a member of the State Legislature and a Judge of the Court of Common Pleas, and Mary (Manlove) Polk; a Protestant. Married to Mary Powell; father of nine, among whom was Charles George Polk. Attended a classical school in Lewes, Delaware; read law with Kensy Johns, Sr. in Newcastle, but never practiced. In 1816 moved to Kent County, where he became the owner of 1,100 acres near Milford. He was elected to the Delaware House of Assembly in 1814, 1815 and 1817, serving as Speaker in 1814; served as a member of the Levy Court of Kent County in 1819; and was a member of the Delaware Senate in 1824. As the Federalist gubernatorial candidate, Polk was elected Governor of Delaware by popular vote on October 3, 1826, defeating the Democratic-Republican candidate, David Hazzard, by a vote of 4,334 to 4,238. He was inaugurated on January 16, 1827. During his administration, construction of the Chesapeake & Delaware Canal was begun and the summit bridge over the canal at the Buck Tavern was completed; a system of common schools was established; and the federal Tariff of 1828 was passed. Because the Delaware Constitution of 1792 prohibited a governor frqm succeeding himself, Polk left office on January 19, 1830. He served as president of the Delaware Constitutional Convention in 1831 and was again elected to the Delaware Senate in 1834, serving as its President in 1836. As President of the Delaware Senate, Polk assumed the Delaware governorship upon the death of Governor Caleb P. Bennett on May 9, 1836 and served until the inauguration of Cornelius P. Comegys on January 17, 1837. He served as Register of Wills for Kent County from 1843 to 1848, as Collector of the Port of Wilmington from 1849 to 1853, and was appointed Commissioner-Judge of the Delaware Supreme Court in August 1857. Polk died on October 27, 1857 at his estate near Milford. Bibliography: John T. Scharf, *History of Delaware,* 2 vols. (Philadelphia, 1888); Paul Dolan, *The Government and Administration of Delaware* (New York, 1956); Congressional Quarterly, Inc., *Guide to United States Elections* (Washington, D.C., 1975); Roy Glashan, *American Governors and Gubernatorial Elections, 1775-1975* (Stillwater, Minnesota, 1975).

HAZZARD, David, 1830-1833

Born on May 18, 1781 in Broadkiln Neck, Sussex County, Delaware, the only son of John, a military officer, and Mary Purnell (Houston) Hazzard; a Protestant. Married to Elizabeth Collins on July 12, 1804; father of John Alexander and David Hazzard. Self-educated. Appointed a Lieutenant in the Second Company of the Delaware militia on October 14, 1807; resigned on May 28, 1808; appointed an Ensign in the Grenadiers attached to the First Battalion, Eighth Regiment of the Delaware militia on July 4, 1812; commissioned a Captain on April 4, 1814. Appointed Justice of the Peace of Sussex County on May 12, 1812, serving until his resignation on December 8, 1817; unsuccessful candidate for Governor of Delaware in 1823 and 1826; elected as a Presidential Elector on November 11, 1828. As the American-Republican gubernatorial candidate, Hazzard was elected Governor of Delaware by popular vote on October 6, 1829, defeating the Democratic-Republican candidate, A. Thomson, by a vote of 4,215 to 4,046. He was inaugurated on January 19, 1830. During his administration, a new State Constitution was adopted, which included the following revisions: the governor was to be elected for a term of four years and serve only one term; no acts of incorporation were to be passed without the concurrence by two-thirds of each branch of the State Legislature; and the office of clerk of the Supreme Court of Delaware was abolished. Because the Delaware Constitution of 1792 prohibited a governor from succeeding himself, Hazzard left office on January 15, 1833 and retired to private life. He was appointed manager under "an Act to improve the navigation of Broadkiln Creek" on May 15, 1843; appointed an Associate Justice of the Delaware Supreme Court to fill the vacancy caused by the resignation of Caleb S. Layton on December 11, 1844; resigned on September 16, 1847; elected to the Delaware Legislature; served as a member of the Delaware Constitutional Convention in 1852; and retired to private life. Hazzard died on July 8, 1864. Bibliography: John T. Scharf, *History of Delaware,* 2 vols. (Philadelphia, 1888); Paul Dolan, *The Government and Administration of Delaware* (New York, 1956); Congressional Quarterly, Inc., *Guide to United States Elections* (Washington, D.C., 1975); Roy Glashan, *American Governors and Gubernatorial Elections, 1775-1975* (Stillwater, Minnesota, 1975).

BENNETT, Caleb Prew, 1833-1836

Born on November 11, 1758 in Chester County, Pennsylvania, son of Joseph, a shipping merchant, and Elizabeth (Prew) Bennett; a Quaker. Married to Catherine Britton on April 5, 1792. Moved to Wilmington, Delaware with his parents in 1761, where he attended the common schools. Entered the Continental Army in 1775; promoted to Sergeant in 1776 and to Ensign in 1777; participated in the battles of Brandywine and Germantown; joined General George Washington at Valley Forge in 1778 and participated in the Battle of Monmouth; promoted to Lieutenant in 1780; participated in the Battle of Camden and the siege of Yorktown; remained in active service until the Continental Army was disbanded in 1783. Appointed a Captain of Artillery during the War of 1812, and later promoted to Major in command of the forces at New Castle, remaining until the treaty of peace was signed. Served as Treasurer of New Castle County from 1806 to 1832. As the Democratic-Republican gubernatorial candidate, Bennett was elected Governor of Delaware by popular vote on October 13, 1832, defeating the American-Republican candidate, Arnold Naudain, by a vote of 4,220 to 4,166. He was inaugurated on January 15, 1833. During his administration, the Delaware Legislature denounced South Carolina's plan to nullify the tariff acts of 1828 and 1832 as unconstitutional; a petition for the restoration of the public deposit to the Bank of the United States was presented to Congress by the people of Delaware; and several companies were incorporated, among which were the Broad Mountain Coal Company, the Powhattan Coal Company, the Newcastle Manufacturing Company, and the People's Steam Navigation Company. Bennett died on May 9, 1836, while still in office. He was buried in the Friends Meeting House Cemetery, Wilmington, Delaware. Bibliography: John T. Scharf, *History of Delaware,* 2 vols. (Philadelphia, 1888); Paul Dolan, *The Government and Administration of Delaware* (New York, 1956); Congressional Quarterly, Inc., *Guide to United States Elections* (Washington,

D.C., 1975); Roy Glashan, *American Governors and Gubernatorial Elections,
1775-1975* (Stillwater, Minnesota, 1975).

POLK, Charles, 1827-1830, 1836-1837

COMEGYS, Cornelius Parsons, 1837-1841

Born on January 15, 1780 in Kent County, Maryland, son of Cornelius, a
Revolutionary War soldier, and Hannah (Parsons) Comegys; a Presbyterian.
Married to Ann Blackiston in 1801; after her death, remarried to Ruhamah Marim
on February 16, 1804; father of seven sons and five daughters, among whom were
Joseph P., Benjamin B., Cornelius G., John M., Mary Elizabeth, and Maria
Comegys. Attended the common schools and was employed as a supercargo by
Colonel Tennent of Baltimore. Moved to Kent County, Delaware, c. 1801. In 1804
settled in Cherbourg, where he engaged in agricultural pursuits. Appointed an
Ensign in the Eighth Company, Fifth Regiment of the Militia on October 30, 1807;
promoted to Major, Second Battalion of the Fifth Regiment on March 29, 1808.
Appointed a Commissioner of Tax, Kent County, on October 6, 1809, serving in
that capacity until January 3, 1811, when he resigned; elected to the Delaware
House of Representatives, serving as Speaker from 1812 to 1816. Reappointed a
Major of the Fifth Regiment of Militia on May 12, 1813; appointed a Major of the
Fifth Regiment of Militia on May 12, 1813; appointed Adjutant General of Militia
on September 5, 1814, serving in that capacity until May 22, 1816, when he
resigned; promoted to Lieutenant Colonel Commandant, Fifth Regiment of the
militia on December 26, 1814. Served as cashier of the Farmers' Bank from 1818 to
1829 and later became a State Director of that institution; served as State
Treasurer from 1818 to 1834; served as a Presidential Elector in 1832. As the Whig
gubernatorial candidate, Comegys was elected Governor of Delaware by popular
vote on November 8, 1836, defeating the Democratic candidate, Nehemiah Clark,
by a vote of 4,693 to 4,276. He was inaugurated on January 17, 1837. During his
administration, Comegys advocated payment by the government of French
spoilation claims; improvement of the penal code; modification of the school-tax
law; and improvement of the common schools. Because the Delaware Constitution
of 1831 limited a governor to one term, Comegys left office on January 19, 1841
and returned to private life. He died on January 27, 1851 in Dover. Bibliography:
John T. Scharf, *History of Delaware,* 2 vols. (Philadelphia, 1888); Paul Dolan, *The
Government and Administration of Delaware* (New York, 1956); Congressional
Quarterly, Inc., *Guide to United States Elections* (Washington, D.C., 1975); Roy
Glashan, *American Governors and Gubernatorial Elections, 1775-1975* (Stillwater,
Minnesota, 1975).

COOPER, William B., 1841-1845

Born on December 16, 1771 near Laurel, Sussex County, Delaware; a Protestant. Attended the common schools. Appointed a Justice of the Peace of Sussex County on August 16, 1797 and served until October 26, 1805. Appointed an Ensign in the Fifth Company of the Ninth Regiment, Third Brigade of the Delaware militia on October 27, 1807. Elected Sheriff of Sussex County on October 7, 1808 and served until October 18, 1812; commissioned a Captain in the Troop of Horse of the Third Brigade on November 24, 1814. Appointed a Judge of the Court of Common Pleas on September 26, 1817 and served in that capacity for more than twelve years. Cooper, a Whig, was elected Governor of Delaware by popular vote on November 10, 1840, defeating the Democratic candidate, Warren Jefferson, by a vote of 5,850 to 5,024. He was inaugurated on January 19, 1841. During his administration, there was a surplus in the State Treasury; Delaware was placed in the Fourth Judicial District of the United States; banks were permitted to suspend specie payments; and a memorial to Congress in favor of an issue of $200 million of government stock was prepared. Because the Delaware Constitution of 1831 limited a governor to one term, Cooper left office on January 21, 1845. He was appointed a superintendent to oversee improvements made in the navigation of Broad Creek in Sussex County, serving from February 25, 1846 until his death. Cooper died on April 27, 1849. Bibliography: John T. Scharf, *History of Delaware,* 2 vols. (Philadelphia, 1888); Paul Dolan, *The Government and Administration of Delaware* (New York, 1956); Congressional Quarterly, Inc., *Guide to United States Elections* (Washington, D.C., 1975); Roy Glashan, *American Governors and Gubernatorial Elections, 1775-1975* (Stillwater, Minnesota, 1975).

STOCKTON, Thomas, 1845-1846

Born on April 1, 1781, the eldest son of John, a Revolutionary War officer, and Ann (Griffith) Stockton; a Protestant. Married to Fidelia Rogerson on June 2, 1804; father of six, among whom was Thomas Stockton. Attended the College of New Jersey. Appointed a Lieutenant in the First Company, Third Regiment, First Brigade of militia on October 28, 1807; commissioned a Captain on May 16, 1808. Appointed Prothonotary, Court of Common Pleas of New Castle County on January 4, 1810, serving in that capacity until his resignation on October 7, 1812. Joined the Delaware Volunteers and was later commissioned a Captain; participated in the capture of Fort George on the Canadian border; transferred to the infantry and brevetted to the rank of Major; commanded a battalion in Lewiston, Maryland and Philadelphia, Pennsylvania until peace was declared; served in both the infantry and artillery until 1825, when he resigned and returned to Newcastle. Appointed clerk of the Peace and Register in Chancery of New Castle County on February 22, 1827, serving in that capacity until his resignation on June 1, 1835; appointed aide-de-camp to Governor Charles Polk on March 13, 1827 and to Governor Cornelius Comegys on April 11, 1837; appointed manager of the lottery authorized for the benefit of Delaware College on June 17, 1842. As the Whig gubernatorial candidate, Stockton was elected Governor of Delaware by popular vote on November 12, 1844, defeating the Democratic candidate, William Tharp, by a vote of 6,140 to 6,095. He was inaugurated on January 21, 1845. During his administration, joint resolutions were passed by the State Legislature opposing the annexation of Texas. Stockton died on March 2, 1846, while still in office. Bibliography: John T. Scharf, *History of Delaware*, 2 vols. (Philadelphia, 1888); Paul Dolan, *The Government and Administration of Delaware* (New York, 1956); Congressional Quarterly, Inc., *Guide to United States Elections* (Washington, D.C., 1975); Roy Glashan, *American Governors and Gubernatorial Elections, 1775-1975* (Stillwater, Minnesota, 1975).

MAULL, Joseph, 1846

Born on September 6, 1781 in Pilottown, Delaware. Resided in Sussex County, Delaware, where he was a doctor. Maull became Governor of Delaware when Governor Thomas Stockton died in office on March 2, 1846, after serving one year and two months of his term. Prior to his succession to the governor's office, Maull was the President of the Delaware Senate. He served as governor from March 2, 1846 to May 1, 1846, when he died in office. A Whig, Maull was replaced by the Whig William Temple, who was the thirty-two year old Speaker of the Delaware Senate. During Maull's short term in office, the Mexican War began in the spring of 1846. As a member of the Whig Party, Maull generally disapproved of President James K. Polk's foreign policy, and argued against the proposal to annex Texas. He died before Polk called for 300 volunteers from Delaware to fight in the war against Mexico. Joseph Maull died on May 1, 1846, at the age of sixty-four. Bibliography: Roy Glashan, *American Governors and Gubernatorial Elections, 1775-1975* (Stillwater, Minnesota, 1975); Henry C. Conrad, *History of the State of Delaware*, 3 vols. (Wilmington, Delaware, 1908); American Guide Series, *Delaware: A Guide to the First State* (New York, 1938); Congressional Quarterly, Inc., *Guide to United States Elections* (Washington, D.C., 1975).

TEMPLE, William, 1846-1847

Born on February 28, 1814 in Queen Anne County, Maryland, son of James, a farmer, and Anne (Kinley) Temple; an Episcopalian. Unmarried. Received a private preparatory education. In 1832 Temple moved to Smyrna, where he became a prosperous merchant. A Whig, Temple became interested in politics. At twenty-one he was elected to the Delaware House of Representatives, serving from 1835 to 1845. In 1844 he was elected Speaker of the House. From 1845 to 1854, he was a member of the State Senate. When Governor Thomas Stockton suddenly died in office on March 2, 1846, Joseph Maull, President of the Delaware Senate, succeeded him. In office barely eight weeks, Governor Maull was also stricken with illness and died on May 1, 1846. As Speaker of the State Senate, William Temple thus became Governor. Governor Temple was inaugurated on May 1, 1846; ten days later, on Monday, May 11, 1846, the Mexican War was declared. The Whig Party in Delaware opposed the war; nevertheless, it agreed to vote money and supplies, since the United States had become involved. Although anti-slavery men and abolitionists in the state saw the conflict as an excuse to gain more slave territory, Governor Temple directed the Assembly to vote as to the state's quota of men and money. After the surrender of Mexico City on September 17, 1846, the prospects of new territory caused further polarization of pro- and anti-slavery forces in Delaware. Since there were fewer than 2,000 slaves in the state, Temple did not fear economic disaster if slavery were to be outlawed, but he attempted to defuse the slavery issue by turning the state's attention to roads, schools, "blue laws," and taxes. Governor Temple left office on January 19, 1847 to resume his seat in the State Senate. In 1862 he was elected as a Democrat to the United States House of Representatives. He died in Smyrna, Delaware on May 28, 1863, before he could take his seat in Congress. Bibliography: Henry C. Conrad, *History of the State of Delaware,* 3 vols. (Wilmington, 1908); Paul Dolan, *The Government and Administration of Delaware* (New York, 1956); Roy Glashan, *American Governors and Gubernatorial Elections, 1775-1975* (Stillwater, Minnesota, 1975); Congressional Quarterly, Inc., *Guide to United States Elections* (Washington, D.C., 1975).

THARP, William, 1847-1851

Born on November 27, 1803 near Farmington, Delaware, in Kent County, son of James, a landowner and farmer, and Eunice (Fleming) Tharp; a Presbyterian. Married to Mary Clark on May 18, 1833; father of a daughter, Ruth. Was privately educated and, while still a young man, took over the management of the large family estate. He personally supervised the development and improvement of the estate. A Democrat, in 1844 Tharp was nominated for the governorship, but he was narrowly defeated by the Whig candidate, Thomas Stockton. The latter received 6,140 votes, a 50.2 percent majority, while Tharp received 6,095. Two years later, however, Tharp ran for the governorship again. In the 1846 election, he received 6,148 votes, a 50.6 percent majority, while his Whig opponent, Peter Causey, received 6,012. Inaugurated on January 19, 1847, Tharp served as governor until January 21, 1851. As governor, he proved to be an excellent administrator, practicing efficiency and frugality. During his term, a problem which had long plagued the state government concerning the ownership of Pea Patch Island off Delaware's coast, which had been claimed by both Delaware and the national government, was finally settled. Protracted negotiations resulted in a settlement in 1848, with Tharp relinquishing the state's claim in favor of the United States government. Governor Tharp also had to face critical national issues. The most important issue was the Mexican War which began in 1846, before Tharp became governor, and ended in 1848, a year after his inauguration. During his campaign for the governorship, Tharp maintained a moderate stance regarding the war. Personally doubting the wisdom of fighting what many Northerners believed was a Southern or "slaveocracy" war, Tharp remained patriotic, arguing that the James K. Polk administration had little choice but to declare war after Mexico had attacked American troops. In 1850 Tharp chose not to seek another term. He moved to Milford, Sussex County, where he continued to supervise his extensive farm lands. He died near Milford on January 1, 1865, at the age of sixty-one. Bibliography: Paul Dolan, *The Government and Administration of Delaware* (New York, 1956); Roy Glashan, *American Governors and Gubernatorial Elections,*

1775-1975 (Stillwater, Minnesota, 1975); Congressional Quarterly, Inc., *Guide to United States Elections* (Washington, D.C., 1975).

ROSS, William Henry Harrison, 1851-1855

Born in Laurel, Delaware on June 2, 1814, son of Caleb and Letitia (Lofland) Ross. Married to Elizabeth E. Hall on June 7, 1840; father of Letitia L., James J., William M., E.C., Sarah H., Mary G. and Laura F. Attended the public schools of Laurel; studied in a Friend's school in Claremont, Pennsylvania for two years. Became clerk in his father's mercantile and commission house; travelled in Europe with his father in 1836; engaged in business for one year in Adams County, Illinois. Returned to Delaware and opened a store in Laurel. Moved to his estate near Seaford, Delaware in 1845. In 1846 he was elected Captain of a company of cavalry which was raised in Seaford, but which disbanded at the close of the Mexican War. On November 12, 1850, William H.H. Ross was elected Governor of Delaware, defeating Peter F. Causey, a Whig, by a vote of 6,001 to 5,978. A Democrat. Governor Ross took the oath of office on January 21, 1851. During his administration, a conflict grew out of the State Constitutional Convention of 1853. Drastic revisions to the constitution were proposed, including greater representation for New Castle County, manhood suffrage, the election of the judiciary, and the abolition of slavery. These proposals were defeated, however, in the popular election of 1853. Governor Ross left office on January 16, 1855. After leaving the office of governor, he declined further political involvement. He was senior partner of the firm of W.M. Ross and Company, importers and manufacturers of agricultural supplies and fertilizers. Ross died in Seaford, Delaware on June 29, 1887. Bibliography: Roy Glashan, *American Governors and Gubernatorial Elections, 1775-1975* (Stillwater, Minnesota, 1975); Congressional Quarterly, Inc., *Guide to United States Elections* (Washington, D.C., 1975); Wilson Lloyd Bevan, ed., *History of Delaware: Past and Present,* 4 vols. (New York, 1929); Paul Dolan, *The Government and Administration of Delaware* (New York, 1956).

CAUSEY, Peter Foster, 1855-1859

Born near Bridgeville, Sussex County, Delaware on January 11, 1801, son of Peter Taylor, a merchant and manufacturer, and Tamzey (Eaton) Causey. Married to Maria Williams in 1825; father of William Frederick and John Williams. Received a good education; entered his father's business. Elected to the State House of Representatives, 1832; elected to the State Senate, 1833; delegate to the Whig National Conventions of 1840 and 1844. Was an aide on the staff of Governor Thomas Stockton in 1846; unsuccessful candidate for governor in 1846 and 1850. On November 14, 1854, Peter Foster Causey was elected Governor of Delaware, defeating William Burton, a Democrat, by a vote of 6,941 to 6,244. A Whig, but elected governor on the American ticket. Governor Causey took the oath of office on January 16, 1855. During his administration, an act abolishing life tenure in office was passed; however, since this law required a change in the State Constitution, the governor's approval was needed. Causey refused, and eventually the reasons which he gave for his decision were accepted by all parties. Although the American Party had been briefly popular, it was not destined to live long. In 1856 it lost control of the state of Delaware because it had been responsible for the passage of a prohibition law. Governor Causey's term in office ended on January 18, 1859. After leaving office, Governor Causey held no position except that of president of the Junction and Breakwater Railroad. Governor Causey died on February 15, 1871 in South Milford, Delaware. Bibliography: Roy Glashan, *American Governors and Gubernatorial Elections, 1775-1975* (Stillwater, Minnesota, 1975); Congressional Quarterly, Inc., *Guide to United States Elections* (Washington, D.C., 1975); *New York Times* (January 19, 1859); Wilson Lloyd Bevan, ed., *History of Delaware: Past and Present,* 4 vols. (New York, 1929).

BURTON, William, 1859-1863

Born near Milford, Kent County, Delaware on October 16, 1789, son of John, a farmer, and Mary (Vaughan) Burton; a Protestant-Episcopalian. Married to Mrs. Eliza (Sorden) Walcott; after her death, remarried to Ann C. Hill in 1830; father of Rhoda. Attended the medical school at the University of Pennsylvania; settled in Lewes, Delaware, but soon moved to Milford, where he established a large practice. Elected Sheriff of Kent County in 1830; unsuccessful Delaware gubernatorial candidate in 1854. On November 2, 1858, Burton was elected Governor of Delaware, defeating John Buckmaster of the People's Party by a vote of 7,758 to 7,554. A Democrat. William Burton was inaugurated on January 18, 1859. Although his efforts ultimately failed, Burton tried to avert the Civil War through his personal and official influence. Delaware was a state which still permitted slavery, and efforts were made to draw it into the Confederacy. These efforts proved futile, and Delaware sent more troops into the Federal army in proportion to population than did any other state. Governor Burton called a special session of the General Assembly on November 25, 1861 to enact funding legislation for Delaware's part in the war effort. Also, unsuccessful attempts were made to pass a law abolishing slavery in the state. Governor Burton's term ended on January 20, 1863. After leaving the office of governor, he returned to his medical practice in Milford. Burton died in Milford on August 5, 1866. Bibliography: Roy Glashan, *American Governors and Gubernatorial Elections, 1775-1975* (Stillwater, Minnesota, 1975); Congressional Quarterly, Inc., *Guide to United States Elections* (Washington, D.C., 1975); J. Thomas Scharf, *History of Delaware, 1609-1888,* 2 vols. (Philadelphia, 1888); Henry Clay Conrad, *History of the State of Delaware,* 2 vols. (Philadelphia, 1908).

CANNON, William, 1863-1865

Born near Bridgeville, Sussex County, Delaware on March 15, 1809, son of Josiah and Nancy (Bowlin) Cannon; a Methodist Episcopalian. Married to Margaret N.B. Laws. Educated in the common schools. At an early age, he began a mercantile career in Bridgeville, Delaware. Was elected to the lower house of the General Assembly in 1844 and 1846; served as State Treasurer in 1851; delegate to the

Peace Congress of 1861. On November 4, 1862, Cannon was elected Governor of Delaware, by defeating Samuel J. Jefferson, a Democrat, by a vote of 8,155 to 8,044. Member of the Union or Republican Party. William Cannon took the oath of office on January 20, 1863. During the election, he had defended the assembling of troops and the arrest of disloyal citizens. The legislature, however, passed a law designed to prevent "illegal arrests." This spurred Governor Cannon to make a patriotic proclamation, which brought about talk of his impeachment by his political opponents. The matter was soon dropped by the State Legislature, but was much discussed in the United States Senate. Governor Cannon established recruiting stations for enlisting black troops under the War Department order of October 26, 1863, which freed all slaves who served in the Union Army. He issued a warning proclamation when the Confederates were on the point of passing through Delaware. Delaware was placed under martial law on July 3, 1864. Governor Cannon died on March 1, 1865, before his term ended. He was buried in Bridgeville, Delaware. Bibliography: Roy Glashan, *American Governors and Gubernatorial Elections, 1775-1975* (Stillwater, Minnesota, 1975); Congressional Quarterly, Inc., *Guide to United States Elections* (Washington, D.C., 1975); J. Thomas Scharf, *History of Delaware, 1609-1888,* 2 vols. (Philadelphia, 1888); Henry Clay Conrad, *History of the State of Delaware,* 2 vols. (Philadelphia, 1908).

SAULSBURY, Gove, 1865-1871

Born in Mispillion Hundred, Kent County, Delaware on May 29, 1815, son of William, Sheriff of Kent County, and Margaret (Smith) Saulsbury; a Methodist Episcopalian. Brother of Eli, Willard, and two others. Married to Rosina Jane Smith on November 1, 1848; father of William and four others. Attended Delaware College; taught for a time, then entered the medical school at the University of Pennsylvania, graduating in 1842. Established a practice at Dover, Delaware. Elected to the State Senate in 1862; became Speaker in the second session of his term. After Governor Cannon died, Saulsbury became Governor of Delaware in accordance with the Delaware Constitution. A Democrat. Governor Saulsbury took the oath of office on March 1, 1865. On November 6, 1866, he was elected to a full term as governor, by defeating J. Riddle, a Republican, by a vote of 9,810 to 8,598. During his administration, he opposed each of the amendments to the federal constitution that arose from the Civil War, and each amendment was rejected by the Delaware General Assembly. He severely criticized the reconstruction measures of the federal government, and believed that the Fifteenth Amendment had been adopted by fraud and coercion. In order to raise money for the state, an act was passed imposing a tax on auctioneers, real estate agents and insurance companies. Each county, in turn, was appointed an assessor for the collection of taxes for the state. Also during his term, improvement in the construction of railroads in Delaware took place. Governor Saulsbury's term ended on January 17, 1871. After leaving the office of governor, he did not hold public office again. He was president of the Board of Trustees for the Wilmington Conference Academy at Dover, which he had helped to found, and served as a delegate to the Democratic National Convention in 1876 and in 1880. Saulsbury died in Dover on July 31, 1881. Bibliography: Roy Glashan, *American Governors and Gubernatorial Elections, 1775-1975* (Stillwater, Minnesota, 1975); Congressional

Quarterly, Inc., *Guide to U.S. Elections* (Washington, D.C., 1975); J. Thomas Scharf, *History of Delaware, 1609-1888,* 2 vols. (Philadelphia, 1888); Henry Clay Conrad, *History of the State of Delaware,* 2 vols. (Philadelphia, 1908).

PONDER, James, 1871-1875

Born in Milton, Sussex County, Delaware on October 31, 1819, son of John, a politician and businessman, and Hetty (Milby) Ponder; a Protestant Episcopalian. Married to Sallie Waples on July 31, 1851; father of Ida, John, James W., and two others. Educated at private schools in Lewes and Georgetown, Delaware; began in business under his father; became owner of the family firm after his father's death in 1863. President of the Farmers' Bank at Georgetown; director of Queen Anne's Railroad and of many companies and corporations. Member of the State Legislature in 1857; elected to the State Senate for four years in 1864; Speaker of the Senate during the session of 1867. On November 8, 1870, Ponder was elected Governor, defeating Thomas Coursey, a Republican, by a vote of 11,464 to 9,130. A Democrat. James Ponder was inaugurated on January 17, 1871. During his administration, he signed bills that restricted fishing by non-citizens of the state; that confined the sales of liquor mainly to hotel keepers; and that increased the legal rights of married women. Governor Ponder's term ended on January 19, 1875. After leaving the office of governor, he returned to his business interests. Ponder died in Milton on November 5, 1897. Bibliography: Roy Glashan, *American Governors and Gubernatorial Elections, 1775-1975* (Stillwater, Minnesota, 1975); Congressional Quarterly, Inc., *Guide to United States Elections* (Washington, D.C., 1975); J. Thomas Scharf, *History of Delaware, 1609-1888,* 2 vols. (Philadelphia, 1888); Henry Clay Conrad, *History of the State of Delaware,* 2 vols. (Philadelphia, 1908).

COCHRAN, John P., 1875-1879

Born in St. George's Hundred, New Castle County, Delaware on February 7, 1809, son of Robert, a landowner, and Rebecca (Ryland) Cochran. Brother of Alice, Robert Thomas, Margaret, William A. and Richard. Married to Eliza Polk on April 14, 1833; after her death, remarried to Mary A. Lumlin on January 6, 1858; father of William R., Juliana and Cyrus. Spent most of his life on his farms and was one of the largest land owners in Delaware. Represented New Castle County in the Levy Court, 1838-1846. On November 3, 1874, John P. Cochran was elected Governor of Delaware, defeating I. Jump, a Republican, by a vote of 12,488 to 11,249. A Democrat. Governor Cochran was inaugurated on January 19, 1875. During his administration a State Board of Education was formed; provision for a State Superintendent of Free Schools was made; and the constitutional amendment of 1873 was ratified, sanctioning a general incorporation law. Governor Cochran's term ended on January 21, 1879. After leaving the office of governor, he retired from public life, and returned to his farming interests. He died at his home in New Castle County on December 27, 1898. Bibliography: Roy Glashan, *American Governors and Gubernatorial Elections, 1775-1975* (Stillwater, Minnesota, 1975);

Congressional Quarterly, Inc., *Guide to United States Elections* (Washington, D.C., 1975); *New York Times* (December 28, 1898); J. Thomas Scharf, *History of Delaware, 1609-1888,* 2 vols. (Philadelphia, 1888).

HALL, John Wood, 1879-1883

Born in Frederica, Kent County, Delaware on January 1, 1817, son of John Hall, a merchant, and Henrietta (Bowman) Wood. Married to Caroline Warren on November 15, 1842; father of four children. Limited education. Began working at the age of sixteen as a clerk; bought a cabinet shop soon thereafter; acquired the shop when he came of age. Extended this business and developed a trade in lumber and grain. He built his own ships and sent them throughout the world; at one time he was the largest shipowner in Delaware. He also owned some very productive farms in Kent County. Entered the State Senate in 1866; delegate to the Democratic National Convention in 1876. In 1878 he was nominated for governor by acclamation. On November 5, 1878, he was elected Governor of Delaware, defeating the National Party candidate, K. Stewart, by a vote of 10,730 to 2,835. A Democrat. John Wood Hall was inaugurated on January 21, 1879. During his term bills were passed to regulate the sale of artificial butter; to provide for the use of a distinguishing stamp; and to provide for the appointment by the governor of an Insurance Commissioner. Another bill authorized the refunding of the state debt to the amount of $8 million at 4½ percent. Governor Hall's term ended on January 16, 1883. After leaving the governor's chair, he returned to his business interests. He was director of the Farmers' Bank of Dover, Delaware for many years. He was once again elected to the State Senate in 1890 and served until his death . Governor Hall died on January 23, 1892 in Frederica, Delaware. Bibliography: Roy Glashan, *American Governors and Gubernatorial Elections, 1775-1975* (Stillwater, Minnesota, 1975); Congressional Quarterly, Inc., *Guide to United States Elections* (Washington, D.C., 1975); J. Thomas Scharf, *History of Delaware, 1609-1888,* 2 vols. (Philadelphia, 1888).

STOCKLEY, Charles Clark, 1883-1887

Born in Georgetown, Sussex County, Delaware on November 6, 1819, son of Jehu, a watchmaker and Register in Chancery for Sussex County, and Hannah Rodney (Kollock) Stockley. Married to Ellen Wright Anderson on December 13, 1857; father of Hannah E. Educated at Georgetown Academy; entered business in Millsboro, Delaware. Appointed County Treasurer in 1852; Sheriff of Sussex County, 1856; elected State Senator, 1873; became Speaker of the Senate in 1875. On November 7, 1882, Charles Clark Stockley was elected Governor of Delaware, defeating the Republican candidate, A. Curry, by a vote of 16,558 to 14,620. A Democrat. Governor Stockley took the oath of office on January 16, 1883. In his inaugural address, he recommended that there be three School Superintendents instead of one; opposed any change in the liquor laws; and recommended amendments to the constitution. During his administration, a law was passed establishing a state library, and another which made the forming of an opinion a disqualification for jury duty in a capital case. Governor Stockley's term ended on January 18, 1887. After leaving the office of governor, he was appointed Register of Wills and Probate Judge for Sussex County in 1891; served as president of the Breakwater and Frankford Railroad; and served as director of the Junction and Breakwater Railroad. Governor Stockley died in Millsboro, Delaware on April 20, 1901. Bibliography: Roy Glashan, *American Governors and Gubernatorial Elections, 1775-1975* (Stillwater, Minnesota, 1975); Congressional Quarterly, Inc., *Guide to United States Elections* (Washington, D.C., 1975); J. Thomas Scharf, *History of Delaware, 1609-1888,* 2 vols. (Philadelphia, 1888); Henry Clay Conrad, *History of the State of Delaware,* 2 vols. (Philadelphia, 1908).

BIGGS, Benjamin Thomas, 1887-1891

Born near Summit Bridge, Pencader Hundred, Newcastle County, Delaware on October 1, 1821, son of John, a farmer. Married to Mary Scott Beekman in 1853; father of two sons and a daughter. Educated at the New Jersey Conference Seminary and at Wesleyan University, Middletown, Connecticut. Engaged in farming and horticulture at his home. During the Mexican War, he was commissioned a Major by Governor William Temple, although he never entered the army. Member of the State Constitutional Convention in 1853; unsuccessful candidate for the United States Congress in 1860; elected to Congress in 1868 and 1870, serving from 1869 to 1873; delegate to the Democratic National Convention in 1872. Returned to farming, and in 1877 to Middletown, Delaware. Director of the Kent and Queen Anne's Railroad. Thomas Biggs was elected Governor of Delaware on November 2, 1886 defeating John R. Hoffecker, on the Temperance Reform ticket, by a vote of 13,942 to 7,732. A Whig and later a Democrat. Governor Biggs was inaugurated on January 18, 1887. Many important bills were signed into law during his administration. Some of the more important were that individuals were allowed to vote on the question of holding a Constitutional Convention; husbands were required to support their wives and children; and three Superintendents of Schools were created rather than two. Also, a state hospital was established for the insane; a new survey of the Pennsylvania-Delaware boundary was conducted; and a Valued-Policy Insurance Law was enacted. Governor Biggs left office on January 20, 1891. He then returned to his business and farming interests. Biggs died in Middletown on December 25, 1893 and was buried in Bethel Cemetery, near Chesapeake City, Maryland. Bibliography: Roy Glashan, *American Governors and Gubernatorial Elections, 1775-1975* (Stillwater, Minnesota, 1975); Congressional Quarterly, Inc., *Guide to United States Elections* (Washington, D.C., 1975); J. Thomas Scharf, *History of Delaware, 1609-1888,* 2 vols. (Philadelphia, 1888); Henry Clay Conrad, *History of the State of Delaware,* 2 vols. (Philadelphia, 1908).

REYNOLDS, Robert John, 1891-1895

Born in Smyrna, Kent County, Delaware on March 17, 1838, son of Robert W., Sheriff of Kent County and Register of Wills, and Sally G. Reynolds. Married to Lovenia L. Riggs in 1862; father of Byron. Educated in the schools of his native state and in Fairfield, New York. Settled in Petersburg, Delaware in 1861 to engage in farming and horticulture. Elected to the General Assembly, 1869; elected State Treasurer, 1879 and 1881. Reynolds was elected Governor of Delaware on November 4, 1890, defeating Henry Richardson, a Republican, by the vote of 17,801 to 17,258. A Democrat. Governor Reynolds took the oath of office on January 20, 1891. During his term, a new boundary line was established between Delaware and Pennsylvania; a constitutional amendment was ratified by the legislature, giving Delaware's citizens the power to call a Constitutional Convention by their vote; and an inland waterway was made between Lewes, on lower Delaware Bay, and Chincoteague Bay, on the eastern shore of Virginia. Governor Reynolds' term ended on January 15, 1895. After leaving the governor's chair, he returned to his farming interests. Reynolds died near Petersburg, Delaware on June 10, 1909. Bibliography: Roy Glashan, *American Governors and Gubernatorial Elections, 1775-1975* (Stillwater, Minnesota, 1975); Congressional Quarterly, Inc., *Guide to United States Elections* (Washington, D.C., 1975); Henry Clay Conrad, *History of the State of Delaware,* 2 vols. (Philadelphia, 1908); *New York Times* (June 11, 1909).

MARVIL, Joshua Hopkins, 1895

Born in Laurel, Sussex County, Delaware on September 3, 1825, son of Joseph, a farmer; brother of five others; a Methodist-Episcopalian. Married to Sarah Ann Sirman in 1849; father of three sons. Received a limited education. Worked on the family farm until coming of age, then went to sea for one year, and engaged in shipbuilding for seven years. Operated a shop for the manufacture of agricultural implements from 1853 to 1865. In 1870 he invented a machine that made peach and berry baskets. After adding steam power to his plant, his business flourished and became the most important industrial plant in Sussex County. Marvil never held public office before running for governor. On November 6, 1894, Joshua Hopkins Marvil was elected Governor of Delaware, by defeating Ebe W. Tunnell, a Democrat, by a vote of 19,880 to 18,659. A Republican. Governor Marvil took the oath of office on January 15, 1895. However, his term of service was cut short by his unexpected death on April 8, 1895. He was succeeded by the Speaker of the Senate, William Thrap Watson. Marvil died in Dover, Delaware on April 8, 1895. Bibliography: Roy Glashan, *American Governors and Gubernatorial Elections, 1775-1975* (Stillwater, Minnesota, 1975); Congressional Quarterly, Inc., *Guide to United States Elections* (Washington, D.C., 1975); Henry Clay Conrad, *History of the State of Delaware,* 3 vols. (Wilmington, 1908); *New York Times* (April 9, 1895).

WATSON, William T., 1895-1897

Born on June 6, 1849 in Milford in Sussex County, Delaware. A businessman. A Democrat, Watson became Governor of Delaware on April 8, 1895, at the age of forty-five, when Governor Joshua H. Marvil died in office at the age of sixty-nine. Prior to assuming the office of governor, Watson had been the President of the Delaware Senate. He served until January 19, 1897, when Ebe W. Tunnell, a fifty-two year-old Democratic businessman from Lewes in Sussex County, Delaware, became governor. During Watson's time in office, a fierce struggle developed in 1895 for the United States Senate seat from Delaware. Anthony Higgins, who had been in the Senate for six years, succeeded in getting a majority of Republican members in the Delaware Assembly to favor his appointment, but failed to get the number necessary for election. The contest went to the floor of a joint meeting of the two houses of the Delaware Legislature. On the last day of the legislative session, and with numerous ballots cast but no victor, Acting Governor Watson claimed that he had the right to cast his vote as a State Senator. He took his Senate seat and cast his vote in the contest. The Speaker of the House refused to accept Watson's vote and declared Henry DuPont the winner. However, the election was protested. After a hearing of several months in the United States Senate, that body refused DuPont the seat and the dispute ended with a senatorial vacancy for Delaware. William T. Watson died on April 14, 1917, at the age of sixty-seven. Bibliography: Roy Glashan, *American Governors and Gubernatorial Elections, 1775-1975* (Stillwater, Minnesota, 1975); Henry C. Conrad, *History of the State of Delaware,* 3 vols. (Wilmington, Delaware, 1908); American Guide Series, *Delaware: A Guide to the First State* (New York, 1938); Congressional Quarterly, Inc., *Guide to United States Elections* (Washington, D.C., 1975).

TUNNELL, Ebe Walter, 1897-1901

Born on December 31, 1844 in Blackwater, Sussex County, Delaware, son of Nathaniel and Maria (Walter) Tunnell; a Presbyterian. Never married. Attended the private schools of Professor Aldred in Milford, Delaware, and Professor Sherman E. Adams in Lewes, Delaware. Began working in the mercantile trade around 1865 in Blackwater. Elected to the Delaware Legislature in 1870. Moved to Lewes, Delaware in 1872 and began a drug and hardware business; was appointed County Clerk of the Peace in 1884, and served until 1889; served as president of the Farmers' Bank of Delaware, Georgetown, Delaware from 1882 to 1917; an unsuccessful Delaware gubernatorial candidate in 1894. On November 3, 1896, Ebe Walter Tunnell won the general election for Governor of Delaware, receiving 16,219 votes to 12,235 votes for John H. Hoffecker, a Republican, and 7,432 votes for John Higgins, an Independent Republican. Governor Tunnell took the oath of office on January 19, 1897. During his administration, a new General Election Law was passed; state lands were given to the federal government to build fortifications in Delaware; and the state courts were reorganized according to provisions in the State Constitution, In 1899 the legislature passed a General Incorporation Act and a general law governing building and loan associations; a State Board of Agriculture was established; and a law was passed permitting a poll tax in Delaware. Governor Tunnell left office on January 15, 1901 and returned to his business interests. Tunnell died on December 13, 1917 and was buried in Lewes, Delaware. Bibliography: Roy Glashan, *American Governors and Gubernatorial Elections, 1775-1975* (Stillwater, Minnesota, 1975); Congressional Quarterly, Inc., *Guide to United States Elections* (Washington, D.C., 1975); Henry Clay Conrad, *History of the State of Delaware,* 2 vols. (Philadelphia, 1908); *New York Times* (December 14, 1917).

HUNN, John, 1901-1905

Born on June 23, 1849 in St. George's Hundred, New Castle County, Delaware, son of John, a farmer, and Mary Jenkins (Swallow) Hunn; a member of the Society of Friends. Maried to Sarah Cowgill Emerson on November 11, 1874; father of Alice. Attended the Friends' School at Camden and in the Bordentown New Jersey Institute. Went to Beaufort, South Carolina with his father in 1861 to do relief work among the freedmen of the South; remained in South Carolina to engage in the phosphate trade; returned to Delaware in 1876; and settled in Wyoming, Delaware as a dealer in grain, lumber, and fruit. On November 6, 1900, John Hunn was elected Governor of Delaware, defeating Peter J. Ford, a Democrat, by a vote of 22,421 to 18,808. A Republican. Governor Hunn took the oath of office on January 15, 1901. During his administration, legislation was passed to provide for the establishment and maintenance of free public libraries. Also, new laws were passed concerning the protection of wild life. He was widely criticized for his appointment of Dr. Caleb R. Layton as Secretary of State, who, however, proved to be very efficient in performing the duties of his office. Governor Hunn's term ended on January 17, 1905. After leaving office he returned to his business interests. He served as vice president of the First National Bank of Dover, Delaware, and as director of the National Building and Loan Association of the same city. Hunn died on September 1, 1926. Bibliography: Roy Glashan, *American Governors and Gubernatorial Elections, 1775-1975* (Stillwater, Minnesota, 1975); Congressional Quarterly, Inc., *Guide to United States Elections* (Washington, D.C., 1975); Henry Clay Conrad, *History of the State of Delaware,* 2 vols. (Philadelphia, 1908); *New York Times* (September 2, 1926).

LEA, Preston, 1905-1909

Born in Wilmington, Delaware on November 12, 1841, son of William, a merchant miller, and Jane Scott (Lovett) Lea; of Quaker ancestry. Married to Adelaide Moore on October 28, 1870; after her death, remarried to Eliza Naudain Corbit on April 29, 1897; father of Claudia Wright, Alice Moore, Ethel Mildred and Louise Corbit. Educated in Lawrenceville, New Jersey. Entered his father's business in Wilmington at age eighteen; upon the death of his father, he became president of the firm in 1876; was elected president of the Union National Bank in 1888. He also served as vice president of the Farmers' Mutual Insurance Company; director of the Philadelphia, Baltimore, and Washington Railroad; president of the Equitable Guarantee Bank; and president of the Wilmington City Railway Company. On November 8, 1904, Preston Lea was elected Governor of Delaware, defeating Caleb S. Pennewill, a Democrat, by a vote of 22,532 to 19,780. A Republican. Governor Lea was inaugurated on January 17, 1905. During his administration, the legislature passed an act authorizing a popular vote on the question of adopting a system of advisory initiative and referendum; the State Constitution was amended to abolish the monetary requirement for voting; and an act was passed approving a new "Great Seal of the State of Delaware." Governor Lea's term ended on January 19, 1909. After leaving the governorship, he returned to his business interests in Wilmington, and retired from public life. Lea died on December 4, 1916. He was buried in Wilmington. Bibliography: Roy Glashan, *American Governors and Gubernatorial Elections, 1775-1975* (Stillwater, Minnesota, 1975); Congressional Quarterly, Inc., *Guide to United States Elections* (Washington, D.C., 1975); Wilson Lloyd Bevan, ed., *History of Delaware: Past and Present*, 4 vols. (New York, 1929); H.C. Conrad, *History of Delaware*, 2 vols. (New York, 1908).

PENNEWILL, Simeon Selby, 1909-1913

Born on July 23, 1867 in Greenwood, Delaware, son of Simeon, a landowner, and Anne (Curry) Pennewill; a Presbyterian. Married to Elizabeth Halsey on December 30, 1920; remarried to Lydia Elder on February 27, 1929; no children. Pennewill was educated in the public schools of Greenwood and at Wilmington Academy; he became a businessman with extensive investment interests. He was elected to the State Senate, serving from 1899 to 1907, representing Kent County. A Republican, Pennewill ran for the governorship in 1908. After receiving his party's nomination, he faced the Democrat Roland G. Paynter in the general election. Pennewill captured 24,905 votes, a 52 percent majority while Paynter, from an old Delaware family, received 22,794 votes (47.6 percent). The minor candidates received 225 votes. Inaugurated on January 19, 1909, Pennewill represented traditional Republican ideals. He practiced thrift in government by limiting governmental expenses and trying to work within a balanced budget. In national politics, he steadfastly supported his party on national issues and was a strong follower of President Taft. During his administration, Pennewill became increasingly concerned about the division within the national party. In 1910 that division became more apparent when ex-President Theodore Roosevelt began challenging Taft for the Republican leadership. Robert LaFollette, a Wisconsin Senator, entered the struggle, which then became one of the progressive Republicans versus traditional or conservative Republicans. Pennewill knew that if the fight continued, the party would be overwhelmed by the Democrats in the national elections of 1912. Despite the fact that Pennewill counseled moderation, his fears proved to be well founded. He watched Roosevelt and Taft struggle through the party convention of 1912. Although Taft won the nomination, Roosevelt bolted the party to found the Progressive or "Bull Moose" Party, a development Pennewill abhorred because it facilitated the election of Woodrow Wilson. In Delaware, however, Pennewill's popularity held the party together and the governor's successor, Charles R. Miller, won for Republicans the gubernatorial election of 1912 by combining the best of Republican and Progressive ideals. Leaving office on January 21, 1913, Pennewill returned to Dover, Kent County, to manage his investments. He died in Dover on September 9, 1935, at the age of sixty-eight. Bibliography: Paul Dolan, *The Government and Administration of Delaware* (New York, 1956); Roy Glashan, *American Governors and Gubernatorial Elections, 1775-1975* (Stillwater, Minnesota, 1975); Congressional Quarterly, Inc., *Guide to United States Elections* (Washington, D.C., 1975).

MILLER, Charles R., 1913-1917

Born on September 30, 1857, near West Chester, Pennsylvania, the son of Robert H. and Margaretta (Black) Miller; an active Episcopalian and a senior warden of the Immanuel Church in Wilmington. Married to Abigail M. Woodnutt of Richmond, Indiana, on December 11, 1884; father of Margaretta M. (wife of Dr. DeForest P. Willard of Philadelphia), Thomas W. and Clement W. Attended the Westtown Friends School; was graduated from Swarthmore College with the degree of Bachelor of Letters in 1879; studied law at the University of Pennsylvania; received the LL.B degree in 1881. In 1884 Miller become an official of the Wilmington Malleable Iron Company; later became an official of the Philadelphia Mortgage & Trust Company in 1886; remained active as officer and director of railway, manufacturing, mining, gas, electric light and waterpower corporations across the United States. He retired from much active management of his business interests in 1911, but retained directorships; corporation president of the Farmers' Bank of Delaware and the Tonopah Mining Co. of Nevada. Entered politics in 1910 when elected to the Delaware Senate for four years; Water Commissioner of Wilmington in 1911; resigned both offices in 1912 when nominated as the Republican gubernatorial candidate. Elected Governor in 1912, polling 22,745 votes to 21,460 cast for Democratic challenger Thomas Monaghan. Miller took office on January 21, 1913. While governor, he urged the establishment of a women's college in connection with Delaware College; advocated better roads; supported revised marriage and ballot laws; and called for improved schools and greater use of scientific farming practices. During his term, legislation was enacted to further these goals. Miller left office on January 17, 1917. He was not a candidate for a second term. Afterwards, Miller remained active in politics, business, and community affairs. He was a member of the executive body of the National Republican Congressional Committee; member of the executive and federal legislative committees of the American Bankers Association; member of the finance committee of Delaware College, of which he was also a trustee; president of the Delaware Hospital, Delaware State Board of Charities, and Delaware Building and Loan Association. Miller was awarded the honorary LL.D. degree from Delaware College. He was a member of the Pennsylvania Society of New York, the Union League, Art, Bachelors, Barge, Down Town, and Germantown Automobile clubs of Philadelphia and the Wilmington County and Delaware Automobile clubs. Miller died on September 18, 1927, in Berlin, New Jersey, at the age of sixty-nine. Bibliography: American Guide Series, *Delaware: A Guide to the First State* (New York, 1938); Paul Dolan, *The Government and Administration of Delaware* (New York, 1956); H. Clay Reed and Marion Reed, eds., *Delaware: A History of the First State* (New York, 1947); Roy Glashan, *American Governors and Gubernatorial Elections, 1775-1975* (Stillwater, Minnesota, 1975).

TOWNSEND, John G., 1917-1921

Born on May 31, 1871 in Bishop Station, Worcester County, Maryland, the son of John G. and Meredith (Dukes) Townsend. Married to Jennie L. Collins of Maryland on July 28, 1890. Educated at a country school in Maryland. Worked for a railroad after completing grade school. Was involved with banking, farming, and business interests in Delaware, where he resided near Selbyville in Sussex County. Was founder in 1903 and president of the Baltimore Trust Company; president of banks at Selbyville, Bridgeville, and Camden (Delaware), Selbyville Manufacturing Company, Peninsula Real Estate Company, Eastern Shore Orchard Company, Delmar Orchard Company, and Atlantic Canning Company; was a partner in John G. Townsend, Jr. & Co. and Melson Brothers & Townsend. He was a member of the General Assembly of Delaware in 1901, and a delegate to the Republican National Convention in all years but one from 1904 to 1960. He was Colonel on the staffs of Governors Preston Lea, Simeon Pennewill, and Charles Miller of Delaware and was the Delaware General Conference M.E. Chairman in 1912. Elected Governor of Delaware in 1916, Townsend defeated Democrat John Hughes, polling 26,664 votes to his opponent's 24,053. He took office on January 17, 1917, at the age of forty-five. As governor, he pushed through laws considered liberal at the time, such as, workmen's compensation, protection for women workers, vocational education, and state income and inheritance taxes. Townsend left office on January 18, 1921, and did not seek a second term as governor. Afterwards, Townsend remained publicly active. He was president of trustees for Wilmington Conference Academy; was trustee for Washington College, Maryland; American University, Washington; and Goucher College. From 1929 to 1942, he was a member of the United States Senate. As senator, he was chairman of the Republican Senate Campaign Committee for nearly a decade, beginning in 1936, and a member of the Banking and Currency Committee. Townsend was defeated for a third term as senator. He was appointed alternate delegate to the United Nations General Assembly and was a member of the Mt. Rushmore Commission. He was a member of the Masons, Odd Fellows, and Young Men's Republican Club. Townsend died on April 10, 1964, at the University of Pennsylvania Hospital, at the age of ninety-two. Bibliography: American Guide Series, *Delaware: A Guide to the First State* (New York, 1938); Congressional Quarterly, Inc., *Guide to United States Elections* (Washington, D.C., 1975); H. Clay Reed and Marion Reed, eds., *Delaware: A History of the First State* (New York, 1947); Roy Glashan, *American Governors and Gubernatorial Elections, 1775-1975* (Stillwater, Minnesota, 1975).

DENNEY, William du Hamel, 1921-1925

Born on March 31, 1873 in Dover, Delaware, the son of William and Anna (du Hamel) Denney; an Episcopalian and a member of the Christ Episcopal Church, Dover, of which he was vestryman from 1905 to 1953, and senior warden during 1940-1953. Married to Alice Godwin in Englewood, New Jersey, on October 27, 1917; father of Anna and Alice Godwin. Educated at Wesleyan Collegiate Institute, Dover, Delaware. Became a clerk in a fire insurance firm in Dover in 1890; worked with Hartford Fire Insurance in various capacities from agent to state agent in the Delaware-Maryland territory, 1905-1925; and established, in partnership with W. Charles Boyer, the Dover Insurance Agency, a firm in which he relinquished his interest to his partner a year later. He began his political career as a Republican member and Speaker of the Delaware House of Representatives, 1905-1907 and was secretary to United States Senator Harry A. Richardson, 1907-1913. Elected

Governor in 1920. Denney defeated Democrat Arthur Lynch, by a vote of 51,895 to 41,038. He took office on January 18, 1921. During his administration, he consolidated several commissions into the State Department of Health and reorganized the State Highway Department. Many new roads were built and incorporated towns were connected by concrete roads. School laws were revised, and a new school code was enacted by the legislature. In 1924 a state constitutional amendment was enacted, leaving a capitation tax on every citizen over twenty-one years of age; a new budget system was created for all state departments; and a State Child Welfare Commission was established. In 1924 a State Health and Welfare Commission was created. Denney left office on January 20, 1925. Afterwards, he remained active in public office and became Acting Secretary of State for Delaware in 1931; became custodian of the State House in 1933; became State Motor Vehicle Commissioner in 1940, resigning in 1941 to accept an appointment as State Librarian, a post he held until 1948. From 1916 until his death, he was state director of the Farmers' Bank, Dover; was a member of the bank's real estate committee, 1941-1953; and was receiver for the International Re-Insurance Corporation of Delaware, 1940-1952. He was active in the Boy Scouts and was one of Dover's first scoutmasters; was a First Lieutenant in World War I, and after the war continued in the U.S. Army Reserves until 1938; was a member of the American Legion and the Sons of the American Revolution, the Masonic Order, IOOF, and the Kent and Maple Dale country clubs of Dover. He was a member of the Republican State Committee from 1920 until his death, having been chairman during 1926-1928. In 1922 and in 1928, Denney was chairman of the Republican State Convention, and he was a delegate to the Republican National Conventions of 1908, 1924, and 1928; in 1916 he was a Presidential Elector. Denney died on November 22, 1953, in Elsmere, Delaware, at the age of eighty. Bibliography: American Guide Series, *Delaware: A Guide to the First State* (New York, 1938); Paul Dolan, *The Government and Administration of Delaware* (New York, 1956); H. Clay Reed and Marion Reed, eds., *Delaware: A History of the First State* (New York, 1947); Roy Glashan, *American Governors and Gubernatorial Elections, 1775-1975* (Stillwater, Minnesota, 1975).

ROBINSON, Robert P., 1925-1929

Born on March 28, 1869 near Wilmington, Delaware, son of Robert L., a financial leader, and Frances (Delaplaine) Robinson; a Presbyterian. Married to Margaret Fouraker on June 9, 1904; no children. Educated in public schools and at Rugby Academy in Wilmington. At the age of nineteen, Robinson began working for the Central National Bank of Wilmington. After thirty years spent learning all aspects of the banking business and after making wise investments in the bank's stock, he became president of that institution. A staunch Republican, Robinson was persuaded by party leaders to seek the governorship in 1924. In the general election, he secured 53,046 votes, a majority of 59.6 percent. His Democratic opponent, Joseph Bancroft, received 34,830 votes (39.2 percent), while minor candidates received 1,063 votes. Inaugurated on January 20, 1925, Robinson was economy-minded and tried to operate within a balanced budget. Few reforms were passed during his administration, but he supported legislation passed in the early

1920s, prior to his administration—legislation which included a pension system for needy mothers; establishment of a state Board of Charities; and the construction of new facilities for many public schools. In national affairs, Robinson supported Calvin Coolidge and his conservative policies. Like Coolidge, Robinson believed that encouragement of American business was best for the country as a whole, and he supported the president's efforts to provide efficient government which benefited capitalists. Likewise, he approved of Secretary of the Treasury Andrew Mellon's move to reduce taxes on the business community and wealthy individuals and to place more of the tax burden on the middle class. A conservative in his personal tastes, Robinson abhorred the development of the "Jazz Age," with its increasing crime rate, "bootleg" gin, speakeasies, and what he saw as a breakdown of the country's morals. Choosing not to seek reelection, Robinson left office on January 15, 1929; heartened by the fact that fellow Republican Herbert Hoover had won the presidency, Robinson retired from politics to become once again the active president of his bank. He died at his home in Christiana Hundred, near Wilmington, on March 4, 1939, at the age of sixty-nine. Bibliography: Paul Dolan, *The Government and Administration of Delaware* (New York, 1956); Roy Glashan, *American Governors and Gubernatorial Elections, 1775-1975* (Stillwater, Minnesota, 1975); Congressional Quarterly, Inc., *Guide to United States Elections* (Washington, D.C., 1975).

BUCK, Clayton Douglass, 1929-1937

Born on March 21, 1890, in Buena Vista, at the family home near New Castle, Delaware, son of Francis N., a landowner, and Margaret (Douglass) Buck; an Episcopalian. Married to Alice du Pont Wilson in 1921; father of two children, C. Douglass, Jr. and Mrs. Dorcas VanDyke Farquhar, and a stepson, Paul Wilson. Attended Wilmington Military Academy, the Friends School, and the University of Pennsylvania. In 1911 he began work on a highway being built by T. Coleman Du Pont. Buck became chief engineer of the State Highway Department in 1916. He served in World War I as a private in the United States Army. A Republican, Buck entered the gubernatorial race of 1928 with his father-in-law's support. He was elected by a vote of 63,215 to 30,994, over the Democratic candidate, Dr. Charles M. Wharton. Renominated by the Republicans in 1932, Buck defeated L. Layton, his Democratic opponent, 60,903 votes to 50,401. He was one of only two Republicans elected Governor in the year that swept Franklin D. Roosevelt into the presidency. Governor Buck was inaugurated on January 15, 1929. The Great Depression of the 1930s put thousands of Delawareans out of work; however, there were no major bank failures. Buck, though a Republican, supported President Roosevelt in those programs designed to help the destitute. He favored the Civil Works Administration rather than the "dole system." The Works Projects Administration poured money into Delaware for reforestation, rural electrification, water works, and flood control. Moreover, the Du Ponts gave millions of dollars to help finance the public schools. Ineligible to run for a third term, Buck left office on January 19, 1937. He then became president of the Equitable Trust Company of Wilmington (the present-day Bank of Delaware.) He served in this position until 1941, when he resigned to become chairman of the board. In 1943 Buck began a term in the United States Senate, and served until 1949. He accepted Governor J. Caleb Bogg's appointment as State Tax Commissioner in 1953, and in 1957 refused reappointment. After an illness of less than a month, Governor Buck died in Buena Vista, Delaware on January 28, 1965, at the age of seventy-four. Bibliography: Paul Dolan, *The Government and Administration of Delaware* (New York, 1956); Roy Glashan, *American Governors and Gubernatorial Elections, 1775-1975* (Stillwater, Minnesota, 1975); Congressional Quarterly, Inc., *Guide to United States Elections* (Washington, D.C., 1975).

McMULLEN, Richard Cann, 1937-1941

Born on January 2, 1868 in Glasgow, Delaware, son of James, a leather worker, and Sarah Louise (Bouden) McMullen; a Methodist. Married to Florence Hutchinson in 1895; father of three children, Laura, Richard and Florence. Attended local schools in Glasgow and Goldey College, Wilmington. In 1888 he began work as a timekeeper for Charles Mullen's leather manufacturing plant. As the business grew, it became the Mullen & Pierson, Daniel Pierson and Amalgamated Leather Companies. McMullen learned the business, went into a partnership, and became vice president and a director of Allied Kid Company. He was also a director of the Industrial Trust Company and an official of the Harrison Street Methodist Church. A Democrat, McMullen became interested in politics and was elected to the Wilmington City Council. He also served as a member of the Delaware Public Utility Commission. In the gubernatorial election of 1936, McMullen defeated his Republican opponent, Harry L. Cannon, 65,437 votes to 52,782. Inaugurated on January 19, 1937, Governor McMullen was the first Democrat to hold the post in forty years. McMullen supported the reelection of President Franklin D. Roosevelt and encouraged the New Deal programs. The Committee for Industrial Organization (later, the Congress of Industrial Organizations) entered Delaware to unionize such industries as the automobile, chemical, and public utilities. By July 1937, John L. Lewis had called a series of strikes across the United States to secure the closed shop and to establish the right of the C.I.O. to represent workers in collective bargaining. Since the "sit-down" strike (the taking possession of the premises and refusing to leave until demands were met) usually led to violence, Governor McMullen successfully appealed to both labor and management to avert a crisis. He favored the Fair Labor Standards Act, which called for an eventual maximum working week of forty hours and a minimum wage of forty cents an hour. In addition, during McMullen's term the legislature amended Delaware's "blue laws," placing fewer restrictions on Sunday activities. McMullen left office on January 21, 1941 to return to his business interests. He died of a heart attack at his home in Wilmington, Delaware on February 18, 1944. Bibliography: Paul Dolan, *The Government and Administration of Delaware* (New York, 1956); Roy Glashan, *American Governors and Gubernatorial Elections, 1775-1975* (Stillwater, Minnesota, 1975); Congressional Quarterly, Inc., *Guide to United States Elections* (Washington, D.C., 1975).

BACON, WALTER W., 1941-1949

Born on January 20, 1879 in New Castle, Delaware, son of John G., an iron worker, and Margaret L. (Foster) Bacon; a Methodist. Never married. Attended the local schools in New Castle, and after graduating from high school, found employment as a timekeeper at the Delaware Iron Works in New Castle. He also worked for the Repauno Chemical Company, E.I. Du Pont de Nemours & Company, the United States Steel Corporation, and General Motors. He became assistant secretary of the Buick Division in Flint, Michigan. Upon his retirement from General Motors in 1931, he returned to Wilmington. A Republican, Bacon entered politics in 1935. He was elected Mayor of Wilmington, pledging to work at the job "full time." Hardworking and popular, Bacon was reelected by a majority of over 9,000 in 1937 and 13,000 in 1939. In 1940 he received his party's nomination for Governor. He won 70,629 votes, and his Democratic opponent, Josiah Marvel, Jr., received 61,237. Renominated in 1944, Governor Bacon defeated Isaac J. MacCollum, the Democratic candidate, by a vote of 63,829 to 62,156. Governor Bacon was inaugurated on January 21, 1941. Although events in Europe seemed to leave little hope that America could continue to remain at peace, the Japanese attack on Pearl Harbor on December 7, 1941 left the United States stunned. Bacon's experience in industry stood Delaware in good stead as he directed the state's war effort. Despite the inconveniences caused by rationing of such items as gas, oil, certain foodstuffs, leather goods and tires, employment in chemical plants, shipbuilding, and other war-related industries was plentiful. Delaware also supplied her share of volunteers for the military, while farmers and fishermen increased production of food and fiber. After the war Bacon supported measures for hospitals, education, bonuses, and rehabilitation for veterans. Governor Bacon left office on January 18, 1949 to retire to private life. Following an illness of over two months, he died on March 18, 1962, in Wilmington, Delaware, of a liver disease. Governor Elbert N. Carvel, who had been Lieutenant Governor during Bacon's second term, ordered all flags over state buildings flown at half staff. Bibliography: Paul Dolan, *The Government and Administration of Delaware* (New York, 1956); Roy Glashan, *American Governors and Gubernatorial Elections, 1775-1975* (Stillwater, Minnesota, 1975); Congressional Quarterly, Inc., *Guide to United States Elections* (Washington, D.C., 1975).

CARVEL, Elbert Nostrand, 1949-1953, 1961-1965

Born on February 9, 1910 in Shelter Island Heights, New York, son of Arnold Wrightson, a businessman, and Elizabeth (Nostrand) Carvel; an Episcopalian. Married to Ann Hall Valliant on December 17, 1932; father of four children, Edwin Valliant, Elizabeth, Ann and Barbara Jean. Attended local schools in Baltimore, Maryland, where the family had moved in 1916. He received his Bachelor's Degree in Engineering in 1928 from the Baltimore Polytechnic Institute and an LL.B. from the University of Baltimore Law School in 1931. He also studied accounting at Johns Hopkins University in Baltimore. He began his business career as a sales engineer with the Consolidated Gas and Electric Power and Light Company of Baltimore; became general manager, treasurer, and director of the Valliant Fertilizer Company in 1936 and its president in 1945. Moving to Delaware in 1936, Carvel helped incorporate the Milford Fertilizer Company, serving first as a director, later as vice president, and finally as chairman of the board. He was also a director of the Sussex Trust Company and the People's Bank and Trust Company in Wilmington. A Democrat, Carvel was so incensed by corrupt election practices in Delaware that he entered politics to fight for reform. From 1944 to 1948 he served as lieutenant governor, and in 1948 he ran for the governorship, defeating his Republican opponent, Hyland P. George, by a vote of 75,339 to 64,996. In 1952 he lost to J. Caleb Boggs, a Republican, by a vote of 88,977 to 81,772. Carvel was first inaugurated on January 18, 1949. During his first term Carvel's programs were blocked in the legislature by the Republican majority there. However, measures to finance new schools and raise teachers' salaries, and appropriations for new roads were passed. The General Assembly authorized an 8 million dollar bond issue for veterans' bonuses; it also created a Public Service Commission and a State Development Department. Carvel left office on January 20, 1953. In 1960, after a period in private life, Carvel once again ran for the governorship, this time against Republican John W. Rollins, whom he defeated by a vote of 100,792 to 94,043. Carvel took office for the second time on January 17, 1961. During his second term he sponsored, and the legislature passed, the Municipal Home Rule Law; he also authorized the Delaware River and Bridge Authority, and ratified the Interstate Compact on Mental Health. The legislature overrode Carvel's veto of a bill reestablishing capital punishment. On January 19, 1965, Carvel left office to return to his business interests. Bibliography: Roy Glashan, *American Governors and Gubernatorial Elections, 1775-1975* (Stillwater, Minnesota, 1975); Congressional Quarterly, Inc., *Guide to United States Elections* (Washington, D.C., 1975).

BOGGS, James Caleb, 1953-1960

Born on May 15, 1909 in Cheswold, Delaware, son of Edgar, a farmer, and Lettie (Vaughan) Boggs; a Methodist. Married to Elizabeth Muir on December 26, 1931; father of two children, James Caleb, Jr., and Marilu. Attended the local schools in Cheswold, Delaware; the University of Virginia, Charlottesville; the University of Delaware, Newark; and Georgetown University Law School, Washington, D.C., where he received his law degree in 1937. He was admitted to the Delaware Bar in 1938, and admitted to practice before the Delaware Supreme Court in 1938 and before the United States Supreme Court in 1946. Beginning his law practice in Dover, Delaware, Boggs moved to Wilmington, Delaware, and became a partner in the firm of Logan, Maruel, and Boggs. While he was serving as a Deputy Judge of the Family Court of New Castle County, World War II broke out. Boggs served in the United States Army as a Colonel in France. Discharged in 1946, he was decorated with the Legion of Merit, the Bronze Star with oak leaf cluster, and the French Croix de Guerre with palm. A Republican, Boggs was elected to the United States House of Representatives in November 1946. Serving until 1953, he favored farm price supports, and opposed the growth of federal power, increased federal spending, and the drift toward socialism. In the gubernatorial election of 1952, Boggs defeated Governor Elbert N. Carvel, the Democratic candidate, 88,977 votes to 81,772. Reelected in 1956, Governor Boggs won 91,965 votes. J.H. Tyler

McConnell, his Democratic opponent, received 85,047. Governor Boggs was inaugurated on January 20, 1953. He advocated municipal home rule; increased salaries for teachers; consolidated school districts; and extensively reorganized governmental agencies. One of Boggs' biggest problems involved the State Board of Education's attempt to comply with the United States Supreme Court's school desegregation order of May 17, 1954. In September 1954, the Milford school board assigned eleven blacks to the local high school. Protest quickly followed, and the school board closed the school. The State Board of Education criticized the Milford board for not submitting its desegregation plan before putting it into effect; the local board resigned; and the state board ordered the school reopened and the blacks to stay. About 60 percent of the whites boycotted, and ill feeling spread. On September 30, Governor Boggs and a newly-elected Milford school board devised a plan which removed the black students. The governor ordered the arrest of Bryant W. Bowles, president of the National Association, for leading the white boycott. On July 25, 1955, the State Supreme Court acquitted Bowles for conspiring to violate school laws. By September 1955, the populace had settled down, and desegregation continued across the state. Boggs left office on December 30, 1960 to take his seat in the United States Senate. He then returned to his law practice. Bibliography: Roy Glashan, *American Governors and Gubernatorial Elections, 1775-1975* (Stillwater, Minnesota, 1975); Congressional Quarterly, Inc., *Guide to United States Elections* (Washington, D.C., 1975).

BUCKSON, David Penrose, 1960-1961

Born on July 25, 1920 in Townsend, Delaware, son of Leon J. and Margaret (Hutchison) Buckson; a Methodist. Married to Patricia Maloney in 1963; father of Brian, David H., Eric, Kent and Marlee. Buckson received his B. A. degree from the University of Delaware in 1941 and attended Dickinson School of Law, where he graduated with an LL.B. degree in 1948. Served in the United States Army from 1941 until 1945, entering as a Second Lieutenant and discharged as a Major. Buckson served in the 198th Coast Artillery and saw service in the southwest Pacific. Buckson returned from active duty and completed his education, subsequently engaging in the practice of law. Served as chairman of the Kent County Republican Executive Committee in 1956. Buckson was elected Judge of the Court of Common Pleas in Dover, Delaware, serving from 1956 to 1957. Elected Lieutenant Governor of Delaware in 1957, and served in that capacity until 1960. A Republican. On December 30, 1960, Governor James Caleb Boggs resigned as governor of Delaware to take a seat in the United States Senate; according to Delaware state law, David Penrose Buckson assumed the duties of the governorship. Governor Buckson took the oath of office on December 31, 1960 and served the remainder of the term, which ended on January 17, 1961. After leaving the governorship, Buckson was elected to the office of Attorney General of Delaware in 1963 and served in that capacity until 1971. In the November 3, 1964 general election for Governor, Buckson was defeated by Charles Terry, Jr. Buckson also lost the August 19, 1968 Republican gubernatorial primary to Russell W. Peterson. Buckson presently lives in Middleton, Delaware. Bibliography: Roy Glashan, *American Governors and Gubernatorial Elections, 1775-1975* (Stillwater, Minnesota, 1975); Congressional Quarterly, Inc., *Guide to United States Elections* (Washington,

Delaware / 245

D.C., 1975); *New York Times* (December 31, 1960); Lester A. Sobel, ed., *Facts on File Yearbook, 1960* (New York, 1961).

CARVEL, Elbert Nostrand, 1949-1953, 1961-1965

.

TERRY, Charles Laymen, 1965-1969

Born in Camden, Delaware on September 17, 1900, son of Charles, a lawyer, and Elizabeth (Maxson) Terry; an Episcopalian. Married to Jessica Irby on June 30, 1924; father of Charles Laymen, III. Received his law degree from Washington and Lee University in 1923; admitted to the Delaware Bar, 1924; member of the law firm of Terry and Terry, Dover, Delaware, 1926-1935; Hughes, Terry and Terry, 1935-1937. Attorney for the Delaware Legislature, 1933-1934; Secretary of State of Delaware, 1937-1938. Became Associate Judge of the Supreme Court of Delaware in 1938; later elevated to Chief Justice. On November 3, 1964, Charles Laymen Terry, Jr. was elected Governor of Delaware, defeating David P. Buckson, a Republican, by a vote of 102,797 to 97,374. A Democrat. Governor Terry was inaugurated on January 19, 1965. A great deal of legislation was passed during his administration, some of which included the establishment of a merit system for state employees; a new Water and Air Resources Department; and a Legislative Council to provide for study of contemplated legislation. Also, new government departments were created for housing, transportation, and justice, and Delaware's first minimum wage law was passed. Terry's term ended on January 21, 1969. He had been unsuccessful in his bid for reelection on November 5, 1968. Governor Terry returned to his law practice in Dover after his service as governor. He died on February 6, 1970 in Dover. Bibliography: Roy Glashan, *American Governors and Gubernatorial Elections, 1775-1975* (Stillwater, Minnesota, 1975); Congressional Quarterly, Inc., *Guide to United States Elections* (Washington, D.C., 1975); *New York Times* (February 7, 1970); Dorothy Kattleman, ed., *Facts on File Five-Year Index, 1966-1970* (New York, 1971).

PETERSON, Russell Wilbur, 1969-1973

Born in Portage, Wisconsin on October 3, 1916, son of John Anton and Emma (Anthony) Peterson; a Unitarian. Married to E. Lillian Turner on June 30, 1937; father of Russell Glen, Peter Jon, Kristin and Elin. Received his B.S. degree from the University of Wisconsin, 1938, and Ph.D., 1942. Employed by E.I. Du Pont de Nemours and Company, Inc., 1942-1969; research director, textile fibers department, 1954-1955, 1956-1959, and merchandising manager, textile fibers, 1955-1956; director of new products division, textile fibers, 1959-1962; director of research and development division, development department, 1963-1969. Textile Research Institute, Princeton, New Jersey, 1956-1969; chairman of the executive committee, 1959-1961; chairman of the board of directors, 1961-1963. On November 5, 1968, Russell Wilbur Peterson was elected Governor of Delaware, defeating Charles L.

Terry, a Democrat, by a vote of 104,474 to 102,360. A Republican. Governor Peterson took the oath of office on January 21, 1969. During his administration, legislation included passage of a Fair Housing Law; a Coastal Zoning Act to prohibit further construction of heavy industry along the Delaware littoral in the Delaware River and Bay and the Atlantic Ocean; and the reorganization of the family court system. Also, a cabinet form of government was inaugurated, giving the governor more authority. Governor Peterson's term ended on January 16, 1973. He had been defeated for reelection by Sherman W. Tribbett on November 7, 1972. After leaving the office of governor, Peterson served as chairman of the United States Council on Environmental Quality. He now lives in Washington, D.C. Bibliography: Roy Glashan, *American Governors and Gubernatorial Elections, 1775-1975* (Stillwater, Minnesota, 1975); Congressional Quarterly, Inc., *Guide to United States Elections* (Washington, D.C., 1975); Henry H. Schulte, Jr., ed., *Facts on File Yearbook, 1973* (New York, 1974); Dorothy Kattleman, ed., *Facts on File Five-Year Index, 1966-1970* (New York, 1971).

TRIBBITT, Sherman Willard, 1973-1977

Born in Easton, Maryland on November 9, 1922, son of Sherman Lawrence and Minnie (Thowley) Tribbitt; a Methodist. Married to Jeanne Cleaver Webb on July 24, 1943; father of James, Carole and Sherman Webb. Received his A.A. degree from Beacom College in 1941. Served with the United States Naval Reserve, 1942-1945. Teller with the Security Trust Company, Wilmington, Delaware, 1941-1942; owner of the Odessa Supply Company, 1947-1973; director of Farmers' Mutual Insurance Company; chairman of the advisory board for Farmers' Bank, Delaware Savings and Loan Company; member of Delaware General Assembly, 1957-1965 and 1970-1972; Lieutenant Governor of Delaware, 1965-1969. Sherman W. Tribbitt was elected Governor of Delaware on November 7, 1972, defeating Russell Peterson, a Republican, by a vote of 117,274 to 109,583. A Democrat. Governor Tribbitt took the oath of office on January 16, 1973. During his term, a law was passed to regulate the uses of the extensive wetland area of the state; a state lottery was authorized; and the custody of adult and juvenile offenders was placed in a newly-created Department of Corrections. Also, a "no-fault" divorce law passed; a proposed new State Constitution was defeated in a bitter battle in the General Assembly in 1974; and the death penalty for some crimes was restored. Governor Tribbitt's term ended on January 18, 1977. Governor Tribbitt was unsuccessful in his bid for reelection in the November, 1976 general election for Governor of Delaware. He was defeated by Pierre S. du Pont, IV, and returned to his business interests. Bibliography: Roy Glashan, *American Governors and Gubernatorial Elections, 1775-1975* (Stillwater, Minnesota, 1975); Congressional Quarterly, Inc., *Guide to United States Elections* (Washington, D.C., 1975); *New York Times* (November 8, 1972); Lester A. Sobel, ed., *Facts on File Yearbook, 1972* (New York, 1973).

DuPONT, Pierre Samuel, IV, 1977-

Born on January 22, 1935 in Wilmington, Delaware, son of Pierre Samuel du Pont, III, an industrialist, and Jane (Holcomb) du Pont; an Episcopalian. Brother of Jane de Doliete and Michele Wainwright. Married to Elsie Ravenel Wood on May 4, 1957; father of Elsie Ravenel, Pierre S., Benjamin Franklin and Eleuthere Irenee. Entered the Navy as an Ensign in 1957 and received his discharge in 1960, holding the rank of Lieutenant. Graduated from Phillips Exeter Academy in 1952; received a B.S.E. in 1956 from Princeton University and an LL.B. in 1963 from Harvard Law School. In 1968 du Pont, a Republican, was elected to the Delaware House of Representatives and served until 1970; elected to the United States House of Representatives in 1971, serving until 1976. Du Pont served as technical representative for Du Pont Nemours and Company from 1963 to 1970. On November 2, 1976, Pierre Samuel du Pont, IV, defeated Sherman W. Tribbitt, a Democrat, 130,566 votes to 97,514 votes, for the governorship of Delaware. Du Pont took the oath of office on January 18, 1977. Bibliography: Gerard Colby Zilg, *Du Pont Behind the Nylon Curtain* (Englewood Cliffs, New Jersey, 1974); *New York Times* (January 19, 1977); Congressional Quarterly, Inc., *Guide to United States Elections* (Washington, D.C., 1975); Charles Monaghan, ed., *Facts on File Yearbook, 1976* (New York, 1977).

FLORIDA

FLORIDA

MOSELEY, William Dunn, 1845-1849

Born on February 1, 1795 at "Moseley Hall," the family homestead in Lenoir County, North Carolina, son of Matthew, a planter, and Elizabeth (Herring) Dunn. Married to Susan Hill in 1822, who died in 1842; father of six children. Attended a local academy; graduated from the University of North Carolina in Chapel Hill, North Carolina in 1818; studied law. Admitted to the bar. Worked on his father's farm; taught school; opened a law practice in Wilmington, North Carolina; bought a plantation on Miccosoukie Lake in Jefferson County, Florida in 1835. Elected to the North Carolina Senate in 1829, and served until 1836; President, North Carolina Senate, 1832-1836; unsuccessful Democratic candidate for Governor of North Carolina in 1834; elected to the Florida Territorial House of Representatives in 1840; elected to the Florida Territorial Senate in 1844. As a Democrat, Moseley was elected Governor of Florida on May 26, 1845, defeating the Whig candidate, Richard Keith Call, 3,292 votes to 2,679. Moseley took office on June 25, 1845. As Florida's first governor, he was faced with implementing the new state government. While he was governor, the Mexican War began, and the federal government started construction of Fort Jefferson on Garden Key in the Gulf of Mexico, and of Fort Clinch in Fernandina, Florida. Though it was thought that the conflict between the Seminole Indians and the white settlers within the state had ended in 1842, skirmishes continued to occur, and in July, 1849, several trading post operators were killed by the Indians. Constitutionally prohibited from seeking reelection for four years after the expiration of his term, Moseley left office on October 1, 1849. Afterward, he returned to his plantation in Jefferson County. In 1851, he moved to Palatka, Florida. Moseley died in Palatka on January 4, 1863. Bibliography: George M. Chapin, *Florida, 1513-1913, Past, Present and Future*, 2 vols. (Chicago, 1914); Harry G. Cutler, *Florida, Past and Present, Historical and Biographical*, 3 vols. (Chicago, 1923); Caroline M. Brevard, *A History of Florida from the Treaty of 1763 to Our Own Time*, 2 vols. (DeLand, Florida, 1924-1925); Roy Glashan, *American Governors and Gubernatorial Elections, 1775-1975* (Stillwater, Minnesota, 1975).

BROWN, Thomas, 1849-1853

Born on October 24, 1785 in Westmoreland County, Virginia, son of William and Margaret (Templeman) Brown. Married to Elizabeth Simpson in 1809; father of seven children. Attended school for a short time in Alexandria, Virginia; attended school in Charleston, Virginia, until 1812. During the War of 1812, Brown enlisted in the United States Army, and served as an aide to General John P. Hungerford; discharged in 1814. Entered the mercantile business in Alexandria, Virginia; became Chief Clerk in the Post Office in Richmond, Virginia; moved to Tallahassee, Florida in 1828; was a large slave owner. Elected to the Virginia Legislature in 1817; elected to the Florida Legislature in 1845. A Mason. As a Whig, Brown was elected Governor of Florida on October 2, 1848, defeating the Democratic candidate, W. Bailey, 4,147 votes to 3,636. Brown took office nearly one year later, on October 1, 1849. During his administration, a public seminary was established in Ocala, Florida. Also while Brown was governor, the transportation within the state began to improve; the Florida Legislature authorized the construction of a plank toll road from Jacksonville to Lake City; and Jacob Brock began a steamship line on the St. Johns River. In 1849, the "Third Seminole War" broke out in Florida; however, the Seminoles were no longer the threat they once were, and the Indian depredations were exaggerated. Nevertheless, the federal government became determined to complete the removal of the Seminoles to Indian Territory. Constitutionally prohibited from seeking reelection for four years after the expiration of his term, Brown left office on October 3, 1853. Afterward, he returned to his home in Tallahassee, where he died on August 24, 1867. Bibliography: George M. Chapin, *Florida, 1513-1913, Past, Present and Future*, 2 vols. (Chicago, 1914); Harry G. Cutler, *Florida, Past and Present, Historical and Biographical*, 3 vols. (Chicago, 1925); Caroline M. Brevard, *A History of Florida from the Treaty of 1763 to Our Own Times*, 2 vols. (Deland, Florida, 1924-1925); Roy Glashan, *American Governors and Gubernatorial Elections, 1775-1975* (Stillwater, Minnesota, 1975).

BROOME, James E., 1853-1857

Born on December 15, 1808 in Hamburg, Aiken County, South Carolina, son of John, an English immigrant, and Jeanette (Witherspoon) Broome; his family background was Protestant. Married five times; father of three children. Received a limited education. Moved to Tallahassee, Florida in 1837, and entered the mercantile business; retired in 1841 from his business; owner of one of the largest plantations in Florida. Appointed Judge of the Probate Court of Leon County, Florida Territory in 1843; remained in office after Florida became a state; resigned from the post in 1848. As a Democrat, Broome was elected Governor of Florida on October 4, 1852, defeating Whig George T. Ward, 4,628 votes to 4,336. Broome did not take office until almost a year later, on October 3, 1853. During his administration, he vetoed more legislative actions than any of the two preceding chief executives; however, the majority of his vetoes were sustained by the State Legislature. He was also an ardent supporter of states' rights, and advocated secession if necessary to secure those rights. One of the most important acts of his administration was his veto of a bill that would abolish the Florida Supreme Court. Constitutionally prohibited from seeking reelection within four years of the expiration of his term, Broome left office on October 5, 1857. Afterward, he remained active in politics, and served four years in the Florida Senate. In 1865, Broome moved to Manhattan in New York City, and later to Brooklyn. He made his home in either Manhattan or Brooklyn for the remainder of his life. Broome died on November 23, 1883, while visiting his son in DeLand, Florida. Bibliography:

George M. Chapin, *Florida, 1513-1913, Past, Present and Future*, 2 vols. (Chicago, 1914); Harry G. Cutler, *Florida, Past and Present, Historical and Biographical*, 3 vols. (Chicago, 1923); Caroline M. Brevard, *A History of Florida from the Treaty of 1763 to our Time* (DeLand, Florida, 1924); Roy Glashan, *American Governors and Gubernatorial Elections, 1775-1975* (Stillwater, Minnesota, 1975).

PERRY, Madison Stark, 1857-1861

Born in 1814 in Lancaster County, South Carolina. Married to Martha; father of Madison Stark, Jr. Moved to Florida and operated a plantation near Micanopy in Alachua County. Became well known as an orator throughout the state. Elected to represent Alachua County in the Florida House of Representatives in 1849; elected to the Florida Senate in 1850. As a Democrat, Perry was elected Governor of Florida on October 6, 1856, defeating the American Party candidate, David S. Walker, 6,208 votes to 5,894. However, it was nearly a year later, on October 5, 1857, that Perry took office. During his administration, several new counties were created within the state; these included Clay, New River—(later the name was changed to Bradford)—Suwannee, Baker, and Polk. Also while Perry was governor, many of the remaining Seminole Indians still living in Florida were removed to Indian Territory; the Florida Railroad was completed; and a long standing boundary question with Georgia was settled. He constantly feared that the rights of the people were being encroached upon by corporations, and called upon the citizens of Florida to give serious consideration to the growth of corporations or else "bow the willing neck to the yoke of unscrupulous monopolists." As a South Carolinian, Perry was in the forefront of the secession movement within Florida. In a message to the State Legislature on November 27, 1860, he recommended that a convention be called to take the state out of the Union. When the legislature approved his request, Perry set December 22, 1860 as the day for electing the delegates. The convention convened in Tallahassee, Florida, and on January 10, 1861, an Ordinance of Secession was adopted. The following day, Governor Perry signed the act. He continued to serve as chief executive during the early months of the Civil War, and did much to mobilize the men and resources of Florida for service with the Confederate troops. He left office at the expiration of his term on October 7, 1861. Afterward, Perry served as a Colonel of the Seventh Florida Regiment in the Confederate Army; however, he was compelled to resign the position because of an illness. He then retired to his plantation. Perry died at his Alachua County plantation in March, 1865. Bibliography: William W. David, *The Civil War and Reconstruction in Florida* (New York, 1913); Caroline M. Brevard, *A History of Florida from the Treaty of 1763 to Our Own Time*, 2 vols. (DeLand, Florida, 1924); W. T. Cash, *The Story of Florida*, 4 vols. (New York, 1938); Roy Glashan, *American Governors and Gubernatorial Elections, 1775-1975* (Stillwater, Minnesota, 1975).

MILTON, John, 1861-1865

Born on April 20, 1807 in Jefferson County, Georgia, son of Homer Virgil, a planter, and Elizabeth (Robinson) Milton. Married to Susan Amanda Cobb on December 9, 1826, who died in 1840; father of one son and two daughters; married a second time to Caroline Howze; father of two sons and seven daughters by his second wife. Educated in the academy in Louisville, Georgia; studied law. Admitted to the bar. Served as a Captain in the Mobile, Alabama Volunteers during the Seminole War from 1835 to 1837. Private law practice in Louisville; moved his practice to Columbus, Georgia; later moved to Mobile and Marion, Alabama, and New Orleans, Louisiana; moved to a plantation near Marianna, in Jackson County, Florida in 1846. Presidential Elector on the Democratic ticket in 1848; elected to the Florida Senate in 1849. As a Democrat, Milton was elected Governor of Florida on October 1, 1860, defeating the Constitutional Union candidate, Edward Hopkins, 6,937 votes to 5,215. However, Milton did not take office until October 7, 1861. In January 1861, Florida left the Union and joined the Confederate States. Milton's administration was concentrated upon the military affairs of the Civil War. He was an advocate of wartime prohibition; approved of the idea of issuing paper money backed by the public lands of the state; and opposed the recruitment of cavalry within Florida, arguing that the topography of the state was not suited to mounted troops. Milton did all that he could to raise troops for the Confederacy, and keep them supplied in the field. He was opposed to any peace with the North that did not result in the independence of the seceding states. So involved was Milton with the idea of an independent Confederacy, that when the South collapsed he became distraught and committed suicide. Milton died in office on April 1, 1865. Bibliography: William W. David, *The Civil War and Reconstruction in Florida* (New York, 1913); George M. Chapin, *Florida, 1513 1913, Past, Present and Future*, 2 vols. (Chicago, 1914); Harry G. Cutler, *Florida, Past and Present, Historical and Biographical*, 3 vols (Chicago, 1923); Roy Glashan, *American Governors and Gubernatorial Elections, 1775-1975* (Stillwater, Minnesota, 1975). Papers of Milton in the Supreme Court Library, Tallahassee, Florida.

MARVIN, William, 1865

Born on April 14, 1808 in Fairfield, Herkimer County, New York, son of Seldon, a farmer, and Charlotte (Pratt) Marvin; from a Protestant background. Brother of Richard P. Married to Harriet Newell in 1846; father of one daughter, Harriet; married a second time to Mrs. Elizabeth Riddle Jewett in 1867. Educated in the local district school in New York; attended Homer Academy; studied law. Admitted to the Bar of the Supreme Court and Court of Chancery of New York in 1833. Taught school; opened a law office at Phelps, New York in 1833. Appointed by President Andrew Jackson as United States District Attorney for the Southern District of Florida in 1835, and moved to Key West, Florida; elected twice to the Florida Territorial Council; delegate to the 1838 Florida Constitutional Convention; appointed Judge by President Martin Van Buren in 1839; after Florida had been admitted to the Union, President James K. Polk in 1849 appointed him United

States District Judge of the Southern District of Florida; he held that post until 1863, when he resigned because of impaired health. Author: *Laws of Wreck and Salvage* and *The Authorship of the Four Gospels*. On July 13, 1865, Marvin was appointed Governor of Florida by President Andrew Johnson for the purpose of reestablishing the state government. He called a State Constitutional Convention to convene in Tallahassee, Florida, on October 28, 1865. On the same day, the Ordinance of Secession was annulled, and on November 7, 1865, the work of the convention was completed. The new instrument of government created the office of Lieutenant Governor, and under its provisions elections were held on November 29, 1865. As a result, Marvin left office on December 20, 1865. Afterward, he was elected to the United States Senate in 1866, but was refused his seat by the Radical Republicans. Thereafter, Marvin refused to be a candidate for any elective office, and he retired to private life. In 1867, he moved to Skaneateles, New York. Marvin died on July 9, 1902. Bibliography: William W. David, *The Civil War and Reconstruction in Florida* (New York, 1913); George M. Chapin, *Florida, 1513-1913, Past, Present and Future*, 2 vols. (Chicago, 1914); Harry G. Cutler, *Florida, Past and Present, Historical and Biographical*, 3 vols. (Chicago, 1923); Roy Glashan, *American Governors and Gubernatorial Elections, 1775-1975* (Stillwater, Minnesota, 1975).

WALKER, David Shelby, 1865-1868

Born near Russellville, Kentucky on May 2, 1815, son of David and May Barbour Walker; an Episcopalian. Married Philoclea Alston, daughter of R. W. Alston; father of Philip J., David S., Jr., Florida and Alston; remarried to Elizabeth Duncan, daughter of the Reverend E. B. Duncan; father of one daughter, Courtney. Attended private schools in Kentucky and Tennessee; studied law before moving to Florida in 1837; practiced law in Leon County. Served in the first State Senate in 1845 and in the lower house in 1848 and 1849. As Register of Public Lands from 1849 to 1854, he became *ex officio* Superintendent of Public Schools, an office which he held from 1851 to 1859. He sponsored several bills for the establishment of a school system, including one creating the seminaries east and west of the Suwannee. He was instrumental in opening the first free school in Tallahassee and served a term as Mayor of that city. In 1858 became a Justice of the Supreme Court of Florida, a position he retained until 1865. At first a Whig in politics, he joined the American (or Know-Nothing) Party in 1856 and ran unsuccessfully for Governor. He was defeated by Democrat Madison S. Perry, 5,407 to 5,027 votes. Walker opposed secession in 1861 and refused to serve in the Confederate Army, but remained in his court position. In the 1865 election, Walker ran for Governor as a Conservative and won without opposition. The struggle between President Andrew Johnson and Congress over Reconstruction policy weakened Walker's authority during his entire term as governor. He and General John G. Foster, the military commander, tried to cooperate, but conflicting instructions from Washington and frequent confrontations between local citizens, made his term a chaotic one. He was succeeded in 1868 by Harrison Reed, the state's first Republican governor. After leaving office, he engaged in private law practice until 1877 when he became a Circuit Court Judge, holding that office until his death in 1891. His private library became the nucleus of the David S. Walker Library which still exists in Tallahassee. Bibliography: "David Shelby Walker: Educational Statesman of Florida," *Florida Historical Quarterly*, v. 34; Rowland H. Rerick, *Memoirs of Florida*, v. 1 (Atlanta, 1902); William Watson Davis, *Civil War and Reconstruction in Florida* (Gainesville, 1964); Jerrell H. Shofner, *Nor Is It Over Yet: Florida in the Era of Reconstruction, 1863-1877* (Gainesville, 1974).

REED, Harrison, 1868-1873

Born in Lowell, Massachusetts on August 26, 1813, Reed moved to Wisconsin with his parents in 1836. Married to Anna Louise Turner of Wisconsin who died in 1862; father of sons, E. H. and H. W.; remarried Chloe Merrick of Syracuse, New York c. 1868; father of one son, Harrison, Jr. For several years, he edited the Milwaukee *Sentinel* before founding the new town of Neenah on the Fox River. After a dispute with his partners, Reed founded Menasha and became editor of the Neenah-Menasha *Conservator*. In 1857 he became editor of the Madison *Wisconsin State Journal*. He served as the first chairman of the County Commission of Winnebago County. First a Whig, he became an early member of the Wisconsin Republican Party. He moved to Washington, D.C. in 1862, and became a Direct Tax Commissioner for Florida. He was removed from that office in 1864, but then was appointed Mail Agent for Florida and Georgia, in order to re-establish the postal system in those states after the Civil War. One of the founders of the Florida Republican Party in 1867, he supported that party's moderate faction and became its gubernatorial candidate in 1868. He won over two other candidates by about 14,170 votes to their combined 10,114 votes. With many white citizens regarding Reed as a "carpetbagger" and opposing the black suffrage upon which his election depended, he had to restore civil government to the state; establish law and order; and put the defunct taxation and finance system on a stable basis. Beset with racial disorder, deficit financing and political factionalism, he nevertheless made progress in all these areas, leaving to his successors a basis on which to build a viable government. Passed over for renomination in 1872, Reed continued to support the Florida Republican Party, promoted economic development and immigration, and improved agriculture in the state. From 1875 to 1878, he edited the Jacksonville *Semi-Tropical Monthly Magazine* and contributed to other journals. He was Jacksonville Postmaster from 1889 to 1893. He died in 1899. Bibliography: Richard N. Current, *Three Carpetbag Governors* (Baton Rouge, 1967); David H. Overy, Jr., *Wisconsin Carpetbaggers in Dixie* (Madison, 1961); William Watson Davis, *Civil War and Reconstruction in Florida* (Gainesville, 1964); Jerrell H. Shofner, *Nor Is It Over Yet: Florida in the Era of Reconstruction, 1863-1877* (Gainesville, 1974).

HART, Ossian Bingley, 1873-1874

Born in Jacksonville, Florida in 1821, son of Isaiah D. and Nancy Nelson Hart; a Presbyterian. Married to Catharine Smith Campbell of New Jersey; father of two adopted girls. Educated in Washington, D.C., Hart read law in Jacksonville offices and was admitted to the Florida Bar. Moved to Ft. Pierce in 1843. Served a term in the legislature from St. Lucie County in 1844. Moved to Key West in 1846, where he lived for ten years. Moved to Tampa in 1856, where he remained until the end of the Civil War. Although a slave owner, Hart remained staunchly loyal to the Union, avoiding Confederate military service by means of a medical exemption. An early member of the Florida Republican Party, Hart was condemned by many of his neighbors as a "scalawag," but others respected him as a man of ability and integrity despite his political views. As Florida Supervisor of Elections under the Reconstruction Act of March 1867, Hart built up a wide acquaintance among black and white Republicans. Supporting the moderate faction of the party during the 1868 constitutional struggle, he was named to the State Supreme Court by Governor Reed. He served in that position until becoming governor in 1873. Acceptable to most Republican factions in 1872, he was a compromise candidate for Governor. He was elected over Democrat William D. Bloxham by a vote of 17,603 to 16,004. Although he was governor for only a few months before succumbing to the illness which took his life, Governor Hart did much to harmonize his party and obtain legislative approval of a positive program in 1873. A limited Civil Rights Act was acceptable to blacks and a majority of whites. A funding measure authorized a bonding program which helped put Florida on an improved financial footing. Building on earlier efforts of Governor Reed, Hart's bond program enabled the administration to end growth of the state debt and even to reduce it slightly before 1877. During an extended illness, he was replaced by Acting Governor Marcellus L. Stearns, who became governor when Hart died on March 18, 1874. Bibliography: *Biographical Sketch of Ossian Bingley Hart* (New York, 1901); William Watson Davis, *Civil War and Reconstruction in Florida (Gainesville, 1964)*; Joe M. *Richardson, The Negro in the Reconstruction of Florida, 1865-1877* (Tallahassee, 1965); Jerrell H. Shofner, *Nor Is It Over Yet: Florida in the Era of Reconstruction, 1863-1877* (Gainesville, 1974).

STEARNS, Marcellus Lovejoy, 1874-1877

Born in Center Lovell, Maine on April 29, 1839. Brother of Timothy, Eckley, Rensalaer, and Granville. Married to Ellen Austin Walker on December 12, 1878. Attended Waterville College (present-day Colby College) from 1859 to 1861. Left school to enlist in 12th Maine Volunteer Infantry. Received battlefield commission, lost an arm at the Battle of Winchester, and was transferred to the Veterans Reserve Corps as a Major. Read law in the office of Josiah H. Drummond of Portland, Maine. Was a Freedmen's Bureau agent in Gadsden County, Florida from 1866 to 1868. Active in organizing the Florida Republican Party under the 1867 Reconstruction Laws; allied with the moderate Republican faction which wrote the 1868 constitution; and was elected to the legislature. Served as Speaker of the House from 1869 to 1873, presiding over seven regular and special sessions. From 1869 to 1873, he was U.S. Surveyor General for Florida. After a disorderly factional struggle, the 1872 Republican Nominating Convention named Stearns as its candidate for Lieutenant Governor. Elected by 17,603 votes to 16,004, he assumed the office in 1873. When a lingering illness forced Governor Ossian B. Hart to enter a hospital, Stearns became Acting Governor. He assumed the office on Hart's death in March 1874. Despite acrimonious opposition, party factionalism, and economic adversity, Stearns balanced the state budget; reduced the debt slightly; and witnessed northern immigration increase and winter tourism begin during his term. His contest for reelection against Democrat George F. Drew was connected with the famous disputed presidential election of 1876 between Rutherford B. Hayes and Samuel J. Tilden. The Florida Supreme Court ultimately awarded the governorship to Drew by the vote of 24,179 to 23,984. After leaving office, Stearns served as U.S. Commissioner in Arkansas from 1877 to 1880. He then resided in Washington and his native Maine for several years, before becoming president of the Atlantic National Bank, Atlantic, Iowa in 1887. Stearns died at Palatine Bridge, New York in 1891, while on his way south for the winter. Bibliography: Sophia A. Walker, "Carpetbaggers," *Journal of Negro History,* v. 14; Claude R. Flory, "Marcellus L. Stearns: Florida's Last Reconstruction Governor," *Florida Historical Quarterly,* v. 44; William Watson David, *Civil War and Reconstruction in Florida* (Gainesville, 1964); Jerrell H. Shofner, *Nor Is It Over Yet: Florida in the Era of Reconstruction, 1863-1877* (Gainesville, 1974).

DREW, George Franklin, 1877-1881

Born on August 6, 1827 in Alton, New Hampshire, son of John Drew, a farmer, and Charlotte (Davis) Drew, both of whom were Episcopalians. Married to Amelia Dickens on April 19, 1853; father of George, Frank, Mrs. L. J. Brush, and Mrs. J. B. Wigginton. Attended school until twelve years old, but financial problems forced his return to the family farm. Became apprenticed at a machine shop in Lynn, Massachusetts, and in 1847 went to Columbus, Georgia with a machinist, Colonel John C. Winter. By 1853 he was the head of a milling business in Albany, Georgia. During the war, he enlisted in the Georgia "Home Guards." He moved to Florida with the end of hostilities in 1865. Drew settled eventually in Ellaville, where he built a prosperous lumbering and saw milling trade. In 1870 he was elected to the County Commission of Madison County and, shortly thereafter, became its chairman. Defeated in a 1872 State Senate race by A. B. Osgood, a black Republican. As an ex-Whig businessman, Drew was viewed by many Democrats as an excellent compromise candidate to win in 1876. He narrowly defeated Republican Marcellus L. Stearns by a vote of 24,179 to 23,984. As on the national level, charges of election fraud clouded the state returns, and the issue was not decided until the State Supreme Court ordered an official recount. Drew's administration marked the return of native white Democratic control to Florida. He stressed the traditional Bourbon themes of retrenchment and reform; in some cases, he cut back taxes and expenditures below the point of fiscal soundness and such areas as education and the penal system thereby suffered. The convict lease system was established as an economy measure in 1877. Drew continued Republican policies of using state lands to support immigration and internal improvements. By 1880 conservative Democrats felt secure enough to nominate William D. Bloxham, from their own ranks. Drew returned to his lumber business in Ellaville and remained until May, 1883, when he moved to Jacksonville and opened a wholesale hardware store. In state politics, he became a leading spokesman for an Independent movement opposed to the conservative Bourbon faction. In 1899 he resumed his lumber operations and he served as the first president of Jacksonville's Board of Trade. He died of a heart attack a few hours after making arrangements for his wife's funeral on September 26, 1900. He was buried in Jacksonville. Bibliography:

Edward Williamson, "George E. Drew, Florida's Redemption Governor," *Florida Historical Quarterly*, vol. XXVII (October, 1948); Jerrell Shofner, *Nor Is It Over Yet: Florida in the Era of Reconstruction, 1863-1877* (Gainesville, 1974); Jerrell Shofner, "A Note on Governor George F. Drew," *Florida Historical Quarterly*, vol. XLVIII (April, 1970). No personal or executive papers of Governor Drew have survived, save a letterbook (dated 1880) in the Florida State Library.

BLOXHAM, William Dunnington, 1881-1885, 1897-1901

Born in Leon County, Florida on July 9, 1835, son of William Bloxham, a planter, and Martha (Williams) Bloxham, both of whom were Methodists. Married to Mary Davis on October 28, 1856; father of William and Martha. Attended William and Mary College and graduated in 1855 with a law degree. Enjoyed the life of a planter near Tallahassee and became active in Democratic Party politics. Campaigned for Buchanan in Leon County, and in 1860 was elected as a member of the State Legislature. Entered the Army shortly afterwards and became Captain of a Leon County Company, but never saw active service. Resumed full political activities after the war, becoming a recognized leader in the Democratic Party. In 1870 he ran for, and was elected to, the vacated post of Lieutenant Governor, but the State Canvassing Board ruled his election invalid. Served as a member of the State Democratic Executive Committee and in 1876 was appointed Secretary of State by Governor Drew. In 1880 he split with Drew and took his conservative faction to victory, defeating Republican Simon B. Conover by a vote of 28,378 to 23,297. Bloxham's first administration is best remembered for a controversial land sale of four million acres to the Philadelphia capitalist Hamilton Disston in 1881. The sale released the Internal Improvement Fund from debt and disencumbered state lands for use in internal improvements and transportation development. It stirred charges of favoritism to special interests and harsh treatment to squatters who had been living on the land. The sale did begin a railroad building boom that continued throughout the decade. After leaving the governorship, Bloxham declined an offer from President Cleveland for the appointment of Minister to Bolivia in 1885. In November, 1885, he became United States Surveyor-General for the District of Florida, a position which allowed him to remain active in state politics. In 1890 he was made State Comptroller. Bloxham won renomination for a second term in the midst of controversy generated by the farmers' revolt. He endorsed bimetallism and easily defeated the Republican Edward R. Gunby and the People's Party candidate, William A. Weeks, in the 1896 gubernatorial race by a vote of 27,172 to 8,290 and 5,270 respectively. Bloxham's second term was notable for his re-establishment of a State Railroad Commission with enhanced powers in 1897 and the passage of a direct primary law. He also guided the state through the Spanish-American War, a conflict which called for an unusual degree of participation from Florida. Bloxham continued state support of drainage and reclamation projects in south Florida. He died in Tallahassee on March 15, 1911. Bibliography: Ruby Leach Carson, "William Dunningham Bloxham—Florida's Two Term Governor," Unpublished Master's Thesis, University of Florida, 1945; Ruby Leach Carson, "William D. Bloxham: The Years to the Governorship," *Florida Historical Quarterly*, vol. XXVII (January, 1949); Kenneth R. Johnson, "The Administration of W. D. Bloxham, 1881-1885," Unpublished Master's Thesis, Florida State University,

1959; Edward C. Williamson, "Independentism: A Challenge to the Florida Democracy," *Florida Historical Quarterly*, vol. XXVII (October, 1948). Bloxham's executive papers are located in the Florida State Archives and his letterbooks for the years 1881-1900 are located in the Florida State Library, Tallahassee.

PERRY, Edward Alysworth, 1885-1889

Born on March 15, 1831 in Richmond, Massachusetts, son of Asa Perry, a farmer, and Philura (Alysworth) Perry, both of whom were Episcopalians. Brother of Albertus, George, David, and Catherine Perry. Married to Wathen Virginia Taylor on February 1, 1859; father of Genevieve, Edward, Jr., Ruby, Ellen, and Frances. He attended Yale University but left in 1852 before receiving a degree; taught school and studied law in Georgia and Alabama; and was admitted to the bar in Montgomery, Alabama, March, 1857. Moved to Pensacola where he practiced law and held various local offices; entered Confederate Army at outbreak of war as Captain of Pensacola Rifle Rangers. In May, 1862 he was made Colonel of the Second Florida Regiment in the Army of Northern Virginia; promoted to Brigadier General after Sharpsburg. Fought in nearly every major engagement of the Virginia front; severely wounded at Frazier's Farm; disabled with typhoid fever at Chancellorsville; and again wounded at the Wilderness. He returned to law practice in Pensacola at war's end in 1865. Perry became known throughout the state for his legal work, his war record, and his criticism of Republican rule in Florida. In a Democratic Party split between the forces of former Governors Drew and Bloxham, Perry represented a compromise candidate. The 1884 campaign featured a strong challenge to Democratic control by an Independent Party, hoping to take advantage of dissension within Democratic ranks. Republicans endorsed the Independent candidate, Frank W. Pope, who lost to Perry by a vote of 32,087 to 27,845. As governor, Perry endorsed a pension law in 1885 which granted a five dollar monthly payment to Confederate veterans unable to work. He supported the calling of an 1885 constitutional convention which drafted a new governing document. The new constitution was ratified in 1886. Perry continued a limited program of reform by recommending that the legislature establish a State Railroad Commission, an act that the body took in 1887. Before he left office, he laid the cornerstone for the state's first agricultural college. Under provisions of the new constitution, Perry was not eligible to succeed himself. He retired to Pensacola and suffered a stroke while on a trip to the West. He died in Kerville, Texas, on October 15, 1889, and was buried in Pensacola. Bibliography: Sigsbee C. Prince, Jr., "Edward Alysworth Perry," Unpublished Master's Thesis, University of Florida, 1949; Sigsbee C. Prince, "Edward A. Perry, Yankee General of the Florida Brigade," *Florida Historical Quarterly*, vol. XXXIX (January, 1951); Herbert U. Feibelman, "E. A. Perry," *Florida Law Journal*, vol. XXII (July, 1949); W. T. Cash, *History of the Democratic Party in Florida* (Live Oak, Florida, 1936).

FLEMING, Francis Philip, 1889-1893

Born on September 28, 1841 in Panama Park, Florida, son of Colonel Lewis Fleming, a soldier and landowner, and Margaret (Seton) Fleming. Brother of Charles and Frederick; half-brother of Lewis and George Fleming and Sophia Fleming Stevens. Married to Floride Lydia Pearson on May 23, 1871; father of Francis, Jr., Charles, and Elizabeth. Educated by private tutors at home. At age nineteen, he entered the Confederate Army and served with the Second Florida Regiment. He took part in numerous major battles of the Virginia theater and was made First Lieutenant in August, 1863. Shortly afterwards, he was transferred to the West where he again fought in major engagements. Fleming returned to Jacksonville after the war, where he studied law and was admitted to the bar on May 12, 1868. Fleming gained a state-wide reputation for his legal work and for extolling the Confederate spirit. He served for many years as a member of the State Democratic Executive Committee and campaigned vigorously for the Democratic ticket in 1876. A factionalized Democratic Party in 1888 took forty ballots to nominate him as its candidate. The campaign was notable for the difficulties the candidates experienced in travelling throughout the state caused by an extensive outbreak of yellow fever. County and municipal authorities established "shot-gun quarantines" which severely limited travelling. Fleming easily defeated Republican V. J. Shipman by a vote of 40,255 to 26,485, the biggest election victory to date. Fleming's first act as governor was to call for a special legislative session to deal with the yellow fever crisis. This session authorized the creation of a much-needed State Board of Health. In 1891 Fleming became involved with a contested United States Senate election in which the Senate refused to seat his nominee and placed instead the incumbent Wilkinson Call. One of his last acts was to appoint a commission to oversee the granting of state lands for an Indian reservation. Unable to succeed himself, Fleming left office and returned to Jacksonville. He refused an offer of appointment to the United States Supreme Court to continue his own law practice. He died after a long illness in Jacksonville, Florida on December 20, 1908. Bibliography: Edward C. Williamson, "Francis P. Fleming in the War for Southern Independence: Letters from the Front," *Florida Historical Quarterly*, vol. XXVIII (July, 1949); "Francis P. Fleming," *Florida Historical Quarterly*, vol. II (April, 1909), *History of the Democratic Party in Florida* (Live Oak, Florida, 1936). Papers of Fleming in the Florida Historical Society Library, University of South Florida, Tampa, Florida.

MITCHELL, Henry Laurens, 1893-1897

Born in Jefferson County, Alabama on September 3, 1831, son of Thomas J. Mitchell, a farmer, and Elizabeth (Starns) Mitchell, both of whom were Methodists. Brother of Samuel, Virginia, George, Thomas, Francis, Robert, Charles, and Edward Mitchell and Caroline Neighbors. Married Mary Eugenia Spencer on April 11, 1866; no children. He was educated in the common schools of Alabama and moved to Tampa, Florida in 1846. Studied law under Judge James A. Gettis and was admitted to the bar in 1849. He entered the Confederate Army in 1861 and rose to the rank of Captain in the Fourth Florida Infantry. After the Vicksburg campaign he resigned his commission to accept a seat in the State Legislature, where he was twice reelected. Interspersed with his service in the legislature, he was employed as editor of the Tampa *Florida Peninsular*, a weekly newspaper. He served as Judge of the Sixth Circuit Court from 1877 to 1888; spent the next two and one-half years as a Justice of the State Supreme Court, and then returned to his former position. His reputation for strict honesty, as well as his support from conservative farmers who split from the Farmer's Alliance, enabled him to defeat in 1892 the Florida People's Party candidate, Alonzo P. Baskin, by a vote of 32,064 to 8,309. Governor Mitchell retained his reputation for honesty, but was not a vigorous leader. He had a non-activist philosophy of the governor's office and initiated few policies. The depression of 1893 further curtailed his effectiveness. In addition to the financial crisis, Mitchell was forced to deal with two great natural disasters. The "Great Freeze" of 1894-95 killed citrus trees in all but the most southern portions of the state and caused great loss; a major hurricane in 1896 added even more property damage, as well as the loss of many lives. Mitchell is probably best remembered for his stand against prize fighting, when he unsuccessfully attempted to prevent an 1894 contest between James J. Corbett and the Englishman Charles Mitchell. After leaving Tallahassee, Mitchell was elected Clerk of the Hillsborough County Circuit Court, a position which he held for four years until January, 1901. In May, 1902 he was elected County Treasurer, his last elective post. He died on October 14, 1903, and was buried in Tampa. Bibliography: George B. Church, Jr., "Henry Laurens Mitchell," Unpublished Master's Thesis, University of Florida, 1969; W. T. Cash, *History of the Democratic Party in Florida* (Live Oak, Florida, 1936). Mitchell's executive papers are located in the Florida State Archives.

BLOXHAM, William, 1881-1885, 1897-1901

JENNINGS, William Sherman, 1901-1905

Born March 24, 1863 at Walnut Hill, Illinois; son of Joseph W., a judge, and Amanda (Couch); Baptists; cousin of William Jennings Bryan. Married twice, to Corinne Jordan and May Mann; one son, Bryan. Attended public school in Illinois, Southern Illinois Normal, and Union Law School in Chicago. Moved to Brooksville, Florida, in 1885 to complete legal studies, and began practicing law there in May, 1886. His positions included appointment as Circuit Court Commissioner in 1887; County Judge, Hernando County, 1888; elected to the Florida House of Representatives from Hernando County, 1893 and 1895; Speaker of House in 1895; and presidential elector in 1896. Jennings received the Democratic nomination for Governor at the State Party Convention (the last one to be held) in Jacksonville, 1900, and won the general election with 29,251 votes to M. B. MacFarlane's 6,238 and A. M. Morton's 631 votes. As governor, Jennings advocated the primary election system to displace the convention method of selecting candidates. The first statewide primary was held in 1902. He saved 3,000,000 acres of public land, and laid the groundwork for other reclamation projects, including the Everglades. Jennings was constitutionally prohibited from succeeding himself. After leaving office he was appointed by Governor Broward as General Counsel of the state's Internal Improvement Fund, which oversaw the reclamation of the Everglades. He was Chairman, Ways and Means Committee, Naval Stores Association, and a member of the federal Reclamation and Drainage Commission. Governor William Sherman Jennings died on February 28, 1920. Bibliography: N. Gordon Carper, "The Convict Lease System in Florida, 1866-1923," Unpublished Ph.D. Dissertation, Florida State University, 1964; J. E. Covell, "The Railroads and the Public Lands of Florida 1879-1905," *Florida Historical Quarterly*, vol. 34 (January, 1956); Alice Strickland, "Florida's Golden Age of Racing," *Florida Historical Quarterly*, vol. 45 (January, 1967). Papers of Jennings on deposit in the Florida State Library, Tallahassee, and the P. K. Yonge Library of Florida History, University of Florida, Gainesville.

BROWARD, Napoleon Bonaparte, 1905-1909

Born on April 19, 1857 in Duval County, Florida, son of Napoleon Bonaparte, a farmer, and Mary Dorcas (Pasoons) Broward. Moved to Hamilton County, Florida during the Civil War. He was orphaned when he was twelve. Married to Carolina Georgia Kemps on January 10, 1883, who died in 1883; married a second time to Annie I. Douglas on May 5, 1887; father of nine children. Attended country schools. Worked in a log camp for an uncle; worked on a farm; employed as a deckhand on a steamboat; became a seaman on sailing vessels and fishing boats; bar pilot on St. Johns Bar in Florida; owner and captain of a steamboat plying between Mayport and Palatka, Florida until 1887; owner of a woodyard in Jacksonville, Florida; engaged in phosphate mining, 1890-1902; operated the steamer *Three Friends* on several filibustering expeditions carrying men and munitions to Cuba; engaged in the towing and wrecking business in Jacksonville. Key West, and Tampa, Florida. Elected Sheriff of Duval County in 1889, 1892, and 1896; member, Florida House of Representatives, 1900; member, Florida State Board of Health, 1900-1904. As a Democrat, Broward was elected Governor of Florida on November 8, 1904, defeating Republican M. B. MacFarlane, 29,251 votes to 6,357. Broward took office on January 3, 1905. During his administration, the state-subsidized institutions of higher education were consolidated into three colleges—The University of Florida, Florida State College for Women, and Florida Agricultural and Mechanical College for Negroes. Also while he was governor the drainage of the Everglades was begun by the state, and the Choctawhatchee National Forest was created. Broward left office on January 5, 1909. He maintained his residence in Jacksonville, and returned to his business investments. In the Democratic primary elections of 1910, he won the nomination for United States Senator. This was virtually equivalent to election, but he died before the general election. Broward died on October 1, 1910. Bibliography: George M. Chapin, *Florida, 1513-1913, Past, Present and Future*, 2 vols. (Chicago, 1914); Harry G. Cutler, *Florida, Past and Present, Historical and Biographical*, 3 vols. (Chicago, 1923); Caroline M. Brevard, *A History of Florida from the Treaty of 1763 to Our Own Time*, 2 vols. (DeLand, Florida, 1924-1925); Roy Glashan, *American Governors and Gubernatorial Elections, 1775-1975* (Stillwater, Minnesota, 1975).

GILCHRIST, Albert Waller, 1909-1913

Born on January 15, 1858 in Greenwood, South Carolina, while his mother was temporarily absent from Florida, son of William E., a planter and State Senator, and Elizabeth (Waller) Gilchrist. Unmarried. Graduated from the Carolina Military Institute in Charlotte, North Carolina; cadet at the United States Military Academy in West Point, New York in the Class of 1882 for three years. Resigned as a Brigadier General in the Florida Militia in June, 1898, and enlisted as a private in Company C, Third United States Volunteer Infantry; served in Santiago, Cuba, during the Spanish-American War; mustered out as a Captain in 1899. A civil engineer; engaged in real estate; orange grower; lived in Punta Gorda, Florida. Member, Florida House of Representatives, 1893, 1895, 1903 and 1905; Speaker of the Florida House of Representatives, 1905. Mason; member, Board of Visitors of the United States Military Academy, 1896. As a Democrat, Gilchrist was elected Governor of Florida on November 3, 1908, polling 33,036 votes to Republican John M. Cheney's 6,453 and the Socialist Party candidate, A. J. Pettigrew's 2,427. Gilchrist took office on January 5, 1909. During his administration, rapid progress was made in the drainage of the Everglades by the State Board of Drainage Commissioners and several new counties were formed. Also while Gilchrist was governor, the overseas railroad, connecting the mainland with Key West, Florida, was completed after eight years of work, and the Montverde Industrial School was established. As governor, he supported legislation establishing a Pure Food Law, a sanitarium for tuberculosis, a hospital for indigent crippled children, and better treatment for state prisoners. He supported the segregation of the races in Florida, but vigorously opposed lynchings. Gilchrist was, however, a less vigorous governor than his predecessors, William Jennings and Napoleon Broward. He opposed interfering in legislative affairs to gain support for his programs. He did not provide dynamic leadership on the Everglades drainage issue, as both Jennings and Broward had. He did, however, block the sale of Everglades land to syndicates, and he supported state drainage of these lands. During his governorship, he also toured the nation seeking tourists, new business, and northern investment for Florida. After his retirement in 1913, he returned to Punta Gorda and the real estate business. He campaigned for the United States Senate in 1916 but was defeated in the Democratic primary. He served as a delegate from Florida to the Democratic National Convention in 1924. He died in New York City on May 15, 1926, and was buried in Punta Gorda. Bibliography: Sister Mary Evangelista Staid, "Albert Waller Gilchrist, Florida's Middle of the Road Governor," Unpublished Master's Thesis, University of Florida, (1950); Daisey Parker, "The Inauguration of Albert Waller Gilchrist: Nineteenth Governor of the State of Florida," *Apalachee*, vol. VI (1963-67). Papers of Gilchrist are housed in the Robert Manning Strozier Library, Florida State University, Tallahassee.

TRAMMELL, Park, 1913-1917

Born in Macon County, Alabama on April 9, 1876, son of John W. and Ida E. (Park) Trammell, both of whom were Baptists. Family moved to Florida during Park Trammell's infancy. Father was a citrus grower and farmer. Brother of Worth W.,

John, Mrs. Walter Jenkins, Mrs. Pere McDougald, Lois, Pearl, and Mrs. Graham Harrison. Married to Virginia Darby on November 11, 1900. She died in 1922, and in 1934 he married Mrs. Louis Mesmer. He studied law at Vanderbilt and Cumberland Universities, receiving his law degree from the latter school in 1899. Trammell served in quartermaster service during the Spanish-American War, 1898. Practiced law in Lakeland; was a citrus grower and newspaper owner-editor. A Democrat. Served two terms as Mayor of Lakeland, 1900 and 1901; elected to State House of Representatives in 1902 from Polk County; elected to State Senate in 1904 and served as President of the Senate in 1905; became Attorney General in 1908 and captured the governorship over Republican William R. O'Neal and Socialist Thomas W. Cox in 1912, 88,977 to 2,646 and 3,467 votes. As governor, he urged passage of a law to control the amount of money spent in election campaigns. In addition, he supported the establishment of a State Tax Commission to equalize property assessments among counties. Trammell also supported many of the progressive reforms of the day including: initiative, referendum and recall; full publicity of state business; establishment of a Labor Commission; and tighter regulation of passenger, freight and express railroad rates. As with most southern progressives, Trammell endorsed the racial segregation of Florida society. He also ignored lynchings of black Floridians when they occurred, thereby encouraging other such acts. Trammell did oppose land frauds in Florida and supported tighter state supervision. Immediately after his retirement as governor, he was elected to the United States Senate in 1916 over William R. O'Neal, 58,391 to 8,774 votes. He served in the Senate for twenty years. He died on May 8, 1936 and was buried in Lakeland. Bibliography: Papers of Trammell in the P. K. Yonge Library of Florida History, University of Florida, Gainesville, and the Florida State Library, Tallahassee.

CATTS, Sidney Johnston, 1917-1921

Born on July 31, 1863 near Pleasant Hill, Alabama. His Baptist father and mother, Samuel W. and Adeline Rebecca (Smyly) Catts, owned a plantation. Sidney's brother and sister, Smiley and Lilian, were both older. Married Alice May Campbell in 1886; father of eight children, seven of whom lived to adulthood; Ruth, Elizabeth, Alice, Sidney, Rozier, Walter and Edward. Although Catts attended Auburn and Howard Colleges, the only academic degree he received was a law degree from Cumberland University in 1882. He practiced law briefly before entering the Baptist ministry. He moved to Florida in 1911, where he was pastor of a church for a short time; he then resigned as pastor to sell insurance, preparatory to running for Governor. He ran in the 1916 Democratic primary, and initially was declared the winner. When the Supreme Court authorized a recount which denied him the gubernatorial nomination, he left the Democratic Party and ran for Governor in the November, 1916 general election as the nominee of the Prohibition Party (nominated by a special caucus), defeating the Democratic nominee 39,546 to 30,343; the Republican candidate received 18,333 votes and the Socialist nominee, 2,470. Although Catts' demagogic campaign attacked the "Roman Catholic" menace, his years in the statehouse were characterized by progressive proposals, many of which were defeated by the Democratic legislature. His notable successes were reforms in the treatment of the mentally ill and convicts; passage of statewide Prohibition; tax and labor reforms; and better roads. He also appointed a woman to his staff and endorsed Women's Suffrage. He altered the structure of the Democratic Party in Florida, when he rejoined it after his election by bringing into the party many new young people. In 1920 Catts could not succeed himself, and ran against incumbent United States Senator Duncan V. Fletcher, losing 25,007 to 62,304. Catts tried several occupations after 1920, including citrus growing and salesmanship but was not very successful. He ran for Governor twice more in 1924 and 1928, losing narrowly both times. In 1928 he led the "anti-Al Smith" forces in Florida. He died on March 9, 1936 and is buried at DeFuniak Springs, Florida. Bibliography: J. Wayne Flynt, *Cracker Messiah: Governor Sidney J. Catts of Florida* (Baton Rouge, 1977); Flynt, "Sidney J. Catts: The Road to Power," *The Florida Historical Quarterly*, vol. XLIX, no. 2 (October, 1970); John R. Deal, Jr., "Sidney Johnston Catts, Stormy Petrel of Florida Politics," Unpublished Master's Thesis, University of Florida, 1949. Correspondence of Catts can be found in the J. B. Hodges Papers at the University of Florida in Gainesville.

HARDEE, Gary Augustus, 1921-1925

Born on November 13, 1876 in Taylor County, Florida, son of James B. and Amanda Catherine (Johnson) Hardee, who were farmers. Hardee was the fourth of ten children; the family were Baptists. Attended public school, but received no higher education. Taught public school until 1900, when he was admitted to the bar, and began to practice law in Live Oak. Later he also became a banker in Live Oak and Mayo. Served as a State's Attorney between 1905 and 1913, and was elected to the Florida House of Representatives from Suwanee and served as Speaker in both 1915 and 1917. He won the Democratic nomination for Governor in 1920 with 54,150 votes to 31,699 for V. C. Swearingen, and 5,591 for Lincoln Hulley. In the general election, Hardee won over George Gay by 103,407 to 23,788 votes. As governor, he fostered legislative reapportionment and a constitutional amendment prohibiting state income and inheritance taxes. The state policy of leasing prisoners to private businesses was finally outlawed. Six new counties were created and the first state gasoline tax enacted. By constitutional provision Hardee was unable to succeed himself. He returned to Live Oak and served as a lawyer and banker. In 1932 he sought the Democratic nomination for Governor, but was defeated. He died of a heart ailment at the age of 81 in Live Oak on November 21, 1957. Bibliography: N. Gordon Carper, "Martin Tabert, Martyr of an Era," *Florida Historical Quarterly*, vol. 52 (October, 1973); Warren A. Jennings, "Sidney J. Catts and the Democratic Primary of 1920," *Florida Historical Quarterly*, vol. 39 (January, 1961); Wayne Flynt, "Florida's 1926 Senatorial Primary," *Florida Historical Quarterly*, vol. 42 (October, 1963). Papers of Hardee in the Florida State Library, Tallahassee.

MARTIN, John Wellborn, 1925-1929

Born in Planfield, Florida on June 21, 1884, son of John M. and Willie (Owens) Martin, both of whom were Baptists. His father was a farmer and citrus grower whose groves were destroyed in the freeze of 1896. Brother of Albert and Marshall Martin, Mrs. Willie M. Tucker, and Mrs. Alice Wither. Married to Charlotte Wilt Pepper, on January 30, 1907; father of John Wellborn Martin, Jr. He attended school for only four years and later continued his education at night. Martin was admitted to the Florida Bar in 1914. He began the practice of law in Jacksonville. A Democrat. Served as Mayor of Jacksonville for three terms from 1917 to 1924; and was elected Governor of Florida in 1924 over William R. O'Neal, Republican, 84,181 to 17,499 votes. Martin became governor during the period of Florida's greatest economic growth known to that time. Tourists descended upon St. Augustine, West Palm Beach, and Miami, using Henry Flagler's East Coast Railroad; speculators bought land in the state, driving prices upward. Martin basked in the economic prosperity while it lasted. He directed a massive road building program; urged the financing of public schools by direct state appropriation and the furnishing of free textbooks to all students through the first six grades; and brought about the first reapportionment of the Florida Legislature in thirty-eight years, although it remained under the control of rural interests. He also established an industrial plant for physically disabled prisoners. When the economic decline began in 1926, Martin offered no recovery programs. Instead he recommended a banking law to supervise state banks. His leadership was similarly lacking following the hurricanes of 1926 and 1928 which left south Florida devastated. Martin ran for the United States Senate in 1928 but was defeated in the Democratic primary. He campaigned for Governor again in 1932 but lost in the Democratic primary to future Governor David Sholtz. He served as co-receiver and trustee for the Florida East Coast Railroad. Martin died and was buried in Jacksonville, February 22, 1958. Bibliography: Victoria H. McDonell, "Rise of the 'Businessman's Politician': The 1924 Florida Gubernatorial Race," *Florida Historical Quarterly*, vol. LII, no. 1 (July, 1973).

CARLTON, Doyle Elam, 1929-1933

Born in Wauchula, Florida on July 6, 1887, son of Albert, a citrus farmer, and Martha (McEwen) Carlton, both of whom were Baptists. Had seven brothers and one sister. Married Nellie Ray on July 30, 1912; father of Martha Ward, Mary Ott, and Doyle Carlton, Jr. He graduated from Stetson University in 1910 and because of special arrangements with the University of Chicago, he received his A.B. degree from the latter school. Carlton received his law degree from Columbia University in 1912; began law practice in Tampa in 1912; and represented the district of Hillsborough and Pinellas Counties as State Senator in 1917-19. He served as City Attorney of Tampa, 1925-27. In 1928, Carlton, a Democrat, defeated Republican W. J. Howey for Governor, 148,455 votes to 95,018. He served as governor during one of the most critical economic periods in Florida's history. The state had four major disasters: the collapse of the land boom; the devastating hurricane of 1928; the infestation of citrus groves by the Mediterranean fruit fly; and the national depression. Economic matters literally engulfed Carlton's administration. Elected on a fiscally conservative platform in which he called for reduced property taxes and debt relief, he asked the legislature to eliminate every unnecessary office. Hundreds of state employees lost their jobs, adding to the widespread unemployment. By 1933, twenty-six percent of the population was out of work. To keep schools and bonds afloat, Carlton increased the gasoline tax by six cents a gallon. He also recommended that the state oversee the banking community to protect depositors. In 1931 he was faced with a legislative revolt. Apparently overwhelmed by the magnitude of the Depression, and under constant criticism by the legislature, he told the legislators to produce their own financial program if they did not like his. Accepting the governor's charge, the legislators raised the gasoline tax again; legalized parimutuel betting at horse and dog tracks over Carlton's veto; and created a State Tax Commission and a State Purchasing Agency to prevent wastefulness in government. Carlton retired to his law practice in Tampa in 1933. He ran for the United States Senate in 1936 but was defeated in the Democratic primary. He was a Special State Attorney in 1947 and bought state ownership of the Ringling Museums at Sarasota. He served as president of the Florida State Chamber of Commerce. Died in Tampa, October 25, 1972. Bibliography: Papers of Carlton in the Florida State Archives, Tallahassee.

SHOLTZ, David, 1933-1937

Born on October 6, 1891 in Brooklyn, New York, son of Michael Sholtz, a businessman and real estate investor, and Anne (Bloom) Sholtz. Brother of two sisters, Rosalee and Ethel. Sholtz was a Congregationalist (converted from Judaism). Married to Alice May Agee on December 28, 1925; father of three children, Michael, Carolyn, and Lois. Attended Yale, and graduated in 1914. Received his LL.B. from Stetson University, 1915. Became a lawyer and businessman in Daytona Beach, Florida, and served as president of both the local and state Chambers of Commerce. Served as Ensign in the Navy during World War I, and remained in the reserves, reaching the rank of Lieutenant Commander. Elected from Volusia County to the Florida House of Representatives in 1917; served as a State's Attorney from 1919-21, and was City Judge in 1921. He won the Democratic gubernatorial nomination in 1932, coming in second behind former Governor John Martin in the first primary, 66,940 votes to 55,406, and defeating Martin in the runoff by 173,540 to 120,805. Sholtz served as governor during the Depression and New Deal, and made use of social welfare programs for unemployment compensation, old age assistance, and temporary relief. He also promoted governmental reorganization. By constitutional mandate, he was prohibited from succeeding himself. After leaving office, Sholtz practiced law in Miami, where he was active in civic and service organizations. He was defeated in 1938 for the Democratic senatorial nomination. Towards the end of his life, he spent much time in New York City. He died of a heart attack in the Florida Keys on March 21, 1953 at age sixty-two. Bibliography: Merlin G. Cox, "David Sholtz: New Deal Governor of Florida," *Florida Historical Quarterly*, vol. 43 (October, 1964); Durward Long, "Key West and the New Deal, 1934-1936," *Florida Historical Quarterly*, vol. 46 (June, 1968). Sholtz' papers are deposited in the Florida State Archives, Tallahassee.

CONE, Frederick Preston, 1937-1941

Born on September 28, 1871 in Benton, Columbia County, Florida, son of William H. and Sarah Emily (Branch) Cone, both of whom were Baptists. Cone was the ninth of thirteen children. Married twice; father of one daughter. Attended Florida Agricultural College and Jasper Normal College. Became a teacher in north Florida and in 1892 was admitted to the Florida Bar; practiced law in Lake City and later became a banker there. Three times he served as Mayor of Lake City; served in the State Senate from 1907-1913, and was President of the Senate in 1911. He was a Florida delegate to the Democratic National Convention in 1924 and 1928, and was chairman of the delegation in 1932. In 1936 he won the Democratic gubernatorial nomination, coming in second of fourteen candidates in the first primary with 46,842 votes to Raleigh Petteway's 51,705, and winning the runoff with 184,540 to Petteway's 129,150. He won the general election with 253,638 votes to E. E. Callaway's 59,832. Cone was the oldest Florida governor in this century, taking office at age sixty-five. As governor Cone oversaw the state's exhibition at the New York World's Fair; urged the licensing of drivers (funds from which were to finance the highway patrol); and fought new taxes. Constitutionally prohibited from succeeding himself, he left office in January, 1941. Cone returned to Lake City where he again became a banker. In 1940, while he was still governor, he was defeated for the Democratic senatorial nomination. He died on July 28, 1948 at the age of seventy-six. Bibliography: Papers of Cone on deposit in the Florida State Archives, Tallahassee.

HOLLAND, Spessard Lindsey, 1941-1945

Born in Bartow, Florida on July 10, 1892, son of Benjamin F. and Virginia (Spessard) Holland, both of whom were Methodists. Father was a citrus grower and abstractor; mother was a school teacher. Brother of Frank Holland and Mrs. Roy T. Gallemore. Married to Mary Alice Groover in 1919; father of four children, Spessard, Jr., William Benjamin, Mrs. Jefferson Lewis, and Mrs. R. B. Craney. Graduated from Emory University in 1912, and from the University of Florida in 1916 with a law degree. Entered the army in 1917 as a First Lieutenant. Transferred to the air force and served with the 24th Flying Squadron in France. Awarded the Distinguished Service Cross for valor. Retired as Captain in July, 1919. Served as Polk County Prosecutor in 1919, and in 1920 was elected Polk County Judge, serving for eight years. Elected to the State Senate in 1932 from Polk County and served in this capacity for eight years. Defeated Francis Whitehair in the 1940 Democratic gubernatorial primary; had no Republican opponent in the November election. Governor Holland established the Game and Fresh Water Fish Commission as a separate agency; increased state assistance to the blind and aged; and supported an increase in gasoline tax revenues to improve highways. He also strengthened the *ad valorem* tax structure; established Everglades National Park; initiated a committee which brought about the Minimum Foundation Program for public schools; and adjusted the bonded debt of the Everglades Drainage District. His administration, however, was principally concerned with World War II and coordinating Florida's defense effort with the federal government. After his retirement from the governor's office, he returned to Bartow·to practice law. He was appointed to the U.S. Senate by Governor Millard Caldwell on the death of Senator Charles O. Andrews in 1946. Subsequently elected to four terms. Retired in January, 1971. Holland died in Bartow on November 6, 1971. Bibliography: Holland's private papers are housed in the P. K. Yonge Library of Florida History, University of Florida, Gainesville, and his public papers are in the Florida State Archives, Tallahassee.

CALDWELL, Millard Fillmore, 1945-1949

Born on February 6, 1897 near Knoxville, Tennessee, son of Millard F., a lawyer and farmer, and Martha Jane (Clapp) Caldwell. Married to Rebecca Harwood; father of two daughters, Sally and Susan. Attended Carson Newman College, the University of Mississippi, and the University of Virginia. During World War I, he served in the army as a Lieutenant, and arrived in Milton, Florida in 1924, where he practiced law. There he served as County Attorney and School Attorney; from 1929-1931 he served in the Florida House of Representatives from Santa Rosa County. Served in the United States Congress from the Third Congressional District from 1933 to 1941, during which time he represented the United States at interparliamentary conferences at The Hague (1938) and Oslo (1939). He retired from Congress to live at Harwood Plantation, near Tallahassee, where he farmed and practiced law. Caldwell won the Democratic nomination for Governor in 1944 over six candidates, winning the first primary by 116,111 over Lex Green's 113,300, and the second primary by 215,485 votes to 174,100. He defeated Bert Acker in the general election by 361,007 votes to 96,321. As governor, Caldwell revised the system of educational finance; established the Minimum Foundation Program; developed the Capitol Center; and expanded state services to meet the postwar population boom. He served as chairman of the National Governors' Conference, 1946-1947, and was president of the Council of State Governments, 1947-1948. By constitutional provision, he could not succeed himself. After leaving office he served as chairman, Board of Control, Southern Regional Education Board, 1948-1951; Administrator, Federal Civil Defense (appointed by President Truman), 1950-1952; Justice of the Florida Supreme Court, 1962-1969 (Chief Justice, 1967-1969). Caldwell retired to practice law in Tallahassee, where he still lives. Bibliography: Caldwell's public papers are on deposit at the Florida State Archives, Tallahassee.

WARREN, Fuller, 1949-1953

Born on October 3, 1905 in Blountstown, Florida, son of Charles R. Warren, a farmer, and Grace (Fuller) Warren, both of whom were Baptists. Brother of Joseph, Richard, Julian and Alma Warren. Married to Sallie Mae Stegall (1929-37); Pat Pacetti (1939-42); and Barbara Manning (1949-54); he had no children by these marriages. He attended the University of Florida and graduated in 1926. At the age of twenty, while finishing his senior year, he was elected to the State House of Representatives as a Democrat from Calhoun County. He served but one term and then studied law at Cumberland University, receiving his degree in 1930 and establishing his practice in Jacksonville. In 1931 he was elected to the Jacksonville City Council and served until 1937. In 1939 he was chosen to represent Duval County in the State House of Representatives. He ran for Governor in the Democratic primary of 1940, finishing third in an eleven-man field. World War II temporarily halted his political ambitions. He served as a navy gunnery officer in the Pacific from 1942-45. After his return to Florida in 1945, he began preparing plans for the 1948 gubernatorial contest. He captured the Democratic primary in a runoff and defeated his Republican opponent, Bert Acker, 381,459 votes to 76,153. As governor, Warren sponsored laws to fence cattle off from the highways; unmask the Ku Klux Klan; revise citrus codes; and develop a flood control program. Warren's administration, however, was handicapped by an empty treasury. To meet pressing postwar social and economic problems, Warren proposed a wide variety of taxes on industry. The breadth of the tax package, however, alienated the entrenched economic interests in Florida, and Warren was not politically adept enough to combat their opposition. His leadership was further impaired when the Kefauver Crime Commission in 1950 linked an aide and a close adviser to organized crime. Thereafter, his sole success came as a salesman for Florida. He toured the nation attracting tourists and business to the state. Constitutionally unable to succeed himself, he retired to practice law in Miami. In 1956 he attempted to win the Democratic nomination for Governor on a segregationist platform but finished fourth in a six-man field. He died on September 23, 1973 and was buried in Blountstown. Bibliography: David Colburn and Richard Scher, "Florida Gubernatorial Politics: The Fuller Warren Years," *Florida Historical Quarterly*, vol. LIII, no. 4 (April, 1975). The Warren Papers are housed in the Robert Manning Strozier Library at Florida State University in Tallahassee.

McCARTY, Daniel Thomas, 1953

Born on January 18, 1912 at Fort Pierce, Florida, son of Daniel Thomas, a land developer and citrus grower, and Frances (Moore) McCarty, both of whom were Episcopalians. Brother of John and Brian McCarty, and Mrs. William Stark. Married to Olie Brown, 1940; father of three children, Frances, Mike and Danny. Attended public schools and graduated from the University of Florida in 1934. Settled in Fort Pierce as a citrus grower and beef cattleman; founded the Indian River Citrus Association. Served in the army in World War II, landing in the south of France on D-Day, receiving numerous decorations, and leaving the service as a Colonel. Served in the Florida House of Representatives from St. Lucie County from 1937-1941, and was Speaker in 1941, the youngest person ever to hold the office. He was defeated for the Democratic nomination for Governor in 1948 by Fuller Warren. McCarty won the nomination in 1952 over five candidates, winning the first primary with 361,427 votes over Brailey Odham's 232,565 and the second by 384,200 to 336,716. He won the general election over Harry Swan by 624,463 to 210,009. As governor he reorganized the Road Department; began a massive state construction program; centralized purchasing; and increased state revenues. McCarty suffered a disabling heart attack on February 25, 1953, and died from another on September 28, 1953. Bibliography: Papers of McCarty on deposit at the Florida State Archives, Tallahassee, Florida.

JOHNS, Charley Eugene, 1953-1955

Born on February 27, 1905 in Starke, Bradford County, Florida, son of Everette E., Sheriff of Bradford County, and Annie (Markley) Johns, both of whom were Baptist. Brother of Markley Johns, who died while Florida Senate President-Designate, 1933. Married to Thelma Brinson; father of Charley and Markley Ann. Attended public schools and the University of Florida, but did not graduate. Returned to Starke where he became a railroad conductor, insuranceman and banker. Served in the Florida House of Representatives in 1935-1937, and the Florida Senate 1937-1966; was Senate President in 1953. Became Acting Governor on September 29, 1953, upon the death of incumbent Dan McCarty. Johns' tenure was marked by controversy over his use of patronage and state contracts. He rapidly expanded state roads and highways. In the three-candidate special eleciton of May, 1954, which was to determine who was to complete McCarty's unexpired term, Johns was defeated by LeRoy Collins, 380,323 votes to 314,198. Johns left office in 1955. After his defeat, Johns returned to the Senate (he had retained his seat while acting governor) and served until 1966. He retired to Starke, where he still lives, as an insuranceman and banker. Bibliography: Terry L. Christie, "The Collins-Johns Election, 1954—A Turning Point," *Apalachee*, vol. 6 (1963-1967); Joseph Tomberlin, "Florida Whites and the Brown Decision of 1954," *Florida Historical Quarterly*, vol. 51 (July, 1972); David R. Colburn and Richard K. Scher, "Race Relations and Florida Gubernatorial Politics Since the *Brown* Decision," *Florida Historical Quarterly*, vol. 55 (October, 1976).

COLLINS, [Thomas] Leroy, 1955-1961

Born on March 19, 1909, in Tallahassee; son of Marvin, a grocer, and Mattie (Brandon) Collins, both of whom werre Episcopalian. He was one of six children. Married in 1932 to Mary Call Darby, who was a great-grandaughter of Richard Keith Call, twice Territorial Governor of Florida. Attended public schools, the Eastman School of Business in Poughkeepsie, New York, and received a law degree from Cumberland University. Elected to Florida House of Representatives from Leon County in 1934, 1936 and 1938. Elected to the State Senate in 1940 and 1942, but resigned to serve in the navy in World War II. Reelected to the Senate in 1946 and 1950. Defeated three candidates in 1954 for the Democratic nomination for Governor in a special election to fill the unexpired term of Dan McCarty. Collins received 222,787 votes in the first primary to Acting Governor Charley Johns' 255,787, but won the second by 380,323 to 314,198; Collins defeated J. Tom Watson in the general election 287,769 to 69,852 (Watson died during the campaign). In 1956 Collins defeated five other candidates for the Democratic nomination, receiving 434,274 votes to Sumter Lowry's 179,019; no runoff was needed. He defeated W. A. Washburn in the general election, 747,753 to 266,980. Collins was the only Florida governor prior to 1974 to serve consecutive terms, and the only candidate since 1920 to win the Democratic nomination without a runoff. As governor, Collins sought to prevent the outbreak of racial hostilities; tried to improve education; and attempted to broaden the state's economic base. He was the first American governor to serve simultaneously as chairman of the Southern

Governors' Conference and the National Governors' Conference (1959). He led a delegation of governors to the Soviet Union in 1959. Collins was the first governor since the Civil War to serve as permanent chairman, Democratic National Convention, 1960. Collins could not ~~suceed~~ succeed himself in 1961. After leaving office he served as president of the National Association of Broadcasters. In 1964 he was appointed by President Johnson as first Director of Community Relations Services in the U.S. Department of Commerce; also in 1965 he was appointed Undersecretary of Commerce. He resigned in 1966 to practice law in Tampa. He received the Democratic nomination for the United States Senate in 1968 but was defeated by Republican Edward Gurney in the general election. Retired to Tallahassee, where he still lives and practices law. Bibliography: Helen Jacobstein, *The Segregation Factor in the Florida Gubernatorial Primary of 1956,* University of Florida Social Sciences Monographs, no. 47 (Gainesville: University of Florida Press, 1972); Terry L. Christie, "The Collins-Johns Election, 1954: A Turning Point," *Apalachee,* vol. 6 (1963-1967); Donald H. Grubbs, "The Story of Florida's Migrant Farm Workers," *Florida Historical Quarterly,* vol. 40 (October, 1961); Joseph Tomberlin, "Florida Whites and the *Brown* Decision of 1954," *Florida Historical Quarterly,* vol. 55 (October, 1976); Robert H. Akerman, "The Triumph of Moderation in Florida Thought and Politics: A Study of the Race Issue from 1954-1956," Unpublished Ph.D. Dissertation, American University, 1967. Papers of Collins on deposit at the University of South Florida, Tampa, and the Florida State Archives, Tallahassee.

BRYANT, [Cecil] Farris, 1961-1965

Born on July 26, 1914 in Marion County, Florida, son of Cecil and Lela (Farris) Bryant, both of whom were Methodists. Brother of Eugene W. and Louise Camp. His father was a farmer and an accountant. His uncle, Ion Farris, twice served as Speaker of the State House of Representatives. Received a business degree from the University of Florida in 1935 and a law degree from Harvard University in 1938. Married to Julia Burnett in 1940; father of three daughters, Julia Lovett, Cecilia Ann, and Allison Adair. Served in the navy from 1942-45 as a Captain in the North Atlantic, Mediterranean, and Pacific. Elected to State House of Representatives in 1946 from Marion County, served five terms and elected as Speaker in 1953. He ran for Governor in 1956, losing the Democratic nomination to LeRoy Collins. In 1960 Bryant defeated Republican George Petersen for the governorship, 849,407 votes to 569,936. As governor, he led the effort to improve funding for higher education and started construction on the cross-Florida barge canal. His ambitious highway program saw the construction of the Sunshine State Parkway from Ft. Pierce to Wildewood and the multi-planning of several state highways. Despite his criticism of the "Brown" decision, and his campaign promise to maintain segregation in the state, he permitted county schools to integrate voluntarily. His support of segregation, however, impeded his effectiveness as governor. During the St. Augustine racial violence of 1963 and 1964, he was unable to alleviate the crisis since he was distrusted by the civil rights forces. Like many Florida governors before him, he toured many states, Europe, and Asia, seeking tourists and new industry for Florida. After retiring as governor in 1965, he returned to Jacksonville to become Chairman of the Board of National Life of Florida Corporation and Voyager Life Insurance Company. On March 23, 1966, President Lyndon Johnson appointed him Director of the Office of Emergency Planning and a member of the U.S. Advisory Commission on Intergovernmental Relations and was chairman in October, 1967. In 1970 he was defeated by Lawton Chiles in the Democratic primary for the U.S. Senate. Bibliography: Papers of Bryant are housed in the P. K. Yonge Library at the University of Florida, Gainesville; [they are presently unavailable to scholars, however.] His public papers are in the Florida State Archives, Tallahassee.

BURNS, Haydon William, 1965-1967

Born in Chicago, Illinois on March 17, 1912, son of Harry Haydon and Ethel (Burnett) Burns, both of whom were Methodists. Family moved to Jacksonville in 1922. Father served as member of the Duval County Commission. Attended Babson College in Massachusetts but left without receiving a degree. Married to Mildred Carlyon in 1934; father of two children, Mrs. Lloyd (Eleanor) Watkins and Bill Burns. Owned and operated a plumbing and electric company, a flying school, and a greeting card company. During World War II, he served in the navy as an aeronautical salvage specialist assigned to the Office of the Secretary of the Navy. Attained the rank of Lieutenant J.G. Returned to Jacksonville in 1945 and ran for Mayor-Commissioner in 1949. Served five terms, retiring in 1964 to become Governor. Burns first ran for the governor's office in 1960, finishing third in the Democratic primary. In 1964, he defeated Republican Charles R. Holley for the governorship, 933,554 votes to 686,297. As governor he proposed to expand the state's manufacturing base; promote the agricultural industry; establish strong trade with South America; and complete a barge canal. He opposed the 1964 Civil Rights Act during his campaign, but did not try to block implementation of the act. He supported increased funding for education; the adoption of the quarter system at state universities; and the creation of the University of West Florida and Florida Technological University. Burns placed his greatest emphasis on a $300 million road bonding bill; the plan was opposed by many legislators, including Lawton Chiles, Reubin Askew and Ralph Turlington, who felt the program was unnecessary and would result in political confusion. Their opposition led to the rejection of the bonding plan by the voters and presaged the defeat of Burns' reelection bid. In 1966, as Florida moved to a non-presidential year gubernatorial election, Burns lost the Democratic nomination to Robert King High, 596,471 to 509,271. He returned to his home in Jacksonville. In 1971 he was defeated in his bid to become Mayor of Jacksonville. Bibliography: Burns' public papers are housed in the Florida State Archives, Tallahassee.

KIRK, Claude Roy, 1967-1971

Born on January 7, 1926 in San Bernardino, California, son of Claude Roy, an operator of Standard Forge and Axle Company and later employed by Alabama State Civil Defense, and Myrtle (McLure) Kirk, a clerk for Alabama House of

Representatives, both of whom were Episcopalians. Brother of Mrs. Richard (Carolyn) Morton. Kirk enlisted in the marine corps at seventeen, was commissioned as Second Lieutenant at nineteen, and ended his three years of service in 1946. Returned to duty in Korea, serving both in combat forces and as a fire control spotter. Married to Sarah Stokes; father of Sarah, Katherine, and twins William and Frank; remarried to Erika Mattfeld in 1967; divorced in 1976; father of one child, Claudia. Received a B.S. degree from Emory University, 1945, and a law degree from the University of Alabama in 1949; never practiced law. Founded American Heritage Life Insurance Company of Jacksonville. Later became vice chairman of the board and partner of the national investment house of Haydon, Stone and Company. In 1960, Kirk led Floridians supporting Richard M. Nixon's presidential campaign. In 1964, he was defeated for the U.S. Senate seat by incumbent Democrat Spessard Holland. In 1966, Kirk defeated liberal Democrat Robert King High for the governorship, 821,190 votes to 668,233, becoming the first Republican governor in Florida since Reconstruction. Kirk's governorship was surrounded by controversy. It began dramatically when he hired a private detective agency—the Wackenhut Corporation—to crack down on organized crime in Florida. The action was condemned by the Democratic legislature and a United States Crime Commission report. Constantly at odds with his Democratic cabinet and the legislators, he had many of his proposals rejected. He seemed to bask in controversy. In 1968 he refused to submit to a statewide teacher walkout over wages and left the state to pursue his vice presidential campaign in California. The legislature was forced to negotiate a settlement and end the strike. In March, 1970 he suspended the school board in Manatee County, directly challenging a court-ordered busing program to achieve integration. Subsequently, he bowed to court order when threatened with contempt and fine. Kirk placed great effort into attracting new business into the state. He achieved his greatest success in the area of conservation by creating the Water Pollution Control Commission; organizing a statewide wilderness system; and halting the cross-Florida barge canal construction project. Also he saw equitable legislative reapportionment instituted during his administration and the adoption of a new constitution in 1968. Kirk was defeated by Democrat Reubin O'D. Askew for the governorship in 1970, 984,305 votes to 746,243. He retired to private business in West Palm Beach. Bibliography: Robert Sherrill, "A Political Happening Named Claude Kirk," *The New York Times Magazine* (November 16, 1967); James Cass, "Politics and Education in the Sunshine State," *Saturday Review*, vol. LI (April 20, 1968); David Halberstam, "Claude Kirk and the Politics of Promotion," *Harper's Magazine*, vol. 236 (May, 1968); Fred J. Cook, "Governor Kirk's Private Eyes," *Nation*, vol. 204 (May 15, 1967). Kirk's public papers are housed in the Florida State Archives, Tallahassee.

ASKEW, Reubin O'Donovan, 1971-

Born on September 11, 1928 in Muskogee, Alabama, son of Leo Goldberg Askew and Alberta O'Donovan. Brother of Leo, Jr., Roy, John, Bonnie Buchanan, and Molly Stewart. Father, an itinerant carpenter, left his family shortly after Reubin Askew's birth and the mother reared the family, working as maid and seamstress. The Askews were Presbyterians. He was a Sergeant and paratrooper in the United States Army, 1946, and a Captain in the air force during the Korean conflict, 1951-

53. Married Donna Lou Harper in 1956; father of two children, Angela Adair and Kevin O'Donovan. Received a B.S. degree in Public Administration from Florida State University in 1951 and a law degree from the University of Florida in 1956; served as president of the student body at both schools. Began public service career by serving as Assistant County Solicitor of Escambia County, 1956-58. Elected to State House of Representatives from Escambia County in 1958 and to the State Senate in 1962. Defeated Republican Governor Claude Kirk for governorship in 1970, 984,305 votes to 746,243; and was reelected in 1974 over Republican Jerry Thomas, 1,118,954 to 709,438. He began his governorship by urging the adoption of a corporate income tax. Despite intense opposition from the business community, the measure was approved by the legislature and submitted to the voters as a constitutional referendum. It won overwhelming approval, due in large part to the governor's campaign effort; it was the first such tax in the state's history. Askew also supported "government in the sunshine" (disclosure by public officials of their income); stricter conservation laws, including the planning and regulation of lands and water, and providing $200 million for the purchase of endangered lands; and the establishment of a Department of Natural Resources. He asked the legislature to reconsider the death penalty and to reduce job discrimination against ex-convicts. In addition, he created a statewide grand jury to investigate organized crime in Florida. Askew has also been a vigorous proponent of integrated schools, and supported a referendum endorsing busing to achieve integration. He has also encouraged the employment of more blacks in state government; he appointed Joseph W. Hatchett, a black Floridian, to the Supreme Court, the first black to sit on the Court since Reconstruction. To aid the poor, he raised the financial limit on the family assistance program. Askew's term will expire in 1978 and he will then be constitutionally ineligible for reelection. Bibliography: Jon Nordheimer, "Florida's 'Supersquare'—A Man to Watch," *The New York Times Magazine* (March 5, 1972); Robert Sherrill, "Best the South Has to Offer This Year," *Saturday Review*, vol. LV (June 17, 1972).

GEORGIA

GEORGIA

WALTON, George, 1789

Born near Farmville, Prince Edward County, Virginia in 1741, son of Robert and Sally (or Mary) (Hughes) Walton; brother of John Walton; a Protestant. Married to Dorothy Camber, 1775; father of two sons. Orphaned at an early age and raised by an uncle; apprenticed to a carpenter; attended the common schools. Moved to Savannah, Georgia in 1769 and studied law; admitted to the bar in 1774; unanimously chosen as secretary of the Georgia Provincial Congress in 1775; elected president of the Council of Safety; served as a member of the Georgia House of Representatives. Elected as a delegate to the Continental Congress on February 2, 1776 and served in that capacity until September 27, 1781, except for the years 1778 and 1779; a signer of the Declaration of Independence; served in the Revolutionary War; commissioned Colonel of the First Regiment of the Georgia militia on January 9, 1778; captured by the British and exchanged for a Captain of the Navy in September 1779. Elected Governor of Georgia, serving from November 1779 to January 1780; commissioned by the Confederation to effect a treaty with the Cherokee Indians of Tennessee in 1783; appointed Commissioner of Augusta by the patriot legislature in 1784 and in that same year was authorized to lay out the city of Washington, Georgia. Served as Chief Justice of Georgia from 1783 to 1789; in 1786 served as a commissioner to settle a boundary dispute with South Carolina; appointed as a delegate to the Philadelphia Constitutional Convention of 1787, but did not attend; a Jeffersonian Republican. Walton was elected Governor of Georgia by a joint ballot of the State Legislature; he was inaugurated on January 7, 1789. During his administration, peace was established with the Creek Indians; a new State Constitution was ratified; and the capital was established in Augusta. Because the Georgia Constitution of 1777 prohibited a governor from succeeding himself, Walton left office on November 11, 1789. He was a presidential elector in 1789 and served as Judge of the Superior Court of the Eastern Judicial Circuit in 1790-1792, 1793-1795, 1799 and 1804; appointed Chief Justice of Georgia, serving from 1793 to 1795; appointed to the United States Senate to fill the vacancy caused by the resignation of James Jackson, serving from November 16, 1795 to February 20, 1796, when a successor was elected; served as a trustee of Richmond Academy and the University of Georgia; appointed Judge of the Georgia Middle Circuit, serving from 1799 until his death. Walton died on February 2, 1804 at his home "Meadow Garden," near Augusta, Georgia; his remains were interred in Rosney Cemetery, and reinterred in 1848 beneath the monument in front of the courthouse in Augusta. Bibliography: George White, *Historical Collections of Georgia* (New York, 1855); George Gilman Smith, *The Story of Georgia and the Georgia People, 1732 to 1860* (Atlanta, 1900); Lucian L. Knight, *A Standard History of Georgia and Georgians,* 6 vols. (Chicago, 1917); Roy Glashan, *American Governors and Gubernatorial Elections, 1775-1975* (Stillwater, Minnesota, 1975); *Who Was Who During the American Revolution* (Indianapolis and New York, 1976). Miscellaneous unpublished material in the Georgia Department of Archives and History, Atlanta.

TELFAIR, Edward, 1789-1793

Born on the Telfair estate, "Town Head," in Scotland *c.* 1735; brother of William Telfair; a Protestant. Married to Sally Gibbons on May 18, 1774; father of three daughters and three sons, among whom was Thomas Telfair. Attended Kirkcudbright Grammar School in Scotland. Emigrated to Virginia *c.* 1758 as an agent of a mercantile house; moved to Halifax, North Carolina and subsequently to Georgia, settling in Savannah in 1766 and engaging in commercial pursuits. Actively engaged in pre-Revolutionary movements of 1774; appointed assistant commander of the up-country militia; elected a member of the Council of Safety, serving in 1775 and 1776. Served as a delegate to the Provincial Congress in Savannah in 1776; served as a member of the Continental Congress from July 13, 1778 to November 1778, at which time he obtained a leave of absence; returned to the Congress on May 15, 1780 and served until the expiration of his term in January 1783; served again from 1784 to 1785 and from 1788 to 1789; one of the signers of the Articles of Confederation; served as Justice and Associate Justice for Burke County at various times during the period from 1781 to 1784. Served as a commissioner to treat with the Creek and Cherokee Indians in 1783; became a commissioner to settle the boundary dispute with South Carolina in 1783; served as Governor of Georgia from January 9, 1786 to January 9, 1787; served as a delegate to the State Convention which ratified the Constitution of the United States in 1788; a Jeffersonian Republican. Telfair was unanimously elected Governor of Georgia by a joint ballot of the State Legislature, defeating the other House nominee, John Houstoun; he was inaugurated on November 11, 1789. During his administration, difficulties arising over the Chisholm *vs.* Georgia case, in which an individual sought a judgement against the state of Georgia, as well as conflict with the federal government regarding the Indian question defined in the Treaty of New York, precipitated the passage of the Eleventh Amendment. Telfair left office on November 7, 1793 upon the inauguration of George Mathews, and retired to private life in August Georgia. Telfair died on September 17, 1807 in Savannah, Georgia and was buried in Bonaventure Cemetery. Telfair County, Georgia was named in his honor. Bibliography: George White, *Historical Collections of Georgia* (New York, 1855); George Gillman Smith, *The Story of Georgia and Georgia People, 1732 to 1860* (Atlanta, 1900); Lucian L. Knight, *A Standard History of Georgia and Georgians,* 6 vols. (Chicago, 1917); Roy Glashan, *American Governors and Gubernatorial Elections, 1775-1975* (Stillwater, Minnesota, 1975). Miscellaneous unpublished material in the Georgia Department of Archives and History, Atlanta.

MATHEWS, George, 1793-1796

Born on September 10, 1739 in Augusta County, Georgia, son of John Mathews, an Irish immigrant; a Protestant. Married a Miss Woods of Albemarle County, Virginia; after her death, remarried to Mrs. Reed of Staunton, whom he divorced; married a third time to Mrs. Flowers of Mississippi; father of four sons and two daughters, among whom were John, William, George, Charles Lewis and Anne Mathews. Self-educated. Was in command of a company of volunteers against the Indians in 1757 and was in the Battle of Point Pleasant on October 10, 1774; participated in the battles of Brandywine and Germantown, where he was wounded and captured by the British; exchanged in December, 1781; became commander of the Third Virginia Regiment. Returned to Georgia in 1784 and was engaged in agricultural pursuits. First elected Governor of Georgia in 1786, serving from January 9, 1787 to January 26, 1788. Elected to the First Congress, serving from March 4, 1789 to March 3, 1791; a Jeffersonian Republican. Mathews was elected Governor of Georgia by a joint ballot of the State Legislature, defeating the other House nominee, Edward Telfair; he was inaugurated on November 7, 1793. During his administration the overriding issue was the Yazoo Land Sale. In 1789, 2,500,000 acres of land were sold for 200,000 dollars to the Virginia Yazoo Company, the South Carolina Land Company and the Tennessee Land Company. Indian titles were to be extinguished by the purchasers and all money was to be paid within two years, but the purchasers failed to comply with these terms and the agreement lapsed. In 1795 five other companies combined to purchase some 35,000,000 acres for 500,000 dollars. Despite Governor Mathews' veto of the sale, the transaction was approved by the State Legislature, which initiated much controversy over Georgia's right to sell this land. Mathews left office on January 15, 1796 upon the inauguration of Jared Irwin. He was nominated as the first Governor of Mississippi Territory in 1798, but withdrew his name from consideration; appointed Brigadier-General in the expedition to capture West Florida in 1811. Mathews died on August 30, 1812 in Augusta, Georgia and was buried in St. Paul's Churchyard. Bibliography: George White, *Historical Collections of Georgia* (New York, 1855); George Gilman Smith, *The Story of Georgia and the Georgia People, 1732 to 1860* (Atlanta, 1900); Lucian L. Knight, *A Standard History of Georgia and Georgians,* 6 vols. (Chicago, 1917); Roy Glashan, *American Governors and Gubernatorial Elections, 1775-1975* (Stillwater, Minnesota, 1975); *Who Was Who During the American Revolution* (Indianapolis and New York, 1976).

IRWIN, Jared, 1796-1798, 1806-1809

Born in Mecklenburg County, North Carolina in 1750; of Scotch-Irish descent; a Protestant. Moved to Georgia, settling in Burke County; was active in the American Revolution; commanded a detachment of the Georgia militia against the Indians on the Georgia frontier. Moved to Washington County in 1788; elected a member of the convention to revise the State Constitution in 1789; served as a member of the first State Legislature convened under the present form of government in 1790; served as a member of the Georgia State Convention of 1795; a Democratic-Republican. Irwin was elected Governor of Georgia by a joint ballot of the State Legislature; he was inaugurated on January 15, 1796. During his administration, Irwin signed a bill rescinding the Yazoo Land Sale; this transaction had created such a controversy that the State Legislature ordered that all record of the act be deleted from official documents. Irwin left office on January 12, 1798 upon the inauguration of James Jackson. He was elected President of the Georgia Constitutional Convention of 1798. As President of the Georgia Senate, Irwin assumed the governorship on September 23, 1806 upon the resignation of Governor John Milledge and served in this capacity until his own inauguration on November 6, 1807, having again been elected Governor of Georgia by a joint ballot of the State Legislature. During his second administration, Georgia was threatened with bankruptcy due to the fact that the demand for cotton and tobacco had ceased with the Embargo and because the Bank of the United States had begun to recall its loans. Consequently, an alleviating act for the relief of debtors was passed, which provided for one-third of a debt to be paid when due, with an extension allowed for payment of the balance of the debt. Irwin left office on November 10, 1809 upon the inauguration of David B. Mitchell. He served several more terms in the Georgia Senate and attained the rank of Brigadier General of the Georgia militia. Irwin died on March 1, 1818 in Union Hill, Washington County, Georgia. Bibliography: George White, *Historical Collections of Georgia* (New York, 1855); George Gilman Smith, *The Story of Georgia and the Georgia People, 1732 to 1860* (Atlanta, 1900); Lucian L. Knight, *A Standard History of Georgia and Georgians*, 6 vols. (Chicago, 1917); Roy Glashan, *American Governors and Gubernatorial Elections, 1775-1975* (Stillwater, Minnesota, 1975).

JACKSON, James, 1798-1801

Born on September 21, 1757 in Moreton-Hampstead, Devonshire, England, son of James and Mary (Webber) Jackson; a Protestant. Married to Mary Charlotte Young on January 30, 1785; father of five sons, among whom was Jabez Young Jackson. Emigrated to Georgia in 1772 and was placed under the protection of John Wereat, a Savannah lawyer. Elected Clerk of the Court of the Provincial Congress in 1776 and 1777; served as a member of the first Constitutional Convention of Georgia in 1777. Served in the Constitutional Army during the Revolutionary War; participated in the unsuccessful defense of Savannah in 1778, the Battle of Cowpens, and the recovery of Augusta in 1781; attained the rank of Lieutenant Colonel; took possession of Savannah after the evacuation of the British; presented with a house by the State Legislature. Studied law with George Walton and established a law practice in Savannah. Appointed Colonel of the Chatham County Militia in 1784 and Brigadier General in 1786. Elected Governor of Georgia in 1788, but declined because of his youth and inexperience; elected to the First Congress, serving from March 4, 1789 to March 3, 1791; contested the election of Anthony Wayne to the Second Congress, whose seat was declared vacant by the House on March 21, 1792; elected to the United States Senate, serving from March 4, 1793 until his resignation in 1795; elected to the Georgia Legislature, where he led the successful fight for the repeal of the Yazoo Act; served as a presidential elector in 1797; a Democratic-Republican. Jackson was elected Governor of Georgia by a joint ballot of the State Legislature and was inaugurated on January 12, 1798. During his administration, Jackson denounced many of the leading men of Georgia as being culpably involved in the Yazoo fraud. John Berrien, State Treasurer, although impeached for embezzlement because of irregularities in the receipt of payment from some Yazoo purchasers, was not convicted. Governor Jackson recommended that the State Legislature pay Phineas Miller and Eli Whitney only a moderate sum for their patent right to the cotton gin or suppress the right entirely. Jackson resigned the governorship of Georgia on March 3, 1801, the day before he took his seat in the United States Senate. He served in the Senate from March 4, 1801 until his death. Jackson died in Washington, D.C. on March 19, 1806, and was interred in the Congressional Cemetery. Bibliography: George White, *Historical Collections of Georgia* (New York, 1855); George Gilman Smith, *The Story of Georgia and the Georgia People, 1732 to 1860* (Atlanta, 1900); Lucian L. Knight, *A Standard History of Georgia and Georgians,* 6 vols. (Chicago, 1917); Roy Glashan, *American Governors and Gubernatorial Elections, 1775-1975* (Stillwater, Minnesota, 1975); *Who Was Who During the American Revolution* (Indianapolis and New York, 1976).

EMANUEL, David, 1801

Born *c.* 1744 in Georgia, son of David Emanuel, a planter; brother of Amos, Levi, Asa, Elizabeth, Rebeckah, Martha and Ruth Emanuel. Served as a Captain and Colonel in the Georgia militia during the Revolutionary War. Appointed one of the commissioners for administering the Test Oath to inhabitants of Burke County, Georgia on May 9, 1780; appointed a magistrate of Burke County in August 1781; appointed Justice for Burke County, January 1782. Took the oath as a member of the Georgia House of Assembly in July 1783; appointed Assistant Justice of Burke County in February 1784; appointed Commissary General on August 15, 1786 and Receiver of Tax Returns of Colonel Lewis' Battalion on April 10, 1792. Served as a delegate to the Georgia State Convention at Louisville, Georgia, May 4, 1795; served as a member of the Supreme Executive Council of Georgia; served as President of the Georgia Senate; a Democratic-Republican. As president of the Georgia Senate, Emanuel assumed the governorship on March 3, 1801, upon the resignation of Governor James Jackson, and served until the inauguration of Josiah Tattnall, Jr. on November 7, 1801, at which time he returned to the Georgia Senate, where he continued his duties as president until his death. Emanuel died on February 19, 1808 at his plantation in Burke County, Georgia. Bibliography: *Augusta Chronicle* (March 3, 1808); National Society of Colonial Dames of America in the State of Georgia, *Abstracts of Colonial Wills of the State of Georgia, 1733-1777* (Atlanta, 1962); Lucian Lamar Knight, *Georgia's Roster of the Revolution* (Baltimore, 1967); Roy Glashan, *American Governors and Gubernatorial Elections, 1775-1975* (Stillwater, Minnesota, 1975).

TATTNALL, Josiah, 1801-1802

Born in 1764 on the family estate, "Bonaventure," near Savannah, Georgia, son of Josiah Tattnall, Sr., a Loyalist; a Protestant. Married to Harriet Fenwick, *c.* 1794; father of Josiah Tattnall. Attended school in Nassau. Accompanied his father to

England at the outbreak of the Revolutionary War; returned to Savannah and enlisted under General Anthony Wayne in 1782; served as Captain of the Chatham Artillery in 1792; commissioned Colonel of the First Georgia Regiment in 1793; promoted to Brigadier General of militia in 1801. Served as a member of the Georgia Legislature from 1795 to 1796; elected to the United States Senate to fill the vacancy caused by the resignation of James Jackson, serving from February 20, 1796 to March 3, 1799; a Democratic-Republican. Tattnall was elected Governor of Georgia by a joint ballot of the State Legislature and was inaugurated on November 7, 1801. His administration was marked by continuing bitterness over the Yazoo affair. Tattnall resigned as Governor of Georgia on November 4, 1802 because of ill health and travelled to Nassau, New Providence, British West Indies, where he died on June 6, 1803; he was interred in Bonaventure Cemetery, Savannah, Georgia. Bibliography: George White, *Historical Collections of Georgia* (New York, 1855); George Gilman Smith, *The Story of Georgia and the Georgia People, 1732 to 1860* (Atlanta, 1900); Lucian L. Knight, *A Standard History of Georgia and Georgians,* 6 vols. (Chicago, 1917); Roy Glashan, *American Governors and Gubernatorial Elections, 1775-1975* (Stillwater, Minnesota, 1975); *Who Was Who During the American Revolution* (Indianapolis and New York, 1976).

MILLEDGE, John, 1802-1806

Born in Savannah, Georgia in 1757, the only son of John and Ann (Robe) Milledge; the family was Episcopalian and among the earliest settlers in Georgia. Married to Martha Galphin, who died in 1811; father of Mary. Remarried to Ann Lamar in 1812; father of John, Ann and Thomas. Attended Bethesda School in Savannah and was studying law at the outbreak of the Revolution. Served both in an unofficial capacity as a "Liberty Boy" and with the army fighting around Augusta and Savannah. Captured by the British, along with another future governor, James Jackson; they escaped, only to be held as spies by American soldiers, and were saved from the gallows at the last minute. Served as State Attorney General from 1780 to 1782; practiced law; and was elected to the General Assembly in 1789. In 1792 he was elected to the United States House of Representatives, serving from 1793 to 1799 and from 1801 to 1802; in 1802 he resigned to become Governor of Georgia. His election by the legislature was apparently without opposition. As governor, Milledge was often occupied with matters dealing with land cessions and the Creek Indians. The terms of the latest treaty were carried out; additional cessions were made; land was surveyed; and a road was built from Tennessee to Augusta. Relations were improved with the Indians and with the federal government. Greatly interested in education, Milledge appointed like-minded men as trustees of academies and served himself as a trustee of the University of Georgia. He was responsible for the sale of land to benefit the university and donated over 600 acres which became its campus. During his second term, Milledge resigned to accept the United States Senate seat vacated by the death of James Jackson. He became a firm supporter of Thomas Jefferson and was made Senate President *Pro Tempore* in January 1809. In November he resigned and returned home to be with his dying wife. For the remainder of his life, he lived in retirement in Augusta, dying at age sixty-one on February 9, 1818; Milledge was buried in Summerville Cemetery. Bibliography: Josephine Mellichamp, *Senators from Georgia* (Huntsville,

Alabama, 1976); *Who Was Who During the American Revolution* (Indianapolis and New York, 1976); W.J. Northen, ed., *Men of Mark in Georgia,* 6 vols. (Atlanta, 1907-12); Harriet Milledge Salley, ed., *Correspondence of John Milledge, Governor of Georgia, 1802-1806,* with a sketch of his life by Victor Davidson (Columbia, S.C. 1949). Papers of Milledge are in the Georgia Department of Archives and History, Atlanta.

IRWIN, Jared, 1796-1798, 1806-1809

MITCHELL, David Brydie, 1809-1813, 1815-1817

Born on October 22, 1766 in Muthill, Perthshire, Scotland, son of John Mitchell. Came to Savannah at the age of seventeen to claim the estate left by his uncle, Dr. David Brydie. Married Jane Mills on January 19, 1792. Studied law and was made clerk of a committee revising the State Criminal Code. Served in the General Assembly, 1794-1796; Solicitor General of his district in 1795; Judge of the Eastern Division of the Superior Court from 1798-1801; Mayor of Savannah, 1801-1802; and United States Attorney General for Georgia from 1803 to 1805. Mitchell joined the state militia in 1793 as a Captain and had risen to Major General by 1804, resigning upon being elected Governor. An ardent Democratic-Republican, in 1809 Mitchell was elected Governor by the General Assembly by a margin of twenty votes over former Governor Jared Irwin. Reelected by fifty-one votes over Irwin two years later, he declined to run in 1813; however, in 1815 he was elected over Governor Peter Early by a margin of seventy-six to forty-nine. As governor, Mitchell emphasized internal improvements and progress was made in improving highways and building new roads. Better banking facilities were established and the militia was strengthened. The University of Georgia was given its first regular appropriation and an act was passed prohibiting dueling (Mitchell himself had killed a man in a duel in 1802). He was an active executive in the prosecution of the War of 1812, actually taking the field to lead a force into Florida. In 1817, Mitchell resigned to become Federal Indian Agent to the Creek Indians, replacing the recently deceased Benjamin Hawkins. As agent he negotiated a treaty in 1818 which resulted in the surrender by the Creeks of 1½ million acres of land. However, his years as agent were filled with controversy, and he was dismissed on March 4, 1821 by President James Monroe as a result of charges that he brought slaves into the country, charges which perhaps were false. Mitchell then retired to his home near Milledgeville and continued his interest in business and politics. Elected to the State Senate in 1836, he died on April 22, 1837 and was buried in Milledgeville. Bibliography: Thomas Henry Rentz, "The Public Life of David B. Mitchell," Unpublished M.A. Thesis, University of Georgia, 1955; G.M. Destler, ed., "Correspondence of David Brydie Mitchell," *Georgia Historical Quarterly,* vol. XXI (1937) and vol. XXVII (1944); W.J. Northen, ed., *Men of Mark in Georgia,* 6 vols. (Atlanta, 1907-12). Papers of Mitchell are in the Georgia Department of Archives and History, Atlanta.

EARLY, Peter, 1813-1815

Born in Madison County, Virginia on June 30, 1793, son of Joel and Lucy (Smith) Early. Attended Lexington Grammar School; graduated from Lexington Academy and from Princeton in 1792. Married fourteen-year-old Ann Adams Smith in 1793; father of a daughter and either two or three sons. While he was studying law in Philadelphia, Early's family moved to Wilkes County, Georgia. Upon completion of his studies, Early began a law practice in Washington, Georgia. Elected to the United States House of Representatives for three terms beginning in 1801; Early was one of the prosecution managers in the impeachment trials of Judges John Pickering and Samuel Chase. While he declined reelection to the House in 1807 for family reasons, Early was appointed Judge of the newly-created Superior Court of the Ocmulgee Circuit. He filled the position until elected Governor in 1813 by the legislature from among several candidates, including future Governor John Clark. With the nation in the midst of the War of 1812, Early energetically tried to prepare the state for war. Unlike most Georgia governors, he cooperated fully with the federal government. However, his veto of the reenactment of the so-called "Alleviating Law," which extended the time permitted debtors under certain conditions, proved unpopular. The veto was overriden, and he was defeated for reelection by David B. Mitchell by twenty-seven votes in the legislature. Early's home county, Greene, promptly elected him to the State Senate in 1816. Before the end of his term, Early died on August 15, 1817, and was buried on the banks of the Oconee River; in 1914 his body was moved to Greensboro. Bibliography: Hugh M. Thomason, "Governor Peter Early and the Indian Frontier, 1813-1815," *Georgia Historical Quarterly,* vol. XLV (1961); W.J. Northen, ed., *Men of Mark in Georgia,* 6 vols. (Atlanta, 1907-12); Stephen F. Miller, *The Bench and Bar of Georgia: Memoirs and Sketches,* 2 vols. (Philadelphia, 1858). Papers of Early are in the Georgia Department of Archives and History, Atlanta.

MITCHELL, David Brydie, 1809-1813, 1815-1817

RABUN, William, 1817-1819

Born on April 8, 1771 in Halifax, North Carolina, son of Matthew and Sarah Rabun. His family moved to Wilkes County, Georgia in 1775; William Rabun was a prominent Baptist layman. Married to Mary Battle on November 21, 1793; father of six daughters and one son, John William. Rabun had little formal education. Appointed Captain of Greene County Militia in 1793, but moved the same year to Hancock County. Rabun served as Justice of the Inferior Court for Hancock County from 1802-1810 and was elected to the General Assembly for one term in 1805. Elected to the State Senate, Rabun served six one-year terms beginning in 1810 and was President of the Senate from 1812 through 1816. When Governor David B. Mitchell resigned in March 1817, Rabun was made *ex-officio* Governor and was elected in November to the post by the General Assembly, defeating John Clark by five votes. Rabun's brief governorship came during a period of general prosperity in the state. At his urging the legislature appropriated money for waterways, canals, roads and other internal improvements, and revised the penal code. The State Penitentiary was completed and a steamboat company was chartered. Rabun died in office on October 25, 1819, and was buried in Milledgeville. Bibliography: *History of the Baptist Denomination in Georgia* (Atlanta, 1881); William J. Northen, ed., *Men of Mark in Georgia,* 6 vols. (Atlanta, 1907-12). Papers of Rabun are in the Georgia Department of Archives and History, Atlanta.

CLARK, John, 1819-1823

Born on February 28, 1766 in Edgecombe County, North Carolina, son of a prominent frontiersman, Elijah Clarke (the son dropped the "e" in the spelling of the family name) and Hannah Arrington. Married to Nancy Williamson, daughter of Colonel Micajah Williamson, a prominent frontiersman and large landowner, in 1787; father of Ann and Wiley P. He had little formal education; his family moved to Wilkes County, Georgia in 1774. Clark joined the army at age fifteen as a Lieutenant; he was made Captain at age sixteen, and fought throughout the course of the Revolution. Remained in the Georgia militia and was appointed Brigadier General in 1793 and Major General in 1811. By virtue of his wife's family and his own efforts, he became the owner of vast acres in the state and was connected with the Yazoo land dealings. In the General Assembly from 1801 to 1803 and in the Senate the following year, Clark was an active figure in state politics. He assumed the leadership of the backcountry faction in opposition to the group led by George M. Troup. Clark engaged in a duel with William H. Crawford; he also was penalized with a large fine for assaulting a judge. As a factional leader, Clark ran unsuccessfully on several occasions. He lost in 1813 and again in 1817, the second time by a margin of five votes. In 1819 he was elected over Troup by thirteen votes; two years later, the legislature chose him by two votes. While Clark was governor, a treaty with the Creeks was signed in 1821, giving the state the area between the Ocmulgee and Flint Rivers, from which five new counties were formed. He also urged the legislature to provide funds for internal improvements and schools. At the end of his second term, he retired from politics. After unsuccessful bids for the governorship in 1823 and in 1825, Clark was inactive in politics. In 1829 he moved to Florida and was appointed Keeper of the Public Forests by President Andrew Jackson. Clark died of yellow fever on October 2, 1832 in St. Andrew's Bay, Florida. He was buried there, and moved in 1923 to the National Cemetery in Marietta, Georgia. Bibliography: Carl Augustus Ross, "The Public Life and Accomplishments of John Clark," Unpublished M.A. Thesis, University of Georgia, 1951; W.J. Northen, ed., *Men of Mark in Georgia,* 6 vols. (Atlanta, 1907-12); George R. Gilmer, *Sketches of Some of the First Settlers of Upper Georgia, of the Cherokees, and the Author* (Americus, Ga., 1926). Papers of Clark are in the Georgia Department of Archives and History, Atlanta.

TROUP, George M., 1823-1827

Born on September 8, 1780 in McIntosh's Bluff on the Toombigbee River (Alabama), son of George and Catherine (McIntosh) Troup. His family moved to Savannah two years later. Married to Anne St. Clare McCormick on October 30, 1803; she died less than a year later. Married to Anne Carter on November 8, 1809; father of George M., Jr., and five daughters. Attended Erasmus Hall Academy on Long Island and graduated from Princeton in 1797. Studied law and was admitted to the bar in Savannah. Elected to the General Assembly in 1801 and was twice reelected to two-year terms. As a Democratic-Republican, Troup served three terms in the United States House of Representatives between 1807 and 1815; he was chairman of the Military Affairs Committee during the War of 1812. Troup did not run for reelection in 1815; he was elected to the United States Senate in 1816, but resigned two years later. By 1815, Georgia's political parties were identified with either Troup or John Clark, evidencing a planter-aristocrat versus backcountry alignment. Troup was defeated by Clark for Governor by thirteen votes in the legislature in 1819, and in 1821 by two votes. Two years later Troup defeated Clark by four votes. In 1825 in the first gubernatorial race decided by popular vote, Troup again defeated Clark, by less than 700 votes of the 40,000 cast. Known as an ardent supporter of States' Rights and internal improvements, Troup served as governor during the removal of the Creek Indians from the state and the making of their land accessible to white settlers. The Treaty of Indian Springs was completed in 1825 during his first term; another treaty was signed in 1827 during his second term, by which the last of the Creek land in the state was ceded. The favorable terms of the latter treaty were a direct result of a clash between Troup and President John Quincy Adams, a clash ending with victory for the governor's view. Troup returned to the United States Senate in 1829, but retired from politics in 1833 due to poor health. Thereafter, he lived in retirement, although continuing to be identified with the extreme States' Rights group in the South. In 1852, he declined a nomination for President offered by the Southern Rights Party of Alabama. Troup died on April 26, 1856 in Montgomery County and was buried on his plantation, "Rosemont." Bibliography: Edward J. Hardin, *The Life of George M. Troup* (Savannah, 1859); Josephine Mellichamp, *Senators from Georgia* (Huntsville, Alabama, 1976); Peter L. Fortune, "George M. Troup: Leading States Rights Advocate," Unpublished Ph.D. Dissertation, University of North Carolina, 1950; James W. Silver, "General Gaines Meets Governor Troup: A State-Federal Clash in 1825," *Georgia Historical Quarterly*, vol. XXVII (1943). Papers of Troup are in the Georgia Department of Archives and History, Atlanta.

FORSYTH, John, 1827-1829

Born on October 22, 1780 in Fredericksburg, Virginia, son of Robert, the first Federal Marshall of Georgia, and Fanny (Johnson) Forsyth; a Methodist. Married to Clara Meigs; father of several children, among whom were John and Julia Forsyth. Graduated from Princeton College in 1799; studied law with Mr. Noel in Augusta, Georgia and was admitted to the bar in 1802. Appointed Attorney General of Georgia in 1808. Three times elected as a Democrat to the United

States House of Representatives, serving from March 4, 1813 to November 23, 1818, at which time he resigned; elected to the United States Senate to fill the vacancy caused by the resignation of George M. Troup, serving from November 28, 1818 to February 17, 1819, when he resigned to accept an appointment as Minister to Spain, serving in that capacity until March 2, 1823; again elected to three terms in the United States House of Representatives, serving from March 4, 1823 to November 7, 1827, at which time he resigned. As the Troup faction's Democratic-Republican candidate, Forsyth was elected Governor of Georgia by popular vote on October 1, 1827. He polled 22,220 votes while his opponent, M. Talbot, died before the election; there was a scattered vote of 9,072. Inaugurated on November 7, 1827, Forsyth denounced the 1828 "Tariff of Abominations" and advocated the possibility of neutralizing it by state action. Forsyth left office on November 4, 1829 upon the inauguration of George R. Gilmer. He was again elected to the United States Senate to fill a vacancy, this time caused by the resignation of John Macpherson Berrien. Forsyth served from November 9, 1829 to June 27, 1834, when he resigned to accept a cabinet post; appointed Secretary of State by President Andrew Jackson and reappointed by President Martin Van Buren, serving from July 1, 1834 to March 4, 1841. Forsyth died on October 21, 1841 in Washington, D.C. and was interred in the Congressional Cemetery. Bibliography: George White, *Historical Collections of Georgia* (New York, 1855); Lucian L. Knight, *A Standard History of Georgia and Georgians,* 6 vols. (Chicago, 1917); Congressional Quarterly, Inc., *Guide to U.S. Elections* (Washington, D.C. 1975); Roy Glashan, *American Governors and Gubernatorial Elections, 1775-1975* (Stillwater, Minnesota, 1975).

GILMER, George Rockingham, 1829-1831, 1837-1839

Born on April 11, 1790 near Lexington, Wilkes (now Oglethorpe) County, Georgia; the fourth child of Thomas Meriwether, a farmer, and Elizabeth (Lewis) Gilmer; brother of eight, among whom were John and Lewis Gilmer; a Presbyterian. Married to Eliza Frances Grattan in 1822. Attended Dr. Wilson's Classical School near Abbeville Court House, South Carolina in 1803; attended the academy of Dr. Moses Wadel from 1804 to 1808; entered the law school of Stephen Upson in Lexington. Served as a First Lieutenant in the Forty-third Regiment of the United States Infantry from 1813 to 1815 in the campaign against the Creek Indians. Resumed his law studies and began his practice in Lexington in 1818. Served as a member of the Georgia House of Representatives in 1818 and 1819; elected as a Democrat to the United States House of Representatives, serving from March 4, 1819 to March 3, 1823; resumed law practice; again a member of the Georgia House of Representatives in 1824. Elected to the United States House of Representatives to fill the vacancy caused by the resignation of Edward F. Tatnall, serving from October 1, 1827 to March 3, 1829; reelected to this position, but failed to take his seat. As the Troup faction's Democratic-Republican candidate, Gilmer was elected Governor of Georgia by popular vote on October 5, 1829, defeating another Democratic-Republican, Joel Crawford, by a vote of 27,398 to 10,946; he was inaugurated on November 4, 1829. Again elected on October 2, 1837 as a States Rights candidate, defeating the Union candidate, William Schley, by a vote of 34,178 to 33,417; inaugurated for his second term on November 8, 1837. During Gilmer's first administration, gold was discovered in the Nacoochee Valley, situated in an area belonging to the Cherokee Indians. The influx of gold seekers to this area, in spite of a proclamation demanding their departure, strained the already tense relations with the Cherokees. Further problems were created by the extension of state laws over the Indian lands, making both Indians and whites subject to Georgia law. Gilmer's second administration was marked by the Panic of 1837. Economic developments resulting from the Panic and the depression which followed included an empty state treasury, the insolvency of the Monroe Railroad and Banking Company, and the bankruptcy of the Bank of Darien, in which the state had invested heavily. Also during Gilmer's second term of office, the Cherokee Indians were removed from Georgia. Gilmer first left office on November 9, 1831, upon the inauguration of Wilson Lumpkin, and next left office on November 6, 1839, upon the inauguration of Charles J. McDonald. He was elected to the United States House of Representatives, serving from March 4, 1833 to March 3, 1835; served as a presidential elector in 1836 and 1840; served as a trustee of the University of Georgia at Athens from 1826 to 1857; and served as president of the Agricultural Association of the Slaveholding States in 1854. He was the author of *Sketches of Some of the First Settlers of Upper Georgia* (1855). Gilmer died on November 16, 1859 in Lexington, Georgia and was interred in the Presbyterian Cemetery. Bibliography: George White, *Historical Collections of Georgia* (New York, 1855); Lucian L. Knight, *A Standard History of Georgia and Georgians*, 6 vols. (Chicago, 1917); Congressional Quarterly, Inc., *Guide to U.S. Elections* (Washington, D.C., 1975); Roy Glashan, *American Governors and Gubernatorial Elections, 1775-1975* (Stillwater, Minnesota, 1975).

LUMPKIN, Wilson, 1831-1835

Born on January 14, 1783 in Pittsylvania County, Virginia, son of John, a private businessman and local politician, and Lucy (Hopson) Lumpkin; brother of William, Jack, George, Henry Hopson, Samuel, Robert, Martha Lumpkin Calloway, Joseph Henry, Thomas Jefferson and James Neville; a Baptist. Married to Elizabeth Walker on November 20, 1800, who died on November 30, 1819; remarried to Ann S. Hopkins on January 1, 1821; father of Lucy, Ann S., Pleiades Orion, Wilson, William, Elizabeth, Samuel Hopkins, John Calhoun and Martha Wilson. Moved with his parents to Oglethorpe County, Georgia in 1784. From 1799 to 1800 he assisted his father in his duties as clerk of the Superior Court of Oglethorpe County. Studied law and became a successful lawyer and planter; taught school in Oglethorpe County from 1803 to 1804. In 1804 he was elected to the State House of Representatives, without any particular party affiliation; reelected in 1805. Appointed Magistrate of the Inferior Court of his district in January 1805, and continued to serve in this office for several years; reelected to the state's Lower House in 1812 and 1813. Elected to the United States House of Representatives in 1815, but was defeated in his bid for reelection in 1817. In 1818 and 1819 President James Monroe appointed Lumpkin a commissioner to determine the boundaries of treaties made with the Creek Indians during those years. Reelected to the State Legislature in 1820 as a representative from Morgan County (having moved there in 1814); he resigned this position in 1821 to accept another appointment as a United

States commissioner to determine the boundary of the Creek Treaty of 1821. Elected by the legislature in 1825 to the Georgia Board of Public Works. In 1826 he was elected to the United States House of Representatives as a Jacksonian Democrat, and was reelected in 1828 and 1830; he resigned his House seat on March 3, 1831 to accept the nomination of the Union Party for Governor. Defeated incumbent Governor George Gilmer by a vote of 27,305 to 25,853, and was sworn into office on November 9, 1831. As governor, Lumpkin's main concern was the removal of the Cherokees from north Georgia. In this effort, he strongly supported the rights of Georgia against what he termed "federal usurpation" and ignored Chief Justice John Marshall's decision in the case of *Worcester vs. Georgia* (1831). Lumpkin ran for reelection in 1833 against Joel Crawford, the States' Rights nominee, and won by a vote of 33,861 to 25,585. He again took the oath of office on November 6, 1833. During his second term, Lumpkin faced a legislature dominated by the opposition party. Nevertheless, he provided aggressive leadership by working for a revision of the state's tax laws, calling for a system of mass education and teacher training; pushing for a railroad to link the Ohio Valley with Georgia's coast; and urging improvements at the State Penitentiary. In July 1836 President Andrew Jackson appointed him a commissioner to assist in carrying out the terms of the Cherokee Treaty of 1835. Lumpkin resigned this position in the fall of 1837 to complete the unexpired term of United States Senator John P. King. In 1841 Lumpkin was appointed distributing agent for the Western and Atlantic Railroad. He retired in 1843 to his home in Athens, Georgia where he spent his time farming, writing his memoirs, and serving as a trustee of the University of Georgia. Lumpkin died on December 1, 1870, and was buried in Oconee Cemetery in Athens. Bibliography: Horace Montgomery, ed., *Georgians in Profile* (Athens, Ga., 1958); Carl J. Vipperman, "Wilson Lumpkin and Cherokee Removal," Unpublished M.A. Thesis, University of Georgia, 1961; Wilson Lumpkin, *The Removal of the Cherokee Indians from Georgia,* 2 vols. (New York, 1907); L.L. Cody, *The Lumpkin Family of Georgia* (Macon, Ga., 1928); James H. Johnston, *Western and Atlantic Railroad of the State of Georgia* (Atlanta, 1931). Papers of Lumpkin are in the Georgia Department of Archives and History in Atlanta, and the University of Georgia Library, Athens.

SCHLEY, William, 1835-1837

Born on December 10, 1786 in Frederick, Maryland, son of John Jacob, a planter, and Anna Maria (Shelman) Schley; brother of Michael, John, Frederick Augustus, Philip Thomas and Catherine; a Protestant. Married to Elizabeth Sarah Hargrove on April 2, 1822, who died on February 11, 1845; remarried to Sophia Kerr on February 25, 1846; father of Anna Maria, William K., George H. and Henry Jackson. Moved with his parents to Jefferson County, Georgia; educated at Louisville Academy in Jefferson County, and at Richmond Academy in Augusta, Richmond County. He served as a private in the Ninth Regiment of the Georgia militia. Studied law and admitted to the Georgia Bar in 1812; practiced law in Augusta until 1825. Appointed in 1823, by the Georgia Legislature to compile a digest of Georgia laws which was published in Philadelphia in 1826. Elected Superior Court Judge for the Middle Circuit in 1825 and served until 1828. Entered the Georgia Legislature in 1830 as a representative from Richmond County. Two years later he was elected to the United States House of Representatives, running as a Democrat. Reelected in 1834, but resigned in 1835 to accept the nomination of the Union Party for Governor of Georgia. Defeated Charles Dougherty, nominee of the States' Rights Party, by a vote of 31,177 to 18,606, and assumed office on November 4, 1835. As governor, Schley supported the construction of the Western and Atlantic Railroad; sponsored improvements in navigation; and advocated the use of state geological surveys to determine the state's mineral resources. He worked for the establishment of a State Supreme Court and an education fund for the deaf and dumb; maintained an insane asylum; introduced conformity to a uniform standard of weights and measures; and urged the use of smallpox vaccinations. For six weeks during his term, he personally conducted a campaign against the Creek Indians who had committed depredations and murders on Georgia's western frontier along the Chattahoochee River. In 1837 he ran for reelection against former Governor George Gilmer, and lost by a vote of 34,178 to 33,417. Schley retired from politics and returned to Augusta. He began a career in private business and spent the last years of his life as the owner of the Richmond Factory, a large cotton and woolen products manufacturing company in Augusta. Schley died on November 20, 1858, and was buried in the family plot at Richmond Hill, near Augusta. Bibliography: Charles C. Jones and Salem Dutcher, *Memorial History of Augusta, Georgia* (Syracuse, N.Y., 1890); Lucian L. Knight, *Georgia's Landmarks, Memorials and Legends*, 2 vols. (Atlanta, 1913-14); Effie G. Bowie, *Across the Years in Prince George's County* (Richmond, Va., 1947); George White, *Statistics of Georgia* (Savannah, 1849); James H. Johnson, *Western and Atlantic Railroad of the State of Georgia* (Atlanta, 1931). Papers of Schley are in the Georgia Department of Archives and History, Atlanta.

GILMER, George Rockingham, 1829-1831, 1837-1839

McDONALD, Charles James, 1839-1843

Born on July 9, 1793 in Charleston, South Carolina, son of Charles, a planter, and Mary (Glas) McDonald; brother of Samuel, Elizabeth McDonald Carter, Anna McDonald Brantley, Alexander, Maria and Catherine; an Episcopalian. His family moved to Hancock County, Georgia in 1794. Married to Anne Franklin on December 19, 1819, who died on October 10, 1835; remarried to Elizabeth Roane Ruffin on October 12, 1839; father of Mary Ann and Ella. Attended South Carolina College in Columbia and graduated in 1816. Served as a Brigadier General, Third Brigade, Sixth Division, Georgia militia from 1823 to 1825. Studied law under Joel Crawford of Macon and admitted to the Georgia Bar in 1817. Opened his own law office in Macon, and in 1830 went into partnership with Benjamin C. Franklin. Elected a trustee of Bibb County Academy and Macon Academy in 1823 and 1833, respectively; in 1824 he was appointed director of the Macon branch of the Bank of Darien. In 1822 McDonald became Solicitor General of the Flint Circuit and served until 1825, when he became judge of this circuit, serving until 1828. Entered the Georgia Legislature as a Democratic representative from Bibb County for the

1830 session; elected to the State Senate in 1834 and in 1837. Nominated as the Union Party candidate for Governor in 1839; he defeated States' Rights candidate Charles Dougherty by a vote of 34,634 to 32,897. He was sworn into office on November 6, 1839. As governor, McDonald faced the difficult problems resulting from the Panic of 1837, as well as a legislature dominated by Whigs. To help alleviate the state's troubled financial condition, he urged: the resumption of specie payments by banks; the suspension of all work on the state-owned Western and Atlantic Railroad, except from Atlanta to Cartersville; and passage of a "stay law" to stop the execution of mortgages. He recommended the establishment of a State Supreme Court, biennial sessions of the legislature, and an adequate educational system. In 1841 McDonald ran for reelection against William C. Dawson, a Whig; he won by a vote of 37,487 to 33,703, and assumed office on November 3, 1841. During his second term, McDonald continued to support the programs of his first administration, concentrating on the state's economy. He called for an increase in taxes until the state debts were cancelled, and when the legislature rejected this unpopular proposal, he ordered the treasurer to use state funds for general expenses first, leaving the legislators' salaries unpaid if need be. At the end of his second term, McDonald moved to Marietta, Georgia where he engaged briefly in planting and other private business pursuits. Keenly interested in the development of Cobb County, he helped to organize the Cobb County and Alabama Plank and Turnpike Road Company in 1850. McDonald was one of the founders of the Georgia Military Institute in Marietta in 1851, and in 1854 was an incorporator of the Mining Company of Northern Georgia. He was a delegate to the Southern Rights Convention in Macon in August 1850, and then served as a vice president of the Nashville Convention later that year. In 1851 he was nominated for Governor for a third term on the States' Rights ticket, but was defeated by Constitutional Unionist Howell Cobb by a vote of 57,397 to 38,824. In 1853, and again in 1857, McDonald unsuccessfully sought a seat in the United States Senate. He became an Associate Justice of the State Supreme Court in 1855 and served until his resignation in 1859. In 1860 he was chosen as an elector-at-large on the Breckenridge presidential ticket. McDonald died at his home in Marietta on December 16, 1860, at the age of sixty-seven. Bibliography: Sarah B. Temple, *The First Hundred Years: A Short History of Cobb County, Georgia* (Atlanta, 1935); John C. Butler, *Historical Record of Macon and Central Georgia* (Macon, 1897; reprinted 1969); Franklin Garret, *Atlanta and Environs,* 3 vols. (New York, 1954); Horace Montgomery, *Cracker Parties* (Baton Rouge, 1950). McDonald's official papers are at the Georgia Department of Archives and History in Atlanta; private correspondence of McDonald is included in the McDonald and Lawrence Papers, the Elizabeth (Furman) Talley Papers, and the Farish Carter Papers, in the Southern Historical Collection, University of North Carolina, Chapel Hill.

CRAWFORD, George Walker, 1843-1847

Born on December 22, 1798 in Columbia County, Georgia, son of Peter, a planter and state politician, and Mary Ann (Crawford) Crawford; brother of Charles, William, Thomas, Eliza, Jane Crawford Torrence, Harriet Crawford Jackson, and

Maria Crawford Rhodes; an Episcopalian. Married to Mary Ann McIntosh on May 4, 1826; father of William Peter, Sarah and Anna. Attended the College of New Jersey and graduated in 1820. Read law in the office of Richard Henry Wilde in Augusta, Georgia, and opened his own law office there in 1822. Second Lieutenant, "Georgia Fensibles," Tenth Regiment, Georgia militia, Richmond County from January 1824 to May 1825. Appointed Attorney General of Georgia in 1827 by Governor John Forsyth to fill a vacancy; elected to a full three-year term in 1828. Entered the Georgia House of Representatives in 1837 as a States' Rights Whig from Richmond County, and was elected to four more terms. Upon the death of United States Representative Richard Habersham of Georgia, Crawford was elected over Democrat Alexander McDougald to fill this vacancy, serving from February to March 1843. In the summer of 1843 Crawford was nominated as the Whig candidate for Governor; after a spirited campaign, he defeated his Democratic opponent, Mark A. Cooper, by a vote of 38,813 to 35,325. Crawford was sworn in as Governor on November 7, 1843, and thus became the state's only Whig governor. When Crawford assumed office, Georgia was beginning to recover from the depression which followed the Panic of 1837. As governor, he favored: sound currency; liquidation of the state bank; payment of the state debt; railroad construction, establishment of a State Supreme Court; and penal reform. Crawford proved to be a popular and successful administrator. In 1845 he was reelected over Democrat Matthew H. McAllister by a vote of 41,514 to 39,763, and was sworn into office on November 5, 1845. Crawford's administration succeeded in accomplishing the payment of a substantial part of the state debt; the completion of much of the state-owned Western and Atlantic Railroad; the reformation of the state penal code and penitentiary; and the establishment of a State Supreme Court. Following the election of Zachary Taylor to the presidency in 1848, Crawford was selected to be Secretary of War. He held this position until Taylor's death in July 1850; he then resigned and returned home to Georgia. In 1860 he was elected as a delegate to the State Secession Convention and was selected as its permanent chairman. Following the convention's adjournment in March 1861, Crawford remained in rigid seclusion at his home in Bel Air, Georgia, pursuing his business interests. Crawford died on July 27, 1872 and was buried in Summerville Cemetery near Augusta. Bibliography: Len G. Cleveland, "George W. Crawford of Georgia, 1798-1872," Unpublished Ph.D. Dissertation, University of Georgia, 1974; Paul Murray, *The Whig Party in Georgia, 1825-1853* (Chapel Hill, 1948); William Y. Thompson, *Robert Toombs of Georgia* (Baton Rouge, 1966); Len G. Cleveland, "The Establishment of the Georgia Supreme Court," *Georgia State Bar Journal,* vol. IX (May, 1973). Crawford's gubernatorial papers are in the Georgia Department of Archives and History in Atlanta; a small collection of personal papers is housed at the Library of Congress.

TOWNS, George Washington Bonaparte, 1847-1851

Born on May 4, 1801 in Wilkes County, Georgia, son of John, a farmer and soldier, and Margaret (George) Hardwick Towns; a Protestant. Married to Miss Campbell of Alabama, and afterwards to Mary Jones; father of seven children by his second marriage. Attended the common schools; studied medicine in Eatonton, Georgia, but was forced to withdraw because of injuries sustained when thrown from a horse.

Studied law in Montgomery, Alabama and was admitted to the bar in 1824. In 1826, he returned to Georgia and settled in Talbot County, where he began the practice of law. Served as a member of the Georgia House of Representatives in 1829 and 1830; served as a member of the Georgia Senate from 1832 to 1834; elected as a Union Democrat to the United States House of Representatives, serving from March 4, 1835 to September 1, 1836, at which time he resigned; again elected to the United States House of Representatives, serving from March 4, 1837 to March 3, 1839; elected a third time to the United States House of Representatives, on this occasion to fill the vacancy caused by the resignation of Washington Poe, serving from January 5, 1846 to March 3, 1847; an unsuccessful candidate for reelection. As the Democratic gubernatorial candidate, Towns was elected Governor of Georgia by popular vote on October 4, 1847, defeating the Whig candidate, Duncan L. Clinch, by a vote of 43,220 to 41,931; reelected on October 1, 1849, defeating the Whig candidate, Edward Y. Hill, by a vote of 46,514 to 43,322; inaugurated on November 3, 1847. During his administration, Towns advocated the use of poll taxes, the revenue from the state railroad, and other sources of revenue to finance the state's common schools. He was an avid supporter of the Mexican War; he also received from the State Legislature the power to call a state convention in the event that the Wilmot Proviso was passed by Congress. In addition, the *ad valorem* system of taxation was adopted and the Western and Atlantic Railroad was completed during Towns' years as governor. He left office on November 5, 1851, upon the inauguration of Howell Cobb, and resumed the practice of law. Towns died on July 15, 1854 in Macon, Georgia and was interred in Rose Hill Cemetery. Bibliography: George White, *Historical Collections of Georgia* (New York, 1855); Lucian L. Knight, *A Standard History of Georgia and Georgians,* 6 vols. (Chicago, 1917); Congressional Quarterly, Inc. *Guide to U.S. Elections* (Washington, D.C., 1975); Roy Glashan, *American Governors and Gubernatorial Elections, 1775-1975* (Stillwater, Minnesota, 1975).

COBB, Howell, 1851-1853

Born on September 7, 1815 in Cherry Hill, Jefferson County, Georgia, son of John A., a planter, and Sarah (Rootes) Cobb; brother of Thomas Reede Rootes, John B., Laura Cobb Rutherford, Mildred Cobb Glenn, Mary Cobb Johnson, and Martha Cobb Whitner; no formal religious affiliation. Married to Mary Ann Lamar on May 29, 1835; father of John A., Lamar, Howell, Andrew Jackson, Mary Ann Lamar, Sarah and Lizzie Craig. Moved with his parents to Athens, Georgia at an early age; attended the University of Georgia, graduating in 1834; studied law and admitted to the Georgia Bar in 1836. Elected Solicitor of Georgia's Western Judicial Circuit in 1837, and in 1842 elected as a Democrat to the United States House of Representatives. Reelected to the House in 1844, 1846, and 1848, and served as Speaker from 1849 to 1851. Nominated as the Constitutional Union candidate for Governor in 1851, Cobb defeated States' Rights candidate Charles J. McDonald by a vote of 57,397 to 38,824; he was sworn into office on November 5, 1851. As governor, Cobb had the support of a Democrat-controlled legislature and entering office after the strife surrounding the Compromise of 1850, generally experienced an uneventful two years. He called for a return to annual legislative sessions; the election of a State Attorney General; Supreme Court sessions in the state capital;

an annual 1,000 dollar appropriation for the State Library; leasing of the state-owned Western and Atlantic Railroad; and financial support of all charitable and educational institutions in Georgia. Despite a popular and successful administration, Cobb was not a candidate for reelection. In 1854 Cobb returned to the United States House of Representatives as a Democrat. He was appointed Secretary of the Treasury by President James Buchanan in 1857; resigned in 1860 upon the election of Abraham Lincoln to the presidency. In 1861 he was a delegate to, and President of, the Provisional Congress of the Confederacy. In July of 1861, he entered the Confederate Army as a Colonel of the Sixth Georgia Regiment, and by September 1861, he had risen to the position of Major General. Following the war, he returned to his home in Athens, where he pursued his legal career. Cobb died on October 9, 1868 while on a business trip to New York; he was buried in Oconee Hill Cemetery in Athens, Georgia. Bibliography: John Eddins Simpson, *Howell Cobb: The Politics of Ambition* (Chicago, 1973); Zachary Taylor Johnson, *The Political Policies of Howell Cobb* (Nashville, 1929); Horace Montgomery, *Cracker Parties* (Baton Rouge, 1950); Horace Montgomery, *Howell Cobb's Confederate Career* (Tuscaloosa, 1959); U.B. Phillips, *Georgia and State Rights* (Washington, D.C., 1902); Richard H. Shryock, *Georgia and the Union in 1850* (Durham, 1926). Cobb's gubernatorial papers are in the Georgia Department of Archives and History in Atlanta; his private papers are housed in the University of Georgia Library, Athens.

JOHNSON, Herschel Vespasian, 1853-1857

Born on September 18, 1812 in Burke County, Georgia, son of Moses and Nancy (Palmer) Johnson. Married to Mrs. Ann (Polk) Walker on December 19, 1833. Attended private schools and Monaghan Academy near Warrenton, Georgia; received his B.A. from Franklin College (now University of Georgia) at Athens in 1834. Studied law under Judge Gould of Atlanta; admitted to the bar in September 1834, and began the practice of law in Augusta; moved to Jefferson County in 1839 and practiced law in Louisville. Served as a delegate to the Georgia Democratic Convention in 1841; declined to be a candidate for the United States House of Representatives in 1841; unsuccessful candidate for the United States House of Representatives in 1843; served as a Democratic presidential elector in 1844; unsuccessful candidate for Georgia gubernatorial nomination in 1847. Appointed as a Democrat to the United States Senate to fill the vacancy caused by the resignation of Walter T. Colquitt, and served from February 4, 1848 to March 3, 1849; was not a candidate for election to this office; served as a delegate to the Democratic National Conventions of 1848, 1852, and 1856; served as Judge of the Superior Court of the Ocmulgee Circuit from November 1849 to August 1853; served as a Democratic presidential elector in 1852. As the States' Rights Democratic gubernatorial candidate, Johnson was elected Governor of Georgia by popular vote on October 7, 1853, defeating the Constitutional Union Candidate, Charles J. Jenkins, by a vote of 47,638 to 47,128; reelected on October 1, 1855, defeating the American Party candidate, G. Andrews, and the Temperance candidate, Mr. Overby, by a vote of 54,136 to 43,358 and 6,333, respectively; inaugurated on November 9, 1853. During his administration, Johnson was a strong advocate of public education and States' Rights. He was also a supporter of the Kansas-Nebraska Act, but deplored the use of force by both proponents and opponents of slavery. Johnson left office on November 6, 1857 upon the inauguration of Joseph E. Brown and returned to his plantation, "Sandy Grove." He was an unsuccessful candidate for Vice President of the United States on the Douglas Democratic ticket in 1860; served as a delegate to the Georgia Secession Convention in 1861; served as a member of the Confederate Senate from 1862 to 1865; served as President of the Georgia Constitutional Convention of October 1865; elected to the United States Senate in 1866, but was denied his seat; resumed law practice in Louisville; appointed Judge of the Middle Circuit of Georgia in 1873 and served in that capacity until his death. Johnson died on August 16, 1880 in "Shady Grove" near Louisville, Georgia. He was interred in the Old Louisville Cemetery. Bibliography: Issac W. Avery, *History of the State of Georgia, 1850-1881* (New York, 1881); Lucian L. Knight, *A Standard History of Georgia and Georgians,* 6 vols. (Chicago, 1917); Congressional Quarterly, Inc., *Guide to U.S. Elections* (Washington, D.C., 1975); Roy Glashan, *American Governors and Gubernatorial Elections, 1775-1975* (Stillwater, Minnesota, 1975).

BROWN, Joseph Emerson, 1857-1865

Born in Pickens District, South Carolina on April 15, 1821, son of Mackey, a farmer, and Sally (Rice) Brown, both of whom were Baptists; Brother of Peggy, Prudence, Mary, Edna, James, William, Aaron, Nancy, Jemima, Sally, John Mackey and John Washington Brown. Married to Elizabeth Grisham in 1847; father of Julius Lewis, Mary Virginia, Joseph Mackey, Franklin Pierce, Elijah Alexander, Charles McDonald, Sally Eugenia and George Marion. Attended Yale Law School and graduated in 1846. Established a law practice in Canton, Georgia and entered politics in 1849 by winning a seat in the Georgia Senate. In 1855 he was elected Judge of the Superior Court, and in 1857 a deadlocked Democratic Party convention selected Brown as a compromise candidate for Governor. In a spirited campaign, he defeated Benjamin H. Hill by 10,000 votes. A popular representative of the people, Brown was reelected in 1859 over Warren Akin by a margin of 22,000 votes; in 1861 he defeated Eugenius Nisbet, 46,493 votes to 32,802, and in 1863 he defeated Joshua Hill and Timothy Furlow, receiving 36,558 votes to 18,222 for Hill and 10,024 for Furlow. Brown is the only Georgian who has served four successive terms as governor. A bold and independent governor, Brown provided strong executive leadership. Through rigid economies and efficient management, he made the state-owned railroad a profitable operation and with the increased revenue began a comprehensive system of public education. An ardent pro-slavery states' righter, Brown advocated secession and exerted strenuous efforts to prepare the state for war. Throughout the Civil War, he quarreled with President Jefferson Davis over conscription, suspension of *habeas corpus,* jurisdiction of troops, taxes and confiscation of property without compensation. His fanatical devotion to state sovereignty weakened the Confederate war effort. Jailed briefly at the end of the war, he resigned the governorship in June of 1865 and urged Georgians to accept Reconstruction. He was bitterly denounced for advocating compliance, and suffered his only defeat in a political campaign when he lost a race for the United States

Senate in 1868. Appointed Chief Justice of the Georgia Supreme Court in 1868, he served until 1870, when he resigned to pursue his many business interests. Through his law practice, real estate investments, and iron, coal and railroad interests, he became one of the state's wealthiest men. From 1880 to 1891, he served in the United States Senate, where he was a leading exponent of the Bourbon philosophy. Brown died on November 30, 1894 and was buried in Oakland Cemetery in Atlanta. Bibliography: Joseph H. Parks, *Joseph E. Brown of Georgia* (Baton Rouge, 1977); Derrell C. Roberts, *Joseph E. Brown and the Politics of Reconstruction* (Tuscaloosa, 1973); Louise Biles Hill, *Joseph E. Brown and the Confederacy* (Chapel Hill, 1939); Herbert Fielder, *Life and Times of Joseph E. Brown* (Springfield, Mass., 1883); I.W. Avery, *The History of the State of Georgia From 1850 to 1881* (New York, 1881); Derrell C. Roberts, "Joseph E. Brown and the Convict Lease System," *Georgia Historical Quarterly,* vol. XLIV (December, 1960); Joseph H. Parks, "States Rights in a Crisis: Governor Joseph E. Brown versus President Jefferson Davis," *Journal of Southern History,* vol. XXXII (February, 1966); William J. Northen, ed., *Men of Mark in Georgia* (Atlanta, 1907-1912). Papers of Brown are on deposit at the Georgia Department of Archives and History in Atlanta, the Atlanta Historical Society and the University of Georgia Library in Athens.

JOHNSON, James, 1865

Born in Robinson County, North Carolina on February 12, 1811, son of Peter and Nancy (McNeil) Johnson, both of whom were Presbyterians. Married to Ann Harris in 1834; father of Walter H. Johnson. Attended the University of Georgia and graduated in 1832. He taught school, studied law, and became an attorney in Columbus. A staunch Whig, Johnson served one term in Congress (1851-1853) but was defeated when he sought reelection. Unlike most Georgians, he opposed secession and remained loyal to the Union throughout the Civil War. On June 17, 1865, Johnson was appointed Provisional Governor of Georgia by President Andrew Johnson for the purpose of enabling the state to form a new government. Following instructions from the president, Governor Johnson called a state convention, which ratified the 13th Amendment, repudiated the Confederate debt, repealed the Ordinance of Secession, and wrote a new state constitution. The convention ordered an election for governor and other state officials, and Charles J. Jenkins was inaugurated Governor on December 14, 1865. Johnson relinquished his position five days later, upon instructions from President Johnson. At the suggestion of the president, Johnson sought a seat in the United States Senate, but was unsuccessful. He was appointed United States Collector of Customs in Savannah, a post he held from 1866 to 1869, when he became Judge of the Superior Court. A learned and courageous jurist, he served on the bench until 1875, at which time he gave up his judgeship and resumed his law practice in Columbus. Johnson's last years were spent in quiet retirement. He died on November 20, 1891 and was buried in the Linwood Cemetery in Columbus. Bibliography: I.W. Avery, *The History of the State of Georgia From 1850 to 1881* (New York, 1881); C. Mildred Thompson, *Reconstruction in Georgia* (New York, 1915); James F. Cook, *The Governors of Georgia* (Huntsville, Ala., 1977); Nancy Telfair, *A History of Columbus, Georgia, 1828-1928* (Columbus, 1929). Papers of Johnson are on deposit in the Georgia Department of Archives and History in Atlanta.

JENKINS, Charles Jones, 1865-1868

Born on January 6, 1805 in Beaufort, South Carolina, the only child of Charles Jones Jenkins, Sr., a planter and local politician; an Episcopalian. His family moved to Jefferson County, Georgia in 1816. Married Sarah Jones on May 24, 1832, who died on August 29, 1849; remarried to Emily Barnes on April 18, 1854; father of Charles, Sarah and Mary. Attended local schools in Chatham, Bryan, and Hancock counties, and Willington Academy in Abbeville, South Carolina. Entered the University of Georgia in 1819, but transferred in 1822 to Union College in Schenectady, New York where he graduated in 1824, winning membership in Phi Beta Kappa. Read law in the Savannah office of John McPherson Berrien and admitted to the bar in 1826; opened law office in Sandersville, Georgia. In 1829 moved to Augusta, where he established his practice. In 1830 entered the Georgia Legislature as a States' Rights representative from Richmond County; in 1831 the legislature elected him Attorney General of Georgia. Resigned in 1834 to run for the State Legislature, but was defeated. Reelected to the Georgia House in 1836 and repeatedly thereafter until 1850, with the exception of a defeat in 1842. Served as Speaker during four sessions. Delegate to the State Convention of 1839 called to reduce the size of the legislature, and to the State Convention of 1850 which drafted the "Georgia Platform." Nominated for the vice presidency by his fellow Georgians in 1852 on the National Constitutional Union Party ticket. In 1853 Jenkins was nominated for Governor by the Constitutional Union Party, but was defeated by Democrat Herschel V. Johnson by 47,638 votes to 47,128. In 1856 he was elected to the State Senate to complete the unexpired term of Andrew J. Miller; in 1860 Governor Joseph E. Brown appointed him to the State Supreme Court, where he served until his resignation in 1865. Elected Governor without real opposition in November 1865 by a vote of 37,500 to 500 for the former Governor Brown, who had declined to run. Assumed office on December 14, 1865. As governor, Jenkins faced the difficult problems of rebuilding the state treasury and renovating state property destroyed as a result of the Civil War. At the end of his administration, there was money in the treasury, and the state railroad had been repaired and put into successful operation. Jenkins was removed from office on January 13, 1868 by General George Meade, commander of the military district of which Georgia was a part. Before he left the State Capitol, Jenkins took the Executive Department Seal, records of his term in office, and approximately 400,000 dollars of the state's money which he deposited in a New York bank (until it was returned in 1872). After a trip to Europe, Jenkins returned to Augusta in 1870, where he continued his law practice and served briefly as president of a local bank and of an Augusta factory. In 1871 he was elected president of the Board of Trustees of the University of Georgia, having been a member since 1839, and he continued to serve until 1883. In 1877 he was elected first as delegate to, and then as President of, the State Constitutional Convention. Jenkins died on June 14, 1883 and was buried in Summerville Cemetery near Augusta. Bibliography: Olive Hall Shadgett, "The Public Life of Charles J. Jenkins, 1830-1865," Unpublished M.A. Thesis, University of Georgia, 1950; Horace Montgomery, ed., *Georgians in Profile* (Athens, 1958); Morton S. Hodgson, Jr., "Georgia Under Governor Charles Jones Jenkins," Unpublished M.A Thesis, University of Georgia, 1934; Elizabeth S. Nathans, *Losing the Peace: Georgia Republicans and Reconstruction, 1865-1871* (Baton Rouge, 1968); Alan Conway, *The Reconstruction of Georgia* (Minneapolis,

1966). Papers of Jenkins are in the Georgia Department of Archives and History, Atlanta.

RUGER, Thomas Howard, 1868

Born on April 2, 1833 in Lima, Livingston County, New York, son of Thomas Jefferson, an Episcopal minister, and Maria (Hutchins) Ruger; an Episcopalian. Married to Helen Lydia Moore in 1857; father of two daughters. Graduated from the United States Military Academy at West Point in 1854; assigned to the United States Army Corps of Engineers, from which he resigned on April 1, 1855. Practiced law in Janesville, Wisconsin; commissioned Lieutenant Colonel of the Third Wisconsin Regiment in June 1861; promoted to Colonel on August 20, 1861 and to Brigadier General on November 29, 1862; served in the Rappahannock campaigns and helped to suppress the New York draft riots in 1863; guarded the Nashville and Chattanooga Railroad in Tennessee until April 1864; brevetted to Major General on November 30, 1864 for gallant and meritorious service at the Battle of Franklin, Tennessee; commanded the Department of North Carolina from June 1865 to June 1866; appointed Colonel of the Thirty-third Infantry, Regular Army on July 28, 1866; brevetted Brigadier General on March 2, 1867 for gallant and meritorious service at the Battle of Gettysburg, Pennsylvania. General Ruger was named Governor of Georgia on January 17, 1868 by Major General George W. Meade, commander of the Third Military District, upon the removal of Charles J. Jenkins from the governorship for his refusal to pay for the State Convention out of state funds. Ruger served in this capacity until June 28, 1868, at which time Rufus Brown Bullock was appointed Governor of Georgia. Ruger was transferred to the Eighteenth Infantry in 1869; appointed as head of a board of United States officers in Atlanta, Georgia inquiring into the eligibility of certain State Senators and Representatives in the Georgia Legislature; served as superintendent of the United States Military Academy at West Point from 1871 to 1876; served as Commander of the Department of the South from 1876 to 1878; served as Commander of Stations of the West and South until 1885, including the Department of Montana; appointed Commander of the Infantry and Cavalry School at Fort Leavenworth, Kansas in 1885; promoted to Brigadier General on March 18, 1886; served as Commander of the Department of Missouri during April and May 1886; appointed Commander of the Department of Dakota in 1888; promoted to Major General on February 8, 1895. Ruger retired from active military service on April 2, 1897; he travelled throughout Europe for two years, and upon his return to the United States, made his home in Stamford, Connecticut. Ruger died on June 3, 1907. Bibliography: Isaac W. Avery, *History of the State of Georgia, 1850-1881* (New York, 1881); Lucian L. Knight, *A Standard History of Georgia and Georgians,* 6 vols. (Chicago, 1917); Congressional Quarterly, Inc., *Guide to U.S. Elections* (Washington, D.C., 1975); Roy Glashan, *American Governors and Gubernatorial Elections, 1775-1975* (Stillwater, Minnesota, 1975).

BULLOCK, Rufus Brown, 1868-1871

Born on March 28, 1834 in Bethlehem, New York, son of Volckert Veeder and Jane Eliza (Brown) Bullock; member of St. Philip's Church. Married to Marie Salisbury of Pawtucket, Rhode Island. Graduated from the Albion Academy in 1850. Became an expert in the field of telegraphy and supervised the construction of telegraph lines between New York and the South for several years; served as a representative of the Adams Express Company in Augusta, Georgia in 1859; became an official of the Southern Express Company. Although opposed to secession, Bullock offered his services as a telegraph expert to the Confederacy at the outbreak of the Civil War, establishing railroad and telegraph lines; he attained the rank of Lieutenant Colonel; paroled at Appomattox as Acting Assistant Quarter Master General. Returned to Augusta, where he resumed his business interests; organized the First National Bank in Augusta; elected president of the Macon and Augusta Railroad in 1867; served as a delegate to the Georgia Constitutional Convention of 1867-1868; a Republican. Bullock was elected Governor of Georgia by popular vote in the election of April 20-April 24, 1868, defeating his Democratic opponent, John B. Gordon, by a vote of 83,146 to 76,099. He was appointed governor by General George C. Meade, Commander of the Third Military District, upon the removal of Thomas H. Ruger from that office on June 28, 1868; Bullock was formally inaugurated to serve his elected term on July 21, 1868. His administration was marked by numerous allegations against his conduct as the chief executive of Georgia. He was charged with purchasing the influence of the press; selling pardons and allowing the state penitentiary to be plundered; and encouraging extravagance and corruption in all departments of state government. The state-owned Western and Atlantic Railroad incurred a debt of 750,000 dollars, as opposed to profits yielded in previous years. Bullock, in an address to the United States Congress, retaliated by declaring that Georgia had not complied with the laws of Congress in its reconstruction. With the return of a Democratic majority to the Georgia Legislature and the possibility of criminal indictment, Bullock resigned the Georgia governorship on October 23, 1871 and left the state. A committee formed to investigate Bullock's official conduct found him guilty of numerous charges of corruption and mismanagement. He was arrested in 1876 and returned to Georgia to be tried on charges of embezzlement of public funds but was acquitted due to lack of evidence. He remained in Atlanta, where he became president of the Atlanta Cotton Mills; president of the Chamber of Commerce; vice president of the Piedmont Exposition; and a director of the Union Pacific Railroad. Author of *Address to the People of Georgia* (1872). Bullock died on April 27, 1907. Bibliography: Isaac W. Avery, *History of the State of Georgia, 1850-1880* (New York, 1881); Lucian L. Knight, *A Standard History of Georgia and Georgians,* 6 vols. (Chicago, 1917); Congressional Quarterly, Inc., *Guide to U.S. Elections* (Washington, D.C., 1975); Roy Glashan, *American Governors and Gubernatorial Elections, 1775-1975* (Stillwater, Minnesota, 1975). Alan Conway, *The Reconstruction of Georgia* (Minneapolis, 1966).

CONLEY, Benjamin F., 1871-1872

Born in Newark, New Jersey on March 1, 1815, of Presbyterian background; brother of Jane, Mary and M.J. Conley. Married to Sarah H. Semmes in 1842; father of John L. Conley and two others. At age fifteen Conley moved to Augusta, Georgia, where he became a successful merchant. After serving twelve years on the City Council, he was Mayor of Augusta from 1857 to 1859. Taking no part in the Civil War, he retired to a plantation in Alabama. Conley returned to Augusta after the war, and became a prominent state political leader during Radical Reconstruction. He served in the State Constitutional Convention of 1867-1868 and in the Georgia Senate. A Republican, Conley became President of the Senate, and when Governor Bullock abruptly resigned, Conley advanced to the governorship on October 30, 1871. Partisan battles raged during the two months and twelve days he served as governor. Although Conley's numerous vetoes usually were overridden by the Democratic legislature, he was praised by his opponents for his honesty and forthrightness, but criticized for disposing of land provided by the Morrill Act for only ninety cents an acre. Conley's brief term marked the end of Republican control of Georgia in the Reconstruction era. In a special election in December 1871, James M. Smith, a Democrat, won without opposition, and was inaugurated on January 12. Appointed Postmaster of the City of Atlanta by President Grant, Conley served from 1875 to 1883. He died in Atlanta in 1885 and was buried in Augusta. Bibliography: I.W. Avery, *The History of the State of Georgia From 1850 to 1881* (New York, 1881); C. Mildred Thompson, *Reconstruction in Georgia* (New York, 1915); Alan Conway, *The Reconstruction of Georgia* (Minneapolis, 1966); Elizabeth Studley Nathans, *Losing the Peace: Georgia Republicans and Reconstruction, 1865-71* (Baton Rouge, 1968); James F. Cook, *The Governors of Georgia* (Huntsville, Ala., 1977). Papers of Conley are on deposit at the Atlanta Historical Society, Duke University in Durham, and the Georgia Department of Archives and History in Atlanta.

SMITH, James Milton, 1872-1877

Born in Twiggs County, Georgia on October 24, 1823, son of a poor farmer-blacksmith and the brother of J.W. Smith. Married in 1848 to Hester Ann Brown (who died in 1877); on September 1, 1881, remarried to Mrs. Sarah Marshall Welborn, a widow; he had no children. After attending local schools, he studied law and began his practice in Columbus. A Democrat, Smith ran for Congress in 1855 and was defeated. He fought with valor in the Confederate Army and attained the rank of Colonel; he also served in the Confederate Congress from May 2, 1864 to March 18, 1865. Elected to the Georgia House of Representatives in 1870, Smith was an outspoken opponent of Radical Reconstruction. He was elected Speaker of the Georgia House of Representatives by a vote of 135 to 21 and was nominated for Governor by acclamation. In the special election of December 1871, the Republican candidate withdrew from the race, thereby giving Smith the victory unopposed. His inauguration on January 12, 1872, marked the return of the Democrats to power after five years of Republican rule. In October 1872, Smith was reelected to a four-year term, defeating Dawson A. Walker, a Republican,

104,256 votes to 45,812. Taking office in the aftermath of Reconstruction, Governor Smith faced serious economic problems. A thorough legislative investigation led to the voiding of 8 million dollars in bonds and the establishment of greater financial stability. During his term the Georgia State College of Agriculture and Mechanical Arts was established in Athens, and the Office of State Geologist and the Department of Agriculture also were created. Although Smith was a powerful and popular executive, his term was characterized by partisan disagreements which led to numerous investigations and bitter litigation. At the expiration of his term, Smith sought a seat in the United States Senate, but was unsuccessful. In 1879 he was appointed to the State Railroad Commission, a position he held for six years. In 1887 he was appointed Judge of the Superior Court of the Chattahoochee Circuit. Smith died on November 25, 1890, and was buried in Alta Vista Cemetery in Gainesville, Georgia. Bibliography: I.W. Avery, *The History of the State of Georgia From 1850 to 1881* (New York, 1881); William J. Northen, ed., *Men of Mark in Georgia* (Atlanta, 1907-12); Judson C. Ward, Jr., "Georgia Under the Bourbon Democrats, 1872-1890," Unpublished Ph.D. Dissertation, University of North Carolina, 1947; James F. Cook, *The Governors of Georgia* (Huntsville, Ala., 1977); Martha E. Mann, "The Public Career of James M. Smith," Unpublished M.A. Thesis, Emory University, 1931. Papers of Smith are on deposit at the Georgia Department of Archives and History in Atlanta.

COLQUITT, Alfred Holt, 1877-1882

Born in Walton County, Georgia on April 20, 1824, son of Senator Walter T. Colquitt and Nancy (Lane) Colquitt, both of whom were Methodists. Colquitt had eleven brothers and sisters. He married Dorothy Tarver in May 1848; after her death in 1855, he married her sister-in-law, Sarah Tarver. Colquitt attended Princeton University and graduated in 1844; he studied law and was admitted to the bar in 1846. After serving in the Mexican War, Colquitt began a long and successful political career with his election to Congress in 1853. He was elected to the Georgia Legislature and served in the Georgia Secession Convention. Entering the Confederate Army as a Captain, he served with considerable distinction and was a Major General when the war ended. A licensed Methodist minister, Colquitt blended religion with politics, law and agricultural interests. In 1870 he was president of both the State Agricultural Society and the Democratic State Convention. In 1876 he was elected to a four-year term as Governor, defeating Jonathan Norcross, a Republican, 111,297 votes to 33,443. He was reelected in 1880 to a two-year term, easily defeating Thomas Norwood, the nominee of dissident Democrats, 118,349 votes to 64,004. During his six years as governor, Colquitt implemented the Bourbon philosophy and was particularly successful in strengthening the state's fiscal affairs. His frugal administration brought reductions in both the floating debt and the bonded debt, reductions in taxes, and the approval of a new State Constitution (which served the state until 1945). Colquitt was governor during a period of agrarian unrest and emotional political divisions. His appointment of ex-Governor Joseph E. Brown to an unexpired Senate seat was highly controversial. Despite numerous legislative accusations and investigations, Colquitt maintained his popular following. He was elected to the United States Senate in

1883 and was reelected in 1888. Regarded as one of Georgia's most outstanding political leaders of the nineteenth century, he died on March 26, 1894, while serving in the Senate. Colquitt was survived by his widow and six children—one son, Walter, three unmarried daughters, Hattie, Dorothy, and Laura, and two married daughters, Mrs. Marshall and Mrs. Thomas Newell. He was buried in Rose Hill Cemetery in Macon. Bibliography: I.W. Avery, *The History of the State of Georgia From 1850 to 1881* (New York, 1881); C. Vann Woodward, *Tom Watson, Agrarian Rebel* (New York, 1938); Judson C. Ward, Jr., "Georgia Under the Bourbon Democrats, 1872-1890," Unpublished Ph.D. Dissertation, University of North Carolina, 1947; Kenneth Coleman, "The Administration of Alfred H. Colquitt As Governor of Georgia," Unpublished M.A. Thesis, University of Georgia, 1940; Allen P. Tankersley, *John B. Gordon: A Study In Gallantry* (Atlanta, 1955); Josephine Mellichamp, *Senators From Georgia* (Huntsville, Ala., 1976); Fleeta Cooper, "The Triumvirate of Colquitt, Gordon and Brown," Unpublished M.A. Thesis, Emory University, 1931. Papers of Colquitt are on deposit at the University of Georgia Library in Athens and the Georgia Department of Archives and History in Atlanta.

STEPHENS, Alexander Hamilton, 1882-1883

Born in Wilkes County, Georgia on February 11, 1812, son of Andrew, a farmer-teacher, and Margaret (Grier) Stephens, both of whom were Presbyterians. Brother of Aaron and Mary, and half-brother of John, Catherine and Linton; Stephens never married. He attended the University of Georgia and graduated first in his class in 1832. After teaching school briefly, he studied law and began his practice in Crawfordville in 1834. Elected to the Georgia House of Representatives in 1836, he served continuously until 1841, when he refused to become a candidate. In 1842 he was elected to the State Senate, and in 1843 was elected to the United States House of Representatives, where he served for the next sixteen years. Although Stephens helped to organize the short-lived Constitutional Union Party, he was nominally a Whig, until the issue of slavery drove him into the Democratic Party. A reluctant secessionist, Stephens was elected Vice President of the Confederacy. His strong belief in states' rights and constitutional law led to numerous conflicts with President Jefferson Davis over the conduct of the war. The suspension of *habeus corpus,* conscription of troops and establishment of military governments particularly distressed him. Arrested by Federal officials on May 11, 1865, he was imprisoned for five months and released. Denied the Senate seat to which he had been elected in 1866, he devoted much time to writing during the Reconstruction era. His most popular book was *A Constitutional View of the Late War Between the States.* Despite frail health and many physical infirmities, Stephens, Georgia's "Great Commoner," continued to serve his state and nation. Defeated for the Senate in 1872, he was elected to the United States House of Representatives and served for a decade. At the end of his distinguished political career, he was elected Governor, defeating Lucius J. Gartrell by 107,253 votes to 44,896. Inaugurated on November 4, 1882, Stephens served for only four months; the demands of the job proved too strenuous for his weakened constitution, and he died on March 4, 1883. He was buried in Atlanta, but his remains subsequently were removed to Crawfordville. Bibliography: E. Ramsay Richardson, *Little Aleck, A Life of*

Alexander Stephens (New York, 1932); James Z. Rabun, "Alexander H. Stephens, 1812-1861" Unpublished Ph.D. Dissertation, University of Chicago, 1949; Richard Malcolm Johnson and William Hand Browne, *Life of Alexander H. Stephens* (Philadelphia, 1884); Lucian Lamar Knight, *Alexander H. Stephens, the Sage of Liberty Hall* (Athens, 1930); Frank Henry Norton, *The Life of Alexander H. Stephens* (New York, 1883); Rudolph Von Abele, *Alexander H. Stephens, A Biography* (New York, 1946); Louis Pendleton, *Alexander H. Stephens* (Philadelphia, 1907); Myrta Lockett Avary, ed., *Recollections of Alexander H. Stephens* (New York, 1910). Papers of Stephens are on deposit at Emory University in Atlanta, the University of Georgia Library in Athens, the University of North Carolina in Chapel Hill, and Duke University in Durham.

BOYNTON, James S., 1883

Born in Henry County, Georgia on May 7, 1833, the seventh of eleven children born to Elijah S., a farmer-carpenter, and Elizabeth (Moffett) Boynton, both of whom were Baptists. Married to Fannie Loyall on December 2, 1852; father of Jessee and Luther. After his first wife's death in 1877, he remarried to Susie T. Harris on April 30, 1883. Boynton studied law, was admitted to the bar in 1852, and opened a practice in Monticello. He served in the Confederate Army and attained the rank of Colonel. After the war, he resumed his practice in Griffin. Boynton served as Judge of the County Court, and was Mayor of Griffin from 1869 to 1872. In 1880 and in 1882 he was elected to the Georgia Senate and was unanimously elected President of the Senate for both terms. Governor Alexander Stephens died on March 4, 1883, and Boynton took the oath as Acting Governor the next day. He immediately ordered an election for April 24 and became a candidate himself for the Democratic nomination. After seventeen ballots, the deadlocked convention chose Henry McDaniel, who subsequently was elected. Boynton served until May 10, 1883. Boynton twice was elected Judge of the Superior Court, serving from 1886 to 1893, when he resigned to accept a position with the Central Georgia Railway Company. Against his wishes, the voters of Spalding County elected him to the Georgia House of Representatives in 1896. Boynton died in his home in Griffin on December 22, 1902. Bibliography: William J. Northen, ed., *Men of Mark in Georgia* (Atlanta, 1907-1912); Amanda Johnson, *Georgia as Colony and State* (Atlanta, 1938); Judson C. Ward, Jr., "Georgia Under the Bourbon Democrats, 1872-1890," Unpublished Ph.D. Dissertation, University of North Carolina, 1947; Raymond B. Nixon, *Henry W. Grady, Spokesman of the New South* (New York, 1943); James F. Cook, *The Governors of Georgia* (Huntsville, Ala., 1977). Papers of Boynton are on deposit at the Georgia Department of Archives and History.

McDANIEL, Henry D., 1883-1886

Born in Monroe, Georgia on September 4, 1836, son of Ira O., a teacher-farmer-merchant, and Rebecca (Walker) McDaniel, both of whom were Baptists. Married to Hester C. Felker on December 20, 1865; father of Sanders McDaniel and Mrs. E.S. Tichenor. Attended Mercer University and graduated with highest honors in

1856. The following year he began to practice law in Monroe. McDaniel served in Georgia's Secession Convention in 1861, fought in the Confederate Army, and was elected to the State Constitutional Convention of 1865. In 1872 he was elected to the Georgia House of Representatives; two years later he was elected to the Georgia Senate, where he served eight years without opposition. Following the death of Governor Stephens, McDaniel was selected by acclamation as the Democratic nominee and was elected Governor, 23,680 votes to 334 miscellaneous votes. In 1884 he was reelected without opposition. As governor, McDaniel was a capable executive. Although supported by the Bourbon faction of the Democratic Party, he did not use the office for personal financial gain. Governor during a period of relative calm between the turbulent era of Reconstruction and the agrarian unrest of the 1890s, his administration was both popular and productive. He strengthened the state's finances, taxed the railroads, supervised the construction of a new Capitol, and improved services for the deaf, blind and insane. After his term expired, McDaniel withdrew from politics, resumed his law practice, and expanded his business interests. He served on the board of directors of several railroads and manufacturing concerns. He died on July 25, 1926, and was buried in Rest Haven Cemetery in Monroe. Bibliography: Helen O. Doster, "The Administration of Henry D. McDaniel As Governor of Georgia, 1883-1886," Unpublished M.A. Thesis, University of Georgia, 1962; Judson C. Ward, Jr., "Georgia Under the Bourbon Democrats, 1872-1890," Unpublished Ph.D. Dissertation, University of North Carolina, 1947; William J. Northen, ed., *Men of Mark in Georgia* (Atlanta, 1907-12); Mrs. William H. Felton, *My Memoirs of Georgia Politics* (Atlanta, 1911); James F. Cook, *The Governors of Georgia* (Huntsville, Ala., 1977). Papers of McDaniel are on deposit in the Georgia Department of Archives and History in Atlanta, and in the University of Georgia Library in Athens.

GORDON, John B., 1886-1890

Born on February 6, 1832 in Upson County, Georgia, son of Reverend Zachariah H., a planter and minister, and Malinda (Cox) Gordon, both of whom were Baptists. Gordon had ten brothers and one sister. Married Fanny Haralson on September 18, 1854; father of Hugh, Frank, Frances, Caroline, Carolina and John. Attended the University of Georgia, but did not graduate. Gordon practiced law in Atlanta and was engaged in coal mining operations in northwest Georgia prior to the Civil War. Though Gordon had no military training, he displayed exceptional leadership qualities in the Civil War and is regarded as one of the greatest untrained soldiers produced by the Confederacy. At the war's end, he was a Lieutenant General, a rank only three Georgians attained. An outspoken opponent of Radical Reconstruction and believed to be the head of the Ku Klux Klan in Georgia, the strikingly handsome Gordon seemed to epitomize the "lost cause." A Democrat, he was defeated in the 1868 gubernatorial race; however five years later, after the Republican regime had been ousted, he was elected to the United States Senate. Rising quickly to a position of leadership, he was easily reelected in 1879, but resigned on May 15, 1880 to accept a lucrative business position. In 1886 Gordon defeated A.O. Bacon, 252 votes to 70, to secure the Democratic nomination for Governor, and was elected without opposition. Again in 1888 he was elected without opposition. A leader of the Bourbon Democrats, Governor Gordon pursued policies favorable to business. Few reforms were enacted during his term, but the state's bonded indebtedness was reduced, and there was an increase in capital, factories, railroads, and population. Gordon spoke out against the convict lease system, but the legislature refused to enact his recommendations. In 1890 Gordon was elected to the United States Senate, and was also elected commander-in-chief of the United Confederate Veterans, a position he held until his death. In his last years he toured the country lecturing on the Confederacy, and in 1903 published *Reminiscences of the Civil War.* Gordon died on January 9, 1904, and was buried in Oakland Cemetery in Atlanta. Bibliography: Allen Pierce Tankersley, *John B. Gordon: A Study in Gallantry* (Atlanta, 1955); Josephine Mellichamp, *Senators From Georgia* (Huntsville, Ala., 1976); Raymond B. Nixon, *Henry W. Grady, Spokesman of the New South* (New York, 1943); C. Vann Woodward, *Tom Watson, Agrarian Rebel* (New York, 1938); I.W. Avery, *The History of the State of Georgia From 1850 to 1881* (New York, 1881); Mrs. William H. Felton, *My Memoirs of Georgia Politics* (Atlanta, 1911); Alice Dunbar, "The Political Life of John Brown Gordon, 1865-1880," Unpublished M.A. Thesis, Emory University, 1939; Fleeta Cooper, "The Triumvirate of Colquitt, Gordon and Brown," Unpublished M.A. Thesis, Emory University, 1931. Papers of Gordon are on deposit at the Georgia Department of Archives and History in Atlanta.

NORTHEN, William J., 1890-1894

Born in Jones County, Georgia on July 9, 1835, son of Peter, a planter, and Louisa (Davis) Northen, both of whom were Baptists. Northen had seven sisters and three brothers. He married Martha Moss Neel on December 19, 1860; father of Thomas and Annie Belle. Attended Mercer University and graduated in 1853. He served as a school teacher, until poor health forced him out of the classroom in 1874. Retiring to a plantation in Hancock County, he became a recognized expert on agricultural matters and served as president of the State Agricultural Society. A Democrat, Northen served two terms in the Georgia House of Representatives, and one term in the Georgia Senate. He was elected Governor in 1890 without opposition, and two years later was reelected over William L. Peek, a Populist, 140,492 votes to 68,900. A conservative, Governor Northen conducted the state's affairs in an efficient and frugal manner, and his administration was free from the demagoguery that characterized many of his contemporaries. His major interest was education, and substantial progress was made in the field. The school term was lengthened from three to five months; the State Normal School was established; and an agricultural and mechanical college for blacks was established. Northen's efforts to create a State Board of Health, reform the penal system, and improve the state's highways, however, were not immediately successful. After leaving office, Northen was engaged in many religious and scholarly activities. He edited *Men of Mark in Georgia,* a seven-volume collection of biographical sketches published from 1907 to 1912; he also served briefly as State Historian, succeeding ex-Governor Allen D. Candler who died in 1910. For many years Northen was one of the South's leading Baptist laymen, serving as president of the Georgia Baptist Convention, the Georgia Baptist Educational Society, the Southern Baptist Convention, the National Baptist Congress, and the Baptist Educational Society. Northen died on March 25, 1913, and was buried in Oakland Cemetery in Atlanta.

Bibliography: William J. Northen, ed., *Men of Mark in Georgia* (Atlanta, 1907-12); Alex M. Arnett, *The Populist Movement in Georgia* (New York, 1922); C. Vann Woodward, *Tom Watson, Agrarian Rebel* (New York, 1938); Mrs. William H. Felton, *My Memoirs of Georgia Politics* (Atlanta, 1911); James F. Cook, *The Governors of Georgia* (Huntsville, Ala., 1977); James Calvin Bonner, "The Gubernatorial Career of W.J. Northen," Unpublished M.A. Thesis, University of Georgia, 1936. Papers of Northen are on deposit at the Atlanta Historical Society and the Georgia Department of Archives and History in Atlanta.

ATKINSON, William Yates, 1894-1898

Born on November 11, 1854 in Oakland, Meriwether County, Georgia, son of John P., a planter and teacher, and Theodora (Phelps) Atkinson; brother of Theodore, Thomas, R.J. and Mrs. D.P. Ellis (his father also had two daughters and a son, John, by a previous marriage); a Presbyterian. Married to Susie Cobb Milton on February 23, 1880; father of John, Lucille, William, Miriam, Bert and Georgia. Attended the University of Georgia and graduated in 1877. Practiced law in Newnan, and served as Solicitor of Coweta County from 1879 to 1882. Elected to the Georgia Legislature in 1886; served four successive terms, the last one as Speaker of the House. Served as chairman of the Georgia Democratic Convention in 1890. Elected Governor in 1894 over Judge James K. Hines, a Populist, 121,049 votes to 96,888; reelected in 1896 in a bitter campaign over Seaborn Wright, a Populist, 120,827 votes to 85,832. Governor during a period of agrarian unrest, Atkinson advocated educational, electoral, and penal reforms; mild reforms were enacted by the legislature during his administration. His efforts to establish the office of Lieutenant Governor and to eliminate lynching failed however. Atkinson stressed industrial expansion and publicized the Atlanta Exposition of 1895; he is also considered to be the founder of the Georgia Normal and Industrial College. After his term expired, he briefly practiced law until his death on August 8, 1899. He was buried in Oak Hill Cemetery in Newnan. Bibliography: Mauriel Shipp, "The Public Life of William Yates Atkinson," Unpublished M.A. Thesis, University of Georgia, 1955; William J. Northen, ed., *Men of Mark in Georgia* (Atlanta, 1907-12); Alex Mathews Arnett, *The Populist Movement in Georgia* (New York, 1922); Bascomb Osborne Quillian, Jr., "The Populist Challenge in Georgia in the Year 1894," Unpublished M.A. Thesis, University of Georgia, 1948; Blanche Alvenia Shehee, "The Movement for the Establishment of a State College for Women in Georgia," Unpublished M.A. Thesis, University of North Carolina, 1953; James F. Cook, *The Governors of Georgia* (Huntsville, Ala., 1977); Mrs. William H. Felton, *My Memoirs of Georgia Politics* (Atlanta, 1911). Papers of Atkinson are on deposit at the Georgia Department of Archives and History in Atlanta.

CANDLER, Allen D., 1898-1902

Born in Auraria, Lumpkin County, Georgia on November 4, 1834, son of Daniel G., a farmer-lawyer, and Nancy (Matthews) Candler, both of whom were Presbyterians. Brother of Margaret, Sarah, Elizabeth, Florida, William, Francis, Nancy, Junius,

Virginia and Ignatius. Married to Eugenia T. Williams on January 12, 1864; father of Eugenia, Florence, Marcus, Thomas, Hortense, Kate, John, Victor, Margaret and Benjamin. Attended Mercer University and graduated in 1859. Candler taught school briefly before enlisting in the Confederate Army; after the Civil War he again taught school until 1870, when he moved to Gainesville and engaged in various businesses. He served in the Georgia General Assembly from 1873 to 1880, served four terms in the United States Congress, and served four years as Georgia's Secretary of State. Candler won the Democratic nomination for Governor in 1898 over Spencer Atkinson and Robert L. Berner, and in the general election defeated J.R. Hogan, the Populist-Republican, 117,455 votes to 50,841. Two years later he was reelected over John H. Traylor, a Populist, 90,445 votes to 23,235. As governor, Candler was a staunch conservative, and his administration was noted more for its honesty and frugality than for any innovations or reforms. The few reforms he advocated were not adopted by the legislature. Candler's most important service to Georgia came after his governorship. From 1903 until his death, he was State Historian. Under his direction twenty-eight large volumes of documents on Georgia's colonial, revolutionary and confederate history were published. He also collaborated with Clement Evans in publishing a three-volume encyclopedia of Georgia in 1906. Candler died of Bright's disease on October 26, 1910, and was buried in Gainesville, Georgia. Bibliography: Elizabeth Hulsey Marshall, "Allen D. Candler, Governor and Collector of Records," Unpublished M.A. Thesis, University of Georgia, 1959; Alton D. Jones, "Progressivism in Georgia, 1898-1918," Unpublished Ph.D. Dissertation, Emory University, 1963; William J. Northen, ed., *Men of Mark in Georgia* (Atlanta, 1907-12); Amanda Johnson, *Georgia As Colony and State* (Atlanta, 1938); James F. Cook, *The Governors of Georgia* (Huntsville, Ala., 1977); Allen Daniel Candler, *Colonel William Candler of Georgia, His Ancestry and Progeny* (Atlanta, 1896). Papers of Candler are on deposit at Emory University in Atlanta and in the Georgia Department of Archives and History in Atlanta.

TERRELL, Joseph M., 1902-1907

Born on June 6, 1861 in Greenville, Meriwether County, Georgia, son of Joel, a doctor and farmer, and Sarah (Anthony) Terrell, both of whom were Baptists. Married to Jessie Lee Spivey on October 19, 1886; father of four sons and one daughter. Admitted to the bar in 1882, he opened his practice in Greenville. A Democrat, Terrell was elected to the Georgia House of Representatives in 1884 and 1886, but was defeated in 1888. He was elected to the Georgia Senate in 1890. Terrell served as Georgia's Attorney General from 1892 to 1902, when he was elected Governor. He won the Democratic nomination with 196 county unit votes to John Estill's 82 and Dupont Guerry's 66; in the general election he defeated the Populist, James K. Hines, 81,344 votes to 4,747. Two years later he was reelected without opposition. As governor, Terrell sponsored numerous progressive reforms, and despite opposition from his conservative legislature, many were adopted. His most important accomplishment was in the area of education. The College of Agriculture was established, and an agricultural and mechanical school for each Congressional district was authorized. Other reforms included the establishment of a State Reformatory for boys and the Court of Appeals; improved election laws; a tax on corporations; child labor legislation; and a law strengthening the Railroad

Commission. When his term expired, Terrell resumed his law practice. Following the death of United States Senator Alexander Clay, he was appointed to the Senate. He served from November 17, 1910 until July 14, 1911, when he resigned to resume his law practice. Terrell died in Atlanta on November 17, 1912, and was buried in Greenville. Bibliography: Alton Dumar Jones, "The Administration of Governor Joseph M. Terrell Viewed in the Light of the Progressive Movement," *Georgia Historical Quarterly,* vol. XLVIII (September, 1964); Josephine Mellichamp, *Senators From Georgia* (Huntsville, Ala., 1976); Amanda Johnson, *Georgia as Colony and State* (Atlanta, 1938); William J. Northen, ed., *Men of Mark in Georgia* (Atlanta, 1907-12); Alton D. Jones, "Progressivism in Georgia, 1898-1918," Unpublished Ph.D. Dissertation, Emory University, 1963. Papers of Terrell are on deposit at the Georgia Department of Archives and History in Atlanta.

SMITH, Hoke, 1907-1909, 1911

Born on September 2, 1855 in Newton, North Carolina, son of Hildreth H., a college professor, and Mary (Hoke) Smith, both of whom were Episcopalians; brother of Frances, Lizzie and Burton Smith. Married to Marion "Birdie" Cobb on December 19, 1883; father of Marion, Hildreth, Mary, Lucy and Calie. Mrs. Marion Smith died on June 7, 1919, and he married Mazie Crawford on August 27, 1924. Tutored by his father, Smith did not attend college but was admitted to the bar in 1873. He taught school briefly and established an extensive law practice in Atlanta. A staunch supporter of Grover Cleveland, Smith was chairman of the Democratic State Convention in 1888 and was a delegate to the Democratic National Convention in 1892. He served as Secretary of Interior from 1893 to 1896. Out of office for a decade, Smith was elected Governor in 1906, winning the Democratic primary over Richard Russell, Sr., Clark Howell, John Estill and James M. Smith, and carrying 104,796 popular votes and 312 county unit votes to his opponents' combined total of 79,477 and 52. As governor, Smith advocated many Progressive reforms which were enacted. The Railroad Commission was strengthened; the convict lease system was abolished; juvenile courts and a parole system were established; a primary election law was passed; appropriations to public schools were increased; at the same time, however, blacks were disenfranchised. Smith sought reelection in 1908, but lost to Joseph M. Brown, 109,806 votes to 98,949. In 1910 Smith defeated Brown, 98,049 to 93,717. In July 1911, the legislature named Smith United States Senator, and on November 15th, he resigned from the governorship. In the Senate, education was his primary interest; two educational reforms bear his name—the Smith-Lever Act and the Smith-Hughes Act. He was reelected to the Senate in 1914 over Joseph M. Brown, but was defeated in 1920 by Tom Watson. Smith then resumed his law practice in Washington and Atlanta and his numerous business and civic activities. He died on November 27, 1931, and was buried in Oakland Cemetery in Atlanta. Bibliography: Dewey W. Grantham, Jr., *Hoke Smith and the Politics of the New South* (Baton Rouge, 1958); Horace Montgomery, ed., *Georgians in Profile* (Athens, 1958); John C. Reed, "The Recent Primary Election in Georgia," *South Atlantic Quarterly,* vol. VI (1907); Alexander J. McKelway, "Hoke Smith: A Progressive Democrat," *Outlook,* vol. XCVI (October 1, 1910); Josephine Mellichamp, *Senators from Georgia* (Huntsville, Ala., 1976); Ted Carageroge, "An Evaluation of Hoke Smith and Thomas E. Watson as Georgia Reformers," Unpublished Ph.D. Dissertation, University of Georgia, 1963; Alton D. Jones, "Progressivism in Georgia, 1898-1918," Unpublished Ph.D Dissertation, Emory University, 1963. Papers of Smith are on deposit at the University of Georgia Library in Athens.

BROWN, Joseph Mackey, 1909-1911, 1912-1913

Born on December 28, 1851 in Canton, Georgia, son of Governor Joseph E. Brown and Elizabeth (Grisham) Brown, both of whom were Baptists; brother of Julius, Mary, Franklin, Elijah, Charles, Sally and George Brown. Married to Cora A. McCord on February 12, 1889; father of Joseph, Charles and Cora. Attended Oglethorpe University and graduated in 1872; entered Harvard Law School, but poor health forced him to withdraw before graduation. Began a long employment with the Western and Atlantic Railroad in 1877. Governor Terrell appointed Brown to the Railroad Commission in 1904. Removed from office by Governor Hoke Smith, Brown ran for Governor in 1908 and defeated Smith in the Democratic primary 109,806 votes to 98,949. Brown went on to defeat Yancy Carter, an Independent in the general election, 112,292 votes to 11,746. He was inaugurated on June 26, 1909. Governor during a period of economic recession, Brown, a staunch conservative, sought rigid economy in government, lower taxes, enforcement of Prohibition, and a reduction in the power of the Railroad Commission. The legislature, however, refused to enact much of his program. In 1910 Brown ran for reelection, but was defeated by Hoke Smith, 98,049 votes to 93,717. When Governor Smith became United States Senator, Brown easily defeated Richard Russell, Sr., and J. Pope Brown for the remainder of the term. He was inaugurated on January 25, 1912. Joseph Brown received 198 county unit votes to Pope Brown's 114 and Russell's 56. Brown conducted the state's affairs in an orderly, businesslike manner, but no major reforms were adopted in either of his administrations. After his term expired, Brown sought a seat in the United States Senate, but he was defeated in 1914 by incumbent Senator Hoke Smith. Brown retired from politics and became an innovative farmer and a prosperous businessman. He wrote numerous articles and two books: *Mountain Campaigns in Georgia* and *Astanax*. Brown died at his home in Marietta on March 3, 1932, and was buried in Oakland Cemetery in Atlanta. Bibliography: William Montgomery Gabard, "Joseph Mackey Brown: A Study in Conservatism," Unpublished Ph.D Dissertation, Tulane University, 1963; Alton D. Jones, "Progressivism in Georgia, 1898-1918," Unpublished Ph.D. Dissertation, Emory University, 1963; Dewey W. Grantham, Jr., *Hoke Smith and the Politics of the New South* (Baton Rouge, 1958); Amanda Johnson, *Georgia as Colony and State* (Atlanta, 1938); William J. Northen, ed., *Men of Mark in Georgia* (Atlanta, 1907-1912); Mary Richards Colvin, "Hoke Smith and Joseph M. Brown, Political Rivals," Unpublished M.A. Thesis, University of Georgia, 1958; Frances Beach Hudson, "The Smith-Brown Controversy," Unpublished M.A. Thesis, Emory University, 1929. Papers of Brown are on deposit in the University of Georgia Library in Athens, Emory University Library in Atlanta, the Georgia Department of Archives and History in Atlanta, and the Atlanta Historical Society in Atlanta.

SMITH, Hoke, 1907-1909, 1911

SLATON, John Marshall, 1911-1912, 1913-1915

Born in Meriwether County, Georgia on December 25, 1866, son of William F., a prominent educator, and Nancy Jane (Martin) Slaton, both of whom were Methodists; brother of William, Lily, Katie, Martha and Lulah. Married to Sarah Frances Grant Jackson on July 12, 1898; they had no children. Attended the University of Georgia and graduated in 1886. Began a law practice in Atlanta, which lasted sixty-eight years and brought him to the forefront of his profession. In 1896 Slaton was elected to the Georgia House of Representatives as a Democrat. He served thirteen consecutive years, and was twice elected Speaker; he advanced to the upper house and served four years as President of the Senate. He became Acting Governor on November 16, 1911, when Governor Hoke Smith relinquished the office to become United States Senator. Slaton served only two months as acting governor and was not a candidate in the special election on January 10, 1912. He was, however, elected Governor in the regular election in 1912, carrying 110,222 votes to Hooper Alexander's 40,947 and Joseph Hill Hall's 24,316, and was inaugurated on June 28, 1913. A conservative, Slaton stressed frugality in government, tax equalization, and strict regulation of public utilities. Additional property was added to the tax digest and the tax rate was lowered. Slaton considered tax equalization one of his greatest achievements as governor; he also succeeded in refunding the state's bonded indebtedness at a substantial savings. Other measures passed during his term included: child labor legislation, the establishment of the Georgia Training School for Girls, and the creation of four new counties. Slaton's popularity ended abruptly shortly before his term expired when he commuted the sentence of Leo Frank, a convicted murderer, to life imprisonment. Frank, a Jew, had been convicted in a sensational trial on questionable evidence. Slaton's courageous act ended his political career and nearly ended his life; the state militia had to be called out to protect him from angry mobs. Slaton sought a seat in the United States Senate, and although he won a plurality in the Democratic primary of 1914, the convention subsequently nominated Tom Hardwick instead. In 1930 Slaton again ran for a Senate seat, but was defeated by William J. Harris. Slaton continued to practice law in Atlanta, and ultimately regained the esteem of his contemporaries. In 1928 he was unanimously elected president of the Georgia Bar Association. He died on January 11, 1955, and was buried in Oakland Cemetery in Atlanta. Bibliography: Amanda Johnson, *Georgia as Colony and State* (Atlanta, 1938); William J. Northen, ed., *Men of Mark in Georgia* (Atlanta, 1907-12); Walter G. Cooper, *The Story of Georgia* (New York, 1938); James F. Cook, *The Governors of Georgia* (Huntsville, Ala., 1977); Harry Golden, *A Little Girl Is Dead* (Cleveland, 1965); Leonard Dinnerstein, *The Leo Frank Case* (New York, 1968). Papers of Slaton are on deposit at the Georgia Department of Archives and History in Atlanta and at Brandeis University, Waltham, Massachusetts.

BROWN, Joseph Mackey, 1909-1911, 1912-1913

SLATON, John Marshall, 1911-1912, 1913-1915

HARRIS, Nathaniel E., 1915-1917

Born on January 21, 1846 in Jonesboro, Tennessee, son of Alexander, a physician and Methodist minister, and Edna (Haynes) Harris; eldest of eleven children. Married to Fannie Burke on February 12, 1873; father of Carrie, Walter, Nat, Fannie, John, David and Nora; after his wife's death on May 3, 1898, remarried to Hattie Gibson Jobe on July 6, 1899. After serving in the Confederate Army, he attended the University of Georgia and graduated in 1870. Practiced law in Macon and in 1882 was elected to the Georgia House of Representatives; served four years in the House and was instrumental in establishing the Georgia Institute of Technology. Harris was elected to the Georgia Senate in 1894. He served less than a year as a Judge of the Superior Court, and declined numerous political positions, preferring to develop his extensive law practice and business affiliations. Elected Governor in 1914, Harris won the Democratic primary with 192 county unit votes to L.B. Hardman's 148, and Randolph Anderson's 32. A capable but unpopular executive, Harris faced the economic dislocations caused by World War I, the resurgence of the Ku Klux Klan, and the divisive issue of Prohibition. The legislature passed, and he signed, five Prohibition bills. He also secured increased pensions for Confederate veterans, a fifty-year lease of the state-owned railroad, and a compulsory education law. Harris sought other reforms including centralized state purchasing, biennial legislative sessions, limitation on campaign spending, and the creation of an Illiteracy Commission; however, these were not adopted by the legislature. In 1916 Harris ran for reelection, but was defeated in the Democratic primary by Hugh Dorsey, 106,680 votes to 70,997. Service to Georgia Tech was Harris' consuming interest in his last years. He served as State Pension Commissioner in 1924-1925. Harris, the last Confederate veteran to serve as governor of Georgia, died on September 21, 1929, and was buried in Rose Hill Cemetery in Macon. Bibliography: Nathaniel E. Harris, *Autobiography* (Macon, 1925); Annie Beth Mobley, "The Public Career of Nathaniel Edwin Harris," Unpublished M.A. Thesis, University of Georgia, 1957; James F. Cook, *The Governors of Georgia* (Huntsville, Ala., 1977); Amanda Johnson, *Georgia as Colony and State* (Atlanta, 1938). Papers of Harris are on deposit in the Georgia Department of Archives and History in Atlanta.

DORSEY, Hugh Manson, 1917-1921

Born on July 10, 1871 in Fayetteville, Georgia, son of Rufus Thomas, an eminent Georgia jurist, and Sarah (Bennett) Dorsey; brother of two sisters and three brothers, among whom were Rufus and Faith Dorsey; a Methodist. Married to Mary Adair Wilkinson on June 29, 1911; father of James Wilkinson and Hugh Manson Dorsey, Jr. Received an A.B. from the University of Georgia in 1893; studied law at the University of Virginia from 1893 to 1894; admitted to the Georgia Bar at Fayetteville in September 1894; began law practice with the firm of Dorsey, Brewster and Howell in 1895, and continued until 1916. Served as a member of the Atlanta Water Board and the Board of Trustees of Grady Hospital of Atlanta for several years; served as a Lieutenant and later Captain of the Atlanta Grays, Company "K," Georgia Volunteers; served as Lieutenant Colonel on the staff of Governor William Atkinson in 1895. Appointed Solicitor General of the Atlanta Judicial Circuit in 1910 to fill the unexpired term of Charles D. Hill; subsequently elected to that position, serving until his resignation in 1916. As the Democratic gubernatorial candidate, Dorsey was elected unopposed as Governor of Georgia by popular vote on November 7, 1916, receiving 59,526 votes; reelected unopposed on November 5, 1918, receiving 70,621 votes. He was inaugurated on June 30, 1917. During his administration, Dorsey was an extremely vocal critic of lynching and of peonage, a system whereby debtors or legal prisoners were forced to work for their creditors or those persons who leased their services from the state. He advocated compulsory education for both blacks and whites; conferences to discuss race affairs; and was author of *The Negro in Georgia,* in which he aroused the public conscience concerning the unjust treatment of blacks in the state. Dorsey left office on June 25, 1921 upon the inauguration of Thomas W. Hardwick, and resumed his law practice. He was an unsuccessful candidate for the United States Senate in 1920; appointed Judge of the City Court of Atlanta in September 1926 and subsequently elected to that position, serving until 1935; served as Judge of the Superior Court of the Atlanta Judicial Circuit from 1935 until his death. Dorsey died on June 11, 1948 in Atlanta. Bibliography: Cullen B. Gosnell and C.D. Anderson, *The Government and Administration of Georgia* (New York, 1956); E. Merton Coulter, *Georgia: A Short History* (Chapel Hill, North Carolina, 1960); Congressional Quarterly, Inc., *Guide to U.S. Elections* (Washington, D.C., 1975); Roy Glashan, *American Governors and Gubernatorial Elections, 1775-1975* (Stillwater, Minnesota, 1975).

HARDWICK, Thomas William, 1921-1923

Born on December 9, 1872 in Thomasville, Thomas County, Georgia, son of Robert William and Zemula Schley (Matthews) Hardwick; a Protestant. Married to Maude Elizabeth Perkins on April 25, 1894. Received an A.B. from Mercer University, Macon, Georgia in 1892 and an LL.B. from Lumpkin Law School, University of Georgia in 1893. Admitted to the bar in 1893 and began the practice of law in Sandersville, Georgia. Served as a member of the Georgia House of Representatives from 1890 to 1899; served as Prosecuting Attorney for Washington County, Georgia from March 1895 until January 1896, at which time he resigned.

Served as a Captain of Company "D," Sixth Regiment Infantry of the Georgia State Troops in 1900 and 1901. Again elected to the Georgia House of Representatives, serving from March 4, 1903 to November 2, 1914, when he resigned; elected to the United States Senate to fill the vacancy caused by the death of Augustus O. Bacon, serving from November 4, 1914 to March 3, 1919. He was an unsuccessful candidate for renomination in 1918. As the Democratic gubernatorial candidate, Hardwick was elected unopposed as governor of Governor of Georgia by popular vote on November 2, 1920, after winning the Democratic gubernatorial primary runoff election with 84,257 votes while his opponent, Clifford M.Walker, polled 68,234. He was inaugurated on June 25, 1921. During the "Red Scare" which developed after World War I, there was a revival of the Ku Klux Klan. Hardwick waged a campaign against this secret organization, demanding that its members unmask and cease their violent activities. Largely through the efforts of the leaders of the Ku Klux Klan, Hardwick was defeated for reelection in the 1922 Democratic gubernatorial primary by 123,784 votes to 86,389; he left office on June 30, 1923, upon the inauguration of Clifford M. Walker. He served as Special Assistant to the United States Attorney General from July 1, 1923 to May 16, 1824, at which time he resigned; was an unsuccessful candidate for nomination to the United States Senate in 1924, and then resumed his law practice; in 1927 moved to Sandersville, Georgia, where he continued the practice of law until his death. Hardwick died on January 31, 1944 in Sandersville, Georgia and was interred in Old City Cemetery. Bibliography: *New York Times* (February 1, 1944); Clement Charlton Moseley, "Political Influence of the Ku Klux Klan in Georgia, 1915-1925," *Georgia Historical Quarterly,* vol. LVII, no. 2 (Summer, 1973); Congressional Quarterly, Inc., *Guide to U.S. Elections* (Washington, D.C., 1975); Roy Glashan, *American Governors and Gubernatorial Elections, 1775-1975* (Stillwater, Minnesota, 1975).

WALKER, Clifford Mitchell, 1923-1927

Born on July 4, 1877 in Monroe, Georgia, son of Billington Sanders and Alice (Mitchell) Walker; a Baptist. Married to Rosa Carter Matthewson on April 29, 1902; father of Clifford, Harold M. and Sanders J. Walker. Attended the Georgia Military Institute; received an A.B. from the University of Georgia in 1897. Admitted to the Georgia Bar in 1897 and began the practice of law, becoming the senior member of the firm of Walker and Kilbride of Atlanta, Georgia. Served as Mayor of Monroe, Georgia, 1905-1907; served as Solicitor General of the Western Judicial Circuit of Georgia, 1909-1913; served as Attorney General of Georgia, 1914-1919. As the Democratic gubernatorial candidate, Walker was elected unopposed as Governor of Georgia by popular vote on November 7, 1922, receiving 75,019 votes; reelected unopposed on November 4, 1924, receiving 152,367 votes. He was inaugurated on June 30, 1923. During Walker's administration, Georgia received national criticism because of the state's cruel treatment of prisoners. He was a proponent of the League of Nations. Walker incurred the wrath of the Ku Klux Klan when the use of the lash was abolished in prison camps. Walker left office on June 25, 1927 upon the inauguration of Lamartine G. Hardman, and resumed his law practice. Served as general counsel for the Georgia Bureau of Unemployment Compensation; served as president of Woodrow Wilson

Law School in Atlanta, Georgia, a position he held at the time of his death. Walker died on November 9, 1954 in Monroe, Georgia. Bibliography: Cullen B. Goshell and C.D. Anderson, *The Government and Administration of Georgia* (New York, 1956); *New York Times* (November 10, 1954); Congressional Quarterly, Inc., *Guide to U.S. Elections* (Washington, D.C., 1975); Roy Glashan, *American Governors and Gubernatorial Elections, 1775-1975* (Stillwater, Minnesota, 1975).

HARDMAN, Lamartine Griffin, 1927-1931

Born on April 14, 1856 in Commerce, Georgia, son of William Benjamin Johnson, a Baptist minister, and Susan Elizabeth (Colquitt) Hardman; a Baptist. Married to Emma Wiley Griffin on March 26, 1907; father of Lamartine Griffin, Josephine Staten, Sue Colquitt and Emma Griffin Hardman. Graduated from the University of Georgia Medical School in 1877; pursued post-graduate studies at the University of Pennsylvania Medical School, Bellevue and New York Polyclinic Hospitals in New York, and Guy's Hospital in London. Began medical practice in Commerce in 1876. Became president of the Harmony Grove Cotton Mills of Commerce, the Northeastern Banking Company, the Commerce Telephone Company and the Hardman Drug Company; served as director of the First National Bank of Commerce; became owner and operator of the Hurricane Shoals Light and Power Plant. Served as a member of the Georgia House of Representatives from 1902 to 1907 and as a member of the Georgia Senate from 1908 to 1910; served as a member of the State Fuel Administration during World War I. As the Democratic gubernatorial candidate, Hardman was elected unopposed as Governor of Georgia by popular vote on November 2, 1926, receiving 47,262 votes; reelected unopposed on November 6, 1928, receiving 202,242 votes. He was inaugurated on June 25, 1927. During his administration, Hardman was an opponent of the repeal of Prohibition; cotton production declined greatly and manufacturing absorbed an increasing percentage of the labor force; and an extremely large number of local acts, dealing with particular counties by name, was passed by the State Legislature. Hardman left office on June 27, 1931 upon the inauguration of Richard B. Russell. He served as a trustee of the Georgia State College of Agriculture and Mechanic Arts, the Southern Baptist Seminary of Louisville, Kentucky, and Shorter College in Rome, Georgia. Hardman died on February 18, 1937 in Atlanta. Bibliography: Cullen B. Gosnell and C.D. Anderson, *The Government and Administration of Georgia* (New York, 1956); *New York Times* (February 19, 1937); Congressional Quarterly, Inc., *Guide to U.S. Elections* (Washington, D.C., 1975); Roy Glashan, *American Governors and Gubernatorial Elections, 1775-1975* (Stillwater, Minnesota, 1975).

RUSSELL, Richard B., 1931-1933

Born in Winder, Georgia on November 2, 1897, son of Richard B. Russell, Sr., a prominent jurist, and Ina (Dillard) Russell, both of whom were Presbyterians; brother of Mary, Ina, Frances, Harriette, Robert, Patience, Walter, Susan, Lewis Carolyn, William, Fielding, Henry, Alexander and Carolyn Lewis. Never married.

Attended the Seventh District Agricultural and Mechanical School, Gordon Institute, and the University of Georgia, where he graduated in 1918. He practiced law in Winder and served as County Attorney for Barrow County. In 1920 he was elected to the Georgia House of Representatives; served ten consecutive years, the last four as Speaker of the House. In 1930 Russell was elected Governor, defeating George Carswell in a runoff in the Democratic primary, 89,966 votes to 40,673; he was unopposed in the general election. Taking office in the midst of the Great Depression, he brought sweeping reforms to state government. Following his energetic leadership, the legislature adopted rigid austerity measures, such as the Reorganization Act of 1931 which reduced the number of state agencies from 102 to 18. The most decisive change was the placing of all state-supported colleges under one Board of Regents. Other reforms included the reapportioning of the state into ten congressional districts and the passing of a constitutional amendment providing for the inauguration of the governor in January, instead of in June. Rather than seeking a second two-year term, as was customary, Russell was elected to the United States Senate in 1932, defeating Congressman Charles R. Crisp. He served continuously in the Senate for the next thirty-eight years. Russell was one of only three men ever to be elected to the Senate for seven consecutive terms, and was the only man to have served more than half of his life in the Senate. A conservative, Russell advocated states' rights and military preparedness. The respected advisor to six presidents, he was, at the time of his death, President *Pro Tempore* of the Senate; chairman of the Senate Appropriations Committee; and third-in-line for the presidency. Russell died of emphysema on January 21, 1971, and was buried in the family cemetery in Winder. Bibliography: Josephine Mellichamp, *Senators from Georgia* (Huntsville, Ala., 1976); *Senator Richard B. Russell: Georgia's Man in Washington* (Atlanta, 1966); *Memorial Services in the Congress of the United States and Tributes in Eulogy of Richard Brevard Russell* (Washington, 1971); Harry Conn, "How Right is Russell?," *New Republic,* vol. 126 (May 12, 1952); Philip A. Grant, "Editorial Reaction to the 1952 Presidential Candidacy of Richard B. Russell," *Georgia Historical Quarterly,* vol. LVII, no. 2 (Summer, 1973). Papers of Russell are housed in the Richard B. Russell Memorial Library, University of Georgia, Athens.

TALMADGE, Eugene, 1933-1937, 1941-1943

Born on September 23, 1884 in Forsyth, Georgia, son of Thomas, a planter, and Caroline (Roberts) Talmadge, both of whom were Baptists; brother of Marylynn, Nettie, Banks, Lucille and Thomas Talmadge. Married to Mattie (Thurmond) Peterson on September 12, 1909; father of Margaret, Vera and Herman; stepfather of John A. Peterson. Attended the University of Georgia and received an LL.B. degree in 1907. Practiced law in Atlanta briefly and then moved to Montgomery County where he farmed, practiced law and operated a saw mill. A Democrat, Talmadge served as Solicitor of the City Court of McRae from 1918 to 1920 and as Attorney for Telfair County from 1920 to 1923. Elected Commissioner of Agriculture in 1926, he served three successive terms prior to his election as Governor in 1932. Talmadge's 116,381 popular votes in the Democratic primary were 45,000 fewer than the total for his opponents, but he won 264 county unit votes to Abit Nix's 94 and Tom Hardwick's 30. A spokesman for the farmers,

Talmadge was a strong executive who often ruled by martial law and executive decree. A bitter critic of the New Deal, he opposed both public welfare and government debt and sought low taxes and frugal government. He lowered utility rates, the cost of license tags, and property taxes, while utilizing federal funds for highway construction and other state services. Always the center of controversy, he ran the state one year without a budget; used troops to suppress a textile strike; and fired professors from the state's colleges. Overwhelmingly reelected in 1934 to second two-year term, Talmadge won 394 county unit votes to Judge Claude Littman's 16. He lost Senate races in 1936 to Senator Richard Russell and in 1938 to Senator Walter George, but was reelected Governor in 1940 over Columbus Roberts and Abit Nix. Talmadge carried 318 county unit votes to Roberts' 80 and Nix's 12. He lost in 1942 to Ellis Arnall, 261 to 149, but came back in 1946 to win a fourth term as governor, defeating James V. Carmichael in the Democratic primary, 242 to 146 county unit votes, even though Carmichael won the popular vote, 313,389 to 297,245. Talmadge died on December 21, 1946 before taking office, and was buried in McRae, Georgia. Bibliography: Allen Henson, *Red Galluses* (Boston, 1945); William Anderson, *The Wild Man from Sugar Creek* (Baton Rouge, 1975); Reinhard Luthin, *American Demagogues* (Boston, 1954); Amanda Johnson, *Georgia As Colony and State* (Atlanta, 1938); Sue Bailes, "Eugene Talmadge and the Board of Regents Controversy," *Georgia Historical Quarterly,* vol. LIII (December, 1969); Sarah McCulloh Lemmon, "The Ideology of Eugene Talmadge," *Georgia Historical Quarterly,* vol. XXXVIII (September, 1954); James F. Cook, "The Eugene Talmadge-Walter Cocking Controversy," *Phylon,* vol. 35 (June, 1974); Alfred Steinberg, *The Bosses* (New York, 1972). Papers of Talmadge are on deposit in the Georgia Department of Archives and History in Atlanta.

RIVERS, Eurith Dickinson, 1937-1941

Born on December 1, 1895 in Center Point, Arkansas, son of James M., a physician, and Millie Annie (Wilkerson) Rivers, both of whom were Baptists; brother of James Rivers. Married to Lucile Lashley on June 7, 1914; father of Eurith D. and Geraldine. Attended Quachita College and graduated from Young Harris College in 1914. Taught school and earned a law degree from LaSalle Extension University in 1923. Became Justice of the Peace, City Attorney for Cairo, and Attorney for Grady County. Edited a newspaper, and was elected to the Georgia Legislature in 1924; elected to the Georgia Senate in 1926. Ran for Governor in 1928, but was defeated by L.G. Hardman; ran again in 1930 and was defeated by Richard Russell. Elected to the Georgia House of Representatives in 1932 and 1934, and served as Speaker in both terms. Elected Governor in 1936, winning the Democratic primary with 372 county unit votes to Charles Redwine's 30 and Blanton Fortson's 8. He was reelected in 1938 with 282 county unit votes to Hugh Howell's 126 and J.J. Mangham's 2. As governor, Rivers gave wholehearted support to Roosevelt's New Deal. With increased federal assistance, state services were vastly expanded, especially in welfare benefits, public health, and public housing; highway construction was increased; electricity was extended to rural areas; and appropriations for the public schools and the eleemosynary institutions were increased. Also, several new state agencies were established to administer the new programs. In his second term, Rivers sought additional taxes to finance his programs, but the General Assembly refused to enact them. Despite efforts to economize, when his term ended the state debt had increased substantially. To a large extent Rivers modernized Georgia's government, but his administration was marred by charges of corruption and mismanagement. In 1946 Rivers sought reelection, but ran a distant third behind Eugene Talmadge and James V. Carmichael. Out of politics, he invested in radio stations in Georgia and Florida and became wealthy. His last years were spent in Miami, Florida. Rivers died in Atlanta on June 11, 1967, and was buried in Lakeland, Georgia. Bibliography: James Walker Herndon, "Eurith Dickinson Rivers: A Political Biography," Unpublished Ph.D. Dissertation, University of Georgia, 1974; Zell Bryan Miller, "The Administration of E.D. Rivers as Governor of Georgia," Unpublished M.A. Thesis, University of Georgia, 1958; Joseph L. Bernd, *Grass Roots Politics in Georgia* (Atlanta, 1960); Joseph L. Bernd, *The Role of Campaign Funds in Georgia Primary Elections, 1936-1958* (Macon, 1958); Michael S. Holmes, *The New Deal in Georgia, An Administrative History* (Westport, Conn., 1975); James F. Cook, *The Governors of Georgia* (Huntsville, Ala., 1977); William Anderson, *The Wild Man from Sugar Creek* (Baton Rouge, 1975); Hal Steed, *Georgia: Unfinished State* (New York, 1942). Papers of Rivers are on deposit in the Georgia Department of Archives and History in Atlanta.

TALMADGE, Eugene, 1933-1937, 1941-1943

ARNALL, Ellis Gibbs, 1943-1947

Born on March 20, 1907 in Newnan, Georgia, son of Joseph G., a grocery store operator, and Bessie Lena (Ellis) Arnall, both of whom were Baptists; brother of Frank Arnall. Married to Mildred Slemons on April 6, 1935; father of Alvan and Alice. Attended Mercer University and the University of the South, where he graduated in 1928; received an LL.B. from the University of Georgia in 1931. Entered law practice with an uncle in Newnan. In 1932 was elected to the General Assembly as a Democrat; elected Speaker *Pro Tempore* in 1933 and 1935, and served as Attorney General of Georgia from 1939 to 1943. Became Governor in 1943, defeating Eugene Talmadge in the Democratic primary, 174,757 to 128,394 in popular votes and 261 to 149 in county unit votes. A liberal and progressive governor, Arnall sponsored numerous reforms which the legislature adopted. The governor was removed from the Board of Regents and accreditation was restored to the state's colleges; prison reforms, including the elimination of the chain gang, were enacted; the poll tax was abolished and Georgia became the first state to lower the voting age to eighteen; the state debt was paid without increasing taxes; and a new constitution was adopted. When his term expired, Arnall resumed his law practice and other business interests. In 1952 he served as director of the Office of Price Stabilization. In 1966 he ran for reelection as governor, but lost in a runoff in the Democratic primary to Lester Maddox, the eventual winner. Arnall has not sought political office since then, and now concentrates on his extensive law practice and numerous corporate interests. Bibliography: Ellis Gibbs Arnall,

Messages and Addresses, 1943-1946 (Atlanta, 1946); Ellis Gibbs Arnall, *The Shore Dimly Seen* (Philadelphia, 1946); Ellis Gibbs Arnall, *What the People Want* (Philadelphia, 1947); Joseph L. Bernd, *Grass Roots Politics in Georgia* (Atlanta, 1960); James F. Cook, *The Governors of Georgia* (Huntsville, Ala., 1977); Thomas Elkin Taylor, "A Political Biography of Ellis Arnall," Unpublished M.A. Thesis, Emory University, 1959; James F. Cook, "The Georgia Gubernatorial Election of 1942," *Atlanta Historical Bulletin,* vol. XVIII (Summer, 1973).

TALMADGE, Herman Eugene, 1947, 1948-1955

Born on August 9, 1913 in Telfair County, Georgia, son of Governor Eugene Talmadge and Mattie (Thurmond) Talmadge, both of whom were Baptists; brother of Margaret and Vera Talmadge, and half-brother of John Peterson. Married to Kathryn Williams in 1937; divorced in 1940; remarried to Betty Shingler on December 24, 1941; divorced on February 18, 1977; father of Herman and Robert. Attended the University of Georgia and received an LL.B. degree in 1936. Practiced law with his father in Atlanta until he enlisted in the Navy at the outbreak of World War II. Following the death of his father, who had been elected Governor in 1946, Talmadge was elected Governor in 1947 by the Georgia Legislature by vote of 161 to 87; the legislature's decision was based on that body's contention that the younger Talmadge had won enough write-in votes in the 1946 gubernatorial election to make him the state's second choice. He served sixty-seven days, until the Georgia Supreme Court ousted him. In 1948 Talmadge defeated M.E. Thompson in the Democratic primary by a popular vote of 357,865 to 312,035 and a county unit vote of 312 to 98, and was elected without Republican opposition. In 1950 he again defeated Thompson (287,637 to 279,137 in popular votes, and 295 to 115 in county unit votes) for a four-year term. As governor, Talmadge greatly expanded state services, especially education. Appropriations for the common schools were nearly tripled during his term, and substantial school construction, financed by a new State Building Authority was undertaken. Also, the Highway Department was reorganized; the State Forestry Commission was established; and a network of hospitals and health centers was constructed. The expanded services were made possible by the introduction of a three percent sales tax in 1951 and by an increase in existing taxes. A noted segregationist and supporter of the county unit system, he backed a constitutional amendment to extend the county unit system to general elections, but it was defeated by the people. An extremely popular chief executive, Talmadge was elected to the United States Senate in 1956, and was overwhelmingly reelected in 1962, 1968 and 1974. Currently chairman of the Committee on Agriculture and Forestry, he is regarded as one of the most powerful members of the Senate. A fiscal conservative, he has consistently opposed expensive foreign and domestic federal programs; he also opposed civil rights legislation and forced busing, and has supported strong defense measures. In 1973 he served on the Select Committee which investigated the "Watergate Affair." The recipient of countless awards and honors, he maintains his residence in Lovejoy, where he has extensive farming interests. Bibliography: Herman E. Talmadge, *You and Segregation* (Birmingham, 1955); Joseph L. Bernd, *Grass Roots Politics in Georgia* (Atlanta, 1960); Josephine Mellichamp, *Senators From Georgia* (Huntsville, Ala., 1976); Numan V. Bartley, *From Thurmond to Wallace*

(Baltimore, 1970); Paul Mayhew, "The Talmadge Story," *New Republic,* vol. 135 (July 23, 1956); Robert Sherrill, *Gothic Politics* (New York, 1968); Harold Lord Varney, "Meet Senator Talmadge," *American Mercury,* vol. 86 (February, 1958).

THOMPSON, Melvin Ernest, 1947-1948

Born on May 1, 1903 in Millen, Georgia, son of Henry J., a farmer, and Eva Inez (Edenfield) Thompson, both of whom were Baptists; the youngest of six children, brother of two sisters, Myrtle, and Nora, and three brothers, H.E., G.B. and W.K. Thompson. Married to Ann Newton on February 3, 1926; father of M.E. Thompson, Jr. Attended Piedmont College, Emory University (B.A. 1926), University of Chicago, University of Alabama, Peabody College and the University of Georgia (M.A., 1935). Having completed most of the requirements for a doctorate, he became an educator, serving successively as a principal and coach, superintendent, State School Supervisor, and Assistant State Superintendent of Schools. Helped to organize Governor Ellis Arnall's successful campaign and served as his Executive Secretary, 1943-1945, and as State Revenue Commissioner, 1945-1947. Elected Georgia's first Lieutenant Governor in 1946, defeating Marvin Griffin in the Democratic primary, 190,332 to 160,082 in popular votes and 192 to 155 in county unit votes. He was inaugurated on January 18, 1947, but two days later became Acting Governor. Since Governor-Elect Eugene Talmadge had died on December 21, 1946, Thompson succeeded to the office after the departure of Governor Ellis Arnall. (Herman Talmadge, however, actually controlled the governor's office for sixty-seven days, until the Georgia Supreme Court ruled that Thompson should be the chief executive.) As acting governor, Thompson, one of Georgia's more liberal governors, emphasized education, succeeded in raising teachers' salaries, and initiated construction of buildings on several college campuses. At his insistence, Jekyll Island was purchased by the state for 650,000 dollars. Thompson advocated the passage of a sales tax, but it was not adopted until Governor Herman Talmadge's administration. In a special gubernatorial election in 1948, Thompson was defeated in the Democratic primary by Herman Talmadge, who won the popular vote, 357,865 to 312,035, and the county unit vote, 312 to 98. In 1950 Thompson again was defeated by Talmadge, and in 1954 he lost to Marvin Griffin; he then retired from politics. Thompson served briefly in 1951 as regional director of the Wage and Price Stabilization Board. Since 1948, Thompson has resided in Valdosta, where he has developed a successful real estate business. Bibliography: Joseph L. Bernd, *Grass Roots Politics in Georgia* (Atlanta, 1960); Joseph L. Bernd, *The Role of Campaign Funds in Georgia Primary Elections, 1936-1958* (Macon, 1958); Numan V. Bartley, *From Thurmond to Wallace* (Baltimore, 1970); James F. Cook, *The Governors of Georgia* (Huntsville, Ala., 1977); Charles Boykin Pyles, "Race and Ruralism in Georgia Elections, 1948-1966," Unpublished Ph.D. Dissertation, University of Georgia, 1967; Robert S. Allen, ed., *Our Sovereign State* (New York, 1949). Papers of Thompson are on deposit in the Emory University Library in Atlanta and the Valdosta State College in Valdosta.

TALMADGE, Herman Eugene, 1947, 1948-1955

GRIFFIN, Samuel Marvin, 1955-1959

Born on September 4, 1907 in Bainbridge, Georgia, son of Ernest Howard "Pat" Griffin, a newspaper publisher, and Josie (Butler) Griffin; a Presbyterian (he followed his mother's religion, while his father was a Baptist); brother of L.H., Rannie Griffin Davis, Josie Mae, Carlyle Patrick and Robert A. Griffin. Married to Mary Elizabeth Smith on July 11, 1931; father of Patricia Ann and Samuel; after his first wife's death on September 25, 1970, remarried to Laura Jane Gibson on September 27, 1971. Attended The Citadel and graduated in 1929. Served as Commandant of Cadets at Randolph-Macon Academy in Front Royal, Virginia, 1929 to 1933. Became editor of the Bainbridge *Post-Searchlight* when his father suffered a stroke. Elected to the General Assembly in 1934 as a Democrat to the seat previously held by his father; lost a Congressional race in 1936; appointed Executive Secretary to Governor E.E. Rivers in 1940. In the United States Army from 1941 to 1944, serving in the Pacific; appointed Adjutant General in 1944 and served until 1947. In 1946 ran unsuccessfully for Lieutenant Governor, but was elected to that office in 1948 and 1950. Griffin was elected Governor in 1954, winning 302 county unit votes in the Democratic primary to M.E. Thompson's 56, Tom Linder's 26, Fred Hand's 22, and Charlie Goven's 4. Griffin's popular vote of 234,690 was 36 percent of the total. Continuing the policies of Governor Herman Talmadge, Griffin stressed segregation and the preservation of the county unit system. He secured increased appropriations to the public schools and the university system; began an 8 million dollar science center at the University of Georgia; built an atomic reactor at Georgia Tech; and paved rural roads through the sale of 100 million dollars in bonds. His administration was marred by charges of corruption in the Purchasing Department and the Highway Department. Prevented from succeeding himself by the Georgia Constitution, he resumed his newspaper business in Bainbridge when his term expired. In a determined bid for reelection in 1962, he waged a racist campaign in the Democratic primary, but was defeated by Carl Sanders, a moderate, 462,065 votes to 305,777. The elimination of the county unit system before the election undoubtedly benefitted Sanders. Griffin has not sought political office since then with the exception of 1968, when he ran briefly as George Wallace's vice presidential running mate. In 1963 he turned over the editorship of the *Post-Searchlight* to his son, but he continues to write two weekly personal columns and other features. Griffin has remained active in local affairs as a public speaker. Bibliography: Joseph L. Bernd, *Grass Roots Politics in Georgia* (Atlanta, 1960); Numan V. Bartley, *From Thurmond to Wallace* (Baltimore, 1970); James F. Cook, *The Governors of Georgia* (Huntsville, Ala., 1977); James P. Wesberry, "Georgia to Stand for Segregation," *Christian Century*, vol. 73 (February 22, 1956); "Silent Moderates," *New Republic*, vol. 134 (March 26, 1956). Papers of Griffin are on deposit in the Bainbridge Junior College Library, Bainbridge, Georgia.

VANDIVER, Samuel Ernest, 1959-1963

Born in Franklin County, Georgia on July 31, 1918, the only child of Samuel E., a farmer and teacher, and Vanna (Osborne) Vandiver; stepbrother of Mrs. Hiram Whitehead and Henry Osborne; a Baptist. Although his mother was a Universalist, and his father belonged to no church, he became a Baptist at age thirteen. Married to Sybil Elizabeth Russell, a Presbyterian, on September 3, 1947; father of Samuel, Vanna Elizabeth and Jane. Attended the University of Georgia and received an A.B. in 1940 and an LL.B. in 1942. After serving as a pilot in World War II, Vandiver began to practice law in Winder. He served as Mayor of Lavonia; aide to Governor Eugene Talmadge; campaign manager for Governor Herman Talmadge in 1948; Adjutant General of Georgia, 1948-1954; State Director of Selective Service, 1948-1954; and Lieutenant Governor, 1955-1959. He was overwhelmingly elected Governor in 1958, winning the Democratic primary with 499,477 votes to William Bodenhamer's 87,830, and Lee Roy Abernathy's 33,099; Vandiver carried 156 of the state's 159 counties and won 400 of the 410 county unit votes. As governor, Vandiver encountered the problems of reapportionment and school integration. An outspoken advocate of segregation and states' rights, he reluctantly accepted the rulings of the federal courts and allowed the public schools to be integrated. Under his leadership, the legislature eliminated the state's segregation laws and the county unit system which had been used to nominate candidates in the Democratic primary; also the Georgia Senate was reapportioned following a federal court ruling. A fiscal conservative, he stressed efficiency in government, development of tourism, expansion of foreign trade, and increased appropriations for education. He inaugurated major reforms in treating the state's mentally ill. Upon completing his term, he resumed his law practice. Vandiver announced his candidacy for Governor in 1966, but was forced to withdraw because of a heart attack. He served as Adjutant General in 1971 and then waged an unsuccessful campaign for a United States Senate seat. Now retired from politics, he practices law in Lavonia and has extensive banking and agricultural interests. Bibliography: Numan V. Bartley, *From Thurmond to Wallace* (Baltimore, 1970); James F. Cook, *The Governors of Georgia* (Huntsville, Ala., 1977); Fred Powledge, "Too Much for Governor Vandiver," *New Republic,* vol. 144, (January 23, 1961); Ann E. Lewis, "S. Ernest Vandiver—73rd Governor of Georgia," *Georgia Magazine,* vol. 2 (February-March, 1959); Charlotte Hale Smith, "The Vandivers of Lavonia," *Atlanta Journal and Constitution Magazine* (August 23, 1964); Charles Boykin Pyles, "Race and Ruralism in Georgia Elections, 1948-1966," Unpublished Ph.D. Dissertation, University of Georgia, 1967.

SANDERS, Carl E., 1963-1967

Born on May 15, 1925 in Augusta, Georgia, son of Carl T., a salesman for Swift & Company, and Roberta (Alley) Sanders, both of whom were Baptists; brother of Robert T. Sanders. Married to Betty Bird Foy on August 6, 1947; father of Carl and Betty. Attended University of Georgia and received an LL.B. in 1947. Practiced law in Augusta and became senior partner of the firm Sanders, Thurmond, Hester, and Jolles. In 1954 was elected to the Georgia Legislature as a Democrat; in 1954 was elected to the Georgia Senate; served as Senate Floor Leader, then as President *Pro Tempore* of the Senate. In the Democratic primary of 1962, he defeated former Governor Marvin Griffin for the gubernatorial nomination, 462,065 votes to 305,777, and was elected without opposition in the general election. A moderate reformer, Governor Sanders established the Governor's Commission for Efficiency and Improvement in Government, the Commission to Improve Education, and the Commission on Science and Technology. He secured additional appropriations for education, highway construction, hospitals and mental health facilities, recreational areas, and community airports. Advances in state services were made possible because state revenues increased from 445 million dollars in 1962-1963 to 617 million dollars in 1965-1966. Education was Sanders' top priority; the Minimum Foundation Program established uniform standards for education, and 6,000 classrooms were constructed and 10,000 additional teachers were hired. Active in regional and national policymaking bodies, Sanders was chairman of the Rules Committee at the Democratic National Convention in 1964; a member of the Executive Committee of the National Governors' Conference, 1964-1965; and chairman of the Appalachian Governors' Conference, 1964-1965. His major disappointment as governor was in constitutional reform. A new constitution was written, but a federal court ruling prevented the people from ratifying it. At the expiration of his governorship, Sanders resumed his law practice. In 1970, when he was eligible to run for governor, he sought reelection. Although considered the frontrunner at the beginning of the campaign, he lost in the Democratic primary runoff to Jimmy Carter, the eventual winner. Now practicing law in Atlanta, Sanders has become a successful businessman, having affiliations with First Georgia Bankshares, Fuqua Industries, First Railroad and Banking Company, and Cousins Mortgage & Equity Investors. Bibliography: Numan V. Bartley, *From Thurmond to Wallace* (Baltimore, 1970); James F. Cook, *The Governors of Georgia* (Huntsville, Ala., 1977); Frank Daniel, ed., *Addresses and Public Papers of Carl Edward Sanders* (Atlanta, 1968); Charlotte Hale Smith, "Boyhood of Gov. Sanders," *Atlanta Journal and Constitution Magazine* (September 13, 1964); Margaret Spears Lyons, "A Comparison of Carl Sanders' Gubernatorial Campaigns, 1962 and 1970," Unpublished M.A. Thesis, University of Georgia, 1971. Papers of Sanders are on deposit at the Georgia Department of Archives and History, Atlanta, Georgia.

MADDOX, Lester Garfield, 1967-1971

Born on September 30, 1915 in Atlanta, Georgia, son of Dean G., a steelworker, and Flonnie (Castleberry) Maddox, both of whom were Baptists. Brother of Howard D., Bethelyn Maddox Wynn, June Maddox Bruce, Thomas W., Allen and Joyce Maddox Kirk. Married to Hattie Virginia Cox on May 9, 1936; father of Linda, Virginia, Lester and Larry. Left high school before graduation and held numerous odd jobs in the Atlanta area. After several business endeavors, Maddox gained economic success with the Pickrick Restaurant, which he opened in Atlanta in 1947. An avid segregationist, Maddox received widespread recognition in 1964 when he closed his restaurant rather than serve blacks. As an outspoken advocate of private property rights, Maddox's one-man campaign against the Supreme Court, President Johnson, Martin Luther King, Jr., the Atlanta newspapers, Communists, and Socialists, made him nationally famous. He was an unsuccessful Democratic candidate for Mayor of Atlanta in 1957 and 1961, and for Lieutenant Governor in 1962. In the 1966 gubernatorial race, Maddox polled 450,626 votes to Bo Callaway's 453,665; since neither candidate had a majority, the election went to the legislature. On January 11, 1967, the legislature elected Maddox, 182 votes to 66. Handicapped by the peculiar circumstances of his election and by a lack of political experience, Maddox implemented few lasting reforms as governor. He released hundreds of prisoners before their terms had expired, revitalized the Department of Industry and Trade, secured substantial salary increases for teachers and other state employees, and, in actuality, appointed more blacks to office than any of his predecessors. Two days a month were designated as "People's Day," and anyone who wished to visit the governor could do so. During Maddox's term the legislature became more independent of the governor. Prevented by the law from succeeding himself, Maddox easily won election as Lieutenant Governor in 1970. A bitter opponent of Governor Jimmy Carter, he opposed Carter's governmental reorganization and managed to block or delay some of his proposals in the Senate. In 1974, he sought the governorship again, but lost in the Democratic primary runoff to George Busbee, the eventual winner. In 1976 Maddox was the presidential candidate of the American Independent Party, but carried less than one percent of the vote. Retiring to private life, he now operates another Pickrick Restaurant in Sandy Springs, an Atlanta suburb. Bibliography: Bruce Graphin, *The Riddle of Lester Maddox* (Atlanta, 1968); Lester Maddox, *Speaking Out* (Garden City, 1975); Frank Daniel, ed., *Addresses of Lester Garfield Maddox* (Atlanta, 1971); Robert Sherrill, *Gothic Politics* (New York, 1968); Charles E. Fager, "Lester Maddox: Showman and Radical," *Christian Century*, vol. 88 (March 31, 1971); Numan V. Bartley, *From Thurmond to Wallace* (Baltimore, 1970). Papers of Maddox are on deposit in the Georgia Department of Archives and History in Atlanta.

CARTER, James Earl, 1971-1975

Born on October 1, 1924 in Plains, Georgia, son of James Earl, a Plains businessman, and Lillian (Gordy) Carter; brother of Gloria, Ruth and William A. Carter, III; a Baptist. Married to Rosalynn Smith on July 7, 1946; father of John William, James Earl, III, Donnel Jeffrey and Amy Lynn Carter. Graduated from Plains High School in 1941; attended Georgia Southwestern College at Americus, Georgia during 1941 and 1942, as well as the Georgia Institute of Technology in Atlanta; admitted to the United States Naval Academy at Annapolis in 1943, graduating in 1946, at which time he was commissioned an Ensign. After attaining the rank of Lieutenant Commander, Carter began work with Admiral Hyman G. Rickover on the nuclear submarine program under the auspices of the Atomic Energy Commission in 1951. Undertook postgraduate studies at Union College of Schenectady, New York and became a senior officer in the pre-commissioning crew of the *Seawolf*, one of the first atomic submarines. Carter resigned from the United States Navy upon the death of his father in 1953 and returned to Georgia to manage the family business interests. Served as chairman of the Sumter County (Georgia) Board of Education and Sumter County Hospital Authority from 1955 to 1962. Successfully contesting the results of the 1962 Georgia state senatorial election, Carter was subsequently reelected to the State Senate, and served from 1963 to 1967. During this time, he served on the Educational Matters Committee and the Highways, Agriculture, and Appropriations Committees. Unsuccessful Democratic gubernatorial primary candidate in 1966; became president of the Plains Development Corporation and the Sumter Redevelopment Corporation; in 1964 Carter assisted in organizing the West Central Georgia Planning and

Development Commission, of which he became the first chairman; served as president of the Georgia Planning Association and the Georgia Crop Improvement Association in 1968 and 1969. As the Democratic gubernatorial candidate, Carter was elected Governor of Georgia by popular vote on November 3, 1970, defeating the Republican candidate, Hal Suit, by a vote of 620,419 to 424,983. He was inaugurated on January 12, 1971. During his administration, the state government was reorganized; capital punishment was reinstated as the penalty for certain crimes, including airplane hijacking and treason; Georgia counties were allowed to vote individually to exempt themselves from the state's "blue laws;" all candidates for public office were required to report the sources of all contributions of 100 dollars or more; and a "no fault" automobile insurance plan was passed by the State Legislature. Carter left office on January 14, 1975 upon the inauguration of George Busbee. Elected President of the United States on November 2, 1976, defeating the incumbent President Gerald R. Ford; he was inaugurated on January 20, 1977. Author of: *People Parables: Pointed Stories for Speakers & Writers* (1973); *Why Not the Best?* (1975); *What Is to Come?* (1976); *A Government as Good as its People* (1977). Bibliography: *New York Times* (December 14 and December 26, 1975); Congressional Quarterly, Inc., *Guide to U.S. Elections* (Washington, D.C., 1975); Roy Glashan, *American Governors and Gubernatorial Elections, 1775-1975* (Stillwater, Minnesota, 1975).

BUSBEE, George Dekle, 1975-

Born on August 7, 1927 in Vienna, Georgia, son of Perry Green and Nell (Dekle) Busbee; a Baptist. Married to Mary Elizabeth Talbot on September 5, 1949; father of Beth Talbot, Jan Guest, George Dekle and Jeff Talbot Busbee. Served with the United States Naval Reserve during World War II. Received a B.B.A. from the University of Georgia in 1949 and an LL. B. from the University of Georgia in 1952; admitted to the Georgia Bar in 1952 and began law practice in Albany, Georgia. Served as a member of the Georgia House of Representatives from 1957 to 1974, holding the positions of Assistant Administration Floor Leader from 1963 to 1965, Administration Floor Leader in 1966, and House Majority Leader from 1967 to 1974. As the Democratic gubernatorial candidate Busbee was elected Governor of Georgia by popular vote on November 5, 1974, defeating the Republican candidate, Ronnie Thompson, by a vote of 646,777 to 289,113. He was inaugurated on January 14, 1975. During his administration, the federal Equal Rights Amendment was defeated by the State Legislature; new revenue sources, including the option of imposing local sales taxes and hotel-motel taxes, were approved for local governments; and an investigation into allegations of massive overcharging by some of Georgia's doctors was initiated by the governor. Tuition to Georgia colleges and universities was raised by an average of fifteen percent, and the Georgia Supreme Court ruled that zoning decisions by local governments were subject to court review, and that the state law requiring open meetings of state agencies did not apply to committee meetings of the Georgia House and Senate. Also, a Georgia constitutional amendment, providing that a governor may succeed himself, was passed by the State Legislature. Busbee's current term as Governor of Georgia will terminate in 1979. Bibliography: *New York Times* (November 6, 1974); Congressional Quarterly, Inc., *Guide to U.S. Elections* (Washington, D.C., 1975); Roy Glashan, *American Governors and Gubernatorial Elections, 1775-1975* (Stillwater, Minnesota, 1975).

HAWAII

HAWAII

QUINN, William Francis, 1959-1962

Born in Rochester, New York on July 31, 1919, son of Charles Alvin and Elizabeth Dorrity Quinn; a Catholic. Married Nancy Ellen Witbeck on July 11, 1942; father of William, Stephen, Timothy, Christopher, Ann, Mary, and Gregory. Quinn grew up in St. Louis, Missouri, graduated from St. Louis University in 1940 and then entered Harvard Law School. World War II interrupted his studies. Quinn served in the United States Navy from 1942 to 1945, being promoted in that time from Ensign to Lieutenant Commander. He worked in naval intelligence in the South Pacific area. Following the war, Quinn graduated from Harvard Law School in 1947. The Quinns moved to Honolulu in 1947 where he entered the legal profession. He was admitted to the bar in 1948. In 1956 he served as a member of the Hawaii Statehood Commission and the Harbor Board. He also ran unsuccessfully for the territorial senate. In 1957, President Dwight Eisenhower appointed William Quinn as Hawaii Territorial Governor, succeeding Samuel P. King. In 1959, statehood was granted to Hawaii, and Quinn led the Republicans against the Democrats' John A. Burns in the first state election. He defeated Burns, 86,215 to 82,054 votes, and was inaugurated on August 21, 1959. Quinn's administration led in the transition from a territorial to a state government. New responsibilities had to be defined and appropriate state offices designated to discharge these duties. Longstanding territorial problems, related to agriculture, land ownership, tourism and social services, remained major state concerns. Quinn, too, was involved in labor disputes involving shipping and the pineapple industry. He sought a second term in 1962, but was defeated this time by John Burns, by a vote of 114,303 to 81,720. Quinn reentered private law practice and remained until 1964 when he became an executive for Dole Pineapple Company. He served as company president from 1965 to 1972. He then joined a Honolulu law firm. In 1976, he received the Republican nomination for the United States Senate, but lost to Democrat Spark Matsunaga in the general election. Bibliography: William F. Quinn, "Papers," Hawaii State Archives, Honolulu, Hawaii; William F. Quinn, *Selected Addresses and Messages of William Francis Quinn* (Honolulu, 1965); Samuel C. Amalu, *Jack Burns: A Portrait in Transition* (Honolulu, 1974); A. Gavan Daws, *Shoal of Time* (New York, 1968).

BURNS, John Anthony, 1962-1974

Born in Fort Assineboine, Montana on November 30, 1909, son of Harry Jacob and Anne F. Scally Burns; a Catholic; brother of Edward, Helen and Margaret. His father an army sergeant major, was transferred to Fort Shafter in Honolulu when

Jack Burns was four years old. Burns graduated from St. Louis High School and attended the University of Hawaii. In the late 1920s, he worked at several odd jobs. On June 3, 1930, he married Beatrice Van Fleet, an army nurse; father of John A., Jr., James S. and a daughter, Mary Beth. In 1934, Burns joined the Honolulu Police Department; by 1940 he was a Vice Squad Captain and during World War II, he was Espionage Bureau Chief. At the war's end, Burns resigned, and subsequently operated a liquor store and engaged in real estate brokering. In 1946, he ran unsuccessfully for the Honolulu Board of Supervisors. He lost in both 1948 and 1954 in bids to become Hawaii's Territorial Delegate to Congress. In 1956 he was successful and served as the territory's last non-voting delegate during the final maneuvering for the statehood bill. He lost to William F. Quinn in his quest to become Hawaii's first state Governor, but in 1962, Burns defeated Quinn, 114,303 to 81,720 votes. Jack Burns was elected two more times. In 1966 he defeated Republican Richard Crossley, 108,840 to 104,324 votes. Burns was elected to a third term in 1970, defeating Samuel P. King by a vote of 137,150 to 109,573. During Burns' twelve years as governor, a social revolution materialized as the state government began to represent a wide range of citizens rather than the territorial planter oligarchy. Burns called for improved educational programs from elementary schools through a system of community colleges and a graduate university. The East-West Center, a brainchild of Burns, aimed to stimulate intellectual and cultural exchange. The governor also strove to make Hawaii the economic and political crossroads of the Pacific. Much of the work of his first two administrations implemented the social revolution and continued the transformation of Hawaii into the fiftieth state. The most visible aspect of the latter was the construction and dedication of the new State Capitol. While many social measures were enacted, perhaps the most controversial one was the abortion bill which moved Hawaii into the forefront ahead of the other states. During his third term, Burns was discovered to have cancer. He entered the hospital in mid-October, 1973 and never really resumed control of the governorship after that. He did complete his term and lived another four months, dying on April 5, 1975 at the age of 66. Bibliography: John A. Burns, "Papers," Hawaii State Archives, Honolulu, Hawaii; John A. Burns Oral History Project, University of Hawaii; Samuel C. Amalu, *Jack Burns: A Portrait in Transition* (Honolulu, 1974); Tom Coffman, *Catch a Wave: A Case Study of Hawaii's New Politics*, rev. 2nd edition (Honolulu, 1973); A. Gavan Daws, *Shoal of Time* (New York, 1968).

ARIYOSHI, George Ryoichi, 1974-

First person of Asian ancestry to be elected a governor in the United States. Born in Honolulu, Hawaii on March 12, 1926, son of Ryozo and Mitsue Yoshikawa Ariyoshi (both immigrants from Japan); his father operated a small shop. Married Jean M. Hayashi on February 5, 1955; father of Lynn, Todd and Donn. George Ariyoshi graduated from McKinley High School in 1942. He attended the University of Hawaii until 1944, when he joined the Army and served as an interpreter in post-war Japan. He then enrolled in Michigan State University, graduating in 1949. He received his LL.B. degree from the University of Michigan Law School in 1952. He joined a Honolulu law firm and was admitted to the bar that year. In 1954 he won a seat in the Territorial House of Representatives as a

Democrat. He served in the House from 1954 to 1958. Elected in 1958 to one last term in the Territorial Senate, he was successfully elected three times to the State Senate. In 1970, he ran for Lieutenant Governor, as John A. Burns sought his third gubernatorial term. On October 16, 1973, with Burns hospitalized for cancer, Ariyoshi became Acting Governor, remaining in that capacity until his own installation as Governor. He met the challenge of Honolulu Mayor Frank Fasi for the Democratic nomination, and then defeated Republican Randolph Crossley in the 1974 general election, 136,217 to 113,351 votes. On December 2, 1974, George Ariyoshi became the first American of Japanese descent to be inaugurated as a state governor. Ariyoshi inherited a factionalized Democratic Party which had held a strong allegiance to Jack Burns. Consequently, the new governor appeared not to be effective, as various legislators now freely espoused their own programs. The state government was confronted with continuing problems in land use, agriculture, housing and health. The Hawaiian situation was particularly complicated by a general decline in the economy and a large influx of new immigrants from Asian countries, many of whom needed state social services. Bibliography: Samuel S. Amalu, *Jack Burns: a Portrait in Transition* (Honolulu, 1974); Tom Coffman, *Catch a Wave: a Case Study of Hawaii's New Politics*, rev. 2nd edition (Honolulu, 1973).

IDAHO

IDAHO

SHOUP, George Laird, 1890

Born on June 15, 1836 in Kittannig, Pennsylvania, son of Henry Shoup, a farmer, and Anne Jane (McCain) Shoup; a Presbyterian. Married to Leona Darnutser in June, 1868; father of Walter, James, George, Lena, Laura, and Margaret. Attended public school intermittently until he was sixteen years of age. In 1852 he moved to Illinois with his parents and spent seven years farming and raising stock with his father. He moved to Colorado in 1859. When the Civil War broke out he enlisted, but soon was given a commission of Second Lieutenant and was promoted to Colonel of the 3rd Colorado Cavalry by the end of the war. He scouted for Indians as well as Confederates in New Mexico, Texas, and Colorado, partaking in the battle of Sand Creek. Obtaining a temporary leave of absence, he became a member of the Colorado Constitutional Convention. After the war he went to Virginia City, Montana but soon moved to Idaho, where he helped found the city of Salmon. He was appointed Commissioner to organize Lemhi County from which he served as territorial delegate to the State Legislature in 1874 and again in 1878. He served as a member of the Republican National Committee from 1880-1884, 1888-1892, 1892-1894, and from 1896-1900. In 1884 he was United States Commissioner for Idaho at the World's Cotton Centennial exposition at New Orleans, Louisiana, where he spent $35,000 of his own money to demonstrate the value of Idaho products. On April, 1889, he was appointed Governor of Idaho Territory and immediately repeated the call of his predecessor for a state constitutional convention. Idaho was admitted to the Union on July 3, 1890 and he was elected as its first governor on October 1, 1890, defeating the Democratic contender, Ben Wilson, by a vote of 10,262 to 7,948. He called the legislature to meet in December, and on the eighteenth of that month they elected him (Shoup) U.S. Senator from the State of Idaho. He spent about two and one half months as elected governor, which gave him little time to do anything of great importance. He took his Senate seat on December 28, 1890. In the Senate, he gave support to all Republican measures. He was an opponent of "free silver" in spite of the fact that Idaho was a great producer of that mineral. His deep interest in territories resulted in his Chairmanship of the Committee on Territories. He was also a member of the Committee on Military Affairs, Indian Affairs, Indian Depredations, Pensions and Education. He advocated liberal (for that time) Indian treatment, believed in liberal pension laws and popular elections of senators. He retired after being defeated in the 1900 election, probably due to his stand on silver. George L. Shoup died December 21, 1904. His statue was placed in the statuary hall at the national capitol by his state in January of 1910. Bibliography: Byron Defenbach, *Idaho, The State and Its People* (Chicago, 1933); J. H. Hawley, ed., *History of Idaho* (Chicago, 1920); H. M. French, *History of Idaho* (New York, 1914); Merrill

D. Beal and Merle W. Wells, *History of Idaho* (New York, 1959) vols. I and II; *The Idaho Daily Statesman* (December 22 and 23, 1904); *The Idaho Daily Statesman* (January 16 and 18, 1910). Papers of George L. Shoup on file at the Idaho Historical Society in Boise, Idaho.

WILLEY, Norman B., 1890-1893

Born on March 25, 1838 in Guilford, New York, son of Hiram and Caroline (Church) Willey; a Protestant. He received his later education at the Delaware Literary Institute, Franklin, New York. He went to the mining districts in California and settled near Dutch Flat in Placer County, where he followed mining with the usual successes and reverses of that occupation. Willey came to Idaho in 1864 and for over thirty years engaged in mining while living at Warrens, Idaho. He was elected to the House of Representatives of the Idaho Territory, serving from 1872 to 1873. He was elected again to the House of Representatives in 1878 and served until 1889. While a Representative he was chosen President of that body—a somewhat memorable event in the political annals of Idaho, as he led a movement against the Mormons of the territory. After the admission of Idaho as a state on July 3, 1890. Willey was elected Lieutenant Governor. With the election of Governor George L. Shoup to the United States Senate in December of 1890, Willey became Governor and held the position until 1893. During his term as governor, the Coeur d'Alene riots occurred and to maintain order, Governor Willey called in federal troops; the "Australian ballot," which applied to all elections except those of school districts, was adopted; and a joint committee of the House and Senate was formed to solicit designs from which a state seal would be selected. His duties as Governor centered mainly upon the "housekeeping chores" of getting Idaho started as a new state. Willey tried to get the Republican nomination to run for Governor in 1893, but the Republicans chose William J. McConnell to run instead. When his term of office was over, Willey went to Blue Canyon, California to superintend a mine which he and General George Roberts owned. His health failed in 1913 and the Idaho Legislature appropriated $1200 to tide him over his financial difficulties. Norman B. Willey never married and spent his last days in Kansas, where he died on October 20, 1921. Bibliography: Merrill D. Beal and Merle W. Wells, *History of Idaho* (New York, 1959); Cornelius Brosnan, *History of the State of Idaho* (New York, 1948); Byron Defenbach, *Idaho, The State and Its People* (Chicago, 1933); *Twenty-first Biennial Report of the Idaho State Historical Department.* Papers of Norman B. Willey at the Idaho Historical Society, Boise, Idaho.

McCONNELL, William John, 1893-1897

Born on September 18, 1839 in Commerce, Michigan, son of James and Mary (Colter) McConnell who were farm immigrants from northern Ireland; a Presbyterian. Married to Louisa Brown of Yamhill County, Oregon in 1870; father of Mary (Mamie) (who later was to marry William E. Borah), Carey, Olive, William, and Benjamin. He had a fairly good education in the common schools. He went to

Oregon in 1860, but in 1863 he came to Fayette, Idaho and built the first irrigation ditch there. He went back to Oregon in 1869, and while living there was elected to the State Senate in 1882, being the presiding officer of that body. Finally he returned to Idaho and in 1884, entered the mercantile business in Moscow, which became his home. He took an active part in the State Constitutional Convention in 1890 and was chosen to serve in the United States Senate in 1890 when Idaho became a state. His election to this office gave satisfaction to northern Idaho as a counter-balance to the political power in southern Idaho. When McConnell drew the short term ending in March of 1891,though, northern Idaho became disturbed. He was elected for two terms as Governor, 1893-1895 and 1895-1897. The Populist candidate, Abraham J. Crook, received 4,865 votes; the Democratic candidate, John M. Burke, received 6,769 votes; and McConnell received 8,178 votes in 1892. For a second term, McConnell received 10,208 votes; his Democratic opponent E. A. Stevenson received 7,057 votes; while the Populist candidate, J. W. Ballantine, received 7,121 votes. The big issues were "hard times," the silver issue, and continuing labor unrest. Idaho's free coinage adherents were divided into a complex pattern of factions distributed through the three political parties (Republican, Democratic, and Populist). Republican McConnell did not "see eye-to-eye" with his Democratic-Populist legislature, but on one issue they did agree—the right of the workers to join a union. The law that they passed was rather an advanced one in the history of labor legislation in the United States. The establishment of two normal schools at Albion and Lewiston was a boost for education in the state. A measure was enacted accepting one million acres of Carey Act Lands (1895) from the federal government. Passage of Idaho's first District Irrigation Law (1895) soon followed. They also passed an act that provided for women's suffrage. After his term had expired, he returned to the mercantile business. He also served as Indian Inspector from 1897 to 1901. McConnell died of influenza on March 30, 1925. He never favored one religion over another. He gave land on which to build a Lutheran Church, but he gave to other churches also. At his funeral, a Presbyterian minister read from the Bible, a Methodist minister gave the prayer, and an ex-governor gave the eulogy. He was listed as a Presbyterian in the newspapers. Bibliography: William John McConnell, *History of Idaho* (Caldwell, Idaho, 1913); Byron Defenbach, *Idaho, The State and Its People* (Chicago, 1933); Merrill D. Beal and Merle W. Wells, *History of Idaho* (New York, 1959); *The Idaho Daily Statesman* (March 31 and April 1, 1925); *Lewiston Morning Tribune*, (April 1, 1925); *Moscow Daily Star Mirror* (March 31, April 1 and 2, 1925). Papers of William J. McConnell at the Idaho Historical Society, Boise, Idaho.

STEUNENBERG, Frank, 1897-1901

Born on August 8, 1861 in Keokuk, Iowa to parents who were immigrants from Holland. Married Belle Keppel of Keokuk, Iowa; father of Julian, Francis, and Frank, Jr.; member of the Christian Church. Moved to Knoxville, Iowa, where he attended the Iowa State Agriculture College at Ames for a while. After working as compositor on various newspapers, in 1864 he purchased the *Knoxville Express* in conjunction with publisher W. J. Casey and retained it for two years. In 1866 he came to Caldwell, Idaho where he formed a partnership with his brother in the publication of the *Caldwell Tribune*. In 1889 he was a member of the Idaho

Constitutional Convention. In 1890 he was elected to the lower house of the State Legislature. He was also Chairman of the Caldwell Town Council for several years. In the 1896 election for Governor, his Republican opponent was Colonel D. H. Budlong, who received 6,441 votes, and Steunenberg won with 22,096 votes. In the 1898 election on a fusion ticket of Democratic and Silver Republican voters, he received 19,400 to 13,800 for A. B. Moss, the Republican candidate, and 5,400 for J. H. Anderson, the New People's Party. The record of Steunenberg's two terms as governor shows that Idaho was still a new state and a good deal of minor legislation was passed. A number of new boards and offices were created, such as the Board of Medical Examiners, the Board of Arbitration of Labor Troubles, a Fish and Game Warden, the Board of Dental Examiners, and a Commissioner of Immigration, Labor, and Statistics. When he became governor, conditions were anything but propitious for a successful administration; Idaho, included with the entire nation, had been in a depression for several years with no signs of amelioration. The Western Federation of Miners, economically troubled, became increasingly restless and rioted. Governor Steunenberg took a firm stand and exercised the power of the state. He called upon federal authorities for protection of property and to aid in the punishment of offenders. This action resulted in federal investigation because of various charges labor brought against his administration's methods of suppressing the strikes. After serving two terms as governor, he returned to Caldwell and the newspaper. It was there that on December 30, 1905 a bomb, which had been planted to go off as he opened the front gate of his home, took his life. Harry Orchard later admitted that he was guilty and that he was an agent of the Western Federation of Miners. Charles H. Moyer, president, William D. Haywood, treasurer, and George A. Pettibone, whom Orchard named as his "contact man," were in Colorado. In close cooperation with that state's authorities and in the utmost secrecy, Idaho officials apprehended the three men on a private train bound for Idaho. They did not convict the three, but William E. Borah and Clarence Darrow emerged from the battle with national reputations. Frank Steunenberg lived for thirty minutes after the bomb went off. His funeral was held at the Christian Church in Caldwell. Bibliography: Cornelius Brosnan, *History of the State of Idaho* (New York, 1948); Byron Defenbach, *Idaho, The State and Its People* (New York, 1933); Hiram T. French, *History of Idaho* (New York, 1914); Merrill D. Beal and Merle Wells, *History of Idaho* (New York, 1914); *The Idaho Daily Statesman* (Nov. 11, 1896); *The Idaho Daily Statesman* (Nov. 13, 1898); *The Idaho Daily Statesman* (Dec. 31, 1905 and January 1 and 3, 1906). Papers of Frank Steunenberg at the Idaho Historical Society, Boise, Idaho.

HUNT, Frank W., 1901-1903

Born on December 16, 1871 in Louisville, Kentucky, son of Thomas Benjamin Hunt, a Captain in the United States Army, and Eugenia (Montmolin) Hunt; an Episcopalian. Married on November 10, 1896 to Ruth Maynard; father of Elizabeth, who died at the age of seven, and Katherine. He was educated in the common schools and moved to Idaho in 1888, where he went into mining. He served in the State Legislature from 1893-94. As a legislator he was very active, especially in securing the passage of a state mining law. With the outbreak of the Spanish American War, he joined the Army and was subsequently appointed First Lieutenant by Governor Steunenberg and eventually made Captain before the war was over. He took part in the Battle of Manila and Topte Bridge on June 13, 1899. Upon his being mustered out, he entered almost immediately into politics, running on the Democratic ticket for Governor. It was actually a fusion ticket as a result of the three parties holding their convention at the same time and place. D. W. Standrod, his opponent on the Republican ticket, received 26,468 votes to Hunt's 28,628 votes. It was a time of great activity with the state emerging from the economic depression and the prosperity brought along with it many immigrants to the state. The eight-hour day was increased to include all people on public financed works as well as workers in factories, smelters and mines. One of the most important acts of his administration was to establish the Academy of Idaho at Pocatello, which was eventually to become Idaho State College. He took a deep interest in the development of commerce. He also took a great interest in agriculture, which was evidenced by his continuous efforts to secure increased investments in irrigation by eastern capital. In the 1902 election, he was defeated by John T. Morrison, Republican, by a vote of 31,874 to 26,021. Of course the Populist, Prohibitionist, and Socialist candidates had some votes, but they were inconsequential; of these, the Socialist candidate, A. M. Slattery, made the best showing with 1,567 votes. After his term had expired, he retired to Emmett, Idaho, where he could once again turn all of his attention to mining. He was chosen vice president and general manager of the Dewey Combination Lease Company which was operating at Goldfield, Nevada. It was while he was travelling in that state, managing the mines, that he contracted pneumonia and died on November 25, 1906. His body was shipped back to his wife in Boise and the funeral was held at the Episcopal Church. Bibliography: Byron Defenbach, *Idaho, The State and Its People* (New York, 1933); Hiram T. French, *History of Idaho* (New York, 1914); Merrill D. Beal and Merle Wells, *History of Idaho* (New York, 1959); *The Idaho Daily Statesman* (November 19, 1900, November 20, 1902, and November 26, 28, and 29, 1900). Papers of Frank W. Hunt at the Idaho Historical Society, Boise, Idaho.

MORRISON, John T., 1903-1905

Born on December 25, 1860 in Jefferson County, Pennsylvania, son of John and Sophia Elizabeth (Tracy) Morrison who were farmers; a Presbyterian. Married to Grace Darling Mackey on July 8, 1886 in Jamestown, New York. He attended the public schools in Pennsylvania. Later. Morrison attended Wooster University, Wayne County, Ohio, where he met William Judson Boone who was to figure so prominently in his future life. He graduated in 1887, receiving his B.A. degree. He taught school for one year and then entered the Cornell Law School, where he received his degree of LL.B. Mr. and Mrs. Morrison came to Caldwell, Idaho in 1890, where he entered the practice of law and soon had an extensive business. He was very active in the Presbyterian Church and was a commissioner to the Presbyterian General Assembly from Idaho at Portland, Oregon in 1892 and again in Winona, Indiana in 1897. He did much of the organizational work in establishing the College of Idaho, a denominational college of the Presbyterian faith, and after it had opened, he became an instructor in English and History there for two years, along with William Judson Boone who was later to become president of the college. Morrison was one of the organizers of the Western National Bank of

Caldwell, as well as the First National Bank at Vale, Oregon. In 1893 he became Chairman of the Board of Trustees of the College of Idaho, a post he held for more than ten years. He acted as Secretary of the Republican State Central Committee and was State Chairman of the Committee from 1897 to 1900. He was an unsuccessful candidate for the State Legislature in 1896 and again in 1900. He ran for Governor in 1902 and won with 31,874 votes to 26,021 votes for Frank W. Hunt, his Democratic opponent. His administration established a Reform School at St. Anthony; issued bonds for a Supreme Court at Lewiston, Idaho; passed the Foreign Corporation Bill, which resulted in increased revenue; and created several state departments. He tried to run for a second term, but after a hard-fought battle in the convention, Senator Borah came out for Frank R. Gooding to run on the Republican ticket and Morrison was defeated. He returned to his law practice at Boise and died of a heart attack on December 20, 1915. He and his wife had spent the day with their daughter and son-in-law, Mr. and Mrs. Wilson, at Meridian which is just a short distance from Boise. He was conscious to the end, sent for his attorney to put his affairs in order, and recommended to his wife that his son, John, should not return from school at Bowdoin College for the funeral. Bibliography: Byron Defenbach, *Idaho, The State and Its People* (New York, 1933); Merrill D. Beal and Merle Wells, *History of Idaho* (New York, 1959); *The Idaho Daily Statesman* (December 22, 24, and 25, 1915); *Twenty-first Biennial Report of the Idaho State Historical Department*, 1947-1948; G. C. Hobson, ed., *The Idaho Digest and Blue Book* (Caldwell, 1935). Papers of John T. Morrison at the Idaho Historical Society, Boise, Idaho.

GOODING, Frank R., 1905-1909

Born on September 16, 1859 in Devonshire, England, son of John and Elizabeth (Wyatt) Gooding, who migrated to Van Buren County, Michigan in 1867, where his father engaged in farming and livestock raising; a Methodist. Married to Amanda Thomas of Red Bluff, California in June of 1879; father of John, Louise, and Maud. Gooding attended the public schools of Michigan, and at the age of eighteen, he moved with his parents to California where they farmed. He came to Idaho in 1881 and was first employed as a contractor for mining companies in the Wood River area. He finally got a homestead and began grazing sheep. He gradually extended the operation and by the time of his death, he was the largest sheep owner in Idaho. Though he was a prohibitionist and hated liquor intensely, politically he was a Republican. He was chairman of the Lincoln County Republicans in 1896 and chairman of the state Republicans for four years. In 1898 he was elected to the State Senate, and again in 1900, when he served as President Pro Tempore of the Senate. He was elected Governor of Idaho in 1904, receiving a vote of 44,872, to Henry Heltfeld's 24,192, his Democratic opposition. He won a second term, receiving a vote of 38,386 to 29,409 for Charles O. Stockslager, his Democratic opposition. There were other parties, such as the Socialist Party, whose candidate received 4,650 votes in 1906, and the Prohibitionist, Silas Luttrell, with 1,037 votes in 1906, but these were not a threat to the candidates of the two major parties. During his first term, ex-Governor Frank Steunenberg was murdered, and Governor Gooding made every effort to punish those responsible, even though numerous threats were made against his life. His administration saw the creation of a State

Banking Department; the organizing of a commission, with the governor as a member, to draft plans for a new Capitol; reorganization of the State Land Department; appropriation for the establishment of a library at the State University at Moscow; and the designation of liberal appropriations for schools. There was also much labor unrest and violence in the Coeur d'Alene mines during his two terms as governor. At the end of his second term, he returned home and continued to raise sheep. He founded the town of Gooding and later (1913) had a county named after him. He was instrumental in getting a Methodist college established, as well as causing a State School for the Deaf and Blind to be located in Gooding. In 1920 he was appointed to fill an unexpired term in the United States Senate, and in 1920 and 1926 he was elected to full terms. He became identified with the farm bloc, working for relief of agriculture and tariffs on farm products. He seemed to be recuperating from an operation, but suddenly on June 24, 1929 death came unexpectedly. He was buried in the cemetery of the town that bears his name. Bibliography: Merrill D. Beal and Merle Wells, *History of Idaho* (New York, 1959); *Twenty-first Biennial Report of the Idaho State Historical Department*, 1947-1948; G. C. Hobson, ed., *The Idaho Digest and Blue Book* (Caldwell, 1935); *The Idaho Daily Statesman* (June 25, 26, 27, and 28, 1929). Papers of Frank R. Gooding at the Idaho Historical Society, Boise, Idaho.

BRADY, James H., 1909-1911

Born on June 12, 1862 in Indiana County, Pennsylvania, son of John Brady, a farmer, and Catherine (Lee) Brady; a Congregationalist. Married Sarah H. Haines on December 25, 1876; father of James and Silas; remarried to Irene Moore of Chicago, Illinois on May 13, 1913. Moved to Kansas with his family in 1865; attended public school at Olathe; went on to get his degree from Leavenworth Normal School, and then taught school for three years while he fitted himself for the law. He edited a semi-weekly newspaper and then embarked on a real estate career with offices in Chicago, St. Louis, and Houston. He moved to Idaho in 1895 and became involved with irrigation and water power companies. Brady was vice president of the National Irrigation Congress in 1896-1898 and was a member of its Executive Committee, 1900-1904. He became active in the Republican Party and was chosen delegate to the National Convention of 1900, 1908 and 1916. He was Chairman of the Republican Central Committee of Idaho in 1904 and in 1906. Elected Governor in 1908 over Moses Alexander, Democrat, who received 41,145 votes to Brady's 47,865. During his administration, funds for a location for Idaho Children's Home Finding and Aid Society were obtained (he was its president until ill health forced him to resign); Direct Primaries were established; Local Option Liquor Laws were enacted; a school for the deaf, dumb, and blind was established at Gooding; the state's Sanitary and Pure Food Department was increased. Brady also sponsored the National Council of Women and was instrumental in calling the meeting which organized the National Council of Women Voters, Boise Chapter. Defeated in 1910 by James H. Hawley, Democrat, 40,856 to 39,961 votes for Brady; S. W. Morley, Socialist, received 5,342 votes. Returning to his Pocatello land, he was chosen by the legislature to complete the unexpired Senate term of Weldon B. Heyburn on January 24, 1913. In 1914 he became the first Senator from Idaho to be elected under the direct primary and for a full six-year term. He supported Wilson in Mexico and in World War I. He was ranking Republican member of the Military Affairs Committee. He was the honorary vice president of the Panama Pacific International Exposition at San Francisco, 1915. Brady died very suddenly in Washington, D.C. on January 13, 1918 of a heart attack. Bibliography: Merrill D. Beal and Merle Wells, *History of Idaho* (New York, 1959); Bryon Defenbach, *Idaho, The State and Its People* (New York, 1933); G. C. Hobson, ed., *The Idaho Digest and Blue Book* (Caldwell, 1935); F. Ross Peterson, *Idaho, A Bicentennial History* (New York, 1976); *The Idaho Daily Statesman* (January 14 and 15, 1918). Papers of James H. Brady at the Idaho Historical Society, Boise, Idaho.

HAWLEY, James H., 1911-1913

Born on January 17, 1847 in Dubuque, Iowa, son of Thomas and Annie (Carr) Hawley; a Catholic. Married Mary E. Bullock of Quartzburg, Idaho on July 4, 1875; father of Edgar T., Jesse M., Emma, Elizabeth, James H., and Harry R. Hawley's mother died in his infancy and after attending the public schools, he followed his uncle, James Carr, to California in 1861. Stirred by the excitement of gold, Hawley journeyed to northern Idaho and engaged in mining. In 1864 he returned to California and entered City College of San Francisco, studying law on the side at the office of Sharpstein and Hastings. In 1868 he returned to Idaho. He spent most of his time in southern Idaho, where among other things, he practiced law at Hailey, Idaho from 1884-1886, when he was appointed United States District Attorney for Idaho by President Cleveland. He moved to Boise in 1890, and in 1902 was elected Mayor of that city. As a result of his interest in public affairs, Hawley also held the following positions: admitted to the bar of the Supreme Court in 1871; County Commissioner, 1876; the main lawyer for the State of Idaho in the trial of those persons accused of assassinating Governor Steunenberg. In 1910 he ran for governor as a Democrat and defeated James H. Brady, a Republican, who received 39,561 votes to Hawley's 40,856. S. W. Motley received 5,342 votes. He ran again in 1912, but this time lost to John M. Haines, a Republican, who received 35,056 votes to Hawley's 33,992. The minority parties, such as the Progressives, headed by G. G. Martin, received 24,325 votes, and the Socialists, headed by L.A. Coblentz, received an unusual 11,094 votes. When Hawley became Governor, it promised to become a stormy period for the legislature. Hawley called a special session to remedy the tax situation and laws were passed which resulted in confusion, as some of the assessors tried to follow the provisions of the new Revenue Law requiring that all property be assessed at its full cash value, while others continued to assess by the old law. The more important acts of the legislature were: creation of Bonneville, Clearwater, Adams and Lewis counties; enactment of the Highway District Law; locating of a site for the State Sanatorium for the Feeble-Minded; the addition of "Pioneer Day" to the list of legal holidays; and stringent search and seizure liquor law enforcement. The State Constitution was also amended to include initiative, referendum, and recall. On leaving the office of governor, Hawley resumed the practice of law at Boise as head of the firm of Hawley, Pluckett, and Hawley. He was also the author of a book, *The History of Idaho, Gem of the Mountains* (Chicago, 1920). Governor Hawley died on August 3, 1929 at the age of 82. Bibliography: Merrill D. Beal and Merle Wells, *History of Idaho*

(New York, 1959); Cornelius Brosnan, *History of the State of Idaho* (New York, 1948); Byron Defenbach, *Idaho, The State and Its People* (New York, 1933); G. C. Hobson, ed., *The Idaho Digest and Blue Book* (Caldwell, 1935); F. Ross Peterson. *Idaho, A Bicentennial History* (New York, 1976); *The Idaho Daily Statesman* (August 4, 5 and 6, 1929). Papers of James H. Hawley at the Idaho Historical Society, Boise, Idaho.

HAINES, John M., 1913-1915

Born on January 1, 1863 in Jasper County, Iowa, son of Isaac and Eliza (Bushong) Haines; a Quaker. Attended public schools and entered Penn College at Oskaloosa, Iowa, a sectarian institution for the Quaker faith; left school after three years due to poor health. Married Mary Symons, daughter of a Quaker minister, on May 20, 1883, in Lynville, Iowa. Afterward they located in Friend, Nebraska, where Haines was connected with the Merchants and Farmers Bank for two years. He migrated to Richfield, Kansas where he met W. E. Pierce and L. H. Cox, and together they entered the real estate business. While there he was a member of the Republican State Central Committee, Deputy Clerk of Morton County, and was elected Register of Deeds in 1889. Reverses came with the depression and drought of the late 1880s. He and his two associates moved to Idaho in 1890, where the three of them formed a life-long partnership in real estate in Boise. He was elected Mayor of Boise for two years in 1907. Haines was nominated to run on the Republican ticket for Governor in 1912, and won the election by a vote of 35,056 to 33,992 for James H. Hawley, his Democratic opponent. G. H. Martin, Progressive, received 24,325; L. A. Coblentz, Socialist, 11,094; and Emmit D. Nichols, Prohibitionist, 1,028 votes. His candidacy was especially trying for the Progressives as they had classified Haines as a "stand-patter," but when he read his message to the legislature, they were surprised at the advanced stand he took on many of the issues. He recommended a Public Utilities Commission and a system of unified control of educational institutions. After the State Legislature defeated a bill for workmen's compensation, it appointed a committee called the Haines Committee to study the measure. As a result a new bill was introduced and passed both houses, but Governor Haines obstinately vetoed it. He also established the State Board of Education. Defalcation of the Treasurer and his assistant, though Haines himself knew nothing about the crime, was the greatest blot on his career; it probably caused him to lose the next election to his Democratic opponent, Moses Alexander, by a margin of 7,269 votes. It was Governor Haines who approved the act appropriating twelve hundred dollars for the benefit of ex-Governor Willey, who was living in California destitute and penniless. After his gubernatorial term was over, he again resumed his real estate business and took an active part in business and civic affairs, until his death on June 4, 1917 at Boise. Bibliography: Merrill D. Beal and Merle Wells, *History of Idaho* (New York, 1959); Byron Defenbach, *Idaho, The State and Its People* (New York, 1933); G. C. Hobson, ed., *Idaho Digest and Blue Book* (Caldwell, 1935); F. Ross Peterson, *Idaho, A Bicentennial History* (New York, 1976); *The Idaho Daily Statesman* (June 5, 1917). Papers of John M. Haines at the Idaho Historical Society, Boise, Idaho.

ALEXANDER, Moses, 1915-1919

Born on November 15, 1853 at Obrigheim, Rheinpfalz, Bavaria, son of Nathan and Eva (Frankel) Alexander. Married Hedwig Keastner of St. Catherine, Missouri on November 5, 1876; father of Emma Amelia, Nettie, Leha, and Nathan. Alexander came to America as an orphan at age fourteen, spent a year in New York City, then went to Chillicothe, Missouri, where he entered the employ of Jacob Berg and Co., a merchandising firm. He was a member of the Chillicothe City Council in 1886 and Mayor of Chillicothe in 1887. In 1891, he moved to Boise, Idaho and established a mercantile business under his own name—Alexander and Co. The business succeeded and he opened a second store in Baker, Oregon. This expansion succeeded without reverses, and eventually he had stores in Vale, Colorado; Ontario, Oregon; and Weiser, Caldwell, Burley and Nampa, Idaho. During 1901-1902 he served as Mayor of Boise. He failed to be elected in his first campaign for Governor in 1908, losing to James H. Brady who won the election by a margin of 6,720 votes. His second attempt to gain the governorship in 1914 on the Democratic ticket proved successful, with Alexander receiving 47,618 votes against his Republican opponent, John M. Haines' 40,349. Hugh E. McElroy, Progressive, received 10,583 votes; L. S. Coblentz, Socialist, 7,967 votes; and E. R. Headley, Prohibitionist, received 1,396 votes. Thus Alexander became the first man of the Jewish faith elected to the rank of Governor by the people of any state in the United States. He was reelected in 1916 with 63,877 votes to 63,305 for the Republican, D. W. Davis. Annie E. Triplow, Socialist, received 7,321 votes. His administration was characterized by a reduction in the tax rate; the consolidation or elimination of offices; the passage (1917) of a state constitutional amendment prohibiting the manufacturing or sale of liquor; and the adoption of an enlightened workingmen's compensation measure. It was also during his administration that a Bureau of Farm Markets was organized, and an extensive highway building program was launched with provisions for issuance of $1,200,000 in bonds for that purpose. Eight new counties were created; 17,000 men were secured for military service; and $52,000,000 for the National Fund was raised. He directed the Criminal Syndicalism Act against the Industrial Workers of the World who were trying to organize the loggers of northern Idaho and declared the advocacy of any armed revolution a criminal offense. His German birth, coupled with his Jewish faith, caused a small amount of criticism, but by and large, the people of Idaho supported him, and he governed well during the period of World War I. Upon completion of his second term, he returned to his business in Boise. He was involved in the Alexander Realty Company of Boise, as well as with irrigation. He was delegate to the Democratic National Conventions in 1920, 1924 and 1928. His party called on him to run for governor in 1922 against his wishes, and he lost by a vote of 36,810 votes to 40,538 for Republican C. C. Moore. H. F. Samuels, Progressive, received 40,516. For the first time the Democratic Party became classified as a minority party. He began to have failing health and a sudden heart attack took his life in Boise on January 4, 1932. Bibliography: Merrill D. Beal and Merle Wells, *History of Idaho* (New York, 1959); G. C. Hobson, ed., *The Idaho Digest and Blue Book* (Caldwell, 1935); F. Ross Peterson, *Idaho, A Bicentennial History* (New York, 1976); *The Idaho Daily Statesman* (January 5, 6 and 7, 1932). Papers of Moses Alexander at the Idaho Historical Society, Boise, Idaho.

DAVIS, David W., 1919-1923

Born on April 23, 1873 in Cardiff, Wales, son of John Wynn and Frances (Lewis) Davis; a Methodist. Married to Florence O. Gilliland, who died in 1903; remarried on April 5, 1905 to Nellie Johnson; father of Margaret Ruth, David William, and Donald J. Davis came to the United States with his parents in 1875. At the age of twelve, he began work in a coal mine in Rippey, Iowa; at fifteen he was a clerk in the mine company's store in Dawson; at twenty-one years of age, he was made manager of the Farmers' Cooperative Association in Rippey; and in 1889 he became cashier of the bank in Rippey. In 1885 he moved West, and after a year as cashier of the Dayton (Washington) National Bank, he settled at American Falls, Idaho. Davis organized the Bank of American Falls, and was president from its inception. He also became in later years joint owner of a newspaper, *The American Falls Press*. Davis became interested in the Republican Party, serving as a delegate to the National Convention in 1912, and as a State Senator from 1913 to 1915. In 1916 he was chosen to run for Governor, but was defeated by Moses Alexander by the narrow margin of 572 votes. In 1918, however, he was elected by a margin of 19,127 votes over his Democratic opponent, H. F. Samuels, who was his only opposition. He was reelected in 1920, receiving 75,748 votes to Ted A. Walters, Democrat, who received 38,509, and Sherman D. Fairchild, Independent, who received 28,752. His terms as governor were known for the following: recodification of Idaho statutes: consolidation of state civil powers in a board of 9 commissioners appointed by the governor to replace the 40-odd administrative agencies which had formerly conducted the state's business; inauguration of a road building program for which a bond of $2,000,000 was voted in referendum; securing legislation for creating a Bureau of Budget and Taxation; creating a teachers' pension system; creating a veterans' welfare program; securing three constitutional amendments which provided for (a) increasing the number of the Supreme Court Justices from 3 to 5, (b) direct appeal from the decisions of the Public Utility Commission to the State Supreme Court, and (c) retaining to the state control of its unused water power. After completing his second term as governor, he was given a presidential appointment in 1923 as special assistant to the Secretary of Interior, and in 1924 as Commissioner of Reclamation and Director of Finance for the Interior Department. For a short time in 1931, he was special advisor to former President Hoover. He died on August 5, 1959, at the age of 86. Bibliography: Merrill D. Beal and Merle Wells, *History of Idaho* (New York, 1959); Byron Defenbach, *Idaho, The State and Its People* (New York, 1933); *Twenty-first Biennial Report of the Idaho State Historical Department, 1947-1948*; G. C. Hobson, ed., *The Idaho Digest and Blue Book* (Caldwell, 1935); *The Idaho Daily Statesman* (August 6, 1959). Papers of David W. Davis at the Idaho Historical Society, Boise, Idaho.

MOORE, Charles C., 1923-1927

Born on February 26, 1866 in Holt County, Missouri to Socrates, a farmer, and Eliza (McCune); a member of the Christian Church. Married Minnie McCoy of Fall City, Nebraska on September 15, 1896 who died in 1909; father of Ira W., George C., Marion S., and Mabel; remarried on June 10, 1915 to Clara E. Wallan of

Adams, Oregon. Moore graduated from high school in Mound City, Missouri, and attended teachers' training schools in the area; taught school in Holt and Atchison County, Missouri, from 1886 to 1895. He was Deputy County Assessor in 1894 and County Auditor and Recorder from 1895 to 1898. He and his family moved to Idaho in 1899 where he taught school at St. Anthony in 1900, and then went into the drug business. He sold it in 1903 and associated himself with H. G. Fuller in farming and the sale of farm lands, forming a partnership that was to last more than thirty-five years without benefit of contract. In 1906 Moore and Fuller plotted and organized the town of Ashton, Idaho. Moore helped create the first independent school district of Fremont County, and was on the Board of Trustees in St. Anthony. He organized the St. Anthony Bank and Trust Company and served as its first president. Moore served as a member of the Idaho House of Representatives for two terms, 1903-1907, and while holding this office was instrumental in founding the Idaho Industrial Training School at St. Anthony. He was appointed Postmaster of St. Anthony in 1908 by President Roosevelt, a post which he held for four and a half years. In 1918 and 1920, Moore was elected Lieutenant Governor of Idaho; in 1922 he ran on the Republican ticket for Governor and won. The primary laws had been changed to combat the Non-Partisan League, and if this had not had the effect of splitting the voters into three factions, the Republicans might have found it more difficult to carry the state on an "anti-primary" platform. As it was, the Non-Partisan League (reorganized as the Progressive Party) was the second largest party in the state, with Moore receiving 50,538 votes, H. F. Samuels, Progressive, 40,516 votes, and Moses Alexander, Democrat, receiving 36,810 votes. In 1924 Moore was reelected, receiving 65,408 votes; Samuels, again running as a Progressive, received 58,163 votes, while A. L. Freehafer, a Democrat, polled 25,081. Moore was an "old line" Republican. He vetoed several appropriation bills, as well as a state primary law. During his term as governor, Idaho was authorized by the Secretary of the Interior to build the American Falls Project, one of the largest projects of its type for the time; the North and South highway, the King Hill reclamation project, and the Black Canyon Dam, were all completed; also the main line of the Union Pacific Railroad into Boise was constructed. He took an active stand in favor of sufficient appropriations for the maintaining of educational institutions in the state. Outstanding in his second administration was the passage of a law for the protection of timber and the perpetuation of the forests. After his second term as governor, he served as United States Land Commissioner under President Hoover, 1929-33. Following this he returned to his real estate and farming business. He died of a stroke on March 19, 1958 at the age of 92. Bibliography: Merrill D. Beal and Merle Wells, *History of Idaho* (New York, 1959); Cornelius Brosnan, *History of the State of Idaho* (New York, 1948); Byron Defenbach, *Idaho, The State and Its People* (New York, 1933); G. C. Hobson, ed., *The Idaho Digest and Blue Book* (Caldwell, 1935); F. Ross Peterson, *Idaho, A Bicentennial History* (New York, 1976); *The Idaho Daily Statesman* (March 21, 1958); *The Chronicle News, St. Anthony* (March 27, 1958). Papers of Charles C. Moore at the Idaho Historical Society, Boise, Idaho.

BALDRIDGE, H. Clarence, 1927-1931

Born on November 24, 1868, in Carlock, Illinois to William John and Caroline (Wright) Baldridge; a Presbyterian. Married Cora McCreighton of Hudson, Illinois on February 1, 1893; father of Marion Claire and Lela Gail. Attended the public schools in Illinois and Illinois Wesleyan University until 1893, when he left to teach school in the winter and farm in the summer. In 1896 he organized the grain dealing firm of O'Hara, Baldridge, and Co. in Carlock and remained there until 1904. Baldridge sold his holdings in Carlock and moved to Parma, Idaho, where he became a member of the firm of E. M. Kirkpatrick and Co., a general merchandise store. Disposing of his interest in 1909, he opened an implement and hardware store in Parma. Being a staunch Presbyterian, he was an elder of the church for over a quarter of a century, and a Sunday School Superintendent for twenty years. Baldridge was Chairman of the Board of Trustees for the College of Idaho at Caldwell, Idaho from 1937 to 1945. Soon after coming to Idaho, he became interested in politics and was elected in 1910 to the Idaho State House of Representatives, and in 1912 to the Senate. He was elected Lieutenant Governor in 1922 and again in 1924. Baldridge, a Republican, won the 1926 election easily, since the Democrats remained separate from the Progressives (largely made up of Non-Partisan League voters) and were the minority party they had been in 1922. But to a great extent, he won the election because he was known as a man of great personal integrity. He received 59,460 votes to Progressive W. Scott Hall's 34,208, and Democrat Asher B. Wilson's 24,837. In the 1928 election, the Progressives did not choose to field a candidate and Baldridge won by 87,681 to 63,046 for C. Ben Ross, Democrat. At the beginning of Governor Baldridge's administration, he warned against indiscriminate expansion of public building programs. Regardless of his warnings, several new buildings were approved for the University of Idaho and various charitable institutions. The Southern Branch of the University of Idaho was established at Pocatello. A prison farm for first time offenders was established, and a gasoline tax was put into effect (the proceeds of which were used to redeem an issue of $1,000,000 in treasury notes used for highway building.) The governor was empowered to take over and hold in trust the water rights of the state's principal rivers until it should be decided where the state needs might be. A constitutional amendment was adopted that gave the state authority to limit water power development on any given stream. Baldridge called an economic conference before he left office and organized the state in its efforts to maintain the wage level, keep the people employed, and stabilize the revenues of the state. During the second term of Governor Bottolfsen (1943), Baldridge was appointed Commissioner of Charitable Returns, from which he retired in 1945. He died on June 8, 1947, five and one-half years after his wife, who died in December, 1941. Bibliography: Merrill D. Beal and Merle W. Wells, *History of Idaho* (New York, 1959); Cornelius Brosnan, *History of the State of Idaho* (New York, 1948); *Twenty-first Biennial Report of the Idaho State Historical Department, 1947-1948*; G. C. Hobson, ed., *The Idaho Digest and Blue Book* (Caldwell, 1935); *The Idaho Daily Statesman* (June 9, 1947); the *Parma Herald* (June 12, 1947). Papers of H. C. Baldridge at the Idaho Historical Society, Boise, Idaho.

ROSS, C. Ben, 1931-1937

Born on December 27, 1876 in Parma, Idaho to John, a stock raiser, miner and freighter, and Jeannette (Hadley); a Congregationalist. Married Edna Reavis of Washington County, Idaho on February 14, 1900; father of four adopted children, Helen, Myra, Dewey and Earl. Attended public schools at Parma and Boise, Idaho and Portland, Oregon; an early interest in agriculture led to his vice presidency of the Riverside Irrigation District, 1900-1905; chairman of the Board of County Commissioners of Canyon County, 1915-1920; president and secretary of the Idaho Farm Board, from 1917 to 1922. He settled in Pocatello, Idaho in 1920 and became Mayor of that city in 1922, and continued to hold that office until he became Governor of Idaho on the Democratic ticket in 1930. Actually Ross had run for governor in 1928, but was defeated by the Republican H. C. Baldridge, who received 87,681 votes to Ross' 63,046. In the 1930 election, Ross received 73,896 votes to Republican John McMurray's 58,002. In the election of 1932, Ross increased his majority even more as Byron Defenbach, Republican, received 68,863 votes and Ross received 116,663. He went on to break precedent in Idaho by running for a third term, defeating Frank L. Stephen, his Republican opponent, by a vote of 93,919 to 75,659. He was also the first native son to be elected as Governor of Idaho. Governor Ross ruled with an iron hand and often disregarded the strict letter of the law "to get things done." His decision to close all relief offices in March of 1935 to pressure the legislature into passing a sales tax was an example of this. It was defeated by referendum in 1936 at the polls, however, and was no doubt part of the reason for his defeat in a bid for Senate election that year. Ross had a plan to eliminate the property tax by substituting other taxes in its place, and he almost succeeded. His administration is known for the passing of laws for an income tax, mine tax, kilowatt tax, beer tax, bank fees, and a tax on corporate stock. During Governor Ross' three terms, the following laws were also passed: the Driver's License Bill; an act making the Governor director of emergency relief in cooperation with the federal government; a law providing for the sale of liquor through state dispensaries; a new Initiative and Referendum Law; and a law creating Idaho's "primitive area." Ross ran again for Governor in 1938 only to lose the election to his Republican opponent, C. R. Bottolfsen, 106,268 to 77,697. During his term as Governor, there were rumors that he was a spiritualist and in later years he admitted this to be true. However he saw nothing about this belief to contradict his Congregational faith. He died at his home in Boise on March 31, 1946. Bibliography: Cornelius Brosnan, *History of the State of Idaho* (New York, 1948); Byron Defenbach, *Idaho, The State and Its People* (New York, 1933); G. C. Hobson, ed., *The Idaho Digest and Blue Book* (Caldwell, 1935); F. Ross Peterson, *Idaho, A Bicentennial History* (New York, 1976); *The Idaho Daily Statesman* (April 1 and 2, 1946); Franklin Girard, Secretary of State, *The Twenty-third Biennial Report of the Secretary of State of Idaho* (December, 1936). Papers of C. Ben Ross at the Idaho Historical Society, Boise, Idaho.

CLARK, Barzilla Worth, 1937-1939

Born on December 22, 1880 in Hadley, Indiana to Joseph Addison and Eunice (Hadley) Clark; a Methodist. Married Ethel Peck of Idaho Falls on October 26, 1905; father of Ferris Hadley, Mary Elizabeth, Alice Salome, and Lois Frances. Clark moved with his family to Idaho and settled at Eagle Rock (later Idaho Falls), where he attended grade school, but went to high school in Terre Haute, Indiana and entered Rose Polytechnic Institute there. He injured a lung while training for the hundred yard dash and consequently had to drop out of school. In 1905 Clark was licensed as an engineer in Idaho, and from then until 1937, he was associated with many reservoir and water developments around Idaho Falls. Possibly the most noteworthy development was the Blackfoot Swamp Project which was taken over by the federal government for irrigation in 1907. A Democrat, Clark was elected Councilman of the city of Idaho Falls, 1908-1912; and Mayor, 1913-1915 and 1926-1936. He believed that public affairs should be run on a cash basis. City taxes were kept at a minimum, even though many new improvements were installed in Idaho Falls during his terms in office. These included the installation of a hydroelectric plant, a new water system, and a storm sewer. Clark was elected Governor in 1936; his Republican opposition, Frank L. Stephan, received 83,430 votes to Clark's 115,098. While in office, he sponsored legislation for the regulation of lumbering activities; advocated public development of phosphate beds in eastern Idaho; encouraged aid to dependent persons; adopted a liberal pardon and parole system; and advocated public ownership of hydroelectric sites, even going so far as endeavoring to have the state develop water sites. The Supreme Court of Idaho overruled him on the development of water sites. Provision for a state tuberculosis hospital and for the creation of junior college districts was made during his administration, and the Department of Public Welfare was reorganized. Clark outlined an ambitious legislative program, but the legislature ignored it. He proposed a moderate budget, but more economy-minded legislators made major cuts. Rejection of the sales tax in a referendum in 1936 had left the state treasury short of funds, and consequently Clark felt obliged to veto the 1.7 million dollar appropriation bill because it exceeded the revenue anticipated for the biennium. Laws pertaining to the "six weeks" divorce law, and fish and game legislation, an amendment of the bank code, as well as an act regulating the manufacture, sale and distribution of narcotics, were passed. Clark ran again for Governor in 1938, but was defeated by C. Ben Ross in the Democratic primary. He was keenly interested in Idaho history and after he left office, he wrote a book, *Bonneville County in the Making*, which he published himself in 1941. He died on September 21, 1943 at the age of 62. Bibliography: Merrill D. Beal and Merle Wells, *History of Idaho* (New York, 1959); Cornelius Brosnan, *History of the State of Idaho* (New York, 1948); F. Ross Peterson, *Idaho, A Bicentennial History* (New York, 1976); Franklin Girard, Secretary of State, *The Twenty-third Biennial Report of the Secretary of State of Idaho* (December, 1936); *The Idaho Daily Statesman* (September 21, 1943). Papers of Barzilla W. Clark at the Idaho Historical Society, Boise, Idaho.

BOTTOLFSEN, Clarence A., 1939-1941, 1943-1945

Born on October 10, 1891 in Superior, Wisconsin to Andrew C. and Mary (Carlson) Bottolfsen; a Lutheran. Married to Elizabeth Hanna on August 26, 1912; no children. Moved in 1902 to Fessenden, North Dakota with his family, where he attended the public schools; later took a course at the National Business College, Minneapolis, Minnesota; and began his career in 1905 as a "printer's devil" with the *Wells County News* in Fessenden. Later the paper consolidated with the *Wells County Free Press* and he continued on with the latter. In 1910 Bottolfsen moved to Arco, Idaho to take over the management of the *Arco Advertiser*, a weekly newspaper which had been established by the *Wells County Free Press* the previous year. He purchased the *Arco Advertiser* in 1912, and published it until it was sold in 1947. He was also editor of the *Daily Bulletin* from 1934 to 1938. On June 27, 1918, he entered the army and was sent to Fort Lewis, where he was discharged 12 months later with the rank of Corporal. Bottolfsen was a member of the Lutheran Church, President of the Idaho Editorial Association in 1929, and Commander of the Idaho Department of the American Legion for 1934 and 1935. His political career began when he was elected State Representative in 1920; he was reelected in 1922, 1926, 1928 and 1930. He was Clerk of the House, 1925-1927, and in 1927 became Speaker of the House. In 1936-1938, he was Chairman of the Republican State Central Committee. In 1938 Bottolfsen ran for Governor and defeated C. Ben Ross, Democrat, by a vote of 106,268 to 77,697. In 1940 he ran again, but was defeated by Chase A. Clark, Democrat, by a vote of 120,420 to 118,117. He ran for Governor again in 1942, however, and managed to win, this time against Chase A. Clark, Democrat, with the votes of 72,260 to 71,826. During his four years in office, the state was put on a cash basis and sufficient funds were accumulated to acquire all outstanding bonds when due. This resulted in the state becoming debt free. Governor Bottolfsen also organized the five northwestern states into the Northwestern Development League. A major event of his second administration was the repeal of the Senior Citizens Grant. At the same time, three constitutional amendments were drawn up for submission to the people of the state. The amendments provided for (a) four-year terms for the Governor of the state, (b) creation of a State Tax Board, and (c) a commission to replace the Board of Equalization and to regulate the taxing of federal property in the state when such taxing was approved by the federal government. These amendments all passed at the next election. After Bottolfsen left the office of Governor, he returned to his newspaper business briefly, but agreed to become Chief Clerk of the Idaho House of Representatives in 1949. He served that year also as co-director of the Interim Committee on Reorganization of State Government. In 1953 he became the Deputy Sergeant-at-Arms of the United State Senate. He served as Executive Secretary for Senator Herman Welker of Idaho in 1955 and 1956. He again served as Chief Clerk in the Idaho House in 1957. Bottolfsen was elected to the Idaho Senate in 1958 and was reelected in 1960. He declined to seek reelection in 1962 because of ill health. Clarence A. Bottolfsen died on July 19, 1964 at the age of 72. Bibliography: Merrill D. Beal and Merle Wells, *History of Idaho* (New York, 1959); Cornelius Brosnan, *History of the State of Idaho* (New York, 1948); F. Ross Peterson, *Idaho, A Bicentennial History* (New York, 1976); Ira H. Masters, *The Report of the State and Roster of State, County, and City Elected Officials and The Judiciary of the State of Idaho, 1937-1938*; George H. Curtis, *The Twenty-fifth*

Biennial Report of the Secretary of State of Idaho, 1939-1940; The Idaho Daily Statesman (July 20, 1964). Papers of Clarence A. Bottolfsen at the Idaho Historical Society, Boise, Idaho.

CLARK, Chase A., 1941-1943

Born on August 20, 1883 in Amo, Hendricks County, Indiana, son of Joseph Addison and Eunice (Hadley) Clark; a Presbyterian. Married to Jean Burnett on January 10, 1906. Chase Clark moved to Idaho and settled with his family in Eagle Rock (later Idaho Falls). He graduated from high school in 1900, took an additional year of high school studies at Terre Haute, Indiana, and subsequently went on for advanced studies at the University of Michigan Law School; he did not remain to graduate, but he did pass the Idaho bar exam in 1904. He settled in Mackay, Idaho, and while building up his law practice, developed interests in mining and stock raising. Clark was elected to the State House of Representatives in 1912 and reelected in 1914. He served in the National Guard from 1915 to 1916, placing that branch of the service on a war footing in preparation for World War I. He served as a Second Lieutenant in a machine gun company in the Mexican border dispute of 1916. Upon his discharge, Clark returned to Mackay and remained there until he moved to Idaho Falls in 1930. He was elected to the Idaho Senate in 1933 and again in 1935. He succeeded his brother, Barzilla W. Clark, as the elected Mayor of Idaho Falls in 1937 and was reelected again in 1938. In 1940 he ran for Governor and was elected by a vote of 120,420 to 188,117 votes for Clark's Republican opponent, C. A. Bottolfsen. In the 1942 election, however, Bottolfsen beat him by the slim margin of a little over 400 votes, 71,826 to 72,260. His administration was the usual wartime administration, with the legislature and people both conscious of inflation, among other things. During Clark's term as governor, the people voted approval on constitutional amendments establishing a nonpartisan State Board of Correction; $10 instead of $5, per acre, was set as the minimum sale price of state-owned land; an Unfair Sales Act was passed; and the Department of Public Health was divided into three parts: the Departments of Public Assistance, of Public Health, and of Charitable Institutions. Also under the terms of the Senior Citizens Act, $40.00 a month was provided to all Idahoans over 65, as well as $8.00 a month medical expenses, and $100.00 for funeral expenses. After he lost the election of 1942, Chase A. Clark became a Federal District Court Judge, a position which he occupied until just before [his] death. Clark came from an illustrious political family. His father ran for Idaho's governorship (unsuccessfully) on the Prohibitionist ticket in 1904. His brother was governor from 1937 to 1939, and his only daughter married Senator Frank Church. Chase A. Clark died on December 29, 1966 in Idaho Falls, Idaho. Bibliography: Merrill D. Beal and Merle Wells, *History of Idaho* (New York, 1959); Cornelius Brosnan, *History of the State of Idaho* (New York, 1948); F. Ross Peterson, *Idaho, A Bicentennial History* (New York, 1976); George W. Curtis, *Twenty-sixth Biennial Report of the Secretary of State of Idaho, 1943-1945; The Idaho Daily Statesman* (December 30 and 31, 1966). Papers of Chase A. Clark at the Idaho Historical Society, Boise, Idaho.

BOTTOLFSEN, Clarence A., 1939-1941, 1943-1945

GOSSETT, Charles C., 1945

Born on September 2, 1888, in Princetown, near Hillsboro, Ohio, to James Watt and Margaret (Finnigan) Gossett; a member of the Christian Church. Married Clara L. Fleming on November 27, 1916 in Ontario, Oregon; father of James Wyatt, Robert Milton, and Charles Elmer. Attended public schools near Princetown, and at the age of 18, went west to Othello, Washington with friends. He worked in Othello for a few years, doing farm work and then homesteaded in the Nyssa-Ontario, Oregon area in 1910. Moving to Nampa, Idaho in 1922, he began farming and raising livestock in the Deer Flat area. Gossett was elected to serve in the Idaho House of Representatives in 1932 and was reelected in 1934. In 1933 he helped form an economy bloc in the Idaho Legislature and was elected its Chairman. During his second term, he was Chairman of the Agriculture Committee. He was elected to the office of Lieutenant Governor in 1936 and again in 1940. Charles C. Gossett was elected Governor of Idaho in 1944 by a vote of 109,527 to 98,532 over his Republican opponent, W. H. Detweiler. The people had chosen a Republican Legislature, so in his message to the legislature he stressed unity and teamwork and pledged his efforts to bring this about. He asked that a program be adopted which would adequately meet the needs of public assistance and this was done. During his administration, a State Teachers' Emergency Salary Aid fund was created; the salaries of the elective state officials were increased; an appropriation of $15,000 was made for the purpose of having a bronze statue of Senator William E. Borah made and placed in Statuary Hall in Washington, D.C. A bill legalizing *parimutuel* gambling was passed in both houses, but Governor Gossett vetoed the bill. An appropriation was made for a survey of the state's schools, which resulted in the Peabody Report recommending a four year college at Pocatello and the consolidation of the public schools. The gasoline tax was increased by one cent and the cigarette tax by a like amount. In November 1945, the year Gossett took office, he resigned and was appointed by his successor, Arnold Williams, to take over the unexpired position of United States Senator, John Thomas, who had died. However, in Gossett's bid for election to a full term, he was defeated. He was a delegate to the Democratic National Convention in 1952; was appointed to the Idaho Tax Commission in 1956; and had run unsuccessfully for State Senator in 1942 and for Governor in 1954. In 1948 Gossett became a director of King Pack Company; eventually he was appointed vice president and manager of the G. K. Livestock Company; and he continued in his executive duties until the firm was sold to the Safeway Stores in 1955. Charles C. Gossett's wife preceded him in death on April 14, 1967, and he passed away on September 20, 1974. Bibliography: Merrill D. Beal and Merle Wells, *History of Idaho* (New York, 1959); F. Ross Peterson, *Idaho, A Bicentennial History* (New York, 1976); Ira H. Masters, *Twenty-eighth Biennial Report of the Secretary of State and Roster of State, County, and Judicial Officials, 1935-1936; Twenty-first Biennial Report of the Idaho State Historical Department, 1947-1948; The Idaho Daily Statesman* (September 20, 1974). Papers of Charles G. Gossett at the Idaho Historical Society, Boise, Idaho.

WILLIAMS, Arnold, 1945-1947

Born on May 21, 1898 in Fillmore, Utah, son of William and Annie (Rutherford) Williams; a Mormon. Married Luella Huskinson on June 2, 1919 in Idaho Falls, Idaho; father of Reed A. and Corine. He received his early education in the public schools in Fillmore and later attended Hennager's Business College at Salt Lake City. He moved to Rexburg, Idaho at the age of 17 and joined the army in 1918, but was discharged soon after the Armistice. After his discharge from the army, he entered the dry cleaning business, which he continued to operate for twenty-five years. Williams was elected to serve as Madison County Commissioner in 1932 and served two terms. In 1936 he was elected to the Idaho State House of Representatives and was reelected in 1938 and 1940. He served as Majority Floor Leader in 1941 and was elected Lieutenant Governor in 1944. When Senator John Thomas died in Washington, Governor Charles C. Gossett resigned and was appointed to fill the unfinished term as Senator. Thus Arnold Williams became Governor of the State of Idaho in 1945. He became the second governor to attain his position by his predecessor's resignation. In 1945 he called a special session of the legislature to enact the Teachers' Retirement Law, which was an attempt to arrest the outward flow of the educators to surrounding states. The law, among other things, permitted retirement at age 60 and made it mandatory at age 70. Ten years later, a provision was added that enabled educators to qualify for social security. Also during this special session, administration of state charitable institutions was reorganized to encourage the development of a professional welfare service. In 1946 Williams was unable to win the election from his Republican opponent, C. A. Robbins, who received 102,233 votes to Williams' 79,131. The Republicans were to retain control of the governorship for the next twenty-four years. Williams retired from public life for a few years and later became Secretary of State in 1959, a capacity in which he served for seven and a half years. He also served as Secretary of the Idaho Senate in 1957. After retiring from public life a second time, Arnold Williams lived quietly in Boise, moved to Idaho Falls in 1968, and died on May 25, 1970 at the age of 72. Bibliography: Merrill D. Beal and Merle Wells, *History of Idaho* (New York, 1959); Cornelius Brosnan, *History of the State of Idaho* (New York, 1948); F. Ross Peterson, *Idaho, A Bicentennial History* (New York, 1976); *The Twenty-first Biennial Report of the Idaho State Historical Department, 1947-1948*; George W. Curtis, *Twenty-fifth Biennial Report of the Secretary of State of Idaho, 1939-1940*; George W. Curtis, *Twenty-sixth Biennial Report of the Secretary of State of Idaho, 1941-1942; The Idaho Daily Statesman* (March 27, 1970). Papers of Arnold Williams at the Idaho Historical Society, Boise, Idaho.

ROBINS, Clarence Armington, 1947-1951

Born on December 8, 1884 in Defiance, Iowa to Charles M. and Rebecca Jane (Burke) Robins; an Episcopalian. At the age of four, Clarence Robins moved with his family to Colorado to live, first in Rocky Ford and then in La Junta where his father became Clerk of the District Court. He graduated from La Junta High School and went on to William Jewell College in Liberty, Missouri, where he received his bachelor's degree in 1907. Robins then taught school for the next six years in a variety of places, including Springfield, Missouri; Billings, Montana; and Laurel, Mississippi. In 1913 he entered Rush Medical School at Chicago University and graduated in 1917; he did his internship at Cincinnati General Hospital. Robins volunteered for the Army Medical Corps in 1918 and was commissioned as a First Lieutenant, but the war ended the year he enlisted and he was discharged at Camp Sherman, Ohio. Married Marguerite Cranberry in 1919 in St. Maries, Idaho; took an active part in building the local hospital. Robins was elected to the Idaho Senate in 1938 and was reelected in 1940, 1942 and 1944. He was President Pro Tempre, Majority Leader, and Chairman of the State Affairs Committee in 1943. After being elected in 1944, he resigned, as another doctor in St. Maries had died and the town was left without enough physicians. In 1946 Robins was drafted to run for Governor on the Republican ticket and he won over his Democratic opponent, Arnold Williams, by a vote of 102,233 to 79,131. Important accomplishments during Governor Robins' administration were: school reorganization, with the number of school districts reduced from 1,063 to less than 200; abolition of the old Board of Pardons and establishment of the Board of Corrections; and creation of Idaho State College at Pocatello as a four-year institution. He recommended the repeal of the slot machine law but the legislature did not follow his recommendation; it also passed the "liquor-by-the-drink" law. Clarence Robins has been called "the governor who moved Idaho into the twentieth century" because of his role in public education, public health, and public welfare. He was the first governor to be elected for a term of four years according to the new constitutional amendment that had been recently passed. The law then read that he could not run for governor again, so he ran unsuccessfully for United States Senator in 1951. Robins was preparing to resume medical practice in St. Maries when he was appointed Director of North Idaho District Medical Service Bureau in Lewiston, a position which he held until May, 1958, when he was forced to retire because of a heart attack. He was a member of many fraternal organizations, a member of the Idaho State Medical Association, as well as the American Medical Association. He died on September 20, 1970 at the age of 85 in Lewiston, Idaho. Bibliography: Merrill D. Beal and Merle Wells, *History of Idaho* (New York, 1959); F. Ross Peterson, *Idaho, A Bicentennial History* (New York, 1976); *Lewiston Morning Tribune* (September 21, and 23, 1970); *The Idaho Daily Statesman* (September 21, 1970); *Twenty-first Biennial Report of the Idaho State Historical Department;* Ira Masters, *Twenty-eighth Report of the Secretary of State and Roster of State, County, Legislative and Judicial Officials, 1945-46;* J. D. "Cy" Price, *Twenty-ninth Biennial Report of the Idaho Secretary of State and the Roster of the State, County, Legislative and Judicial Officials, Correct as of December 1, 1942.* Papers of Charles Armington Robins at the Idaho Historical Society, Boise, Idaho.

JORDAN, Leonard Beck, 1951-1955

Born on May 15, 1899 to Leonard Eugene, an accountant, and Mary Irene (Beck) Jordan in Mount Pleasant, Utah; a Methodist. Married to Grace Edgington on December 30, 1925 in Bend, Oregon; father of Patricia Jean, Joseph Leonard, and Stephen Edgington. The family moved to Enterprise, Oregon when Leonard (Len) B. Jordan was a child. He went to high school there and in 1917 he entered

Utah State College in Logan, Utah. He took military training in school and went to summer training with his unit at O.T.S. Presidio in San Francisco, California in 1918. He was transferred to Camp Hancock, Georgia in September of 1918 to undergo machine gun training and remained there until January 1919, earning the rank of Second Lieutenant. He was transferred to Camp Grant, Illinois and was discharged on January 13, 1919. Returning to Oregon, Jordan entered the University of Oregon in the fall of 1920. He received his Bachelor of Arts degree and was elected to Phi Beta Kappa. He returned to the university to begin studies toward a master's degree in economics, but instead went to work in Portland, Oregon. In the spring of 1926 he returned to Wallowa, Oregon, and went into ranching for himself. After selling his interests in his ranch at Wallowa four years later, he moved to the Snake River and bought ranching interests there. He was eventually to give this up and move to Grangeville, Idaho, for the education of his children. He was elected to the State Legislature in 1946 and was appointed by Governor Robins as chairman of an Interim Committee on Highway Problems. In 1948 he was defeated for reelection to the State Legislature. Jordan won the nomination for Governor in 1950 and eventually the election, by a margin of 107,642 votes to 97,150 for his Democratic opponent, Calvin E. Wright. Jordan served only one term, since at that time governors could not succeed themselves. His administration saw the adoption of the State Highway Commission which removed highways from political patronage. The law also provided tenure and professional status for the personnel. Governor Jordan worked vigorously for an improved long-range highway program. He also worked for greater emphasis on teaching the fundamentals in the elementary and high schools of the state. During his administration, the State Board of Education adopted a sixty-five percent formula for the transportation costs to be included in the School Equalization Program; a law creating a ton gross weight of one ton mile tax was passed; slot machines were outlawed; unemployment insurance, employment and job training services were consolidated. In 1954 President Eisenhower appointed Governor Jordan Chairman of the International Joint Commission of the United States and Canada to take effect as soon as his term as governor expired in 1955. He was to hold this position until 1957. In 1956 he was granted a leave of absence in order to survey the water resource development in the Helmud River Valley of Afghanistan for the Tudor Engineering Company of San Francisco. Jordan was a member of the International Development Advisory Board between Canada and the United States, 1957-1958. He was elected to the United States Senate in 1962 and was a member of that body until 1973. Since retiring to his home in Boise, Idaho, he has served on various corporate boards, and has been an active member of his community. He is a Methodist and has served on the church board, both before and after going to Washington, D.C. Bibliography: Merrill D. Beal and Merle Wells, *History of Idaho* (New York, 1919); F. Ross Peterson, *Idaho, A Bicentennial History* (New York, 1976); J. D. "Cy" Price, *The Thirtieth Biennial Report of the Idaho Secretary of State, 1949-1950; The Idaho Daily Statesman* (November 7 and 8, 1950). Personal correspondence with Leonard B. Jordan. Papers of Leonard B. Jordan at the Idaho Historical Society, Boise, Idaho.

SMYLIE, Robert E., 1955-1967

Born on October 31, 1914 in Marcus, Iowa to Lorne Francis, a schoolmaster, and Ida Mae (Stevens) Smylie; a United Methodist. Married Lucille Caroline Strong, nee Irwin on December 4, 1943; father of Robert William and Richard Steven. Robert Smylie came to Idaho and attended the College of Idaho at Caldwell; he received his Bachelor of Arts degree in 1938. He received his Degree of Juris Doctor from George Washington University in 1942. He was admitted to the bar in the District of Columbia and began his law practice there. From 1942 to 1946, he was a member of the Coast Guard and attained the rank of Lieutenant. In 1947 he became Assistant Attorney General at Boise, Idaho, and ten months later, he was appointed as Attorney General to fill a vacancy. In 1950 he was elected to the position. As a lawyer, he belongs to the Order of the Coif and Phi Alpha Delta, as well as to the state and national bar groups. Robert E. Smylie was the first person to succeed himself in the governorship of Idaho since the term of office had been lengthened to four years. He won against his Democratic opponent, Clark Hamilton, by a score of 124,033 votes to 104,647 in 1954. He won by the smallest majority in 1958 against A. M. Derr with a vote of 121,180 to 117,236, but in 1962, he was clearly victorious against Vernon K. Smith, with a vote of 139,577 to 115,876. There were many changes during his twelve years as governor. His administration was responsible for the following: perfection of the Employment Security Law in 1955, 1957, 1959, 1961 and 1963; maintenance of a balanced budget through the years 1955-1967; implementation of a state minimum wage law for 1957; acquisition of Farragut State Park and Harriman State Park; construction of buildings at state universities, 1955-65; Permanent Building Fund Act, 1961; Public Employees' Retirement System, 1963; State Personnel Commission, 1965; creation of the State Parks Department, 1965; Fiscal Responsibility Acts, including the sales tax, 1965. A State Board of Health was also established, as well as a State Department of Commerce and Development. The State Income Tax Law was amended to provide a plan for withholding salaries. Also in keeping with the mood of the country, a loyalty oath was adopted in the mid-1950s. In addition, Northern Idaho College of Education was reopened as a two-year school, with its name changed to "Lewis-Clark Normal." Governor Smylie chose to run for reelection again in 1966, but he lost the nomination for a fourth term in the primary. Since Robert Smylie's term as governor, he has been a member of the Advisory Commission on Inter-Governmental Relations and a counsel to the Idaho Legislative-Executive Reorganization Commission for 1975-1976. He is a partner in the law firm of Langroise, Sullivan, and Smylie in Boise, Idaho. In addition, he is a lecturer, author, investment counselor, and a corporate acquisitions consultant. He resides, with his wife, in Boise, Idaho. Bibliography: Merrill D. Beal and Merle Wells, *History of Idaho* (New York, 1959); F. Ross Peterson, *Idaho, A Bicentennial History* (New York, 1976); Ira H. Master, *The Thirty-Second Report of the Secretary of State, 1953-1954;* Jas. H. Young, *The Thirty-Third Biennial Report of the Secretary of State, 1955-1956;* Jas. H. Young, *Thirty-fourth Biennial Report of the Secretary of State of Idaho, 1957-1958;* Arnold Williams, *Report of the Secretary of State of Idaho, 1961-1962; The Idaho Daily Statesman* (November 2 and 3, 1954, November 4 and 5, 1958 and November 6 and 7, 1962). Papers of Robert E. Smylie at the Idaho Historical Society, Boise, Idaho; personal correspondence with Robert E. Smylie.

SAMUELSON, Donald William, 1967-1971

Born on July 27, 1913 in Woodhull, Illinois to Fred W. and Nellie M. (Johnson) Samuelson; a Methodist. Married to Ruby A. Mayo on February 22, 1936; father of Stephen Lee and Donna Jean. Don Samuelson graduated from high school in 1932 and attended Knox College in Galesburg, Illinois. He served in the United States Navy during World War II as a Gunner's Mate, Instructor, and Small Arms Gunsmith at Camp Farragut, a naval base outside of the small town of Sandpoint, Idaho. Upon his discharge from the navy, Samuelson returned to Iowa for a brief time and then went to Idaho to make his home in Sandpoint. His early years on his father's farm influenced him as an adult into being an "outdoor man"; his private business from 1946-1966 was for 14 years a retail sporting goods store and then was a construction equipment business covering the states of Idaho, Montana and ten counties in eastern Washington. He was also responsible for starting the first hunter safety course in Idaho, was vice president of the State Wildlife Association, and Chairman of the Sandpoint Recreation Board. He was elected to the Idaho State Senate in 1960 and served for three terms, 1961-1967. While on that body, Samuelson served as Chairman of the Public Resources Committee, was on the Public Recreation Committee, and served on the Senate Finance Committee. In the 1966 election, the Democrats were split among several factions due to the fact that their candidate, Charles Herndon, was killed in a plane crash shortly before the November election. Cecil D. Andrus got the approval of the party and though he polled 93,744 votes in the general election, it was the Republican Samuelson with 104,586 votes who was the winner. His administration reorganized many branches of the state government, such as the State Land Department, State Finance Department, State Insurance Department. Also, a beginning was made on the reorganization of the State Mental Health Program; the first Inventory of State Chattel Property was developed; and a procedure was set up to modernize the state's emergency equipment. The State Budget Office and the State Auditor's Office were modernized and brought under the direct supervision of the governor. Samuelson's administration also brought many professionally trained people and many modern business methods into the Idaho state government. Governor Samuelson ran for reelection in 1970, but was defeated by Cecil D. Andrus by a vote of 128,004 to 117,108. Since retiring from the position of Governor, Samuelson was appointed Secretarial Representative of the Secretary of Transportation for Region 10, covering Idaho, Washington, Oregon, and Alaska. He retired from this position in 1976 and presently makes his home in Sandpoint, Idaho. Bibliography: Department of Transportation [provided by Governor Samuelson] "Don Samuelson"; Louis E. Clapp, Secretary of State, *Compiled Annual and Biennial Reports, 1965-1966*, Vol. II; Pete Cenarrusa, Secretary of State, *The "Gem State," Idaho Blue Book of 1971-1972* [*with the 1970 Election Returns*]. Personal correspondence with Governor Samuelson; Papers of Don Samuelson at the Idaho Historical Society, Boise, Idaho.

ANDRUS, Cecil Dale, 1971-1977

Born on August 25, 1931, in Hood River, Oregon, to Hal and Dorothy Mae (Johnson) Andrus; a Lutheran. Married to Carol M. May in Reno, Nevada on August 27, 1949; father of Tana, Tracy, and Kelly. Cecil Andrus grew up on a farm in logging country, where he worked in the woods and sawmills. After a year at Oregon State University, Andrus joined the United States Navy and saw duty during the Korean War. He came to Orofino, Idaho in 1955 where he was a sawmill owner and operator; he also sold life insurance, eventually moving to Lewiston, Idaho, to become State Director for Paul Revere Life Insurance Company. He served as Senator in the Idaho State Legislature from Clearwater County from 1960 until 1966 and from District 5 (Nez Perce and Lewiston) from 1968 until 1970. In 1966 Andrus was chosen to run for governor after Charles Herndon, the Democratic candidate for Governor, was killed in a plane crash. He lost to Don Samuelson, Republican, 104,586 votes to 93,744. Andrus ran for governor against Don Samuelson again in 1970, and won the election by a vote of 128,004 to 117,108. His Senate career had already shown a marked evidence of responsibility in his strong support for education, his sense of fiscal accountability, and his work for legislation in the fields of conservation, social services, business, and agriculture. His governorship simply carried this on to a further degree. An executive reorganization measure he spearheaded in 1972 streamlined the state bureaucracy from 270 agencies, boards, and commissions to 19 state departments. He had been a strong advocate of locally controlled, state-assisted, land-use planning. He strongly supported such things as regional approaches to the delivery of health services, better funding of education by the state, and fiscal solvency. Under his leadership, he brought about a reduction in property taxes in both 1973 and 1974. He managed to do this while keeping a financially sound position, with no debts and no encumbrances carried over into new fiscal years. Cecil Andrus was reelected in the 1974 gubernatorial election by defeating his Republican opponent, Jack M. Murphy, by a vote of 184,142 to 68,731. He was named to the Executive Committee of the National Governors' Conference and served from 1971 to 1972. He served as Chairman of the Rocky Mountain Federation of States from 1970 to 1972. It was through that organization that Cecil Andrus brought an educational satellite into use for isolated Idaho communities. He was elected Chairman of the National Governors' Conference in 1976 and resigned when he was nominated Secretary of the Interior. Upon being appointed Secretary of the Interior by President Carter in 1977, Cecil Andrus resigned his position as governor. Bibliography: *Biographical Sketch of Cecil D. Andrus, 42nd Secretary of the Interior*, January, 1977; Pete Cenarrusa, Secretary of State, *"The Gem State," The Idaho Blue Book, 1971-1972* [*with the 1970 Election Returns*]; Pete Cenarrusa, Secretary of State, *"The Gem State," The Idaho Blue Book, 1975-1976* [*with the 1974 Election Returns*]. Personal correspondence with Cecil D. Andrus; Papers of Cecil D. Andrus at the Idaho Historical Society, Boise, Idaho.

EVANS, John V., 1977-

Born on January 18, 1925 in Malad City, Idaho to David Lloyd and Margaret (Thomas) Evans; a Mormon. Married Lola Daniels in Malad City on April 29, 1945; father of David L., John Victor, Martha Anne, Susan Dee, and Thomas Daniels. He has lived virtually his entire life in Malad City, except for army service during World War II (when he rose to the rank of Technical Sergeant) and when he was studying for his bachelor's degree in Business and Economics at Stanford University. In Malad City, he has engaged in farming, ranching, and various business enterprises. He has always been greatly interested in conservation, as shown by his service as president of the Bear River Water Users Association, his membership on the National Legislators Committee on Natural Resources, and by his six years as president of the Oneida County Resources, Conservation and Development Committee. Following in the footsteps of his grandfather, who served as Speaker of the Idaho House of Representatives in 1953, Evans began his legislative career at the age of 27 when he was elected to the Idaho Senate. Except for the two terms he was Mayor of Malad City in the early 60s, he served continuously from 1953 to 1974. He was Senate Majority Leader, 1957-1969, and Minority Leader, 1969-1974. He received the Distinguished Service Award from the Association of Idaho Cities in June, 1974 for meritorious performance during his legislative career. He was elected Lieutenant Governor of Idaho in 1974 and was elected in August, 1975 to the Executive Board of the National Conference of Lieutenant Governors. When Governor Cecil Andrus was appointed United States Secretary of the Interior, John V. Evans became Governor of Idaho on January 24, 1977. His swearing in marked the second time that Idaho has had a member of the Church of Latter Day Saints (Mormon) as governor. (The first was Governor Arnold Williams, 1945-1946.) This represents substantial progress for the Mormons since the 1890s when the state of Idaho tried to disenfranchise all Mormons. It is impossible to evaluate Governor Evans' term, since he stepped into office during the middle of a legislative session. He has spent considerable time getting many executive proposals enacted into law. His biggest problem to date was the 1977 drought, the most serious for the state in its history. The water shortage poses problems with agricultural irrigation and with generation of hydroelectric power. Bibliography: Pete Cenarrusa, Secretary of State, *The "Gem State," the Idaho Blue Book, 1975-1976 [with the 1974 Election Returns]; The Idaho Daily Statesman* (January 23, 24, 25, 1977). Personal correspondence with John V. Evans; the file of John V. Evans has just been started at the Idaho Historical Society, Boise, Idaho.

ILLINOIS

ILLINOIS

BOND, Shadrack, 1818-1822

Born on November 24, 1773 in Fredericktown, Frederick County, Maryland; son of Nicodemus, a landowner, and Rachel (Stevenson) Bond; a Methodist-Episcopalian. Brother of nine, among whom was Benjamin Bond. Married to Achsah Bond on November 27, 1810; father of five daughters and two sons, among whom were Julia Rachel, Mary Achsah, Isabella Fell, Thomas Shadrach, and Benjamin Nicodemus Bond. Attended common schools in Frederick County, Maryland. Moved to present-day Monroe County, Illinois in 1794, where he was engaged in agricultural pursuits. Served as a member of the Indiana Territory Legislative Council from 1805 to 1808; appointed Lieutenant Colonel Commandant of militia on May 3, 1809; appointed Justice of the Peace of St. Clair County on December 9, 1809; appointed an aide-de-camp to the Commander-in-Chief of the Illinois Territorial Militia on March 7, 1812; appointed Judge of the Court of Common Pleas for St. Clair County on April 4, 1812; elected as a Democratic delegate from Illinois Territory to the United States House of Representatives on October 10, 1812, and served from December 3, 1812 to October 3, 1814; appointed Receiver of Public Moneys in the General Land Office at Kaskaskia, Illinois on October 3, 1814 and served in that capacity until 1818. As the Democratic-Republican gubernatorial candidate, Bond was elected Governor of Illinois by popular vote in the election held from September 17 to September 19, 1818, receiving 3,426 votes; he was unopposed. Inaugurated on October 6, 1818, Bond recommended a revision of the newly created state laws. He urged the importance of a canal to connect Lake Michigan with the Illinois River; called attention to the subject of education; advised that provisions for the leasing of salt springs be made. Legislation passed during his term included the enactment of a revenue law which provided for the raising of money for state purposes by taxing the lands of non-residents; the state capital was moved from Kaskaskia to Vandalia; and the State Bank of Illinois was chartered. Because the Illinois Constitution of 1818 prohibited a governor from succeeding himself, Bond left office on December 5, 1822 and returned to his farming interests. Appointed Register of the Land Office for the District of Kaskaskia on December 5, 1823, serving in this capacity until his death. Bond died on April 12, 1832 at Kaskaskia, Randolph County, Illinois; buried in Evergreen Cemetery, Chester, Randolph County, Illinois. Bibliography: Alexander Davidson and Bernard Stuve, *A Complete History of Illinois from 1673 to 1873* (Springfield, 1874); State Centennial Commission, *Centennial History of Illinois*, 5 vols. (Springfield, 1917-1920); Kinnie A. Ostwig, "Life of Shadrack Bond, The First Governor of Illinois under Statehood," *Transactions of the Illinois State Historical Society*, no. 36 (1929); Roy Glashan, *American Governors and Gubernatorial Elections 1775-1975* (Stillwater, Minnesota, 1975).

COLES, Edward, 1822-1826

Born on December 15, 1786 at "Enniscorthy," Albemarle County, Virginia; son of John, a Revolutionary War officer, and Rebecca (Tucker) Coles; a Protestant. Brother of nine. Married to Sally Logan Roberts on November 28, 1833; father of one daughter and two sons, one of whom was Edward Coles, Jr. Privately educated; attended Hampden-Sydney College and the College of William and Mary. Served as private secretary to President James Madison from 1809 to 1815; sent to St. Petersburg on a diplomatic mission in 1816. Coles settled in Edwardsville, Illinois in 1818 after returning from Russia. He was appointed Register of the Land Office in Edwardsville on March 5, 1819, serving in that capacity until 1822. As the Democratic-Republican gubernatorial candidate, Coles was elected Governor of Illinois by popular vote on August 5, 1822, defeating his fellow Democratic-Republican opponents, Joseph Phillips and Thomas C. Browne, by a vote of 3,854 to 2,687 and 2,443, respectively; inaugurated on December 5, 1822. During his administration, Coles recommended that the Black Laws be revised and that adequate laws to repress kidnapping be enacted; the legislature reorganized the judiciary by creating both circuit and supreme courts; the effort to make Illinois a slave state was defeated. Because the Illinois Constitution of 1818 prohibited a governor from succeeding himself, Coles left office on December 6, 1826 and retired to private life. He was an unsuccessful candidate for the U.S. Senate in 1824 and for the U.S. House of Representatives in 1831. He moved to Philadelphia, Pennsylvania in 1833, where he resided until his death. Coles died on July 7, 1868 in Philadelphia, Pennsylvania. Bibliography: Alexander Davidson and Bernard Stuve, *A Complete History of Illinois from 1673 to 1873* (Springfield, 1874); State Centennial Commission, *Centennial History of Illinois*, 5 vols. (Springfield, 1917-1920); Theodore Pease, *Illinois Election Returns, 1818-1848* (Springfield, 1923); Roy Glashan, *American Governors and Gubernatorial Elections, 1775-1975* (Stillwater, Minnesota, 1975).

EDWARDS, Ninian, 1826-1830

Born on March 17, 1775 at the Edwards farm "Mount Pleasant," Montgomery County, Maryland; eldest child of Benjamin, United States Senator from Kentucky, and Margaret (Beall) Edwards; a Baptist. Married to Elvira Lane in 1803; father of Ninian Wirt Edwards. Attended private schools; graduated from Dickinson College, Carlisle, Pennsylvania in 1792; studied law. Moved to Bardstown, Kentucky in 1795; member of the Kentucky House of Representatives in 1796 and 1797; admitted to the bar in 1798 and began law practice in Russellville, Kentucky. Served as Judge of the General Court of Kentucky in 1803; served as a Democratic presidential elector in 1804; served as Judge of the Court of Appeals in 1806 and Chief Justice of Kentucky in 1808. Appointed Governor of Illinois Territory by President James Madison, serving from 1809 to 1818, at which time Illinois became a state. Elected to the U.S. Senate, serving from December 3, 1818 to March 4, 1824, at which time he resigned to accept the appointment of Minister to Mexico; recalled to testify before a select committee of the U.S. House of Representatives appointed to investigate charges made by him against William H. Crawford,

Secretary of the Treasury. Resumed law practice; engaged in mercantile pursuits. As the Democratic-Republican gubernatorial candidate, Edwards was elected Governor of Illinois by popular vote on August 7, 1826, defeating the Jackson-Democratic candidate, Thomas Sloo, Jr., by a vote of 6,280 to 5,833; inaugurated on December 6, 1826. During his administration, Edwards waged an attack on those responsible for the administration of the State Bank at Edwardsville, Illinois; the circuit court system was repealed; and the governor urged removal of Indians from the state, insisting that the state had the right to that part of the public domain lying within its borders. Because the Illinois Constitution of 1818 prohibited· a governor from succeeding himself, Edwards left office on December 6, 1830, retiring to his home in Belleville, Illinois. Edwards died on July 20, 1833; buried in Belleville, Illinois. Reinterred in Oak Ridge Cemetery, Springfield, Illinois in 1855. Bibliography: Ninian W. Edwards, *History of Illinois from 1778 to 1833; and Life and Times of Ninian Edwards* (Springfield, 1870); State Centennial Commission, *Centennial History of Illinois*, 5 vols. (Springfield, 1917-1920); W. G. Norton, "Ninian Edwards," *Journal of the Illinois State Historical Society*, vol. XVII, no. 1-2 (April-July, 1924); Roy Glashan, *American Governors and Gubernatorial Elections, 1775-1975* (Stillwater, Minnesota, 1975).

REYNOLDS, John, 1830-1834

Born on February 26, 1788 near Philadelphia, Montgomery County, Pennsylvania; son of Robert, an Irish immigrant, and Margaret (Moore) Reynolds; a Protestant. Eldest of six children. Married first to Madame Catherine (Dubuque) Lacroix Manegle in 1817; remarried after her death, to Sarah Wilson in 1836; no children. Moved with his family to Tennessee in 1789; moved to Illinois in 1800, settling near Kaskaskia. Attended the school of Reverend Isaac Anderson in Knoxville, Tennessee; read law with John McCampbell. During the War of 1812, served with Captain William B. Whiteside's company, earning the title of "Old Ranger." Admitted to the Illinois Bar and began law practice in Cahokia, Illinois in 1814. Elected a Justice of the Illinois Supreme Court, serving from 1818 to 1824; unsuccessful candidate for the U.S. Senate in 1823; served as a member of the Illinois House of Representatives from 1827 to 1829. As the Democratic-Republican gubernatorial candidate, Reynolds was elected Governor of Illinois by popular vote on August 2, 1830, defeating the Jacksonian-Democratic candidate, William Kinney, by a vote of 12,837 to 8,938; inaugurated on December 6, 1830. During his administration, the criminal code was adapted to the penitentiary system; notes of the old State Bank were redeemed; the "Wiggins Loan" of $100,000 was authorized; several charters were granted for the incorporation of railroad companies; and the Illinois militia cooperated with Federal troops during the Black Hawk War. Reynolds resigned the Illinois governorship on November 17, 1834, having been elected to the U.S. House of Representatives to fill the vacancy caused by the death of Charles Slade; subsequently reelected to the Twenty-Fourth Congress, serving from December 1, 1834 to March 3, 1837; unsuccessful candidate for reelection in 1836. Again elected to two terms in the U.S. House of Representatives, serving from March 4, 1839 to March 3, 1843. Served as a member of the Illinois House of Representatives from 1846 to 1848, and from 1852 to 1854, being elected Speaker during the latter term; unsuccessful candidate to the Illinois Senate in 1848; unsuccessful candidate for Illinois Superintendent of Schools in 1858; selected as an anti-Douglas delegate to the Democratic Convention of 1860, but was denied a seat. Author of *Remarks on the Civil and Diplomatic Appropriation Bill* (1840); *Pioneer History* (1852); *Sketches of the Country on the Northern Route from Belleville to the City of New York and Back by the Ohio Valley, Together with a Glance at the Crystal Palace* (1854); *Friendship's Offering* (1858); *The Old Line Democracy Forever* (1858); *Anti-Insurrection Meeting* (1859); *The Political Olive Branch* (1860); *The Balm of Gilead* (1860); *John Reynolds, My Own Times* (1855). Reynolds died on May 8, 1865 in Belleville, St. Clair County, Illinois. He was buried at Walnut Hill Cemetery. Bibliography: Alexander Davidson and Bernard Stuve, *A Complete History of Illinois from 1673 to 1873* (Springfield, 1874); State Centennial Commission, *Centennial History of Illinois*, 5 vols. (Springfield, 1917-1920); Jessie McHarry, "John Reynolds," *Journal of the Illinois State Historical Society*, vol. VI, no. 1 (April, 1913); Roy Glashan, *American Governors and Gubernatorial Elections, 1775-1975* (Stillwater, Minnesota, 1975).

EWING, William Lee Davidson, 1834

Born on August 31, 1795 in Paris, Bourbon County, Kentucky; son of the Reverend Finis, one of the founders of the Cumberland Presbyterian Church, and Peggy (Davidson) Ewing; a Presbyterian. Married to a daughter of Elijah E. Berry, first State Auditor of Illinois. Privately educated; studied law; admitted to the bar and began the practice of law in Shawneetown, Illinois. Appointed Receiver of Public Monies in the Land Office at Vandalia, Illinois in 1820 by President James Monroe. Served as Brigadier General of the Illiniois State militia and as a Colonel of the "Spy Battalion" during the Black Hawk War. Served as clerk of the Illinois House of Representatives from 1826 to 1828; served as a member and Speaker of the Illinois House of Representatives in 1830; served as a member of the Illinois Senate from 1832 to 1834, having been chosen President Pro Tempore of that body in 1832. Commissioned acting Lieutenant Governor of Illinois on March 1, 1833 to fill the vacancy caused by the resignation of Zadoc Casey. Ewing assumed the Illinois governorship on November 17, 1834 upon the resignation of Governor John Reynolds, and served until December 3, 1834, at which time Joseph Duncan was inaugurated. Appointed as a Jacksonian Democrat to the U.S. Senate to fill the vacancy caused by the death of Elias K. Kane, serving from December 30, 1835 to March 3, 1837; unsuccessful candidate for reelection. Elected to the Illinois House of Representatives in 1838 and 1840, having been chosen Speaker over Abraham Lincoln during both sessions; elected clerk of the Illinois House of Representatives in 1842; appointed Auditor of Public Accounts in March, 1843 and served in that capacity until his death. Ewing died on March 25, 1846 in Vandalia, Illinois; buried in Oak Ridge Cemetery, Springfield, Illinois. Bibliography: Alexander Davidson and Bernard Stuve, *A Complete History of Illinois from 1673 to 1873* (Springfield, 1874); Newton Bateman and Paul Selby, ed., *Historical Encyclopedia of Illinois*, 2 vols. (Chicago, 1916); State Centennial Commission, *Centennial History of Illinois*, 5 vols. (Springfield, 1917-1920); Roy Glashan, *American Governors and Gubernatorial Elections 1775-1975* (Stillwater, Minnesota, 1975).

DUNCAN, Joseph, 1834-1838

Born on February 22, 1794 in Paris, Bourbon County, Kentucky; son of Joseph, a United States military officer, and Anna Maria (McLaughlin) Duncan; a Presbyterian. Married to Elizabeth Caldwell Smith on May 13, 1828; father of James Caldwell, Henry St. Clair, Mary Louise, Ann Elizabeth, Joseph, Julia Smith, Smith, Hannah Caldwell, Ellen Marian, and Catherine Clay Duncan. Self-educated; during the War of 1812 was commissioned an Ensign in the Seventeenth Infantry on March 12, 1812; promoted to Second Lieutenant on March 13, 1813; promoted to First Lieutenant in the Forty-sixth Infantry on July 16, 1814 and transferred to the Seventeenth Infantry; honorably discharged on June 15, 1815; received the testimonial of a sword for his part in the defense of Fort Stephenson, Ohio by a resolution of Congress on February 13, 1835. Moved to Illinois in 1818, settling in Kaskaskia; engaged in agricultural pursuits. Served as Justice of the Peace of Jackson County from 1821 to 1823. Commissioned Major General, Illinois Militia in 1823; served as Brigadier General of the Illinois volunteer forces during the Black Hawk War. Served as a member of the Illinois Senate from 1824 to 1826; as a Jacksonian Democrat, was four times elected to the United States House of Representatives, serving from March 4, 1827 to September 21, 1834, at which time he resigned, having been elected Governor of Illinois. As the Whig gubernatorial candidate, Duncan was elected Governor of Illinois by popular vote on August 4, 1834, defeating the Democratic candidate, William Kinney, and the Jacksonian Democratic candidate, Robert H. McLaughlin, by a vote of 17,330 to 10,224 and 4,315, respectively; inaugurated on December 3, 1834. During his administration, Duncan recommended that a system of public education be devised; urged the establishment of colleges; advocated the initiation of a general system of internal improvements; and advocated the construction of a canal to connect the Great Lakes with the Mississippi River. Because the Illinois Constitution of 1818 prohibited a governor from succeeding himself, Duncan left office on December 7, 1838, retiring to private life. He was defeated for the Illinois governorship by Thomas Ford in 1842. Duncan died on January 15, 1844 in Jacksonville, Morgan County, Illinois and was buried in Diamond Grove Cemetery. Bibliography: State Centennial Commission, *Centennial History of Illinois*, 5 vols. (Springfield, 1917-1920); Elizabeth Duncan Putnam, "The Life and Services of Joseph Duncan, Governor of Illinois, 1834-1838," *Transactions of the Illinois State Historical Society for the Year 1919*, no. 26 (1920); Elizabeth Duncan Putnam, "Diary of Mrs. Joseph Duncan (Elizabeth Caldwell Smith)," *Journal of the Illinois State Historical Society*, vol. XXI, no. 1 (April, 1928); Roy Glashan, *American Governors and Gubernatorial Elections 1775-1975* (Stillwater, Minnesota, 1975).

CARLIN, Thomas, 1838-1842

Born on July 18, 1789 near Frankfort, Kentucky; son of Thomas Carlin. Married to Rebecca Hewitt in 1814; father of thirteen children. Self-educated. Served as a volunteer under General Howard during the War of 1812; commanded a battalion during the Black Hawk War. Served as a member of the Illinois House of Representatives; was elected twice to be a member of that legislative body;

elected to two terms in the Illinois Senate; appointed Receiver of Public Monies at Quincy, Illinois in 1834 by President Andrew Jackson, serving in that capacity until his election as Governor of Illinois. As the Democratic gubernatorial candidate, Carlin was elected Governor of Illinois by popular vote on August 6, 1838, defeating the Whig candidate, Cyrus Edwards, by a vote of 30,648 to 29,722; inaugurated on December 7, 1838. During his administration, the Sangamon and Morgan railroad was opened to traffic; a loan of $4,000,000 was negotiated to aid in the construction of the Illinois and Michigan Canal; the Mormons immigrated into Illinois and founded the city of Nauvoo; the state judiciary system was reorganized; and both the State Bank of Shawneetown and the Illinois Bank failed. Because the Illinois Constitution of 1818 prohibited a governor from succeeding himself, Carlin left office on December 8, 1842 and retired to his farm at Carrollton, Illinois. He served as a member of the Illinois House of Representatives in 1842, filling the vacancy caused by the death of J. D. Fry. Carlin died on February 14, 1852 at Carrollton, Illinois. Bibliography: Alexander Davidson and Bernard Stuve, *A Complete History of Illinois from 1673 to 1873* (Springfield, 1874); Newton Bateman and Paul Selby, eds., *Historical Encyclopedia of Illinois*, 2 vols. (Chicago, 1916); State Centennial Commission, *Centennial History of Illinois*, 5 vols. (Springfield, 1917-1920); Roy Glashan, *American Governors and Gubernatorial Elections 1775-1975* (Stillwater, Minnesota, 1975).

FORD, Thomas, 1842-1846

Born on December 5, 1800 near Uniontown, Fayette County, Pennsylvania; son of Robert and Elizabeth (Logue) Forquer Ford; no religious preference. Half-brother of George Forquer. Married to Frances Hambaugh on June 12, 1828; father of Anna, Mary Frances, Julia, Seuel, and Thomas Ford. Attended Transylvania University for one year; studied law; began law practice in Waterloo, Illinois; formed law partnership with George Forquer and practiced in Edwardsville, Illinois from 1825 to 1829; served as State's Attorney of the Fifth Judicial District, Galena and Quincy, Illinois from 1829 to 1835; enlisted in Colonel Sam Whiteside's "Spy Battalion" during the Black Hawk War; elected Judge of the Sixth Illinois Circuit on January 14, 1835 and served until March 4, 1835, at which time he resigned to become Judge of the Chicago Municipal Court; elected Judge of the Ninth Illinois Circuit on February 23, 1839; elected to the Illinois Supreme Court on February 15, 1841, resigning in May, 1842 to run for the Illinois governorship. As the Democratic gubernatorial candidate, Ford was elected Governor of Illinois by popular vote on August 1, 1842, defeating the Whig candidate, Joseph Duncan, by a vote of 46,507 to 39,020; inaugurated on December 8, 1842. During his administration, the peaceful termination of the state banks was secured; the Illinois and Michigan Canal was completed, the tolls from which were to be applied to the liquidation of the state debt; the militia was called out to maintain order between the Mormons and Gentiles in western Illinois. Because the Illinois Constitution of 1818 prohibited a governor from succeeding himself, Ford left office on December 9, 1846 and resumed his law practice in Peoria, Illinois. Author of *History of Illinois from its Commencement as a State in 1818 to 1847* (posthumously published in 1854). Reynolds died on November 3, 1850 in Peoria, Illinois. Bibliography: Alexander Davidson and Bernard Stuve, *A Complete History of Illinois from 1673 to 1873* (Springfield, 1874); State Centennial Commission, *Centennial History of Illinois*, 5 vols. (Springfield, 1917-1920); J. F. Snyder, "Governor Ford and His Family," *Journal of the Illinois State Historical Society,* vol. III, no. 2 (July, 1910); Roy Glashan, *American Governors and Gubernatorial Elections 1775-1975* (Stillwater, Minnesota, 1975).

FRENCH, Augustus C., 1846-1853

Born on August 2, 1808 in Hill, Merrimack County, New Hampshire; brother of five, four brothers and one sister. His father died when he was a child, and his mother died when he was nineteen years of age. Never married. Attended a district school irregularly; entered Dartmouth, but was unable to complete his studies because of financial difficulties; studied law and was admitted to the New Hampshire Bar in 1823. Emigrated to Albion, Edwards County, Illinois in 1824; moved to Paris, Edgar County, Illinois in 1825 and established a law practice there. Served as a member of the Illinois Legislature from 1837 to 1839. Appointed Receiver of Public Monies, Land Office of Palestine, Illinois; served as presidential elector in 1844. As the Democratic gubernatorial candidate, French was elected Governor of Illinois by popular vote on August 3, 1846, defeating the Whig candidate, Thomas M. Kilpatrick, and the Liberty candidate, Richard Eels, by a vote of 67,828 to 37,033 and 5,157, respectively; reelected under the Illinois Constitution of 1848 on November 7, 1848, defeating the Whig candidate, W. S. D. Morison, and Liberty candidate, Charles V. Dyer, by a vote of 67,828 to 5,659 and 4,692, respectively; inaugurated on December 9, 1846. During his administration, the last of the Mormons left Illinois; the Illinois and Michigan Canal was completed; a new state constitution was adopted; a township organization act was passed; expenses were reduced and the state debt was liquidated. Because the Illinois Constitution of 1848 prohibited a governor from succeeding himself, French left office on January 10, 1853 and became Professor of Law at McKendree College in Lebanon, Illinois. He was appointed Bank Commissioner by Governor Joel Matteson; was an unsuccessful candidate for State Superintendent of Public Instruction in 1858; and served as a member of the 1862 Illinois Constitutional Convention. French died in Lebanon, Illinois on September 4, 1864. Bibliography: Alexander Davidson and Bernard Stuve, *A Complete History of Illinois from 1673 to 1873* (Springfield, 1874); Newton Bateman and Paul Selby, eds., *Historical Encyclopedia of Illinois*, 2 vols. (Chicago, 1916); State Centennial Commission, *Centennial History of Illinois*, 5 vols. (Springfield, 1917-1920); Roy Glashan, *American Governors and Gubernatorial Elections 1775-1975* (Stillwater, Minnesota, 1975).

MATTESON, Joel Aldrich, 1853-1857

Born on August 2, 1808 in Watertown, New York; only son of Elnathan, a farmer, and Eunice (Aldrich) Matteson. Married to Mary Fish on October 7, 1832; father of three sons and four daughters. Attended the local schools; taught school in Brownsville, New York; in 1834 worked as a foreman on the first railroad built in South Carolina; moved to Kendall County, Illinois in 1833 and was engaged in farming; sold his land and moved to Joliet in 1836; secured contracts for construction on the Illinois and Michigan Canal in 1838; elected to the Illinois Senate in 1842, 1844, and 1846, serving from 1842 to 1853. As the Democratic gubernatorial candidate, Matteson was elected Governor of Illinois by popular vote on November 2, 1852, defeating the Whig candidate, E. B. Webb, and the Free Soil candidate, D. A. Knowlton, by a vote of 80,789 to 64,408 and 9,9024, respectively; inaugurated on January 10, 1853. During his administration, much of the state debt was liquidated; a system of free schools was introduced; the State Agricultural Society was incorporated; the construction of one hundred and fifty additional prison cells at the Alton Penitentiary was authorized; old canal claim damages were settled; the state railroad network was greatly increased; the "Maine Law," prohibiting the sale and manufacture of liquor, was enacted. Because the Illinois Constitution of 1848 prohibited a governor from succeeding himself, Matteson left office on January 12, 1857 and retired to private life. Afterwards he served as a lessee and president of the Chicago and Alton Railroad, and was an unsuccessful candidate for the United States Senate in 1855. Matteson died on January 31, 1873 in Chicago, Illinois. Bibliography: Alexander Davidson and Bernard Stuve, *A Complete History of Illinois from 1673 to 1873* (Springfield, 1874); Newton Bateman and Paul Selby, eds., *Historical Encyclopedia of Illinois*, 2 vols. (Chicago, 1916); State Centennial Commission, *Centennial History of Illinois*, 5 vols. (Springfield, 1917-1920); Roy Glashan, *American Governors and Gubernatorial Elections 1775-1975* (Stillwater, Minnesota, 1975).

BISSELL, William Henry, 1857-1860

Born on April 25, 1811 in Hartwick, Otsego County, New York; son of Luther and Hannah Bissell; a Roman Catholic. Married first to Emily James on November 14, 1840. After her death, remarried Elizabeth Kane on November 26, 1851; father of Josephine and Rhoda Bissell from first marriage. Attended local schools; entered Cooperstown Academy; graduated from Jefferson Medical College, Philadelphia in 1835; graduated from the Law Department of Transylvania University in 1841. Practiced medicine in Chemung County and Steuben County, New York; in 1837, moved to Waterloo, Monroe County, Illinois, where he taught school. Served as a member of the Illinois House of Representatives from 1840 to 1842. Admitted to the Illinois Bar in 1843 and began law practice in Belleville, St. Clair County, Illinois; became Prosecuting Attorney for the Second Illinois Judicial District in 1844. Served in the Mexican War as Colonel of the Second Regiment, Illinois Volunteer Infantry. Three times elected as a Democrat to the United States House of Representatives, serving from March 4, 1849 to March 3, 1855; was not a candidate for reelection. As the Republican gubernatorial candidate, Bissell was elected Governor of Illinois by popular vote on November 4, 1856, defeating the Democratic candidate, William A. Richardson, and the American (or Know-Nothing) Party candidate, Buckner S. Morris, by a vote of 111,466 to 106,769 and 19,078, respectively; inaugurated on January 12, 1857. During his administration, the "Illinois and Michigan Canal scrip fraud" was uncovered; appropriations for the northern penitentiary and the asylums at Jacksonville were approved; payment for the semi-annual interest on the state debt was authorized; judges were permitted to receive their salaries on vouchers certified from the governor to the auditor. Bissell died on March 18, 1860 in Springfield, Sangamon County, Illinois, while still in office. He was buried in Oak Ridge Cemetery. Bibliography: Alexander Davidson and Bernard Stuve, *A Complete History of Illinois from 1673 to 1873* (Springfield, 1874), State Centennial Commission, *Centennial History of Illinois*, 5 vols. (Springfield, 1917-1920); William U. Halbert, "William Henry Bissell, Eleventh Governor of Illinois," *Journal of the Illinois State Historical Society* vol. XXXVI, no. 1 (March, 1943); Roy Glashan, *American Governors and Gubernatorial Elections 1775-1975* (Stillwater, Minnesota, 1975).

WOOD, John, 1860-1861

Born on December 20, 1798 in Moravia, Cayuga County, New York; son of Daniel, a surgeon and Revolutionary War officer, and Catherine (Crouse) Wood; a Presbyterian. Married first to Ann M. Streeter in January, 1826; after her death, remarried to Mrs. Mary A. Holmes in June, 1865; father of Anna E., Daniel C., John, Joshua, James T., Sarah L., and two others by his first marriage. Moved to Illinois in 1819, settling in Pike County; in 1822 purchased land and built the first cabin in present-day Quincy; initiated the movement for the organization of Adams County, of which Quincy was designated as the county seat; in 1824 was instrumental in defeating those who agitated for a new state constitution recognizing slavery. Served as a private during the Black Hawk War. Served as town trustee of Quincy from 1834 to 1840 and was elected Mayor of Quincy seven times; served as a member of the Illinois Senate from 1850 to 1854; elected Lieutenant Governor of Illinois in 1856, serving from January 12, 1857 to March 21, 1860. As the Lieutenant Governor of Illinois, Wood assumed the governorship on March 21, 1860 upon the death of Governor William H. Bissell; a Republican. During his administration, the investigation of the "Illinois and Michigan Canal scrip fraud" continued. Wood left office on January 14, 1861 upon the inauguration of Richard Yates. Appointed as one of the five delegates to the Peace Convention in Washington, D.C. in February, 1861; appointed Quartermaster-General of Illinois in May, 1861; commissioned Colonel of the One Hundred and Thirty-seventh Illinois Volunteers in June, 1864; honorably mustered out in September, 1864 and returned to his business interests in Quincy, Illinois. Wood died on June 11, 1880 in Quincy, Illinois. Bibliography: Alexander Davidson and Bernard Stuve, *A Complete History of Illinois from 1673 to 1873* (Springfield, 1874); State Centennial Commission, *Centennial History of Illinois*, 5 vols. (Springfield, 1917-1920); Cora Agnes Benneson, "The Work of Edward Everett of Quincy in the Quarter-Master's Department in Illinois during the first year of the Civil War," *Transactions of the Illinois State Historical Society for the Year 1909*, no. 14 (1910); Roy Glashan, *American Governors and Gubernatorial Elections 1775-1975* (Stillwater, Minnesota, 1975).

YATES, Richard, 1861-1865

Born on January 18, 1818 in Warsaw, Gallatin County, Kentucky; son of Henry, founder of Warsaw, and Millicent (Yates) Yates; a Methodist-Episcopalian; brother of nine. Married to Catharine Geers on July 11, 1839; father of five, among whom were Catharine, Henry, an assistant postmaster of Jacksonville, and Richard, Governor of Illinois from 1901 to 1905. Moved with his family to Sangamon County, Illinois in 1831. Graduated from Illinois College at Jacksonville in 1835; studied law at Transylvania University, Louisville, Kentucky; admitted to the bar in 1837 and began law practice in Jacksonville, Illinois. Served as a member of the Illinois House of Representatives from 1842 to 1845, 1848, and 1849. Twice elected as a Whig to the U.S. House of Representatives, serving from March 4, 1851 to March 3, 1855; unsuccessful candidate for reelection in 1854; served as a delegate to the Illinois Republican Convention in 1854 and to the Republican National Convention in Chicago in 1860. As the Republican gubernatorial candidate, Yates was elected Governor of Illinois by popular vote on November 6, 1860, defeating the Democratic candidate, James C. Allen, by a vote of 172,218 to 159,293; inaugurated on January 14, 1861. During his administration, Yates was a zealous supporter of President Abraham Lincoln and did much to aid the Union cause during the Civil War. In response to Lincoln's call for troops, Illinois provided almost double its quota of volunteers. Ulysses S. Grant was appointed Mustering Officer for Illinois and later commissioned Colonel of the Twenty-First Regiment of Illinois Volunteers. In 1863 the Illinois House of Representatives embarrassed Yates by passing a resolution which recommended that a compromise be made with the seceded states and that a national convention be convened in order to restore peace. Exercising his constitutional powers, Governor Yates prorogued the state legislature and conducted the state's war efforts until the following year. Because the Illinois Constitution of 1848 prohibited a governor from succeeding himself, Yates left office on January 16, 1865. He was elected as a Union Republican to the United States Senate, serving from March 4, 1865 to March 3, 1871; was not a candidate for reelection; was appointed a U.S. Commissioner to inspect land subsidy railroads. Yates died on November 27, 1873 in St. Louis, Missouri; buried in Diamond Grove Cemetery, Jacksonville, Illinois. Bibliography: *History of Morgan County, Illinois: Its Past and Present* (Chicago, 1878); State Centennial Commission, *Centennial History of Illinois*, 5 vols. (Springfield, 1917-1920); "Richard Yates, War Governor of Illinois," *Transactions of the Illinois State Historical Society for the Year 1923*, no. 30 (1924); Roy Glashan, *American Governors and Gubernatorial Elections, 1775-1975* (Stillwater, Minnesota, 1975).

OGLESBY, Richard James, 1865-1869, 1873, 1885-1889

Born on July 25, 1824 in Floydsburg, Oldham County, Kentucky, son of Jacob, a farmer and member of the Kentucky Legislature, and Isabella (Watson) Oglesby; an Episcopalian. Brother of three, two brothers and a sister. Married first to Anna White in 1859; after her death, remarried to Emma (Gillett) Keyes in November, 1873; father of seven by his second marriage, among whom were Felicite, John Gillett, and James Oglesby, Jr. Orphaned at the age of eight; moved to Decatur,

Illinois with an uncle and attended the local schools; studied law in the office of Silas W. Robbins in Springfield, Illinois; admitted to the bar in 1854 and began law practice in Sullivan, Illinois until the outbreak of the Mexican War; commissioned a First Lieutenant in Company C, Fourth Illinois Infantry on June 13, 1846 and honorably discharged on May 25, 1847. Graduated from Louisville Law School in 1848; from 1849 to 1851, mined for gold in California; returned to Decatur, Illinois in 1851 and resumed the practice of law. Unsuccessful candidate for the U.S. House of Representatives in 1858; elected to the Illinois Senate in 1860, serving for one session, at which time he resigned to join the Union Army. Commissioned as a Colonel of the Eighth Regiment, Illinois Volunteer Infantry on April 25, 1861; became Commander of the First Brigade, First Division, Army of West Tennessee in February, 1862; promoted to Brigadier General of Volunteers on March 21, 1862 and to Major General on November 29, 1862; resigned on May 26, 1864. As the Republican gubernatorial candidate, Oglesby was elected Governor of Illinois by popular vote on November 8, 1864, defeating the Democratic candidate, James C. Robinson, by a vote of 190,376 to 158,711; inaugurated on January 16, 1865. During his administration, the Thirteenth and Fourteenth Amendments were ratified; the "Black Laws" were repealed; the Southern Illinois Penitentiary was constructed; a home for the children of deceased soldiers and a school for the retarded were established. Because the Illinois Constitution of 1848 prohibited a governor from succeeding himself, Oglesby left office on January 11, 1869 and returned to private law practice. As the Republican gubernatorial candidate, Oglesby was again elected Governor of Illinois by popular vote on November 5, 1872, defeating the Liberal Republican candidate, Gus Koerner, by a vote of 237,774 to 178,084. Inaugurated on January 13, 1873, Oglesby resigned the governorship on January 23, 1873 because of his election to the United States Senate. Served as a member of the U.S. Senate from March 4, 1873 to March 3, 1879; declined to be a candidate for reelection and retired to private life. As the Republican gubernatorial candidate, Oglesby was elected to an unprecedented third term as governor of Illinois by popular vote on November 4, 1884, defeating the Democratic candidate, Carter H. Harrison, by a vote of 334,234 to 319,645; inaugurated on January 30, 1885. During this administration the Citizens' Election Bill, providing that no election district shall include more than four hundred and fifty voters, was passed; a Soldiers' and Sailors' Home and a home for juvenile delinquents were established; a revenue commission was created; and various pension funds were established. Oglesby left office on January 14, 1889 upon the inauguration of Joseph W. Fifer, retiring to private life. He died on April 24, 1899 in Elkhart, Illinois, and was buried in Elkhart Cemetery. Bibliography: Alexander Davidson and Bernard Stuve, *A Complete History of Illinois from 1673 to 1873* (Springfield, 1874); Newton Bateman and Paul Selby, eds., *Historical Encyclopedia of Illinois*, 2 vols. (Chicago, 1916); State Centennial Commission, *Centennial History of Illinois*, 5 vols. (Springfield, 1917-1920); Roy Glashan, *American Governors and Gubernatorial Elections 1775-1975* (Stillwater, Minnesota, 1975).

PALMER, John McAuley, 1869-1873

Born on September 13, 1817 in Eagle Creek, Scott County, Kentucky; son of Louis D., a farmer, and Ann Hansford (Tutt) Palmer; a Baptist. Brother of seven, among whom were Elihu and George Palmer, and one sister. Married first to Malinda Ann Neely on December 20, 1842; after her death, remarried to Hannah (Lamb) Kimball on April 4, 1888; father of ten, among whom were Betty, Mary, Lucy, Tom, Susie, and John Mayo Palmer. Moved to Madison County, Illinois with his family in 1831; attended the local schools; entered Shurtleff College at Upper Alton, Illinois in 1834 and attended for two years; taught school; studied law in the office of John S. Greathouse and was admitted to the bar in December, 1839; practiced law in Carlinville, Illinois from 1839 to 1861; served as Probate Judge of Macoupin County, Illinois in 1845 and 1847; served as a delegate to the Illinois Constitutional Convention in 1847; elected a County Judge under the new Constitution of 1848; served as a member of the Illinois Senate from June, 1852 to July, 1854, at which time he resigned because of political differences; reelected in 1855 and resigned in 1856; served as a delegate to the Republican National Convention in Philadelphia in 1856; served as a Republican presidential elector in 1860; served as a delegate to the Peace Convention of 1861 held in Washington, D.C. Commissioned a Colonel in the Fourteenth Regiment, Illinois Volunteer Infantry on May 25, 1861; promoted to Brigadier General of Volunteers on December 20, 1861, and to Major General on November 29, 1862; honorably mustered out on September 1, 1866. Resumed law practice in Springfield, Illinois in 1867. As the Republican gubernatorial candidate, Palmer was elected Governor of Illinois by popular vote on November 3, 1868, defeating the Democratic candidate, John R. Eden, by a vote of 249,912 to 199,813; inaugurated on January 11, 1869. During his administration, Palmer advocated a return of "states' rights" by the federal government, since the Civil War had ended and the need for such a usurpation was no longer necessary. In his conflict with General Sheridan over the stationing of federal troops in Chicago after a fire had destroyed much of that city, Palmer reinforced his "states' rights" position. As a supporter of Horace Greeley for the presidency in 1872, Palmer shifted his allegiance to the Democratic Party. Since Palmer was elected Governor of Illinois under the Constitution of 1848, which prohibited a governor from succeeding himself, he left office on January 13, 1873 and resumed his law practice in Springfield, Illinois. He served as a delegate to the Democratic National Convention at Chicago in 1884; was elected as a Democrat to the United States Senate, serving from March 4, 1891 to March 3, 1897; was not a candidate for reelection; returned to Springfield and resumed his law practice; and was an unsuccessful candidate for President as a Gold Democrat in 1896. Palmer died on September 19, 1900 in Springfield, Illinois, and was buried in Carlinville City Cemetery, Carlinville, Illinois. Bibliography: State Centennial Commission, *Centennial History of Illinois*, 5 vols. (Springfield, 1917-1920); "John M. Palmer," *Transactions of the Illinois State Historical Society for the Year 1923*, no. 30 (1924); George Thomas Palmer, *A Conscientious Turncoat, the Story of John M. Palmer, 1817-1900* (New Haven, 1941); Roy Glashan, *American Governors and Gubernatorial Elections 1775-1975* (Stillwater, Minnesota, 1975).

OGLESBY, Richard James, 1865-1869, 1873, 1885-1889

BEVERIDGE, John Lourie, 1873-1877

Born on July 6, 1824 in Greenwich, Washington County, New York; son of George, a farmer, and Ann (Hoy) Beveridge; a Methodist. Married to Helen Mar Judson on January 20, 1858; father of Alla May and Philo J. Beveridge. Moved to Illinois in 1842 with his family, settling in Somonauk in DeKalb County; attended Granville Academy and Rock River Seminary; moved to Tennessee in 1845 and studied law, while teaching in Wilson and Overton Counties; subsequently admitted to the bar. Returned to Illinois in 1851 and practiced law in Sycamore, DeKalb County until 1854, at which time he settled in Evanston; engaged in law partnership with John F. Farnsworth in Chicago from 1855 until the outbreak of the Civil War. Appointed Major of the Eighth Illinois Cavalry on September 18, 1861; promoted to Colonel of the Seventeenth Illinois Cavalry on January 28, 1864; brevetted Brigadier General on March 7, 1865 and honorably mustered out on February 7, 1866. Elected Sheriff of Cook County, serving from 1866 to 1870; served as a member of the Illinois Senate in 1871; resigned to become a member of the United States House of Representatives; elected as a Republican to the Forty-second Congress to fill the vacancy caused by the resignation of John A. Logan, serving from November 7, 1871 to January 4, 1873, at which time he resigned. Elected Lieutenant Governor of Illinois on November 5, 1872. As lieutenant governor of Illinois, Beveridge succeeded to the governorship on January 23, 1873, upon the resignation of Governor Richard J. Oglesby, who had been elected to the United States Senate. During his administration, twelve charitable and reformatory institutions were funded; the payment of the state debt was authorized; the state militia was increased; the new capitol in Springfield was occupied by government offices. Beveridge left office on January 8, 1877 upon the inauguration of Shelby M. Cullom. Appointed Assistant Treasurer of the United States in Chicago in December, 1881, and served in that capacity until September, 1884, at which time he resigned. In 1895, moved to Hollywood, California, where he resided until his death. Beveridge died on May 3, 1910 in Hollywood, California, and was buried in Rose Hill Cemetery, Chicago, Illinois. Bibliography: Newton Bateman and Paul Selby, eds., *Historical Encyclopedia of Illinois*, 2 vols. (Chicago, 1916); State Centennial Commission, *Centennial History of Illinois*, 5 vols. (Springfield, 1917-1920); Rev. John O. Foster, O.D., "The First Des Plaines Camp Meeting, Des Plaines, Illinois, August, 1860," *Journal of the Illinois State Historical Society*, vol. XXIV, no. 4 (January, 1932); Roy Glashan, *American Governors and Gubernatorial Elections 1775-1975* (Stillwater, Minnesota, 1975).

CULLOM, Shelby Moore, 1877-1883

Born on November 22, 1829 in Monticello, Wayne County, Kentucky; seventh child of Richard Northcraft, a member of the Illinois Legislature, and Elizabeth (Colley) Cullom; a Methodist. Brother of eleven. Married first to Hannah M. Fisher on December 12, 1855; after her death, remarried to his sister-in-law, Julia Fisher, on May 5, 1863; father of Ella and Carrie Cullom. Moved with his family to Tazewell County, Illinois in 1830; attended the local schools; was a student at Mount Morris Seminary for two years; studied law in the office of Stuart and Edwards in Springfield, Illinois in 1853; admitted to the bar in 1855. Elected City Attorney of Springfield in 1855 and presidential elector in 1856; elected to the Illinois House of Representatives in 1856, 1860, and 1861, serving as Speaker in 1861; in 1862, appointed to a commission by President Abraham Lincoln to settle claims against the federal government for property purchased by commissary officers and quartermasters in the volunteer service; three times elected as a Republican to the U.S. House of Representatives, serving from March 4, 1865 to March 3, 1871; again elected to the Illinois House of Representatives in 1872 and 1874, serving as Speaker in 1873; served as a delegate to the Republican National Convention at Philadelphia in 1872. As the Republican gubernatorial candidate, Cullom was elected Governor of Illinois by popular vote on November 6, 1876, defeating the National candidate, Lewis Steward, by a vote of 279,263 to 272,495; reelected on November 2, 1880, defeating the Democratic candidate, Lyman Trumbull, by a vote of 314,565 to 277,562; inaugurated on January 8, 1877. During his administration, $80,000 was appropriated to pay the military for services rendered in suppressing the riots of 1877; a Board of Fish Commissioners was established; the rate of interest paid or collected on written contracts was reduced to eight percent; polls were required to be open from eight a.m. to seven p.m. in all city, town, or village elections; taxation laws were revised; the Bureau of Labor Statistics was created; the state debt was liquidated; the State Board of Health was organized; the Illinois and Michigan Canal was ceded to the United States; and Illinois was apportioned into senatorial and congressional districts. Cullom, having been elected to the U.S. Senate, resigned the Illinois governorship on February 5, 1883. Subsequently reelected four times, serving from March 4, 1883 to March 3, 1913; served as a delegate to the Republican National Convention at Chicago in 1884 and Minneapolis in 1892; served as Regent of the Smithsonian Institution from March 24, 1885 to March 3, 1913; served as chairman and resident commissioner of the Lincoln Memorial Commission in 1913 and 1914. Cullom died on January 28, 1914 in Washington, D.C., and was buried in Oak Ridge Cemetery, Springfield, Illinois. Bibliography: Henry A. Converse, "The Life and Services of Shelby M. Cullom," *Transactions of the Illinois State Historical Society for the Year 1914*, no. 20 (1915); Newton Bateman and Paul Selby, eds., *Historical Encyclopedia of Illinois*, 2 vols. (Chicago, 1916); *State Centennial Commission, Centennial History of Illinois*, 5 vols. (Springfield, 1917-1920); Roy Glashan, *American Governors and Gubernatorial Elections, 1775-1975* (Stillwater, Minnesota, 1975); James W. Neilson, *Shelby M. Cullom: Prairie State Republican* (Urbana, 1961).

HAMILTON, John Marshall, 1883-1885

Born on May 28, 1847 in Ridgewood, Union County, Ohio; son of Samuel, a farmer, and Nancy (McMorris) Hamilton; a Methodist. Married to Helen; father of Alethia and Leonard. Moved to Illinois with his family in 1854, settling near Wenona, in Marshall County. Enlisted in Company I, One Hundred and Forty First

Illinois Infantry in 1864; graduated with honors from Ohio Wesleyan University in 1868; tutored in an academy in Henry, Illinois from 1868 to 1869. While studying law, became Professor of Languages at Wesleyan University, Bloomington, Illinois; admitted to the bar in 1870 and formed a law partnership with Captain J. H. Powell which lasted until 1882; elected to the Illinois Senate in 1876; elected Lieutenant Governor of Illinois on November 2, 1880, serving from January 10, 1881 to February 16, 1883. As the lieutenant governor, Hamilton assumed the governorship on February 16, 1883, upon the resignation of Governor Shelby M. Cullom; a Republican. During his administration, a Compulsory Education Act for children between the ages of eight and fourteen was passed; an appropriation for the completion and furnishing of the State House was made; foreign insurance companies, involved with fire, marine, and inland navigation insurance, and doing business in the state were made subject to state regulations; railroads organizing or conducting business in the state were required to maintain a public office where transfers of stock could be made. Hamilton left office on January 30, 1885 upon the inauguration of Richard J. Oglesby, and resumed law practice in Chicago, Illinois until his death. Hamilton died on September 22. 1905 in Chicago, Illinois. Bibliography; Newton Bateman and Paul Selby, eds., *Historical Encyclopedia of Illinois*, 2 vols. (Chicago, 1916); State Centennial Commission, *Centennial History of Illinois*, 5 vols. (Springfield, 1917-1920); Roy Glashan, *American Governors and Gubernatorial Elections, 1775-1975* (Stillwater, Minnesota, 1975); Congressional Quarterly, Inc., *Guide to U.S. Elections* (Washington, D.C., 1975).

OGLESBY, Richard James, 1865-1869, 1873, 1885-1889

FIFER, Joseph Wilson, 1889-1893

Born on October 28, 1840 in Staunton, Augusta County, Virginia; son of John, a farmer, and Mary (Wilson) Fifer; a Methodist. Married to Gertrude Lewis on June 15, 1870; father of Herman W. and Florence Fifer. Moved with family to McLean County, Illinois in 1857; attended the local schools. Enlisted as a private in the Thirty-third Illinois Infantry in 1861; severely wounded in 1863, but continued to serve; entered Illinois Wesleyan University at Bloomington in 1864 and graduated in 1868; studied law in the office of Prince and Bloomfield and was admitted to the bar in 1869; elected as Corporation Counsel to the city of Bloomington in 1871; elected State Attorney in 1872, serving in that capacity until 1880; elected to the Illinois Senate in 1880, serving until 1884, at which time he resigned; resumed law practice. As the Republican gubernatorial candidate, Fifer was elected Governor of Illinois by popular vote on November 6, 1888, defeating the Democratic candidate, former Governor John M. Palmer, by a vote of 367,860 to 355,313; inaugurated on January 14, 1889. During his administration, a revision and codification of the State Public School Law was enacted; the Primary Election Law of 1885 was repealed; an annexation act, providing for the consolidation of cities if approved by a vote of the residents, was passed; an act requiring bank directors to own at least ten shares in the stock of their banks was initiated; the State Historical

Library was established; the Act of 1887, ceding the locks and canals in the Illinois River to the United States, was repealed; a Ballot Reform Act, providing for the printing and distributing of all ballots in every election for public officers at the public's expense, was enacted; the right to vote for school officers at all elections was granted to women; a stringent act for the suppression of pools, trusts, and combines was passed; an act providing for the election of U.S. Senators by a direct vote of the people was passed. Having lost the election of November 8, 1892 by a vote of 402,676 to 425,558, Fifer left office on January 10, 1893, upon the inauguration of John P. Altgeld. He resumed law practice in Bloomington, Illinois; served as a member of the Interstate Commerce Commission from 1899 to 1906; and served as a delegate to the Illinois Constitutional Convention in 1920. Fifer died on August 6, 1938 and was buried in Bloomington, Illinois. Bibliography: Newton Bateman and Paul Selby, eds. *Historical Encyclopedia of Illinois*, 2 vols. (Chicago, 1916); State Centennial Commission, *Centennial History of Illinois*, 5 vols. (Springfield, 1917-1920); Congressional Quarterly, Inc., *Guide to U.S. Elections* (Washington, D.C., 1975); Roy Glashan, *American Governors and Gubernatorial Elections 1775-1975* (Stillwater, Minnesota, 1975).

ALTGELD, John Peter, 1893-1897

Born on December 30, 1847 in Niedersellers, Nassau, Germany, son of John Peter, a German immigrant, and Mary Altgeld; a Catholic. Married to Emma Ford; no children. Accompanied his parents to America, where they settled in Richland County, Ohio; attended the local schools. Enlisted in the One Hundred and Sixty-Fourth Ohio Infantry in 1863 and served until the end of the Civil War. Obtained a legal education in St. Louis and Savannah, Missouri; served as Prosecuting Attorney for Andrew County, Missouri from 1874 to 1878; moved to Chicago, Illinois in 1878 and practiced law; elected to the Superior Court of Cook County in 1886, serving until his resignation in August, 1891. As the Democratic gubernatorial candidate, Altgeld was elected Governor of Illinois by popular vote on November 8, 1892, defeating the Republican candidate, Governor Joseph W. Fifer, and Populist candidate, N. Barnett, by a vote of 425,558 to 402,676 and 20,103, respectively; inaugurated on January 10, 1893. During his administration, Altgeld pardoned the three surviving prisoners accused of participation in the Haymarket Riots; appointed a woman, Florence Kelley, as a factory inspector; the Compulsory Education Law of 1889 was repealed; and the Insurance Department of the State Auditor was made a separate state department under the control of a superintendent appointed by the governor. Also a State Home for Juvenile Offenders was established; the naval militia was established; a commission to promote uniformity in state law was created; the Illinois Farmers' Institute and State Board of Pardons were created; and the employment of children under fourteen years of age in factories, workshops, laundries, offices, and stores was prohibited. Having lost the election of November 3, 1896 by a vote of 474,256 to 587,637, Altgeld left office on January 11, 1897 upon the inauguration of John R. Tanner. He resumed his law practice in Chicago; was an unsuccessful candidate for Mayor of Chicago in 1899; and was the author of *Our Penal Machinery and Its Victims* (1884). Altgeld died on March 12, 1902, and was buried in Graceland Cemetery, Chicago, Illinois. Bibliography: Newton Bateman and Paul Selby, eds.,

Historical Encyclopedia of Illinois, 2 vols. (Chicago, 1916); State Centennial Commission, *Centennial History of Illinois*, 5 vols. (Springfield, 1917-1920); Harvey Wish, "John Peter Altgeld and the Election of 1896," *Journal of the Illinois State Historical Society*, vol. XXX, no. 3 (October, 1937); Roy Glashan, *American Governors and Gubernatorial Elections 1775-1975* (Stillwater, Minnesota, 1975).

TANNER, John R., 1897-1901

Born on April 4, 1844 near Booneville, Indiana; son of John, a farmer, and Eliza (Downs). Brother of Albert, Frederick, and James. Married to Lauretta Ingraham on December 25, 1866; after her death in 1887, remarried Cora E. English on December 30, 1896. He enlisted as a private at the age of nineteen in the 98th Illinois Regiment and served from 1863 to 1865. He was elected Clay County Sheriff in 1870 and served until 1872. From 1872 to 1876, he served as clerk of the Circuit Court, after which he resumed farming and his real estate business. He was elected State Senator in 1880 and served until 1883, when he was appointed U.S. Marshal for the Southern District of Illinois. He was elected State Treasurer in 1886 and served until 1889. He was appointed Railroad Commissioner in 1891. He was Assistant United States Treasurer for Chicago from 1892 through 1893. Tanner, a Republican, was elected Governor of Illinois by defeating the incumbent Democratic governor, John P. Altgeld, by a vote of 587,637 to 474,256. He assumed office on January 11, 1897. One of the most important events in the Tanner administration was a coal strike in which the governor refused to send troops to protect strikebreakers. After violence occurred, troops were sent, but with orders not to allow strikebreakers to enter the mines. Tanner also signed the Allen Bill which allowed city councils to grant fifty-year franchises to street railway companies. These two actions made Tanner very unpopular in Illinois and account for his failure to win a second term. After Tanner took office, he was faced with a financial crisis. There was no money in the treasury to pay the state bills. Tanner secured an agreement with companies supplying the state to sell at wholesale prices and to wait for payment until the state had the money. He also secured a loan that allowed the state to meet its immediate needs. By the end of his term, the financial crisis had passed and the state's credit restored. Also during his term, the Spanish-American War began and the governor was responsible for seeing that Illinois quota of ten equipped regiments was met. Before his term ended, Tanner had decided that his renomination would be impossible and decided to challenge U.S. Senator Shelby Cullom for his seat; however, after a bitter political fight which cost Tanner his health, he lost at the Republican convention. Tanner died on May 23, 1901 and was buried in Springfield, Illinois. Bibliography: State Centennial Commission, *Governors of Illinois, 1818-1918* (Springfield, 1918); William Hutchison, *Lowden of Illinois: The Life of Governor Frank O. Lowden*, 2 vols. (Chicago, 1957); James W. Neilson, *Shelby M. Cullom: Prairie State Republican* (Urbana, 1961); Roy Glashan, *American Governors and Gubernatorial Elections 1775-1975* (Stillwater, Minnesota, 1975).

YATES, Richard, Jr., 1901-1905

Born on December 12, 1860 in Jacksonville, Illinois; son of Richard, who served as Governor of Illinois from 1861 to 1865 and as United States Senator from 1865 to 1871, and Catherine (Geers); a Methodist. Brother of Henry and Katie. Married to Helen Wadsworth on October 23, 1888; father of Catharine and Dorothy. He graduated from Illinois College in 1880 with a Bachelor of Arts degree and in 1883 he received a Master of Arts degree from the same college. He served in the Illinois National Guard from 1885 to 1890. In 1884 he received his law degree from the University of Michigan. From 1885 to 1890, he served as City Attorney of Jacksonville. In 1892 he ran as the Republican nominee for the United States Congress but lost. In 1894 he was elected Judge of Morgan County, serving until 1897 when he resigned to accept appointment as United States Collector of Internal Revenue at Springfield. He held this post until 1900. In 1900 Yates was elected Governor of Illinois, defeating the Democratic candidate, Samuel Alschuler, by a vote of 580,199 to 518,966. He assumed office on January 14, 1901. Yates' administration was characterized by economy; he vetoed a bill appropriating money for the repair and improvement of the Executive Mansion. He also vetoed legislation that would have legalized race tracks in Illinois. In June 1902 a race riot occurred in Saline County, and Yates immediately sent troops into the county to protect black citizens and to restore order. Yates had hoped for a second term, but he was opposed by Frank O. Lowden (supported by the Illinois Republican boss, William Lorimer) and Charles S. Deneen, the candidate of Cook County. The Republican Convention of 1904 was deadlocked, and after some fifty-eight roll call votes, Charles Deneen was nominated. Yates left office on January 9, 1905. Following his term of office, Yates ran again for the Republican nomination for Governor in 1908 and 1912 but lost. He served as a member of the State Public Utilities Commission from 1914 to 1917; was Assistant Attorney General from 1917 to 1918; was elected to the United States House of Representatives in 1918, serving from 1919 to 1933. He lost the Republican nomination in 1928, but when the winner, Henry Rathbone, died, he was appointed the nominee and won. In 1932 he was defeated in the general election and retired from politics. Yates died on April 11, 1936 and was buried at Jacksonville, Illinois. Bibliography: Robert P. Howard, *Illinois: A History of the Prairie State* (Grand Rapids, Michigan, 1972); Roy Glashan, *American Governors and Gubernatorial Elections, 1775-1975* (Stillwater, Minnesota, 1975); State Centennial Commission, *Governors of Illinois, 1818-1918* (Springfield, 1918); John H. Krenkel, *Serving the Republic, Richard Yates* (Danville, 1968).

DENEEN, Charles S., 1905-1913

Born on May 4, 1863 in Edwardsville, Illinois, son of Samuel H. and Mary F. (Ashley); a Methodist. Married Bina Day Maloney on May 10, 1891; father of Charles Ashley, Dorothy, Frances and Bina Day. Graduated from McKendree College in 1882 and received his law degree from Union College of Law in 1888. Deneen practiced law in Chicago from 1890 to 1904. He was elected to the Illinois House of Representatives in 1892; from 1895 to 1896, he served as attorney for the

Sanitary District of Chicago; from 1896 to 1904, he served as State's Attorney for Cook County, Illinois. Deneen, a Republican, was elected Governor of Illinois in 1904, defeating the Democratic candidate, Lawrence B. Stringer, by a vote of 634,029 to 334,880. He assumed office on January 9, 1905. He was reelected in 1918, for a second term, defeating Adlai E. Stevenson, the Democratic candidate, by a vote of 550,076 to 526,912. During his term of office, Deneen supported the passage of a Presidential Preference Primary Law in 1912, which was the first in the nation. He also was instrumental in obtaining dramatic increases in appropriations for higher education and the common schools. Deneen was defeated in his attempt for a third term by Democrat Edward F. Dunne by a vote of 443,129 to 318,469. He left office on February 3, 1913. Following his term of office, he resumed the practice of law in Chicago. In 1925 he was appointed to the United States Senate to fill the unexpired term of Medill McCormick; he served until 1931. Following his Senate service, he practiced law in Chicago until death. Deneen died on February 5, 1940 and was buried in Chicago. Bibliography: Robert P. Howard, *Illinois: A History of the Prairie State* (Grand Rapids, Michigan, 1972); Theodore Calvin Pease, *The Story of Illinois* (Chicago, 1929); State Centennial Commission, *Governors of Illinois, 1818-1918* (Springfield, 1918); Roy Glashan, *American Governors and Gubernatorial Elections 1775-1975* (Stillwater, Minnesota, 1975).

DUNNE, Edward F., 1913-1917

Born on October 12, 1853 in Waterville, Connecticut, son of P. W., a member of the Illinois General Assembly, and Delia M. (Lawler); a Catholic. Married to Elizabeth J. Kelly on August 16, 1881; father of thirteen children; Edward P., Gerald, Charles P., Edward F., Geraldine, Jennette, Richard J., Eugene, Robert J., Dorothy, Maurice F., Mona, and Eileen. He received his law degree from Union College of Law in 1877 and practiced law until he was elected judge of the Circuit Court of Cook County in 1892. He served until 1905 when he was elected Mayor of Chicago, 1905-1907. From 1907 to 1913, he resumed his law practice. In 1913 Dunne, a Democrat, entered the race for Governor, defeating the incumbent Republican governor, Charles Deneen, by a vote of 443,120 to 318,469. He was inaugurated on February 3, 1913. His administration was successful in winning legislative approval of a bipartisan commission to regulate public utilities, and a law allowing cities and localities to acquire electric and gas plants. In his attempt for a second term, Dunne was defeated by the Republican candidate, Frank Lowden, by a vote of 696,535 to 556,654. He left office on January 8, 1917. Following his term as governor, he was appointed attorney for the Cook County Board of Election Commissioners in 1930. In 1933 he completed a history of Illinois. Dunne died on May 14, 1937 and was buried in Chicago. Bibliography: Edward F. Dunne, *Illinois, the Heart of the Nation*, 5 vols. (Chicago, 1933); Roy Glashan, *American Governors and Gubernatorial Elections 1775-1975* (Stillwater, Minnesota, 1975); Edward F. Dunne, *Dunne: Judge, Mayor, Governor* (Chicago, 1916); Robert P. Howard, *Illinois: A History of the Prairie State* (Grand Rapids, Michigan, 1972); Secretary of State, *Illinois Blue Book, 1913-1914* (Springfield, 1914).

LOWDEN, Frank O., 1917-1921

Born on January 6, 1861 in Sunrise, Minnesota; son of Lorenzo C., village blacksmith, farmer, and Justice of the Peace, and Nancy Elizabeth (Breg). Brother of May, Eugene, Eva, Caroline, Alice, Eleanor, and Isabel. Married Florence Pullman on April 29, 1896; father of Pullman, Florence, Harriet, Frances. He graduated from the University of Iowa in 1885 and received his law degree from Union College of Law in 1887. He practiced law in Chicago from 1887 to 1906 and was appointed professor of law at Northwestern University in 1899. Lowden was a Lieutenant Colonel in the 1st Infantry, Illinois National Guard during the Spanish-American War. He was a delegate to the Republican National Convention in 1900 and 1904, and served on the Republican National Committee from 1904 to 1912. Lowden entered the Republican primary for governor in 1904, but was defeated by Charles Deneen. He was elected to the United States House of Representatives in 1906, serving until 1911. Lowden was elected Governor of Illinois in 1916, defeating the incumbent Democratic governor, Edward Dunne, by a vote of 696,535 to 556,654. He assumed office on January 8, 1917. During his term of office, Lowden pushed through the state legislature an administrative reorganization plan that combined 128 overlapping agencies into nine departments. One of these departments was the Department of Finance, which was given the power to systematize and supervise the operation of the other eight and to prepare a biennial executive budget. This reorganization saved the state at least $1,000,000 a year. Lowden was able to reduce taxes by $7,000,000, while accumulating by 1921 a surplus of $15,000,000. Lowden also doubled state aid to public schools; increased the University of Illinois' budget by 33 percent; began construction of a $57,000,000 hard road construction program; and began a $20,000,000 waterway to link the Great Lakes with the Gulf of Mexico. After race riots occurred between June 8-11, 1917, Lowden supported antirace and antireligious discrimination legislation. He also appointed a non-partisan commission to revise the state's election laws. Lowden's reforms also included the replacement of the State Board of Equalization by a three-man State Tax Commission. His reorganization of Illinois government made the state the model for the rest of the nation to follow. Lowden chose to serve only one term, leaving office on January 10, 1921. Following his term, he returned to his farm and estate which was a legally protected bird sanctuary. He also supervised his cotton plantations in Arkansas. He received over 300 votes for the presidential nomination in the Republican National Convention in 1920. He declined the vice presidential nomination in 1924. Lowden died on March 20, 1943. Bibliography: Robert P. Howard, *Illinois, a History of the Prairie State* (Grand Rapids, Michigan, 1972); Roy Glashan, *American Governors and Gubernatorial Elections, 1775-1975* (Stillwater, Minnesota, 1975); William T. Hutchinson, *Lowden of Illinois: The Life of Governor Frank O. Lowden*, 2 vols. (Chicago, 1957); Secretary of State, *Illinois Blue Book, 1917-1918* (Springfield, 1918).

SMALL, Lennington, 1921-1929

Born on June 16, 1862 in Kankakee, Illinois; son of Abram, a doctor, and Calista (Currier). Married Ida Moore on November 21, 1883; father of Budd, Leslie, and

May. He attended public schools and Northern Indiana Normal School. He was a member of the Illinois State Senate from 1901 to 1905; he was elected State Treasurer in 1904 and served until 1908. From 1908 until 1912, he was assistant treasurer in charge of the United States Subtreasury at Chicago. From 1917 to 1919, he was again State Treasurer. Small, a Republican, was elected governor in 1920, defeating Democrat James H. Lewis by a vote of 1,243,148 to 731,551. He was elected to a second term in 1924, defeating Norman L. Jones by a vote of 1,366,436 to 1,021,408. He assumed office on January 10, 1921. Small's administration is best remembered for the fact that he was indicted and tried in 1921 on charges of embezzlement and conspiracy during his tenure as State Treasurer. Though he was found not guilty by a jury, Small was forced to pay $650,000 to settle a civil suit. The Small administration was also known for its active highway building program. He spend over $200,000,000 for some 7,000 miles of concrete-paved roads, which gave Illinois at that time the best road system in the United States. The roads were paid for by a $100,000,000 bond issue to be retired by auto license fees. Small left office on January 14, 1929. Following his term of office, Small ran for Governor two more times. In 1932 he won the Republican nomination but lost to Democrat Henry Horner by a vote of 1,930,330 to 1,364.043. In 1936 he lost the primary by C. Wayland Brooks by a vote of 596,445 to 268,903. Between, and after, his political campaigns, Small lived on his farm and was owner of the Kankakee *Daily Republican*. Small died on May 17, 1936 and was buried in Kankakee, Illinois. Bibliography: Robert P. Howard, *Illinois, A History of the Prairie State* (Grand Rapids, Michigan, 1972); Roy Glashan, *American Governors and Gubernatorial Elections 1775-1975* (Stillwater, Minnesota, 1975); William Stuart, *The Twenty Incredible Years* (Chicago, 1935); Carroll H. Woody, *The Case of Frank L. Smith: A Study in Representative Government* (Chicago, 1931).

EMMERSON, Louis L., 1929-1933

Born on December 27, 1883 in Albion, Illinois; son of Jesse E. and Fannie (Saurdet); a Presbyterian. Married Anna Mathews in 1887; father of Aline and Dorothy. He attended the public schools in Albion, and in 1879 entered business as a clerk in a local hardware store. In 1883 he moved to Mount Vernon where he was a partner in a retail dry goods business. In 1901 he helped to organize the Third National Bank of Mount Vernon. In 1912 he ran for State Treasurer but lost. In 1916 he was elected Secretary of State and served until 1929. Emmerson was elected Governor of Illinois as a Republican in 1928, defeating the Democratic candidate, Floyd Thompson, 1,709,818 votes to 1,284,897. He assumed office on January 14, 1929. During his administration, Emmerson had to face the problems created by the Great Depression. The burdens of taxpayers were eased by legislation that changed the penalty dates on overdue taxes and permitted the issuance of bonds to meet emergencies. Also due to the Depression, the first Unemployment Commission was created. A tax on motor fuel was enacted to pay for the expansion of the public highway system from 1,340 miles to 4,761 miles. Emmerson also sought and received federal funds to complete the Lakes-to-the-Gulf Waterway. Emmerson decided that a Republican's chances for electoral victory were not hopeful during the Great Depression and he therefore decided to retire from politics. He left office on January 9, 1933. Following his term of office, Emmerson returned to his business affairs and did not take an active role in politics again. Emmerson died on February 4, 1941 and was buried in Mount Vernon. Bibliography: Robert P. Howard, *Illinois, A History of the Prairie State* (Grand Rapids, Michigan, 1972); Roy Glashan, *American Governors and Gubernatorial Elections 1775-1975* (Stillwater, Minnesota, 1975); Secretary of State, *Illinois Blue Book, 1929-1930* (Springfield, 1930); Edward F. Dunne, *Illinois, The Heart of the Nation* (Chicago, 1933).

HORNER, Henry, 1933-1940

Born on November 30, 1879 in Chicago, Illinois; son of Solomon A. Levy and Dilah (Horner); Jewish. His parents separated when Horner was a young boy and his mother resumed her maiden name which Henry also used. Never married. He attended the Chicago public schools, the Chicago Manual Training School, and the University of Chicago, receiving his law degree from the Chicago-Kent College of Law in 1898. He practiced law in Chicago from 1899 until 1914. In 1914 he was appointed Judge of the Probate Court of Cook County, and served in this position until 1933. Horner was elected Governor of Illinois as a Democrat in 1932, defeating former Republican Governor, Len Small, 1,930,330 votes to 1,364,043. After surviving a bitter primary election, in which he defeated the candidate of the "Chicago machine" by 161,092 votes, Horner won a second• term in 1936 by defeating C. Wayland Brooks by a vote of 2,067,861 to 1,682,685. He assumed office on January 9, 1933. During his term of office, Horner had to contend with the Great Depression and the bitter fighting between his supporters and the "Chicago machine" led by Mayor Edward J. Kelly. To help the state rebound from the Depression, Horner pushed through the legislature a two percent sales tax levy for relief, and a bill abolishing the state tax on real estate and personal property. He also signed into law the repeal of state prohibition and presided over the formal ratification of the Twenty-first Amendment repealing national prohibition. In the attempt to restrict the power of the "Chicago machine," Horner supported a law requiring permanent registration, a system by which voters were required to match signatures kept on file by election officials. Horner had already decided not to seek a third term when he died on October 6, 1940. He was succeeded by the Lieutenant Governor, John Stelle. Horner died on October 6, 1940 and was buried in Winnetka, Illinois. Bibliography: Thomas B. Littlewood, *Horner of Illinois* (Evanston, 1969); Robert P. Howard, *Illinois, A History of the Prairie State* (Grand Rapids, Michigan, 1972); Roy Glashan, *American Governors and Gubernatorial Elections 1775-1975* (Stillwater, Minnesota, 1975); Secretary of State, *Illinois Blue Book, 1933-1934* (Springfield, 1934).

STELLE, John H., 1940-1941

Born on August 8, 1891 in McLeansboro, Illinois; son of a county judge in Hamilton County, Illinois. Married Wilma Wiseheart in 1912; father of John Albert and Russell. He attended Western Military Academy and in 1916 received a law degree from Washington University. In 1917 he enlisted in the Illinois National

Guard and in 1919 was discharged as a Captain. From 1913 to 1931, he served as assistant State Treasurer; from 1933 to 1934, he served as assistant State Auditor; from 1934 to 1936, he served as State Treasurer; and in 1936 he was elected as Lieutenant Governor. When Governor Horner became ill on April 2, 1940, Stelle named himself Acting Governor, but failed to win recognition of his claim. He entered the 1940 Democratic primary for Governor but lost. Stelle became Governor of Illinois on October 6, 1940 when Governor Horner died. His short term was distinguished only by his firing of Horner's appointees and the appointment of his friends. Stelle left office on January 13, 1941. Following his term of office, Stelle served as national commander of the American Legion from 1945 to 1946. He had also been the chairman of the Legion committee that had drafted the "GI Bill of Rights" and lobbied for its passage. In 1941 Stelle became president and owner of Arketex Ceramic Corporation; he was also president of the Evansville Coal Company, Inc., and the McLeansboro Shale Products Company. Stelle died on July 5, 1962 and was buried in McLeansboro. Bibliography: Robert P. Howard, *Illinois, A History of the Prairie State* (Grand Rapids, Michigan, 1972); Roy Glashan, *American Governors and Gubernatorial Elections 1775-1975* (Stillwater, Minnesota, 1975); Secretary of State, *Illinois Blue Book, 1939-1940* (Springfield, 1940).

GREEN, Dwight H., 1941-1949

Born on January 9, 1897 in Ligonier, Indiana, son of Harry and Minnie (Gerber); an Episcopalian. Married Mable Victoria Kingston on June 29, 1926 and was the father of two girls, Nancy and Gloria. He attended Wabash College from 1915 to 1917, when he entered the United States Army Air Service. From 1917 to 1918, he was a 2nd Lieutenant in the Air Service; and from 1918 to 1919, was an army pilot and flying instructor. After studying at Stanford in 1919, he attended the University of Chicago where he received his law degree in 1922. From 1922 to 1926, Green practiced law in Chicago; in 1926 he was appointed Special Attorney for the Bureau of Internal Revenue. In 1927 he was appointed as special assistant to the United States Attorney for the Northern District of Illinois in charge of income tax matters. In this position he prosecuted Al Capone for income tax evasion. Green served as United States District Attorney for the Northern District of Illinois from 1932 to 1935. In 1939 he was the Republican candidate for Mayor of Chicago, but lost. Green entered the 1940 Republican gubernatorial primary election and defeated former Governor John Stelle by 256,945 votes. Green was elected Governor of Illinois in the general election, receiving 2,197,778 votes to Democrat Harry Hershey's 1,940,833 votes. He was reelected in 1944, receiving 2,013,270 votes to Democrat Thomas Courtney's 1,940,999 votes. He was inaugurated on January 13, 1941. His administration was noted for its program of re-employment, retraining, and rehabilitation for veterans and corrective treatment for those rejected for physical disabilities. During his term, a law was approved that required all educational institutions supported by public funds to teach American history, and the principles of republican government and the secret ballot. Green also appointed an interracial commission to investigate racism, especially in the areas of housing and employment. Also the public purchase of Chicago's transit system and the creation of publicly-owned port authorities was approved during his term. In his attempt for an unprecedented third term, Green was defeated by Adlai Stevenson by a vote of 2,250,074 to 1,678,007. He left office on January 10, 1949. Following his term as governor, Green returned to his private law practice. Green died on February 20, 1958 and was buried in Chicago. Bibliography: R. J. Casey and W. A. S. Douglas, *The Midwesterner* (Chicago, 1948); Roy Glashan, *American Governors and Gubernatorial Elections 1775-1975* (Stillwater, Minnesota, 1975); Robert P. Howard, *Illinois: A History of the Prairie State* (Grand Rapids, Michigan, 1972); Secretary of State, *Illinois Blue Book, 1941-1942* (Springfield, 1942).

STEVENSON, Adlai E., 1949-1953

Born on February 5, 1900 in Los Angeles, California, son of Lewis Green and Helen Louise (Davis); a Unitarian. Brother of Elizabeth. Married to Ellen Borden in December, 1928; father of Adlai E., 3rd, Borden, and John P. In 1918 Stevenson served as an apprentice seaman in the United States Naval Reserve. He graduated from Princeton in 1922 and received his law degree from Northwestern University in 1926. From 1924 through 1926, he served as assistant managing editor of the Bloomington *Daily Pantagraph*; in 1927 Stevenson joined the law firm of Cutting, Moore, Sidley. In 1933 he served as special counsel for the Agricultural Adjustment Administration; in 1934 he was assistant general counsel for the Federal Alcohol Control Administration. From 1941 to 1944, he served as special assistant to the Secretary of the Navy; in 1943 he was appointed head of the Italian Section of the Foreign Economic Mission. In April 1945 he served as press spokesman for the American delegation to the United Nations Conference on International Organization. In 1946 Stevenson was the senior advisor to the American delegation to the first United Nations General Assembly. Stevenson was elected Governor of Illinois as a Democrat in 1948, defeating the Republican incumbent, Dwight Green, by a vote of 2,250,074 to 1,678,007. He assumed office on January 10, 1949. During his term of office, Stevenson sponsored proposals that revised mining laws; put the state police under the merit system; and increased the state gasoline tax to finance the public highway system. He did not seek a second term as governor, since he was chosen in 1952 as the Democratic presidential nominee. Stevenson was also the Democratic presidential candidate in 1956, but he was defeated in both 1952 and 1956 by Republican Dwight D. Eisenhower. From 1955 through 1960, he was a partner of the law firm of Stevenson, Rifkind, and Wirtz. From 1961 to his death in 1965, Stevenson was the American Ambassador to the United Nations. Stevenson died on July 14, 1965 and was buried in Bloomington, Illinois. Bibliography: Stuart G. Brown, *Conscience in Politics: Adlai E. Stevenson in the 1950's* (Syracuse, 1961); Noel P. Busch, *Adlai E. Stevenson of Illinois: A Portrait* (New York, 1952); Bert Cochran, *Adlai Stevenson: Patrician Among the Politicians* (New York, 1969); Patricia Harris, *Adlai, the Springfield Years* (Nashville, 1975); Roy Glashan, *American Governors and Gubernatorial Elections, 1775-1975* (Stillwater, Minnesota, 1975); Secretary of State, *Illinois Blue Book, 1949-1950* (Springfield, 1950).

STRATTON, William G., 1953-1961

Born on February 26, 1914 in Ingleside, Illinois; son of William J. and Zula (Van Wormer); a Methodist. Married Shirley Breckenridge on December 27, 1950; father of Sandra, Diane, and Nancy. He graduated from the University of Arizona in 1934. From 1944 to 1946, he served in the United States Navy. In 1940 Stratton was elected to the United States House of Representatives where he served one term. From 1942 to 1946, he served as Illinois State Treasurer. In 1946 he was again elected to the United States House of Representatives and served until 1950. He was then elected State Treasurer in 1950. Stratton was elected Governor of Illinois as a Republican in 1952, defeating Sherwood Dixon, the Democratic candidate, 2,317,363 votes to 2,089,721. He was reelected for a second term in 1956, defeating Richard B. Austin, the Democratic candidate, by a vote of 2,171,786 to 2,134,909. He assumed office on January 12, 1953. During his term of office, Stratton named in 1953 the first woman to cabinet rank; pushed through a bond issue to finance expressways; and removed a requirement that referendum approval had to precede adoption of a city sales tax, greatly aiding the financial situation of the cities. In 1959 the state sales tax was increased to raise money for the schools. He also pushed reform in the state hospitals to provide beds for inmates. He was defeated in his attempt at a third term by the Democratic candidate, Otto Kerner, by a vote of 2,594,731 to 2,070,479. He left office on January 9, 1961. Following his term of office, Stratton returned to his Black Angus cattle farm. In 1968 he attempted to win the Republican nomination for Governor but finished third in the primary race. Bibliography: Robert P. Howard, *Illinois, A History of the Prairie State* (Grand Rapids, Michigan, 1972); Roy Glashan, *American Governors and Gubernatorial Elections, 1775-1975* (Stillwater, Minnesota, 1975); Secretary of State, *Illinois Blue Book, 1955-1956* (Springfield, 1956); Secretary of State, *Illinois Blue Book, 1959-1960* (Springfield, 1960).

KERNER, Otto, 1961-1968

Born on August 15, 1908 in Chicago, Illinois; son of Otto, a lawyer and Circuit Court Judge, and Rose (Chmelik); member of Glenview, Illinois Community Church. Married Helena Cermak on October 20, 1934; father of Anton and Helena. He received his Bachelor of Arts Degree from Brown University in 1930; attended Trinity College, Cambridge University, England from 1930 to 1931; and received a law degree from Northwestern University in 1934. From 1934 to 1936, he was a member of the Illinois National Guard; in 1936 he joined the United States Army and by 1946 had risen to the rank of Major General. From 1947 to 1954, he served as United States District Attorney for the Northern District of Illinois. From 1954 to 1961, he was County Judge for Cook County. Kerner was elected Governor of Illinois in 1960, defeating the incumbent Republican governor, William G. Stratton, by a vote of 2,594,731 to 2,070,479. He was reelected for a second term in 1964, defeating Charles Percy by a vote of 2,418,394 to 2,239,095. He assumed office on January 9, 1961. While in office Kerner supported an increase and widening of sales tax coverage and an increase in corporate taxes. He supported the passage of a fair employment practices law, consumer credit law, and a new criminal code. On May 22, 1968 Kerner resigned as governor to become a judge on the United States Court of Appeals in Chicago. While on the bench, Kerner was indicted and convicted of bribery, conspiracy, income tax invasion, mail fraud, and perjury. He resigned from the Court of Appeals in 1974. Kerner died on May 9, 1976 and was buried in Arlington National Cemetery. Bibliography: Robert P. Howard, *Illinois, A History of the Prairie State* (Grand Rapids, Michigan, 1972); Roy Glashan, *American Governors and Gubernatorial Elections 1775-1975* (Stillwater, Minnesota, 1975); Secretary of State, *Illnois Blue Book, 1960-1961* (Springfield, 1961); Secretary of State, *Illinois Blue Book, 1964-1965* (Springfield, 1965).

SHAPIRO, Samuel H., 1968-1969

Born on April 25, 1907 in Kankakee, Illinois; son of Joseph and Tillie (Bloom); Jewish. Married Gertrude Adelman on May 21, 1939. He attended Saint Victor College and received his law degree from the University of Illinois in 1929. From 1929 to 1933, he practiced law in Kankakee. In 1933 he became City Attorney for Kankakee, serving until 1936, when he was appointed State's Attorney for Kankakee County. He was elected Lieutenant Governor in 1960 and was reelected in 1964. Shapiro became Governor of Illinois when Governor Otto Kerner resigned on May 22, 1968 to accept a judgeship on the United States Court of Appeals. His short administration was characterized by his attempt to win election as governor in his own right. He did win the Democratic nomination for governor, but was defeated in the general election by the Republican nominee, Richard B. Ogilvie, by a vote of 2,307,295 to 2,179,501. The Democratic National Convention was held in Chicago during his term of office. He left office on January 13, 1969 and returned to his law practice. Bibliography: Robert P. Howard, *Illinois, A History of the Prairie State* (Grand Rapids, Michigan, 1972); Roy Glashan, *American Governors and Gubernatorial Elections, 1775-1975* (Stillwater, Minnesota, 1975); Secretary of State, *Illinois Blue Book, 1965-1966* (Springfield, 1966); *Facts on File 1968* (New York, 1969).

OGILVIE, Richard Buell, 1969-1973

Born on February 2, 1923 in Kansas City, Missouri, son of Kenneth S. and Edna May (Buell); a Presbyterian. Married Dorothy Shriver on February 11, 1950; father of one daughter, Elizabeth. Ogilvie was a student at Yale University when he enlisted in the United States Army in 1942. He was discharged in 1945 after suffering face and jaw wounds in France as a tank commander. Ogilvie graduated from Yale in 1947 and received a law degree from Chicago-Kent College of Law in 1949. Between 1950 and 1958, he practiced law in Chicago, and also served a year, 1954-1955, as an Assistant United States Attorney. From 1951 to 1961, he led the legal battle against Chicago-area mobsters as a special assistant to the United States Attorney General, heading a specal midwest office on organized crime. Running as a Republican, he was elected in 1962 as Cook County Sheriff and in 1966 was elected president of the Cook County Board of Commissioners. After winning the 1968 Republican gubernatorial primary election, Ogilvie was elected

Governor of Illinois in the general election, receiving 2,307,295 votes to Democrat Sam Shapiro's 2,179,501. He was inaugurated on January 13, 1969. During his administration the state's first income tax law was passed; law enforcement and corrections procedures were modernized; state aid to local schools was nearly doubled; direct revenue-sharing for cities and counties was established, helping to revitalize local government financing; and a massive road-building program for the state was initiated. In his attempt for a second term, Ogilvie was defeated by Democrat Daniel Walker by a vote of 2,371,303 to 2,293,809. He left office on January 8, 1973. Following his term as governor, he was appointed as chairman of the Young Republican Organization for Cook County. Bibliography: Roy Glashan, *American Governors and Gubernatorial Elections, 1775-1975* (Stillwater, Minnesota, 1975); Robert P. Howard, *Illinois: A History of the Prairie State* (Grand Rapids, Michigan, 1972); Secretary of State, *Illinois Blue Book, 1969-1970* (Springfield, 1970); *Facts on File 1968* (New York, 1969).

WALKER, Daniel, 1973-1977

Born on August 6, 1922 in Washington, D.C.; son of Lewis W., a chief radioman for the United States Navy, and Virginia (Lynch). Married Roberta Dowse on April 12, 1947; father of Kathleen, Daniel, Julie Ann, Roberta Sue, Charles, Margaret Ann, and William. He served as a seaman in the United States Navy from 1939 to 1942, and in 1945 graduated from the United States Naval Academy. He attended Northwestern University Law School from 1947 to 1950. In 1950 he served as law clerk to Supreme Court Justice Fred M. Vinson; in 1951 he served as administrative assistant to Illinois Governor Adlai Stevenson. In 1953 he joined the law firm of Ross, McGowan, O'Keefe; in 1954 he joined the law firm of Hopkins, Sutter, Owen, Mulroy, Wentz, and Davis. In 1966 he became vice president, secretary, and general counsel for Montgomery Ward; in 1968 he became vice president and general counsel for MARCOR, Inc. He failed to win the Democratic primary for State Attorney General in 1960. From September 27, 1968 to November 18, 1968, he served as chairman of the commission which investigated the confrontation between Chicago police and anti-war demonstrators. The "Walker Report" won him wide publicity. Walker won the Democratic primary for Governor by defeating the candidate of the "Chicago machine," Lieutenant Governor Paul Simon, with fifty-two percent of the vote. In the general election, he defeated the incumbent governor, Richard B. Ogilvie, by a vote of 2,371,303 to 2,293,809. He assumed office on January 8, 1973. During his term of office, Walker trimmed the state payroll by ten percent; instituted zero base budgeting; and won approval for a Regional Transit Authority. In his attempt to win a second term, Walker was defeated in the Democratic primary by the "Chicago machine" candidate, Secretary of State Michael J. Howlett, by a vote of 792,393 to 678,495. He left office on January 10, 1977. Bibliography: Roy Glashan, *American Governors and Gubernatorial Elections, 1775-1975* (Stillwater, Minnesota, 1975); Secretary of State, *Illinois Blue Book, 1973-1974* (Springfield, 1974); Secretary of State, *Illinois Blue Book, 1975-1976* (Springfield, 1976); *Facts on File 1974* (New York, 1975).

THOMPSON, James Robert, 1977-

Born on May 8, 1936 in Chicago, Illinois, son of James Robert and Agnes Josephine (Swanson); a Presbyterian. Married to Jayne Carr in 1976. Attended the University of Illinois from 1953 to 1955; Washington University, St. Louis in 1955-1956; attained his J.D. degree from Northwestern University, 1959; admitted to the Illinois Bar that same year. Served as Assistant State's Attorney for Cook County, Illinois from 1959-1964. Taught law at Northwestern University from 1964-1969; lectured at the Davis Campus of the University of California, and at the Michigan State University, 1968. Served on the committee that revised the Illinois criminal code from 1959 to 1963; was a member of the President's task force on crime in 1967. He also was on the committee that drafted handbooks for the use of petit jurors in criminal and civil cases in 1959. Assistant Attorney General for Illinois in 1969-1970; served as chief of the Criminal Division in 1969; as chief of the Department of Law Enforcement and Public Protection in 1969-1970; First United States Attorney for the Northern Division of Illinois in 1970-1971; and was United States Attorney for the Northern Division from 1971-1976. In the November 21, 1976 general election, James R. Thompson, Jr. was elected Governor of Illinois defeating Michael J. Howlett, a Democrat, by a vote of 2,963,247 to 1,580,769. A Republican. Governor Thompson took the oath of office on January 9, 1977. In March 1977, the Equal Rights Amendment suffered a setback as the Illinois Legislature voted to require a three-fifths vote for passage. Governor Thompson will only serve a two year term, to enable Illinois to prevent its gubernatorial elections from coinciding with presidential elections. Bibliography: *New York Times*, (November, 1976, January, 1977); Congressional Quarterly Inc., *Congressional Quarterly Yearbook* (Washington, 1976).

INDIANA

INDIANA

JENNINGS, Jonathan, 1816-1822

Born in 1787; birthplace not definitely known, but was probably Hunterdon County, New Jersey. Son of Jacob Jennings, minister of the Dutch Reformed Church, and Mary Kennedy Jennings, daughter of a Presbyterian minister; brother of Samuel, Jacob, Ebenezer, Obadiah, David, Sarah Jennings Simonson and Ann Jennings Mitchell. Married Ann Gilmore Hay, August 8, 1811, who died in April 1826; remarried to Clarissa Barbee on October 19, 1827. No children. Obtained common school education, and attended grammar school in Canonsburg, Pennsylvania. Jennings came to Clark County, Indiana Territory in 1806 and settled in Vincennes in 1807, where he was admitted to the bar. Served as clerk in the land office and on the board of Vincennes University, 1807-1808. Returned to Clark County in 1808. In 1809, Jennings was elected delegate to Congress from Indiana Territory, defeating Thomas Randolph, then Attorney General of the territory. The major issue of the campaign involved whether slavery should be introduced into the territory, and Jennings was the antislavery candidate. He was reelected territorial delegate in 1811, 1812, and 1814. Jennings was mostly concerned with the affairs of his constituents, such as land purchases, protection from Indian raids, and internal improvements, and in December 1815, he presented a petition to Congress from the Territorial Legislature requesting statehood. On April 11, 1816, the Enabling Act, which provided for a constitutional convention, was passed, and Jennings was elected from Clark County to serve as president of the convention. His government services were during a period of personal, rather than party, politics. He was one of the "Adams and Clay" men, who called themselves National or Jeffersonian Republicans. They opposed the Jacksonian party, but were never as closely organized as their opponents, nor were they as party-conscious. Jennings was elected Governor of Indiana in 1816, defeating Thomas Posey, the Territorial Governor since 1813. He advocated the organization of an educational system, a banking system, and laws to protect legally free blacks. In 1818, he was a member of several commissions to negotiate treaties with the Potawatomi, Wea, Delaware and Miami Indians. Jennings served two terms as governor, and left office on September 12, 1822, following his election to Congress. He was reelected to Congress in 1824, 1826, and 1828, and was defeated in 1830 by General John Carr, a soldier in the War of 1812. He retired to his farm near Charlestown, Clark County. In 1832, he was again a member of the commission to negotiate with Potawatomi and Miami Indians. He died on July 26, 1834 and was buried in Charlestown. No church affiliation in Indiana is known. Bibliography: Logan Esarey, ed., *Messages and Papers of Jonathan Jennings, Ratliff Boon, William Hendricks* (Indianapolis, 1924), Jonathan Jennings, *Unedited Letters*, with notes by Dorothy Riker (Indianapolis, 1943); Dorothy Riker, "Jonathan Jennings," *Indiana Magazine of History*, XXVIII, 4 (December, 1932). Letters of Jennings in the Indiana State Library, the Indiana Historical Society Library, Indianapolis, and the National Archives, Washington, D.C.

BOON, Ratliff, 1822

Born on January 18, 1781, probably in Franklin County, North Carolina; son of (probable) parents, Jesse and Kessiah Boon; a Presbyterian. Married on August 13, 1801 to Deliah Anderson; father of Malinda, Matilda, Minerva [Boon(e)] Luce, Maria, Perry, Allen, and Baily Hart. Boon attended public schools in Danville, Kentucky and then learned the gunsmith's trade. He moved to Warrick County, Indiana Territory about 1809; was elected the first Treasurer of Warrick County in 1813; was a member of the Indiana House of Representatives, 1816-1817, and of the Indiana Senate, 1818. He was elected Lieutenant Governor on the ticket with Jonathan Jennings, August 2, 1819. His opponent was John De Pauw. Boon received 7,397 votes to De Pauw's 3,882. When Jonathan Jennings resigned as Governor of Indiana to take a seat in the United States Congress on September 12, 1822, Boon completed the unexpired term. Boon was again elected Lieutenant Governor, with William Hendricks as Governor, on August 5, 1822. There were four candidates for Lieutenant Governor, William Polke being the closest contender. Boon received 6,614 votes to Polke's 3,469. He served as Lieutenant Governor until the close of the legislative session, January 30, 1824, resigning to run for Congress. He was elected to Congress on August 2, 1824 as a Jacksonian Democrat, where he served until 1839 (with the exception of the term 1827-29, when he was defeated for reelection by Thomas H. Blake, by eighty-four votes). In 1836 he was a candidate for the United States Senate, but was defeated by Oliver H. Smith. While in Congress, he worked for legislation concerning public lands. Boon moved to Pike County, Missouri in 1839, where he was again active in politics. He led a revolt against Thomas H. Benton, but lost. He died in Louisiana, Missouri on November 20, 1844 and was buried in Riverview Cemetery there. Bibliography: Logan Esarey, ed., *Messages and Papers of Jonathan Jennings, Ratliff Boon, William Hendricks* (Indianapolis, 1924); Hazel A. Spraker, *The Boone Family* (Baltimore, 1974); William W. Woollen, *Biographical and Historical Sketches of Early Indiana* (Indianapolis, 1883). Letters of Boon in the Indiana Historical Society Library and the Indiana State Library, Indianapolis.

HENDRICKS, William, 1822-1825

Born November 12, 1782 on a farm in Westmoreland County, Pennsylvania, son of Abraham and Ann Jamison Hendricks; a Methodist. Brother of Thomas, Daniel, Rachel Hendricks Pollock, Abraham, Jamison, Mary Hendricks McHarg, John and Ann Hendricks Henderson. Married on May 19, 1816 to Ann Parker Paul; father of William, Sarah Ann Hendricks Hendricks, John Abraham, Josiah Grover, William Parker, Paul, Thomas, Mary and Ellen Corry Hendricks Weyer. Hendricks was educated at Canonsburg, Pennsylvania, and later settled in Cincinnati where he read law and was admitted to the bar. He moved to Madison, Indiana Territory in

1812 and practiced law there. From 1813 to 1815, he published the newspaper *Western Eagle* with Seth M. Levenworth. (The paper was later published in Lexington, Indiana Territory.) He was elected to the House of Representatives of Indiana Territory in 1814, and served as Secretary of the Indiana Constitutional Convention in June 1816. In August 1816 Hendricks was elected the first representative to Congress from the state of Indiana after defeating Allen Thom. He served three successive terms in Congress, and was particularly interested in legislation that concerned the building of canals and roads. He was appointed Major General of the 5th Division, Indiana Militia, January 21, 1820. Hendricks was elected Governor of Indiana on August 5, 1822. He was unopposed in the election, and received 18,340 votes. He took office on December 5, 1822. During his administration, there was a great influx of settlers into the state, since settlers were moving north from the Ohio River area. The capital was moved from Corydon to Indianapolis in 1824. On January 12, 1825 Hendricks was elected United States Senator by the legislature, and he resigned from the governorship on February 12, 1825. He was reelected to the Senate on December 18, 1830 and served until 1837. He was an unsuccessful candidate for reelection in 1836, losing to Oliver H. Smith. A Democratic-Republican, he was a firm believer in the internal improvements program. Upon retirement from public office, he spent much of his time managing his large estate in Jefferson County. He died on May 16, 1850 in Jefferson County and was buried in Springdale Cemetery in Madison. In early life he was a Presbyterian, but in later years he joined the Methodist Church. Bibliography: Logan Esarey, ed., *Messages and Papers of Jonathan Jennings, Ratliff Boon, William Hendricks* (Indianapolis, 1924); William P. Hendricks, *Sketches of the Family of Abraham Hendricks of Ligonier Valley, Westmoreland Co. Pa.* (Madison, 1892); William W. Woollen, *Biographical and Historical Sketches of Early Indiana* (Indianapolis, 1883). Hendricks Papers in the Archives and Indiana Division, Indiana State Library. Scattered letters of Hendricks in the Indiana Historical Society Library, Indianapolis.

RAY, James Brown, 1825-1831

Born in Jefferson County, Kentucky, on February 19, 1794, son of William Ray, a Revolutionary War veteran, and Phebe Ann Brown Ray. Married Mary Riddle in December 1818, who died July 4, 1823; father of James G. and Mary Ann; remarried Esther Booker in September 1825; father of Indiana, Eliza Jane Ray Garver, Virginia, Sarah and John W. Ray had little formal education. He read law in Cincinnati and in 1818 moved to Brookville, Indiana where he was admitted to the practice of law. In 1821 he was elected to the Indiana House of Representatives, and in 1822 to the Indiana State Senate. When Ratliff Boon resigned as Lieutenant Governor on January 30, 1824 to run for Congress, Ray was elected President Pro Tempore of the Senate and was reelected the next year. A year later Governor William Hendricks resigned upon his election to the United States Senate, and Ray assumed the governorship on February 12, 1825. He was elected Governor in his own right on August 1, 1825, after defeating Isaac Blackford. Ray received 13,852 votes to Blackford's 12,165. His term of office began on December 7, 1825. He was reelected on August 4, 1828, receiving 15,131 votes to Dr. Israel T. Canby's 12,251 and Harbin H. Moore's 10,898. Ray was a Democratic-Republican.

During his administration, two internal improvement programs were of prime interest, the Michigan Road—a road to run from the Ohio River to the Michigan border—and the Wabash and Erie Canal. He also served as one of the commissioners to negotiate treaties with the Potawatomi and Miami Indians for further land concessions in October 1826. Ray's second term was plagued by difficulties with the legislature. He was unsuccessful in his attempt to get a revised penal code passed, and a bitter battle ensued over his appointments to the Indiana Supreme Court. After his retirement from the governor's office, he resumed the practice of law in Indianapolis. On several occasions he was a candidate for public office, but was defeated. In 1833 he started a newspaper, *The Hoosier*, in Greencastle with W. M. Tannehill, but it was short-lived. He owned property of considerable value throughout the state. Ray died in Cincinnati, August 4, 1848, of cholera, and was buried in Spring Grove Cemetery near Cincinnati. Bibliography: John H. Nowland, *Early Reminiscences of Indianapolis* (Indianapolis, 1870); Dorothy Riker and Gayle Thornbrough, *Messages and Papers Relating to the Administration of James Brown Ray, Governor of Indiana, 1825-1831* (Indianapolis, 1954); William W. Woollen, *Biographical Sketches of Early Indiana* (Indianapolis, 1883); Papers from the Ray administration in the Archives Division, Indiana State Library.

NOBLE, Noah, 1831-1837

Born in Berryville, Frederick (now Clarke) County, Virginia on January 14, 1794, son of Dr. Thomas and Elizabeth Claire Sedgwick Noble; a Methodist. Brother of Benjamin Sedgwick, James, Maria Noble Lindsey, Elizabeth Noble Winston, Louise Noble John, Lazarus, Mary Ann Noble Bush, Amelia, Martha Noble Tyner, Thomas George, George Thomas, Lucinda Noble Houston, Lavina Noble Sedgwick and Arthur Vance. Married to Catherine Stull Van Swearington on November 8, 1819; father of Thomas Enoch and Catherine Mary Noble Davidson. Dr. Thomas Noble moved in about 1800 to Kentucky where Noah Noble grew to manhood, and where he probably attended the common schools. Noah Noble moved to Brookville, Indiana in 1816. In 1817 he was commissioned a Lieutenant Colonel in the 7th Regiment of the Indiana Militia, and a Colonel in 1820. He was engaged in a number of business enterprises in Brookville, including land speculation and the running of a fulling mill and wool carding machines. He was elected Sheriff of Franklin County in 1820 and reelected in 1822. In 1824 he was elected to the Indiana House of Representatives and in 1825 was appointed Receiver of Public Monies for the Indianapolis Land Office, a position he held until 1829. In 1830 he was appointed a commissioner to locate the Michigan Road which was to run from the Ohio River across Indiana to the Michigan border. On August 1, 1831, Noble was elected Governor as a "Clay man." He received 25,518 votes against 21,002 for Daniel G. Read, campaigning on the Jackson ticket, and 6,984 for Milton Stapp, running as an Independent. During his first administration, a state bank was created. Noble attempted to improve the common school system, although the bill passed by the legislature was far from what he had wanted. On August 4, 1834, Noble was reelected Governor as a Whig. Daniel Read, a Democrat, was again his opponent. Noble received 36,773 votes to Read's 27,257. During Noble's second administration, a revised tax law was passed, and an extensive internal improvements program, calling for construction of roads and canals, was begun. Noble was a candidate for United States Senator in 1836 and in 1838, but was defeated both times. He served on the Internal Improvements Board, 1839-40, and was appointed Fund Commissioner in February, 1841, a post he held until it was abolished in 1842. He died in Indianapolis, February 8, 1844, and was buried in Greenlawn Cemetery. His remains were later moved to Crown Hill Cemetery, Indianapolis. Bibliography: Lucius Boltwood, *History and Genealogy of the Family Thomas Noble of West-field, Massachusetts* (Hartford, Conn., 1878); Dorothy Riker and Gayle Thornbrough, *Messages and Papers Relating to the Administration of Noah Noble, Governor of Indiana, 1831-1837* (Indianapolis, 1958); William W. Woollen, *Biographical and Historical Sketches of Early Indiana* (Indianapolis, 1883). Papers of Noah Noble in the Indiana State Library.

WALLACE, David, 1837-1840

Born in Mifflin County, Pennsylvania, on April 4, 1799, son of Andrew and Eleanor (or Ellen) Jones Wallace. Brother of Thomas J., John Thomson, William Harrison, John Milton, Benjamin F., Catherine Wallace Lewis and Washington. Married Esther French Text on November 10, 1824, who died July 14, 1834; father of Lewis (Lew), John T., Edward T., William W.; remarried Zeralda Sanders on December 25, 1836; father of Mary, Agnes Wallace Steiner and David Wallace, by his second marriage. By 1807 Andrew Wallace had moved with his family to Miami County, Ohio where he was a surveyor and served as County Treasurer. David Wallace attended school in Troy, Ohio, and enrolled in West Point in September, 1817. He was graduated in 1821 with the rank of Second Lieutenant, and remained in West Point as an instructor until he resigned at the end of May, 1822. He then joined his family, who resided in Brookville, Indiana. He studied law and was admitted to the bar. Wallace was elected Lieutenant in the 7th Regiment, Indiana Militia, shortly after his arrival in Brookville; he was later elected Captain in 1825 and Colonel in 1827. Wallace served in the Indiana House of Representatives, 1828-1831. In 1831 he ran for Lieutenant Governor with Noah Noble as the gubernatorial candidate. In the election held on August 1, Wallace's opponents were Ross Smiley, a Democratic-Republican, and James Gregory, an Independent. Wallace received 22,801 votes to Smiley's 17,502 and Gregory's 7,163. He was reelected on August 4, 1834 as Lieutenant Governor, again with Noble as Governor on the Whig ticket. Wallace defeated David Culley, a Democrat, 38,018 votes to 20,364, but resigned on February 6, 1837 to run for Governor. He was elected on August 7, 1837, defeating John Dumont, also a Whig. The vote was Wallace 46,067, and Dumont 36,915. Wallace's term as governor began December 6, 1837. Wallace's administration was confronted with economic disaster due to the breakdown of the state's internal improvement program. The removal of the Potawatomi Indians was accomplished in 1838. Wallace also advocated school reform, but the legislature failed to pass any school laws. After his term as governor had ended, Wallace opened a law office in Indianapolis. On May 3, 1841, he defeated Nathan B. Palmer for Congress, but was himself defeated in 1843 by William J. Brown. He returned to Indianapolis, and in 1850 served in the Indiana Constitutional Convention. He was Judge of the Marion County Court of Common Pleas from 1856 until his death in Indianapolis on September 4, 1859. He was buried in Crown Hill Cemetery in Indianapolis. Bibliography: *Biographical History of Eminent and Self Made Men of the State of Indiana* (Cincinnati, 1880); Dorothy Riker, ed., *Messages and Papers Relating to the Administration of David Wallace, Governor of Indiana, 1837-1840* (Indianapolis, 1963); William W. Woollen, *Biographical and Historical Sketches of Early Indiana* (Indianapolis, 1883). Scattered letters of Wallace in the Indiana State Library and Indiana Historical Society Library, Indianapolis.

BIGGER, Samuel, 1840-1843

Born in Warren County, Ohio on March 20, 1802, son of John Bigger, a pioneer and for many years a member of the Ohio Legislature; a Presbyterian. Brother of Finley Bigger. Married Ellen Williamson, May 25, 1830. Bigger attended Ohio University, Athens, Ohio, receiving an A.B. degree in 1825 and an A.M. in 1830. He studied law in Lebanon, Ohio, and in 1829 moved to Liberty, Indiana, remaining there for only a short time. Later he settled in Rushville. He was elected to the Indiana House of Representatives in 1833 and 1834. In 1836 he was elected by the legislature as Presiding Judge of the Sixth Judicial Court, a post he resigned after his nomination for Governor, March 29, 1840, on the Whig ticket. His opponent was General Tilghman A. Howard, a Democrat. In the election of August 3, 1840, Bigger received 62,932 votes to Howard's 54,274. Bigger took office on December 9, 1840. He was a candidate for reelection on August 7, 1843, but was defeated by James Whitcomb, a Democrat, 60,784 to 58,721. Elizur Deming of the Liberty Party received 1,683 votes. Governor Bigger's defeat was thought due to his having opposed on religious grounds legislation pertaining to the establishment of Asbury College, a Methodist institution. Whitcomb was a Methodist, while Bigger was a Presbyterian. During Bigger's administration, the state was overwhelmed with debt. Indiana's internal improvements program had broken down, but little was done during his administration to relieve the financial difficulties. Bigger advocated a revision of the state's laws, which was adopted by the legislature. After leaving office on December 6, 1843, Bigger moved to Fort Wayne, and resumed his practice of law. He died in Fort Wayne on September 9, 1846 and was buried in the old Broadway Cemetery, Fort Wayne. Bibliography: *Samuel Bigger: Fort Wayne's Forgotten Man* (Fort Wayne, 1953); Gayle Thornbrough, ed., *Messages and Papers Relating to the Administration of Samuel Bigger, Governor of Indiana, 1840-1843* (Indianapolis, 1964); William W. Woollen, *Biographical and Historical Sketches of Early Indiana* (Indianapolis, 1883). Bigger's Papers in the Indiana State Library.

WHITCOMB, James, 1843-1848

Born on a farm near Windsor, Vermont on December 1, 1795, son of John and Lydia Parameter Whitcomb; a Methodist. Brother of John, Almira, Asa, David, Susan, Sally, Simon, Lydia and Joanna. Married Ann Renick Hurst on March 24, 1846, who died on July 17, 1847; father of Martha Whitcomb Matthews. Whitcomb graduated from Transylvania University, studied law and was admitted to the bar in Fayette, Kentucky in March 1822. In 1824 he moved to Bloomington, Indiana where he practiced law. He was elected to the Indiana Senate in 1830 and reelected in 1833. In October 1836, he was appointed Commissioner of the General Land

Office by President Andrew Jackson, and later reappointed by President Martin Van Buren. He served until 1841, when he returned to Indiana and settled in Terre Haute. In 1843 Whitcomb was nominated for Governor by the Democrats. His opponents were Samuel Bigger, a Whig and the incumbent governor, and Elizur Deming, the Liberty Party candidate. Whitcomb won the election on August 7, 1843, the vote being Whitcomb 60,784, Bigger 58,721, and Deming 1,683. Three years later, on August 3, 1846, Whitcomb defeated Joseph G. Marshall, Whig, 64,104 to 60,138; Stephen C. Stevens, Liberty Party, received 2,301 votes. Much of Whitcomb's work during his administration was concerned with adjusting the debts incurred by the internal improvements program. Under Whitcomb, the Indiana Hospital for the Insane and the Indiana Asylum for the Education of the Deaf and Dumb were established in 1844, and the Indiana Institute for the Education of the Blind was founded in 1847. State finances were in a bad condition, and the governor appealed to the branches of the State Bank. Most of the branches responded with loans, and through this aid, five regiments of infantry were organized and mustered into service in 1846 for the Mexican War. On December 14, 1848, the State Legislature elected Whitcomb to the United States Senate. He resigned as Governor on December 27, 1848. His health was poor during most of the time he was in the Senate, and he died in New York on October 4, 1852 before the completion of his term. He was buried in Greenlawn Cemetery, Indianapolis, and his remains were later moved to Crown Hill Cemetery, Indianapolis. Bibliography: Oran Perry *Indiana in the Mexican War* (Indianapolis, 1908); George I. Reed, *Encyclopedia of Biography of Indiana* (Chicago, 1895); Charlotte Whitcomb, *The Whitcomb Family in America* (Minneapolis, 1904); William W. Woollen, *Biographical and Historical Sketches of Early Indiana* (Indianapolis, 1883). Whitcomb's Papers in the Archives Division, Indiana State Library.

DUNNING, Paris C., 1848-1849

Born on March 15, 1806 near Greensboro, North Carolina, son of James and Rachel North Dunning; a Methodist. Brother of William, John and Thomas. Married Sarah Alexander on July 6, 1826, who died on May 19, 1863; father of Martha E. Dunning McBride, Mary C., Rachel J., Paris C. and James A.; remarried Mrs. Ellen Lane Ashford on September 27, 1865; father of Smith Lane Dunning by his second marriage. Dunning was educated at the academy at Greensboro, North Carolina. Following the death of his father, his family moved to Bloomington, Indiana in 1823. Dunning studied medicine in Louisville, Kentucky, but was attracted to law and studied in the office of James Whitcomb (Governor of Indiana, 1843-48) at Bloomington. He was elected to the Indiana House of Representatives on August 5, 1833, and was reelected in 1834 and 1835, serving from 1833 to 1836. On August 1, 1836, he was elected to the Indiana Senate where he served until his retirement in 1840. In 1846 Dunning was nominated for Lieutenant Governor by the Democrats on the ticket with James Whitcomb. Dunning was elected on August 3, 1846, defeating Alexander C. Stevenson, a Whig, and Stephen S. Harding of the Liberty Party. The vote was Dunning 62,965, Stevenson 59,766 and Harding 2,305. Governor Whitcomb resigned on December 27, 1848 upon being elected to the United States Senate, and Dunning became Governor, serving until December 5, 1849. Dunning returned to Bloomington in 1850. In 1863 he was again elected to the Indiana Senate. He was on the Board of Trustees of Indiana State College (which later became Indiana University) 1838-41; he also served as President of the Board from 1838-41. He died in Bloomington on May 9, 1884, and was buried in Rose Hill Cemetery. Bibliography: *Biographical History of Eminent and Self Made Men of the State of Indiana* (Cincinnati, 1880); Burton D. Myers, *Trustees and Officers of Indiana University 1826-1950; Portrait and Biographical Record of Boone and Clinton Counties* (Chicago, 1895). Dunning's Papers are in the Archives Division, Indiana State Library.

WRIGHT, Joseph A., 1849-1857

Born in Washington, Pennsylvania on April 17, 1810, son of John and Rachel Seaman Wright; a Methodist. Brother of George Grover, Rebecca Wright Kennedy, William Seaman, Hannah Wright Benton, John Rogers, Rachel Wright Baldwin and Amy Wright Puett. Married Louisa Cook on November 31, 1831, who died on May 21, 1852; father of John Cook Wright. His second marriage was to Harriett Burbridge on August 15, 1854, who died, October, 1855; father of Joseph Albert, Jr., Harriett Burbridge Wright Brinton, and an adopted daughter, Nannie Bryant Wright Manning. Wright's third marriage was to Caroline Rockwill in 1863. When Wright was young, his family moved to Bloomington, Indiana, where he assisted his father in his brickyard. He attended Indiana Seminary, later Indiana University, in 1828. He studied law and was admitted to the bar in 1829, and then practiced law in Rockville, Parke County. Wright was elected to the Indiana House of Representatives in 1833 and 1836, and in 1839, was elected to the Indiana Senate. He served in the United States Congress, 1843-1845, but was defeated for reelection the next two sessions. In 1849 Wright was nominated by the Democrats as their gubernatorial candidate. In the election on August 6, 1849, he received 76,996 votes to defeat John Matson, Whig, 67,218 and James Cravens, Free Soil Party, 3,076. He was reelected in 1852, receiving 92,576 votes to Nicholas McCarthy, Whig, 73,641 and Andrew L. Robinson, Free Soil, 3,303. The election was held under Indiana's new constitution and was for a term of four years. Wright's terms of office saw the state adopt a new constitution; schools were placed under the township trustee; a State Board of Education was formed; and cities were authorized to levy taxes for schools. A State Board of Agriculture was organized in 1852, and Wright was chosen as its president. The first Indiana State Fair was held in 1851. When Governor Wright's term was completed in 1857, he was named U.S. Minister to Prussia and served until 1862. In 1862 he was appointed to the United States Senate, serving from February 24, 1862 until January 14, 1863. In 1863 Wright was appointed Commissioner to the Hamburg Exposition, and in 1865 he was again sent as Minister to Prussia, where he remained until his death on March 11, 1867. His remains were brought to New York for burial. Bibliography: *Biographical History of Eminent and Self Made Men of the State of Indiana* (Cincinnati, 1880); Phillip Crane, "Governor Jo. Wright: Hoosier Conservative," Ph.D. Dissertation, Indiana University, Bloomington, 1963; William M. Seaman, *Seamon-Hunt-Wright Genealogy* (Indianapolis, 1957); William W. Woollen, *Biographical and Historical Sketches of Early Indiana* (Indianapolis, 1883). Joseph Wright Papers in the Indiana State Library.

WILLARD, Ashbel P., 1857-1860

Born on October 31, 1820 in Oneida County, New York, son of Colonel Erastus Willard, who served for a time as sheriff of Oneida County, and Sarah Parsons Willard. Married Caroline C. Cook on May 31, 1847; father of James H., Caroline C., Ashbel P. Educated at Hamilton College, graduated in 1842, and studied law in his home county. He emigrated to Marshall, Michigan, then to Texas, and finally settled in Kentucky, where he taught school. In the campaign of 1844, Willard campaigned for James K. Polk, and spoke at New Albany, Indiana, where he so impressed the first men of the town that they asked him to settle there. He moved to New Albany in 1845 and began the practice of law. In 1850 he was elected to the Indiana House of Representatives and served from 1850 to 1851. In 1852 he was nominated for Lieutenant Governor by the Democrats on a ticket with Joseph A. Wright, and was elected to that office. His opponents were William Williams, Whig, and James P. Milliken, Free Soil. Willard received 90,239 votes to Williams' 75,094 and Milliken's 3,086. In 1856 Willard was the Democratic candidate for Governor, opposing Oliver P. Morton, Republican. Willard received 117,971 votes to Morton's 112,039. Willard's administration was marked by difficulties with the legislature. The legislature ignored state issues and debated national questions instead. When the legislature adjourned without making appropriations for defraying governmental expenses, Willard borrowed sufficient funds to pay the interest on the state's debt so that the state's credit would not be threatened. John E. Cook, brother of Governor Willard's wife, was arrested for participating in John Brown's raid on Harpers Ferry. Willard went to his aid, but Cook was found guilty and executed. Willard's efforts on behalf of John Cook did much to increase his popularity at home. In 1860 Willard's health failed and he went to Minnesota to try to recuperate. He died in St. Paul on October 3, 1860 and was buried in New Albany. Bibliography: *Biographical History of Eminent and Self Made Men of the State of Indiana* (Cincinnati, 1880); Gerald A. Haffner, "Ashbel Willard's Town," *Indiana History Bulletin*, vol. 52, no. 2 (February, 1975); William W. Woollen *Biographical and Historical Sketches of Early Indiana* (Indianapolis, 1883).

HAMMOND, Abram A., 1860-1861

Born in Brattleboro, Vermont, on March 21, 1814, son of Nathaniel and Patty Ball Hammond. Brother of David, William and John G. Married Mary B. Amsden; father of Georgie Hammond Sweeney Voorhies. Hammond moved to Indiana when he was six years old and settled in Brookville, later studying law there. He practiced law in Greenfield and in Columbus, Indiana where he served as Prosecuting Attorney. In 1846 he moved to Indianapolis and the following year to Cincinnati, Ohio. He returned to Indianapolis in 1849, and served as Judge of the Court of Common Pleas for Marion County. Hammond left Indiana in 1852 for San Francisco, California, but returned in 1855 to settle in Terre Haute. In 1856 he was elected Lieutenant Governor on the Democratic ticket with Ashbel P. Willard, the gubernatorial candidate. Opposing Hammond in the election was Conrad Baker, running on the People's Party ticket. Hammond received 116,717 votes to Baker's 111,620. When Governor Willard died on October 3, 1860, Hammond became Governor and served until January 14, 1861. In his one message to the legislature, he recommended legislation to protect the ballot box, and the establishment of a house of refuge for juvenile offenders, an institution which was eventually established years later. Hammond's health began to fail about the time he left office, and he remained in poor health for the remainder of his life. He died in Denver, Colorado, August 27, 1874 and was buried at Crown Hill Cemetery, Indianapolis. Bibliography: *Biographical History of Eminent and Self Made Men of the State of Indiana* (Cincinnati, 1880); George I. Reed, *Encyclopedia of Biography of Indiana* (Chicago, 1895); William W. Woollen, *Biographical and Historical Sketches of Early Indiana* (Indianapolis, 1883).

LANE, Henry S., 1861

Born on a farm in Montgomery County, Kentucky on February 11, 1811, son of James Hardage Lane, Jr. and Mary Higgins Lane; a Methodist. Brother of William, Higgins, John, Mary Lane Carrington, James H., Elizabeth Lane Goodloe, Nancy Lane Riggs, Evelina Lane Reed and Sarah Lane Stone. Married Pamela Bledsoe Jameson on December 24, 1833, who died in 1842; remarried Joanna M. Elston on February 11, 1845. Lane received a classical education from his tutors. He studied law and was admitted to the bar. In 1835 he settled in Crawfordsville, Indiana and practiced law there. In 1837 he was elected to the Indiana House of Representatives, and served in 1837-38. Tilghman A. Howard resigned from the United States Congress in 1840, and in a special election held on August 3, 1840, Lane, a Whig, defeated Edward A. Hannegan, a Democrat. In 1841 he defeated John Bryce, a Democrat, who opposed him for his congressional seat. Lane ran again for Congress in 1849, but was defeated by Joseph McDonald. At the outbreak of the Mexican War, Lane raised a company of volunteers, and on June 25, 1846, he was chosen Major of the First Indiana Regiment. On October 22, 1847, he was promoted to Lieutenant Colonel and served until July 28, 1848. Lane was active in the formation of the Republican Party in Indiana, and in the convention of 1860, was nominated for Governor, with Oliver P. Morton for Lieutenant Governor. The Democratic contenders were Thomas A. Hendricks for Governor and David Turpie for Lieutenant Governor. Lane defeated Hendricks by 136,736 votes to 126,767, and was sworn in as Governor on January 14, 1861. Two days later he was elected United States Senator by the legislature; he resigned as Governor on January 16, 1861. As a United States Senator, he voted for Union Party policies. At the end of his term in the Senate in 1867, he returned to Crawfordsville. His only other government services were as Special Indian Commissioner (1869-71) and Commissioner for Improvement of Mississippi River (1872). He died at Crawfordsville on June 19, 1881 and was buried in Oak Hill Cemetery, Crawfordsville. Bibliography: *Biographical History of Eminent and Self Made Men of the State of Indiana* (Cincinnati, 1880); George I. Reed, *Encyclopedia of Biography of Indiana* (Chicago, 1895).

MORTON, Oliver P., 1861-1867

Born in Salisbury, Indiana on August 4, 1823, son of James T., a shoemaker, and Sarah Miller Morton. The family name was originally Throckmorton, but his father shortened it to Morton. Brother of Maria Morton Hart, William R. and James. Married Lucinda M. Burbank on May 15, 1843; father of John Miller, Mary Elizabeth, Sarah Lillian, Walter Scott and Oliver Throckmorton. Belonged to no church. Morton attended Miami University, Oxford, Ohio, 1843-45. He studied law at Centreville, Indiana and was elected Circuit Court Judge in 1852. He was one of the organizers of the Republican Party in Indiana, and in 1856 was nominated for Governor, but was defeated by Ashbel P. Willard, a Democrat, 117,971 votes to 112,039. In 1860 Morton was nominated for Lieutenant Governor on the Republican ticket with Henry S. Lane. Morton was elected over his Democratic opponent, David Turpie with 136,470 votes to Turpie's 126,292. On January 14, 1861, Lane was sworn in as Governor, and Morton as Lieutenant Governor. Two days later, on January 16, Lane was elected United States Senator by the legislature and resigned the governor's chair. Morton was sworn in as Governor the same day. In 1864 Morton ran for Governor against Joseph E. McDonald, a Democrat. Morton received 152,273 votes to McDonald's 131,200. Morton was Indiana's Civil War governor, and he was immediately faced with a tremendous task after war was declared. Indiana had no money for war purposes, and many residents of the state were opposed to the conflict. There was also continual strife between the governor and the legislature. Nevertheless, under Morton's leadership, Indiana had a fine recruitment record. When the legislature failed to appropriate funds for the war effort, Morton borrowed more than a million dollars from various banks to equip and pay the soldiers. In 1865 Morton suffered a paralytic stroke. During his recuperation, he turned over the executive duties to Lieutenant Governor Conrad Baker. In 1867 after having regained his health, Morton was elected to the United States Senate, resigning as Governor on January 24, 1867. He was reelected to the Senate in 1872. Morton died in Indianapolis on November 1, 1877 and was buried in Crown Hill, Indianapolis. Bibliography: William D. Foulke, *Life of Oliver P. Morton* (Indianapolis, 1889); George I. Reed, *Encyclopedia of Biography of Indiana* (Chicago, 1895); Russell M. Seeds, *History of the Republican Party of Indiana* (Indianapolis, 1899); William W. Woollen, *Biographical and Historical Sketches of Early Indiana* (Indianapolis, 1883). Papers of Morton in the Indiana State Library.

BAKER, Conrad, 1867-1873

Born on a farm in Franklin County, Pennsylvania on February 12, 1817, son of Conrad and Catherine (or Mary) Winterheimer Baker; a Presbyterian. Brother of William and John. Married to Matilda Escon Sommers on October 31, 1838, who died, November 4, 1855; father of Albert and William Bratton; remarried Charlotte Frances Chute on January 9, 1858; father of Alice Nancy Baker Woollen, Florence Baker Holliday, Elizabeth Baker Anderson and Thaddeus. Baker was educated at Pennsylvania College, Gettysburg and studied law in Gettysburg, where he practiced law for two years. He settled in Evansville, Indiana in 1841. In 1845 he was elected to the Indiana House of Representatives and served one term, 1845-46. In

1856 Baker was nominated for Lieutenant Governor on a Republican ticket which had Oliver F. Morton as the gubernatorial candidate; Ashbel Willard and Abram Hammond were their Democratic rivals. Baker was defeated by Hammond, 116,717 votes to 111,620. On August 20, 1861 Baker was commissioned Colonel of the First Cavalry (28th Regiment of Indiana Volunteers) for Civil War service. He was mustered out on September 12, 1864. In 1864 he was again nominated for Lieutenant Governor on a ticket with Oliver P. Morton. Mahlon D. Manson was Baker's Democratic opponent for Lieutenant Governor, and on this occasion Baker received 147,795 votes to Manson's 131,656. In 1865 Morton's health became impaired, and he turned over the chief executive's duties to Conrad Baker. On January 24, 1867, Governor Morton chose to resign after his election to the United States Senate, and Baker became Governor. Baker was elected Governor in his own right in 1868, defeating Thomas A. Hendricks, 171,505 votes to 170,554, and was sworn in as Governor on January 11, 1869. During Baker's term, funds were appropriated for a state normal school at Terre Haute, a soldiers' home, a house of refuge for juvenile offenders, and a women's prison. Following his term of office, he practiced law in Indianapolis. Baker died in Indianapolis on April 28, 1885 and was buried in Evansville. Bibliography: Jacob P. Dunn, *Greater Indianapolis* (Chicago, 1910); Arnold E. Mueller, "Conrad Baker; Former Governor of Indiana," M.A. Thesis, Butler University, Indianapolis, 1944; John H. Nowland, *Early Reminiscences of Indianapolis* (Indianapolis, 1870). Papers of Baker in the Indiana Historical Society Library and in the Archives Division, Indiana State Library.

HENDRICKS, Thomas, 1873-1877

Born near Zanesville, Ohio on September 7, 1819, son of John and Jane Thompson Hendricks; at first a Presbyterian, but in later life an Episcopalian. Brother of Abraham, Jane Hendricks Webb Pierce, Ann Hendricks Pierce, John and James. Married to Eliza C. Morgan on September 26, 1845; father of a son, Morgan, who died at the age of three. Hendricks entered Hanover College in 1837 and graduated in 1841. He studied law in Chambersburg, Pennsylvania, then settled in Shelbyville, Indiana. In 1848 Hendricks was elected to the Indiana House of Representatives, and in 1850 he was a member of the Indiana Constitutional Convention. Hendricks was elected to Congress in 1851; was reelected under the new state constitution in 1852, but was defeated in 1854. He was appointed Commissioner of the General Land Office in 1855, an office he held until 1859. In 1860 he was the Democratic nominee for Governor, but was defeated by Henry S. Lane, 136,736 votes to 126,767. In the same year, he moved to Indianapolis, and in 1863 was elected to the United States Senate and served until 1869. In 1868, he was defeated by Conrad Baker for the governorship, 171,505 votes to 170,554. After retiring from the Senate, Hendricks returned to Indianapolis. In 1872 he was elected Governor, defeating Thomas M. Browne, a Republican, 189,424 votes to 188,276. During Hendricks' administration, he was called on to deal with labor riots in Logansport and in Clay County. Hendricks had been supported by the temperance forces in his election, and in 1873 he signed the Baxter Prohibition Law, which was repealed two years later. In 1876 Hendricks was the Democratic vice presidential candidate on the ticket with Samuel J. Tilden, and in 1884 he was nominated as Grover

Cleveland's running mate and elected. On November 25, 1885, less than nine months after his inauguration as Vice President, he died in Indianapolis and was buried in Crown Hill Cemetery. Bibliography: *Biographical History of Eminent and Self Made Men of Indiana* (Cincinnati, 1880); William P. Hendricks, *Sketches of the Family of Abraham Hendricks of Ligonier Valley, Westmoreland County, Pa.* (Madison, 1892); J. W. Holcombe and H. M. Skinner, *Life and Public Service of Thomas A. Hendricks* (Indianapolis, 1886). Papers of Hendricks in the Archives Division, Indiana State Library.

WILLIAMS, James D., 1877-1880

Born in Pickaway County, Ohio on January 16, 1808, son of George Williams, a farmer; a Methodist. Married to Nancy Huffman on February 24, 1831; father of Sarah Williams McCoy, John, George and Eliza Williams Dunn. In 1818 moved to Indiana and settled on a farm in Knox County; attended common schools. After his marriage, Williams settled on a farm south of Wheatland. In 1843 he was elected to the Indiana House of Representatives, serving in 1843-44, 1847-48, 1851-52, 1857 and 1869. He served in the Indiana Senate, 1859-65, 1871, and 1875. Williams was a member of the Indiana State Board of Agriculture, 1856-1872. In 1872 Williams was the Democratic nominee for the United States Senate, but was defeated by Oliver P. Morton. In 1874 he was elected to Congress. During his term, he was elected Governor of Indiana and resigned from Congress on December 1, 1876. He had been nominated for Governor in April 1876 by the Democrats, and defeated Benjamin Harrison, a Republican, 213,219 votes to 208,080, in the election held on October 11. Henry W. Harrison, a Greenbacker, received 12,710 votes. Williams won the nickname "Blue Jeans" because he wore a fine quality of blue jeans nearly all his life, except during the summer months. He took office as Governor on January 8, 1877. During Williams' term as governor, a railroad strike crippled the Midwest and there were labor troubles in Indianapolis in 1877. The present Indiana State House was begun in 1878. Williams was a member of the Patrons of Husbandry and was particularly interested in agriculture. Williams died in office on November 20, 1880. Bibliography: *History of Knox and Davies Counties, Indiana* (Chicago, 1886); John B. Stoll, *History of the Indiana Democracy, 1816-1916* (Indianapolis, 1917); William W. Woollen, *Biographical and Historical Sketches of Early Indiana* (Indianapolis, 1883). Papers of Williams in the Archives Division, Indiana State Library.

GRAY, Isaac P., 1880-1881, 1885-1889

Born in Chester County, Pennsylvania on October 18, 1828, son of John and Hannah Worthington Gray; a Quaker. Married to Eliza Jaqua on September 8, 1850; father of Pierre and Bayard (sons Lyman and Warren died as children). Gray had a common school education. The family moved to Montgomery County, Ohio in 1839, and in 1855 Gray settled in Union City, Indiana, where he entered the dry goods business. Later he was a banker, and subsequently studied law. In the Civil War, Gray was a Colonel of the 4th Indiana Cavalry from September 4, 1862 until his resignation on February 11, 1863. On July 10, 1863, he was made Colonel of the

106th Regiment ("The Minute"), which participated in the raid across Indiana in July 1863 against John H. Morgan. The regiment was mustered out, July 17, 1863. Gray later recruited and organized the 147th Regiment in March 1865. Gray was nominated for the United States Congress in 1866 but was defeated by George W. Julian. He was elected to the Indiana State Senate in 1868 as a Republican, and served until 1872. Gray joined the Liberal Republican movement in 1872, and later became affiliated wth the Democratic Party. In 1876 he was nominated for Lieutenant Governor by the Democrats on the ticket with James D. Williams. Gray defeated Robert S. Robertson, Republican, and Richard Gregg, Greenbacker. The vote was Gray, 212,076, Robertson, 206,641, Gregg, 15,388. Governor Williams died on November 20, 1880 and Gray completed his term, serving until January 10, 1881. He was again nominated for Lieutenant Governor in 1880 but was defeated by Thomas Hanna, a Republican, 229,642 votes to 224,872. In 1884 he was the Democratic candidate for Governor, defeating William H. Calkins, a Republican, 245,140 to 237,748. Robert Wiggins, a Prohibitionist, received 3,868 votes and Hiram Z. Leonard, a Greenbacker, 8,338. Appropriations for the Indiana Soldiers and Sailors' Monument in Indianapolis were made during Gray's administration. Funds were also appropriated to build a "school for the feeble-minded" in Fort Wayne and to rebuild the Soldiers' Orphan Home at Knightstown. Following his term of office, Gray practiced law in Indianapolis. In 1893 he was appointed United States Minister to Mexico, where he served until his death in Mexico City on February 14, 1895. He was buried in Union City, Ohio. Bibliography: *Biographical Sketches of Members of the Indiana State Government, 1885* (Indianapolis, 1885); George I. Reed, *Encyclopedia of Biography of Indiana* (Chicago, 1895); John B. Stoll, *History of the Indiana Democracy, 1816-1916* (Indianapolis, 1917). Scattered letters and papers of Gray in the Indiana Historical Society Library.

PORTER, Albert G., 1881-1885

Born in Lawrenceburg, Indiana on April 20, 1824, son of Thomas and Miranda Tousey Porter. Brother of Omer T. and Andrew D. Married to Minerva Virginia Brown on November 30, 1846, who died November 5, 1875; father of Omer Tousey, George Tousey, Edward B., Ray and Annie Porter Mason; remarried to Cornelia Stone on January 5, 1881. As a boy Porter helped his father operate a ferry between Lawrenceburg and the Kentucky shore. He attended Hanover College in Hanover and graduated from Indiana Asbury College (now DePauw University) in 1843. He moved to Indianapolis in 1843 and began the practice of law. He served as a reporter for the Indiana Supreme Court, 1853-57. Porter left the Democratic Party in 1854, and as a Republican was elected to the United States Congress in 1858 and reelected in 1860. From 1878-80, he was Controller of the United States Treasury. In 1880 Porter was elected Governor on the Republican ticket, defeating Franklin Landers, a Democrat, 231,405 votes to 224,452. Richard Gregg, a Greenbacker, received 14,881 votes. During Porter's administration, the Kankakee swamp and other marshlands were drained, adding 80,000 acres of land to Indiana. The State Board of Health was created, and hospitals for the insane were built at Logansport, Richmond and Evansville. Porter served as United States Minister to Italy from

1889 to 1892. He died in Indianapolis, May 3, 1897, and was buried in Crown Hill Cemetery, Indianapolis. Bibliography: Theodore C. Rose, *The Tousey Family in America* (Elmira, N.Y., 1916); Russell Seeds, *History of the Republican Party of Indiana* (Indianapolis, 1899); J. Sutherland, *Biographical Sketches of the Members of the 41st General Assembly* (Indianapolis, 1861); Charles W. Taylor, *Biographical Sketches and Review of the Bench and Bar of Indiana* (Indianapolis, 1895). Papers of Porter in the Archives Division and the Indiana Division, Indiana State Library.

GRAY, Isaac P., 1880-1881, 1885-1889

HOVEY, Alvin P., 1889-1891

Born in Posey County, Indiana on September 6, 1821, son of Abiel, a farmer, and Frances Peterson Hovey. Brother of Frances, Eliza, Amanda, Charlotte, Charles and Minerva. Married to Mary Ann James on November 24, 1844, who died November 6, 1863; father of Esther Hovey Menzies, Enoch James, Charles James and Mary Anne; remarried to Mrs. Rose Alice Smith Carey in 1865. Hovey attended the common schools, studied law and practiced in Mount Vernon, Indiana. At the outbreak of the Mexican War, he was commissioned a First Lieutenant in a company assigned to the 2nd Indiana Regiment; however, it was never mustered into service. He was a member of the Indiana Constitutional Convention in 1850, and from 1850-54 he served as a Circuit Court Judge. He was appointed to the Indiana Supreme Court to fill a vacancy, serving from May 8, 1854 to December 10, 1855. In 1856 he was appointed United States District Attorney and served until 1858. In approximately 1858, Hovey left the Democratic Party and became a candidate for Congress on the Republican ticket, but was defeated by W. E. Niblack. Early in the summer of 1861, Hovey organized the 1st Regiment, 1st Brigade (Posey County) Indiana Legion, and was made Colonel. He resigned when he was commissioned Colonel of the 24th Indiana Regiment on July 31, 1861. He was promoted to Brigadier General on April 28, 1862. In July 1864, he was brevetted Major General and on August 25, 1864, he took command of the Military District of Indiana. He resigned from the service on October 7, 1865. From December 1865 until 1870, Hovey was United States Minister to Peru. He then resumed the practice of law in Mount Vernon. In 1872 he refused the Republican nomination for Governor. He was elected to Congress in 1886, and in 1888 he was his party's candidate for Governor. Hovey defeated Courtland C. Matson, a Democrat, 263,194 votes to 260,994. As governor, he had difficulties with the Democratic-controlled legislature over appointive powers. Also during his administration, the Australian ballot was adopted in 1889, and the State Board of Education was made responsible for the selection of textbooks. Hovey died on November 23, 1891, before the end of his term, and was buried at Mount Vernon. Bibliography: Elfrieda Lang, "Autobiography of Alvin P. Hovey's Early Life: Introduction and Notes," *Indiana Magazine of History*, XLVIII, 1 (March 1952); John C. Leffel, *History of Posey County, Indiana* (Chicago, 1913); Charles M. Walker, *Lives of General Alvin P. Hovey and Ira J. Chase* (Indianapolis, 1888). Papers of Hovey in

Lilly Library, Indiana University, Bloomington and the Archives Division, Indiana State Library.

CHASE, Ira J., 1891-1893

Born on December 7, 1834 in Monroe County, New York, son of Benjamin and Lorinda Mix Chase; a member of the Disciples of Christ Church. Married on March 24, 1859 to Rhoda Jane Castle; father of Emma Chase Holland, Frank E., Electa Chase Murphy and Benjamin. When Chase was twelve years old, the family moved to Milan, Ohio where he attended Milan Seminary; later he attended Medina Academy in New York State. In 1855 the family moved to a farm near Barrington, Illinois where Ira Chase began to teach school. On June 17, 1861, he enlisted in the 19th Illinois Regiment. His health declined after his first year in military service, and he received his discharge papers on November 7, 1862. He returned to Barrington and opened a hardware store, but the business failed. He then entered the ministry of the Christian Church and served congregations in LaPorte, Mishawaka, Wabash and Danville in Indiana, Pittsburgh, Pennsylvania and Peoria, Illinois. In 1886 he was Chaplain of the Indiana G.A.R. and in 1887 he was elected Department Commander. In 1888 Chase was the Republican candidate for Lieutenant Governor on the ticket with Alvin P. Hovey. Chase defeated his Democratic opponent, William R. Myers, 263,166 votes to 261,011. John W. Baxter, a Prohibitionist, received 10,066 votes and Hiram Mainee, Union Labor Party, 2,737. Governor Hovey died on November 23, 1891, and Chase was sworn in as Governor on November 24. He was the Republican candidate for Governor in 1892, but was defeated by Claude Matthews, a Democrat, 260,601 votes to 253,625. During his administration he strongly advocated the construction of better roads. After retiring from office, he devoted his time to preaching and lecturing. He died in Lubec, Maine on May 11, 1895 and was buried at Crown Hill Cemetery, Indianapolis. Bibliography: *Portrait and Biographical Record of Boone and Clinton Counties, Indiana* (Chicago, 1895); Commodore W. Cauble, *Disciples of Christ in Indiana* (Indianapolis, 1938); Charles M. Walker, *Lives of General Alvin P. Hovey and Ira J. Chase* (Indianapolis, 1888). There is a small collection of Chase's papers in the Indiana Division, Indiana State Library.

MATTHEWS, Claude, 1893-1897

Born in Bethel, Kentucky on December 14, 1845, son of Thomas and Eliza Ann Fletcher Matthews; a Presbyterian. Married on January 1, 1868 to Martha Renick Whitcomb, daughter of former Governor James Whitcomb; father of Mary Matthews Ewing, Helen Matthews Krekler and Renick Seymour. Matthews graduated from Centre College, Danville, Kentucky in 1867. Shortly after his graduation, he settled on a farm in Vermillion County, near Clinton, Indiana, where he became interested in the breeding of fine livestock. In 1876 he was elected to the Indiana House of Representatives, and in 1882 he ran for the Indiana State Senate, but was defeated. He served as Indiana Secretary of State from 1891-1893. In 1892 he was the Democratic candidate for Governor, defeating his Republican opponent, Ira J. Chase, 260,601 votes to 253,625. Aaron Worth, a Prohibitionist, received 12,960 votes and Leroy Templeton, People's Party, 22,017. Governor Matthews, in the face of bitter opposition, succeeded in suppressing an organization promoting racing, prize fighting and other amusements. During his administration there was also labor unrest, and a strike of coal miners was settled only after the governor called out the National Guard. Matthews died on April 28, 1898 and was buried at Clinton. Bibliography: *Biographical and Historical Record of Vermillion County, Indiana* (Chicago, 1888); George I. Reed, *Encyclopedia of Biography of Indiana* (Chicago, 1895); John B. Stoll, *History of the Indiana Democracy, 1816-1916* (Indianapolis, 1917). Papers of Matthews in the Archives Division, Indiana State Library.

MOUNT, James A., 1897-1901

Born on March 24, 1843 on a farm in Montgomery County, Indiana, son of Atwell and Lucinda Fullenwider Mount; a Presbyterian. Brother of Thomas R., Catherine, Jacob, Elijah, William H., Ann Elizabeth, Mary Jane, Harriet N., Arvenia F., Samuel B. and Lucinda. Married to Catharine Boyd on November 12, 1867; father of Hallie Lee Mount Butler, Helen Mount Nicely and Harry W. Mount. Attended common schools, and after the Civil War, attended Presbyterian Academy, Lebanon, Indiana for one year. He enlisted in Company D of the 72nd Indiana Regiment on July 22, 1862, was promoted to Sergeant on August 1, 1863, and was mustered out on June 26, 1865. Following his marriage in 1867, Mount settled on a farm in Montgomery County. He was a successful farmer, and became widely known through his lectures to farmers' institutes. He was elected to the Indiana State Senate in 1888 and ran for the United States Congress in 1890, but was defeated by E. V. Brookshire. In 1896 he was the Republican candidate for Governor, receiving 320,932 votes to Benjamin Shively, Democrat, 294,855; Leander M. Crist, Prohibitionist, 2,997; Thomas Wadsworth, Populist, 8,626; James H. Kingsbury, National Prohibitionist, 2,500; Philip H. Moore, Socialist, 283. During Mount's term as governor, the prison system was remodeled; the office of Labor Commissioner established; and a Medical Examining Board set up. Mount was governor during the Spanish-American War. He died in Indianapolis, January 16, 1901, a few days after he had completed his term of office. He was buried at Oak Hill Cemetery, Crawfordsville. Bibliography: *Centennial Memorial, First Presbyterian Church, Indianapolis* (Greenfield, 1925); William E. Henry, *State Manual of Indiana, 1899-1900* (Indianapolis, 1899); Russell M. Seeds, *History of the Republican Party of Indiana* (Indianapolis, 1899). Papers of Mount are in the Archives Division, Indiana State Library.

DURBIN, Winfield, 1901-1905

Born in Lawrenceburg, Indiana on May 4, 1847, son of William Sappington and Eliza Ann Sparks Durbin; a Methodist. Brother of John Weaver, Samuel Weaver, David Sparks, Hosier Hamlet, Henry Clay and William Nunn. Married to Bertha McCullough on October 6, 1875; father of Fletcher and Marie. While a boy, his parents moved to New Philadelphia, Indiana, where his father operated a tannery. Durbin attended common schools; he also studied at a commercial college in St. Louis in 1865. Durbin served in the 139th Regiment in the Civil War from April 23, 1864 to September 29, 1864. He was Colonel, 161st Indiana Regiment in the Spanish-American War, serving from July 15, 1898 to April 30, 1899. Following his Civil War service, Durbin taught school in Washington County during the winter months, and worked in his father's tannery in the summer. In 1869 he moved to Indianapolis, and worked in a dry goods firm. He moved to Anderson in 1879, where he was instrumental in establishing the Citizens' Bank and where he operated a paper mill. Durbin was active in the Republican Party, and in 1900 was the party's candidate for governor. He defeated his Democratic opponent, John Worth Kern, 331,531 votes to 306,368. Durbin was an advocate of better highways, believing that the industrial growth of the state depended on good roads. He also clashed with his own party over legislation which he judged to be for the economic benefit of only a few individuals, and not for the state as a whole. Durbin was again nominated for Governor by the Republicans in 1912, but was defeated by Samuel M. Ralston, a Democrat, 275,357 to 142,850. Albert J. Beveridge, the Progressive candidate, received 166,124 votes; Stephen N. Reynolds, Socialist, 35,464; William Hickman, Prohibitionist, 18,465; and James Matthews, Socialist Labor, 2,861. Following his term as governor, Durbin returned to Anderson where he died on December 18, 1928. He was buried at Crown Hill Cemetery, Indianapolis. Bibliography: *Commemorative Biographical Record of Prominent and Representative Men of Indianapolis and Vicinity* (Chicago, 1908); George I. Reed, *Encyclopedia of Biography of Indiana*, vol. 2 (Chicago, 1895); Russell M. Seeds, *History of the Republican Party of Indiana* (Indianapolis, 1899). The Durbin Papers are in the Archives Division, Indiana State Library.

HANLY, James Franklin, 1905-1909

Born on a farm in Champaign County, Illinois on April 4, 1863, son of Elijah, a cooper, and Ann Eliza Calton Hanly; a Methodist. Married on December 3, 1881 to Eva Augusta Rachel Simmer; father of Ethel Elfrida Hanly Gorman. J. Frank Hanly, as he was known in political circles, had a meager education in rural schools, since from his boyhood he had worked on farms to help support the family. He settled in Williamsport, Warren County, Indiana, in 1879, taught common school, and took a six-weeks course at Eastern Illinois Normal School at Danville. He continued to teach school in the winter and to work at manual labor in the summer until 1889, when he was admitted to the Warren County Bar and began the practice of law at Williamsport. In 1890 he was elected to the Indiana State Senate, and in 1894 to the United States Congress, serving from 1895 to 1897. In 1904 he was the Republican candidate for Governor, defeating his Democratic opponent, John Worth Kern, 359,362 to 274,998. Felix T. McWhirter, Prohibitionist, received 22,690 votes; Matthew Hallenberger, Socialist, 10,991; Leroy Templeton, Populist, 2,065; and E. J. Dillon, Socialist-Labor, 1,437. During Hanly's gubernatorial term, the Industrial School for Girls was built at Clermont; the Coliseum was constructed at the Indiana State Fairgrounds; and a tuberculosis hospital was built near Rockville. Hanly attempted to check vice and gambling in the state, and several state officials were forced to resign due to a financial scandal.

Temperance legislation was also passed; on September 18, 1908 Hanly called a special session of the legislature, which passed a county local option bill. Following retirement from office, Hanly organized the "Flying Squadron," a group of anti-saloon advocates, and lectured throughout the country against saloons. He was the Prohibition candidate for President of the United States in 1916. Hanly was killed on August 1, 1920, when the automobile in which he was riding was struck by a train near Denison, Ohio. He was buried at Williamsport. Bibliography: Leander Monks, *Courts and Lawyers of Indiana* (Indianapolis, 1916); Russell M. Seeds, *History of the Republican Party of Indiana* (Indianapolis, 1899); Charles W. Taylor, *Biographical Sketches of the Bench and Bar of Indiana* (Indianapolis, 1895). Papers of Hanly in the Archives Division, Indiana State Library.

MARSHALL, Thomas R., 1909-1913

Born on March 14, 1854 in North Manchester, Indiana, son of Dr. Daniel and Martha Patterson Marshall; a Presbyterian. Married to Lois I. Kimsey on October 2, 1895; father of an adopted son who died in infancy. Due to his mother's ill health, the family lived in Illinois, Missouri, and Kansas before they finally settled in Pierceton, Indiana, where Marshall attended public schools and high school at Warsaw and at Fort Wayne. He graduated from Wabash College in 1873; studied law at Fort Wayne and at Columbia City, where he was admitted to the bar. Marshall was active in Democratic Party affairs, and acquired a reputation as a public speaker. In 1908 he was nominated by the Democrats for Governor. He defeated his Republican opponent, James Watson, 348,849 votes to 334,040. Sumner W. Haynes, Prohibitionist, received 15,926; Frank S. Goodman, Socialist, 11,948; Fred J. S. Robinson, Populist, 986; Oliver P. Stoner, Socialist-Labor, 573; and James M. Zion, Independent, 383. While governor, Marshall tried to have a new state constitution adopted, since he felt the business of the state had made the old one obsolete. Nothing came of this attempt. However, a Child Labor Law, described as "a start in the right direction," was passed. Marshall unsuccessfully sought protection for depositors in banks and trust companies and also failed in his attempts to have building and loan companies examined by the state. The enforcement of state laws against gambling occupied much of Marshall's time. In 1912, and again in 1916, he was elected Vice President of the United States as Woodrow Wilson's running mate. Following his retirement as vice president, Marshall returned to Indianapolis. He gave lectures throughout the country and worked on his *Recollections* (published in 1925). He devoted much time to his duties as a member of the Board of Trustees of Wabash College. He died in Washington, D.C., June 1, 1925 and was buried in Crown Hill Cemetery, Indianapolis. Bibliography: Thomas R. Marshall, *Recollections of Thomas R. Marshall* (Indianapolis, 1925); John B. Stoll, *History of the Indiana Democracy, 1816-1916* (Indianapolis, 1917); Charles Thomas, *Thomas Riley Marshall, Hoosier Statesman* (Oxford, Ohio, 1939). Papers of Marshall are in the Indiana State Library.

RALSTON, Samuel, 1913-1917

Born on a farm near New Cumberland, Tuscarawas County, Ohio on December 1, 1857, son of John and Sarah Scott Ralston; a Presbyterian. Brother of Boyd M. and Sarah Ralston Bayliss. Married to Mary Josephine Backous in 1881, who died in 1882; remarried Jennie Craven on December 30, 1889; father of Emmet Grattan, Julian Craven and Ruth Ralston La Rue. In 1865 Ralston's parents moved to Owen County, Indiana. He attended common schools, began teaching school in 1876, and graduated from Central Normal College at Danville, Indiana in 1884. He then studied law in Spencer, Indiana and was admitted to the bar in 1886; in June of that year, he moved to Lebanon, Indiana, where he practiced law. In 1898 he was the Democratic candidate for Secretary of State, but was defeated by his Republican opponent, Union B. Hunt. He was a candidate for Governor at the Democratic convention in 1908 but was defeated for the nomination by Thomas R. Marshall. In 1912 he was the successful Democratic nominee for Governor, and went on to win the general election. Ralston received 275,357 votes; Albert J. Beveridge, Progressive, 166,124; Winfield T. Durbin, Republican, 142,850; Stephen N. Reynolds, Socialist, 35,464; William H. Hickman, Prohibitionist, 18,465; James Matthews, Socialist-Labor, 2,861. During his administration, Ralston advocated flood control legislation following the flood of 1913. He appointed a non-partisan highway commission to study the building and maintenance of public roads; a Public Service Commission was created to regulate public utilities; the State Park System was begun with the acquisition of Turkey Run; a state farm for short-term offenders was established; and industrial aid for the blind was provided. The legislature passed a Workmen's Compensation Law, and Ralston helped draw up measures to insure better safety and health conditions in housing under construction in the cities. In 1922 Ralston was elected to the United States Senate, after defeating former Senator Albert J. Beveridge. He died October 14, 1925, while still serving in the United States Senate, and was buried in Lebanon. Bibliography: L. M. Crist, *History of Boone County, Indiana* (Indianapolis, 1914); Jacob P. Dunn, *Memorial and Genealogical Record of Representative Citizens of Indiana* (Indianapolis, 1912); John B. Stoll, *History of the Indiana Democracy, 1816-1916* (Indianapolis, 1917). Papers of Ralston in the Lilly Library, Indiana University, Bloomington, and the Archives Division, Indiana State Library.

GOODRICH, James P., 1917-1921

Born in Winchester, Indiana on February 18, 1864, son of John Bell and Elizabeth Putnam Edger Goodrich; a Presbyterian. Brother of Edward S., Percy E. and William W. Married to Cora I. Prist on March 15, 1888; father of Pierre F. Goodrich. Attended public schools in Winchester, and attended DePauw University, Preparatory Department, 1885. Goodrich was admitted to the bar in 1887 and practiced law in Winchester. In 1910 he moved his office to Indianapolis. He held large investments in farms, coal mines, grain elevators and banks. He was active in Republican politics, and served as Republican State Chairman, 1901-1910, and Republican National Committeeman, 1912-1916. In 1916 Goodrich was elected Governor, after defeating John A. M. Adair, Democrat, 337,831 votes to 325,060.

William Farmer, Socialist, received 22,156 votes; Alfred L. Mondy, Prohibitionist, 15,454; Thomas A. Dailey, Progressive, 4,573; and Joe B. Trunks, Socialist-Labor, 1,553. Goodrich was governor during World War I. During his term, revised highway laws were passed; the Department of Conservation was established; state parks were developed; and a law providing for the World War Memorial was passed. In 1921 Goodrich toured Europe as a member of Hoover's American Relief Administration investigating famine conditions, and in 1922 he was appointed to the commission responsible for the purchase and distribution of American food to Russian famine districts. In 1923 he became a member of the Indiana Deep Waterway Commission studying means of securing a deep water channel between the Great Lakes and the Atlantic Ocean, and in 1924 he was appointed to the International St. Lawrence Waterways Commission. In his later years, Goodrich became a prominent philanthropist, and several Indiana colleges benefited from his generosity. He died in Winchester, August 15, 1940, and was buried at Fountain Park Cemetery. Bibliography: *Indianapolis Men of Affairs, 1923* (Indianapolis, 1923); Leander Monks, *Courts and Lawyers of Indiana* (Indianapolis, 1916); Indiana Synod of the Presbyterian Church, *Minutes* [June 16-19, 1941] (LaPorte, Indiana). Papers of Goodrich in Archives Division, Indiana State Library.

McCRAY, Warren T., 1921-1924

Born near Kentland, Indiana on February 4, 1865, son of Greenberry Ward and Martha Jane Galey McCray; a Presbyterian. Brother of Fannie McCray Comparet. Married to Ella M. Ade on June 15, 1892; father of Lucille McCray Evans, George and Marian. When McCray was four years old, the family moved to Kentland, where his father was connected with the Discount and Deposit Bank. At the age of fifteen, McCray became a clerk in the bank and at the death of his father in 1913, he succeeded him as president. He also operated a chain of grain elevators in northern Indiana, and was a nationally known breeder of Hereford cattle. He served on the Indiana Board of Agriculture, 1912-16, and was treasurer of the Board of Trustees, Northern Hospital for the Insane, 1904-12. During World War I, he was chairman of the Food Conservation Committee of Indiana, and the Livestock Advisory Board. He was a trustee of Purdue University, 1917-18. In 1920 McCray was elected Governor on the Republican ticket after defeating Carleton B. McCulloch, a Democrat, 683,253 votes to 515,253. Andrew J. Hart, Socialist, received 23,228 votes; James M. Zion, Farmer-Labor, 16,626; Charles M. Kraft, Prohibition, 12,235. A number of public buildings were erected during McCray's administration, including the reformatory at Pendleton, which had been moved from Jeffersonville, and several buildings at the Indiana State Fairgrounds. On April 29, 1924, McCray resigned from the governorship following his conviction in a mail fraud case. After serving three years in federal prison, he was released and worked to regain the respect of his fellow Hoosiers and to rebuild his Orchard Lake Farm. He received a pardon from President Herbert Hoover in 1930. McCray died on December 19, 1938 at his farm near Kentland, and was buried in Fairhaven Cemetery. Bibliography: *Indianapolis News* (December 20, 1938); Thomas R. Johnson, and Helen Hand, *The Trustees and the Officers of Purdue University, 1865-1940,* (Lafayette, Indiana, 1940); Kate Milner Rabb, and William Herschell,

An Account of Indianapolis and Marion County [Vol. 3 of Logan Esarey's *History of Indiana*] (Dayton, Ohio, 1924). Papers of McCray in the Archives Division and the Indiana Division, Indiana State Library.

BRANCH, Emmett F., 1924-1925

Born in Martinsville, Indiana on May 16, 1874, son of Elliott F. and Alice Parks Branch; member of the Disciples of Christ. Brother of Olive, Leafy and Frank Oaks. Married to Katherine Bain on August 30, 1905; father of James Elliott. Branch graduated from Indiana University in 1896, studied law and was admitted to the bar in 1899. With the outbreak of the Spanish-American War, he enlisted in Company K, 158th Regiment, on April 27, 1898, and was discharged on November 4, 1898, with the rank of First Lieutenant. He served as a Lieutenant Colonel on the Mexican border in 1916-17, and was a Colonel in World War I, in the 151st Infantry, from October 1, 1917. Later he commanded the 165th Depot Brigade at Camp Travis, Texas. He was discharged from the service on December 5, 1918. Branch served in the Indiana House of Representatives, 1903, 1905, and 1907. In 1920 he was elected Lieutenant Governor on the Republican ticket, with Warren T. McCray as Governor. He received 684,627 votes to defeat Samuel T. Foster, a Democrat, who polled 512,084. Branch was sworn in as Governor on April 30, 1924, after the resignation of Governor Warren McCray and served until January 12, 1925. Governor Branch called the first State Safety Conference through the Public Service Commission, October 14, 1924. He was an advocate of better roads and schools, and emphasized these themes in his keynote address to the Republican State Convention in 1924. Branch died in Martinsville on February 23, 1932, and was buried there. Bibliography: *Indianapolis Star* (February 24, 1932); *Legislative and State Manual of Indiana, 1905* (Indianapolis, 1905); Charles Roll, *Indiana. One Hundred Fifty Years of American Development* (Chicago, 1931). Papers of Branch in the Archives Division, Indiana State Library.

JACKSON, Edward L., 1925-1929

Born on a farm in Howard County, Indiana on December 27, 1873, son of Presley, a millworker, and Mary E. Howell Jackson; member of the Disciples of Christ. Married to Rosa Wilkinson on February 20, 1897, who died on October 29, 1919; father of Helen E. and Edith Jackson Beatty; remarried to Lydia Beaty Pierce on November 23, 1920; father of an adopted son, Edward L. Jackson, Jr. Jackson attended public schools in Howard County, studied law, and opened a law office at Kennard in Henry County. He was Prosecuting Attorney for Henry County, 1901-1906, and on July 13, 1907 was appointed Judge of the Henry County Circuit Court. He was elected to a full term in 1908, serving until 1914. In 1916 Jackson was elected Indiana Secretary of State. He resigned from office on November 27, 1917 to enlist in the military service in World War I. He was commissioned Captain on November 27, 1917 and later Major, and was stationed at Lafayette, where he was Commandant of the S.A.T.C. at Purdue University. He was discharged from the service on February 11, 1919. After his military career had ended, Jackson began the practice of law at Lafayette, but on January 21, 1920, he was appointed Secretary of State of Indiana. He was elected to the office in November, 1920, and reelected in 1922. In 1924 Jackson was the Republican candidate for Governor, defeating his Democratic opponent, Carleton B. McCulloch, 654,784 votes to 572,303. Francis M. Wampler, Socialist, received 5,984 votes; Basil L. Allen, the Prohibitionist candidate, polled 3,808. During Jackson's administration, several parks were added to the State Park System, and preparations were begun for the George Rogers Clark Memorial at Vincennes. Following his term of office, Jackson opened a law practice in Indianapolis. In 1937 he moved to his farm near Orleans, Indiana, where he died on November 18, 1954. He was buried at Green Hills Cemetery, Orleans. Bibliography: *Indianapolis News* (November 19, 1954); Leander Monks, *Courts and Lawyers of Indiana* (Indianapolis, 1916); Kate Milner Rabb, and William Herschell, *An Account of Indianapolis and Marion County* [Vol. 3 of Logan Esarey's *History of Indiana*] (Dayton, Ohio, 1924). Papers of Jackson in the Archives Division, Indiana State Library.

LESLIE, Harry G., 1929-1933

Born in West Lafayette, Indiana on August 6, 1878, son of Daniel and Mary Ann Burkhardt Leslie; a Methodist. Brother of Frank and Amy Leslie Hivon. Married Martha Morgan on August 16, 1910; father of John Morgan, Richard Morgan and Robert Warner. Leslie graduated from Purdue University in 1905 and Indiana University Law School in 1907. He opened a law office in Lafayette, and in 1912 was elected Treasurer of Tippecanoe County, serving 1913-17. He served in the Indiana House of Representatives, 1923-27, and was Speaker of the House in 1925 and 1927. Leslie was elected Governor on the Republican ticket in November, 1928, defeating Democrat, Frank C. Dailey, 728,203 votes to 683,545. Albert Stanley, a Prohibitionist, received 5,096 votes; Clarence E. Bond, Socialist, 3,258; Cassimer Benward, Socialist-Labor, 424; Harry W. Garner, Workers, 319; and Henry O. Shaw, National, 168. During his term as governor, Leslie was faced with labor problems and unemployment. In 1932, as the Great Depression worsened, he called a special session of the legislature to reduce property taxes. Following his term of office, he helped organize the Standard Life Insurance Company of Indiana at Indianapolis, and was president of the firm when he died in Miami, Florida on December 10, 1937. He was buried at Lafayette. Bibliography: *History of Tippecanoe County and the Wabash Valley* [Vol. 4 of Logan Esarey's *History of Indiana*] (Dayton, Ohio, 1928); Ken Hubbard, ed., *A Book of Indiana* [Indiana Biographical Association]; *Indianapolis Star* (December 11, 1937). Papers of Leslie in the Archives Division, Indiana State Library.

McNUTT, Paul V., 1933-1937

Born in Franklin, Indiana on July 19, 1891, son of attorney John C. and Ruth Neely McNutt; a Methodist. Married Kathleen Timolat on April 20, 1918; father of Louise. The McNutt family moved to Martinsville, Indiana in 1899, where Paul attended public schools. He graduated from Indiana University in 1913 and

Harvard University Law School in 1916, and then returned to Martinsville to practice law with his father. In the fall of 1917, he accepted a position as Assistant Professor at Indiana University Law School. He enlisted in the army on November 27, 1917, where he became a Captain in the Field Artillery; he was promoted to Major on August 22, 1918. McNutt was discharged on March 14, 1919 and commissioned a Major in the Field Artillery, Officers Reserve Corps on April 22, 1919, promoted to Lieutenant Colonel on August 18, 1919, and a full Colonel on January 8, 1923. Soon after his discharge from the army, McNutt resumed teaching at Indiana University Law School. He was appointed Dean of the Law School on August 1, 1925, a position he held until 1933. He served as Commander of the Indiana Department, American Legion in 1927, and in 1928-29 served as National Commander of the Legion. Paul McNutt was elected Governor of Indiana on the Democratic ticket in November, 1932. He received 862,127 votes to defeat Raymond Springer, the Republican candidate, who polled 669,797; other candidates included Fessenden W. Lough, Prohibitionist, 9,273; Powers Hapgood, Socialist, 18,735; Charley Lynch, Socialist-Labor, 1,796; Theo Luesse, Communist, 2,129; Ward B. Hiner, National, 3,052. McNutt became Governor in the midst of the Great Depression. He sponsored a reorganization of state government. Emergency relief laws were passed, and laws to control the operation of banks, building and loan companies, and insurance companies were enacted. The Gross Income Tax Law was passed, and in 1936 McNutt called a special session of the legislature to enact legislation consistent with the Federal Social Security Act, Unemployment Compensation Act, and welfare programs. Paul McNutt served as High Commissioner to the Philippines, 1937-39. In July, 1939, he was appointed Administrator of the Federal Security Administration, a post he held until October, 1945. He was also Chairman of the War Manpower Commission, 1942-45. He was again appointed High Commissioner to the Philippines in 1945, and was the first United States Ambassador to the Philippine Republic, serving from June 15, 1946 to May 8, 1947. Following his return from the Philippines, he established a law practice in New York City, but retained his partnership in his father's old firm at Martinsville. McNutt died in New York City on March 24, 1955, and was buried in Arlington Cemetery. Bibliography: George I. Blake, *Paul V. McNutt. Portrait of a Hoosier Statesman* (Indianapolis, 1966); C. Walter McCarty, ed., *Indiana Today* (New Orleans, 1942); Charles Roll, *Indiana, One Hundred and Fifty Years of American Development* (Chicago, 1931). Papers of McNutt in the Lilly Library, Indiana University, and in the Archives Division, Indiana State Library.

TOWNSEND, M. Clifford, 1937-1941

Born on a farm on August 11, 1884 in Blackford County, Indiana, son of David and Lydia Glancy Townsend; a Methodist. Brother of Myrtle Townsend Hoover. Married Nora Adele Harris on December 25, 1910; father of Helen Townsend Duncan, Lucille Townsend Marshall and Max. Educated in common schools in Blackford County, and graduated from Marion (Indiana) College in 1907. Townsend was a school teacher and a farmer. He was superintendent of the Blackford County schools, 1909-19, and of the Grant County schools, 1925-29. In 1929 he was made Educational Director of the Indiana Farm Bureau. He served in the Indiana

House of Representatives in 1923, and in 1928 was an unsuccessful candidate for the United States Congress. Townsend was elected Lieutenant Governor in 1932 on the Democratic ticket with Paul V. McNutt as Governor. His Republican opponent was Joseph B. Kyle. The vote was Townsend, 860,924, Kyle, 666,943. The 1933 legislature made the Lieutenant Governor a full-time employee, and Townsend was given the duties of Commissioner of Agriculture. In 1936 Townsend became Democratic nominee for Governor. He defeated Raymond E. Springer, Republican, 908,494 votes to 727,526. Marion B. Tomisch, Socialist, received 3,871 votes; Wenzell Stocker, Communist,1,182. Outstanding achievements of the Townsend administration were the establishment of a pension for firemen in several of the larger cities; the decision to require examinations for drivers' licenses; and the creation of the Division of Labor. Also Governor Townsend set up a flood disaster program during the 1937 flood, which helped to provide for the flood refugees. During World War II, Townsend served as Director, Office of Agricultural War Relations, 1941-42; Administrator, Agricultural Conservation and Adjustment Administration, June, 1942-January, 1943; Director, Food Production Administration, 1943. He was defeated in his bid for the United States Senate in 1946 by William E. Jenner. Townsend died on November 11, 1954 at Hartford City, Indiana, and was buried in the I.O.O.F. Cemetery there. Bibliography: Indiana State Library, *Biography of Members of the Indiana Legislature* (1923); *Indianapolis Star* (November 11, 1954); Benjamin G. Shinn, *Blackford and Grant Counties, Indiana* (Chicago, 1914). Papers of Townsend in the Archives Division, Indiana State Library.

SCHRICKER, Henry F., 1941-1945, 1949-1953

Born on August 20, 1883 in North Judson, Indiana, son of Christopher, a grocer, and Magdalena Meyer Schricker; a Lutheran. Married Maude L. Brown on October 21, 1914; father of Margaret Schricker Robbins, Henry F., Jr. and George. Schricker attended common schools in Starke County, Indiana. In 1908 he bought the *Starke County Democrat*, a weekly newspaper published at Knox, Indiana. He sold the paper in 1919, and joined the Farmers' Bank and Trust Company, Knox. He was elected to the Indiana State Senate in 1932, and in 1936 was the Democratic candidate for Lieutenant Governor with M. Clifford Townsend as the gubernatorial candidate. Schricker's Republican opponent was Joseph B. Kyle. The vote was Schricker, 902,228, Kyle, 705,964. In 1940 Schricker was elected Governor, defeating Glenn R. Hills, Republican, 889,620 votes to 885,657. Omer S. Whiteman, Prohibitionist, received 4,869 votes; Mary Hapgood, Socialist, 1,455; Herman B. Barefield, Socialist-Labor, 651. Schricker was affiliated with the Fletcher Trust Company, Indianapolis, from 1945 to 1948. He was nominated in 1944 for the United States Senate, but was defeated by Homer E. Capehart. In 1948 he was again the Democratic nominee for Governor. He defeated Hobart Creighton, Republican. The vote was Schricker, 884,995; Creighton, 745,892; Clinton W. Spiecher, Prohibitionist, 13,582; Walter Frisbie, Progressive, 6,259; William Rabe, Sr., Socialist, 985; Charles Ginsberg, Socialist-Labor, 608. In both of Schricker's administrations, he was challenged by Republican-controlled legislatures. The 1941 legislature repealed the 1933 laws which had centralized the state government under the governor, and tried to strip Schricker of appointive powers. The Indiana Supreme Court declared most of the "ripper" bills unconstitutional, and returned patronage power to the Governor. In Schricker's term, the legislature attempted to open welfare rolls to the public. Schricker called a special session of the legislature to try to avoid the loss of federal funds to Indiana. The difficulty was eventually solved by Congressional action. After retiring from office, Schricker was affiliated with the Wabash Fire and Casualty Company, Indianapolis. He died on December 28, 1966 at Knox, and was buried there in Crown Hill Cemetery. Bibliography: John D. Barnhart and Donald F. Carmony, *Indiana: From Frontier to Industrial Commonwealth* (New York, 1954); Charles F. Fleming, *The White Hat: Henry F. Schricker; A Political Biography* (Indianapolis, 1966); C. Walter Mc-Carty, ed., *Indiana Today* (New Orleans, 1942). Papers of Schricker in the Archives Division, Indiana State Library.

GATES, Ralph F., 1945-1949

Born in Columbia City, Indiana on February 24, 1893, son of Benton E. and Alice Fessler Gates; a Presbyterian. Brother of John, Scott and Benton E. Married on October 30, 1919 to Helene Edwards; father of Robert E. and Patricia Gates McNagney. Received an A.B. degree from the University of Michigan, 1915, and an LL.B. degree in 1917 from the same institution. Enlisted in the United States Naval Reserve Force, and commissioned an Ensign in the Pay Corps on August 8, 1917. Gates was promoted to Lieutenant, J.G., and for some time was connected with the War Risk Insurance Bureau. He served overseas from December 14, 1917 to April 7, 1919. After military service, Gates returned to Columbia City to practice law with his father. He served as Commander, Indiana Department, American Legion, 1931. He was active in Republican Party politics, serving as State Chairman, 1941-44. In 1944 Gates was the Republican nominee for Governor. He defeated his Democratic opponent, Samuel D. Jackson, 849,346 votes to 802,765. Waldo E. Yeater, Prohibitionist, received 12,358 votes; William Rabe, Sr., Socialist, 1,770. During Gates' administration, the Department of Revenue, the Flood Control Commission, the Department of Veteran Affairs, and the Traffic Safety Commission were established. Also, a Public Employees Retirement Pension was begun. Following his term as governor, Gates returned to his law practice in Columbia City and continued to have an influential role in Republican politics. Bibliography: John D. Barnhart and Donald F. Carmony, *Indiana: From Frontier to Industrial Commonwealth* (New York, 1954); C. Walter McCarty, ed., *Indiana Today* (New Orleans, 1942); John B. Martin, *Indiana: An Interpretation* (New York, 1947). Papers of Gates in the Archives Division, Indiana State Library.

SCHRICKER, Henry F., 1941-1945, 1949-1953

CRAIG, George N., 1953-1957

Born on August 6, 1909 in Brazil, Indiana, son of Bernard and Clo Branson Craig; a Methodist. Married Kathryn L. Heiliger on August 29, 1931; father of John David and Margery Ellen. Attended Culver Military Academy. Received an LL.B. degree from Indiana University in 1932, and practiced law with his father in Brazil, Indiana, and in Indianapolis. Served in World War II, 1942-46, and was discharged as a Lieutenant Colonel. Most of his service was in the European theater of the war. He was active in the American Legion on the local and state level, and served as National Commander, 1949-50, being the first World War II veteran to win that post. He practiced law in Indianapolis from 1946 to 1953. In 1952 Craig was the Republican candidate for Governor. He defeated his Democratic opponent, John A. Watkins, 1,075,685 votes to 841,984. Lester N. Abel, Prohibitionist, received 12,554 votes; Samuel Boorda, Progressive, 920; and Charles Ginsberg, Socialist-Labor, 726. Craig's administration saw the creation of the Department of Corrections to oversee all penal institutions, and the reorganization of the State Department of Health, centering on mental health facilities. Plans were begun for an Indiana port on Lake Michigan. Highway construction emphasized safety by replacing narrow "killer" bridges, and by widening roads. Also, the Indiana Toll Road across northern Indiana was constructed. Upon retirement from the governor's office, Craig opened a law office in Washington, D.C. and in 1965 moved to California. In 1967 he returned to Indiana to practice law in his home city, Brazil. Bibliography: John D. Barnhart and Donald F. Carmony, *Indiana: From Frontier to Industrial Commonwealth* (New York, 1954); *Indiana University Alumni Magazine*, vol. 12, no. 2 (October, 1949); "Welfare on the Wabash," *Time*, vol. LXV, no. 10 (March 7, 1955). Papers of Craig in the Archives Division, Indiana State Library.

HANDLEY, Harold W., 1957-1961

Born in LaPorte, Indiana on November 27, 1909, son of Harold L. and Lottie Margaret Brackbill Handley; a Presbyterian. Brother of Kenneth Edward and Stanley Dwight. Married Barbara Winterble on February 17, 1944; father of Kenneth David and Martha Jean. Handley received an A.B. degree from Indiana University in 1932. After graduation he assisted his father, who was general manager of the Rustic Furniture Company at LaPorte. He was a sales representative for Unagusta Furniture Corporation, Hazelwood, N.C., 1940-53. Handley served in the Indiana State Senate, 1941, 1949-52. He resigned after the 1941 session to enter military service. He served in the 85th Division, U.S. Army, from 1942-46, and was discharged with the rank of Lieutenant Colonel. In 1952 he was elected Lieutenant Governor on the Republican ticket with George N. Craig as Governor. Handley defeated his Democratic opponent, E. Spencer Walton, 1,069,780 votes to 839,360. In 1956 he was his party's candidate for Governor. The vote was Handley, 1,086,868; Ralph Tucker, Democrat, 859,393; J. Ralston Miller, Prohibitionist, 6,791; and Merle L. Miller, Socialist-Labor, 1,238. In 1958, while still serving as governor, Handley ran for the United States Senate, but was defeated by R. Vance Hartke. During Governor Handley's administration, a thirteen-floor state office building was constructed; a veterinary school was established at Purdue; funds were appropriated for land at the Lake Michigan port site; and a "right to work" law took effect without the governor's signature. After leaving office in 1961, Handley was president of a public relations firm in Indianapolis. He died on August 30, 1972 at Rawlins, Wyoming, and was buried at Pine Lake Cemetery, LaPorte. Bibliography: Thomas H. Cannon, *History of Lake and Calumet Regions of Indiana* (Indianapolis, 1927); *Indiana Business and Industry,* vol. 5, no. 5 (May-June, 1961), vol. 9, no. 4 (April, 1965); *Indiana University Alumni Magazine,* vol. 35, no. 2 (October, 1972); *Indianapolis News* (August 30, 1972). Papers of Handley in the Archives Division, Indiana State Library.

WELSH, Matthew E., 1961-1965

Born in Detroit, Michigan on September 15, 1912, son of Matthew and Inez Empson Welsh; member of the Disciples of Christ. Brother of Mary, Virginia, John Edward and Margaret Welsh Clark. Married Virginia Homann on September 25, 1937; father of Janet and Katherine. The family moved to Vincennes, Indiana in 1924, where Welsh attended public schools. He received a B.S. degree from the University of Pennsylvania in 1934 and a J.D. degree from the University of Chicago Law School in 1937. Welsh returned to Vincennes in 1937 to practice law. He served in the Indiana House of Representatives, 1941 and 1943, resigning in 1943 to join the navy. He was a Lieutenant in the USNR, 1943-46. Welsh served as United States Attorney for the Southern District of Indiana, 1950-51. In 1954 he was elected to the Indiana State Senate, serving in the sessions from 1955 through 1959. In the 1957 and 1959 sessions, he was Democratic Minority Leader. He was defeated for the Democratic nomination for Governor in 1956, but was nominated in 1960. Welsh defeated his Republican opponent Crawford Parker, 1,072,717 votes to 1,049,540. J. Ralston Miller, Prohibitionist, received 5,892 votes; Herman Kronewitter, Socialist-Labor, 816. The need for more revenue was the pressing problem when Governor Welsh took office. Subsequently, a two percent sales tax was enacted, and the Department of Administration was created to oversee business transactions of state government. Welsh, a civil rights advocate, created the Indiana Fair Employment Commission and established Youth Training Centers at state parks under the Department of Corrections. At the close of his gubernatorial term, Welsh joined a law firm in Indianapolis. He served as Chairman of the United States-Canada International Joint Committee, 1966-70. He was an unsuccessful candidate for Governor in 1972, losing to Dr. Otis R. Bowen, Republican, 1,203,903 votes to 900,489. Bibliography: John D. Barnhart, and Donald F. Carmony, *Indiana: From Frontier to Industrial Commonwealth* (New York, 1954); Hubert H. Hawkins, and Robert R. McClarren, *Indiana Lives* (Hopkinsville, Ky., 1967); *Indiana Business and Industry,* vol. 3, no. 5 (May, 1959). Papers of Welsh in the Archives Division and in Indiana Division, Indiana State Library.

BRANIGIN, Roger D., 1965-1969

Born in Franklin, Indiana on July 26, 1902, son of Elba L. and Zula Francis Branigin; a Baptist. Brother of Gerald F., Edgar M. and Elba L., Jr. Married Josephine Mardis on November 2, 1929; father of Roger and Robert M. Branigin received an A.B. degree from Franklin College in 1923, and an LL.B. degree from Harvard University in 1926. Branigin practiced law in Franklin, 1926-29, and was Counsel for the Federal Land Bank and Farm Credit Administration, Louisville, Kentucky, 1930-38. He moved his law practice to Lafayette in 1938. Branigin served as Lt. Colonel, JAGD, 1942-46, and was Chief, Legal Division, Army Transport Corps. At the end of his military service, he returned to his law practice in Lafayette. He was a trustee of Franklin College, 1937-75, Purdue University trustee, 1950-55, member of the Conservation Commission, 1948-50, and chairman, Indiana Revolutionary War Bicentennial Commission, 1971-1975. Branigan was elected Governor on the Democratic ticket in 1964, defeating Richard Ristine, Republican, 1,164,620 votes to 901,342. Gordon A. Long, Socialist-Labor, received 1,182 votes; Chester G. Bohannan, Prohibitionist, 5,771. Some of the accomplishments of the Branigin administration were the abolition of the poll tax and personal property tax on household goods; the enactment of the state's first taxpayer-paid college scholarship program; the repeal of the controversial "right to work" law; the expansion of the powers of the Civil Rights Commission; the creation of the Department of National Resources through the merger of the Water Resources and the Conservation Agencies; and enactment of legislation to provide a mandatory program for law enforcement officers. Following his term as governor, Branigin returned to the practice of law at Lafayette. He died in Lafayette, November 19, 1975, and was buried in Franklin. Bibliography: John Barnhart and Donald F. Carmony, *Indiana. From Frontier to Industrial Commonwealth* (New York, 1954); Hubert H. Hawkins and Robert R. McClarren, *Indiana Lives* (Hopkinsville, Ky., 1967); *Indiana Business and Industry*, vol. 3, no. 6 (June, 1959); *Indiana University Alumni Magazine,* vol. 38, no. 5 (January-February, 1976). Papers of Branigin in Franklin College Library, Franklin, Indiana.

WHITCOMB, Edgar D., 1969-1973

Born in Hayden, Indiana on November 6, 1917, son of John W. and Louise Doud Whitcomb; a Methodist. Brother of Charles, Laura Whitcomb Showalter and Sarah Whitcomb Lieurance. Married Patricia Dolfuss on May 20, 1951; father of Patricia, Linda, Shelley, Alice and John. Whitcomb attended Indiana University in 1936, but dropped out due to lack of funds. He served in the USAFR during World War II, 1940-46. He graduated in the first class of navigators to be trained for air force bombers, and was sent to the Philippine Islands in October, 1941. Whitcomb was taken prisoner by the Japanese at the fall of Corregidor, May 7, 1942, and escaped from a Japanese prison on May 22, 1942. He was recaptured, and forced to spend time in other enemy prisons; finally, he was extricated from enemy territory. He arrived back in the United States in December, 1943, and then flew transport missions to the European theater of the war. He returned to combat duty in the Philippines in May, 1945. His war experiences are related in his book, *Escape from*

Corregidor (Chicago: Regnery, 1958). Following his release from the army, he returned to Indiana University to study law, and received his LL.B. degree in 1950. Whitcomb was admitted to the bar in 1952. He practiced law in North Vernon, Seymour and Indianapolis from 1952 to 1966. He served in the Indiana State Senate, 1951-54, was Assistant United States Attorney for the Southern District of Indiana, 1955-56, and Indiana Secretary of State, 1966-68. Whitcomb was the Republican candidate for Governor in 1968. He defeated his Democratic opponent, Robert Rock, 1,080,271 votes to 965,816. Melvin E. Hawk, Prohibitionist, received 2,985 votes. Governor Whitcomb was elected on a platform which promised to hold the line on taxation, and during his administration, there was no general state-wide increase in taxes. He appointed a Governor's Economy Team, which reviewed the work of state departments with the intent of eliminating waste and duplication in government. Better enforcement of collection procedures for the State Department of Revenue were adopted. The "pocket veto," which had been used by governors for many years, was declared unconstitutional. A number of new ideas for the correction program were implemented, and state highways and bridges were built with an emphasis on safety. Since his term as governor, Whitcomb has been Director of Mid-America World Trade Association, Indianapolis. Bibliography: Alton J. Ritchie, *The Whitcomb Years* (Indianapolis, 1973); Donald E. Thompson, *Indiana Authors and Their Books, 1917-1966* (Crawfordsville, Ind., 1974); Edgar D. Whitcomb, *Escape from Corregidor* (Chicago, 1958). Papers of Whitcomb in the Archives Division, Indiana State Library.

BOWEN, Otis R., 1973-

Born near Rochester, Indiana in February 26, 1918, son of Vernie, a school teacher, and Pearl Wright Bowen; a Lutheran. Brother of Esther Bowen Bremer, Evelyn Maxine Bowen Amacher, Richard and Sarah Jane Bowen Marvin. Married Elizabeth A. Steinmann on February 25, 1939; father of Richard H., Judith I., Timothy R. and Robert O. Bowen received his A.B. degree from Indiana University in 1939 and his M.D. from Indiana University Medical School in 1942. He served as a First Lieutenant and a Captain in the United States Army Medical Corps, 1943-46. From 1946 to 1972, he was a physician at Bremen, Indiana. Dr. Bowen served in the Indiana House of Representatives, 1957-72. He was Republican Minority Leader for the House, 1965-66, and Speaker of the House, 1967-69, 1971-72. In 1972 Bowen was the Republican candidate for Governor, and defeated his Democratic opponent, Matthew E. Welsh, 1,203,903 votes to 900,489. John M. Morris, Socialist-Labor, received 1,652 votes; Berryman S. Hurley, Indiana American Independent, 8,525, and Finley C. Campbell, Peace and Freedom, 6,278. An amendment to the Indiana Constitution adopted in 1972 permitted a governor to succeed himself in office and in 1976 Governor Bowen was reelected, defeating Democrat Larry Conrad, 1,236,555 to 927,234. Bowen was elected on a platform calling for tax restructuring, which was accomplished during the first legislative session of his administration. Property taxes were reduced, and the sales tax increased. The Task Force on Position Classification and Salary Administration was appointed and made recommendations on state employee salaries and duties, with a view towards providing more efficient governmental service. A more adequate governor's mansion was purchased and the old mansion sold. Bibliography: Hubert Hawkins and Robert McClarren, *Indiana Lives* (Hopkinsville, Ky., 1967); *Indiana Publisher*, vol. 38, no. 3 (March, 1973); Shirley Willard, *Fulton County Folk* (Marceline, Mo., 1974).

INDEX

Each Governor's name is followed by a two-letter state abbreviation, a roman numeral (I, II, III, IV) denoting the volume in which the entry appears, and page number.

A

Index

Ames, Oliver, MA, II, 716
Ammons, Elias Milton, CO, I, 141
Ammons, Teller, CO, I, 147
Andersen, Elmer Lee, MN, II, 794
Anderson, C. Elmer, MN, II, 793
Anderson, Charles, OH, III, 1210
Anderson, Forrest Howard, MT, III, 885
Anderson, Hugh Johnson, ME, II, 605
Anderson, John, KS, II, 499
Anderson, Sigurd, SD, IV, 1457
Anderson, Victor Emanuel, NE, III, 913
Anderson, Wendell Richard, MN, II, 796
Andrew, John Albion, MA, II, 707
Andrews, Charles Bartlett, CT, I, 182
Andrus, Cecil Dale, ID, I, 360
Ansel, Martin Frederick, SC, IV, 1427
Anthony, George Tobey, KS, II, 465
Anthony, Henry Bowen, RI, IV, 1344
Apodaca, Jerry, NM, III, 1064
Ariyoshi, George Ryoichi, HI, I, 332
Armstrong, Samuel Turell, MA, II, 700
Arn, Edward F., KS, II, 495
Arnall, Ellis Gibbs, GA, I, 319
Arnold, Lemuel Hastings, RI, IV, 1338
Aronson, J. Hugo, MT, III, 882
Arthur, Harold John, VT, IV, 1612
Ashe, Samuel, NC, III, 1113
Askew, Reubin O'Donovan, FL, I, 275
Atkinson, George Wesley, WV, IV, 1697
Atkinson, William Yates, GA, I, 308
Austin, Horace, MN, II, 777
Avery, William Henry, KS, II, 500
Aycock, Charles Brantley, NC, III, 1148
Ayers, Roy Elmer, MT, III, 880

B

Babbitt, Bruce, AR, I, 60
Babcock, Tim, MT, III, 884
Bachelder, Nahum Josiah, NH, III, 982
Bacon, Walter W., DE, I, 242
Badger, William, NH, III, 952
Bagby, Arthur Pendleton, AL, I, 11
Bagley, John Judson, MI, II, 750
Bailey, Carl Edward, AR, I, 90
Bailey, Thomas L., MS, II, 828

Index

Index

Index

Index

Index

C

Index

Index

Index

Index

Cross, Burton M., ME, II, 637
Cross, Wilbur Lucius, CT, I, 198
Croswell, Charles Miller, MI, II, 751
Crothers, Austin Lane, MD, II, 678
Crounse, Lorenzo, NE, III, 896
Cruce, Lee, OK, III, 1242
Culberson, Charles Allen, TX, IV, 1529
Cullom, Shelby Moore, IL, I, 377
Culter, Nathan, ME, II, 598
Cummins, Albert Baird, IA, II, 442
Cunningham, Russell McWhortor, AL, I, 28
Curley, James M., MA, II, 729
Currier, Moody, NH, III, 975
Curtin, Andrew Gregg, PA, III, 1310
Curtis, Kenneth M., ME, II, 641
Curtis, Oakley Chester, ME, II, 628
Cutler, John Christopher, UT, IV, 1548
Cutler, Nathan, ME, II, 598

D

Dale, Charles Milby, NH, III, 997
Dalton, John M., MO, II, 867
Dalton, John Nichols, VA, IV, 1670
Dana, John Winchester, ME, II, 604
Daniel, Price, TX, IV, 1540
Darden, Colgate Whitehead, VA, IV, 1663
Davey, Martin Luther, OH, III, 1231
Davidson, James O., WI, IV, 1741
Davie, William Richardson, NC, III, 1114
Davis, Cushman Kellogg, MN, II, 778
Davis, Daniel Franklin, ME, II, 618
Davis, David W., ID, I, 347
Davis, Deane C., VT, IV, 1617
Davis, Edmund Jackson, TX, IV, 1524
Davis, Harry L., OH, III, 1228
Davis, James Houston, LA, II, 588
Davis, Jefferson, AR, I, 80
Davis, John, MA, II, 700
Davis, John Edward, ND, III, 1185
Davis, John William, RI, IV, 1358
Davis, Jonathan, McMillan, KS, II, 484
Davis, Westmoreland, VA, IV, 1657
Dawes, James William, NE, III, 893
Dawson, William Mercer Owens, WV, IV, 1699
DeBaca, Ezequiel Cabeza, NM, III, 1050

Index

E

Index

Index

Index

G

Index

Index

H

Index

Index

Henderson, James Pinckney, TX, IV, 1515
Henderson, Thomas, NJ, III, 1008
Hendricks, Thomas, IN, I, 406
Hendricks, William, IN, I, 396
Henry, John, MD, II, 648
Herbert, Thomas J., OH, III, 1234
Herreid, Charles N., SD, IV, 1449
Herrick, Myron, OH, II, 1222
Herring, Clyde L., IA, II, 446
Herschler, Edgar J., WY, IV, 1784
Herseth, Ralph, SD, IV, 1459
Herter, Christian A., MA, II, 733
Heyward, Duncan Clinch, SC, IV, 1426
Hickel, Walter Joseph, AK, I, 44
Hickenlooper, Bourke Blakemore, IA, II, 448
Hickey, John Joseph, WY, IV, 1781
Hicks, Thomas Holliday, MD, II, 667
Hiester, Joseph, PA, III, 1298
Higgins, Francis Wayland, NY, III, 1094
Higgins, James Henry, RI, IV, 1366
Hildreth, Horace A., ME, II, 635
Hill, David B., NY, III, 1090
Hill, Isaac, NH, III, 953
Hill, John Fremont, ME, II, 624
Hinkle, James Fielding, NM, III, 1052
Hoadly, George, OH, III, 1217
Hoard, William Dempster, WI, IV, 1736
Hobby, William Pettus, TX, IV, 1534
Hoch, Edward Wallis, KS, II, 478
Hockenhull, Andrew W., NM, III, 1055
Hodges, George Hartshorn, KS, II, 480
Hodges, Luther Hartwell, NC, III, 1162
Hoegh, Leo A., IA, II, 451
Hoey, Clyde Roark, NC, III, 1157
Hoff, Philip Henderson, VT, IV, 1616
Hoffman, Harold Giles, NJ, III, 1040
Hoffman, John Thompson, NY, III, 1085
Hogg, James Stephen, TX, IV, 1528
Holbrook, Frederick, VT, IV, 1580
Holcomb, Marcus Hensey, CT, I, 194
Holcomb, Silas Alexander, NE, III, 897
Holden, William Woods, NC, III, 1138
Holland, Spessard Lindsey, FL, I, 269
Holley, Alexander Hamilton, CT, I, 176
Holliday, Frederick William Mackey, VA, IV, 1649
Hollings, Ernest Frederick, SC, IV, 1440
Holloway, William Judson, OK, III, 1246

Index

Index

I

Ingersoll, Charles Roberts, CT, I, 181
Iredell, James, NC, III, 1124
Ireland, John, TX, IV, 1527
Irwin, Jared, GA, I, 281
Irwin, William, CA, I, 109

J

Jackson, Charles, RI, IV, 1342
Jackson, Claiborne Fox, MO, II, 847
Jackson, Edward L., IN, I, 416
Jackson, Elihu Emory, MD, II, 674
Jackson, Frank Darr, IA, II, 440
Jackson, Hancock Lee, MO, II, 845
Jackson, Jacob Beeson, WV, IV, 1695
Jackson, James, GA, I, 282
Jacob, John Jeremiah, WV, IV, 1693
James, Arthur Horace, PA, III, 1323
James, William Hartford, NE, III, 890
Jarvis, Thomas Jordan, NC, III, 1142
Jay, John, NY, III, 1070
Jeffries, Richard Manning, SC, IV, 1436
Jelks, William Dorsey, AL, I, 26
Jenison, Silas H., VT, IV, 1570
Jenkins, Charles Jones, GA, I, 299
Jennings, Jonathan, IN, I, 395
Jennings, William Sherman, FL, I, 262
Jensen, Leslie, SD, IV, 1455
Jerome, David H., MI, II, 751
Jester, Beauford Halbert, TX, IV, 1539
Jeter, Thomas Bothwell, SC, IV, 1420
Jewell, Marshall, CT, I, 180
Johns, Charley Eugene, FL, I, 272
Johnson, Andrew, TN, IV, 1478
Johnson, David, SC, IV, 1406
Johnson, Edwin Carl, CO, I, 145
Johnson, Henry S., LA, II, 558
Johnson, Herschel Vespasian, GA, I, 296
Johnson, Hiram, CA, I, 118
Johnson, Isaac, LA, II, 562
Johnson, James, GA, I, 298
Johnson, James Neely, CA, I, 103
Johnson, John Albert, MN, II, 785

Index

K

Index

L

Index

Index

M

Index

Index

Index

Index

N

Index

O

Index

Orr, James Lawrence, SC, IV, 1415
Osborn, Chase Salmon, MI, II, 757
Osborn, Sidney Preston, AZ, I, 54
Osborn, Thomas Andrew, KS, II, 464
Osborne, John Eugene, WY, IV, 1766
Owen, John, NC, III, 1124
Owsley, William, KY, II, 519

P

Pacheco, Romualdo, CA, I, 109
Packer, William Fisher, PA, III, 1309
Padelford, Seth, RI, IV, 1352
Page, Carroll Smalley, VT, IV, 1592
Page, John, NH, III, 954
Page, John, VA, IV, 1627
Page, John B., VT, IV, 1582
Paine, Charles, VT, IV, 1571
Palmer, John McAuley, IL, I, 376
Palmer, William Adam, VT, IV, 1569
Pardee, George Cooper, CA, I, 116
Park, Guy B., MO, II, 863
Parker, Joel, NJ, III, 1021
Parker, John Milliken, LA, II, 580
Parkhurst, Frederick Hale, ME, II, 629
Parnell, Harvey, AR, I, 89
Parris, Albion Keith, ME, II, 597
Parsons, Andrew, MI, II, 746
Parsons, Lewis E., AL, I, 17
Pastore, John Orlando, RI, IV, 1376
Paterson, William, NJ, III, 1007
Patterson, Isaac Lee, OR, III, 1277
Patterson, John Malcolm, AL, I, 36
Patterson, Malcolm Rice, TN, IV, 1495
Patterson, Paul Linton, OR, III, 1285
Patteson, Okey Leonidas, WV, IV, 1709
Pattison, John M., OH, III, 1223
Pattison, Robert Emory, PA, III, 1313
Patton, John Mercer, VA, IV, 1639
Patton, Robert Miller, AL, I, 18
Paulen, Benjamin Sanford, KS, II, 484
Payne, Frederick G., ME, II, 635
Paynter, Samuel, DE, I, 220
Peabody, Endicott, MA, II, 735
Peabody, James Hamilton, CO, I, 138
Pease, Elisha Marshall, TX, IV, 1517

Index

Index

Q

Index

R

Index

Index

Index

Index

Index

Index

T

Index

Index

Index

Index

Index

Y

Z